ANGLO-VATICAN RELATIONS, 1914-1939:

CONFIDENTIAL ANNUAL REPORTS OF THE BRITISH MINISTERS TO THE HOLY SEE

Her Majesty's Stationery Office

London, England

GREAT BRITAIN . LEGATION
''' (HOLY SEE)

Edited by

Thomas E. Hachey

Department of History

G. K. HALL & CO., 70 LINCOLN STREET, BOSTON, MASS.

1972

Library of Congress Cataloging in Publication Data

Great Britain. Legation (Holy See).
   Anglo-Vatican relations, 1914-1939.

   "Annual reports of the British Ministers to the
Vatican from the F. O. General Correspondence (Political)
held in the Public Record Office (F0371)"
   1. Catholic Church--Relations (diplomatic) with
Great Britain. 2. Great Britain--Foreign relations--
Catholic Church. I. Hachey, Thomas E., ed. II. Title.
BX1493.A5   261.8'7   72-5361
ISBN 0-8161-0991-5

This publication is printed on permanent/durable acid-free paper.

BX
1493
A5

942.083

G 786

Part I: Introduction

© Thomas E. Hachey 1972

Part II: Annual Reports of the British Ministers to the
Vatican from the F. O. General Correspondence (Political)
Held in the Public Record Office (F0371)

© British Crown copyright 1972

Published by permission of the Controller of Her
Brittanic Majesty's Stationery Office.

ISBN 0-8161-0991-5

DEDICATION

For my mother and father, Margaret and Leo.

ACKNOWLEDGMENT

I am indebted to the Marquette University Committee on Research for the generous grant which made it possible for me to spend a summer in London collecting and preparing materials for both this book and a related study.

TABLE *of* CONTENTS

INTRODUCTION

Students of twentieth century history owe a
debt of gratitude to the British Government for its
Public Record Act of 1967 which introduced on
January 1, 1968 a "thirty-year rule," thus opening
all official records to the end of 1937 and making
provision thereafter for the annual advancement of
the open date on January 1 of each year. With few
exceptions, the archival holdings of the London Government for the period between World War One and the
outbreak of the Second World War were referenced and
made available by 1972. Few of the major nations of
the world have authorized public access to official
governmental papers and correspondence for this
critical era in contemporary history. None of the
major world powers except Britain was diplomatically
accredited at the Holy See during this quarter century. The documents contained in this volume,
therefore, are a unique source on the personnel and
policies of the Vatican, as well as on its activities throughout the world. Each of the documents is
a comprehensive annual report to the London Foreign

Office by the British Minister at the Holy See; collectively they cover the period from 1916 through the year 1939.

In December 1914 Sir Henry Howard was sent as British envoy on a special mission to the Holy See. The purpose of this mission was to extend congratulations to Pope Benedict XV on his election to the papacy, to lay before him the motives which compelled His Majesty's Government to intervene in the War, and to inform him of the British attitude towards the various questions arising therefrom. After three and a half centuries without a fully accredited representative at the Vatican, England was prompted to make this dramatic break with tradition because of the considerable influence which Germany was known to enjoy at the Holy See. The British Mission was, therefore, conceived as a war-time expedient; it was given the status of a legation and became a regular part of the British Foreign Service in 1926. England's diplomatic representation at the Holy See has been maintained without interruption to the present day.

Anglo-Vatican relations were never entirely suspended in the period following the Reformation

although the contact which did exist was often
irregular and always unofficial. In the forecourt
of the church of San Gregorio in Rome, from which
the Pope sent St. Augustine on a mission to England
in 596 A.D., there is a memorial tablet to Sir Edward
Carne, the last British diplomatic envoy to the Holy
See before relations were severed during Queen
Elizabeth's reign. Thereafter, until King James II's
unhappy experience, English law prohibited foreign
jurisdiction in either church or state, establishing
Royal Supremacy in religion and rendering illegal
any link between London and Rome.[1] During the reign
of the Stuarts there were occasional and informal
communications between the British Court and the Vatican. In 1621 a representative of the British Roman
Catholics, George Gage, arrived in Rome ostensibly
with a request from his co-religionists to Pope
Gregory XV for a dispensation for the marriage of
the Spanish Infanta and Prince Charles. The dispensation request was coupled with the condition
that it not be granted until British Roman Catholics
had received freedom of worship. George Gage's
primary mission at Rome, however, was to conduct

matrimonial negotiations with the Vatican on behalf of the British Crown.[2]

Charles I ultimately married a Catholic from French royalty, Henrietta Maria, who was also the godchild of the Pope. The marriage afforded His Holiness, Gregory XV, with an excellent opportunity to send to England a papal agent, Gregorio Panzani, a priest of the Roman Oratory, who was charged with the delicate task of resolving disputes between the secular and regular clergy, and of exploring the possibility of establishing diplomatic relations between England and the Holy See. He was succeeded by George Conn, a Scotsman and a Dominican, who stayed in England from 1636 to 1639 and, being on good terms with the King, was able to do much for his fellow Catholics. Meanwhile, another Scotsman, Sir William Hamilton, served in the capacity of Queen Henrietta Maria's agent at Rome. Count Carlo Rossetti succeeded Conn as the papal envoy to England in 1639 but, after 1640, the influence of the Roman Church and the plight of English Catholics rapidly deteriorated with the rising power of the Puritan Parliamentarians and the intervention of the Scottish Covenanters in English affairs. The Restoration

produced a more tolerant atmosphere for a time, and
later brought the last Catholic King of England to
the throne. James II dispatched Earl Castlemaine as
his personal ambassador to the Holy See in 1686. His
Majesty also agreed to receive Count Fernando D'Adda
as the Pope's envoy with the title of Nuncio Apostolic. The Glorious Revolution of 1688 ended James'
reign and virtually terminated Anglo-Vatican relations for more than a century.[3]

Great Britain and the papacy shared a common
interest in resisting French aggression during the
revolution in that country and, in 1792, the British
Government sent Sir John Coxe Hippisley to the Holy
See for the purpose of discussing the political consequences of the war against the French Republic.
Hippisley, a non-Catholic, had previously been sent
to Rome in 1779-80 to explore prospects for improving Britain's relations with the Holy See. Following Hippisley's second assignment to the Vatican,
Monsignor Charles Erskine, Dean of the College of
Consistorial Advocates, was received as a papal
agent by King George III. Both the King and his
chief minister, William Pitt, expressed satisfaction
with the circumspect manner in which Erskine conducted

himself, respecting the royal wish that the mission of the Pope's representative not assume a public character. Erskine subsequently was assigned to other duties and left England in 1801. London's relations with the Vatican were certainly improved by the success of this collaboration, but official English diplomatic accreditation at the Holy See was still more than a century away.

When Leo XII became Pope in 1823, he sent a courteous letter announcing his accession to King George IV. The letter was received by George Canning, British Foreign Secretary, who was unable to reply on behalf of His Majesty when the law officers of the Crown ventured the opinion that such direct correspondence with the Pope would imply recognition of his claims as the spiritual head of Christendom. Canning, who was anxious to solicit the Holy See's opinion as to the best method by which His Majesty's Government might reconcile Irish and English Catholics to the British Crown, attempted indirect contact with the Vatican through Lord Burghersh who was then British Minister to Tuscany.[4] Following the passage of legislation which provided for Catholic emancipation in 1829, the law officers of the Crown ruled

that the Government could enter into official correspondence with the Holy See, but George Canning was no
longer Foreign Secretary and no new initiatives were
undertaken.

A new era in Anglo-Vatican relations was introduced in 1832 when an attaché at the British Mission
in Florence was ordered by Lord Palmerston to take
up residence in Rome for the purpose of reporting on
activities at the Holy See. Several British agents
subsequently served their Government in this fashion
at the papal Court, the last of whom was Clarke
Jervoise whose duties were terminated in 1874 when
the international status of the Vatican could not be
clarified.[5] The new kingdom of Italy incorporated
Rome and the Roman provinces within its realm in 1870
and limited the Pope's sovereignity to the confines
of the Vatican and his official residences.

Earlier, the British Parliament had passed an
act in 1848 authorizing Queen Victoria to accredit a
minister to the Sovereign of the Roman States, and
also to receive any diplomatic agent from such Sovereign who was not in holy orders. London's law
officers had deemed that such representation would
not be in violation of the statutes and Her Majesty's

Government had begun gradual preparations for the establishment of formal diplomatic relations. With the Pope no longer temporal Sovereign of the Roman States, however, the British Statute Law Revision Committee ruled in 1875 that the act of 1848 was obsolete and the law was repealed.

Britain waited another forty years before finally sending an official envoy to the Vatican. During that period relations between the two Courts were friendly, if infrequent. Between 1881 and 1885 Sir George Errington sometimes served as an unofficial medium of communication between the London Government and the Holy See. Two years thereafter, in 1887, the Duke of Norfolk was sent on a special mission to the Vatican to express Queen Victoria's appreciation for the courtesy shown her by the Pope; the latter had sent a personal representative to congratulate Her Highness on the occasion of her jubilee. In 1889 Sir Linton Simmons was sent on a special mission to the Holy See in connection with certain religious questions which had assumed political overtones on the island of Malta. And in 1902, Lord Denbigh was sent to Rome to convey King Edward VII's congratulations to the Pope at the time of His Holiness' jubilee.

The appointment of an official British envoy at the Vatican was an inevitable development over the course of time but doubtlessly it was hastened by the outbreak of a general European war in 1914. The Central Powers' representation at the Holy See outclassed the Allies in both the number and quality of their diplomatic missions. While Imperial Russia did have a minister at the papal Court, his influence was seriously hampered by the Czarist religious policies in Russian Poland. France had broken relations with the Holy See in 1904 so that Belgium remained the only Allied nation in a position to challenge Germany's considerable influence at the Vatican before Britain instituted diplomatic relations in December 1914.[6] By contrast, the Austro-Hungarian Ambassador, Prince Johann Schönburg, enjoyed much prestige at the Curia. While Germany had no imperial minister accredited to the Vatican, the Reich benefited from the services of the Prussian minister, Otto Muhlberg, who was a competent diplomatist, and the Bavarian minister, Otto Ritter, who was widely known in Rome as a devout Catholic. All three of these envoys labored to win the sympathies of the ecclesiastical hierarchy for the Central Powers.[7]

London's Foreign Office became convinced during the early months of hostilities that the success of German and Austrian propaganda at the Holy See could result in serious political and moral consequences for the Allied cause.[8] The election and coronation of a new Pope, Benedict XV, provided the British with an appropriate opportunity to undertake a new diplomatic initiative vis-à-vis the Vatican. England felt it necessary, however, to reassure the Italian Government that the Mission to the Holy See was temporary and intended only for the duration of the War. Moreover, the British Foreign Secretary also promised the Italians there was no truth to rumors alleging that London had promised to support a Vatican bid for official representation at any post-war peace conference in appreciation for the Holy See's acceptance of the Mission.[9]

Sir Henry Howard was chosen in December 1914 to serve as British Envoy Extraordinary and Minister Plenipotentiary to the papal Court. Howard, who was seventy-two years of age, had served for nearly fifty years in the diplomatic service. His previous responsibilities had included that of Minister at The Hague and at Luxemburg. Educated at the Benedictine College near Bath, Sir Henry Howard was a member of one of England's most prominent Catholic families and, at the time of his appointment to the Vatican, he was residing in Rome where he was well known to a number of cardinals and leading churchmen. The element of timidity which had always characterized British relations with the Vatican appeared, perhaps for the last time, in the decision to withhold the news of the British Mission from the press.[10] The Times of London did, however, report the story on December 12 and for a time the Government's apprehensions appeared unwarranted when there were few immediate protests in either the press or Parliament over Howard's appointment. In retrospect it would seem that the London Government's emphasis upon the temporary nature of the Mission, and its argument that the critical circumstances of the War necessitated official access to so important a neutral as the Holy See, caught those opposed to relations with the papacy off balance.

Britain's anxiety was not misplaced since the Vatican often subscribed to views and policies which were not in harmony with the interest of the Allies. Indeed, the Holy See avoided any official condemnation of German, Austrian, or Turkish conduct of the

War partly because such a declaration would compromise the Pope's neutrality, but also because the Vatican feared that an Allied victory would result in the pre-dominance of Russia in Europe.[11] The Holy See had historical ties to Austria and the Allies were dis-tressed to learn in 1915 that the Vatican was pressing Austria to concede contested differences with Italy in order to preserve the latter's neutrality in the War. And the Vatican had more discreet reasons for prefer-ring the Central Powers to the Allies. Pius X had been such a poor financial manager that the Vatican Treasury was substantially depleted at the time of his death. His successor, Benedict XV, accepted mone-tary contributions collected for the Holy See by Matthias Erzberger from wealthy German Catholics and Protestants. This liaison understandably gave the Allies pause since Erzberger was Germany's director of propaganda activities in the neutral states.[12]

From the time of the establishment of the British Mission to the papal Court in December of 1914, many people and organizations in England either remained unconvinced of the need for retaining the Vatican's goodwill or were opposed under any circumstances to diplomatic ties with the Holy See. The London Foreign

Office received numerous letters and petitions protesting the Mission from such groups as the Protestant
Alliance, the Loyal Orange Institutions of England,
and the United Protestant Council.[13] Moreover, there
were inquiries in the House of Commons as to whether
the costs of the Mission were a justifiable expense.
To all these critics the Government gave the same
reply: the British Minister to the Holy See was performing a necessary and useful service in the nation's
interest. It was also argued that the expenses of
the Mission were hardly extravagant since the entire
staff numbered only five: the minister, a diplomatic
secretary, an attaché, a shorthand-typist and a
porter-messenger.

Controversy over the British Mission to the Holy
See extended to the press where some London newspaper
editorials scathingly attacked the alleged pro-German
sympathies of Pope Benedict XV. By way of a reply,
John Duncan Gregory prepared a memorandum for the
Foreign Secretary on November 30, 1917. Gregory, an
assistant to the British minister at the papal Court,
was a Catholic and a career diplomat. His repudiation of the allegations against the Pope was not
prompted by any sectarian sympathies but rather by a

frank consideration and analysis of the situation as
he saw it. Gregory wrote:

> . . . The present Pope is a very
> decided mediocrity. He has the
> mentality of a little official,
> the inexperience of a parochial
> Italian who has hardly travelled
> at all and a tortuous method of
> conducting affairs which arises
> from years of office work con-
> nected with a fifth rate diplo-
> macy [the Vatican]. He is cap-
> able neither of rising to great
> heights nor of efficiently con-
> trolling the ordinary routine
> of his administration. He is
> without any particular charm or
> personality and he is obstinate
> and bad-tempered to a marked
> degree. But I am convinced that
> he is not either temperamentally
> or politically pro-German.[14]

Throughout the First World War, the British Government continued to defend the Mission with specific
examples of the contributions it was reputed to have
made. London felt certain that its Minister to the
Holy See had been partly responsible for having the
Vatican withdraw its objections to Italy's joining
the Allies in 1915. The British also felt that diplomatic presence at the Holy See had permitted them
the opportunity to restrict the activities of enemy
[German] controlled religious orders in India and
other parts of the British Empire. Finally, although

angered by the anti-conscription position of the
Irish Catholic hierarchy in 1918, the London Foreign
Office determined that conditions in Ireland would
have been worse had not the British Minister at the
Holy See sought the Pope's assistance.

With the termination of the War on November 11,
1918 the agitation against the British Mission intensified. London, for years having stressed the war-
time justification and temporary nature of the Mission, now suggested that its removal might offend the
millions of Roman Catholic British subjects throughout the Empire. If the Government were depending
upon the Dominions to provide support for this contention, it must have been disappointed. When asked
for advice in 1919 respecting the possible retention
of a British Minister to the Holy See, the Dominion
Governments offered no consensus. Newfoundland
mildly favored the idea; Canada, Australia, and
South Africa confessed to no feeling on the matter,
or replied that their interests were not involved;
New Zealand thought the continuance of a British
Mission at the Vatican unnecessary.

On November 4, 1920, the British Cabinet met
and decided that "the Secretary of State should have

authority to retain the British Diplomatic Representation at the Vatican." No indication was given in
the subsequent public announcement of this decision
as to whether the Mission's continuance would be temporary or permanent. The evidence would suggest that
nearly all of His Majesty's chief ministers were in
favor of rendering it permanent but hesitated, despite the proven usefulness of the Mission, because of
the opposition such a step might possibly provoke.
The British Cabinet finally agreed in February 1923
to accede to Sir Odo Russell's request that the title
of the Mission be changed from "Special Mission to the
Vatican" to "His Majesty's Legation to the Holy See."
Budgetary considerations postponed action on this
matter until fiscal 1925-26 when the Government
dropped the pretense of a temporary Mission and the
Legation to the Holy See was duly entered among the
published Foreign Office lists.

It was not until 1938 before an Apostolic Delegate, Monsignor William Godfrey, was appointed to
London. This step did not make Anglo-Vatican relations reciprocal since the position is without any
diplomatic character. Moreover, a nuncio [papal
ambassador] was and remains equally as unwelcome to

the Roman Catholic hierarchy in England as to the
Government. Cardinal Henry Edward Manning perhaps
best represented the view of the former when he declared that a papal nuncio would import strange and
unwelcome Latin traditions and might even prove harmful to the Roman Church in England. For its part,
the London Foreign Office would never consent to the
practice of recognizing the papal ambassador as the
doyen of the diplomatic corps at the Court of St.
James. Godfrey's appointment did reflect, however,
the satisfaction which the Vatican had derived from
the return of a British minister to the papal Court
in 1914. The abundant information contained in the
recorded observations of His Majesty's Ministers to
the Holy See testifies to the fact that the unilateral diplomatic tie was indeed useful to Great Britain.

The reports contained in this volume were prepared at the end of each calendar year and were forwarded via diplomatic carrier to the London Foreign
Office during the first weeks of the following new
year. They provide an annual summary of proceedings
at the Holy See, together with considered judgments
and opinions on Vatican subjects which often were
communicated only in a fragmentary fashion, if at

all, by the British ministers in their dispatches, telegrams, and memoranda to the Foreign Office. It will be noted that the first British minister accredited to the papal Court, Sir Henry Howard, served for less than two years before being succeeded by another Catholic diplomat, Count John de Salis, in October, 1916. Howard did not leave a summary report of his brief tenure, nor did Count de Salis initiate the practice until 1922. Hence, the first report was not forthcoming until 1923 when de Salis submitted a dispatch to the Foreign Office which reviewed the course of events at the Vatican from the date of his appointment to the Holy See in 1916 through the year 1922. Thereafter, an Annual Report by the British Minister to the Holy See became the accepted practice until 1939 when the outbreak of World War Two suspended their continuation. The brief outline of events which was substituted for the regular Annual Report in 1939, the first year of hostilities, is here included. Collectively, these documents comprise a unique diplomatic diary of the Vatican's involvement in global affairs as seen by skilled observers who enjoyed privileged access to the Holy See throughout this troubled era.

There is no standard format for the Annual Reports which vary both in length and in subject matter, but some features are more constant than others. Many of the reports contain some commentary on changes in the Sacred College of Cardinals, the Curia, and the Vatican administration generally. Others include an analysis of the Roman Catholic press, both in Italy and throughout the world. A few reports specualte about the policy implications which might be drawn from the published views of the Vatican's official newspaper, <u>Osservatore</u> <u>Romano</u>. The greater part of each report, however, is devoted to the activities of the Holy See and/or to the Vatican's interests in the British Empire, North America, Latin America, Western and Eastern Europe, Africa, the Middle East, China, and Japan. Indeed, the universality of the Roman Church is nowhere more apparent than in these accounts of its comprehensive undertakings throughout the world.

Aside from the purely ecclesiastical interests of the Holy See, the reports also contain a substantial amount of information about Vatican personalities and policies which is often more political in character. For example, Count John de Salis' initial report affords a perceptive and candid description of the prominent personalities in the papal Court of Pius XI. It also reveals how anxious the Holy See was that Soviet Russia not gain control over Constantinople and how Britain was preferred to the Turks, or any other power, as an administrator of Palestine. Moreover, the Church of Rome is seen to have had a keen mistrust of Zionism during World War One while harboring an open distaste for France because of that country's official anti-clericalism. The British found themselves in the difficult position of seeking the goodwill of both the Quirinal and the Holy See as they disputed the Roman question. London supported Italy's territorial claims but was clearly opposed to that Government's gaining any control over the Vatican itself during the post-war period. Especially interesting is the section pertaining to the Irish College in Rome and the manner in which the British sought the assistance of the Holy See in moderating the Irish hierarchy during the period of armed rebellion in Ireland. Pope Benedict XV is alleged to have described the hunger strike of Terence MacSwiney, Irish patriot and Lord Mayor of Cork City, as "a farce." The story suggests that the papacy was even less sympathetic with Ireland's war of independence than has been assumed by students of this period.

In December 1922 Britain appointed a Protestant, Sir Odo Theophilus Russell, as Count de Salis' successor. The selection of a non-Catholic as British Minister to the Holy See proved perfectly agreeable to the Pontiff; it also satisfied the wishes of those Englishmen whose support of the British Mission hinged upon such a condition, and doubtlessly made it easier for His Majesty's Government to raise the diplomatic status of the Mission to that of a legation a few years thereafter. The year 1923 was perhaps no more troubled nor less typical than any other for Anglo-Vatican relations: there were both pleasant and trying times. On the one hand, the year was highlighted by King George V's state visit to Italy during which he also paid a much-publicized visit to the Pope. Despite vociferous protests on the part of some Protestants in England, the meeting between King and Pope was a huge success and it strengthened Anglo-Vatican ties. Moreover, the Holy See used its good offices during 1923 in an effort to persuade Eamon de Valera that he should help end the Irish Civil War. On the other hand, the British Mission's Annual Report for the year describes the irritating problems which feuding Catholic clerics in Palestine caused His Majesty's Government.

Other sections of this same report serve to illustrate the diverse and multiple global activities of the Holy See. The British Minister described the papal role in attempting to moderate the French and Belgian occupation of Germany's Ruhr district. Also included are insights into the Vatican's meddling in the internal affairs of the Spanish Government and Monarchy; the Pontiff's response to religious persecution in Russia; the futile attempt of the Argentine Government to prevent Rome from selecting the chief prelate of that Andean nation; the favorable disposition of the Holy See toward the prospect of a Japanese Minister at the papal Court because of the Vatican's inclination to view Japan as a bulwark against Bolshevism. On a different note, His Majesty's Minister reported that the Roman Catholic Church was estimated to have some 70,000 missionaries, many of them in Asian and African possessions of the British Empire.

No less newsworthy are the Annual Reports for 1924 and 1925. In noting the increasing influence of New World prelates among Vatican circles, the British

Minister concluded that United States gold was not un-related to the creation of more American cardinals. With equal frankness, Vatican officials characterized the fall of the French Socialist Government in the spring of 1925 as an "Easter egg" for the Holy See. Details of the Vatican's secret conditions for possible recognition of the Soviet Government are included, together with a few interesting examples of how the Holy See deferred to the British on all matters affecting Ireland despite that nation's new status as the Irish Free State.

By 1926 the British Minister to the Holy See was proclaiming the Vatican as a formidable deterrent to Communism and a moderating influence upon excessive nationalism. England, he reported, was held in high esteem by the Roman Church because of the humanitarian manner in which the British handled the General Strike of 1926. The United States was also regarded favorably by the Vatican because of that country's religious tolerance. France, however, had earned the displeasure of the Holy See which protested vehemently against the pagan doctrines of the Action Française movement in that nation. Nowhere was the re-emergence of Germany as a great power more evident than at the Vatican where Berlin's influence grew substantially. The Soviet Union was still regarded as reprehensible by the Holy See in 1927, an attitude which was keenly reflected in the Vatican's congratulatory message to London following a rupture in Anglo-Soviet relations over a propaganda issue. The papacy appeared more conciliatory toward Italian fascism as it scrupulously avoided condemning the system whenever attacking fascist theorists such as Gentile or Rocco.

Vatican officials were not unaware of the implications and possible consequences which could derive from the unprecedented candidacy of a Roman Catholic, Alfred E. Smith, for the presidency of the United States in 1928. Cardinal William O'Connell of Boston confided to the British Minister at the Holy See that some Vatican officials believed Smith's election as president could prove embarrassing since they thought him unequal to the task and therefore likely to invite abuse upon the Church by his political shortcomings. At the same time, O'Connell conceded that the same parties were hopeful that Herbert Hoover's election to office would not produce a new wave of anti-Catholic nationalism in America.

Italian-Vatican relations were finally normalized with the Lateran Treaty of 1929 and Henry G. Chilton, British Minister to the papal Court, afforded the London Foreign Office with an expansive report on the behind-the-scenes treaty deliberations. Anglo-Vatican relations, however, suffered during this period owing to the complex church-state entanglements on the island of Malta where a serious misunderstanding developed between the Roman Catholic hierarchy and British civil authorities. The dispute, which began in 1929 and continued for three years thereafter, was provoked by clerics who openly opposed the Government of Lord Strickland, the Maltese Prime Minister. The latter publicly condemned Church leaders for their political interference, an action which so offended the Vatican that it subsequently refused to grant Lord Strickland a papal audience. His Majesty's Government made known its displeasure by allowing the British Minister to the Holy See, Henry Chilton, an indefinite leave and by placing the Legation in the hands of a chargé d'affaires. The publication of a British Blue Book on the affair was answered by the release of a Vatican White Paper. Several of the Annual Reports of the British Legation contain

descriptive accounts of the controversy, all of which
contribute to a first-hand analysis of an interesting
but intricate chapter in the brief history of recent
Anglo-Vatican affairs. Differences were resolved in
1932 to the general satisfaction of both sides and
Sir Robert Henry Clive was announced on March 25, 1933
as the new British Minister to the Holy See.

Nazi Germany signed a concordat with the Vatican
in 1933 and the British Minister, in summarizing the
proceedings, stated that the agreement had infuriated
the French. Paris was said to be particularly incensed by a secret clause in the concordat by which
the Nazi Government agreed not to require military
service of clerics in the event that conscription was
re-introduced. French officials viewed that provision as tantamount to recognition by the Holy See of
Germany's right to rearm. Vatican relations with the
Italian Government, although certainly not harmonious,
had improved to the point where the Pope left Rome in
1933 for his mountain retreat at Castel Gondolfo, the
first Pontiff to leave the Eternal City since 1870.
Even by the following year the British Minister
thought the Holy See to be on reasonably good terms
with the fascist government. Indeed, the

international development which seemed to cause the
Vatican the greatest irritation was the admission of
the Soviet Union into the League of Nations.

Perhaps no single event alienated Anglo-Vatican
relations quite so profoundly during the nineteen-
thirties as the Ethiopian War. At one point in 1935,
British Minister Sir Charles Wingfield appears to
have concluded that Pius XI reluctantly condoned
Mussolini's African adventure because of a fear that
Italy might be taken over by the Communists. Wingfield observed that the Holy See was so convinced
Soviet Russia was its mortal enemy that Vatican
spokesmen did not hesitate to quote Dr. Goebbels on
the dangers of Bolshevism. London became angered
when the Holy See urged that Great Britain negotiate
with Mussolini during the battle for Ethiopia; the
British tersely advised the Vatican that the issue
was more legitimately the concern of the League of
Nations. Relations were scarcely improved when the
Holy See openly deprecated the British Government's
renunciation of the Hoare-Laval agreement. The
British Minister at the Holy See began to wonder if
papal support for the Italians in Ethiopia might
not suggest that the Vatican's action was simply a

matter of preferring to see a Catholic power, Italy, benefit at the expense of a Protestant power like England. He even suggested that there was common ground between fascists and Roman Catholics:

> It is true that fascism and pop-
> ular catholicism rest upon prin-
> ciples which are to some extent
> similar. Both admit no question-
> ing of their creed; both insist
> upon the submission of the indi-
> vidual to the system, encourage
> large families, attach importance
> to external ceremonies, and to
> mass psychology.

Seldom had an Annual Report by a British Minister to the Holy See adopted such a critical tone toward the Roman Church. The report concludes with a descrip- tion of the incremental fashion in which the Vatican assumed a strong pro-Italian stance vis-à-vis Britain by the end of 1935.

Francis D'Arcy Godolphin Osborne was named Bri- tish Minister to the Holy See on January 23, 1936. He observed that the Holy See, while appalled by the Popular Front Government of France, openly favored the forces of General Francisco Franco in the Spanish Civil War. While this was a further instance of the Vatican's siding with Italy instead of England, Osborne reported that the Holy See's motives were more religious than political. In the view of the Church, the struggle in Spain was one between a godless political system and the defenders of conservative religion. The British Minister found encouragement in the sympathy which Pius XI expressed privately for London's attitude toward the Ethiopian question, and in His Holiness' wish for an Anglo-Italian rapprochement that would serve as a counterweight to a resurgent Germany.

British Foreign Secretary Anthony Eden resigned from Prime Minister Neville Chamberlain's Government in February 1938, and the Vatican, which thought Eden's alleged Italopholia an obstacle to Anglo-Italian amity, welcomed his departure. London's Minister to the papal Court noted that the Holy See was far less pleased with the German occupation of Austria. The Vatican Under Secretary of State told Osborne that the Anschluss was a disaster which had resulted from German arrogance, Italian folly, and Anglo-French weakness. Pius XI also reminded the Italian Government that its imitation of Nazi anti-Semitism infringed upon the provisions of the Concordat of 1929, under which the State was pledged to accord civil recognition to any marriage celebrated

by Catholic rite. The Pope gave orders to close the
Vatican museums at the time of Hitler's visit to Rome
when it was learned that members of the Fuehrer's
party were claiming the right of access on the
strength of passes issued by the Italian Government.

The appointment of an Apostolic Delegate to Great
Britain in the autumn of 1938 was interpreted by His
Majesty's Minister at the Holy See as a concrete
expression of the respect and admiration which Pius
XI had for England and her Sovereigns. Prime Minister
Chamberlain's action in flying to see Hitler at
Berchtesgaden in an effort to resolve the Sudeten
Deutsch problem made a most favorable impression at
the Vatican. The British Minister to the papal Court
noted, however, that the Holy See was not optimistic
over England's prospects for success in negotiating
a settlement in Czechoslovakia. The Czechs, said
the papal Under Secretary of State to a member of His
Majesty's Legation, were a slow and obstinate people.
Their nation lacked a natural principle of unity, was
militarily indefensible, and was surrounded by countries with claims to parts of its territory. Following the Munich Conference, the Pope broadcasted an
appeal to the whole Catholic world to join him in

prayer for the preservation of peace, offering his own
life to God as a sacrifice in seeking this goal. The
Anglo-French acceptance of the dismemberment of
Czechoslovakia at Munich was heartily approved by
the Vatican which took the position that if peace
failed now it would not be England's fault. The
Osservatore Romano wrote that Prime Minister Chamberlain was a statesman of the first order to whom the
world owed its salvation from the appalling disaster
of war.

Pius XI died in 1939, six months before the outbreak of a war he had hoped would never come. His
Secretary of State, Cardinal Eugenio Pacelli, succeeded him as Pius XII. In a diplomatic dispatch
entitled Political Review for 1939, introduced as a
substitute for the Annual Reports during the period
of hostilities, the British Legation to the Holy See
summarized highlights of that momentous year. The
British took particular interest in the exchange of
formal visits between the Italian Sovereign and the
Pope, and the manner in which His Holiness' unexpected
and unprecedented return visit to the Quirinal was
given the greatest publicity and significance in both
the Italian press and in the Vatican's official organ.

English observers thought these events possibly compromised Italy's relations with her anti-Catholic German ally.

President Franklin Roosevelt announced on December 23, 1939 that he was sending Myron C. Taylor as his "personal representative" to the Pope with the rank of ambassador. The purpose of Taylor's mission was also disclosed: to further the parallel peace efforts of the President and the Holy Father. From the Political Review for 1939 we also learn that Pius XII revealed his personal satisfaction over Mr. Roosevelt's initiative to members of the British Legation. Francis Osborne reported to London that "the Vatican is now much more of an active political force that it was under the late Pope. And I do not anticipate that we shall have any reason to regret this." The British Foreign Office took a more cautious position as seen in the following minute from its records:

> . . . I agree with Osborne that
> on the whole this will be to our
> advantage, but it is also not
> without its dangers, more especi-
> ally because Pius XII has not up
> to the present shown such frank
> courage in standing up to the
> dictators as did his predecessor;
> I would not wish to imply that

the Pope is a weak man, but he
had only been Pope for a few
months and perhaps has not yet
quite found his feet; also his
training [as a diplomatist] may
make him generally readier to
compromise.

Recalling the recent friendly exchange between the Holy See and the Italian Government, and the appointment of a personal peace ambassador to the Vatican by the President of the United States, Osborne concluded his 1939 report with the earnest hope that the new year might bring a peace initiative sponsored by the Pope, the President, and the Duce. But Pius XII and Franklin Roosevelt failed in their bid for world peace, Mussolini never made the effort, and World War Two convulsed the world for the next five and a half years.

These trials and tribulations of a troubled quarter century were witnessed by a succession of British ministers from the singularly unique perspective of the Vatican. The Annual Reports of these ministers to the Holy See provide an informative and frequently intriguing chronicle of the Vatican's ecclesiastical, diplomatic, and political involvements throughout the world.

References

1. Sir Alec Randall, "British Diplomatic Representation at the Holy See," Blackfriars, 37 (September, 1956), 356.

2. Sir Stephen Gaselee, "British Diplomatic Relations with the Holy See," The Dublin Review, 204 (January, 1939), 1-2.

3. Gordon Albion, "England and the Holy See. A Survey of Diplomatic Relations," The Month, 171 (January, 1939), 76-77.

4. Harold Temperley, "George Canning, the Catholics and the Holy See," The Dublin Review, 193 (July, 1933), 10-11.

5. Robert A. Graham, S.J., Vatican Diplomacy: A Study of Church and State on the International Plane (Princeton, 1959), pp. 72-73.

6. Graham, Vatican Diplomacy, pp. 76-77.

7. William A. Renzi, "The Entente and the Vatican During the Period of Italian Neutrality," The Historical Journal, XIII, 3 (1970), 492-493.

8. Sir Alec Randall, Vatican Assignment (London, 1956), p. 11.

9. Sir Edward Grey to Sir J. Rennell Rodd, London, 20 November 1914, F.O. 371/2007, P.R.O. Rodd, the British Ambassador accredited to the Italian Government, has provided an interesting personal account of this period in his published memoirs. See James Rennell Rodd, Social and Diplomatic Memories, 1902-1919 (London, 1925).

10. H. A. Smith, "Diplomatic Relations with the Holy See, 1815-1930," The Law Quarterly Review, 38 (July, 1932), 392.

11. Randall, Vatican Assignment, p. 13.

12. The Italian Government was aware of Erzberger's financial aid to the papacy even before May 1915. See Renzi, "The Entente and the Vatican," _The Historical Journal_, p. 496. Sir Henry Howard reported this information to London from his post at the Holy See. Sir Henry Howard to Sir Edward Grey, 27 May 1915, F.O. 371/2377, P.R.O.

13. For a representative sampling of these voluminous protest letters and petitions, see the Foreign Office correspondence at the London Public Record Office among the following files: F.O. 371/1858, 1874, 1880, 1999, and 2007.

14. Confidential Memorandum, November 30, 1917. J. D. Gregory to the London Foreign Office, F.O. 371/3086.

CONFIDENTIAL.

(12014)

Report on Mission to the Holy See.

Count de Salis to the Marquess Curzon of Kedleston.—(Received October 25.)

My Lord,   *Travellers' Club, October* 25, 1922.
    I HAVE the honour to submit to your Lordship herewith a confidential report on the mission to the Holy See.

                               I have, &c.
                                J. DE SALIS.

Enclosure.

Report on Mission to the Holy See.

CONTENTS.

THE SPECIAL MISSION.

    IN the latter part of 1916 I was appointed to succeed Sir Henry Howard* as chief of the special mission to the Vatican, and presented my letters of credence to the Pope on the 2nd December.
    Before leaving London I had the advantage of learning, through conversation with Mr. Gregory, much with regard to the manner in which the work of the mission had been carried on, especially as regards propaganda in favour of the aims and objects of the *Entente.* It appeared to me that the task to be undertaken in the domain of foreign policy must in all probability meet with special difficulty on some

---

   * The special mission to the Vatican under Sir Henry Howard was despatched at the end of the year 1914. Its work during the first months after its arrival is recorded in a memorandum by Mr. Gregory, dated April 1, 1915.

half-dozen points, to which I allowed myself to call Lord Grey's notice on taking leave of him before starting. The points were :—

(*a*.) The distrust which the Vatican must feel as to the use which their enemy, the Russian Government, would wish to make of victory; (*b*) the future of Poland, at that time considered by His Majesty's Government to be an internal Russian question; (*c*) the interests at Constantinople of the Church which might be seriously menaced by a transfer to Russian sovereignty; (*d*) the future of the Catholic South Slavs (Croats and Dalmatians) : (*e*) the Bohemian question and the substitution of Czech for Austrian rule; (*f*) the Irish question.

THE SITUATION IN 1916.

An extract from a private letter written by a foreign diplomatist* in the month of September 1916, insisted that the dispositions of the Vatican towards the Allies were unfavourable. The Pope himself was declared to have used to a high ecclesiastic belonging to a neutral country language hostile to the *Entente*, and blaming them for the continuance of the war. The situation was depicted as bad. A more detailed statement, marked strictly confidential and declared to be from a good source, which was not disclosed to me, reached the Foreign Office shortly after my arrival in Rome. The Vatican were described as sympathising with the Central Powers as the representatives of order, discipline, organisation and religious spirit, though it was added that this leaning could only be detected by people with whom they were on confidential terms. The Irish College were conspiring (" had become a nest of conspiracy ") against the Allies in favour of the Central Powers, while Cardinal Gasparri was in relation with President Wilson with a view to stop the war by measures to be taken against the Allies, and was declaring that the threatened Muscovite hegemony in Europe was incompatible with the liberty, civilisation and independence of the peoples of Europe. Also, in another paper of February 1917 the Vatican were stated, on the authority of a good source not revealed to me, to be in close touch with Count Bernstorf and the Irish in order to prevent the United States from doing anything to help the Allies. The Foreign Office learnt, equally from one of the papers to which I have alluded, that immediately after Mr. Wilson's note of the 18th December, 1916, Cardinal Gasparri conveyed to the American President that he had the possibility of putting an end to the European conflict almost immediately by having recourse to either of the following measures :—

(*a*.) Prohibiting despatch of supplies of arms and ammunition to the Allies or exacting that the same trade should be allowed with the Central Powers.
(*b*.) Making relations between America and Japan so strained as to justify the United States putting an embargo on all supplies, and preventing Japan helping the Allies.

An explanation of this given to me locally was that the American Ambassador, Mr. Page, received three successive visits from persons he had good reason to regard as (I think the words used were " had no difficulty in identifying as ") emissaries from Cardinal Gasparri, asking him to urge his Government to stop munition supplies to the Allies; but no information was forthcoming as to who the persons in question might be.

The Foreign Office also learnt, apparently on some other occasion, that, according to an opinion given by the Cardinal Secretary of State, the German submarine blockade was justifiable in international law. Count Horodicki, a Polish-American gentleman, who was at that time very active in these quarters but who has subsequently not been seen here, was very ready to furnish information, but his presence in Rome was opposed by the Italian authorities. From another source, equally not revealed, information reached the Foreign Office† that in the view of the Cardinal Secretary of State the submarine blockade was justifiable in international law. The presence of M. Caillaux in Rome was a cause of further disquieting rumours; positive information was given to me by a Belgian ecclesiastic, whose good faith was beyond question, that M. Caillaux had certainly been to the Vatican and seen the Cardinal Secretary of State, if not the Pope himself.

In the first weeks after my arrival the situation might have seemed anything but encouraging; the task which appeared to lie before the mission was to sift the value

---

* Prince Ghika to Mr. Gregory, September 1, 1916.
† February 21, 1916.

of the endless stories which were being put into circulation respecting the Vatican; clearing rubbish out of the way, to arrive at a correct understanding of the aims of the Holy See; and to watch how far they might be in correspondence with British interests. For this purpose support and assistance from the various organs of the British Government which might be concerned was very desirable.

THE LEANINGS OF THE VATICAN.

As to the leanings of the Vatican, it would be hard to say that there was any great mystery about them. At the time of my arrival, and for many months during the year 1917, the situation was entirely dominated by the question of Russia. Never in his conversation did Cardinal Gasparri make any secret of his distrust of the Government of Petrograd. Never. in his opinion, could the Russians alone take Constantinople, and he trusted that, if victorious elsewhere, we should not go on fighting to put them there. He would be perfectly happy to see the British there, or even the French, in spite of the anti-clerical tendencies of their Government of the day. Under Russian rule, rights, laboriously acquired in the course of centuries, would be valueless in twenty years. The Russian Government had never respected the rights of the Church or kept a promise made to her. Proceedings in Galicia afforded ample proof that their ways had not been changed by the war, and the policy of the Allies, by which the whole of Poland was to pass under Russian supremacy, had no attraction for the Holy See. Cardinal Falconio, the head of the Franciscans, was equally decided in holding the same opinion, while the Father-General of the Jesuits, Father Ledochowski, though speaking well of their relations with the Russian people, insisted of the impossibility they found of dealing with the Russian Holy Synod. On all sides the same views were expressed, that the Russian programme would be disastrous to Catholic interests; nor, if the published evidence of such authorities as M. Nekludof* be correct, was it easy to combat this impression, unless it were that a continuance of Ottoman rule might leave these interests in the hands of such opponents as newly-roused Moslem fanaticism or the Masonic organisation of the Young Turks.

Obviously the Vatican had no reason to wish for the destruction of an independent Austria. either by the Allies or, just as little, at the hands of Berlin in pursuance of the schemes known generally as Mittel-Europa. There was no mystery on the point which Cardinal Gasparri alluded to more than once in the course of his conversations, nor might there have been any ground for reticence on his part, since the ideas put forward by him would scarcely seem to have differed from those held in 1917 by His Majesty's Government themselves.† At the same time the then existing constitution of the monarchy by no means represented, in their opinion, conditions incapable of improvement. In Austria the increasing encroachments of officialism, the' tendency to treat the Church as a mere, department of the State, a spirit of "Josephismus,"‡ of which the Cardinal complained more than once, were creating friction. The predominance of Hungary, with its chauvinism and strong Calvinist element,§ was not too favourable to the Church, which had a better position among the Croats; "Trialism" or any such solution which would have given autonomy to the Slavs could not therefore be unwelcome, especially if it helped to realise the aspirations of the Poles. Above all, though the matter was never directly alluded to before me, the interference of the Austro-Hungarian Government in the Papal election on the death of Leo XIII had not been forgotten. "Once," so in August 1918 ran an article in a Catholic newspaper, "it was Austria which personified Catholicism in face of the Slav world, but the policy of Metternich and his successors identified Catholicism with reasons of State. . . . Thus arose the legend that Austria was a bulwark of Catholicism. Well! Official Austria, the Austria of Francis Joseph, the Austria of the famous veto opposed to the election of Cardinal

---

* " Diplomatic Reminiscences," by A. Nekludof, formerly Russian Minister at Sofia and Stockholm and Ambassador at Madrid. P. 327 (1920):—

". . . . Austria-Hungary dismembered and replaced by an agglomeration of independent States, which would be obliged by the force of circumstances to form a confederation, naturally under the auspices and presidency of Russia; this confederation extending from the Carpathians to Constantinople and from Danzig to the Adriatic, embracing Orthodox countries—because Russia is Orthodox; Slav countries—because Russia is Slav; and finally the Hungarians—because they could not exist otherwise. That was the programme!"

† *E.g.*, speech of Mr. Lloyd George to the trade unionists, January 5, 1918 (reported in the " Times " of January 7, 1918).

‡ A reference, it is probably unnecessary to explain, to the reforms of the Emperor Joseph II.
§ The Tiszas, Banffy, Horthy, Gratz—in fact, most of the stronger men.

Rampolla, this Austria is showing to-day its impotency in presence of Germany. She contributes to the pan-German league, takes Mahomet V by the hand, sends guns against the liberators of Jerusalem and massacres Poles, Czechs and South Slavs."* This appeared in the "Corriere d'Italia"; the author (Mgr. Bianchi Cagliese) was not in a position to carry with his views the direct responsibility of the Vatican, but sufficiently near to it to require that later on an ill-timed interference on his part in Irish affairs should be stopped.

Cardinal Gasparri's ideas during the war, up to October 1918, are, I think, fairly summed up in the following notes. Poland, in justice, should be independent, its frontiers being fixed according to the aspirations of the populations in question, and full freedom being given to minorities. A republican Constitution was inopportune, as the country was not ripe for it; a monarchy with the Emperor of Austria as Sovereign offered advantages, but only a personal union should be created. Galicia would accordingly cease to be part of an Austro-Hungarian State, which was to be based in future on a federal system with the widest autonomy for the separate nationalities, except the Italians on the frontier, who should go to Italy, since the legitimate claims of Italy in this respect could easily be met. The complete liquidation of Austria would leave nothing but small political groups incapable of holding their own against invasion on the part of 100,000,000 Germans.

Both in Croatia and among the Slovenes the Nationalist movement has owed much of its success to the clergy; in Dalmatia the clergy are practically all Slavs and opposed to the Italians. The Vatican had no reason to oppose the free development of these countries. But the Jugoslavia advocated in the English and French press seemed to them, I gather, something of a Utopia, difficult to realise, which, in practice, might mean, for a time at least, Serbian domination, half civilised and orthodox, in more civilised Catholic countries; or else meant the success of a revolutionary movement with the possible help of French or even Italian anticlericalism. Objections of the same order no doubt inspired a certain scepticism whether the heterogeneous elements within the boundaries of Czechoslovakia could be the basis of a durable State. But as soon as any sort of a Government was set up in either, the Vatican instructed their representative at Vienna to enter into friendly relations with it. The Vatican were, in fact, among the first to deal with the new States.

THE POLICY OF BENEDICT XV.

Benedict XV was elected on the 3rd September, 1914.

A fortnight had elapsed since Pius X had died. A popular figure in some respects, his simplicity and modest origin appealing to the sympathies of many, his reign of eleven years could claim little real success. His very election had been indirectly due to outside interference with the conclave, to an incident which had done grave injury to the prestige due to the ability of Leo XIII. This blow, deeply resented in Rome, had been followed by the rupture of relations with France and by the gradual estrangement of the Vatican from the political life of Europe. Nor were the religious reforms of his reign of a nature to interest the outside world, unconcerned with changes in the Breviary, in the administration of the Sacraments, with the codification of the Canon Law, and on the whole inclined to be hostile to the attitude adopted by the Pope and his advisers towards the Modernists. The political situation of the Papacy, so high in the preceding century, had dropped again to nothing; this was the cheerless prospect which confronted Benedict XV after his hasty and almost unceremonious coronation in the semi-privacy of the Sistine Chapel on the 6th September, 1914, the third day after his election. What steps, if any, his predecessor had taken with regard to the outbreak of war we do not know. There are circumstantial stories of a remonstrance urging the Emperor of Austria to abstain from war, whatever the wrong he might have suffered, but the Vatican have published nothing and are inclined to keep their correspondence to themselves.

From the very first the new Pope might seem to have made up his mind as to a line of policy to which he steadily adhered to the day of his death. Two days after his coronation appeared a solemn exhortation, prescribing to the faithful prayers for the termination of the scourge of war and urging rulers to put a stop to bloodshed and make peace—*properent igitur pacis inire consilia et dextras miscere*. The first Encyclical *Ad beatissimi*,† not published till the 1st November, followed the same theme : " We beseech princes and rulers that . . . . they delay not to bring back to

---

* To Foreign Office, No. 97 of August 30, 1918.
† " Ad beatissimi Apostolorum principis . . . ," diei 1 Novembris, 1914.

their peoples the life-giving blessings of peace. . . . If their rights have been violated, they can certainly find other ways and other means of obtaining a remedy.'' The allocution to the cardinals of the following January* still further defines the attitude already decided on. If it is not to be given to him, the Pope declared, to hasten the end of so much evil, it may at least be possible for him to mitigate the woes which result from it. It is not committed to him to do more than this at the present moment. It belongs chiefly to the Pope to proclaim that nobody may, on any plea whatever, offend justice and every injustice, by whatever side it may be committed, is condemned, but to involve the Pontifical authority in the contentions of the belligerents is neither appropriate nor useful; the Holy See must remain impartial. In a letter of the following June 1915, the Cardinal Secretary of State† declared that the invasion of Belgium is directly included in the words used in this allocution. A fresh exhortation appeared on the 28th July, 1915,‡ at the end of the first year of the war. As before, the subject is peace, the need to put a stop to the carnage, but for the first time there is a slight indication of peace terms. The rights and lawful aspirations of peoples should be weighed; nations do not die. The allocution of December 1916,§ while following the same line as the former ones, contained obvious allusions to the proceedings of the Russians in Galicia and to the deportations carried out in Belgium by the Germans, but it was not until August 1917 that the Pope brought forward his peace proposals; these have been treated at some length in a separate section.

The foregoing is, of course, but a brief notice of the principal utterances of the Pope with regard to his policy; it could, of course, be amplified considerably. The Vatican claimed‖ that it was in these acts that the ideas of the Pope were to be sought and not in publications by private persons, such, I gather, as stories reproduced in the " Revue de Paris," which attributed pro-German sentiments to two Roman priests, Angelucci and Lucantonio, neither connected with the Vatican, and to a Benedetto Governa, never identified. There was also a pamphlet by a certain Henri Bafile, " La formola della pace," a copy of which was given to me by one of the French (M. Gonse), with an assurance that it was inspired by the Vatican. It was another Frenchman (Mgr. Le Floch)¶ who pointed out the absence of any ground for the supposition; the pamphlet itself contained no reference to religion or moral considerations : neither God nor even the Pope was mentioned. Much greater trouble was raised by a French journalist, M. Latapie, who, contrary to usual practice, was allowed an interview and published an account of it, which was contradicted. Here we have a conflict as to what passed, the Pope on one side and M. Latapie on the other.

These pronouncements of the Holy See are practically all outside my personal experience which dates only from the very end of 1916. By that time the Pope's policy had been repeatedly affirmed and defined. The peace proposals of the following August were in a measure but the logical development and consequence of it. This was the situation with which, as far as I am concerned, the mission was called upon to deal.

Strict impartiality was therefore the declared attitude of the Pope towards the belligerents; the neutral position thus assumed was to be turned to account in efforts to alleviate the sufferings caused by the war, an intention first indicated in the

---

* Allocutio habita in Consistorio diei 22 Januarii, 1915.
† Cardinal Gasparri to M. van den Heuvel, June 1915.
‡ Apostolica Exhortatio ad populos belligerantes eorumque rectores (July 28, 1915).
§ Allocutio . . . . die 4 decembris, 1916.
‖ Cardinal Gasparri to M. van den Heuvel, July 6, 1915 :—

"A votre pénétration ne peut certainement pas échapper que la vraie pensée de Sa Sainteté doit être puisée dans ses actes publics et officiels, et non dans les publications ou narrations privées ; souvent la passion politique fait mal entendre les mots, qui, ensuite, répétés de bouche en bouche, prennent quelquefois des proportions fantastiques."

A somewhat similar letter was sent to the Archbishop of Paris a few days later. To the Archbishop of Lyons the Cardinal Secretary of State had already written in November 1914 :—

"Votre Eminence n'ignore pas que, dès le début de la guerre actuelle, le Saint-Siège, embrassant dans une même sollicitude les pasteurs et les fidèles de l'Église universelle, s'est proposé de garder et a constamment maintenu l'impartialité la plus stricte et la plus absolue à l'égard des différentes nations belligérantes, et qu'il l'a recommandé d'une façon péremptoire à la presse catholique et à celle de Rome en particulier. . . . Je puis vous assurer que ces directions et ces conseils du Saint-Siège ont été fidèlement suivis soit par l' Osservatore Romano,' qui est sous sa dépendance directe, soit par le ' Corriere d'Italia,' principal organe de la Societá editrice " (the Catholic group of papers).

When Italy came into the war, the " Corriere," using its liberty, took its stand on the side of the Entente.
¶ " La Politique de Benoît XV," by Mgr. Le Floch.

Pope's address to the Cardinals on Christmas Eve, 1914,* and, as mentioned above. some days afterwards in a Consistorial Allocution (the 22nd January, 1915).

Could the Pope's attitude have been different? Subject to criticism on points of detail, could his policy in general have been other than it was? An ardent Catholic might, indeed, be inspired by the thought of a supreme moral and divinely constituted authority judging, and if necessary condemning the faults, the crimes committed by nations and their rulers in the pursuit of their aims, legitimate and other. Consciously or not, such a feeling on the part of a Catholic would be strengthened by the prestige to be acquired by his Church, should it thus vindicate a right to be regarded, not only within, but without its fold, as the supreme arbiter of Governments, the sanction necessary to the most decisive of their acts. But reflection might hesitate to entrust such a task to the co-operation of a State Department, subject to the limitations common to even the best intentioned bureaucratic organisations. We are dealing with political questions, questions which touch the interests of millions who are not of the Pope's allegiance, owing no obedience to him. What trouble has there not been in the past at the mere suggestion of authority being exercised in such cases!

No Pope, not even a Gregory VII, succeeded in establishing such a power, and that in a world which professed submission to him. None have apparently ever taught with authority that such a power existed.†

But support for a forward policy on the part of the Pope was by no means solely Catholic. What are we to make of the advocacy, let us say, of the leader writer of the "Times"? What was wanted there might well seem to have been an act which would have hampered the military efficiency of the enemy, have rendered it difficult for some of his subjects to fight for him. It must have been evident before the mission reached Rome, that any idea of the kind was out of the question. And it is Geneva, of all places, which puts forward in a few lines one of the best defences of Benedict XV and his policy.

"En résumé, pour apprécier avec équité la politique du Saint-Siège, il faut en comprendre la raison profonde. Ne pouvant aspirer, en plein vingtième siècle, à être le juge suprême et l'arbitre de l'humanité—que ses adversaires les plus résolus, les anticléricaux, lui reprochent, par un paradoxe singulier, de ne pas être—le Pape s'est fait partout le protecteur des catholiques, individus et collectivités. Lorsque le recul de l'histoire permettra d'apprécier toutes les

---

* Allocutio XXX habita die XXIV Decembris, MDCCCCXIV, ad collegium purpuratorum patrum . . . . :—

"We intend to use every effort to hasten the end of this unparalleled disaster, or at least to alleviate its sad consequences. . . . . *Clama, ne cessa.*"

The Pope's efforts, often involving negotiations with the various Powers concerned, were in many instances successful. They included:—

The exchange of prisoners of war unfit for further military service.
Liberation and exchange of detained civilians.
Hospital treatment for sick and wounded. As the result of protracted negotiations, arrangements were made by which, in certain conditions, sick and wounded could be transferred to Switzerland.
Sunday rest for prisoners of war.
A variety of services, such as the Vatican as a neutral was in a favourable position to render: The Vatican Bureau of Information for enquiry about missing soldiers, conservation of graves, forwarding of correspondence to and from invaded countries, food in relief of war-stricken countries benevolence to prisoners of war, &c.

The intervention of the Vatican did not always lead to a happy result. On the initiative of the Archbishop of Cologne, where an aerial bombardment on May 18, 1918, had caused a number of casualties, the Vatican proposed a cessation of attacks during the Feast of Corpus Christi. The proposal was conveyed officially to His Majesty's Government, and formally accepted; through the Archbishop of Paris it reached the French Government, which gave no formal acceptance. The understanding was observed as between British and Germans on May 30 (Thursday). The French did not bombard Cologne on May 30, and the Germans, by order of Field-Marshal von Hindenburg, did not bombard Paris on June 2, but a shot from the German long-range gun struck the Madeleine Church on the afternoon of May 30. The French Government accused the Germans of bad faith. It appears that the legal date for observing the feast in France is not the Thursday, according to the liturgical calendar, but the following Sunday (in this case, June 2), as fixed by the concordat between Pius VII and the First Consul in 1801. But there was an angry attack from M. Pichon all the same.

† "Les Moines d'Occident": par le Comte de Montalembert. Edition 1882. Tome VII, chapitre 7 St. Grégoire VII, moine et Pape:—

" . . . . Dans tout cela Grégoire VII a triomphé et son triomphe s'est prolongé jusqu'à nous. Le seul point où son œuvre n'ait pas duré, bien que continuée avec autant de courage que de constance par ses successeurs pendant trois siècles; le seul point où l'avenir ne lui ait point donné complètement raison, ç'a été dans l'établissement du pouvoir d'arbitrage suprême entre les couronnes et les peuples. . . . Il n'avait du reste jamais prétendu lier la conscience des chrétiens par aucun décret solennel au sujet de ce pouvoir qui pouvait être un bienfait pour la société temporelle, mais qui n'était absolument nécessaire ni à l'autorité, ni à la liberté de l'Eglise."

complexités infinies de cette guerre, il est probable que nos descendants seront moins sévères pour Benoît XV—chef hiérarchique, ne l'oublions pas, du noble et courageux Cardinal Mercier*—que ne le sont aujourd'hui ses contemporains et ses fidèles eux-mêmes."—(" Journal de Genève," the 24th August, 1918.)

The Pope's policy of working for the alleviation of suffering caused by the war met in some cases with the co-operation of the British Government; notably, though the proposal was rejected when first put forward by the Vatican, as regards the internment of wounded in Switzerland. To my recollection, intervention on behalf of individuals was regularly rejected in England, though on our side we reaped benefit, as, for instance when the Hadfield brothers condemned to death by the Turks were saved with the help of the Apostolic Delegate at Constantinople. On one or two occasions an opportunity for enlisting the moral support of the Vatican against inhumanity on the part of the enemy seems to have been lost. At our request the same delegate opened negotiations on our behalf with the Turks about the exchange of prisoners and was left in the lurch. Much the same occurred when we invoked the intervention of the Holy See with regard to the torpedoing of hospital ships. In the first case, our change of attitude would seem to have been due to the Quai d'Orsay†; possibly also in the second.

Stories and Reports.

M. Caillaux's visit to Rome was made the occasion for numerous attacks on the Pope; in connection with it a regular campaign was carried on throughout the year 1917, originated by the French Embassy, where M. Barrère, with the support of Baron Sonnino, was working against the re-establishment of diplomatic relations between France and the Holy See. The Vatican were perfectly well aware of these proceedings and the situation was poisoned by them. On the collapse of the accusations—a detailed account of the business is given further on—the air became clearer. The story of the alleged justification by the Vatican of the German submarine blockade was found to have its alleged origin in a statement attributed to the Spanish Ambassador, who was represented as having repeated a statement made to him by Cardinal Gasparri. An enquiry from Señor Calbeton and his indignant denial were enough to show that the whole story had been invented. It is less easy to demonstrate that the reported intrigues with the United States Government on the part of Cardinal Gasparri could not have taken place; according to the stories, clumsy and childish methods were adopted for carrying out a most dangerous policy, the exposure of which would have hopelessly compromised the Church in half the Catholic world. That is not my experience of the ways of the Vatican. Nor is it easy to deal with the anonymous revelations respecting their inner thoughts; there might be reason for identifying the source of this information with a person whom I think to have been mistaken more than once in his ideas and still more mistaken as to the degree of confidence which he inspired here.

Much information came from Switzerland. The Pope's peace note of August 1917, had not been published for many days before a secret report traced it to a committee composed of the Father General of Jesuits (Count Ledochowski); the Papal representative (M. Marchetti) and the Bishop of Coire. Immediately after the revelation in the early spring of 1918, about the negotiations of Prince Sixtus of Bourbon, a "well-informed source" revealed that the terms of the Emperor Charles's letter had been drawn up with the help of Herr Erzberger, by the General of the Jesuits, Mgr. Marchetti and the Bishop of Coire. The story might pass muster for once; but twice? Following on this came an official statement that the Papal representative in question was a most dangerous German agent. The late Pope may well have been the last ruler in the world to employ agents to carry out a policy other than his own; few representatives can have had less latitude for pursuing personal fads and fancies. Here then was an assertion which, if it could be shown to be true, would have thrown instructive light on the real attitude of the Holy See and might have been of invaluable help to the work of this mission. But the source was too secret for communication.

Had we, then, really here a valuable clue, turned to little account? Or merely another story like the inventions of the Caillaux-Vatican revelations? Rome was the one place where the matter might have been sifted, where the information to be gained would have been of real value.

---

* It was Cardinal Mercier who, in 1920, advocated an independent inquiry into the acts of the British Government in Ireland. There was no echo in Rome of this idea, which was clearly quite foreign to the policy of the Pope

† See my despatch to Foreign Office, No. 12, Consular, of April 9, 1917.

Much of all this bore indications of coming from military or quasi-military sources, of having been collected with much industry but less discrimination. This was not least required in the case of the contributions of foreign colleagues with their own ends in view. One finds, too, pretended revelations of dead secrets,* coupled with errors as to facts easily ascertainable, well known to a slight acquaintance with the subject.

In the course of 1920 we have an account, possibly from the same sources, of a committee formed in Switzerland to decide the policy to be followed by the Vatican in the affairs of Ireland. There was, if I remember right, as I have not the reference under my hand, a German Monsignore, the Bishop of Lausanne (a French Swiss) and a few other impossibilities, none of whom, as far as I know, had ever had anything to do with the country. The only Irish name given was Kelly.† The story was nonsense. Vatican business is not done in that way, and an account of the consultation which actually took place, of course at Rome, is given elsewhere. This must have been about the last of the stories of the kind; the supply ceased on the withdrawal of the improvised organisations of the war and the return of business to the charge of the Legation.

One rather fruitful source of gossip was an Italian institution describing itself as the "Difesa Interna," carried on privately for patriotic motives by a certain Signor Pietro Lanino. Some slight service or civility, credited to me in the Balkans by the family—they were interested in schemes for Italian penetration there—was rewarded by an abundant supply of their memoranda, which required many grains of salt. Signor Lanino tendered himself as a witness in the trial in March 1919 of one Cavallini, mixed up in the intrigues here of Caillaux, but was laughed out of court, though Italian procedure as to admitting evidence is not that of the Old Bailey. It might have been unnecessary to refer to him if some of his information without indication of source had not come back to me from the Foreign Office, which it had reached by another channel. I feel sure that he was honest and, on his own subjects, Italian economic interests and a commentary of Machiavelli, well informed.

THE POPE'S PEACE PROPOSALS OF AUGUST 1917.

The autumn of 1916 was drawing to an end. The Allied offensive on the Somme had not led to decisive results, except to great losses on both sides, but in the preceding twelve months the Central Powers had swept over a large part of South-East Europe and, though brought no nearer to breaking the force of their principal opponents, had thus acquired valuable assets in the event of discussion with them. On this account there was some anxiety in London at the time I was leaving lest the Pope, in his well-known desire for the speedy return of peace, should be led to support schemes which, however much they might be disguised, would necessarily be founded on the recent German successes in the field. In fact, shortly afterwards Herr von Bethmann-Hollweg put forward his peace proposals,‡ drawn up in conjunction with Count Burian, the note to the Cardinal Secretary of State by the Prussian Minister being dated the 12th December, 1916. Cardinal Gasparri urged on Lord Balfour that it would be a mistake to oppose a flat refusal; such a course might prejudice the cause of the Allies in the eyes of neutrals and, perhaps, even of their own people. If the Germans were called upon to state their terms, and if these were impossible, the moral advantage in the continuance of the struggle would be on the side of the Allies. He believed the terms would be moderate. With this the action of the Vatican ended; the Pope himself told me that the moment did not appear to him suitable for making suggestions to the belligerents, a conclusion which may well have been confirmed by the cold reception given to President Wilson's intervention in the discussion.

During the summer of 1917 the situation had changed. The submarine campaign, after six months, had not given the results hoped for in Germany, and in the Reichstag, Erzberger, challenging the figures of the German Admiralty, demanded the conclusion of peace by agreement. A few days afterwards, on the 19th July, Fehrenbach, of the Centre Party, carried a resolution in favour of such a peace. In Austria the general feeling was even more pessimistic. In the spring

---

* *E.g.*, confidential print, "The War," November 19, section 1 (1915).

† There were at least three or four of the name, connected to various degrees with the movement. I think, for what it is worth, they are correctly sorted out in my reply. One at least was known to me personally.

‡ "The tone of the peace proposal was very arrogant." So Count Czernin, who succeeded Count Burian some ten days afterwards (see "In the World War," p. 139). The reply of the Allies merely termed it "illusory."

various efforts had been made by the Emperor Charles and Count Czernin to bring about peace; details may or may not have been known to the Vatican; but, in any case, they were well acquainted with the general situation in the monarchy.* It was in these circumstances that the Cardinal Secretary of State, sending for me on the 9th August, asked me to forward to His Majesty's Government the Pope's peace proposals with the request that they would also communicate them to the Allied States not represented at the Vatican. Briefly, the proposals were :—

Moral force of law to take the place of material force of arms. Simultaneous and reciprocal reduction of armaments. Arbitration.

Once the supremacy of law established, removal of any obstacle to free communication between nations; true freedom and community of the seas.

Complete and reciprocal condonation as regards reparations and war indemnities, a solution justified by the immense benefits of disarmament. If in certain cases there are special reasons to the contrary, they are to be weighed with justice and equity.

Reciprocal restitution of territories at present occupied. Total evacuation of Belgium by Germany with guarantee of absolute political, military and economic independence as regards every Power. Evacuation of French territory by Germany and restitution of German colonies by other belligerent Powers.

Examination in a conciliatory spirit of territorial questions, as, for example, those in dispute between Italy and Austria, and Germany and France, taking into account the aspirations of the peoples concerned.

Examination in the same spirit of equity and justice of the other territorial and political questions at issue, notably Armenia, the Balkan States and Poland.

Hopes of the Pope for the early conclusion of a terrible struggle which appeared more and more to be a useless massacre.

On handing the proposals to me, the Cardinal Secretary of State made some observations in explanation. Although the belligerents were still far apart, recent declarations had brought their points of view nearer together. The Reichstag had voted in favour of peace without indemnity or annexation, while English statesmen were speaking of reparation rather than of annihilation. The belligerents were certainly nearer, and it was the Pope's desire to see whether they could be brought into agreement on the basis of these recent utterances. The words with regard to freedom of the seas had been taken from the speeches of Mr. Wilson and Mr. Winston Churchill. As regards reparation and indemnities, the clause respecting " special reasons in certain cases " was meant to apply, and he thought to apply solely, to Belgium. Germany had declared her desire for peace, but without stating her terms; the sincerity of this declaration would now be tested.

The proposals were met by violent attacks in the English press. To the " Times " they were anathema from beginning to end, the outcome of German inspiration, an accusation from which even the special mention of the reconstitution of the ancient Kingdom of Poland did not save them. More from the same source followed in the " New Europe," in which the revelations of an anonymous Allied Catholic diplomatist played a part. In the German press they scarcely fared any better. According to the " Kölnische Zeitung," the Pontiff " had allowed himself to be used as a tool by the Allies, and especially by England through the British Minister to the Vatican."

A courteous reply, received with satisfaction at the Vatican, was at once sent by Lord Balfour. The King had gladly complied with the Pope's wishes, and had transmitted at once copies of the proposals to the heads of Allied States with whom the Holy See was not in diplomatic relation; the King had received these proposals with the most sincere appreciation of the lofty and benevolent intentions which animated the Pope, and His Majesty's Government would study them with the closest and most serious attention. The message did much to counteract the annoyance caused by the tirades of the " Times." It was followed within a week by a further message; His Majesty's Government had not so far had an opportunity of consulting their Allies as to a reply. In their opinion no progress was likely to be made until their enemies had announced the objects for which they were carrying on war, the restoration and reparation they were prepared to make, and the means by

---

* Count Czernin's report to the Emperor on the desperate condition of the monarchy was in Erzberger's hands, and was not kept secret by him. See Czernin, " In the World War," p. 155.

which the world could be guaranteed against a repetition of the present horrors. They had owned themselves in the wrong in the case of Belgium, but even then there was no clear intimation of an intention to restore its independence or repair the injuries they had inflicted. The Allies had made a statement in reply to President Wilson; no corresponding statements had been made by Germany or Austria, and it appeared useless to attempt to bring the belligerents into agreement until the points on which they differed were clearly known.

These views were to be expressed on behalf of His Majesty's Government, but M. Ribot, on hearing of them, sent an urgent communication through the French Embassy, expressing regret that he had not been consulted, and stating that the French Government were anxious to associate themselves in the *démarche* that I had been instructed to make. I made a careful translation of the telegram in the same form, that is, in the form of a message addressed to me; it was essential that the cogent arguments employed should lose none of their force when repeated, while it was necessary to avoid danger of misunderstanding lest, if they were not precisely adhered to and understood, the Cardinal Secretary of State should be led to look on them as an overture towards the acceptance of the Vatican's mediation. I read the message to the Cardinal, who listened with attention, and asked if he might make a note of what I had said; as a matter of courtesy, and to save him trouble, I handed to him the note which I had used. He then remarked that Germany had already announced her intention of restoring Belgium to independence. I demurred and the Cardinal appealed to the resolution of the Reichstag in favour of peace without annexations. I answered that the Reichstag did not command in Germany;* moreover, we had no authoritative text. The following day the Cardinal asked me to give Lord Balfour the following reply :—

> "The Cardinal Secretary of State reserves to himself to answer the telegram after having received from the German Government an official declaration relative to Belgium which he has asked them for."

Some conversation followed, and the Cardinal asked me for an opinion on his reply and the reception it might meet with. As I pointed out in my report to Lord Balfour of the conversation, I was anxious (in the absence of any instruction which would have allowed me to act otherwise) to avoid saying anything which might appear to give encouragement to discussions with the German Government; at the same time, it was not for me to take exception to the answer he wished me to send to London. I therefore confined myself to pointing out that, as stated in the telegram sent to me, a declaration of the policy of the Central Powers as regards Belgium appeared to be called for; his Eminence, I added, would, however, remember that Belgium was one of many issues between the belligerents.

With the desire of acting with the strictest loyalty towards the French, I called on M. Barrère, the French Ambassador, and telling him that the French Government had associated themselves in the *démarche* that I had been instructed to make, showed him the translation of the telegram sent to me. Subsequently M. Ribot took exception to what had occurred; the communication should have been verbal, but had taken the form of a written document which had opened a discussion on the fate of Belgium.† Can either of these statements, rather obviously inspired by M. Barrère, be considered as being in accordance with the facts? A circular telegram, sent on the 30th August, shows that His Majesty's Government looked on the instructions as an expression of the view that it was for the Central Powers first to send a reply to the proposal made by the Pope. At the Vatican there was no misapprehension; there was no question, it was declared in a communiqué to the Agence Havas, of an overture‡—quite the contrary. The brief communication made to Cardinal Gasparri enumerated, in his opinion, with particular insistence on the Belgian question, the reasons why peace was considered by His Majesty's Government to be impossible.

---

* The Reichstag majority resolution of July 19, 1917.
It is not the Cardinal's view which is supported by Count Czernin " In the World War," p. 165 :—

  "The peace resolutions passed in the Reichstag proved nothing, or at any rate not enough, for the Reichstag is not the real exponent of the Empire in the world war."

† No such view was taken by the Vatican. On the contrary, a communiqué of the Secretariate of State ran as follows :—

  "C'est le 24 août 1917 que le Comte de Salis, Ministre d'Angleterre auprès du Saint-Siège se rendit au Vatican pour y transmettre verbalement le contenu d'un télégramme reçu de son Gouvernement. Il ne laissa pas une note au vrai sens du mot, mais il se borna à préciser par écrit les termes de sa communication."

‡ See " Figaro " of July 30, 1919, and elsewhere.

Within three weeks President Wilson's reply was received and communicated by this mission to the Vatican. It was argued that the Pope proposed a return to the *status quo ante bellum*, which would not be a sound basis for carrying out the programme he put forward. The object of the war was the delivery of the peoples of the world from the menace of an irresponsible Government, between which and the German people a sharp distinction was drawn. The word of the present rulers of Germany could not be accepted as a guarantee without conclusive evidence of the will and purpose of the will of the German people. After some discussion between the Allies, including, I understand, the consideration of a French suggestion for a reply which was not found acceptable, it was decided by the Great Powers to express concurrence with President Wilson's views, and not to make a further reply. Belgium answered separately. Meanwhile, notes were received by the Vatican from the German Government, Austria-Hungary, Bavaria, Bulgaria and Turkey. The German reply did not go beyond generalities, and, in particular, no reference was made to war aims or to Belgium.* In the Pope's judgment it was not explicit, but left the door open for further discussion, a view which was recorded in Cardinal Gasparri's note of the 28th September, 1917. This was certainly true as regards the letter of the Emperor Charles, but Herr von Kühlmann's speech of the 9th October, 1917, as well as papers subsequently published, such as the letter of the German Chancellor Michaelis to Count Czernin of the 17th August, 1917† or to the Papal Nuncio Pacelli at the end of September,‡ show conclusively that the German Government were in no way prepared to state their war aims or to come to any agreement on such fundamental questions as either Belgium or Alsace-Lorraine. All along both the Russian and Italian Foreign Ministers had shown themselves opposed to joining in any reply on the part of the Allies, and at the end of October Baron Sonnino at last showed his hand by pronouncing in the Chamber an offensive diatribe against the Vatican. His object in doing so is difficult to define. Whatever satisfaction he may have given to his own, he placed several supporters of the Government in a humiliating position and weakened the coalition on which it rested. But the speech was hardly pronounced before the Italian troops had begun to give way at Caporetto, and, in presence of the disaster which followed, all other considerations were apparently forgotten.

At the National Assembly in Weimar, Herr Erzberger, at the end of July 1919 delivered a speech attacking the preceding German Governments for having persisted in the war and for having failed to try to make peace when they could quite well have done so. Notably, he declared, in August 1917 the British Government had made an offer, to which the French Government had adhered; it was a well-founded and carefully thought-out step with a view to peace§ well calculated to bring forward the idea of reconciliation between nations. For four weeks no answer had been given, and then there was a refusal to give the desired explanation (respecting Belgium); it was in this way that the English attempt was disposed of. The speech created some sensation, and accounts were published in various papers, purporting to relate the truth. None of them seem to me to have been quite accurate, the French accounts in particular being faulty.‖ Finally, the Foreign Office published a Blue Book with the principal documents, the telegrams being, of course, paraphrased. I have accordingly given in some detail my experience of what occurred. Whatever may have been the hesitations in the United Kingdom and the opposition on the part of its Allies to diplomatic action, the effect at the Vatican of the various published documents appeared to me on my return to Rome to have been very favourable to British interests. His Majesty's Government, said Cardinal Gasparri, had nothing to conceal; they had played a most honourable part in the matter. The Nuncio at Munich, Mgr. Pacelli, spoke to me in the same sense; the peace proposals had shown that the real obstacle to peace lay in the ambitions of the German military party.

* " Cette réponse ne contenait pas un mot relatif à la Belgique."—Benoît XV. By M. van den Heuvel (Belgian Minister), p. 23.
† " In the World War." p. 157.
‡ " Écho de Paris," July 29, 1919, and other papers. The letter seems to have been dated on or about September 24, 1919.
§ " . . . . eine wohlbegründete, wohlüberlegte Friedensaktion. . . ."
I was away in Montenegro when the speech was made, with little communication with the outside world, and for some time the only information available was a rather garbled version of the story in a Croat newspaper of Agram.
‖ Among these might be included a rather poisonous attack in the " Paris-Midi " of July 31, 1919, which I may be wrong to think of attributing to M. Canet or his superiors. The editor, M. Millet, was at that time, according to a report from His Majesty's Embassy at Paris, employed at the Quai d'Orsay. (Lord Hardinge to Lord Curzon, No. 918 of April 11, 1922.)

Since the termination of the war various publications have dealt with the question*—Herr Scheidemann, Dr. Helfferich, Dr. Martin Spahn and Herr Erzberger. Scheidemann's pamphlet, though short, gives important details, especially the comment of the Chancellor Michaelis on the British communication acknowledging receipt of the Pope's proposals :—

"In my opinion our efforts should be directed to throwing on to our opponents the odium for any failure of the Pope's mediation and to putting them in the wrong, as was the case with our peace action last December. I intend, therefore, to treat the business in a dilatory manner. . . . ."

The Vatican would not have known this at the time, though the pamphlet was brought to their notice later on, but they were, of course, well aware by the latter half of September 1917, from the instructions given to the Prussian Minister at Munich, that, if they had up to then believed, from Herr Erzberger or others, in the desire of Berlin for a peace in possible conditions, they were in the wrong. According to his own account, Herr von Bethmann Hollweg, on the 26th June, 1917, *i.e.*, a few days before his fall, replied to the Nuncio in Munich, Mgr. Pacelli, that Germany was prepared to restore the complete independence of Belgium.† A similar enquiry must have been put to the new Chancellor, Herr Michaelis, at an interview which took place on the 24th July, 1917, but I do not think we have any direct evidence on the point. The account just published in the Emperor William's Memoirs of the audience given to Mgr. Pacelli in June 1917 has been met by a statement issued by the Nunciature, which is said to be substantially different.‡ The Nuncio, it says, handed to the Emperor a letter from the Pope, in which the latter expressed the anguish caused to him by the continuation of the war, and the Nuncio himself, without entering into details, then warmly exhorted the Emperor to put an end to these evils, even at the cost of renouncing one or other of Germany's war aims. The Emperor's reply was to the effect that the war was one of defence against British aims of destruction.

THE POPE AND THE PEACE CONFERENCE.

Much was printed and said of the desire of the Pope to take part in the Peace Conference; in the pursuit of its attainment considerations of the gravest moral character were alleged to be put aside. Accusations of this kind were freely made by Baron Sonnino and others. I cannot speak from personal experience of the years 1915 and 1916, but the attitude consistently maintained towards me from first to last by Cardinal Gasparri was that the Holy See were most anxious to afford any possible help as intermediaries towards the negotiation of peace; by a mediation which could only be efficacious with the consent of both parties. On no account could they or would they take part in any conferences at which one group would dictate its conditions to the other. This policy applied equally to every stage of the war; to the earlier part of it, when it seemed likely that Germany would get the upper hand, or to the latter part of it, when the Allies were victorious. There might seem little reason to cast doubt on this definition of their views, since the Holy See could scarcely put its signature to an instrument which imposed loss or humiliation to any considerable group of members of the Church. The declared policy of the Pope, pursued on every possible occasion, was the restoration of peace by agreement, since for years no other solution of the struggle appeared to Rome to be attainable. This policy was steadily adhered to from the moment of Pope Benedict's accession, and in pursuit of it the Pope refused to do anything which would have brought about a breach of the Holy See with any of the belligerents, either with Germany, for example, over the invasion of Belgium or with Russia in connection with their proceedings in Galicia. Nor was the Pope's decision to be shaken by a storm of adverse criticism, by repeated accusations of the readiness to subordinate morality to political aims. A troublesome situation was the result, as British policy was not prepared to accept the Pope's

---

* "Papst, Kaiser und Sozialdemocratie in ihren Friedensbemühungen im Sommer 1917"; von Philip Scheidemann. Berlin, 1921.
  "Die päptliche Friedensvermittelung"; von Martin Spahn. 1919.
  "Die Friedensbemühungen im Weltkrieg"; von Staatsminister Dr. Helfferich. 1919.
  M. Erzberger. "Erlebnisse im Weltkriege. . . . ." 1920.
† Th. von Bethmann Hollweg, "Betrachtungen zum Weltkrieg," Part II, p. 212 :—

    "In reply to a question with regard to our aims in Belgium, I answered that we should restore her complete independence. It was incompatible with this complete independence, should Belgium fall politically, militarily and financially under the domination of England and France. . . . ."

‡ "Pall Mall Gazette," October 17, 1922, and elsewhere. (I have not seen the original.)

attitude as conducive to its aims. Newspaper articles in London,* some full of imputations of base motive, but poor in argument, made matters worse, and throughout the best part of the year 1917 there were indications of an impression at the Vatican that, if peace should get within reach, the obstacles would be raised by the Allies rather than by Germany. All this changed after the Pope's peace proposals; the brief comments of His Majesty's Government resulted in proving to the Vatican that the *sine quâ non* of the Pope's suggestions, justice to Belgium, was not conceded by the ruling authorities at Berlin. From that time on no further move was made in the direction of mediation until the moment when in October 1918 the Vatican supported the offer of a separate peace on the part of Austria.

The armistice followed; the war was over and peace, the object for which the Pope had worked, was in sight, but a great Empire had fallen and it was not for the Pope to join in rejoicings which marked the humiliation of so many of his people. No invitations were, of course, issued by the Vatican, but it was known that there would be a service, to be held forthwith at the Church of Ara Coeli on the Capitol. A long wait—we are in Rome—in the chilly November evening, and the Duke of Genoa, Lieutenant-General of the Kingdom, was escorted to his place under the direction of Mgr. Respighi and his assistants, the Pope's chief master of ceremonies, while the Cardinal-Vicar, the Pope's representative in Rome, intoned the *Te Deum*, taken up in the church by the choir sent from the Sistine Chapel and in the dense crowd outside. The occasion, the unequalled surroundings, the significance of not a few details, might make such a scene difficult to forget.

The official celebration of the victory took place a few days after at the Altar of the Fatherland, recently instituted on the other side of the Capitol. There were speeches, but no religious ceremony and little or no reference to Allies or assistance, human or other. Cardinal Gasparri told me subsequently how the Pope had remarked that on the announcement of the armistice the House of Commons, with the Prime Minister at their head, had adjourned to the neighbouring church to hold a service of thanksgiving.

THE DEATH OF BENEDICT XV AND ELECTION OF PIUS XI.

In the latter half of January 1922 the Pope fell ill. His malady, apparently at first a cold, soon turned to disquieting symptoms, and within a week, on the 22nd January, he was dead. A frail-looking man, small and giving rise to suspicion that some defect in his growth had at an early age hindered the proper development of lungs or even heart, he had shown in the seven years of his reign an astonishing power of resistance, but there was little reserve of force, and he died with very little struggle, worn out and exhausted.

His career had been political. His first appointment in the Secretariate of State was due to Mgr. Rampolla, whom he subsequently accompanied to the Nunciature in Spain, returning to Rome later when Rampolla became Cardinal and the Minister of Leo XIII. Rampolla's exclusion at the following conclave by the veto of Austria and the intrigues of Berlin must have been a severe blow to his hopes, though he remained for some time longer in the Vatican till promotion to the See of Bologna seemed to exile him definitely from any further chance of playing a part in political affairs. In speculations with regard to alleged pro-German leanings, it is well to remember that he stood for the policy of Leo XIII and Rampolla and was elected on that ground. The lack of sympathy between Rampolla and the Triple Alliance need not be dwelt upon here; one striking piece of evidence of it, the vulgar abuse heaped on Rampolla by Cardinal Hohenlohe in his letters to his brother the Chancellor,† was never published in regular book form.

Such were his antecedents. His training had been under the two ablest politicians whom the Vatican have had for a very long time. Might it be maintained, however, that to the end he was but the pupil of his masters./ Popularity of any sort he did not enjoy, but his Genoese tenacity won by slow degrees a measure of success for him; the best proof might seem the determination of the Cardinals and of his successor that his policy was to be continued. No Papal election, by all accounts, was ever followed by so few changes.

The Cardinals went into conclave on the 2nd February, as soon as the nine days' funeral ceremonies were over. By the Constitutions of Pius X, drawn up with a view to prevent outside interference such as that of the Central Powers at his own election, the procedure had become very strict and brief. No one could say with

* " Times," " Morning Post," " Spectator." I have not thought it necessary to give the references.
† Published, I think, in a periodical. *Query* " Oesterreichische Rundschau."

certainty what was going on, but there could be no secret as to the existence of two tendencies, as indeed on almost every similar occasion, one party described, according to the sympathies of the narrator, as religious or reactionary, the other as political or progressive. " Zelanti " and " Politici " were the old Roman names. The former centred round Cardinal Merry del Val, who was supported by Cardinal Boggiani, a Dominican monk, who had just resigned the Archbishopric of Genoa, where his disciplinary measures had provoked too much friction and Cardinal De Lai, head of the Consistorial Congregation. The life and soul of the latter was Cardinal Gasparri; as Camerlengo he became the executive organ of the Holy See the moment the Pope had breathed his last, and his strong personality seemed to dominate the situation from that moment till the peremptory order *Extra omnes!* left us with nothing but guesswork. Was there ever any question of his candidature, and why not ? Age, perhaps, but he is not really an old man, though at times with doubtful health ; or the tradition of the Holy See that neither the Camerlengo nor the Secretary of State are ever elected. And he was both. The first place among the group with him would be that of Cardinal Maffi, Archbishop of Pisa, already much favoured at the time of the last election and credited with advanced ideas as to the advantages of an understanding with the Italian Government and Court; not acceptable, in conse- quence to the opposing side or indeed to many of the neutrals. After him the new Archbishop of Milan, Cardinal Ratti. It may seem unnecessary to discuss what might have happened if he had not been chosen; we should then have come to the compromise candidates, the Patriarch of Venice, Cardinal La Fontaine, or perhaps Cardinal Lualdi, sent not unsuccessfully to Palermo to put things in order. There was also the Archbishop of Benevento, Ascolesi, the youngest of the Cardinals; he is mentioned as he may be heard of again.

The moment had not yet come for a non-Italian Pope, though not so distant as many seem to think. Report will have it that from the start there was a strong group for Cardinal Merry del Val, but there was no chance of its increase. Cardinal van Rossum, Prefect of Propaganda, was one of the foreigners having a thorough knowledge of the Vatican administration; ascetic, unpopular as being strict and unyielding, he would have been a far stronger candidate than, let us say, Cardinal Mercier, whose name, it may be without much reflection, was talked of among those of the *Entente*. But, though poles apart in everything, neither the last Spaniard, Alexander VI* nor Dutch Adrian† have left Rome with any desire to renew the experiment.

From the outer balcony overlooking the great square before St. Peter's the newly elected Pope gave his first blessing; this was repeated a few days afterwards on his coronation, which took place with the least possible delay, as the new reign only dates from that moment. Not for fifty years‡ had this been done, and the act was hailed at once as an important step towards a solution of the question between the Vatican and the Quirinal. Not necessarily a reconciliation on the basis of the Law of Guarantees; outside Italy there seems to be no wish to see the Papacy fall under the control of an Italian Government; of that the " Times "§ is good evidence. Nothing further has occurred, but, whatever the differences in principle, relations in practice are perfectly smooth. In external affairs the Pope has given open support to the policy pursued by His Majesty's Government at Genoa, and it was in accord- ance with his wishes that the Belgian Government should have done the same at the subsequent meeting in London.

THE PAPAL COURT AND ADMINISTRATION.

The foregoing pages will explain to your Lordship better than any expression of opinion the leading part in the affairs of the Holy See taken by Cardinal Gasparri during the last few years. For some years professor of Canon Law at Paris, where he was frequently consulted in vexed questions, he was brought back to Rome by Pius X and entrusted, as by far the most competent authority, with reform and codification of the Canon Law; this work, which entailed great labour, has been completed in spite of hindrances due to the war. Benedict XV appointed as his Secretary of State Cardinal Ferrata, who was marked out for the post by a distinguished career abroad, ending up at the Nunciature in Paris, and, on his sudden death within two months, put in his place Cardinal Gasparri, to the surprise

---

* Alexander VI (Roderigo Borgia), 1492-1503.
† Adrian VI (of Utrecht), 1522-3.
‡ No doubt since Easter 1870. Not, as stated in many papers, since the election of Pius IX, whose conclave was held in the Quirinal, and who must have blessed the crowd in the space in front of the Consulta.
§ " Times," February 1922.

of many, as he had no previous experience of the work and it was not thought that his heart was in it. Since then the policy followed was his just as much as the late Pope's. The possibility of better relations with the Italian Government has been steadily kept in view, and neither Sonnino's attacks nor the shifting opportunism of some of his successors were allowed to discourage these hopes. The breach with France was to be made good, in spite of M. Barrère and his supporters, while all the time an attitude of strict neutrality was to be maintained towards the belligerents. The programme was difficult of execution; realisation in one particular threatened to be fatal to any other, and yet there has been a measure of success in all. Relations have been renewed with France, Sonnino and his policy have gone, and so, for the matter of that, President Wilson, distrusted at the Vatican because not understood, while at Genoa the conciliatory attitude of the Holy See has met with approbation from the British Prime Minister. In ecclesiastical matters the Cardinal has come in for criticism; in some mouths "Gasparri's methods" are another name for laxity, in others for broad views. Offenders escape lightly, and suspected modernists, if they have not had theological approbation, have had posts. A Roman priest, Bonaiuti, an incorrigible type of *enfant terrible*, was at last laid by the heels by the Holy Office and put outside, to the satisfaction of stricter minds; on the Cardinal's intervention the late Pope quashed everything and again gave him a fresh start.

Careless in dress and impatient of formalism, Cardinal Gasparri would seem in many respects to be in contrast to the Secretary of State of Piux X, Cardinal Merry del Val, brother of the Spanish Ambassador in London. The event has shown that in the Conclave there was little desire to return to the former régime, credited with aloofness from France and Italy and scant desire to co-operate with Governments such as that of the United Kingdom. But on other grounds Cardinal Merry del Val commands support, standing for strict administration in religious matters and for suppression of abuses.

For a short time from my arrival the head of the Secretariate of State was Mgr. Pacelli. His relations with this mission, such as I found them, were excellent, though at the time in question, the earlier part of 1917, he was unduly influenced by the idea that there were sincere tendencies on the part of the German Emperor and Government towards peace in possible conditions. He went as Nuncio to Munich in the spring of 1917 and learnt much there; after the peace he removed to Berlin. His successor, Mgr. Cerretti, was for long in Australia and America; he knows English well. If anything, his experience in those countries, not shared by many here since the death of Cardinal Falconio, may have been too complete and have led him to overestimate the importance of certain elements in them. He went as Nuncio to Paris last year. More than once rumours, probably from French sources, have indicated him as being on the point of succeeding Cardinal Gasparri as Secretary of State. No regular successor was appointed, but his place has been taken, without corresponding rank, by Mgr. Borgongini Duca, who so far seems to have justified his appointment. For many years the Under-Secretary, known as the "Sostituto," was Mgr. Tedeschini, a protégé of Benedict XV, and generally liked as obliging and helpful; he has gone as Nuncio to Madrid.

The "Maestro di Camera" for years was Mgr. Sanz de Samper, a Spanish-American, who, it must be supposed, owed his appointment to the need for finding at least one post of some sort for his countrymen who have no Cardinal or other recognition in Rome of their numbers. His business is more or less that of a Lord Chamberlain, ceremonies, audiences, tickets for functions and such like. In no circumstances would a foreigner of his race, not loved in Rome, have had an easy task, but Mgr. Samper was constantly in trouble, until the accusations of inefficiency and corruption levelled at his Department, especially in connection with the funeral of the late Pope, led to his substitution, as soon as Pius XI was elected, by a Milanese, Mgr. Caccia. Nothing but the tenacity of the late Pope would have kept him so long in his post. He is now Maggiordomo, in charge of the Pope's household, perhaps to a rather nominal extent.

Prefect of the Archives for some time past, Cardinal Gasquet received during the reign of the late Pope the post, specially created for him, of Librarian of the Church, the archives, library and much else in the Vatican being thus placed under his direct charge. The interest and importance of these collections, unequalled in so many respects, are not matters for this report, but the prestige which the Cardinal's qualities have given to his country requires to be taken into account. As Cardinal Gasquet is the most prominent member of the Benedictine Order, so the Dominicans are represented by Cardinal Frühwirt, an Austrian, from Linz, I think, one of the few foreigners who have held appointments as Nuncios; he was accredited by Pius X to Munich. For all that, it is difficult to associate his name with political affairs; in my time it has hardly been mentioned in connection with them. His own occupation he described as bad books, *i.e.*, black-listing works of unsound theology. Two Franciscan Cardinals have died in the last few years, Falconio and Serafini; both were influential, the former being well acquainted with both America and the Near East, the latter being till his death the Prefect of Propaganda, known to Roman slang as the "Red Pope." His place was taken by Cardinal van Rossum, a Dutchman. His jurisdiction extends over countries in which there is no regularly established hierarchy and thus includes a large part of the British Empire, *i.e.*, India, several colonies, particularly in Africa, Palestine, Egypt, &c. Some 60 per cent. of the students trained under him in Rome are British subjects, and an even larger proportion must be destined to work under the British flag. In view of this I have had reason to regret that suggestions and representations from Propaganda have so rarely found favourable consideration either in the India Office or the Colonial Office, and that, in the rather strained situation thus created, it was often difficult for me to carry out the wishes of His Majesty's Government in matters in the Near East and elsewhere which were of consequence to us. The clergy in countries with an organised hierarchy are dealt with by the Consistorial Congregation under Cardinal De Lai, able, but, I am under the impression, rather feared as a disciplinarian. The Cardinal-Vicar, *i.e.*, the Pope's representative in Rome itself, is Cardinal Pompili. I think he dates from Piux X and enjoys, anyhow, some of his popularity with the people.

Though no longer, as far as is known, weighing in the counsels of the Vatican, Cardinal Vannutelli can scarcely be omitted from any description of affairs here. As dean of the Sacred College he is in any case the figurehead, and in spite of his advanced age—he must be over 90—well able on account of his commanding appearance to take the foremost part at ceremonies, especially during the interval between the death of the late Pope and the election of his successor. His extreme kindness of heart, triumphing better than any other quality over the advance of years, has made him liable to be the victim of the adventurers who seek a hunting ground in Rome.

As in the case of the Benedictines, Dominicans and Franciscans, the Jesuits have also a representative in the Sacred College, Cardinal Billot, a Frenchman, who has reached an advanced age. I hardly know what influence he has. The head of the Jesuits, the "Black Pope," is Fr. Ledochowski, a Pole, the nephew of Cardinal Ledochowski, Archbishop of Posen-Gnesen, the opponent of Bismarck, who died at Rome in exile from his diocese. Elected shortly after the outbreak of the war in place of Fr. Wernz, he took up his quarters at Zizers in the Grisons, near Coire, in order the better to carry on from neutral territory his functions as head of an international body. As such, he explained to me, the Jesuits could not and would not take part in the politics of the moment; personally he was a Pole,* and looked forward to the freeing of his country as a result of the war. Whether because they could make no use of him or because they would have wished to see Cardinal Billot or another Frenchman in his place, in the belief that the influence of the society would thus have been at their disposal, the French treated him from the first with hostility, hampering as much as possible his communications with his people. The Italian Government, on the other hand, did all they could to help him. Elsewhere I have alluded to the stories attributing to him a share in the authorship of Pope Benedict's Peace Proposals and the Emperor Charles's letter to Prince Sixtus of Bourbon. All this may well have come from a French source, perhaps their military intelligence.

But for the reports from Switzerland alluded to elsewhere, it might scarcely have occurred to me to make mention here of the Bishop of Coire. The See was once of considerable importance, its holder was a Prince of the Empire,† but it fell on evil times; Calvinist reformers, peasant land hunger, a contested election in the 16th century. The present bishop, quite incorrectly stated to be a German, is from the Grison Oberland, and author of poems and other literary work in Romantch. Energetic and patriotic, he took, from his first appointment years ago, energetic steps to stop the missions to the Italian stonecutters and casual labourers in his diocese serving the ends of the insidious propaganda promoted by Italian

---

* Why in a part of the Foreign Office he was written down a German, I cannot say; perhaps in confusion with his predecessor.

† Balzac levelled his jokes at it. In his time it could boast of neither wealth nor learning, and as local feeling would not tolerate an outsider, the saying had it that the only qualifications required for a bishop were to be Grison, speak Romantch and know the Pater.

"Irredentist" associations for the annexation of territory to Italy on the ground of "Latinità," a Latin origin of the original inhabitants. On this account he seems for long to have been the *béte noire* of Italian military intelligence and propaganda people, stories against him being all the more readily invented as the true cause of dislike could not be told to Allied colleagues or others in Switzerland.* The idea of representing the Bishop of Coire as directing the policy of Benedict XV was curious. His friction with the Italian authorities estranged him rather than otherwise from the Vatican and from Father Ledochowsky of the Jesuits. I note that since my appointment he only once came to Rome, the minimum required from a bishop being a visit *ad limina* once in five years.

M. CAILLAUX.

I had been but a short time here, before Rome was thrown into a great state of excitement in connection with the visit of M. Caillaux to Rome. Every sort of story was circulated on the subject of intrigues with the pro-German press, elements in the country and negotiations and interviews at the Vatican. It was with the latter that I was of course concerned. It seemed to me that in view of the high position he had held in France, M. Caillaux,† if he chose to present himself, could not lightly be refused access to the Vatican, but that it by no means followed that the Holy See would give him their confidence or run the risks which participation in any common action with him must entail. At the same time very confident assertions were made to the contrary; irrefutable proofs were forthcoming, should the Vatican seriously challenge enquiry. So the matter dragged on a whole year till December 1917, when the "Petit Temps" published a series of "Documents émanés de l'Ambassade de France à Rome," the first of these being a letter addressed by the French naval attaché, Admiral de Saint-Pair, to the Chief of the Staff of the Navy. The information was stated to come from sources which were absolutely sure and to be, moreover, confirmed (the word used was the naval term "recoupés,") by the Ambassadors of England and Russia, by Baron Sonnino, by Signor Salandra and the Roumanian Minister, while the account given was a "reflet exact des choses." Mme. Caillaux had seen Cardinal Gasparri several times and M. Caillaux himself had seen Mgr. Pacelli (then the head of the Secretariate of State), and other "pacifist monsignori," urging them to work *more than ever* for a separate peace with Italy which would ultimately detach also France. In a second document a certain Leprestre, described elsewhere as a Canadian horse dealer, related how two Vatican prelates, delegated by the Holy See, discussed an alliance between France, Italy and the Central Powers against England and Russia, the support of the Vatican being assured by the offer of diplomatic relations and a concordat as soon as M. Caillaux should get back into power; Leprestre had had under his eyes in the United States Embassy and had been able to read at his leisure a memorandum brought there by an Irish prelate respecting this interview. All this was communicated to the "Temps" by the French authorities.

Once the accusations published, the Vatican was able to make short work of them. Signor Salandra declared in the Senate that "what was to be read in Saint-Pair's letter with regard to the Holy See was pure fantasy." Baron Sonnino‡ denied that he had ever confirmed the statements. His Majesty's Ambassador had no recollection of any conversation with Admiral de Saint-Pair on the subject and realised that there was no foundation for the rumours. The Russian Government

---

* The principal story I can remember was that the bishop was engaged in selling the Emperor of Austria's pictures, in order to provide funds for a restoration of the dynasty. The truth, I believe, to be as follows:—

In the old episcopal palace at Coire, known perhaps to some travellers as containing some good *baroque* work, there is a picture gallery—nothing very extraordinary perhaps: such work as a pupil or imitator of a Gaudenzio Ferrari, an Antonio Campi, known to those parts, might have done rather than the masters themselves. The gallery had been there for a very long time, since already in the middle of the 18th century a handy man, workman rather than artist, by name Kaufmann, was engaged to repair, and his little child Angelica got, no doubt, her first ideas of form and colour. Times being difficult, the bishop obtained leave to alienate some of the episcopal property and journeyed with pictures to London and New York, but quite in vain. I cannot bring myself to admit that our National Gallery were offered any of the masterpieces once in possession of the Habsburgs, and recognised neither their value nor their origin.

† Cardinal Gasparri, when I had become better acquainted with him, subsequently summed up the situation to me. "Mme. Caillaux has had at least two husbands at a time; she has shot a man; she is now living with Caillaux; she would not be received by anyone here." "And Caillaux?" I asked. "Caillaux! Is he not an ex-Prime Minister? Providentially he did not ask."

‡ A note from Baron Sonnino to the French Embassy of December 16, 1916, put in in evidence at the Caillaux trial, spoke of the relations which Caillaux had had with the Vatican. He must have forgotten.

wrote to say that the Ambassador had only recorded the impressions of the French Embassy; the confirmation given by the Roumanian Minister proved to be merely founded on deductions which his brother, Prince Vladimir Ghika, thought he could draw after a conversation with Mgr. Pacelli, the head of the Secretariate of State, and was abandoned. If any doubt were still possible, it was put an end to by the evidence given at the Caillaux trial in the spring of 1920 by M. Barrère, the French Ambassador, who saved himself by throwing everything overboard.

There remained Leprestre. His story was flatly contradicted by the American Ambassador, who used the strongest language with regard to him. The man put up no sort of defence and disappeared from Rome and diplomatic society.

The incident has been related at greater length than might seem justified, but these attempts to involve the Vatican in the Caillaux scandals were a serious obstacle throughout the year 1917 to frank relations between any Allied representative and the Vatican, who were well aware of the persistent efforts made by the French Embassy, with the support of Baron Sonnino, and Russian hostility. Once this unsatisfactory business was liquidated, the situation improved rapidly.

MGR. GERLACH.

If the Vatican came out of the Caillaux affair with flying colours, so much can hardly be said as regards some other scandals which arose during the earlier months of the year 1917. At the time of my arrival here, and actually on duty, when I presented my letters of credence, as one of the chamberlains in office at the Vatican, was a certain Mgr. von Gerlach. Educated at Rome in the Collegio dei Nobili Ecclesiastici, into which, according to hostile sources, he had introduced himself by an unjustified claim of kinship with an honourable family of the same name, he had managed to profit by the strong interest shown in that institution by Mgr. della Chiesa some time before he became Pope, and to have convinced his patron of his fitness for discharging diplomatic duties, for which suitable candidates were not always to be found. There was a question of attaching him to the Nunciature in Munich, but the Nuncio at the time, the present Cardinal Frühwirt, an Austrian, shrewd, straightforward, and no doubt a better judge of character as regards his own race, saw through him and refused to admit the appointment. Nevertheless, under the late régime he attained to the privileged position of a chamberlain in regular attendance in the Papal antechamber, and was further entrusted with the care of the Vatican wardrobe—that is to say, the hats and other insignia conferred on Cardinals and high dignitaries—the position being one which brought him into close contact with the Pope and the highest placed persons in the Vatican.

Gerlach's activities before the date of Italian participation in the war, his relations with German representatives and politicians, such as Herr Erzberger, had already attracted attention, so that his frequent appearances in public during the winter of 1916–17 began to provoke comment. Some friendly, but pressing, hints are understood to have been conveyed by the Italian authorities to the Vatican, at whose direction he left Italy at the end of February 1917, being escorted with great care and deference to the Swiss frontier by Italian gendarmes.* Scarcely had he been put safely over the border before he was indicted for high treason, tried by the military court of Rome, in company with some half-dozen rogues suspected of relations with the enemy, and sentenced *in contumaciam* to penal servitude for life. Of the other accused, one, a spy working in Switzerland, who could not be caught, was condemned to be shot, while the rest were sent to prison for various terms. It is difficult to give an opinion, as the proceedings were conducted *in camera*. The court affirmed that, according to the evidence, the criminal acts under consideration were not carried out in places occupied by the Holy See, and that these acts had no connection with the Holy See or with the ecclesiastical offices which Gerlach filled. But this passage in the judgment was suppressed by the military censorship. Nevertheless, a few days afterwards one of the principal counsel engaged published in full book form an account of the trial and of his defence of the accused, while proceedings instituted against him on this account by the military court before the disciplinary authority of the Bar led to a triumphant acquittal. The evidence against Gerlach offered by one of the other accused (a certain Valente) was subsequently retracted, and the principal witness, an unfrocked priest named Bruno Tedeschi, is being prosecuted by the civil authorities for perjury. Rome was pleased: the Government had shown adroitness of a sort to appeal to its critical faculty. Exemplary sentences

* The humorists at Rome represented him as the only person who at the time had succeeded in travelling on an Italian railway in comfort and decency.

had been passed; enough to silence the French and English, with their complaints about the Italian attitude towards Germany; but as Gerlach had been carefully put out of the country first, no awkward complications could arise out of the execution of the sentence. The prosecution of a Vatican monsignore had given satisfaction to the anti-clericals, but the suppressed clause in the judgment was there in order to evade any possible trouble with the Vatican, especially in connection with the question of jurisdiction in its borders. As Gerlach was not represented at the trial and was out of reach, he could not appeal; there was no means, therefore, of dealing with the doubts created by the withdrawal of much of the evidence accepted against him. There were smiles here at the idea of punishment for giving money to newspapers, but doubtless the effect abroad of such a sentence could not but be salutary. And, lastly, the law courts were delighted; military justice, which had invaded their sphere, had been flouted and rendered ridiculous. As to Gerlach. whatever the legal aspects of his case, there seems little doubt that he was an unscrupulous adventurer. Cardinal Merry del Val warned the Pope against him before the Conclave of 1914 had broken up, and his view was supported by both Mgr. Zonghi, the rector of his college, and Mgr. Maglione, the present Nuncio in Switzerland, at that time employed in the Secretariate of State. Of Cardinal Frühwirt I have already spoken. Cardinal Gasparri was known to be opposed to Gerlach's retention in Rome, so there can be little doubt as to where the responsibility lies. At the time in question, it may be remembered, both the British and Belgian Ministers and numerous ecclesiastics of the Allies had free access to the highest authorities at the Vatican, while the diplomatists and others of the Central Powers could only correspond in writing from Lugano or through the Papal representative at Berne. The Pope, no doubt inspired with the desire of impartiality. wished to redress the balance by retaining at least one German at his court, but the tenacity with which His Holiness adhered to this decision involved a misplaced confidence which brought no small discredit on the Holy See.

Gerlach retired to Switzerland; in the circumstances there could be no extradition for a political offence, nor would any have been sought. The last news of him* was that he had thrown his cassock to the nettles and married a divorced lady. Between the claims of civil and ecclesiastical authority he will scarcely be heard of again in Rome.

The Pact of London of April 1915.

At the end of 1917, Trotsky, the Russian People's Commissioner for Foreign Affairs, began to publish various documents found by the revolutionaries in the archives at Petrograd; among these was the secret treaty between Great Britain, France, Russia and Italy, signed at London on the 26th April, 1915. A text in Russian appeared in the Soviet organ, the " Isvestia,'' on the 28th November, 1917; a version in English, evidently leaving something to be desired, was published by the " Manchester Guardian " of the 18th January, 1918, and another and poorer translation appeared in the " New Europe " dated the day before. The true text ran :—

  " La France, la Grande-Bretagne et la Russie appuieront l'opposition que l'Italie formera à toute proposition tendant à introduire un représentant du Saint Siège dans toutes les négociations pour la paix et pour le règlement des questions soulevées par la présente guerre.''

The translation published by the " Manchester Guardian " was worded :—

  " France, Great Britain and Russia pledge themselves to support Italy in not allowing the representatives of the Holy See to undertake any diplomatic steps having for their object the conclusion of peace or the settlement of questions connected with the present war.''

The " New Europe '' version gave :—

  ". . . . to support Italy in so far as she does not permit the representatives of the Holy See to take diplomatic action with regard to the conclusion of peace and the regulation of questions connected with the war.''

The Cardinal Secretary of State spoke of the painful impression which this publication had made on the Pope. According to the text, any proposal of the Holy See, relating not only to the conclusion of peace, but to any question connected with the war was excluded in advance from consideration; suggestions, whether good or

* November 1920.

bad, could not be considered on their merits, but were to be condemned in advance *in odium auctoris.* In a subsequent note the Cardinal suggested that the article accounted for the lack of reply to the Pope's peace note and for the rejection of certain proposals for revictualling Syria, the Lebanon, Montenegro, &c., whereas, humanitarian proposals on the part of the Holy See before the date of the treaty had always been crowned with success. The Holy See protested against the article. Lord Balfour pointed out to the Italian Prime Minister that the Vatican protest was based on the "Manchester Guardian" version of the article; if the correct text were shown to them, there was reason to hope that they would allow the matter to drop, but M. Orlando refused to move, alleging that the Allies thus had in their possession a "useful lever" with which to work upon the Vatican in the event of their desiring to secure the assistance of the Holy See in detaching Austria from her allies. In reply to a further defence of the article by M. Orlando, during a short stay in London, Lord Balfour insisted that he was not reconciled to the article in its present or, perhaps, in any shape. His Majesty's Government could not insist on their views, but he wished Baron Sonnino to understand that the removal of this quite unnecessary cause of offence might be advantageous to the common cause. Baron Sonnino remained obdurate and refused to recede from the position he had taken up. A proposal from the Belgian Government suggesting that, by a modification of the text, all neutrals should be excluded from peace negotiations was equally rejected. The matter then dropped, with the help no doubt of the explanation given by Lord Balfour to Cardinal Mercier, that the Bolshevik text was inaccurate, that the clause was no special interest of His Majesty's Government, who would be glad to see it modified, and were not without hope that this would eventually be done.

PALESTINE.

The news of the taking of Jerusalem at the end of 1917 was received with expressions of considerable satisfaction at the Vatican; a solemn *Te Deum* was sung in the Church of Santa Croce in Gerusalemme. To indignant criticism from the other side that this was little in accord with the Papal policy of political neutrality, reply was made that in such a matter as the recovery of the Holy Places from the domination of the infidel the Holy See could not fail to take sides. Praise and blame were distributed as was considered due, without regard to the grouping of the Powers at the particular moment. England, so ran an inspired article in the "Osservatore,"[*] had twice merited well of the Church: now by saving these shrines from the profanation of the Turk, and, in the last century, by opposing the advance towards the East of intolerant Russian bureaucracy. The language of the Vatican organ was direct enough, but was confronted with a letter to the "Times" over the signature of "Civis Britannicus," who professed to know that Cardinal Gasparri expressed regret at the rescue of the Holy City by a Power not of the true faith.

Two difficult questions had now to be dealt with: Zionism and the French protectorate of the Church in the East.

For Zionism the Vatican showed, from the first, great mistrust. British rule, it was frequently repeated, would give them every satisfaction, but they were afraid of anything like Jewish supremacy at Jerusalem. Dr. Sokolof came to Rome, and the moderation of his views left a good impression; still more the visit of Sir Herbert Samuel on his way out to Palestine, and his personal efforts to hold the balance fairly, it being well known to the Vatican, from their own and from the experience of others, that missions to Jerusalem are of great difficulty.[†] Still there was anxiety lest the interests of the Church should be placed in danger by the policy pursued, and a pointed reference was made to the fears of the Holy See in the Pope's allocution to the Cardinals of the 13th June, 1921. In the following March Dr. Weizmann came to Rome, with the object of removing difficulties as far as possible; his visit was not altogether unsuccessful; some misconceptions were put aside, and if no actual agreement was reached on the main issue, the policy of the Zionists, the Vatican were reassured on hearing from Dr. Weizmann that there was no desire on his part to interfere in the Holy Places which were entirely outside the scope of the movement. I reported on the situation in April.[‡] the meeting of the League of Nations took place at Geneva in the middle of May, and owing principally to the

---

[*] "Osservatore Romano" of December 1917.

[†] Cum autem rex interrogasset Heliodorum quis esset aptus adhuc semel Jerosolymam mitti, ait: Si quem habes hostem, aut regni tui insidiatorem, mitte illuc, et flagellatum eum recipies, si tamen evaserit.—Liber II Machabaeorum, cap. III, vv. 37 et 38.

[‡] Count de Salis to Foreign Office, No. 58, of April 13, 1922.

opposition of the Vatican* the consideration of the Palestine mandate had to be put off till the next meeting, which took place in London on the 15th July. A fresh draft of article 14 dealing with the commission for the Holy Places had meanwhile been prepared; the original text, in the opinion of His Majesty's Government, reproduced in substance article 95 of the Treaty of Sèvres, but to meet criticism it was recast in such a way as clearly to lay down that the main function of the commission was the definition of the existing rights which the mandatory was to preserve and protect. This the French Government refused to accept,† on the ground that sufficient count was not taken of the moral interests of France in the Holy Places, and that the Pope did not approve of it. On the first point only the French were entitled to speak; they were trying to recover some of the lost protectorate by securing a right to the chairmanship of the commission. In this they were not supported by the Vatican, which appreciated the new draft, but finding it a little vague were concerned about the means of dealing with disputes which might arise in the future. Though putting forward officially no suggestion on this point, Cardinal Gasparri, though conscious of the drawbacks, was inclined towards the solution of forming the commission from the consular corps at Jerusalem.

The correspondence between the British and French Governments is continuing. Besides working for the chairmanship of the commission, the French claim that certain sanctuaries respecting which, it is asserted, there is no conflict should be outside the competency of the commission, while in the case of the mixed sanctuaries, the Franciscan Custodia should of right be under the control of the French Government, to whose representative honours are accordingly due. His Majesty's Government have opposed a decided refusal to these pretensions.‡

Based on Capitulations concluded between the French monarchy and the Sublime Porte, the French protectorate has been for centuries the mainstay of French influence in the East. With the decay of Turkish rule French claims were advanced to extreme lengths and nowhere further than in Egypt where, in the anomalous conditions of the occupation, it was a constant thorn in the side of the British administration. What then was the position in Palestine on the expulsion of the Turks? Cardinal Gasparri, the author of a study on the subject written some years before,§ laid down at an early date after the taking of Jerusalem the views of the Holy See. The protectorate had been established a long time ago in order to secure the interests of the Church from the oppression of a hostile and semi-barbarous Government. Various States had obtained similar rights under Capitulations, but France was best able at the time to give the required protection to religious interests But now authority in Palestine had passed into the hands of a civilised Government which practised the rule of justice in its actions. The French protectorate was never intended to apply to such conditions; there was no reason for its continuance nor was there any right to it, the moment the Turks had left. In a word, the protectorate had gone and there was no reason to revive it. Orders were accordingly given to the Custos to the effect that the Turkish domination having ceased, the French protectorate with all its privileges had ceased also.

The French were by no means disposed to acquiesce in this decision without a struggle. The first step was to prevent the discontinuance of the liturgical honours rendered to the French representative in virtue of the protectorate. The Vatican were informed that Lord Allenby accepted as just the claims of M. Picot, the French representative, that the honours should be continued, and that both the British and Italian Governments had endorsed Lord Allenby's decision. These statements were anything but the truth; as far as the Italians were concerned, Baron Sonnino gave a denial described by the Vatican as violent. The Foreign Office, though really in agreement with the Vatican, were not prepared to raise the question at that moment with the French and I was told to say that His Majesty's Government did not desire to intervene in a question of ceremonial. So the French, by a piece of sharp practice, scored the first point in the struggle. The honours were continued; to our detriment, as ceremonial, especially in the East, has its importance. In the next month, May 1918, M. Picot was giving out that the Holy See had recognised and consecrated anew the French protectorate in the East.

* The Earl of Balfour to the Secretary to the Cabinet, May 17, 1922.
† Lord Hardinge, No. 1609, of July 11, 1922.
‡ The Earl of Balfour to Count de Saint-Aulaire, August 5, 1922.
§ " Il protettorato cattolico della Francia nell' Oriente e nell' estremo Oriente "; studio storico giuridico di un prelato Romano. 1904.
The author was Cardinal Gasparri, the present Cardinal Secretary of State, at that time Professor of Canon Law at Paris. He told me so on giving me a copy.

Without being discouraged by the rebuff they had met with, the Vatican continued throughout 1919 to press the matter on the attention of His Majesty's Government, and the opportunity of Mgr. Cerretti's journey through London in the spring of that year was taken to repeat that it was to them as the ruling authority rather than to protectorates that the Holy See trusted for the security of its rights in Palestine. In the spring of 1920 a decided step was taken at the conference at San Remo, when M. Millerand was understood to have agreed that on the assumption of a mandate by Great Britain, all French claims to a protectorate over Catholics would be abandoned and withdrawn. The view taken in London was that the French renunciation of their protectorate over Catholics in territories ceded by Turkey was absolute and complete and covered all special rights and privileges. The French on their side continued to urge the Vatican to give orders for the maintenance of the honours, doubt being thrown on the binding character of the San Remo Agreement, which, moreover, to the exclusion of the Vatican, merely concerned France and Great Britain.

The Christmas ceremonies at Bethlehem at the end of the year put the matter to the test, since the French Government, ignoring the negotiations of San Remo, claimed from the Vatican that, as the Treaty of Sèvres had not been ratified and as the Palestine mandate had not been approved, the *status quo* should be maintained. To this the Vatican thought they were obliged to assent, especially as they had had no official communication of the San Remo Agreement, though the Consulta had kept them privately informed at the time, of what was going on.

A *requiem* held at Constantinople on the death of Pope Benedict XV again raised the question, and in a wider aspect, the British and Italian representatives abstaining from attending the service owing to the claim of the French representative to a special position. The French Government took the line that the San Remo decisions applied only to Palestine and did not, even there, apply the liturgical honours, which could only be regulated by ecclesiastical authority. On this Cardinal Gasparri again defined the attitude of the Holy See.[*]

The French protectorate is based on—

1. The Capitulations, *i.e.*, a treaty between France and Turkey.
2. The orders given by the Holy See to the local religious authorities. The liturgical honours are an accessory to the protectorate: *accessorium sequitur principale.*

It therefore follows that—

In territory still under the Turk (and subject to the Capitulations) the protectorate and honours continue, unless there is any agreement on the subject.

In territory no longer under the Turk, the protectorate, or the only effective part of it, remains until the Treaty of Sèvres is ratified. In such cases the honours are the only effective part of the protectorate.

As regards San Remo, the British and Italian Governments affirm that the protectorate has gone; the French affirm the contrary. The Vatican is obliged to wait till the Governments are agreed on this point.

A further question which still awaits settlement is that of the Cœnaculum, traditionally the place of the Last Supper and of the day of Pentecost. The account given of it is that it was acquired in 1333 from the Sultan of Egypt by Robert of Anjou; that by the patronage of the Crown of Naples it was placed in the occupation of the Franciscans, who kept it, though not without some interruption, till 1552, when they were expelled by the Turks who professed to be then convinced that it was the tomb of David. The Italian Government have raised a claim to be put into possession, on the grounds that they are the heirs of the Angevin Kings of Naples,[†] and that in 1919 the Sultan of Turkey (who was no longer reigning in Palestine) gave them a lawful title: propositions which seem to be as much open to question the one as the other. The Vatican have not committed themselves to the support of either, but urge that on general grounds Christianity and the Franciscans have the better right to the place.

IRELAND.

There is an Irish College in Rome, as also English, Scottish and Canadian. The Irish College was founded in former times when the legislation of the English

---

[*] Cardinal Gasparri to Count de Salis, February 14, 1922.
[†] A rival claim, put forward on behalf of the Spanish crown, is presumably sounder in law.

Government was openly hostile to priests. The traditions of the college are what might be expected; they have tended to soften, but there are still recollections of the struggles of the 18th and 19th centuries, disabilities, tithe wars, emancipation, &c. It is the principal channel of communication with the Vatican for the Irish bishops and jealous of its position; hence a lack of co-operation with the Archbishopric of Westminster in such matters as army chaplains. The policy of the Irish bishops has been to hold themselves aloof from the Government of Dublin Castle and especially not to participate in any of its ceremonies or public functions. In this respect the attitude of the bishops is reflected by the college.

The information which had reached the Foreign Office was that the college was " a nest of conspiracy against England, against the Allies and in favour of the Central Empires; anonymous pamphlets had been published with this object, including a certain so-called Red Book." The statement appeared to me at the time to be too sweeping and the reasoning loose. One pamphlet only had been printed; it was not published, and could not be published, since it was printed for private circulation without the printer's name. It was a defence of the attitude of the Irish clergy, especially in relation to the Dublin rising of 1916, on which the Royal Commission of Enquiry had commented. The pamphlet defended them, though it did not profess to speak in their name; it quoted from official documents and from the evidence of Mr. Birrell himself. The pamphlet was no doubt damaging to the prestige of the British Government, but Irish affairs only were dealt with; there was nothing about the Allies or the Central Empires. No direct attempt, as far as I know, was made by Dublin Castle to refute any of the statements, but a proposal was made to issue and circulate as a reply an anonymous pamphlet,* the proofs of which were shown to me, but it was very poor stuff and worse than useless.

Of anything that might be strictly termed conspiracy I knew nothing. According to one story which was supplied to the Foreign Office, the college declared that they would wreck the mission to the Vatican. How they proposed to do so unless helped by the Foreign Office, or by mistakes of the mission, was not stated. The dispositions of His Majesty's Government at the time of my appointment were favourable to the Irish; there was even an idea of attaching an Irish M.P. to the mission, while it was, of course, evident that the whole weight of Vatican authority must be on the side of conciliation and opposed to the display of hostility within its hearing. Mgr. O'Riordan, the rector, called on me on my arrival and my personal relations with him continued to be good down to his death in the course of 1919. It proved impossible, however, to present any representatives of the college to the Prince of Wales on the occasion of His Royal Highness's visit in 1920. At the Vatican annoyance was not concealed at an attitude which appeared to them to be at variance with a claim limited to autonomy, their severe methods of logic condemning what possibly passed as natural to the Irish, if not to the English. I may add that my relations with Cardinal Logue have all along been satisfactory and even cordial. The task, therefore, before the mission in this respect was delicate rather than difficult, and I do not think that after 1916 the Foreign Office had much cause for preoccupation on account of the college; but this does not mean that throughout that period there were no troubles in connection with Ireland.

In the spring of 1918 the application of the Military Service Act to Ireland aroused a storm. The Royal Assent was given on the 18th April and already on the same day a meeting of the bishops assembled at Maynooth issued a public declaration of opposition to the measure; on the following Sunday meetings were held all over Ireland, those present, including the clergy, pledging themselves to resist conscription. These proceedings were supported by public utterances from the Cardinal Archbishop of Armagh, the Archbishop of Cashel, the bishops of Raphoe, Cloyne, Killaloe, Kilmore and others; it is to be presumed that as the reports in the papers were not contradicted, they were more or less correct. Statements, for which official responsibility was taken, were made respecting the proceedings of priests in Mayo, Kerry, Tipperary, &c., advocating forcible resistance to conscription. No official complaint was to be made to the Vatican, but the facts were to be brought to their notice. Cardinal Gasparri's answer was that the clergy in Ireland had taken action without any previous reference to Rome and the matter caused much anxiety; conscription, like Home Rule, was a purely political question, into which the Vatican did not intend to enter, but that the Pope would certainly intervene, and with severity, should it appear that religious and political questions had been unduly mixed up together. On this latter point the principal evidence sent from Ireland was an extract from a

* The pamphlet was subsequently published under the title : " England, Germany and the Irish Question," by an English Catholic.

communication in private form,* stated to be views taken from a reliable source and containing assertions of a sweeping character; the use in it of certain forms of expression did not point to the Catholic origin which Dublin Castle claimed for its information. This, and the fact that Dublin Castle were putting forward anonymous views in order to depict the disorder in the country under their direct administration, were not likely to escape the attention of the Vatican. If there was a strong case, it was not well represented. The result was rather what was to be expected. Cardinal Logue deplored that among the numerous clergy of Ireland there should be some who did not observe prudence and moderation, but suggested that the reports of the speeches must have been made by policemen unable to write shorthand and obviously ignorant of Catholic matters. Neither in London nor at the Vatican was the reply considered satisfactory, nor was persuasion required to convince the Secretariate of State that it was not in harmony with the gravity of the situation. The matter was referred back to Ireland; an open letter was addressed to the bishops, urging the need of the greatest prudence and moderation, while a private admonition was understood to have accompanied it. As to the latter nothing can, of course, be known; the rather stiff, academic phrases of the former were no doubt sufficient to have conveyed the Pope's views to Italian or French bishops. But what of other races? In his reply to me Cardinal Gasparri, satisfied that the incriminated words would extend to the extreme limit of sedition, urged that if the Irish Government really had satisfactory proof of utterance, the offenders should be prosecuted according to civil law, sedition being a civil offence. Meanwhile, it was announced that Father O'Flanagan had been suspended *a divinis* by his bishop for disobedience in not abstaining from making political speeches. Even this severe measure would not appear to have had much effect anywhere, as later on, in 1919, we find Father O'Flanagan negotiating as a representative of the Sinn Feiners with the Prime Minister.

While these events were occurring in Ireland, trouble in the same connection arose in Australia. In 1913 Dr. Mannix, head of Maynooth College, was appointed auxiliary to Archbishop Carr, of Melbourne, and subsequently succeeded him. A taste for politics brought him into collision with the Prime Minister, Mr. Hughes; a bitter personal quarrel ensued, the first act of which was the wrecking of Mr. Hughes's conscription Bill. Very violent language in the course of the campaign was attributed to Dr. Mannix, and both the departing Apostolic delegate, Mgr. Cerretti, and his successor, Mgr. Cattaneo, addressed warnings recommending prudence and moderation. When in London in the summer of 1918, Mr. Hughes insisted on my asking for Dr. Mannix's recall from Australia; otherwise the Australian Government would be compelled to take action themselves. To this the assent of the Vatican was by no manner of means to be obtained. Though his language was disapproved in Rome, Dr. Mannix had not brought himself within reach of deprivation under the Canon Law; his employment in Rome was out of the question, while his transfer to Ireland was scarcely the solution desired by anyone. The Cardinal Secretary of State insisted that the further use of violent language after the receipt of the Vatican warnings was not supported by evidence. On that, as nothing further reached me on that point, the matter dropped till the summer of 1920, when the Archbishop left his diocese with the sanction of the Vatican in order to pay the visit (due by every bishop at least once in five years) *ad limina Aposto lorum*. Already during the journey the Archbishop succeeded in getting himself talked about, while reports of a speech delivered on the way through New York caused His Majesty's Government to forbid his landing in Ireland. In an inspired press communication the Vatican expressed its disapproval of the language, and agreed to the exceptional course of allowing it to be known that the Archbishop had been admonished by the Consistorial Congregation, the competent authority in such matters. The Archbishop came on to Rome; since then nothing further has been said to me about his political activities. The conclusion may be drawn. A mischievous story was put on the Foreign Office that the Vatican intended to make him Archbishop of Dublin, but, as Cardinal Gasparri protested, Archbishop Walsh was then

---

* A telegram conveying my doubts as to the sufficiency of the report produced in time a reply merely to the effect that it was official, and that there was no ground for questioning it. Neither assertion helped very far. I have reason to know that a complete statement was subsequently drawn up for the Irish Government by a Catholic source, but for some reason or another it was never put forward. The most useful résumé of *primâ facie* evidence that in a purely political question pressure had been exercised through religious means was not official at all, but in the form of a letter from Lord Curzon to the "Times" of June 27, 1918. As much could not be maintained for a memorandum prepared for the Lord Chancellor of Ireland some time before. There was presumably an original in English, but a rendering into Killaloe French before it got here made it useless.

still alive, and there was an auxiliary,* whose claims to the succession were. it may be added, when the See became vacant, considered to be well-founded.

In the course of the year 1920 the situation of Ireland grew worse. Organised resistance to authority increased, open attacks and ambushes were carried out against the forces of the Crown, while officers were murdered. The Irish Constabulary, which suffered severely, had to be reinforced by elements without previous training for their duties, and a policy of reprisals promised neither a permanent solution nor even a temporary restoration of order.

In the summer of 1920 the Prime Minister, speaking in the House of Commons. put forward the minimum conditions on which he was prepared to deal with any responsible persons : separate treatment for Ulster; no secession; no detraction from the security of the British Isles. At that moment a very active propaganda was being carried on at Rome on behalf of a republican solution by men such as Mr. Sean T Kelly. Mr. Gavan Duffy and others. Noisy demonstrations were held at the Grand Hotel, banquets, meetings, to which the extreme Left of the Partito Popolare were invited. Recourse, even, was had to threatening letters, an occurrence of unhappy frequency in Ireland, but not understood here. Then came the MacSwiney affair, in connection with which the late Pope employed in conversation the word " farce." For all this was little to the taste of the Holy See, thoroughly Latin in its conception of external dignity and decorum; it defeated its own object and alarmed the Vatican. instead of gaining its support. Mgr. Salotti, a Vatican official, was severely taken to task earlier in the year for taking part in a demonstration at the Irish College. while the Rector was understood to have been reprimanded by the Pope himself and reminded that he was in Rome. As to this I cannot speak with certainty, but, as regards Mgr. Salotti, the blame inflicted on him was rendered to a certain degree public by the address to me of a strongly-worded note, sent within a couple of days of the occurrence. At one moment the despatch of a special delegate to Ireland to report on the situation came under consideration, but here there was considerable reluctance on the part of Cardinal Gasparri himself. The facts seemed to be sufficiently notorious. and enquiry by a delegate would go very near to an investigation into the political conditions of the country. Ultimately, after a delay, the whole question was submitted to the Congregation of Foreign Affairs. As to what happened I do not profess to be able to speak with certainty. On the one hand, the matter was, in its very essence, political; as such it was outside the scope of religious authority. On the other. crimes had been committed, crimes for which there was no palliation, no saving clause. Was it not right to warn the faithful that they could not take part in a political movement unless and until such sinful methods were abandoned ? Such was, more or less, the view favoured in London, and, as far as I can form an opinion, the Congregation was not inclined to reject it; in that case, it would be due to higher authority that it was not definitely adopted. Such an explanation is at least plausible. The attitude consistently maintained by Benedict XV, the conviction, the fixed idea of his policy that the part of mediator was the one which the Pope could best play, may well have stood in the way of his taking a step which his advisers favoured.

The action taken by some of the bishops in the disturbed districts left nothing to be desired, notably the Archbishop of Tuam and the Bishop of Cork, though both were understood to hold advanced Irish views in politics. They were followed by others. though in one or two cases one waited in vain for news. In London a collective declaration of the bishops was missed. Why was it not forthcoming ? Here we are on rather more delicate ground, it might seem. Collective action is, of course, at times taken by the bishops of various countries—at any rate, in the transaction of current business—but it would need great knowledge of Church history to analyse whether this took place as a rule on the initiative of the Holy See, or whether the Vatican was not usually at pains to insist rather on the individual responsibility of each bishop towards the Pope for the affairs of his diocese. In restoring the Church in France after the revolution. the First Consul, for his own purposes, proposes (I think in the Organic Articles, not in the Concordat itself) that there should be no collective action by bishops, and to this the Pope seems to raise no objection whatever. In Ireland, too, unlike England, decisions are by unanimity, and not by majority, I believe, so the chain is no stronger than the weakest link. And one or two are not strong.

* Mgr. Byrne, who became archbishop on the death of Cardinal Walsh. His appointment was understood to be satisfactory from all points of view.

In December 1920 Cardinal Gasparri made his first enquiry on behalf of the Pope; whether there was anything which the Holy See could do to contribute to a peaceful settlement and whether the moment was opportune; some step of course which would be received with satisfaction by the English and without dissatisfaction by the Irish. A similar enquiry was repeated in March 1921, with reference to a statement made by the Prime Minister in the House of Commons. This was followed by the declaration made by Cardinal Logue in April; if the people in Ireland abandoned crime, they could obtain everything that was necessary for the country; an Irish Republic they would never achieve. The Vatican might have wished that a statement of this importance, the genesis of which is obvious, should have been made with greater solemnity than at the confirmation service at Clonoe, but this was perhaps the earliest occasion which could be found. Then followed an open letter from the Pope to Cardinal Logue, urging the abandonment of violence and resort to peace by mutual agreement. The resumption of negotiations in the following October was welcomed by the Pope in a telegram addressed to the King, no notice being taken at the time of the effort made by De Valera to compromise the situation, though the tone of his telegram to the Pope was resented, and on the first suitable occasion an inspired article in the " Corriere " repudiated in very definite terms any sympathy with him and his ideas.[*]

Extreme caution must ever have characterised the dealings with Ireland of the Holy See, caution based not only on secular traditions of prudence but on contact with a mentality which, if a mystery to the Englishman, is no open book to the closer reasoning of the Latin. Down to our own time the legend still survived that the Pope of the day,[†] claiming, it is said, a special interest in the fate of islands, had for the benefit of true religion and peace assigned Ireland to the sovereignty of Henry II, while Irish writers were reduced to pleading that the good faith of the one English Pope had been deceived by his countrymen. Only in recent times has the story been exploded,[‡] the evidence being to the effect that the Holy See refused to commit itself, in fact, that the traditions of the oldest diplomacy in Europe were as well guarded in the hands of the Englishman as of any Italian. Mr. Froude insists, on historical grounds, that the Holy See have attempted but twice to intervene in Irish affairs, and never without regretting it;[§] in any case, I am inclined to urge that disinclination to do so is a very old policy, rooted in pre-Reformation times, long before there were Orangemen and other complications.

In many respects there might seem to the neutral to be close analogy between our Irish question and some of the numerous racial struggles within the borders of the Austro-Hungarian Monarchy. The Vatican might have considered it had reason to favour the Catholic Croats rather than the Hungarians guided by the strong Calvinist element in the country, but while insisting that such political questions were not the concern of the Holy See, Cardinal Gasparri was of opinion that a large measure of autonomy, which in all these cases had become inevitable, would be the best solution. In this respect the ideas of the Vatican would not always coincide with those of the local hierarchies, who, though free to hold their own political views, were exhorted to remain within the limits of prudence and moderation. More than that, it was thought, could scarcely be done;[||] throughout, the Vatican were at pains

---

[*] " Corriere d'Italia "

[†] Adrian IV, Nicolas Brakespeare, 1154-1159.

[‡] John of Salisbury was sent by Henry II on a mission to Rome. Acting, it may well be, with a view to preferment, and counting, perhaps, on ignorance of local circumstances on the part of his superiors, he claimed to have attained to the highest degree of influence and intimacy with the Papal Court, to the extent of eating off the same plate with the Pope. His reports might have been buried; it was Giraldus Cambrensis, a contemporary writer of history and propaganda, who revealed some time after, that among the fruits of a mission which may have been criticised as barren, was a Papal sanction for the conquest of Ireland. Giraldus was either grossly deceived or as great a liar as my predecessor and quasi-namesake; he is honest in one respect, in announcing that the object of his history is the glorification of his master, Henry II. Cardinal Gasquet deals with the subject in his " Essays."

[§] In his " History of the English in Ireland." I cannot say whether he is strictly accurate in affirming that a Papal Legate perished in the bogs. I cannot give the reference. Was it at the time of the Armada or in the rebellion of 1641 ?

[||] A story, originating with an obscure paper or press agency, was to the effect that Mgr. Jeglić, Bishop of Laibach, was being prosecuted by the Nuncio at Vienna for sedition. It was taken up by the " Times," and attracted attention in the Foreign Office. A Nuncio is a diplomatist, and in no conceivable circumstances could he be called upon to prosecute the subjects of the country to which he is accredited for breaches of its civil law. The reply of the Vatican was that they had not thought such a story worth contradicting. Canon Law does not, of course, deal with such matters. It is understood that Mgr. Jeglić, who had placed himself at the head of the nationalist movement, received the same counsels which were given elsewhere, to moderate his language. But such matters are not made public.

to maintain, what seemed to them, a consistent attitude, while we were hampered in our diplomacy by the conflicting tendencies of our interests.*

The Roman Question.

For the first few months of the war the Vatican were able to continue, as before, their relations with the various Powers involved, but as soon as the Italian Government ceased to be neutral, a difficulty at once arose in regard to the diplomatic representatives of the hostile belligerents; had they the right to remain in Rome, at least within the precincts of the Vatican? It was decided to raise no question on the subject, and the three missions, Austrian, Prussian and Bavarian, withdrew to Lugano, while the Pope, in accordance with his policy of neutrality, sought to remedy the inequality in which the Central Powers were placed, by maintaining relations through a member of the Secretariat of State sent for the purpose to Switzerland, and by keeping a German chamberlain in office at the Vatican. The disastrous choice made in the latter case is dealt with elsewhere under the name of Gerlach; as regards the former, the mission of Mgr. Marchetti to Berne and his functions, to give to the Central Powers the same opportunities of intercourse as were enjoyed in Rome at the Vatican itself by our side, would have been well known to the diplomatic missions of the *Entente* in Switzerland.† At the same time public declarations were made drawing attention to the difficulty in which the Pope was placed by not being able to communicate with the bishops of enemy countries, but repudiating any idea of desiring to see a solution imposed by force of arms from outside. " The Holy See, being neutral, will not create difficulties for the Italian Government, and places its confidence in God, awaiting a suitable settlement, not from foreign arms, but from the triumph of those sentiments of justice which, it is to be hoped, are spreading more and more among the people of Italy, in accordance with its true interests."‡

It may be doubtful whether these protests aroused much attention at the time. Not until the war was over, and the resumption of relations with France became a possibility, became likely, and then was actually realised, did the Italian press take up the matter. If France, without sacrificing, as was understood, any sovereign right within her own territory, could deal diplomatically with the Holy See, why should not Italy do the same? The answer was given in the " Osservatore "; because, unlike other countries, Italy has a question at issue with the Holy See which must first be settled.

What is the nature of this question, and what solution of the conflict to the mutual benefit of both parties is possible? If these are accepted as the terms of the problem, we need not pause to consider extreme views, such, on the one hand, as the restoration of the Papal dominions as before; on the other, the destruction of the Papacy, or at least its transformation into a subordinate institution under the supremacy of the Italian State. Why should not the situation as it is be accepted? Will the new Pope come out of the Vatican, was the question of the tourist at the last Conclave? It is all nothing but a comedy, was once the answer.§

The brief military operations of September 1870 were brought to an end by an armistice signed by the opposing commanders, which left a part of the Leonine city in the hands of the Papal authorities. Subsequently, the Royal troops occupied the rest of the city, with the consent, it is understood, of the Pope, in order to stop looting on the part of the mob, which was out of control. No attempt was made to assert possession over the Vatican, on which the Papal flag continued to be hoisted. No further agreement of any sort was ever reached, but in the following May (1871) a law was voted, the well-known Law of Guarantees, dealing by a unilateral act of authority with the Pope and his position. Its defects from the point of view of the Vatican are due to this fact: it purports to confer by law certain rights and certain sovereign honours on the Pope, but nowhere recognises them as already his. None are recognised as his subjects, and in a well-known case the Italian tribunals successfully

* The " Times " of May 9, 1916, contained on the same page a brief account of trials by court-martial in Dublin. followed by executions, and an eloquent denunciation, signed by Mr. R. W. Seton Watson, of the judicial proceedings instituted at Banjaluka against certain Serbs for sedition.

† But not apparently to others. In February 1917, months, I think even years, after Mgr. Marchetti had been established in Berne, an agency, secret service or other, is able to report that a person named Maghetti, of whose identity there seems to be no knowledge, has had an interview with Professor Spahn and Herr Erzberger.

‡ Declaration of Cardinal Gasparri, June 28, 1915.

§ " Lealtà italiana," di Gilbert Murray, Professore regius nell'università di Oxford; p. 6. (This was one of the publications of the Propaganda Bureau in Rome.)

upheld a claim to cite before them the Master of the Pope's household and call him to account for his dealings with the servants in the Vatican. No territory is allowed to him; not a square yard on which sovereign rights can be exercised. One hears about the Vatican being extra-territorial—not long ago a correspondent of the "Daily Telegraph,"* sent specially to write on the Roman question, led off with this assertion—but no such right is guaranteed. On the contrary, the Palace and garden are not even recognised as the private property of the Holy See, but, set aside for the Pope's use, are treated as the property of the Italian Crown. By article 5 the Pope merely has the enjoyment of them (" continua a godere "), with certain privileges as regards immunity from entry by agents of the public force, perquisitions, sequestration of papers, &c., while the preceding article suggests that at some future date the Italian Government may undertake the maintenance and custody of the museums and library.

To queries as to what the Papacy wants in order to settle the dispute, the answer given from the more authoritative sources has been that the absolute requirement is independence, real and apparent. Real, because the Pope cannot carry on his functions without it; apparent, because even the suspicion that he was under the control of any Government might be fatal to his discharge of them in other countries. That independence was formerly assured (very badly assured at times) by the possession of a certain territory; now it is no longer assured by anything, unless it be by manifest dissidence between the Quirinal and the Vatican. To an enquiry in London, Mgr. Cerretti answered,† what the Pope requires is the estate of an English Lord. This was the line also taken by Father Ehrle,‡ predecessor and at one time superior of the present Pope in the Vatican Library, to whose articles on the point much authority was attributed. But the Pope must be recognised as a sovereign in virtue of his office and not in virtue of a law which, although spoken of as organic and fundamental, can be altered or repealed like any other. In guarded language the " Osservatore "§ of last September made something like an offer on these lines. It was taken up at once on the other side. Most Italian Liberals, answered the " Tempo,"‖ feel the need of an agreement; the Vatican, let us say so frankly, have defined the minimum required in order to be free. Could an Italian Government embark on a settlement of this nature? The makers of Italy as at present constituted thought they could not. They were basing themselves on the identity of State and nation, carrying out to its extreme logical conclusion the theory of national unity, as a justification for what they had done already, for what they aspired to do in the near future. Their principles admitted of no concession; least of all, that of a square yard of sovereignty sufficient to establish that their doctrine was not of absolute truth. . . . In the past fifty years much of this has changed: the doctrinaire Liberalism of the past century, though still represented, is no longer an all-powerful factor in Italian political life, while in the day of its triumph elsewhere the principle of nationalism has been found to admit of many modifications, strategic frontiers, economic needs, access to the sea, and when these are exhausted there is historical claim to which the monuments of the past, in default of the population, bear witness. A collection of articles from the Italian press of all shades of opinion,¶ appearing during the three weeks subsequent to M. Jonnart's arrival, is a striking witness to the difference in the views of to-day; the most remarkable fact in connection with it is that it should have been published by the Italian Government.

On both sides, therefore, it is publicly admitted that a settlement by mutual concession would be advantageous; thence to agreement is still a very long step. Are there Italian statesmen who would concede as of right real independence to the Holy See, who would give up the hope that, though there may have been little success in the past, some development in the political situation, some pact of London due to the needs in other matters of foreign States, may not put into their hands a "useful lever," the means of making the Vatican subservient to the requirements of Italian policy. To them the Vatican is an Italian institution, though the Consulta may be at pains to persuade the foreigner that there is no understanding with it.

On the side of the Vatican it is an Italian majority which elects the Pope. This

* " Daily Telegraph," July 28, 1922.
† Lord Curzon to Count de Salis, No. 30, of March 24, 1919.
‡ " Benedikt XV und die Lösung der römischen Frage," " Die römische Frage " (both articles in " Stimmen der Zeit " for 1916).
§ " Osservatore Romano," September 2, 1921.
‖ " Tempo," September 24, 1921.
¶ " Ministero degli Affari Esteri; " ufficio stampa. " Una nuova discussione sui rapporti tra Chiesa e Stato in Italia." (Articles from the Italian press between May 29 and June 20, 1921, with an appendix of articles from the foreign press.)

has been thought essential in the past; would it be so in the future if the Italian Crown and Government, with all the advantages derived from their presence on the spot, enjoyed at the Vatican the same rights as others? Would not the independence claimed by the Holy See be in such circumstances more marked under the reign of a non-Italian Pope, by the nomination of a College of Cardinals more nearly corresponding to the number of Catholics in the various countries? There may well be many in the Vatican who hesitate before the first step in the direction of such far-reaching changes.

Various formulas have been devised in the past on the part of Italian statesmen to define the object to be attained. A spectator of Italian affairs might find fault with them all, as failing to distinguish between two distinct ideas, the sovereignty of the Pope over the Catholic world and the local organisation of the Church in Italy. "*Libera Chiesa in Stato libero*—a free Church in a free State. So was the Cavour programme. As a promise not to interfere with the Pope's authority over the faithful in general, it may have been sound politics, but the grant of complete independence to any religious organisation within its borders is more than any modern State has been ready to give; least of all Italy since 1870. The new State wanted money, the hen roosts were there and the new order of things had secured for the claims of the Exchequer the support of strong majorities in the Chambers. A period of confiscation set in; Church property of all sorts was seized, lands, buildings, books, till the sequestration of the great Benedictine library brought into the field, with others, such a singular champion of monasticism as Mr. Gladstone. "*Chiesa libera in rapporti do buon vicinato con lo Stato sovrano*—free Church in relations of good neighbourship with the sovereign State," is scarcely an improvement in substance while clumsy in form. For this, Signor Giolitti substituted his "parallel lines." Was he happier than the others? The lines meet, rather often.

And then there is a great change in Italy itself. Hitherto the Chambers have been dominated by parties which repudiated the existence of a Roman question, any thought of revising the Law of Guarantees. But the war brought strong Catholic elements into close touch with Italian public life. The Vatican decided that there was not to be a Catholic Party in the Chamber, but admitted that a party might be formed of Catholics, independent of the Vatican as regards purely political matters, but bound to conform to the teaching of the Church in matters of faith and morals.* The "Popular Party" has already only a rival in the Socialists as the strongest group in the Chamber: in recent times no Government could be formed without it. With their presence in power the system of trying to exercise leverage on the Vatican by means of anti-Church legislation has been stopped and has been replaced by the need for coming to an understanding. On the other hand there is a strong opposition outside. Two powerful organisations are understood to offer uncompromising hostility to any settlement other than the unconditional surrender of the Vatican, the Grand Orient of Italy with its headquarters in the Palazzo Giustiniani and the Ancient Scottish Rite established in the Piazza del Gesù. The former, the stronger of the two, was showing considerable activity in the summer of 1917. A congress with the French Grand Orient and the Serbian masons was held in July and a programme for the settlement of Europe drawn up. But outcry was raised in Italy that under French pressure Italian interests were being sacrificed to the Slavs, it being alleged that the offices of the Serbian propaganda in France were established at the headquarters of the Grand Orient in the Rue Cadet in Paris. The Italian Grand Master had to resign, and since then there has been much less publicity as to the views of his successors. In attempting to settle with the Vatican an Italian Government would have to reckon with them.

DIPLOMATIC RELATIONS WITH THE UNITED KINGDOM, FRANCE, GERMANY, RUSSIA, ITALY, BELGIUM AND SWITZERLAND.

The United Kingdom.

For three centuries and a half, down to the war of 1914, no regular, fully accredited representative of a King of England had resided in Rome; the last envoy must be Carne, *eques auratus*, who, finding it as well not to return to England on the conclusion of his mission, lies buried in San Gregorio since 1571. Not that there have been no relations at all in that period. It would seem that some time in the first half of the year 1792 the English Government found it necessary to open official

---

* *E.g.*, the party might support female suffrage, although I believe that the Cardinal Secretary of State thought there was little good in it for Italy. It could not support a divorce law, as divorce is banned by the Church.

communications with Pope Pius VI regarding the political situation which had arisen in consequence of the war with the French Republicans. For this purpose choice was made of Sir John Hippisley, who had previously served in India, and who had already, whilst residing in Italy in 1779 and 1780, been entrusted with confidential communications in Rome and elsewhere. After a stay of some months in Rome, occupied in surveying the general situation, Mr. Hippisley, as he then was (it may be noted, he was not a Catholic), came to the conclusion that the best interests of England would be served by having a Papal envoy in London. Mgr. Erskine, who was subsequently made a Cardinal for his services, was chosen for the task; he had been brought up at the Scots College in Rome under the protection of the Cardinal Duke of York, but this does not seem to have been held to disqualify him for a mission to the Court of King George. Erskine reached England about November 1793, and was well received. The Cardinal Secretary of State is informed that the "great and powerful Mr. Burke" was favourable,* and Lord Grenville, Windham and Stuart, even Lord Thurloe, to whom Erskine described himself as the Devil's advocate, was civil. Among other matters arranged was the supply to the English fleet of provisions and of some thousands of quintals of gunpowder of Papal manufacture, a detail which would give support to the point of view occasionally maintained that our diplomatic relations of the past were with the temporal ruler of a petty Italian State and not with the head of the Roman Catholic Church.†

As in 1792, it was the occasion of a European catastrophe which induced His Majesty's Government in 1914 to renew relations with the Holy See. With formal congratulations to the new Pope on his elevation, Sir Henry Howard was to lay before His Holiness the motives which compelled His Majesty's Government, after exhausting every effort in their power to preserve the peace of Europe, to intervene in the war, and to inform him of their attitude towards the various questions which arise therefrom. The scope of the mission was, therefore, in the first instance, work in connection with the war, but very soon, and that before Sir Henry Howard's retirement, it was occupied with many other matters. A long-standing cause of friction in India was the Portuguese Padroado, or right of presentation to certain bishoprics in Bombay, which, as part of the dowry of Catherine of Braganza, fell to the English Crown in the time of Charles II. Not only in these cases was it thought desirable by the India Office to ensure the appointment of a larger number of British subjects to sees in India, the occupants of which have generally been chosen among missionaries, priests of foreign nationality. In Canada, troubles in connection with the language question in schools provoked the intervention of the Vatican in the sense desired in London. The taking of Jerusalem and of Mesopotamia raised questions in connection with the Holy Places and the claims of France to a religious protectorate in the East. Ireland, the rebellion of 1916, the anti-conscription agitation and the spread of the republican movement have never ceased to require attention. These and other questions were not directly affected by the termination of the war, and the mission was not withdrawn on the conclusion of peace. The moment might hardly have appeared propitious; before long a German Ambassador had been appointed; a French Ambassador, with interests by no means identical with British, followed; the number of lesser States to be represented increased rapidly, while in the background were unofficial and indistinct figures whose arrival promised no particular good to us.

If these relations are to be continued, on what footing should they be maintained? To whom should the task be entrusted? Sir Henry Howard, under whom the mission was despatched in 1914, had had a distinguished career and many qualifications by birth and experience for rendering him both *persona grata* at the Vatican and a most suitable representative of His Majesty. But, for all that, it should be borne in mind that to the Vatican the value of diplomatic relations with a Government lies in the possibility of direct communication with it, of learning its views through a properly authorised agent, competent to speak on its behalf.

---

* Mr. Burke said :—

"If the thing depended on me, I should certainly enter upon diplomatic correspondence with the Court of Rome, in a much more open and legitimate manner than has been hitherto attempted. If we refuse it, the bigotry will be on our side, and most certainly not on that of His Holiness. Our unnatural alienation has produced, I am convinced, great evil and prevented much good. If the present state of the world does not make us learn something, our error is much more culpable."

(Mr. Hippisley to Cardinal De Zelada; quoted by Cardinal Gasquet in " Great Britain and the Holy See," 1792-1806.)

† Notably in the time of the temporal power, when the late Lord Ampthill was sent to Rome as Chargé d'Affaires.

Hitherto the mission has been composed of Catholics, a disposition which secures some obvious advantages here in Rome, but this condition is not indispensable. Neither the Russian nor the Prussian Governments conformed to it in the past. Not that it would be well that in the future His Majesty's Government should copy either the bitter hostility of the former or the methods of the latter. " If you only knew," said the ex-head of the secretariate, Mgr. Pacelli, " what we have had to put up with from Herr von Mühlberg." At present there are Greek and Roumanian representatives who are Orthodox, as well as a German Ambassador, Herr von Bergen, who is a Lutheran. The part he can play at present cannot but be in the background, so it is hard to say how far the German Government is the loser by their choice, except from the plain disadvantage due to the lack of confidence and of co-operation between the Embassy and the best German asset, the German ecclesiastics, who by their work and learning have won for themselves an influential position in the Church. As a set-off to this, the choice of a regular Prussian may make for better support on the part of subordinate elements in the Wilhelmstrasse.

Nor does the establishment of regular relations necessarily imply that there need be a Nuncio in London. For years there were Russian and Prussian Ministers in Rome without any corresponding Papal representatives in their respective countries, though Nuncios have been sent to Russia, as to England, on special occasions on missions of a complimentary character. Relations with Switzerland and Holland in the past were also unilateral, but in these cases Nuncios were sent without any corresponding representatives being accredited to Rome. Whether the Vatican would wish in present conditions to have a Nuncio in London is another matter. If ever there is one, it will surely be because the British Government desire it; because, perhaps, whatever the final solution applied to it, there is an Irish question.

More than once during the war it was proposed that an ecclesiastic, an English prelate, should be attached to the mission in some sort of capacity, with a view to exercising influence in the ecclesiastical world or dealing, it was suggested, with lesser matters. I can throw no light on the source of these proposals; they were pressed with great persistency and efforts made to enlist the sympathies of the Prime Minister on their behalf.* There seemed to be very little to be said for such an idea and a great deal against it. It is not true that other missions have a similar functionary attached to them; one or two only, who, unlike the British Government, have to treat with the Holy See over such things as Church Temporalities, have an expert for such purposes. The duties of the mission, representing the Sovereign of the British Empire with its many and complicated interests in these matters, must necessarily be delicate. There would seem to be an evident advantage in having these duties discharged by servants of the Government responsible solely to the Secretary of State and acting solely under his orders. If advice in ecclesiastical affairs is required, it is sufficient to mention such names as Cardinal Gasquet, and after him Mgr. Prior and others who exercise real influence here owing to the position they hold, whose aid would always be at the disposal of a British representative.

Whatever the solution favoured, it should be borne in mind that the problem to be solved concerns our relations with what is practically a first-class Power, possessing an organisation throughout the world which is as complete in many ways as that of any great State, which, whatever the degree of ability of which it, like any other Government, can at any given moment dispose, brings to the discharge of its business the widest experience and the oldest traditions of Europe. At random, I would cite an opinion such as that of Lord Lansdowne in 1840 :—

> " The condition of the Pope's sovereignty is quite peculiar; as a temporal sovereign he is of the fourth or fifth order; as a spiritual sovereign he is not only of the first order, but enjoys a sovereignty unparalleled."

France.

At the time of my arrival here there was, in consequence of the rupture of diplomatic relations in July 1904, no regular French representatives. But on the outbreak of war M. Charles Loiseau, an able writer and contributor to the " Revue de Paris," was attached to the French Embassy with the mission of keeping unofficially in touch with the Cardinal Secretary of State; his wife, with literary capacity and great devotion to the Church, being the sister of Count Vojnovitch, the Dalmatian poet, and of his brother, Louis (Lujo), the confidential adviser of King Nicolas of Montenegro during the Scutari crisis of April–May, 1913. With M. Loiseau, much

* The matter was dealt with in a memorandum, dated July 25, 1918, sent direct to the Secretary of State, and also communicated to the Department in November, 1919.

interested in Balkan affairs and the author of a study on the Adriatic question written in opposition to the views of the Italian. Vico Mantegazza, and the Austrian. Baron Chlumecky, I had been acquainted for some years; my relations with him were always friendly. At the same time a member of the French Diplomatic Service. M. Gonse, had been told off to keep his eye on what might be going on at the Vatican, with a certain M. Canet as his assistant. With the former I had had some slight previous acquaintance—a rather typical French functionary. His work, I understand, was to collect information. good, bad or indifferent, and consign it to voluminous *dossiers.* The system had its obvious failings; the gossip of Rome requires sifting. and these gentlemen were not in a position to get impressions from both sides. Their methods were crude and too much was known of them. At the time of my arrival there were jokes circulating respecting their *dossier* of the intrigues of Mgr. Aversa with the American Government. It had escaped attention that that prelate had not been sent to Washington, but to Brazil.

During the whole of 1917—the first year I spent here—the French Embassy were constant in their endeavours to convict the Vatican of participation in the proceedings of M. Caillaux. The Vatican were perfectly well aware of this underground work directed against them, and relations were accordingly bad. At the turn of the year an open attack was made. the reports of the French Embassy being published in the hostile "Temps." The result was a fiasco; the accusations collapsed as on one point after another neither confirmation nor the witnesses . invoked were forthcoming. For some time after this there was a cessation in M. Barrère's campaign, but a fresh cause of dissension arose in the summer of 1918, on an attempt being made to establish direct diplomatic relations between the Vatican and the Chinese Government. The French Government took their stand on the Treaty of· Tien-tsin, to which the Pope was not a party, and on their rights as protector of the Church in the Far East, while they appealed to the help of the Allies on the ground that the Vatican's candidates were Germanophile. I have dealt with the incident elsewhere. For the moment the Quai d'Orsay were able to prevent anything being done, but even their success accentuated the anomaly of pretending to protect the Church, while refusing to have official relations with its head and maintaining a hostile attitude towards him. The same dilemma arose in connection with Palestine, as soon as the Turks had been driven out and the British authorities installed at Jerusalem; it was difficult to combine non-intercourse as regards the Vatican with an attempt to recover the religious privileges which for so long had been the foundation of French influence and prestige in the East. Public opinion, moreover, in France was moved; Radical Deputies began to criticise the policy of abstention. and M. de Monzie's book "Rome sans Canossa," excited attention. May it have been with the object of combating these tendencies that in the " Revue de Paris " of the 15th October and the 1st November, 1918. a bitter and insulting attack was made on the Pope and his surroundings? It was common belief that the author was M. Canet. to whom I have referred above, and that the articles were written in the French Embassy. I have little doubt on the subject. A detailed refutation was prepared by Mgr. Le Floch, the rector of the French Seminary at Rome, and. after a refusal on the part of the " Revue de Paris," appeared in the "Correspondant" of the 10th March, 1919. For another year the question lay dormant, but with the opening of 1920, the agitation began again. Might it be that the return to Rome of the two German representatives helped to hasten a decision? In March 1920 cordial telegrams were exchanged between the Vatican and M. Deschanel on his election to the Presidency of the Republic, and within a week a Bill was introduced into the Chamber of Deputies for meeting the cost of an Embassy. Without waiting for a decision the Quai d'Orsay despatched a Chargé d'Affaires to the Vatican before the end of the month. At that a dead point was again reached until in May 1921. M. Jonnart arrived and presented his letters. No pains were spared to give importance to the new Embassy. the best residence that could be found, a large staff and all else that might seem suitable. Already in his opening speech the Ambassador made a pointed reference to the part played by the French Government as protector of Catholics in the East and the Far East; the rivalry of other Powers suggested that it might not alone be in these distant countries that the French aimed at predominance. An active policy was started with a view to securing ecclesiastical appointments agreeable to the Government. not only on French soil, but much further afield, on neutral ground, such as Copenhagen or even in British spheres such as Bagdad. After the lapse of more than a year it might seem that so far success had been far from complete. that the high hopes that the re-establishment of

* Reprinted under the title " La Politique de Benoît XV."

relations would alone be sufficient to ensure to France all she desired, have not been fulfilled. On the main point at issue, the *status* of the Church in France, agreement has not been reached, the protectorate in the East has not been recovered while on the occasion of the recent conference at Genoa and in London, the influence of the Holy See has been cast in no uncertain manner in favour of the English rather than the French thesis.

Germany.

Before the war there were diplomatic relations between the Vatican and Bavaria of the usual character; a Bavarian Minister in Rome and a Papal representative, a Nuncio, in Munich. There were also relations with Prussia, but on a unilateral basis; no Papal representative in Berlin, but a Prussian Minister in Rome. The latter was Herr von Mühlberg, an able and energetic official, understood to be a member of the Prussian State Church, well known, no doubt, to many of us owing to a long tenure of office at the Wilhelmstrasse. He seems to have been well provided with money and with the help of it to have stood socially in close relations with a wide circle of persons connected in one way or another with the Vatican. The Bavarian Minister was Baron Ritter, who has since returned; a man of good family and acceptable to the Vatican. This double representation of German interests suggests a certain flexibility, according as it might be desired to profit by insistence on the importance of the Catholic element in the Empire or on the disagreeable results which might follow resistance to a Government backed by the latent hostility of North and East Germany. In the spring of 1915, while Prince Bülow was dealing with the Quirinal, Herr Erzberger was doing what he could at the Vatican, but beyond relating that he was able to settle some secondary questions, his memoirs do not record any particular success before the declaration of war by Italy put an end to his visits. The two Ministers left for Lugano and kept in contact with the Holy See either by communications transmitted by the Swiss Federal authorities or through the Papal representative, who had been sent to Berne with the object of keeping the Vatican in touch with those who on account of the war could not come to Rome. Throughout the year 1916 the services of Mgr. Gerlach as chamberlain were retained in Rome, with a view, it was understood, of affording some compensation to the Germans for the more advantageous position which free access to the Vatican conferred on the diplomatic representatives of the Allies.

No action was taken by the Vatican on the German peace note of the 12th December, 1916. Peace, says Erzberger, quoting from a neutral diplomatist, was not offered, it was threatened. The aid of the Vatican was invoked, but, as remarked by the German press, no sign was given; still an impression may be justified that the attitude of the Vatican throughout most of the year 1917 was influenced by the view that in the end Germany would offer terms acceptable in the circumstances to the Allies. On the death of Mgr. Aversa his place at Munich was filled by Mgr. Pacelli, who as head under Cardinal Gasparri of the Secretariate of State was in the closest relation to the Pope and his views. The new Nuncio set off in the spring of 1917, rather sanguine, it might seem, of success, but giving the impression that an acquaintance with Germany derived from ecclesiastical circles might prove a scanty equipment for dealing with the real masters of the situation. The result was the reply given to the Pope's peace proposals by Herr Michaelis at the bidding of the Military Party. Would the proposals have ever been presented at all if the Nuncio had correctly gauged the situation? On this there was a very evident change in the attitude of the Vatican. In the early days of 1918 the Cardinal Secretary of State spoke with appreciation of the speech delivered by the Prime Minister, Mr. Lloyd George, on the 5th January; he had been much impressed by the importance of these declarations, which were clear and precise, and it was now for the other side to speak. Two semi-official articles in the " Osservatore " published the Cardinal's views as being those openly held by the Holy See.

The Nuncio summed up to me, on the occasion of a visit to Rome early in 1920, his experiences in Berlin. The Emperor was much less intelligent than his reputation; Bethmann Hollweg was the least bad of all of them; Michaelis was impossible, a mere functionary under the orders of the General Staff; Hertling was an honest man but much too old for governing; one could speak to the Wilhelmstrasse, but the General Staff were impossible, and understood nothing of politics. There is nothing very original in these views; merely the fact that they were not apparently the impressions which the Nuncio had taken with him to Berlin.

According to Herr Erzberger, the practical inconvenience to the Imperial Government in having to deal through a Nuncio resident in Munich had given rise to discussion; in former times it was understood that one of the principal elements of opposition to a change was the dislike of the Empress to the presence of a Nuncio in Berlin. In January 1920, after the conclusion of peace, the Prussian and Bavarian Legations returned to Rome, and three months later the former presented fresh credentials as German Ambassador, while the Nuncio at Munich was transferred to Berlin. This prompt action on the part of the Germans rather discounted the effect of the long-promised and long-delayed appointment of a French representative; at Berlin the arrival before his colleagues of a Papal representative upset a plan under which the first place in the Diplomatic Body was to go to the French Ambassador. The French were annoyed, especially as they had already been put to some trouble in order to prevent precedence going to the Italian. The matter was after all of very secondary importance, but such advantage as was to be got out of it was for the Germans.

I have not the material for giving anything like a comprehensive account of the attitude during the war of the German press towards the Vatican. Besides the quotation already made, there were attacks in the " Hamburger Fremdenblatt " early in 1917, it being remarked that the one belligerent Power against which the Vatican had officially spoken was Germany. The " Vossische Zeitung " preached after the fashion of Tante Voss on the anti-German Romanism of the Vatican. Too much importance need not be attributed to the German comic papers; some very scurrilous things were published against the Vatican in the " Kladderadatch," " Ulk," " Jugend," the " Muskete " and " Simplicissimus." A small collection of them was published here.

Russia.

At the end of 1916 relations between the Vatican and the Russian Legation were frankly bad. The Russian Minister, M. Nelidof, was the son of a well-known Russian Ambassador in Constantinople more than thirty years ago; he was anything but *persona grata*. Russia, said the Cardinal Secretary of State, had never respected a right, had never kept a promise which concerned the interests of the Church; the last thing in the world which the Holy See could desire was the extension of Russian rule either in Poland or at Constantinople. Controversy had arisen over the policy of the Russian authorities, and notably of Count Bobrinsky, during the Russian occupation of Galicia. Among other causes of complaint, the Ruthenian Uniate Archbishop of Lemberg, Count Szepticki, had been maltreated and imprisoned. The vexatious laws against the Church were maintained and enforced; no communication was allowed between the Vatican and the bishops except through the Russian Administration, while even prayers in the books sent from Rome were clumsily censored and altered in transmission.

M. Nelidof soon left, and during the long interval till his successor, M. Lyssakowsky, arrived the new Liberal régime had been installed. All the old laws were swept away, complete religious freedom was guaranteed, extending to liberty for religious orders to teach. The Vatican declared themselves delighted with the new order, but sceptical of its continuance. After the victory of Bolshevism the Minister still remained.

Italy.

Even from the possibilities of Italian politics good relations between the Vatican and Baron Sonnino seemed to be excluded; his anti-clerical professions and Jewish origin seemed to debar him from any of those understandings which are a common solution in Italian political life to wide divergences of principle. As a condition to Italy's adhesion to the cause of the Allies, he had armed himself in April 1915 with his Pact of London. Clause 15 provided as follows :—

> " La France, la Grande-Bretagne et la Russie appuieront l'opposition que l'Italie formera à toute proposition tendant à introduire un représentant du Saint-Siège dans toutes les négociations pour la paix et pour le règlement des questions soulevées par la présente guerre."

What was the object of the clause? France was not at the time in diplomatic relation with the Holy See; Great Britain was scarcely indicated as its champion in such matters, while the hostility of Russia was a foregone conclusion. None of them stood to gain by the admission of a Papal delegate to a peace congress. A League of Nations would, it is true, have acquired in the eyes of many of their subjects strong moral support from the Pope's signature, but at the time the contracting parties were scarcely thinking of the League. The treaty was to remain secret, but in the course of discussions on the subject early in 1918, after the revelations made in Russia, it was frequently insisted by the Italian Government that the Vatican were aware of it. Is it possible that Baron Sonnino should himself have seen to it that this should be the case, that the Vatican should clearly understand that, whatever relations they might establish with other Powers, they were entirely dependent in this matter on his good-will? More than once the Italian Government justified their refusal to modify the article by urging that it was a " useful lever," but they gave no security that the leverage should be used in the interests of all the Allies rather than of the Consulta alone.

Communication between the Vatican and the Quirinal is carried on through the director of the " Fondo pel Culto," an Italian Government Office for administering certain ecclesiastical funds. The director, Baron Monti, is a *persona grata* at the Papal Secretariate of State, a friend of childhood of the late Pope, a school companion, and chosen for his present responsible and delicate functions on that account In some ways, therefore, relations with the Italian intermediary are of a more intimate and cordial character than those maintained with many a regular diplomatic representative whose appointment has been submitted to the usual perfunctory *agrément*. More than one report from this mission has drawn attention to the point. Taking an instance or two at random, one might recall the revelations respecting Prince Sixtus and his negotiations. Baron Monti, Cardinal Gasparri told me, had been hastily despatched by the Italian Government to make a friendly and confidential enquiry whether the Vatican were concerned in the business. The Cardinal, according to his own account, returned an equally friendly reply : " Whatever else we may be, we are neither lunatics nor children." In his turn the Cardinal, when in need of information, sends for Baron Monti in order to learn what had been agreed to at San Remo about the French protectorate at Jerusalem. It is unnecessary to insist that in these circumstances communications between Vatican and Quirinal do not require to be carried on either in private houses or at strange hours of the night, and that stories to that effect did not come from well-informed sources. Baron Monti, it may be noted, does not report to the Consulta, but direct to the Prime Minister, as his business is not considered as belonging to foreign affairs; he once showed me the file of his daily correspondence with the Vatican, conducted, it is true, on quarto, and not on foolscap, paper. So much for official etiquette. Baron Sonnino and Signor Orlando were by no means at one in their opinions. While in 1917 the former was assuring His Majesty's Embassy of the pro-German character of the Pope's policy, Germany and Austria being responsible for his peace proposals,[*] the Prime Minister was declaring such an idea to be nonsensical.[†] Baron Sonnino's diatribe of October 1917, described by his colleague, Signor Scialoja, as cretinism,[‡] was about the last open attack made by a Minister on the Pope. Before the end of the year the Government were loud in their thanks for the patriotic work done by the bishops in face of the enemy's invasion and in the interest of the national loan, the tirades of Mr. Bagot and others in England, who attributed the Caporetto disaster to the Vatican,[§] finding little or no echo in any responsible quarter in Italy. The ex-Prime Minister, Salandra, was the first to give an unqualified repudiation to the accusations brought by the French Embassy against the Vatican in connection with M. Caillaux, the published reports being described as " pure fantasy." Since then relations have steadily become more and more cordial. A step towards a lasting improvement was made by the Encyclica " Pacem, Dei Munus Pulcherrimum " of the 1st June, 1920, in which it was declared that the work of reconciliation among nations could be aided by the meeting of princes and heads of States; the Pope, therefore, considering the changed conditions of the times and the perilous trend of events, with a view to co-operation in the re-establishment in the fraternity of nations, would not be averse to modifying the conditions rightly laid down by his predecessors with regard to the visits of Catholic sovereigns to Rome. In other words, one standing cause of friction between Vatican and Quirinal is apparently to be removed in future. Visits of the King of Spain and the King of the Belgians were at once announced; so far the former has not taken place, but for reasons other than the long-standing controversy between Pope and King.

* Sir R. Rodd, telegram No. 760 of September 3, 1917; telegram No. 925A of November 11, 1917.
† To Foreign Office, No. 74 of November 23, 1917.
‡ To Foreign Office, No. 82 of December 16, 1917.
§ The Italian Commission of Enquiry expressly repudiated any such idea.

Belgium.

In July 1880 the Belgian Minister to the Holy See was recalled, and passports were given to the Nuncio, Mgr. Serafino Vannutelli, the reason invoked by the Liberal Prime Minister, M. Frère Orban, being the attitude of the Belgian bishops towards his law concerning primary education. Five years afterwards, under the next Ministry, the quarrel was made up, and the task of renewing relations was entrusted to Mgr. Ferrata, subsequently successful in Paris in maintaining relations which were broken off under his less skilful successor, Mgr. Lorenzelli. Cardinal Ferrata died in 1914 after a very brief tenure of office as Secretary of State to the late Pope. Since then relations with Belgium have been normal. On the outbreak of war the Nuncio in Brussels was Mgr. Tacci, whose attitude seems to have come in for criticism, be it fair or unfair. He was subsequently removed, a post being found for him at the Vatican without the usual promotion to a Cardinal's hat, for which he had to wait some years. The Belgian Minister was M. van den Heuvel, a lawyer and ex-Minister of Justice. Without losing his head he kept up a steady pressure of argument on the Vatican, and was rewarded by acquiring a position of considerable influence due to his patience.

Switzerland.

A controversy, ending in the dissolution of the diocese of Bâle in October 1873, brought about a rupture between the Federal Government and the Holy See. Whatever the actual cause of the breach, feeling was, in any case, running high; in Switzerland there was, in the closing years of the reign of Pius IX, the same wave of hostility to the Vatican which led to the Falck laws in Prussia and to the troubles under the Frère Orban Government in Belgium. The actual cause of dispute over the diocese of Bâle, and a further trouble in connection with the Ticino, were settled by succesful negotiations conducted in 1884 by Mgr. Ferrata, but for some years anti-clerical feeling was dominant at Berne until a Catholic, in the person of M. Zemp, could take his place in the Federal Council. Since then relations have steadily improved. A semi-official agent was kept at Berne during the war, principally to keep in touch with the representatives and clergy of the Central Powers who were unable to come to Rome. This arrangement seems to have given satisfaction in Switzerland, since, in the summer of 1920, after the conclusion of peace, Mgr. Maglione, who had acted as agent for some two years, was, after some negotiation with the Federal Council, formally accredited as Nuncio. In these respects times have changed considerably. In the middle of the last century civil war broke out in order to enable the Central Government to expel the Jesuits, in violation of the sovereign rights then enjoyed by the separate States; in the first year of the present war the General of the Jesuits took up his quarters at Zizers, in Switzerland, in order the better to discharge his functions without interference.

Proposed Establishment of Relations with China.

The desire of the Vatican to enter into diplomatic relations with the Chinese Government, in order the better to work for the interests of the numerous missions in the Chinese Empire, led to a conflict with the French Government. The Vatican maintained that the number and importance of the missions in China, and their increase in recent years, rendered necessary the presence of a Papal representative, in the same way as in India, Canada, Australia, the United States, &c.: they had their own representative at Constantinople and had never admitted that in protectorate countries they were diplomatically represented by the French. There was certainly an obvious absurdity in the Church being represented in China by the French, who at that time were refusing to have relations with the Pope. The situation was intolerable, and the Vatican, in endeavouring to deliver themselves from it, had the goodwill of the Belgians, the Italians and the Spaniards. The Germans were not, I believe, much interested at any time, and had already, for many years, refused to allow missionaries of German nationality to have recourse to French protection. With a poor case to defend, unwilling to join issue on the ground of the protectorate and the legitimate or illegitimate extension of its rights, the Quai d'Orsay was forced to have recourse to indirect means in order to defeat a distasteful proposal. At first it was given out that Mgr. Petrelli,* designated as Nuncio, was a friend of Prince Bülow, or, alternatively, of Admiral von Hintze. But there were difficulties in making out a plausible story, especially as Mgr. Petrelli had been in

* A Reuter's telegram from Peking was reproduced in the " Times " of August 10, 1918, with a headline in large letters : " German Intrigue through the Vatican."

the Philippines since 1903. Anyhow, the nomination was withdrawn in deference, as the Cardinal Secretary of State told me, to the *Entente*, and Mgr. Pisani was designated. To this the French raised objection on the ground that Mgr. Pisani entertained friendly sentiments towards the enemy, and was a *protégé* of Cardinal de Lai, whom they declared to be anti-*Entente*. It was at the same time admitted that the choice of candidate had little to do with the matter; the French Government based themselves on the right of protectorate secured by the Treaty of Tien-tsin.† while the object of the Vatican in opening up relations with countries like China was stated to be a plan to enable them, as soon as peace negotiations were near, to work behind the scenes for those of the belligerents whom they wished to help. With this, on the exercise of pressure by the French on the Chinese Government—His Majesty's Government did not join in it—the proposed relations were abandoned, the Vatican still maintaining, however, in a correspondence conducted through the Archbishop of Paris, their refusal to admit that the French protectorate included a right of diplomatic representation. Other work was found for Mgr. Pisani, the important post of Apostolic delegate in India. He was well known to me, and I do not know on what the charge of pro-Germanism on his part could be based. It is true, and the Cardinal Secretary of State admitted it to me, that he may not have been a *persona grata* to the French, since he had the confidence of the Italian Government, and, when I first knew him, held an appointment of a delicate character as member of a commission for looking after the interests of Italian subjects, mostly of the working classes, over the Italian frontier, *i.e.*, Switzerland, France, and in earlier times, Austria.

NOTE ON THE PRESS.

(By Mr. L. Wood.)

The only Vatican newspaper is the "Osservatore Romano." But it has no telegraphic service from abroad. It publishes correspondences from numerous countries; they appear very late; some are sent by Vatican people, secretaries of Nunciatures or Apostolic delegations or other ecclesiastics; some are sent by independent Catholics in those countries; some are made up here, translated from Catholic papers of the countries. I have heard Dalla Torre (the present editor) say to a Frenchman that they get any amount sent (independent) from Germany, and would be glad to have more from France to prevent appearing pro-German. I have been asked to let them have English Catholic news (in Italian—they have no one now who can translate), but what I have supplied has not been put in properly on account of their ignorance of English matters or possibly prejudice in the office. The office is hopelessly unbusinesslike and slow. *Temp.* Cerretti, I know that nothing verging on the political was allowed to be inserted without being passed by the Secretariate of State.

As regards amount of news appearing, there is hardly any English at all. Nor do I know where they get the occasional scraps they do publish. Possibly the Rev. Nicola, recently in the office, now at the Catholic University, Milan, who was at Washington and knows English, translates and sends to them.

There is a good deal that might be said—and with advantage—on news about the Vatican sent from here.

Ordinarily, English Catholic correspondents here do not send telegrams except occasional short ones on something interesting English Catholics. The "Universe" correspondent alone has got press rates, their go-ahead policy desiring some telegrams, but he does not send much.

Most of the news goes to England through Reuter, Cortesi or his people. For years Cortesi has been given a pull at the Vatican; he gets what other people cannot and gets it earlier. Michael Williams, of the N.C.W.C. American press service, told me he had found that Mgr. Pucci (of the "Corriere") was in with Cortesi, to whom he passed all the news he had. (But one does not yet know how things are going to be under Pius XI.) Cortesi's service has been generally sound, but it is not so personal as it used to be, and his people are not so reliable as he was.

It is hardly necessary here to dwell on the proper sources of official Vatican information and the way in which pronouncements, &c., get falsified through misunderstanding, prejudice or a desire for sensationalism.

In actual fact, it would be a very good thing if there were in Rome an English

----

† The Vatican were not, of course, a party to the treaty.

Catholic layman who could supply to the "Osservatore" true English Catholic news of interest and could get from the Vatican and supply quickly to the English press the truth about important political Vatican things here.

But it would be necessary (1) to have some commonsense in the "Osservatore" office; (2) to make the Vatican realise how valuable it would be for them to have a trustworthy means of disseminating the truth and preventing misunderstanding. Also you have got to get the English press to publish such news, which they will not do because it would be simple truth, not sensational.

o

CONFIDENTIAL.

(12421)

HOLY SEE.

Annual Report, 1923.

[C 3566/3566/22]

Sir O. Russell to Mr. MacDonald.—(Received March 3.)

(No. 25. Confidential.)   *British Legation to the Holy See,*
Sir,   *Rome, February 25, 1924.*
    I HAVE the honour to transmit herewith the annual report on the Holy See for the year 1923, which I have drawn up with the collaboration of Mr. Dormer, first secretary to His Majesty's Legation.

                  I have, &c.
                  ODO RUSSELL.

Enclosure.

Annual Report on the Holy See for 1923.

CONTENTS.

I.—INTRODUCTION.

    THE year 1923, the second year of the Pontificate of Pius XI, will ever remain memorable in the annals of the Papacy as having witnessed the visits of the British and Spanish Sovereigns to the Pope. From the purely Church point of view there were doubtless events of more abiding importance; but the visits of the Protestant

2111 [11454]
                B

King of England and of His Most Catholic Majesty of Spain to the Vatican were so significant of altered conditions and struck the public imagination to such a degree as to ensure them for ever a predominant place in the records of the past year. Edward VII was the first reigning King of England to visit the Pope since Canute in 1027 (unless we reckon Edward I, then Prince of Wales, who was passing through Rome on his return from Palestine when the news arrived of his father's death); but in Edward VII's case there was no British Legation to the Holy See, and His late Majesty's appearance at the Vatican was of an entirely private and unofficial character. King George and Queen Mary, on the other hand, were received in royal state with the tacit approval of the Italian Government and encouraged by the sympathetic interest of the vast majority of His Majesty's subjects.

2. The Spanish visit was an even more unique occurrence. Visits of heads of Roman Catholic States have not been possible since 1870 owing to the ban against the journeys of such personages to Rome. This was removed only in 1921 by the late Pope; and before that date, in spite of their privileged position, there is no record of a King of Spain, since the Emperor Charles V, having paid homage in person to the head of his Church. King Alfonso's journey to Rome aroused, therefore, much enthusiasm throughout the Catholic world.

3. In turning to matters of the Church the first event of importance was the Pope's encyclical on the "Peace of Christ in the Reign of Christ," which was followed by a series of brilliant letters throughout the year of which, perhaps, the most notable was the encyclical in July on St. Thomas Aquinas, the great authority on Catholic doctrine. Among other pronouncements, each with its special value, were the encyclical on St. Francis of Sales, the encyclical on the Eastern Church, the letters on St. Bernard of Menthon, on St. Columbanus of Bobbio, on the centenary of Luis Pasteur, on the spiritual exercises of St. Ignatius, as well as exhortations addressed to a continual flow of pilgrims from different countries in Europe and America embracing a wide field of religious activities and devotions. Words were not unaccompanied by action. A year's unremitting philanthropic labour has gone to lighten the lot of the hapless sufferers of Russia, of the Middle East and of South-Eastern Europe, whatever their religion. As a notable instance, I might quote the grant of the Papal villa at Castle Gandolfo as a refuge for 400 Armenian children orphans. The state of the Catholics in Germany, particularly in the west, has been the subject of continuous and anxious negotiation. The Beatification of Sœur Thérèse, Cardinal Bellarmino and Michael Garicoits were among the solemn festivities held. Remarkable, too, has been the revival of religion in Italy, so sensationally illustrated in the Eucharistic Congress at Genoa, the efforts to organise Catholic lay action in the religious and social spheres, and the insistence that such action must be kept distinct from anything approaching party politics.

4. In turning lastly to the political activity of the Vatican it will here suffice to note but the one great effort on the part of the Pope to reconcile the differences of the struggling nations. Although the chaotic state of Europe since the early days of the year had been viewed by the Vatican with ever-growing anxiety, it was only towards the end of June that Pius XI decided to take diplomatic action. On the 24th of that month His Holiness addressed a letter to the Cardinal Secretary of State defining the Papal attitude with regard to the problem of reparations. It was hoped that when everything else had failed an appeal from the chair of St. Peter addressed to Cardinal Gasparri and communicated to the Governments of the Great Powers would not be made in vain. That this appeal had little or no effect was mainly due to the action of France, who was not in a mood at that moment to tolerate interference of any description. Though the Governments of the other States were inclined to regard the step taken by the Pope as a valuable contribution towards the cause of peace, they were powerless without French approval to take up the discussion on the lines set forth in the Papal letter. The effort therefore failed, though it may be that some seed, as hinted by the Pope in his encyclical at the end of the year, may have fallen on good ground and that where there was apparently no result subsequent negotiations were not entirely uninfluenced by the appeal from Rome.

5. For subsequent reference and in order to make clear the Pope's attitude it will be necessary to quote the principal passages of His Holiness's letter. It ran as follows:—

"\. . . . At the beginning of our Pontificate . . . . we asked all to consider how very much worse would be the condition of Europe, already so miserable and threatening, if the attempts to reach sincere pacification and a lasting agreement should fail once again.

"Little more than a year has gone by and it is needless to point out how justified our fear was; in the short time that has intervened international relations have not only not improved, as there was every right to hope would result from the Genoa Conference, rather have they become worse, so as to justify anxiety and no small fear for the future. . . . .

"Therefore, while we endeavour with all our power and all the means which our children entrust to us to this end to alleviate the sufferings, so serious and so general, of the present time, it is our duty to take advantage of every occasion that offers to co-operate as best we may in the work incumbent of pacification and restoration in Christ longed for by peoples and individuals.

"Now that among the Governments of the Powers most closely concerned in the war new diplomatic conversations are in view, based on new proposals, in order to reach a friendly solution of the questions which are troubling Central Europe and inevitably recoiling on all the nations, we believe it to be our duty to raise again our voice, disinterested, impartial and of goodwill towards all, as the voice of the common father must be. Considering the grave responsibility lying at the moment on us, and on those who hold in their hands the destinies of the peoples, we conjure them once again to examine the different questions, and particularly the question of reparations, in that Christian spirit which does not set a dividing line between reasons of justice and the reasons of social charity on which the perfection of civil society is based. If and when the debtor, with the intention of paying reparation for the most serious damage suffered by populations and places once so prosperous and flourishing, gives proof of his serious will to reach a fair and definite agreement, invoking an impartial judgment in the limits of his own capacity to pay and undertaking to hand over to the judges every means of true and exact control, then justice and social charity, as well as the very interests of the creditors and of all the nations wearied of strife and longing for peace, seem to require that no demand shall be made from the debtor that he cannot meet without entirely exhausting his resources and his capacity for production, with irreparable damage to himself and to his creditors, with danger of social disturbances which would be the ruin of Europe and with resentment which would be a perpetual means of new and worse conflagrations. In equal measure, it is just that the creditors should have guarantees in proportion to their credits to ensure the payments on which depend interests vital for them too; we leave it, however, to them to consider whether for that purpose it is necessary to maintain in every case territorial occupations which impose heavy sacrifices on occupied and occupiers, or whether it would not be better to substitute for them, possibly by degrees, other guarantees equally effective and certainly less obnoxious.

"If these pacific arguments be agreed to by both sides, and in consequence the bitterness caused by the territorial occupation is eliminated and by degrees the occupation itself is reduced until it comes to an end entirely, it will be possible to reach that true pacification of the peoples which is also a necessary condition for the economic restoration which all keenly desire. Such pacification and restoration are of such great benefit for all the nations, conquerors and conquered, that any sacrifice seen to be necessary ought not to seem too great in order to obtain them."

*　　　*　　　*　　　*　　　*　　　*

6. No less than twenty-six States now have diplomatic representatives to the Pope as against twelve before the war. In the subsequent paragraphs, the relations of the Holy See being world-wide, unrepresented States where outstanding events have occurred are included, while a number of those who maintain Ministers here are omitted owing to the absence in their cases of exceptional occurrences in the course of the year.

II.—Foreign Relations.

(1.) *Great Britain.*

7. " If the thing depended on me, I should certainly enter upon diplomatic correspondence with the Court of Rome in a much more open and legitimate manner than has hitherto been attempted. If we refuse it, the bigotry will be on

our side, and most certainly not on that of His Holiness. Our unnatural alienation has produced, I am convinced, great evil and prevented much good. If the present state of the world does not make us learn something, our error is much more culpable.''

The above words, uttered by the great Burke in 1792, when, after the war with the French Republicans, it was found expedient to establish relations with the Holy See, apply with equal, if not greater, force to-day. His Majesty's Government were the first to realise this during the recent great war, and other States were not long in following the example set by them in 1914.

In the month of January 1923 my mission to Berne terminated on my appointment to succeed Count de Salis as British Minister to the Holy See, and, as the Secretary of State happened to be in Switzerland at that moment presiding over the Conference at Lausanne, I took the opportunity of visiting him there in order to receive instructions before taking up my new duties in Rome. After laying stress on .the importance of the post for purposes of observation and information, Lord Curzon told me that the mission, which had only borne a temporary character during the war, was now, in virtue of a Cabinet decision, to be converted into a permanent Legation. This might encounter a certain amount of opposition among ultra-Protestant circles in the United Kingdom, but these circles possessed no great influence, and the value of having a Minister where twenty-five other nations were represented outweighed any inconvenience which might be provoked by their protests. The affairs of Europe being in a disastrous condition, no authority could justifiably be ignored capable of contributing towards a settlement, and it was quite possible that the Pope's influence, thrown, as it would be, into the scale for peace, might prove some day of immense value. Moreover, the British Empire contained 14 million Catholics, who would regard with satisfaction the establishment of a permanent Legation to the Holy See.

8. I arrived in Rome on the 1st February, and on the 5th February presented my letters of credence to the Pope. After the official reception, Pius XI led me into his private library for a private conversation. There I was pleased to observe, as I have continued to observe subsequently, that the fact of not being a Catholic in no way detracted from His Holiness's kindly benevolence and frank demeanour towards His Majesty's representative. He talked freely and openly, and this same attitude, in an even more extended degree, has been consistently observed by the Cardinal Secretary of State. It will, I trust, not be deduced from the above that in my opinion His Majesty's Government would be better served by a Protestant than a Roman Catholic Minister in Rome. In many ways, indeed, the latter might be of greater use, and I only raise the point in the desire to prove that the attitude of the Vatican in this respect will leave the Secretary of State a perfectly free hand in the future to select a Minister irrespective of his religious denomination. It certainly was no light task to follow in the footsteps of Count de Salis, who occupied a unique position in Rome, but, thanks largely to the good words he himself put in on my behalf in high quarters before vacating his post, and possibly also to the fact that I was known to be imbued with Vatican traditions (being the third member of my family to represent an English Sovereign at the Papal Court), the path throughout has been made smooth.

9. In the series of interviews which I have had with Cardinal Gasparri in the course of the year he has made it abundantly clear that the Vatican have pinned their whole faith on His Majesty's Government for the task of restoring order in Europe. Every step taken in that direction has evoked their outspoken admiration and approval; and it was only towards the end of the year, when they realised that words were not always translated into acts, that their confidence showed signs of waning. But even then when they realised the difficulties—which I was not slow to accentuate—the Vatican continued in their idea that Great Britain alone among the Powers was honestly striving for a just settlement of European affairs. His Majesty's Government, on the other hand, were the first to acknowledge and approve the Pope's great effort in the interests of peace.

10. When in July His Holiness's letter on the European situation to Cardinal Gasparri was communicated to the Powers, His Majesty's Government lost no time in instructing me to inform His Eminence of "the appreciation with which they had learnt of this fresh evidence of interest taken by the Pope in the re-establishment of peace and tranquillity; an object which His Majesty's Government, in common with the Pope, have much at heart.''

11. The cordiality of the relations was destined in the course of 1923 to be still further enhanced by an event of transcendent importance. In the early part of the

year it was announced that the King and Queen were coming to Rome, and that an official visit to Pius XI at the Vatican would be included in their Majesties' programme. This visit took place on the 9th May; and in view of the historical significance of the ceremony, and for purposes of record, it may be of interest to quote *in extenso* the report sent to the Foreign Office on the evening of that memorable day :—

" . . . . The visit of their Majesties to the Vatican took place this morning.

" His Majesty arrived in full uniform, accompanied by the Queen, at the Legation from the Quirinal at 10·35 A.M.   At 10·45 they left the Legation, accompanied by the Royal suite, myself and Mr. Dormer, in private cars provided by the Vatican. This part of the programme was purely private, and consequently Prince Massimo, who accompanies Sovereigns to the Vatican when Papal State carriages are used, was not deputed to wait on their Majesties at the Legation.

" The streets were lined with dense crowds, and their Majesties had a very cordial reception as they drove along. It is to the credit of the Italian Government that, unlike on the occasion of King Edward's visit, military escorts were by special request from His Majesty's Ambassador conspicuous by their absence.

" Their Majesties arrived at 11·15 A.M. at the Gate of the Zecca, announced by a flourish of trumpets; and as they drove through the courtyards into the Cortile S. Damaso the band of the Palatine played ' God Save the King,' and a company of the Palatine guard and Pontifical gendarmerie rendered military honours. Inside the Vatican precincts the full programme for the State visit was carried out with a pageantry which will not easily be forgotten by those who were privileged to witness it.

" Their Majesties were accompanied through the last room by the Maestro di Camera, and the Pope received them alone in the Sala del Tronetto. The conversation, which ranged over general topics, lasted about twenty minutes, and at the end the Pope presented his photograph in silver frames and their Majesties gave him theirs.

" The King then presented the Royal suite to His Holiness, and later the high dignitaries of the Pontifical Court were presented to their Majesties, as well as a number of British prelates of the Court and heads of the various British colleges.

" The cortège which had accompanied their Majesties on their arrival in the Vatican Palace was then re-formed and their Majesties proceeded to pay the customary visit to the Cardinal Secretary of State. Their Majesties then graciously shook hands with a few British clerical students representing the different British colleges in Rome.

" The departure from the Vatican took place at 11·55, and as their Majesties drove out through the Cortile del Papagallo the students of the English college presented to Her Majesty, on behalf of and amidst the respectful cheers of the 400 British students who lined the entrance, a bouquet of roses tied with red, white and blue ribbons.

" Their Majesties reached the Legation at 12·30, and, after changing into the Quirinal carriages, proceeded to the Quirinal Palace to change into blue undress. Their Majesties returned to the Legation at 12·50, and at 12·55 the Cardinal Secretary of State returned their visit. At the conclusion of this interview His Majesty presented His Eminence with a massive silver inkstand.

" The luncheon which followed at 1 o'clock was given · by their Majesties. . . . .

" At 2·15 P.M. their Majesties proceeded in Vatican cars to visit privately St. Peter's, where they were conducted round by Cardinal Merry del Val, and thence by the Scala Regia direct into the Vatican, where a visit was made to the galleries and museums.

" Their Majesties were accompanied by Mgr. de Samper, the Maggiordomo, and by Commendatore Professor Nogara, Director-General of the Museums, as well as by other experts.

" Cardinal Gasquet met their Majesties at the Borgia apartments and accompanied them round the library.

" Their Majesties returned to the Legation at 4·30, and at 4·50 received Cardinals Vannutelli, Merry del Val and Bisleti, as representing the three orders of the College of Cardinals. This visit was returned a few minutes later on Cardinal Vannutelli, Dean of the Sacred College, by Admiral Sir Charles

Madden and General Lord Cavan, who thanked His Eminence on their Majesties' behalf for the visit.

"The visit, an historical one which will not quickly be forgotten by those who were privileged to assist, can, I venture to think, be termed a complete success. Fanatics may continue to protest, but the two greatest Sovereigns on earth have met all the same, and it is difficult to imagine anything but good resulting from the visit of their Majesties to the Vatican. The most bitter opponent of the Papacy could hardly have remained unmoved at the simple, and at the same time impressive, manner with which the Pope invoked God's blessing on their Majesties and the Royal Family, on their suite, on England and the whole Empire."

12. Apart from the larger political aspect of the Legation, enhanced to a marked degree by the Royal visit, there arose during the year a variety of questions of common interest to Great Britain and the Holy See calling for attention and negotiation. The Vatican appealed to the good offices of His Majesty's Government on behalf of the unfortunate Chaldeans, of Christian schools in Turkey and, above all, on behalf of Catholics in Russia. This latter question is more fully treated under the chapter relating to Russia.

(a.) *Palestine.*

13. *The Latin Patriarchate.*—The efforts of this Legation have been continually directed to bring about a better state of things at the Latin patriachate in so far as their relations with the British authorities are concerned. The present Latin patriarch is wholly unsuited to the post, a fact which is realised by the Vatican as well as by ourselves. The difficulty is how to dispose of him. There is every reason to believe that he will be removed as soon as a post can be found for him. In the ordinary course of events a patriarch would eventually be created a cardinal; but so far the Pope has shown himself unwilling to promote Mgr. Barlassina.

14. In the circumstances it was felt that the next best thing was to secure the appointment of an English auxiliary bishop, or, failing that, of an English secretary to the patriarchate. The obvious candidate was Father Paschal Robinson, who stood in high favour not only with His Majesty's Government, but also with the Vatican and propaganda. The insuperable obstacle against his selection, however, was that he was a Franciscan, which would have involved difficulties with other religious orders. His appointment being found impossible, the Cardinal Secretary of State asked Cardinal Gasquet if he knew of another English priest who would be acceptable to His Majesty's Government. He, in his turn, consulted the Bishop of Salford, who recommended Father Godric Keane. Though this solution caused disappointment, I was instructed to intimate that His Majesty's Government saw no objection, and I understand that Father Keane has now been made secretary. The Franciscan Order, however, were somewhat alarmed at what might be the scope of his duties; but I was able to assure them that neither officially nor officiously would he act as intermediary in any question affecting the Holy Places.

15. The vacancy at Turin caused by the death of Cardinal Richelmy gave rise to hopes that that see would be offered to Mgr. Barlassina, and that Father Paschal Robinson would be made patriarch at Jerusalem. I was instructed to intimate to the Vatican that this latter appointment would be welcomed by His Majesty's Government and acquiesced in by the French Government; and that we, on our side, should raise no objection to the appointment of one of the French White Fathers as auxiliary bishop. I broached the subject to Cardinal Gasparri, and, as I anticipated, he said that there was no likelihood of either appointment.

16. The service held in the Anglican Cathedral of St. George at Jerusalem on the occasion of the the King's birthday gave rise to a serious incident. Invitations to the service were sent to Mgr. Barlassina and to the Consular Corps. Mgr. Barlassina did not attend, and apparently used his influence to induce the Catholic representatives to adopt a similar attitude.

17. Lord Curzon took so serious a view of this incident that the Legation was instructed to make a strong representation to the Vatican, and to add that, unless satisfactory assurances were given, the mission might have to be withdrawn. These instructions were subsequently modified in so far as Mgr. Barlassina's action in not attending the service himself was concerned (this, as was pointed out, was, in any case, out of the question).

18. The representations were made, and Cardinal Gasparri at once expressed

his regret at Mgr. Barlassina's interference in the actions of foreign representatives, and gave implicit assurances as to his future conduct. His Eminence followed this up with an official note, in which these regrets and assurances were renewed. The incident thus terminated satisfactorily.

19. Mgr. Barlassina has created trouble all round. Not only are his relations strained with His Majesty's Government in Palestine, but he has also incurred the hostility of the Arabs, who have demanded an Arab patriarch, making a delicate situation still more difficult.

20. The problem of what will be done when he leaves Jerusalem and who will be his successor is not yet solved. The question was at one time considered of handing the patriarchate over to the Greek Uniates, but I hear that it was found unfeasible. As a successor to Mgr. Barlassina, the most likely candidate at present is perhaps Mgr. Vallega, until recently Archbishop of Smyrna. He is a diplomatist, and from what I have heard should prove entirely suitable from our point of view.

21. As regards other questions with which, at times, this Legation has had to deal, such as Zionism and the Holy Places, there have been no developments during the year. The question of the Holy Places is regarded, of course, by the Vatican as of the highest importance, and the difficulty of putting through any schemes regarding the Holy Places Commission which has not their concurrence has already been seen; as, for instance, in the case of Lord Balfour's project, submitted to the Council of the League of Nations in 1922.

22. The alleged activities of some Protestant missionary bodies and the assertion that they are conducting an anti-Catholic propaganda have, in the Italian press and, I understand, in other Catholic countries, led, at times, to some bitter criticism of British rule in Palestine. Similarly, the incident which is said to have taken place in December, when the Copts attacked the Latins and inflicted loss of life, was met with a storm of indignation in Italian newspapers. But neither in this nor as regards propaganda have the Vatican made any comment. Nevertheless there is no disguising the fact that the jubilation which greeted the British occupation of Palestine has given place to a noticeable feeling of uncertainty and suspicion; a feeling, too, that there was greater liberty for the Church and religion under the régime of the Turks.

23. It is calculated that there are altogether some 70,000 Catholic missionaries scattered throughout the world, a large proportion of whom carry on their work in British possessions. The present Pope takes the keenest interest in the foreign missions, and has centralised their headquarters in Rome. That great importance is attached to their work is evident; and one can hardly open a Catholic newspaper or parish magazine anywhere without seeing an item of missionary news.

24. Many of the questions affecting the Empire that have arisen during the year have been of a local character; but when viewed as part of a collective whole they assume a considerable importance.

25. In the case of India, the country chiefly concerned, it was decided that German and Austrian missionaries should, as a general measure, be excluded for a period of five years after the conclusion of the war, although exemptions might be granted under certain conditions in the case of individuals belonging to " recognised societies.'' This period of five years will soon expire, and the difficulties which at times have been encountered should gradually disappear. Some welcome modifications affecting neutrals were introduced in June and again extended in December. It is now possible for missionaries of neutral nationality to obtain visas for India without their applications having to be dealt with by the India Office, so long as they are submitted to Cardinal Bourne. It would undoubtedly help matters and smooth the path if, in urgent cases, applications could be dealt with by this Legation; delay in reference to London is, indeed, the main source of complaint.

26. In the case of ex-enemy nationals, exceptions have been made and the Government of India agreed, in August, to the admission of four or five German sisters into the United Provinces, although they were not on the list of " recognised " societies.

27. During the year questions were raised affecting Catholic missions in the Tanganyika Territory and Nyasaland. These concerned the division of " spheres of influence " among the missionaries of different denominations. Representations were made by the Vatican in the first case, with the result that these divisions were removed as affecting Catholic missions. As regards Nyasaland, the result is not yet known.

(b.) *Ireland.*

28. Considering the historical attachment of Ireland to the Holy See, it is not surprising that she should be strongly represented in Rome. Two important religious orders, the Carmelites (of the old observance) and Redemptorists have Irishmen at their head, and in addition to the Irish church of St. Patrick's and the Irish College there is a house of Irish Dominicans, Irish Franciscans and the Christian Brothers.

29. The disturbed state of Ireland had of course its repercussion in Rome, and it was doubtless with great relief that the Vatican learned of the establishment of the Free State Government and the gradual return to more normal conditions.

30. The action of the Irish bishops at the beginning of the year in prohibiting access to the sacrament to anyone taking part in the Republican campaign of murder and arson led to widespread petitions and protests addressed to the Holy See from different parts of the world. It was argued that men fighting in the Republican cause were entitled to their political opinions, and there was no justification for the bishops' intervention. So many conflicting accounts poured in of what was taking place that the Pope decided in March 1923 to send a mission to make enquiries on the spot and to aid so far as possible the cause of pacification. The prelate chosen was Mgr. Luzio, who had spent some ten years in Ireland as a professor at Maynooth. The fact that he knew Mr. de Valera well was hoped to be an advantage, as, it was felt, it might be easier for a friend to influence him rather than a stranger. Mgr. Luzio took with him a secretary, but the latter became ill and the substitute that was found for him was a deplorable selection. Mgr. Luzio was led into a Republican atmosphere, with the inevitable result that he became identified with the Republican cause and aroused suspicion both among the Irish hierarchy and the Free State Government. I happened to be visiting Cardinal Gasparri one day towards the end of April, when a telegram arrived from Mgr. Luzio announcing the decision of the Republicans to abstain from further hostilities. To my surprise two days later I received a visit from Mr. Desmond FitzGerald, the Free State Minister for External Affairs. He explained that he had come to Rome in order to discuss the mission and its objects with the Cardinal Secretary of State and to remove the misunderstanding which had been aroused through the action of an unscrupulous press campaign. Mr. FitzGerald's conversation with the Cardinal cleared the air, as His Eminence succeeded in convincing him that the mission was only designed to assist, if possible, in pacification; and that the various irritating instructions that the Vatican were supposed to have sent to Mgr. Luzio had no existence in fact. Amongst other things, the Vatican had been accused of sending the Pope's blessing to Dr. Con Murphy, who had been on hunger-strike in a Dublin prison. The accusation proved to be unfounded, as no such message had ever been sent.

31. Mgr. Luzio was eventually recalled. It was, I think, realised that his mission had been badly conducted; and it was deplored that the feeling should have been allowed to grow that the Vatican had any sympathy for the Republican movement or that they had been actuated by unfriendly feelings towards the Free State.

32. Happily, the agitation which was formerly carried on in Irish circles in Rome against England is now practically dead; and with one or two exceptions I find that the Irish here (at least, those who are British subjects) are now entirely friendly.

33. In reviewing the events of the past year as affecting Ireland, I cannot omit to mention the festivities held at Bobbio in September in honour of an Irish saint, St. Columbanus. The celebrations, which were attended by President Cosgrave and other members of the Free State Government, as well as by a number of Irish pilgrims under the leadership of the Archbishop of Dublin, were carried out in solemn manner. The Pope was specially represented by a Cardinal Legate, who paid a warm tribute to Irish devotion to the Catholic faith and to the Holy See, and the civil authorities showed every courtesy and attention.

34. The Irish pilgrims came on afterwards to Rome and were received by the Pope. In the allocution delivered at the last consistory held on the 21st December, the Pope referred briefly to Ireland, "nostra Irlanda," as he termed it, expressing the pleasure with which he had learnt from Cardinal Logue's pastoral letter and from other sources that conditions there were becoming more settled.

(2.) *Italy.*

35. Though the Holy See and Italy are still unreconciled, Signor Mussolini may fairly claim that he has done more than any Italian statesman since 1870 to restore the Catholic faith to its natural place in the nation's life. Unlike his predecessors, he has not hesitated to proclaim that an Italian can be true to the State whilst being true to the Church, that the two are not incompatible. Both by words and by deeds he has shown his appreciation of religion as an essential element in the task of reconstruction. The Crucifix has been restored to the schools, religious instruction has been made compulsory, and certain festivals of the Church have been made a holiday; while the civil and military authorities have not only shown due respect to the many public religious celebrations held during the year, but they have also co-operated in their success. This was notably the case at Genoa, where ten Cardinals attended the Eucharistic Congress in September and a procession was formed, 15 kilom. in length. The desire, moreover, to avoid anything unfriendly to the Holy See was made manifest in the extremely moderate tone adopted by the official speakers on the occasion of the anniversary of the occupation of Rome. The perfunctory character of the ceremony paled before the elaborate festivities arranged a fortnight later in honour of the first anniversary of the Fascista march on Rome.

36. On the other side, the Vatican has shown a conciliatory disposition. Cardinal Gasparri's announcement during the war that for the settlement of the Roman question he placed his faith in the Italian sense of justice is constantly quoted; and the present Pope's first act was one of conciliation when, on his election, for the first time since 1870, he gave his blessing *urbi et orbi* from the loggia of St. Peter's and again at Christmas 1922 in his first encyclical, when, in renewing the protest of Pius IX and the succeeding Popes, he referred to his native country in the warmest tones of affection.

37. That Signor Mussolini has pleased the Vatican by his attitude towards religion is evident from the chorus of praise and approval which his various acts have evoked from ecclesiastical authorities. But whenever on either side an act of courtesy and deference was shown its effect was marred by a portion of the press in Italy and abroad, especially in France, acclaiming it as the final step towards reconciliation. The Roman question, it was declared, had finally settled itself and had died a natural death. The Law of Guarantees had at last come into its own, and there was no longer any reason why the Pope should not leave the Vatican, and, as a good Italian citizen ("Papa cittadino"), join in the Canzone del Piave and indulge in *italianità* with the rest of them.

38. The "Osservatore Romano," the official Vatican organ, has proved itself more than a match for its opponents of the Liberal press. Though unbending as regards the main problem dividing the two Powers, its articles have been uniformly courteous in tone and have succeeded in keeping the main issue before the public. It has never wearied of pointing out that, however meritorious might be the attitude of the new Italy towards religion, the situation created for the Papacy by the occupation of Rome was a juridical problem which still remained untouched and was as much awaiting solution to-day as in 1871 or in 1915. This was the line taken by Cardinal Gasparri in discussing the attitude of the Italian Government with me one day. Signor Mussolini himself had deserved well of the Church, on the whole; but no one could speak of the attitude of those who would come after him. The Roman question, which is perhaps the most arduous problem of the century, is so often misunderstood that it may not be out of place to give here a brief description of its main features from the Catholic standpoint.

39. Before September 1870 the guarantee of the Pope's sovereignty and independence lay in his territorial dominion over the Papal State. By conquering that state Italy destroyed the guarantee. In the changed conditions of the times, and for the better discharge of his spiritual ministry, the Pope could renounce the *summum jus* of a return pure and simple to his temporal power of old. But he cannot, in virtue of his very office, renounce the right and duty of demanding something which in the eyes of the Catholic world will adequately substitute the lost guarantee. Either he must remain a sovereign as before 1870 or become a subject; and if he is a subject he cannot be independent. The same reasons which impelled Pius VII in 1813 to resist becoming the "chaplain" of Napoleon prevent Pius XI from accepting the situation created by the Law of Guarantees of 1871. This law was probably founded on the Napoleonic guarantees, but was even less acceptable.

c

Apart from some of its provisions, it had the radical defects of being a unilateral instead of a bilateral act, and of having the character of an internal law. It was thus an act of State sovereignty and as such was no guarantee of the liberty and independence of a Power both super-national and itself sovereign. What the Vatican will consider sufficient for its purpose has not transpired. It seems quite certain that it would not wish in these days for the return of territory of any size.

40. There are few who will deny that a settlement would benefit Italy. There are some who fear that it would not benefit the Papacy. To these, however, the reply has been that, as in the past the Holy See has preserved its independence, so now it would be failing in its duty if it accepted any settlement which did not keep this independence intact and visible. The respect which the Pope owes to the national conscience of the Italians he owes equally to the national conscience of the French, Portuguese and of all his spiritual subjects.

(3.) *France*.

41. Diplomatic relations between France and the Vatican, which had been broken off in 1904, were resumed on the 4th May, 1920; and on the 1st May, 1921, M Jonnart, who had been Governor of Algeria, presented his letters of credence as Ambassador. As the foreign policy of his Government as well as their attitude towards the Church in France were thoroughly distasteful to the Vatican, his task was no easy one. Towards the end of the year under review he decided, mainly on the grounds of ill-health, to resign his appointment, which he had only held with reluctance. As the relations during his mission were more or less consistently strained, it may perhaps be well to record in the first instance the few successes he was able to achieve before mentioning the two main causes of political difference between the French Government and the Holy See. After the occupation of the Rhineland and later on of the Ruhr, M. Jonnart obtained with no small difficulty the recognition by the Vatican of Mgr. Rémond as Aumônier général of the Rhineland and the substitution of his jurisdiction for that of the German bishops as far as French troops, French officials and French religious schools were concerned. In Morocco he induced the Vatican to create two religious zones to correspond to the two political zones; and at the same time to wrest from the Spanish Archbishop of Cadiz and from the Spanish Franciscans the right they had arrogated to themselves of nominating the secular clergy in the French one. Finally, though he did not actually have the satisfaction of signing the agreement with the Vatican for the creation of the diocesan associations which was to regulate the status of the Church in France, he bore the whole brunt of these protracted negotiations. Before quitting Rome, thanks to his unremitting labours in this direction, they had reached a point when the French jurists were able to declare that the project as framed by the Vatican was in conformity with French legislation. After this there remained but the adjustment of details, and it can be confidently anticipated that his successor, M. Doulcet, will have the good fortune to witness the entry into force of an arrangement which will serve in a large measure to ameliorate the relations, as far as Church questions, at any rate, are concerned, between France and the Holy See.

42. The situation with regard to foreign policy which M. Jonnart was called upon to face entailed even more delicate handling than Church and domestic questions, and here his diplomacy can be said to have failed. In justice to him it must be stated that no one else could have done better, owing to the conviction on the part of France that the Vatican were imbued with pro-British and pro-German sentiments, and the conviction on the part of the Vatican that France, by her determination to destroy and dismember Germany, was delaying the recovery of Europe and increasing thereby the distress and sufferings of the German people. Those views were not unnaturally accentuated by the Pope's letter on reparations quoted in the introduction to this report. It aroused in Paris feelings of perturbation and resentment, and finally became the subject of a debate in the Chamber of Deputies. In the course of this debate, M. Poincaré stated that it was the duty of the Government to speak of the letter of His Holiness without exaggerating the incident or speaking with heat. Cardinal Gasparri had informed the French Ambassador that the letter had been written in a spirit of pacification and universal charity. The Pope has recognised the right of the creditors. M. Jonnart had replied that there seemed no justification for the Pope's intervention and that France would be astonished at his action. M. Jonnart on instruction from Paris had then sought an audience of the Pope, who himself stated that the letter had been issued solely

for the public well-being; and that it incidentally presupposed the good faith of Germany. The Belgian victims of the German outrage which followed proved to His Holiness that France was right, and the Pope invited his representative at Munich to express his reprobation of such acts of sabotage. As to the letter itself, M. Poincaré declared that no matter how high the authority by which it was written that authority had no power of intervention in the internal or external policy of France. The republic had a lively respect for all religious beliefs; but the intervention of a spiritual power in political questions weakened his authority.

43. The attitude of France, as voiced by the Prime Minister, had the effect of nipping in the bud the Pope's intervention in the interests of peace; and the year rolled by without any further attempt being made from Rome. Apart from the mutual distrust engendered by the war, another cause of dissension was the strong objection on the part of the Holy See to the historic protectorate over the Roman Catholics in the East exercised for several centuries by France. The thesis of the Vatican was that this right had lapsed; and Cardinal Gasparri practically told my predecessor Sir Henry Howard that he preferred Protestant England to Catholic France as ruler of Palestine. According to the logical view of the Holy See, if the protectorate depends on treaties concluded with the Turk, it lapses like all other treaty rights in places out of which the Turk has been ejected as he was at San Remo and Sèvres. But in spite of this the French clung tenaciously to their claims, while bitterly and unjustifiably resenting the lack of support on the part of the Vatican. Towards the end of the year M. Jonnart departed and M. Doulcet was appointed to succeed him. Being *persona grata*, it is possible, nay, even likely, that he will be able to place the relations, at any rate in some respects, on a more satisfactory footing.

(4.) *Spain.*

44. In the year which has passed Spain's position as the foremost Catholic country has been brought into prominence by two outstanding events : the bestowal by the Pope in May of the Golden Rose on the Queen, and the visit of the King and Queen in November to the Vatican.

45. The decision to send a mission with the Golden Rose was come to by the Pope early in the year. But a hitch occurred in March, and for a time it looked as if the gift would be withheld. Under the pressure of the extreme left wing of the then Liberal Coalition, the Government apparently contemplated in March a modification of article 11 of the Spanish Constitution dealing with the Roman Catholic religion of the country. Strong opposition was shown by the Cardinal Archbishop of Zaragoza, and the Nuncio, Mgr. Tedeschini, is said to have felt such indignation that he proposed to ask for his passports. In the beginning of April the Pope received a large Spanish pilgrimage, and, in addressing the pilgrims, His Holiness let it be plainly seen that he expected the King to show no hesitation in defending the Catholic faith, to which he owed his own greatness and his hopes for the future.

46. Whatever had been the intentions of the Government, the proposal was dropped, and the mission, headed by the Marchese Sacchetti as special envoy, left Rome in May. The practice of bestowing the Golden Rose dates from about the 13th century. It was usually awarded in return for some special service rendered to the Church, and among the recipients have been many Sovereigns, cities and generals of historic fame. His Majesty's Ambassador at Madrid reported that the ceremony was conducted with great magnificence in the presence of all the members of the Royal Family, the Ministers, Grandees of Spain and the whole Diplomatic Body.

47. The long-expected visit of the King and Queen to Rome took place in November. The difficulties to be faced in connection with the Roman question on such occasions are at all times vexatious and delicate, but they were doubly so in the case of the Spanish visit. No secret was made of the fact that King Alfonso attached greater importance to his visit to the Vatican than to his visit to the Quirinal, and there is ground for believing that the latter showed no very accommodating dispositions. Their Majesties arrived in Rome at midday on the 18th November and proceeded almost immediately from the Quirinal to the Spanish Embassy to the Holy See and thence to the Vatican. The King read a stirring address, in which, while emphasising his Catholic sentiments and devotion to the Holy See, he took occasion to put forward a number of requests. The Pope was asked to use his influence to bring about greater unity among the Spanish people, to remember Spanish claims and privileges in the Holy Land, and to give to the Spanish American

republics larger representation in the College of Cardinals. He concluded by proclaiming himself ready to march at the head of his army and nation to the Pope's assistance should a new crusade ever be raised against the enemies of the Church. The Pope's reply was cordial and affectionate, but extremely guarded, and the King was reminded that no one can expect to obtain all he wants on this earth. On the whole, the visit was indubitably a great success. The efforts of a portion of the Liberal press to stir up ill-feeling between the Vatican and the Quirinal had little effect, and both the King and Queen of Spain, by their tact, charm of manner and general attitude, contributed in no small degree to the enhancement of their country's prestige in the eyes of the Catholic world.

(5.) *Germany*.

48. Before the war there were Prussian and Bavarian Ministers in Rome and a Papal Nuncio at Munich. The importance attached to closer relations was promptly demonstrated after the conclusion of the armistice by the appointment of a Papal Nuncio at Berlin, by transferring the Prussian Legation into an Embassy and by the retention of a Nuncio in Munich and a Bavarian Minister to the Holy See. This double representation of German interests suggests a certain flexibility, according as it might be desired to profit by insistence in the importance of the Catholic element in the Empire or on the disagreeable results which might follow resistance to a Government backed by a latent hostility of North and East Germany. As a matter of fact, with the actual representatives the system is working smoothly, the Bavarian Minister, a devout Catholic, being content to confine his activities to the problems of the Church and to leave political questions to be dealt with by the Ambassador. The post-war relations between Germany and the Holy See cannot, however, be said to be running as yet in any very definite channel. This is due partly to the unsettled state of Germany and to the frequent change of Ministries, and, above all, to an all-pervading feeling of sympathy at the Vatican for the sufferings of the German people, which has had the effect during the past year of obscuring political questions, or, at any rate, of relegating them to a secondary position. This has greatly facilitated the task of the German representatives, and it was only after the Papal letter on reparations in June, quoted in the introduction, that the Ambassador had cause to protest at what his Government considered to be unfair treatment on the part of the Vatican. Germany, it is true, could take no exception to the terms of the letter itself, which in France was even stigmatised as a pro-German document, but, when a few days after its publication, at the instance of the French and Belgian Ambassadors, the Apostolic Nuncio at Berlin was instructed to warn the German authorities against all acts of sabotage, the German Ambassador lodged an indignant protest with the Cardinal Secretary of State. He affirmed emphatically that his Government were not responsible for acts of sabotage, that the German population in the occupied territories were living under intolerable conditions, and that it was therefore the troops of the occupying Powers who should in the first instance be called upon by the Pope to revise their conduct. In order to counteract the unfortunate impression created in Germany, he was instructed to persuade the Cardinal to send fresh instructions to the Papal representatives in Paris and Brussels to exhort the French and Belgian Governments to exercise moderation in the occupied territories. As the suggestion was adopted, he may be said to have had the last word in the controversy which raged round the Papal letter. In the following July the German Ambassador handed in a memorandum at the Vatican containing the conditions on which the German Government would abandon passive resistance in the Ruhr and the proposals which they would offer if negotiations could be resumed. As a similar document was communicated to the Foreign Office by the German Ambassador in London, a correspondence ensued, in which the Vatican offered to lend their co-operation should it be needed by His Majesty's Government, but, as shortly after this passive resistance witnessed its last struggle, neither His Majesty's Government nor the Vatican were called upon to intervene. Though political mediation both on this occasion and at other periods was withheld, the Holy See were able during the year to render various services to Germany both by sending material aid to the distressed districts and by despatching a delegate, Mgr. Testa, to the occupied area to report on abuses and to exercise whenever possible a pacificatory influence. By these acts and many others it was apparent that the rehabilitation of Germany, the relief of distress and the return to normal conditions were matters of absorbing concern to the Holy See throughout 1923.

(6.) *Portugal*.

49. The relations between the Holy See and Portugal during the past year have been normal; and I am informed that nothing but routine matters arose. The Portuguese Minister told me that he seldom has to consult Lisbon, that he is more guided by what he knows to be the feelings of the people than by those of his constantly changing Governments.

50. Evidence of the good relations with the Vatican was afforded when the Pope agreed with the President in conferring the red hat on Mgr. Locatelli, the Papal Nuncio at Lisbon, who had been created Cardinal in December 1922. In the days of the monarchy the King of Portugal performed this ceremony, but the privilege lapsed with the separation of Church and State under the republic. The concession to the late President was, I understand, for that one occasion and was not necessarily to constitute a practice. The separation of Church and State in Portugal does not apply to Portuguese possessions abroad, or even in countries such as India, where Portugal has retained the " padroado." From our point of view this is apt to be an inconvenience, as those who have had to deal with the " padroado " question in the Bombay Province well know. The agitation carried on by the British East Indian community against the jurisdiction of the Bishop of Damaun is not entirely a religious grievance, but partly economic. It is a source of annoyance to the Vatican as well as to ourselves, but, as this Legation has pointed out, their hands are tied by the concordat. So far the Portuguese Government appear to cling to their ancient position; but the Apostolic delegate in India told me when he was in Rome recently that he hoped, in conjunction with the Holy See, to reach a solution without touching the concordat.

(7.) *Austria*.

51. Vienna, though bereft of its importance by the suppression of the monarchy, remains a valuable post of observation for the Vatican, whence the many complicated religious problems agitating the succession States can be studied. An able diplomat, Mgr. Sibilia, has been sent there for the purpose; and the Austrian Republic, with great foresight and wisdom at the outset of its career, selected as its representative to the Holy See the famous Dr. Pastor, whose history of the Popes is destined to supersede all other writings on that subject; who enjoys the personal friendship of the present Pontiff; and is altogether a *persona grata* at the Vatican. In the month of April Mgr. Seipel, the Austrian Prime Minister, visited the Pope to discuss among other things the conclusion of a new concordat, the old one, limited " ad Principem," having lapsed with the disappearance of the Habsburgs. These discussions, being conducted in a friendly and sympathetic spirit on both sides, are likely to produce satisfactory results in the near future.

(8.) *Poland*.

52. Poland, although Slav, being strongly Roman Catholic, enlisted the interest of the Papacy in a special degree when she re-embarked on an independent existence after a long period of thraldom. The Vatican has been on the side of the Poles in the darkest hours of their history. Clement XIII protested against the iniquitous partition of Poland, while both Gregory XVI and Pius IX remonstrated on various occasions with the oppressors of the Poles. Benedict XV at the conclusion of the war sent a message of comfort and hope to the Polish nation, and later on showed his sense of the importance by selecting as his Nuncio at Warsaw so eminent a man as Mgr. Ratti (now Pius XI). One of the first acts of his Pontificate was to congratulate the Poles upon their victory over the Bolsheviks. Though it is perhaps of advantage to Poland that the Pontiff should have had personal experience of Polish affairs, the Papacy has been obliged to observe a certain caution. Thus in July 1921 the late Pope sent a strongly worded letter to Warsaw warning the Polish bishops and clergy against interference in Polish internal politics; adding that they would greatly aid the resurrection of Poland by keeping within the limits of the Church's mission. As it turned out, this warning was not superfluous, for Polish politics have involved the Holy See in various disputes during the past year and notably in the case of Mgr. Szeptyzki, Archbishop of Leopoli. This prelate, head of the Ruthenian Church, who was alleged by the Polish Government to have indulged

in political activity hostile to the Polish State and to the rights of Poland in Eastern Galicia, was arrested by them on his way from Vienna to Lemberg. The Polish Government demanded that he should clearly declare his allegiance in a pastoral letter before entering Galicia, and public opinion supported the Government in this attitude. As the Vatican were naturally annoyed at this indignity and endeavoured to insist on Mgr. Szeptyzki being allowed to return to his diocese, the relations became somewhat strained. Finally, the Archbishop having been induced to make a verbal declaration of fidelity to the Polish Republic, he was allowed to return to Lemberg, and the incident was considered closed.

(9.) *Hungary.*

53. Though the relations of the Vatican with the Hungarian Government are nominally close and cordial, a certain amount of tension has been caused during the year by differences of opinion over ecclesiastical appointments. In virtue of an ancient right, the Kings of Hungary have for centuries past enjoyed the right to nominate archbishops and bishops after informing Rome and obtaining the *agrément* of their nominee. When, on the Crown becoming vacant, the Vatican withdrew this ancient privilege, the Hungarian Government took the first opportunity of attempting to assert their right to nominate. In the beginning of the year the Archbishop of Kalocsa—the richest bishopric in Hungary—died and the choice of the Hungarian Government fell upon Mgr. Prahaszka, Bishop of Szekesfehnvar, but Rome refused to sanction the appointment on account of a book he had written on Christian philosophy, which had been placed on the index. After this two other names were suggested, both of which failed to satisfy the Vatican, who maintained that the Hungarian Government were too much influenced by the political colouring of candidates for high ecclesiastical appointments. The Hungarian Government, on the other hand, take the view that as it is they who provide the bishops with their revenues, it is they who have the right to appoint; and if this right be denied them, then they have the right to withhold the revenues. These divergent views are apt to promote continual trouble; but as it is in the interest of both parties to preserve good relations, a compromise will almost always be devised for adjusting these differences. There are no three men better adapted for the delicate work of mediation than the Prince Primate, the Papal Nuncio and the Hungarian Minister to the Holy See.

(10.) *Roumania.*

54. After the war Roumania was one of the first States to inaugurate diplomatic relations with the Holy See. In the early days of 1919, an Apostolic Nunciature was established at Bucharest and a Roumanian Legation at the Vatican, while negotiations were commenced for the conclusion of a concordat. The main reason for those steps was to be found in the fact that the Catholic population of Roumania had been largely increased by the new territories incorporated into the kingdom. In Transylvania, where the vast majority of the people are Catholic, the Hierarchy of the Roman Church had been established for centuries. The greater Roumania now embraces nine Catholic dioceses instead of only two, seven having been added by the annexation of Transylvania. This being so, the Government felt impelled to enter into direct relations with the Head of the Roman Catholic Church, and, if possible, to come to an understanding which would be acceptable to all. At the start the matter seemed simple enough, but difficulty succeeded difficulty, and the concordat is, at the moment of writing, no nearer being signed than it was at the commencement of the negotiations. Moreover, a great anti-Catholic campaign is raging. The Orthodox of Roumania, in conformity with their traditional aversion to Roman Catholicism, are proclaiming loudly against the Pope and the Nuncio, and are, at the same time, voting for the expulsion of the religious orders, while the Catholics of Transylvania, writhing under the domination of Bucharest, will do nothing to assist a settlement with the Holy See. For the moment, therefore, the Roumanian Government are powerless. It must be admitted that all through they have shown no hostility themselves to the Church of Rome. On the contrary, they have indulged in various interchanges of courtesies of the most friendly description, testifying to their goodwill to the Vatican, which culminated in the visit of the Crown Prince to the Pope. It is difficult to see, though, how they will emerge from the present deadlock, which is impeding the signature of the concordat.

(11.) *Jugoslavia.*

55. When, by the third Treaty of Bucharest in 1913, a certain number of Roman Catholics, mostly Albanians, were included in the southern frontiers of Serbia, the Serbian Government lost no time in concluding a concordat with the Holy See. The wisdom of this course was apparent some years later when the Vatican showed its appreciation by recognising the new Serb-Croat-Slovene State at a time when Italy had still declined to do so. That diplomatic relations should now subsist is of importance to the Vatican from many points of view, but more especially on account of the fact that the Catholic population nearly equals the Orthodox, and because the Catholic Croats, though less numerous, are more highly educated than the Serbs, and, as such, are likely to acquire influence in the counsels of the Triune State. The negotiations for the enlargement of the concordat between the Holy See and Serbia into a concordat with the whole new Kingdom of the Serbs, Croats and Slovenes appear to have been unduly delayed. M. Bakotìc, before vacating his post in September last, told me that a preliminary scheme was still under the consideration of his Government, and that it had not yet reached the stage of negotiations with the Vatican. There are not likely to be any serious points of difference over the concordat, and the Belgrade Government have already informed the Vatican that they hope to find an amicable solution to their protest concerning the confiscation of twenty convents, the Roman Catholic gymnasium at Novi Sad, seventy schoolmasters' houses and a certain quantity of ecclesiastical land. The change in the person of the Minister towards the end of the year did not in any way, I gather, denote any deterioration in the good relations subsisting between the two Governments.

(12.) *Czechoslovakia.*

56. The programme of Czechoslovakia, after gaining its independence, was to found a modern lay State with non-religious education in public schools; and one of the first events after the armistice was the substitution of a statue of the Virgin by one of Huss, the famous Bohemian reformer. Then the German-speaking Benedictines were expelled, though in this act racial and national considerations had perhaps more weight than anti-Catholicism. Nevertheless, a Nuncio was appointed to Prague. In 1920 the late Pope had to deal with a serious schism of a section of the Bohemian clergy from the Roman Church. The seceders not only drew up a programme, but acted on it. They celebrated Masses in Czech in the Church of St. Nicholas at Prague; and, on the 8th January, formally proclaimed separation from Rome and the constitution of a Czech National Church, on the basis of a vernacular liturgy and permission to marry. Though the Vatican maintained that the secessionists numbered only 150 out of a total priesthood of 2,000, they were seriously perturbed. As time went on the influence of the Church would appear to have prevailed; and in the course of the year under review no progress was made with the policy of separating Church from State. Those Deputies who were formerly most in favour of the schism, such as the free-thinkers and socialists, no longer wished to carry the measure through. The *bourgeois* parties, the National Democrats and Agrarians, considered it a movement towards the Left, and were inclined to lose all interest now that the nation was showing signs of reacting towards the Right after the socialistic period following the late war. The Catholic Church has been steadily and silently regaining its former influence. The Holy See, always well informed, has little apprehension as to the future, and, in the meantime, can afford to excommunicate such priests as adhered to the National Church. At the end of August, M. Benes appeared in Rome, bringing with him a long list of subjects which he wished to discuss with the Vatican. These concerned chiefly the question of the limits of different ecclesiastical jurisdictions, and the question of a concordat, which is still unsettled. As regards this last point, the difficulty is that the Vatican refuse to extend to Czechoslovakia certain privileges enjoyed under the concordat by the former Dual Monarchy. These privileges were personal to the Habsburg Monarchy and lapsed with its downfall. The Vatican, on the whole, were satisfied with the interview and with the complete frankness with which the various questions were approached by M. Benes.

(13.) *Russia.*

57. Even in the time of the Empire the Vatican were treated with sparse consideration in Russia, but those were indeed halcyon times in the history of the

Church when compared with the year just terminated, when the implacable hostility of the Bolsheviks to all religions rendered civilised intercourse, let alone diplomatic relations, useless. Having been compelled by inexorable facts to abandon economic Communism, the Bolsheviks believed they could use the political despotism they still retained to extirpate those religious habits, those deep-rooted spiritual instincts which they regard as the chief obstacle to the triumph of Communism in the future. With this campaign in full force, the year presented a melancholy record of Christian persecutions with which the Church was powerless to cope. The persecution of the Roman Catholics in Russia dated back to December 1922, when a Roman Catholic church in Petrograd was closed by the Bolsheviks. A few days later ten other churches were closed. The reason given by the Bolsheviks was the refusal of the Roman Catholic clergy to recognise a decree for the lease and use of Church property. The effect of this decree was to recognise the ownership by the State of Church property in contravention of the laws of the Roman Catholic Church. Mgr. Cieplak, Archbishop of Petrograd, appealed to the Pope through the Papal Nuncio at Warsaw, on the 6th December, 1922. In January 1923, the Archbishop, together with a number of other priests, was arrested for opposing the confiscation of sacred vessels by the Soviet. The Vatican thereupon requested M. Chicherin to intervene on the ground that Mgr. Cieplak had acted in good faith, knowing that the Vatican had offered to redeem the property. This appeal had no effect as the Soviet authorities were determined to proceed with the trial. It was held in March, and, to the horror of the whole civilised world, terminated with the condemnation to death of Archbishop Cieplak, Mgr. Budkiewicz and a number of other Roman Catholic priests. Mgr. Budkiewicz was actually shot; but the execution of the Archbishop was postponed, and when the year closed he was still languishing in prison. Oppressed by these melancholy events, a profound gloom prevailed throughout the Vatican with regard to the position of the Church in Russia, which, however, did not hamper the activity with which they persisted in distributing funds and provisions among the poor and starving through the medium of Father Walsh, their intrepid delegate at Moscow.

(14.) *Japan.*

58. The budget estimate for 1923 laid before the Diet contained an item of 114,000 yen for the provision of diplomatic representation at the Vatican, but this was subsequently omitted owing to Buddhist protests. An organisation containing some 3,000 priests of various Buddhist sects demurred on the ground that the proposed appointment was "contrary to the principles of international law to acknowledge the Pope of Rome as a sovereign." The movement spread rapidly. Certain Shintoists and Protestant Christians also took part, and eventually a special organisation was formed under the leadership of Count Otani, Chief Abbot of the Hongwanji Temple of Kyoto, to secure the rejection of the proposal. In the meantime the Ministry for Foreign Affairs issued a statement laying emphasis on the necessity for Japan keeping herself fully informed of the course of events in all quarters of the globe, and on the great importance of maintaining diplomatic contact with the Vatican. The precedents of 1885, 1906 and 1916, when Papal envoys were received by Japan and Japanese envoys were sent to the Holy See, were referred to, and stress was laid on the recent visit which the Crown Prince paid to the Pope. Though the Japanese Government had considered it wiser to pause, they evidently had no intention of abandoning the idea of establishing diplomatic relations with the Holy See; for not only were the Vatican assured privately that a representative would appear in course of time, but the Government continued to make a variety of enquiries with regard to our Legation in Rome, notably at our Foreign Office in London, calculated to assist them in pursuing a similar course. The Cardinal Secretary of State alluded to this matter several times in the course of the year, laying special stress on the point that the Japanese Government had realised that the Roman Catholic Church was the most effective breaker to stem the rising tide of Bolshevism, and that to attach an anchor to this breaker, even though it was situated in another hemisphere, seemed well worth while. The opposition to the proposal evidently weakened towards the end of the year, and advocates of the mission even appeared in the ranks of the Buddhists themselves, who actually sent a Buddhist abbot to Rome to study at its central point the organisation of the Catholic Church. That the relations of the Vatican with the

Imperial House are of the most cordial character was evidenced by the fact that the Pope appointed a special mission to represent him at Tokyo on the occasion of the marriage of the Crown Prince, and had sent personal presents to the bride and bridegroom.

(15.) *China.*

59. The year witnessed the establishment of an Apostolic delegation in China, Mgr. Constantini having been selected by the Pope for this post. This event terminated an old-standing question. France, on the basis of ancient treaties, had for long claimed protectorate of religion in the Far East, objecting, not only to the presence of a Papal Nuncio in China, but to the direct supervision of religious matters on the part of the Holy See through an Apostolic delegate. Three or four years ago the question was discussed, and the solution postponed; but the very direct statement here at the time that nothing could interfere with the right of the Holy See to immediate control of its religious affairs made it evident that the solution, if for a moment delayed, would in time come on the lines now seen. The Church in China, organised in Apostolic vicariates and prefectures, now has the guidance of Rome for its development in the person of the Apostolic delegate.

(16.) *Argentine Republic.*

60. In the month of June of the past year there was no cloud on the relations of the Argentine with the Holy See; and the Government, anxious to emulate the example of the neighbouring republics of Brazil, Chile and Peru, seized the opportunity to ask Congress to vote sufficient funds to raise their Legation in Rome to the status of an Embassy. Unluckily, on the very eve of the promotion of the Argentine Minister, an incident occurred which not only menaced his personal position, but even contained elements calculated to bring about a complete rupture of diplomatic relations. At the time of the visit of the President of the Republic to the Pope he let it be known privately that he was opposed to the appointment of a certain prelate to the vacant Archbishopric of Buenos Aires; and as the Vatican view coincided with that of Dr. Alvear it was decided in principle that the archbishopric would, in due course, be conferred on another. In the meantime, the Argentine Government, either unaware of this private agreement or perhaps anxious to assert their own authority and independence, not only submitted the name of this very prelate for preferment to the highest ecclesiastical position in the republic, but also treated his appointment as a *fait accompli*, which did not even call for confirmation. The Vatican were not slow to resent this interference with their prerogatives, and promptly informed the Argentine Government that the appointment was their concern, and that they had no intention whatever of adopting the Government candidate. The Argentine Government retorted by a threat to recall their Minister, and to break off relations. Happily more prudent counsels appear to have prevailed, for when the year closed the Minister was still at his post in spite of the fact that neither side had yielded or had shown any disposition to yield. The problem will probably only be solved with a change of Government at Buenos Aires.

(17.) *Brazil.*

61. The Brazilian Legation to the Holy See was raised to an Embassy in 1919; and the cordiality of the relations was seen in 1922 when the Pope appointed a Legate to attend the centenary celebrations of Brazilian independence, and conferred the highest Papal order, the Order of Christ, on President Pessoa. Following on this came the visit of Cardinal Gasquet, who was received with high honour, and when overtaken by an illness lasting several weeks, was shown the utmost attention and kindness by the President's family. The action, therefore, of the Brazilian Government in conferring on Cardinals last summer the rank and precedence of Royal Heirs Apparent was no isolated one, and merely corresponds to their friendly attitude towards the Holy See.

(18.) *Other South American Republics.*

62. Of the other South American Republics cordial relations have been maintained throughout the year with Peru, Colombia and, on the whole, with Chile. The visit paid to these three countries in October by Cardinal Benlloch, Archbishop of

Burgos, as the special Ambassador of the Pope and the King of Spain, was made the occasion of many festivities, each country vieing with the other in according him welcome; although in Chile the spontaneity was somewhat marred by the President, who largely owed his election to the anti-clericals, having to blow hot and cold alternately. In Chile there are clouds on the horizon now that the Radicals have made the separation of Church and State the principal plank in their platform at the approaching elections. The Chilean Government suffered a loss in December through the death of the Chilean Ambassador to the Holy See, M. Errazuriz, who had won for himself a fairly prominent position in Rome.

63. In Colombia, where the Government and still more the people are on the best of terms with Rome, some friction occurred between the Minister of Education and the Nuncio, Mgr. Vicentini, who only the year before had shown want of tact at The Hague. The incident had no serious consequences, but it was sufficient to create temporarily an embarrassing situation all round.

64. The relations with Venezuela have improved noticeably now that President Gómez is more favourably disposed. He won much flattering praise when he gave his encouragement to the founding of missions in the more uncivilised parts of the interior and allowed foreign missionaries to enter the country. The Nuncio and the Archbishop of Caracas have in the past had a difficult part to play, but their efforts have been rewarded. New dioceses have been created and the President appears to have realised the importance which religion must play in developing a backward race. The Vatican are on good terms with Bolivia, but with Ecuador the rupture of relations continues, and further trouble may be ahead if the anti-clericals secure the election of their candidate, Signor Cordova, to the Presidency.

65. With regard to Central America, Panamá had expressed the desire to establish diplomatic relations with the Holy See, and consequently Mgr. Rotta, the Inter-Nuncio in Central America, now represents the Holy See also at Panamá.

66. The other Central American republics are on the friendliest terms with the Vatican with the exception of Mexico, who expelled the Apostolic delegate in a ruthless manner, and Guatemala, where the Catholic Church is undergoing a veritable persecution.

III.—THE SACRED COLLEGE.

67. The Sacred College at the end of the year 1923 was composed of 64 cardinals out of the full complement of 70. Of these, 33 are of Italian nationality and 31 of the nationality of foreign States. Of the latter, France heads the list with 7, followed by the British Empire with 4, Germany 4, Spain 4, Austria 2, United States 2, Poland 2, Portugal 1, Brazil 1, Belgium 1, Holland 1, Hungary 1, Czechoslovakia 1. There are 5 Italian cardinals in diocese and 28 in curia, and 26 foreign cardinals in dioceses and 6 in curia. These are Cardinals Merry del Val, van Rossum, Billot, Gasquet, Frühwirth and Ehrle. The prelates with whom His Majesty's Legation are primarily concerned are Cardinal Gasparri, the Secretary of State; Mgrs. Borgongini-Duca and Pizzardo, the Under-Secretaries of State; Mgr. Samper, the Maggiordomo; Mgr. Caccia-Dominioni, the Maestro di Camera; Cardinal Vannutelli, the Dean of the Sacred College; Cardinal van Rossum, Prefect of Propaganda; and Cardinal Gasquet, Prefect of the Archives, the only English cardinal in the Roman Curia.

IV.—PRESS.

68. The "Osservatore Romano," the only Catholic paper officially representing the Holy See, can hardly yet be called a newspaper, but it seems to be endeavouring to move in that direction. It publishes more "news," short messages from the Italian Stefani agency, on current events in Italy and abroad, and its own notices on religious events in Italy and its own correspondence from all over the world, sent usually by people in the Papal Nunciatures or delegations, giving an account of religious conditions in the various countries. From England it publishes colourless messages from the Catholic News Service. The "Osservatore" is less a semi-official guide to the views of the Roman Curia than it used to be; there are fewer semi-official articles over the signature-initial of its director. It is always prompt with a short note to correct any false impression that might be produced by something appearing in Italian or foreign papers. It is careful, for instance, to reiterate the Papal case if the "Roman question" is mooted in the press; and it will not allow to pass any suggestion that the Holy See or any Catholic organisation as such are

engaged in Italian politics; but, generally speaking, the deliberation and reserve seen in the present Pontificate are reflected in the official organ. If the Holy See wishes to say something it more often uses the means of an article in the most widely circulated ordinary Catholic paper here, the "Corriere d'Italia," written under guidance from the Secretariate of State, but in appearance quite unofficial.

69. As regards the Catholic press generally, there has been a change, which, however, only covers home affairs. When the Popular party was formed, almost entirely of Catholics, in 1919, nearly all the Catholic papers were affiliated to it. That party is now going through a bad time and practically all those papers have given up or been expelled from affiliation, becoming again just newspapers run by Catholics on Catholic principles. This does not change their attitude towards foreign affairs, except, possibly, in a very small degree, in that, as regards England, the Popular party point of view was always jaundiced against England and ready to accept and print in their papers any of the anti-English propaganda rampant a few years ago. Since the Irish settlement this has died down, and there has been little opening for attack on England, save for an occasional reference to Palestine and Zionism. Even here, however, the virulence of a few years ago is not now seen, though it cannot be said that there is any real attempt to understand English foreign policy; and when a moment of exasperation happens to come the Catholic press, with the exception of the "Osservatore Romano," is as strong as the rest of the press; instance the Greece League of Nations incident of last summer. These moments, however, soon pass.

70. On the occasion of their Majesties' visit the "Osservatore Romano" published a really very remarkable article, more eulogistic than anything ever written before, particularly with regard to a non-Catholic Power, during the last fifteen years. And the tone of the whole Catholic press was very good. It is true that on these occasions one expects flattering references; but it is also true that the Catholic press did show quick and sincere appreciation of the perfectly correct light in which their Majesties' visit to the Supreme Pontiff was regarded and the way in which it was carried out.

71. On the whole it may be said that Catholic papers here are following the trend noticeable in Catholic circles in losing slowly that anti-English bias which used to characterise them, which was largely due to ignorance, and was, during the difficult times, fostered by Irish propaganda.

o

CONFIDENTIAL.

(12706)

HOLY SEE.

Annual Report, 1924.

[C 3342/3342/22]

Sir Odo Russell to Mr. Austen Chamberlain.—(Received March 9.)

(No. 39. Confidential.)   *British Legation to the Holy See,*
Sir,   *Rome, February 28, 1925.*
    I HAVE the honour to transmit herewith my annual report on the Holy See for the year 1924.

                                 I have, &c.
                                    ODO RUSSELL.

Enclosure.

Annual Report on the Holy See for 1924.

CONTENTS.

I.—INTRODUCTION.

    ALTHOUGH the year 1924 was unmarked by any event of outstanding importance it was a period of steady progress in every sphere of Papal activity. Happily the Pope, upon whose word and initiative everything depends, enjoyed throughout the year the health and strength which the fulfilment of his high task demanded, and was thus able to pay personal and unremitting attention to the manifold problems which were daily submitted for his decision. The third year of the Pontificate of Pius XI not only shows a record of great achievement in religious, social and political affairs, but also an undoubted extension of the influence of the Holy See.

    2. There were three public pronouncements from the Chair of St. Peter :—

    (1.) The encyclical *Maximam* of January, which dealt with the organisation of the " Associations diocésaines " recently instituted in France.

    (2.) The allocution of the 24th March, *Amplissimum consessum*, which spoke, among other things, of the Russian maltreatment of clerics, and the relief

2751   [12859]   B

afforded to destitute Europe by the United States in connection with the creation of two American cardinals. It expressed satisfaction at the replacing of the crucifix in the Italian schools, and preoccupation at acts of violence committed by political factions in Italy. It dealt also with economic conditions in Europe, the approaching synod in China, and the inauguration of the Holy Year.

(3.) The allocution of the 18th December, *Nostis qua,* recalled the China Council, the Amsterdam and Palermo Eucharistic Congresses. It spoke of the desolate condition of Russia and of the perils of Socialism and Communism.

3. Among many notable events were the opening of the Missionary Exhibition in the Vatican, due entirely to the initiative of the Pope; the celebration of the 16th centenary of the Lateran Basilica; the consecration of two new basilicas in Palestine; the Eucharistic Congress at Amsterdam. Almost every month decrees were issued for beatifications, and hardly a day passed without audiences, private or public, or without some speech or address on the part of His Holiness. These were not confined alone to spiritual matters. Science, art, letters, intellectual progress, all received an impetus from the discourses of Pius XI, whose earlier career as a student enabled him to appreciate the requirements of the times, and to make his now powerful influence felt.

4. In purely political questions the future relations of the Holy See with France and the Argentine gave rise to intricate and anxious negotiations throughout the year; while those with Russia, with the sole redeeming feature of Archbishop Cieplak's release, showed, in spite of much patient handling, no sign of amelioration. With other States good relations were maintained and consolidated. Among the many personages received in audience by the Supreme Pontiff in the course of the year were the Prince Regent of Abyssinia, the Queen of Roumania, the Jugoslav Prime Minister, special missions from Chile, Portugal, Hungary and Poland; Sir Herbert Samuel, the High Commissioner of Palestine; Mr. Austen Chamberlain, His Majesty's Principal Secretary of State for Foreign Affairs, and 300 British sailors from the Mediterranean Fleet.

II.—RELATIONS WITH FOREIGN POWERS.

Great Britain.

5. An Italian cardinal was recently heard to say that the Vatican would rather deal with England and Germany than with any of the Latin countries. So far as England is concerned this remark is quite intelligible. In the first place, there are few countries where the Catholic Church enjoys so much liberty; and, secondly, as the past year has shown, His Majesty's Government have given the Vatican every proof of their readiness to examine questions on their merits and to display an accommodating spirit. The visit of Mr. Chamberlain to the Pope and to Cardinal Gasparri last December, the message of good wishes which the King bade me give to Cardinal Gasquet on the occasion of his jubilee, and the official reception given by His Majesty's High Commissioner to Cardinal Giorgi on his visit to Palestine as Papal Legate, were acts all highly appreciated at the Vatican. They reflect, moreover, the harmonious relations which exist between Great Britain and the Holy See. An excellent impression was created too, when some 300 Catholic sailors from the Mediterranean Fleet were given permission last July to come to Rome to be received in audience by the Pope.

6. The policy of Great Britain on the continent and her influence in the cause of pacification have been an added factor in inspiring confidence. Proof of this was forthcoming when the Cardinal Secretary of State appealed exclusively for British support in Russia on behalf of Archbishop Cieplak and of the priests and nuns imprisoned or deported to Siberia, and again on behalf of the inhabitants in Georgia.

7. The only quarter from which difficulties may conceivably arise is Palestine, with its ever delicate problem of the Holy Places. As there has been correspondence with the Vatican on a variety of points affecting Palestine during the year, this question will be dealt with separately. It will suffice here to say that, from the Pope downwards the greatest importance is attached to Catholic claims to the Holy Places and, indeed, to every development that may affect the future of the Holy Land.

8. As regards other parts of the Empire, all questions that have arisen between His Majesty's Government and the Vatican have been or are on the road to being

adjusted smoothly. As they are not of general interest, only a brief allusion to some of them need be made :—

Malta.—In April, the attention of the Vatican was called to an arrangement which had been come to between Sir L. Simmons and Cardinal Rampolla respecting nominations to the sees of Malta. The Vatican recognised the validity of the arrangement, and enquired unofficially whether His Majesty's Government had any objection to the appointment of Mgr. Gonzi as Bishop of Gozo. The reply was favourable and the appointment took place.

9. *Cyprus.*—The law of 1923 regarding marriages in Cyprus had led to complaint from the Vatican, and came under discussion in London on the return there in March of Cardinal Bourne from Palestine and Rome. Mgr. Bidwell was appointed to treat with the Colonial Office direct and as a result a new law was to be drafted and submitted to London for approval. The news was received by the Vatican with expressions of satisfaction.

10. *Irak.*—Mgr. Berré, the Apostolic delegate at Bagdad, was in Rome in the early spring of 1924, and begged me to acquaint the Foreign Office of his only grievance, viz., in regard to certain school-books in use in Catholic schools of the Chaldean and Syro-Chaldean rites. The matter was referred to the local authorities and a reassuring statement made to Mgr. Berré on receipt of their report.

His Majesty's High Commissioner at Bagdad reported at the end of April that a bad effect had been caused among the local Catholics by the transfer of Mgr. Habra, Archbishop of Mosul, to Damascus. The reason was said to be partly on account of his alleged pro-British and insufficiently pro-French sentiments. On enquiry being made in Rome, it transpired that the reason for his removal was that he had infringed Canon Law in regard to the administration of the finances of the diocese; and that he was being sent to Damascus because the Holy See did not wish to deal too harshly with him on account of his advanced age. They promised, however, that British interests would not be overlooked in choosing a successor. There were further difficulties in store at Mosul when a temporary administrator of the diocese, in the person of Mgr. Dallal, endeavoured to take over from Mgr. Habra. Some of the latter's supporters had taken possession of the archbishop's house and refused to surrender it. The authorities appeared to have held aloof, and the representative in Rome of the Patriarch asked that Mgr. Dallal should be afforded official recognition, as otherwise he would be unable to take up his duties or hold the "elections" for a new archbishop. The case was referred to London and is not likely to prove difficult of solution.

Palestine.

11. With regard to questions in Palestine which have been directly treated with the Vatican, the past year shows some satisfactory results. Agreement was reached on the subject of the King's birthday celebrations, which had caused friction the year before. It has now been arranged that instead of the celebrations being confined to an official service at the Anglican Cathedral, His Majesty's High Commissioner will also hold a civil reception which the Catholic hierarchy and consular representatives can attend to pay their respects. A British subject, in the person of Mgr. Kean, has been appointed auxiliary bishop to the Latin Patriarchate. He had been acting for a year previously as secretary to the Patriarch, and according to His Majesty's High Commissioner had contributed in no small measure to an improvement in the relations with the Civil Administration. Mgr. Barlassina's own attitude has improved, partly as a result, no doubt, of strict injunctions from the Vatican, partly because he has acquired a genuine feeling of respect for the high qualities of Sir H. Samuel, with whom he claimed, when he was recently in Rome, to be on the best of terms. That this feeling is shared by the Vatican was evident when, in October, Sir H. Samuel himself visited the Cardinal Secretary of State. In view of the delicate questions which may arise in Palestine, the personal element must long remain an important factor. A further cause for satisfaction was the final abolition at Easter of the liturgical honours hitherto accorded to the French representative at Jerusalem. The Vatican had sided with His Majesty's Government on the principal question, but later, under French pressure, supported a compromise limiting the honours to French churches on specified occasions. When His Majesty's Government, however, insisted on complete abolition the Vatican readily acquiesced; and in the teeth of strong French opposition despatched the necessary instructions to the Catholic ecclesiastical authorities concerned.

12. Not the least important event in the year was the visit to Palestine of Cardinal Giorgi, who as Papal Legate was to consecrate the new basilicas on Mount Tabor and at Gethsemane. He was received officially by the Government authorities; and before departing expressed his gratification for the courtesy which had been extended to him. The visit was carefully watched by the Italian press, and the fact that everything passed off smoothly was therefore all the more satisfactory. The same may be said of Cardinal O'Connell's visit at the head of an American pilgrimage early in the year. He was followed shortly afterwards by Cardinal Bourne, who led an English pilgrimage, and who had been charged by the Pope to report to him on the situation there as affecting the Church. The most noteworthy result of Cardinal Bourne's visit was that from being formerly opposed to Mgr. Barlassina he became convinced that it would not now be expedient to work for his recall.

13. Although, as the above account may show, various difficulties have been overcome during the past year, there are still rocks ahead. The feeling continues to prevail that with the establishment of the British mandate Protestants, Orthodox and Zionists are combining in hostility to the Catholic Church, and that the two former are organising resistance to Catholic claims in the Holy Places. That such a feeling exists was made clear after the unfortunate episode at Easter, when disturbances occurred during Catholic religious services. The representations made at the time by the Vatican were very mild as compared with the outburst of the Italian and incidentally of the French press. Much of the agitation is doubtless the work of political wire-pullers, and no great significance attaches to the activity of such bodies as the *Unione pro Luoghi Santi*, who addressed a petition to the League of Nations at Geneva in favour of the protection of Catholic rights at the Holy Places. The fact, nevertheless, remains that there is a large body of Catholic opinion which appears to be genuinely alarmed at the uncertainty of the future and at the continued non-settlement of the question of the Cenacle. It is noteworthy that in announcing the opening of the Holy Year the Pope included among the intentions for which he wanted prayers the safeguarding of Catholic rights in Palestine. His words were addressed *urbi et orbi*.

Italy.

14. During the year there has been no pronouncement of importance bearing directly on the Roman question, but, nevertheless, indications have shown that with the lapse of time the desire for reconciliation between the Vatican and the Quirinal increases, although the conditions on which the Holy See could accept a settlement remain in principle unchanged. Meanwhile, there has been a steady improvement in the relations between Church and State, which is the necessary preliminary to any pourparlers on the main question.

For a time in the early part of the year, both before and after the Italian political elections, it looked as if the clock would be set back. Party feeling ran high, and, disappointed perhaps at the election results in some of the country districts, the Fascisti or others masquerading as Fascisti, attacked a number of Catholic lay institutions supposed to be supporting the Popular party. In some places there were acts of sacrilege and profanation, causing a wide-spread feeling of revulsion.

The Pope had, as early as February, given the strictest orders publicly and privately that religious activity must remain outside of and above any political party and avoid "dangerous identifications." Special warning was given to priests and religious, and every care was taken to prevent the use of the designation Catholic from being applied to any one political group. It was with all the more reason, therefore, that the Vatican resented the Fascisti acts of violence, and it was immediately made known that the Pope had contributed 500,000 lire to repairing the material damage done. The Fascisti organs protested, and at the moment the Vatican were accused of having gone over to Signor Nitti and Don Sturzo; but this tone was almost immediately dropped, doubtless on the orders of the Government. In the peculiar conditions of Italy any serious developments in the political or social situation affects the Vatican far more closely than those occurring in other countries; and the nervous depression which filled the nation after the murder of Signor Matteotti was also noticeable on the other side of the Bronze Doors.

15. The appeal made by the "Osservatore Romano" that recriminations against this or that individual and party should cease and the administration of the law be left to those responsible, had a wholesome effect and was used by

Signor Mussolini himself to enforce his arguments in the Chamber. The chaos to which the country seemed to be heading during the summer amidst the burst of indignation, partly genuine, partly artificial, brought out the fact that if Signor Mussolini opposed Socialism so did the Pope. There was, at any rate, that in common. On the one hand, as Cardinal Gasparri told me, although Signor Mussolini could not be acquitted of some measure of responsibility for the system of violence, it was realised at the Vatican that he was the only man who could steer the ship of State into smoother waters and give Italy the strong hand that she needed. This fact and the evident readiness of the Popular party to co-operate with the Socialists in overturning the Government led the Pope to utter severe warnings on the duties of Catholic citizens to the State. His example was followed by the leading Catholic press and by the leaders of the Catholic Action Association.

16. On his side Signor Mussolini appears to have become more and more convinced of the necessity of conciliating the Church and winning the support of as many Catholics as possible Already in March, on the eve of the elections, the decision was announced of increasing the annuities paid by the State to the clergy, and of making concessions to priests and students regarding military service. In September fresh proof was given of the desire of the Government to conciliate Catholic opinion when at the Porta Pia celebrations on the anniversary of the occupation of Rome the tone of the speeches was almost one of veneration for the Holy See. Signor Mussolini himself followed this up at Vicenza when he made a public—and much applauded—profession of his religious convictions; and later in having the cross restored on the Capitol, whence it had been removed after 1870. Of such minor acts numerous instances could be quoted, not the least being the facilities provided by the authorities in connection with the Holy Year, which opened on the 24th December. The streets leading to St. Peter's were repaired—none too early, it is true—and great improvements were made in the communications between the four chief basilicas, measures which would have been unthinkable under former Governments, and which were warmly appreciated in Catholic circles.

France.

17. As foreshadowed in my last annual report, the negotiations between the Vatican and the French Government on the status of the Church in France were brought to a successful conclusion early in January, when the Pope issued the encyclical *Maximam* permitting the formation of special diocesan associations, which were " to provide for the cost and maintenance of religious worship," and which were to be recognised by the State as possessing juridical personality. A section of the French hierarchy viewed the terms of settlement with misgivings, and the Pope himself stated in the encyclical that the arrangement was not a perfect one; and that though he wished it to be given a trial, he would not order the bishops to form the associations. His wishes, however, were promptly obeyed; and for the moment it looked as if a new era was opening in the relations between France and the Holy See in so far as domestic questions were concerned. Causes of friction still remained over M. Poincaré's foreign policy. The French Government resented the Pope's reiterated appeals for pacification as implying that they were to blame; and the resentment was increased when, at Easter, liturgical honours ceased to be rendered to the French representative in Palestine. The Holy See had been spoken of as pro-German; it was now accused of being pro-English.

18. To the Vatican M. Poincaré had all along been a thorn in the flesh; and his defeat at the elections in the spring was viewd with no great sorrow. Worse was, however, to follow.

From the start, M. Herriot had made no secret as to his attitude towards the Holy See or to the Church, and one of the early acts of his Government was to forbid participation in religious observances by the navy. In spite, however, of public declarations and rumours the Vatican appeared convinced that there would be no rupture of diplomatic relations. It was not, they said, the Holy See who raised a finger to re-establish relations, but the French Government and the French people for their own political ends. After all the trouble that had been taken to pick up the discarded threads it was inconceivable that these threads should so soon again and so lightly be cast aside. Whatever M. Herriot's Government and party wished, they could not fly in the face of French Catholics and of the population of Alsace-Lorraine.

In September it was announced that the credits for the French Embassy to the Holy See no longer figured in the budget presented to the Chamber. But not even this announcement seemed to alarm the Vatican, or for that matter, the French Embassy either. M. Herriot was known to have no great personal feelings one way or the other, and the only danger in the eyes of the Cardinal Secretary of State to the maintenance of relations lay in his having to yield to the pressure of his extremist followers, and in including the suppression of the Embassy in a general programme, which would be voted by the Chamber *en bloc.*

Meanwhile, the rumours afloat regarding the Government's intentions led to protests from the French hierarchy and to heated replies. The Nuncio himself came in for attack from M. François-Albert, the Minister for Public Instruction, in a speech at Valence. The atmosphere was highly charged, but to the end of the year the situation remained unchanged.

Spain.

19. In spite of the special appeal put forward by the King of Spain on the occasion of his visit to Rome, the year 1924 rolled by without the creation of either a Spanish or South American Cardinal; from which it may be gathered that not even from Spain, a privileged daughter of the Church, will an initiative of such a nature be tolerated. Apart from this, which not unnaturally had a somewhat disturbing effect, the relations between Spain and the Holy See preserved a friendly aspect.

20. Amongst the special privileges accorded to the Spanish Crown on account of its secular efforts at furthering the Catholic faith is that of the royal right to nominate candidates for episcopal sees, for minor benefices and ecclesiastical preferments in general, a privilege which represents the ancient and continual goodwill of the Church towards the Spanish Crown.

In practice, however, this relegation to the Crown of powers of the Church often allowed Governments which were hostile to the Church to use the prerogative for party purposes, thus perverting the fundamental principle of the privilege conferred solely on the Crown, which should be above and foreign to all such infringements of justice and equity in its conferring of ecclesiastical property. The Military Dire orate has attempted to remedy this abuse by a decree royal, which is one of the mc important proclaimed by the Directorate. The " junta delegated by Royal patronage " is practically an entirely ecclesiastical commission, since it is composed of the Primate (Archbishop of Toledo), of a Spanish archbishop and two bishops, a prebendary and a canon.

The propositions of the junta represent the highest guarantee for the Minister of Justice, who is responsible to His Majesty: but they leave the Government free to follow or refuse the decisions of the junta, which has no powers in the transferments or nominations of the metropolitans, and in the nominations, rare indeed, made by the Holy See or by the bishops.

21. Conde de la Vinosa was appointed Spanish Ambassador to the Quirinal; this is the first time that a Spanish Ambassador. formerly accredited to the Vatican, has been appointed to the Court of the King of Italy.

Germany.

22. Throughout the year the Vatican continued to evince a lively interest in the task of promoting a return to normal conditions in Germany. While Mgr. Testa, the delegate of the Holy See, was, with the co-operation of the authorities, achieving results which were much appreciated by the German population of the Ruhr, Mgr. Pizzardo was despatched by the Pope to Munich to hand over to the Papal Nuncio funds for the relief of sick and starving Catholics; and at the same time to bring back a first-hand account of conditions prevailing in Germany. On his return, in reply to my enquiry as to the impressions he had formed, Mgr. Pizzardo, who hitherto had been inclined to think that the whole country was on the verge of starvation, was constrained to admit that there was a large section of the population living in affluence. The trouble was that the rich had disregarded the needs of their poorer brethren. The Nuncio, it appears, was dismayed at the utter callousness displayed by opulent Germans towards the sufferings of their own countrymen.

23. Apart from the above assistance rendered to Germany by the Holy See, the Papal Nuncio in Paris. Mgr. Cerretti, in the early part of the year was instructed by the Pope to make representations at the Quai d'Orsay in favour of German prisoners confined in France. His reception was not unfriendly, and he was promised that, apart from the fact that a certain proportion of prisoners not actually guilty of crime would be released, an attempt would be made to improve the position of the

remainder. He had also spoken to the President of the Republic, who promised that he would do what he could to meet the Nuncio's wishes.

24. After the Ludendorff trial. when the general's attacks on the Papacy and the Church had excited much indignation in Italy, Herr Brauns, the Prussian Premier, made ample amends by writing to the Papal Nuncio in Berlin, Mgr. Pacelli. In this letter he expressed the regret of the Prussian Government for the attacks against the Pope made by General Ludendorff during his trial. The Government, said the Premier, knew how unfounded these attacks were, and what warm thanks Prussia owed to the Holy See for its efforts for peace and for the welfare of the Prussian people during and since the war. A peaceful atmosphere was thus restored, and with a friendly advance on both sides for concluding the negotiations for the concordat with Bavaria. The relations between the Holy See and Germany rested on a most cordial footing as the year closed.

Austria.

25. The choice of Dr. Pastor, the eminent historian of the Popes, to be Austrian Minister to the Holy See was a clever move on the part of the Austrian Government, and proved to be no small factor in consolidating friendly relations. On the occasion of his seventieth birthday, not only did the Pope send him a long autograph letter and a medal to commemorate the anniversary, but a brilliant reception was also organised in his honour, which was attended by the Cardinal Secretary of State and a number of other members of the Sacred College. Another occasion presented itself later in the year for the Pope to show his affection and concern for the Austrian people. Just as His Holiness was receiving an Austrian pilgrimage on the 1st June, news came of the attempt on the life of the Austrian Chancellor, Mgr. Seipel; and from the Papal Throne, with moving word, he instantly gave striking proof to the pilgrims of his love and sympathy for this portion of the old Dual Monarchy and for their leading statesmen. For the inauguration of the new and magnificent cathedral at Linz, the ancient capital of Upper Austria, the Pope sent a special Legate, in the person of Cardinal Frühwirth, to represent him, thus again demonstrating his interest and his desire to honour Austrian aspirations.

26. The negotiations for the concordat progressed but slowly during 1924, but this was more due to the pressure of other questions and preoccupations than to any great divergence of opinion over the terms of a future agreement.

Poland.

27. My Polish colleague, in discussing with me last summer the possibility of a rupture of relations between France and the Holy See, deplored the fact that the French Government could not see eye to eye with Poland on this question. In his country, he said, very special value was attached to close relations with Rome. Not only were these essential from the purely Church point of view, but great store was also laid on them politically for the preservation of contact with the only effective bulwark against revolutionary Bolshevism with which Poland as a State was surrounded. Those doctrines were powerless to contend against the doctrines of the Church, which were professed by the great majority of his countrymen, and who would, therefore, always insist on close relations with the Holy See.

28. Several events in the course of 1924 served to cement these relations, so highly valued by both parties. These were the raising of the status of the missions to ambassadorial rank; a very friendly exchange of telegrams between the Pope and the President on the occasion of the silver wedding of the latter; a decided advance in the concordat negotiations, which rendered signature a certainty in the early part of the New Year; and the gift of a house to the Papal Nuncio, for which the Polish nation had subscribed.

Hungary.

29. The question of ecclesiastical appointments continued to be a source of contention between Hungary and the Holy See, although in not so marked a degree as in the preceding year. When the Crown became vacant, the Vatican withdrew from the Hungarian Government the ancient privilege enjoyed by the Kings of Hungary of nominating archbishops and bishops, but they were not on such firm ground as they were with the other succession States who had become republics, and Hungary, conscious of the difference of her position as a potential kingdom, was constantly struggling to maintain relations with the Vatican on the old basis. This

caused difficulties, but the relations on the whole were cordial. Only one incident temporarily threatened to impair this cordiality, and that was the sudden recall of Count Somssich, the Hungarian Minister, who was *persona gratissima* to the Cardinal Secretary of State. It appears that the Minister for Foreign Affairs considered Count Somssich to be too outspoken a Royalist, and that he failed to persuade the Vatican to see eye to eye with his own Government on the question of ecclesiastical appointments. Another grievance which hastened his recall was his failure to frustrate certain dispositions in Transylvania which were to be concluded in the concordat with Roumania, and which were obnoxious to the Hungarians as former overlords in that province. On this question, the Cardinal told me, no Hungarian Minister, however influential, could have intervened between the contracting parties, and that it was, therefore, unfair to have made Count Somssich a scapegoat.

  With the retirement of the Minister for Foreign Affairs at Budapest and the appointment of Baron Bornemisza as Minister in Rome, which followed shortly after this occurrence, the clouds blew over, and a friendly atmosphere prevailed again as the year closed.

Roumania.

  30. The Catholic population of Roumania having been largely increased by the new territories incorporated into the kingdom after the war, the need for a concordat with the Holy See soon became apparent, but the negotiations which were attempted spasmodically throughout the year revealed so many difficulties that it was not possible to reach a definite agreement. As the Government, however, have all along evinced a friendly disposition and a desire to quell the disturbing elements, and as there have been various exchanges of courtesy, including a visit of the Queen to the Pope, there is a distinct possibility that no untoward incident may delay signature beyond the current year.

  31. I gathered from Cardinal Gasparri that one of the stumbling-blocks so far had been the Roumanian Government's demand that they should appoint teachers in the seminaries for other than religious subjects. This was a point, His Eminence said, that had only once been asked for before by the former Tsarist Government for Polish seminaries. The Vatican had refused point-blank then, as they were refusing now. There were one or two other demands which the Vatican could not admit, but there was no difficulty over the teaching of Roumanian in schools and seminaries.

  32. M. Banu, late Minister of Public Worship, was entrusted by the Roumanian Government to conduct the negotiations in Rome with a representative of the Pope.

  33. During the session of the Senate in November a complaint was made by Dr. Biano in regard to the attitude of Cardinal Schioppa, the Apostolic Nuncio at Budapest, who was reported to have opened a meeting of Catholics in Hungary with a speech professing irredentist sentiments hostile to Roumania. Dr. Biano demanded that representations should be made to the Vatican with a view to the punishment of the Nuncio. The Minister for Foreign Affairs protested against the remarks of Dr. Biano, who had expressed suspicion of the Pope's absolute impartiality. He regretted that words of the kind could have been said in the Roumanian Parliament.

  As regards the action of Cardinal Schioppa, he had called for a report from the Roumanian Legation in Budapest, and had already called the attention of the Vatican to the improper attitude of the prelate in question towards Roumania.

Jugoslavia.

  34. On the 28th January, M. Pachitch and M. Ninchitch, Premier and Foreign Minister of Jugoslavia, were received by the Pope, who congratulated them on the agreement between their country and Italy over the Fiume question. It would, he said, be beneficial to both countries and to the cause of international peace. The Pope also expressed a hope that a concordat between the Vatican and Jugoslavia would be included within the year.

  35. It will be recalled that a concordat had already been signed in 1913. The present negotiations, therefore, are being conducted for the enlargement of that concordat into a concordat with the whole new Kingdom of the Serbs, Croats and Slovenes, in which the Catholic population nearly equals the Orthodox. The hope expressed by His Holiness to the Jugoslav Minister was not destined to be realised before the end of the year, as the negotiations turned out to be far more intricate than

was originally anticipated, but I have been assured that they are running a smooth course and that no insuperable difficulties are likely to arise.

36. Among the principal points to be discussed is, I understand. the election of bishops. The Vatican no longer concedes the *jus presentandi*, and is likely to abide by the stipulations concluded with Latvia. Then there is the question of the delimitation and erection of new dioceses, especially in the annexed territories; the question of Church property and maintenance of the clergy, &c. (as regards this latter point, the Government spent in 1922 roughly £1,500,000 on the Orthodox Church and only £180,000 on the Catholic); the question of seminaries, religious orders, the juridical position of Catholic institutions and of the clergy, and, more particularly, the immunity from military service. Scholastic questions will also have to be discussed, such as the recognition and safeguarding of confessional schools and religious instruction in State schools.

Present indications are that the Serb-Croat-Slovene Government are well disposed, but the Vatican are likely to be firm on all the questions mentioned above.

Czechoslovakia.

37. Among the succession States to the Dual Monarchy the relations of Czechoslovakia to the Holy See have been by far the least cordial; though comparing 1924 with previous years, the situation of the Catholic Church has shown a visible improvement, while the influence of Catholics on public affairs has increased. In spite of this improvement there were many shadows obscuring the horizon, and the Church has constantly to be on the alert against the attacks of Socialists, Atheists and Freethinkers. These are numerically few, but they are influential and liable to dominate public opinion by means of the press, the schools and even the Government.

38. Early in the year, during a meeting of the Foreign Affairs Committee, an attack was made on the policy of the Vatican by Deputy Hrusovsky, a member of the Nationalist Socialist party, who is generally considered as the mouthpiece of Dr. Benes in the Chamber. He complained that the Vatican openly supported every movement directed against the republic, and that it ignored the proposals of the Czechoslovak Government with regard to the nomination of bishops, as was evident by the appointment of Bishop Jantausch to the diocese of Trnava. The latter, he insisted, encouraged agitation in Slovakia, and the Vatican policy made a separation of Church and State essential within the republic. He strongly advocated the withdrawal of the mission to the Vatican.

Dr. Benes, while returning a temporising reply to the speaker, showed plainly that he sympathised with the attacker. On general questions of ecclesiastical policy, he continued, the most important problems remained to be solved, but these lay in the realm of internal rather than of foreign affairs.

39. At the Vatican it is considered that a separation of Church and State is almost inevitable, and such a contingency is regarded with equanimity. The Cardinal Secretary of State considers that from the moment that Czechoslovakia had gained independence after the war, the new Government of the republic, while anxious to retain the privileges accorded by the Church to the Dual Monarchy, had taken every occasion to show their hostility to the Church. The Vatican had no intention of ceding any of their rights; and in an interview with Dr. Benes the cardinal explained that Czechoslovakia could not profit by the concordat with Austria-Hungary any more than she could by the treaties concluded with other States before the war. Dr. Benes did not seem inclined to agree with this view.

40. The Czechoslovakian Minister, M. Pallier, told me that he, too, was entirely pessimistic about the situation. He complained of the intransigence of the Vatican and of their business methods; and even considered the continuation of his mission futile.

Russia.

41. It will be recalled that the Bolshevik persecution of Christians, which had raged during the whole of 1923, culminated in the arrest, trial and condemnation to death of Mgr. Cieplak, Archbishop of Petrograd. The execution was postponed, and when the year closed the unfortunate prelate was still languishing in prison. On the 24th January Cardinal Gasparri sent for me by the orders of the Pope, who had seen in the accession to office of the Labour Government an opportunity which might not recur of repairing the great injury which had been done to priests in Russia. As their policy was to renew diplomatic relations with Russia, His

Holiness hoped that in negotiating terms with the Soviet Government the latter could at the same time be urged to release Archbishop Cieplak. I lost no time in forwarding this request to the Foreign Office, and soon received a reply from the Prime Minister saying that he would certainly bear in mind the Pope's wishes and do all that lay within his power to obtain the release whenever a fitting moment arrived. In the meantime, he hoped that the mere fact of recognition would conduce to a condition of affairs in Russia which might lead to a greater measure of toleration than in the past. In the beginning of April, largely thanks to the pressure brought on M. Rakovski by Mr. MacDonald in London, Archbishop Cieplak was released. The Vatican were immensely relieved, and I was charged to transmit the expression of the Pope's grateful thanks to His Majesty's Government. The Cardinal Secretary of State thoroughly realised the difficulty of the task undertaken by Mr. MacDonald, and hardly dared anticipate success at so early a date. He also thoroughly realised that the only pressure capable of producing any result on the Soviet authorities was that exercised by the British Foreign Office at that critical juncture. A few days later I met Mgr. Cieplak himself at the Polish Legation, and he hurried up to me from the crowd with which he was encircled in order to beg me to thank the Prime Minister from the bottom of his heart for his powerful intervention on his behalf.

42. In July, when it was rumoured that the Vatican would be disposed to recognise the Soviet Government, the cardinal told me that there was little or no chance of this, as Russia was not in a mood to admit the Vatican conditions. In reply to my enquiry as to the nature of these conditions, His Eminence replied that they were : (1) release of Catholics now in prison or exiled to Siberia; (2) arrangement as to handing back the confiscated Catholic churches; (3) liberty to teach the Catechism to persons under 18 years of age, at least in church; (4) liberty for the Pope's representative to communicate freely with the Catholic clergy.

43. In August the Pontifical Relief Mission in Moscow was ordered out of the country in a peremptory manner; and I was informed at the Vatican that this action was undoubtedly due to the attitude of the Holy See in the matter of recognition. The policy of the Holy See certainly appeared to be reasonable and justified; there was at the moment no Catholic bishop in Russia, and the Church, therefore, had no one to guide it. The Vatican had asked that the Apostolic delegate should be allowed to go and be able to communicate freely with those under his jurisdiction. If after a few months he found that the conditions were tolerable he would take up the negotiation for recognition with the Soviet Government. The latter, however, insisted that recognition must come first, and that they would then discuss the degree of liberty to be accorded to the Catholic Church. This, of course, meant that the Vatican would be surrendering their chief weapon in return for vague assurances; and all further negotiation was thereupon abandoned.

Holland.

44. In the early part of the year the question of the continuance of the Netherlands Mission to the Vatican was discussed in the States General. An amendment to the Foreign Office vote was proposed by certain members of the Christian Historical party, providing for the abolition of this mission. The motion was discussed but did not receive a very large amount of support from the other groups represented in the Chamber, and was officially rejected by 61 votes to 24.

45. On the 23rd July the Twenty-seventh International Eucharistic Congress was opened at Amsterdam, attended by Cardinal van Rossum as Papal Legate, accompaned by six other cardinals, forty archbishops and bishops, and many other prelates. The congress has been described as one of the most impressive gatherings which has ever assembled in the Netherlands. Over 70.000 persons are alleged to have been present, the Papal Legate being escorted by a guard of honour of twenty knights of the Order of Malta. A resolution was passed by the congress to the effect that the Council of the League of Nations should be asked by the congress to invite the Holy See to join the League; a resolution which received the support of Cardinal Dubois, who argued that it is anomalous that the majority of countries should be represented at the Holy See whilst the latter should not be represented in the League of Nations.

46. Cardinal van Rossum read the Apostolic Message from the Pope in which the latter referred to the desire in the Netherlands for the restoration of complete freedom for Catholic ceremonies which had been lost. It has been suggested that

the Pope's message might incite the Catholic parties in the States-General to press for the repeal of the prohibition to hold religious processions.

There are about 2 million Catholics in Holland, a third of the total population.

China.

47. Though regular diplomatic relations have not yet been established between the Holy See and China, the gradual elimination of the French Protectorate of Catholics in the Far East is causing a closer connection and understanding. These have made appreciable progress in the course of the past year.

48. The new President of the Republic, on assuming office, not only notified this fact to the Pope, but supplemented the announcement with a letter, in which he gave an assurance that he meant to do all in his power to render more intimate and intense the friendship between the Holy See and China.

49. Another incident, testifying to the growing cordiality and progress of the Catholic Church in China, was the appointment of the Rev. P. Odoric Tcheng, of the Order of the Friars Minor, as Prefect Apostolic in Eastern Hupé. The Vicariate Apostolic of that province has been divided, and a portion has been assigned to native clergy. This is said to be the first appointment of a native Prefect Apostolic in China.

50. On the 15th May the first general synod was solemnly inaugurated at Shanghai. As a further indication that the relations between China and the Holy See, in spite of French opposition, are likely to assume a more direct character in the future, this ceremony was not without significance. Judging from a remark made to me by the Cardinal Secretary of State, I am inclined to think that the status of Mgr. Costantini, who is one of the ablest of the Vatican representatives, may not inconceivably be raised to that of an Apostolic Nuncio in the not distant future.

Japan.

51. On the 13th December the Cardinal Secretary of State informed me that the Japanese Government, having requested by telegram the establishment of diplomatic relations, the Pope had immediately responded by giving the Apostolic delegate at Tokyo the rank of Nuncio. The reason for this urgent request has not yet transpired; but the development was not unexpected, and it is felt that the moment is not far distant when the Emperor of Japan will have his representative to the Holy See. From the day the Japanese Crown Prince visited the Pope three years ago, the idea of the necessity of diplomatic relations has become engrained, not only in the minds of the Japanese Imperial Family, but also in the minds of Japanese statesmen. There is a certain opposition, but it is anticipated that with time and patience this will be overcome, possibly in the course of 1925.

The Argentine.

52. The relations between the Holy See and the Argentine Government were marked by severe and constant tension, so much so that it is surprising that the year should have closed without an actual rupture. The controversy, as it will be recalled, rages round the appointment to the vacant archbishopric of Buenos Aires. The nomination of Mgr. Andrea by the Argentine Government was not confirmed by the Pope, and neither side had any intention of receding from the position they had taken up. In order to get out of this *impasse* the Argentine Minister in Paris, undei instructions from his Government, suggested to the Nuncio that Mgr. Andrea should be summoned to Rome, and kept there till the trouble had blown over. The Pope, however, disliked this arrangement, and it was finally decided, with the approval of the Argentine Government, that Mgr. Andrea should be appointed an Apostolic visitor to Latin South America, excluding the Argentine, and start off on a mission which would take at least a year, if not two. Everything was arranged accordingly, and the nomination was duly despatched to Buenos Aires, when the Argentine Government suddenly said that Mgr. Andrea could not leave without their *placet*. They also demanded to see the instructions which the Holy See had sent him, a request to which the Vatican declined to submit. From this it was obvious that the Argentine Government wished to cause trouble, and that the personal hostile sentiments of the Minister for Foreign Affairs would always have to be reckoned with as well as those of certain party politicians, who were working for a rupture of diplomatic

relations. In September the Senate at Buenos Aires approved a motion to the following effect :—

   (*a*.) The Government notify the Holy See that Mgr. Cardinale is no longer *persona grata.*
   (*b*.) That Señor García Mansilla be superseded.
   (*c*.) That when this has been done the Holy See be asked to make an official statement of its policy.
   (*d*.) That no appointments by the Holy See of ecclesiastics having jurisdiction in the Church in Argentina be approved by the Government until a solution of the present conflict be reached.

   As the year closed both the Nuncio and the Argentine Minister were still at their posts awaiting further developments.

Mexico.

   53. It will be recalled that Mgr. Filippi, the Apostolic delegate, was summarily expelled from Mexico for holding a religious service in the open air (two years ago), although on private property, the occasion being the laying of a foundation stone of a monument. The year 1924 witnessed a renewal of relations. In December the " Osservatore Romano " announced that, " as a result of an exchange of views between the Holy See and the Mexican Government, and of the acceptance by the latter of the Holy See's conditions, the Pope has appointed the Rev. Father Serafino Cimino, Order of Friars Minor, to be Apostolic delegate to that republic, creating him at the same time titular Archbishop of Cyrrhus." In reply to an enquiry I made at the Vatican I was informed confidentially that the Holy See insisted that, after the treatment to which Mgr. Filippi, the last Apostolic delegate was subjected, they would only appoint a successor on definite assurances being given that he would be able to communicate freely with the Holy See and with the hierarchy of Mexico; and generally, that he should receive the consideration befitting his dignity. To these conditions the Mexican Government gave their assent.

United States.

   54. Through the whole year friendly relations existed between the Holy See and the United States of America, in spite of the fact that there is no diplomatic representation. The Church now counts four American cardinals : O'Connell, Dougherty, Hayes and Mündelein. The Apostolic delegate co-operated harmoniously with the whole American episcopate. No cloud obscured the serene nature of these relations, and Catholics continued to give substantial proof of their filial attachment to Rome (their contributions, for instance, to the foreign missions, surpass those of all other countries put together). The Government, too, took a sympathetic interest in their development, as a proof of which it may be noted that the President himself attended and addressed a recent great Catholic assembly at, I think, St. Louis. Thanks to their generous contributions to the Holy See, the four cardinals, and especially Cardinal O'Connell and Cardinal Mündelein, enjoy great influence in Rome. They both passed several years here as ecclesiastical students, and speak Italian fluently.

   55. American Catholics have now a national church in Rome, which has already eclipsed the English church of San Silvestro in attracting English-speaking Catholics. Their college, too, is yearly increasing in numbers; and being plentifully supplied with funds is contemplating the purchase of a wide strip of land on a hill near St. Peter's, a part of which will be handed over as a gift to the College of Propaganda Fide. The increasing strength of the Catholic Church in America means increasing influence at the Vatican; and it is not so much of an exaggeration to say that the United States is now looked up to as if it were the leading Catholic nation.

League of Nations.

   56. At the Eucharist Congress at Amsterdam in July a resolution of the Argentine Delegation was passed to the effect that the Council of the League of Nations should be asked by the Congress to invite the Holy See to join the League. This resolution is stated to have received the special support of Cardinal Dubois, who argued that it is anomalous that the majority of countries should be represented at the Holy See, whilst the latter has no voice in the League of Nations.

57. This same question of the representation of the Holy See at the League of Nations was urged at various Catholic Congresses, such as the International Catholic Association at Lugano, the German National Congress at Hannover, the Belgian Catholic Youth Society at Brussels and spasmodically throughout the year in the columns of the press.

58. In May the British representative on the League discussed with the secretary-general at Geneva the possibility of bringing the Vatican into direct touch with the League's work; and with that possibility in view suggested to the Foreign Office that the Papal Nuncio in Berne should be furnished with any papers concerning subjects in which the Vatican were likely to be interested. It was further suggested that it might be possible to arrange that the Papal Nuncio should express to the Council of the League of Nations the view of the Vatican on any matter in which the Papacy took a particular interest. There could be no question of a League representative to the Vatican as such a proposal would be resented by the Italian Government; and would in any case in itself be quite impracticable. In replying to these suggestions the Prime Minister took the line that the adoption of such a procedure would be tantamount to assigning to the Vatican the position of informal assessor to the council and should not be pursued. The matter then dropped. As a matter of fact the Vatican know full well that the wording of article 1 of the covenant was specially designed to exclude the possibility of their obtaining membership: and I am bound to admit that in the many conversations I have had on the subject I have never observed a trace of a desire to gain admittance.. The fear of this, therefore, if fear there be, is groundless. With regard to the charge that the Vatican is hostile to the League I am convinced that this lacks all foundation. They may be indifferent, but even this indifference will vanish when the League becomes a real League with the participation of the United States, Germany and Russia.

III.—THE SACRED COLLEGE.

59. The Requiem Mass for the cardinals who have died during the year, which it is customary to celebrate early in November, did not take place, as death had made no claims on the Sacred College during the past year. In the latter part of November, however, the news reached Rome of the death of Cardinal Logue. I took an early opportunity of presenting my condolences to the Cardinal Secretary of State at the death of such a distinguished member of the Sacred College; and expressed my satisfaction to his Eminence that the Pope had directed that a Requiem Mass should be said in the Sixtine Chapel. The service took place on the 27th, and was attended by His Holiness in person, by the Sacred College, the Diplomatic Body and the Roman nobility. Obituary notices in the Italian press all paid tribute to Cardinal Logue's integrity and learning, as well as to his efforts in the cause of Irish peace and reconciliation. On the last day of the year Cardinal Giorgi succumbed to an attack of pneumonia. He was Protector of the Franciscan Order; and, in June. as will be recalled, he visited Palestine as Papal Legate when he consecrated the new basilicas of Mount Tabor and Gethsemane. On his return he spoke in high terms of the courtesy and attention with which he had been received by His Majesty's High Commissioner and the British authorities; and the visit was undoubtedly productive of good results.

60. On the 21st March the Pope held a consistory at which he created two new American cardinals, Mgr. Mündelein, Archbishop of Chicago and Mgr. Hayes, Archbishop of New York. It was declared in Rome, and probably with some truth, that American gold had something to do with the promotion of the two archbishops; and also with the fact that the consistory was held in St. Peter's instead of in the regular Consistory Hall. With regard to the latter assertion I was assured at the Vatican that the Consistory Hall was under repair, and that though the ceremony at St. Peter's would permit of a larger number of Americans being present—and there were a vast amount in Rome at the time—it was not to be regarded as an exceptional honour to the American prelates. This is no doubt true, though America has deserved well of the Holy See, seeing that she has furnished vast sums for distribution among the poor in Russia and Germany, and especially for foreign missions. Apart from special collection the Catholics of New York and Chicago are by far the greatest contributors towards Vatican funds. It is, indeed, difficult to see how the present administration could be preserved without their support.

61. In December, Cardinal Gasquet, the only English cardinal in the Roman Curia, celebrated his golden jubilee in the priesthood. The Pope marked the occasion by raising his Eminence from Cardinal Deacon to the dignity of Cardinal Priest;

and in addition presented him with a chalice and other gifts, including a substantial sum for the benefit of his titular church of Santa Maria in Campitelli. The celebrations held throughout the week concluded with the party given in the cardinal's honour at the Legation, when I was privileged to deliver to his Eminence a gracious message of congratulation from His Majesty the King. The demonstrations of which Cardinal Gasquet was the centre were a pleasing testimony to the high regard and esteem in which he is held in all circles, from the Pope downwards. His personality, learning and eminent qualities have won for him a foremost place among his colleagues in the Sacred College, where he is the worthy representative of the Catholics in the British Empire.

IV.—THE PRESS.

62. In previous reports the "Osservatore Romano," the only Catholic paper officially representing the Holy See, has been depicted as a somewhat colourless and uninfluential organ of the press. A distinct improvement in this position was made in the course of the year, and this journal can now hold up its head with any and all contemporaries. A number of young leading lights in the Azione Cattolica now contribute articles to it; and its news from abroad is often supplied by the staff of Nunciatures. On the 24th June its article regarding the murder of the Deputy Matteotti was cited by Signor Mussolini the following day in order to enforce his own arguments when facing in the Chamber the deputies of a justly exasperated nation. Considering that the "Osservatore" is not sparing of criticism of the Italian Prime Minister when it sees the need the latter showed by his allusion that he holds the paper in high respect, and recognises its impartiality and authority.

63. Later on the "Osservatore Romano" was destined to receive a further pat on the back worth recording, and this time from a London contemporary, the "Morning Post," which contained the following paragraph :—

"It would appear that the only really independent paper published to-day in Italy is the 'Osservatore Romano,' the Vatican organ, which presumably shares in the extra-territoriality of the Pope. It is, as is fitting, a serious little paper, well-written and not at all biassed, and it is indispensable even in normal times to the student of Italian affairs."

64. The "Unità Cattolica" of Florence is a daily paper with a small but serious minded clientèle. It is subsidised by the Vatican. Its articles, which are often well written and quoted by other papers, deal mainly with politico-religious questions. By many it is considered as superior to the "Osservatore Romano." The "Civiltà Cattolica" run by the Jesuit fathers is a fortnightly magazine and carries great weight in higher Catholic circles. It is on much the same level as the "Month," edited by the Jesuits in England and covers an equally wide field.

o

(12998)

HOLY SEE.

Annual Report, 1925.

[C 5004/5004/22]

Sir O. Russell to Sir Austen Chamberlain.—(Received April 26.)

(No. 68.)　　　　　　　　　　　*British Legation to the Holy See,*
Sir,　　　　　　　　　　　　　　　　*Rome, April 21, 1926.*

I HAVE the honour to transmit herewith my annual report on the Holy See for 1925, drawn up for this year of exceptional interest with the able co-operation of Mr. Randall, secretary to His Majesty's Legation.

2. Immediately following the introduction I have included a chapter on the organisation of the Vatican, my motive being that this historical feature, which was included in reports from other missions when the annual reports were inaugurated, has not hitherto found a place in reports from this Legation.

I have, &c.
ODO RUSSELL.

Enclosure.

Annual Report on the Holy See for 1925.

CONTENTS.

I.—INTRODUCTION.

FOR the Holy See the year 1925 was of exceptional importance and activity. It was, first of all, a year of jubilee. The celebrations in connection with this event, otherwise called the Holy Year, will be described in a later section of this report. It is sufficient to say here that, although there were many who prophesied failure, or at least the non-attainment of the results which the Vatican organisation had made its goal, the success of the undertaking grew more pronounced and striking as the year progressed, reaching a high-water mark twice; first, on the canonisation of Blessed Teresa of the Child Jesus, a 19th century Saint, who again proved the ability of French Catholicism to produce pious personalities of the most extraordinary universal appeal; second, with the celebration on the 15th November of the 16th hundredth anniversary of the Council of Nicaea, which was marked by a remarkable simultaneous celebration in St. Peter's of masses in all the principal non-Latin rites and by a demonstration of the vitality, much renewed under the present Pontificate, of the connection between the Roman See and the Catholics of the East.

2. In addition to the canonisation just mentioned, there were several other canonisations during the year, among which may be mentioned St. Peter Canisius, a Dutch Jesuit scholar of the 16th century, whose celebration attracted numerous Dutch, German and Scandinavian pilgrims to Rome. There were also several beatifications. These ceremonies have a more than purely religious significance, since each person raised to the altars of the Church, to employ the Catholic formula, constitutes a further bond of sentiment and devotion between the Holy See and the country from which the person canonised or beatified comes. Of particular interest to British visitors was the ceremony of beatification of the Canadian Jesuit martyrs of the 17th century which took place on the 21st June, attended by a number of representative Canadians.

3. Apart from the large number of public speeches to pilgrims, which averaged more than one a day throughout the year and were often of more than passing interest, as, for instance, a long address to the Bulgarian pilgrims in July in which special mention was made of the goodwill of the ex-Czar Ferdinand, His Holiness the Pope made three official pronouncements during the year, namely :—

(1.) *The Allocution of the* 30*th March*, issued in connection with the promotion of two Spanish Cardinals to the Sacred College. This document, after describing the qualities of the two new Cardinals, paid a special tribute to the poor pilgrims who were making such sacrifices to pay their jubilee visit to Rome; and referred to the approaching celebration of the sixteenth centenary of the Nicene Council.

(2.) *The Allocution of the 14th December*, made on the occasion of the consistory at which four more Cardinals were created. This comprehensive document began with a lengthy reference to the Holy Year, paid a cordial tribute to the way in which the Italian civil authorities had assisted in facilitating the visits of the pilgrims, and expressed the Pope's abhorrence at the criminal attempt on the Italian Prime Minister; this being followed by a reminder of the anomalous and unsatisfactory position of the Papacy. Then came a moderate criticism of the principle of the Fascist trade-union legislation and a condemnation of the licence and anarchy to which Liberalism and Socialism lead society. Finally, His Holiness passed in review the condition of the Church in various parts of the world; not quite satisfactory in Chile, where the separation of State and Church, although not anti-clerical, was not in accordance with Catholic teaching; far worse in Mexcio, where the situation might seem well nigh hopeless. Conditions in the Argentine, in Czechoslovakia and Jugoslavia were also not satisfactory. Brighter were the prospects in France, and the conclusion during the year of concordats between the Holy See and Bavaria and Poland was likely to be productive of good. The Papal utterance ended with an announcement that the privileges of the Holy Year would in 1926 be extended to the whole world in view of the approaching celebration of the seventh centenary of St. Francis of Assisi.

(3.) *The Encyclical " Quas primas "* of the 24*th December*, by which His Holiness proclaimed the institution of a new feast of the Church, called the feast of Christ the King, and emphasised the overlordship of the Saviour in civil society. The first celebration of the new festival was impressively conducted by the Pope himself in St. Peter's on the last day of the year.

4. Comprehensive as was the review of the activities of the Church throughout the year contained in the Papal Allocution summarised above, it did not cover all the ground. If the Church abroad suffered a certain political set-back in two or three countries, in particular Czechoslovakia, Holland and Lithuania, it made

considerable progress elsewhere. Of this progress an obvious criterion was the number of new dioceses or Apostolic Delegacies. Three new dioceses were established in Bolivia and Brazil respectively, one in Italy (Fiume), one in Great Britain (Lancaster), and one in the Caroline Islands. Five new Apostolic prefectures were set up, one in Bolivia, one in the Congo and three in China—these last in spite of depressing news from Catholic missions in that troublous country. A new ecclesiastical province was formed in Cuba and an Apostolic Delegacy established for Indo-China.

5. This introductory record of the activities of the Holy See during 1925 would be incomplete without a reference to the contributions to learning and research made by the Holy See during the year. First comes the Petrine Museum, opened near St. Peter's and destined to be a mine of information for all students of the great basilica. Then the continued interest of the Pope in the Milan Catholic University has to be chronicled. This now has the official recognition of the Italian Government, but is financially dependent on the support of the Holy See and the faithful. Lastly, a word must be said of the recent archæological discoveries made in and about Rome, which have an important bearing on Catholic apologetic, and are of interest to students of Christian archæology and the early history of Christian art. The developments were considered of such moment by the Holy See that it contributed a large sum for the purpose of buying a site on which a new and ambitious institute of Christian archæology is to be built.

II.—The Organisation of the Vatican.

6. As a preliminary to an examination in detail of the activities of the Holy See during 1925 and its relations with foreign States, I venture to give, in the hope that it may be of some use for reference, a summary account of what may be called the administrative machinery of the Vatican. The remarkable organisation of the Holy See is a commonplace which is always taken for granted, but not very often analysed. Without the necessity, or, even in modern times, the desire, of interfering in a country's foreign or internal politics or giving, unless in exceptional circumstances, political " directives " to the faithful, the Holy See is, however, intimately concerned with civil government when it touches the faith or moral principles of its millions of adherents, and for this reason a general knowledge of the administrative agencies through which the faith is preserved or diffused seems to be a desirable adjunct to the education of a politician or diplomatist.

7. The Roman administration of the Holy See may be conveniently divided as follows :—

    (1.) The Pontiff himself.
    (2.) The Cardinal Secretary of State.
    (3.) The Sacred College.
    (4.) The Congregations.

The Pontiff.

8. Little need be said about the Pope as the Head of the Administration of the Holy See. By the very constitution of the Catholic Church he is the human source of all authority, and, although much of this, naturally, is delegated, His Holiness fills no small or easy part in the actual day-to-day government of the Church. Every head of a congregation has a regular time, once a week, or once a fortnight, rarely less frequently, for personal consultation with the Pope, and has the right of access at other times, as have all bishops and heads of all religious orders and colleges. The result is that the Pope is in fairly complete control of the vast and complicated organisation, and is the final authority before whom every decision of major importance must go before it can be executed. Not a new diocese or college or foreign mission can be established, not an ex-communication take effect, not a Catholic marriage be annulled, not an Apostolic delegate be appointed or withdrawn, without at least the formal approval of the Pope.

The Cardinal Secretary of State.

9. Next to the Pope comes the Cardinal Secretary of State. This office is sometimes spoken of as more or less equivalent to that of Secretary of State for Foreign Affairs, subject to an authority similar to that of Prime Minister. The

analogy is not quite correct. The Pope, although elected by a democratic system in the sense that wealth or title, or even intellectual ability, have nothing necessarily to do with the choice, and that the poorest parish priest can be, and has been, chosen for this highest office, once he achieves his exalted position, assumes the rôle of an absolutely autocratic sovereign, and the Cardinal Secretary of State, chosen by him, becomes, so to speak, his *alter ego*, the one Cardinal of the Sacred College who is in daily consultation with His Holiness, his most intimate counsellor, chief interpreter of his will, the reflection of the Pope's mind. This alone should dispose of the rumours, heard from time to time, that there were serious differences of opinion between the Pope and the Cardinal Secretary of State. The exact functions of the Secretary of State—the title became official in 1560—were laid down in modern times by Pope Pius IX in the year 1850, when it was decreed that the holder of this high office should not only represent the Pontiff-King in all relations with foreign States, but should be the agent of the sovereign for legislative acts, supreme over the other five ministries. These ministries were abolished, of course, after the collapse of the Temporal Power, and their functions were taken over, so far as they continued to exist, by the Cardinal Secretary of State. In his reform of the Congregations, which he carried through by his encyclical *Sapienti concilio* in June 1908, Pope Pius X again defined the office of Cardinal Secretary of State, dividing it into three parts: Extraordinary Affairs, Ordinary Affairs, and the despatch of Apostolic Briefs, each of which is presided over by a secretary, all subject to the Cardinal Secretary of State. This organisation is now embodied in Canon Law, according to which—in particular, article 255—all appointments to sees necessitating negotiations with civil Governments—and in practice this covers almost the entire world—are subject to the Congregation of Extraordinary Ecclesiastical Affairs, over which the Cardinal Secretary of State presides. It will thus be seen that the powers of the Cardinal Secretary of State far exceed the constitutional functions of a Minister for Foreign Affairs, and much more resemble those of a Prime Minister, subject to a supreme authority with which he is always in the closest contact and on terms of the most intimate confidence.

The Sacred College.

10. From the year 1586 the number of cardinals has been fixed at seventy. In origin, these ecclesiastics were the immediate assistants of the Supreme Pontiff in the task of governing Rome and its immediate neighbourhood, and to this day, however remote the place from which a cardinal may come, he still has the title of a particular Roman parish. Thus, His Eminence Cardinal Bourne, Archbishop of Westminster, has as his titular church that of Sta. Pudentiana, in Rome. The full complement of the Sacred College is as follows: six cardinal-bishops, fifty cardinal-priests, fourteen cardinal-deacons.

11. Of these, the first and last classes reside permanently in Rome, and, together with a certain number of the cardinal-priests, who are also given apartments in the city, constitute the Cardinals in Curia; the remainder of the cardinal-priests are in charge of important arch-dioceses in all parts of the world, and proceed to Rome only on important occasions—above all, on the death of a Pope, or when specially summoned. The Sacred College does not act as a body except at the election of a new Pontiff, and the Cardinals in Curia also do not act as one committee, but function through the various Congregations, over each of which a cardinal, or the Pope himself, presides as prefect, having under him such other cardinals or monsignori or simple priests who may be selected to serve as active members or "consultori," in virtue of special gifts or knowledge.

The Sacred Congregations.

12. The congregations of the Roman Curia, as reorganised, with one exception, by Pope Pius X, and established, with a definition of the functions of each, by the Canon Law of the Church, are twelve in number, as follow :—

(1.) *The Holy Office* (formerly the Holy Inquisition), which is charged with the duty of preserving the doctrines and dogmas of the Church touching faith and morals. The well-known organisation of the Index Expurgatorius is subject to this Congregation.

(2.) *The Consistorial Congregation.*—This is concerned with the supervision of dioceses and the selection of new bishops.

(3.) *The Congregation of the Sacraments*, which supervises all administration or discipline connected with the seven sacraments of the Church.

(4.) *The Congregation of the Council*, which deals with the summoning of councils of the Church and ecclesiastical assemblies in general.

(5.) *The Congregation of the Religious*, which supervises the affairs of the religious orders.

(6.) *The Congregation of Propaganda*, which supervises the affairs of Catholic missions in countries that are largely non-Catholic. It used to supervise Roman Catholic missions in Slav countries until this function was taken from it and confided by Pope Benedict XV, in the year 1917, to a new and special Congregation, namely—

(7.) *The Congregation of the Eastern Church*, whose importance in the organisation of the Holy See increases with the prospect of the reclamation of Russian orthodox to the Roman obedience.

(8.) *The Congregation of Rites* supervises the rites and ceremonies of the Church, and questions of canonisation.

(9.) *The Ceremonial Congregation*, which is self-explanatory.

(10.) *The Congregation of Extraordinary Ecclesiastical Affairs* which supervises all questions of relations with foreign Governments, arranges concordats, and is responsible for the appointment of nuncios having diplomatic rank.

(11.) *The Congregation of Seminaries, Universities and of Studies*, which is self-explanatory.

(12.) *The Congregation of the Fabric of St. Peter's*, which administers the basilica.

13. In addition to these Congregations there are numerous subordinate or, one should say, executive offices, the most important of which are the *Cancelleria*, which sees to the despatch of Apostolic Letters; the *Dateria*, which has charge of letters of appointment; the *Secretariat of State*, through which functions the Cardinal Secretary of State; and the *Rota*, which deals with legal questions affecting Catholics, such as petitions for nullification of marriage. Most of these multifarious organs of the Church are liable to affect civil Governments in any country where Roman Catholics are present in appreciable numbers.

III.—THE HOLY YEAR.

14. The year 1925 stood out prominently in the history of the Church, being a Holy Year or jubilee. This is a celebration instituted by Pope Boniface VIII in the year 1300, and now taking place every twenty-five years. During its course the faithful all over the world are enjoined to visit Rome and pray in the principal churches for certain " intentions " of the Pope, an act of devotion to which special indulgences are attached. The Holy Year of 1925 was opened on Christmas Eve 1924 by the Pope himself, who performed the symbolic act of breaking down the sealed Holy Door leading into St. Peter's, and so inaugurated the jubilee A similar ceremony was performed in the other three basilicas, Santa Maria Maggiore, San Giovanni Laterano, and San Paolo fuori le Mura, by cardinals specially delegated for this duty.

15. Primarily, of course, the Holy Year was of religious and particularly Catholic interest. The principal " intentions " for which the pilgrims were exhorted to pray were for peace—the motto taken by the present Pontiff being " Pax Christi in regno Christi "—and for a settlement of conditions in Palestine in accordance with Catholic aspirations. The fervent prayers that were offered for the first " intention " were held by many pious Catholics here to have led to the Locarno Treaty. The latter " intention " might have been thought likely to stir up a certain political controversy, but nothing of the kind was observed by this Legation; and the whole year, especially towards the end, provided on the whole a singularly striking and edifying illustration of the piety and loyalty of Catholics from all parts of the world. Complete statistics have been difficult to collect, as in addition to the organised pilgrimages, which are easily controlled, there were numerous private pilgrimages, and large numbers of individual pilgrims, many of whom, at first, did not take advantage of the cheap tickets and so escaped statistical observation. From the reports issued by the Holy Year organising committee in Rome and the Italian State railways, however, it is possible to frame a fairly

accurate estimate of the number of pilgrims. Italy, naturally, stood at the head of the organised pilgrimages with 212,000 pilgrims. Germany, who made a characteristically efficient and imposing effort, came next with 42,000. Next came Spain with 13,000, then France with 12,000. Great Britain and Ireland were, in proportion to the size of their Catholic population, well represented with official pilgrimages totalling 6,300. The principal Irish pilgrimage arrived in October, and was led by Mr. Cosgrave, President of the Free State Parliament. There were also pilgrimages from other dominions, in particular, Australia and Canada. It is unnecessary to enumerate the other countries, for the list would include most nations in the world. Altogether, according to the official figures of organised national pilgrimages only, there were 1,180 groups totalling something over 600,000 pilgrims, who visited Rome. It is a fair estimate, on the basis of the railway and tourist companies' returns, to say that this represented about one-half of the total number of pilgrims, this giving a very probable estimate of about a million and a quarter pilgrims for the whole of the year. The part played by the Pope himself in receiving this large number deserves special mention. A collective audience was accorded to all the official national pilgrimages, and to most of the private ones; and this, in addition to a constant succession of private audiences, imposed an enormous burden on His Holiness, who delived during the year about 380 regular speeches. To say that this prodigious task was carried through with success would be an under-statement. The vigorous and spontaneous way in which His Holiness sustained his part was remarkable, and made a great impression on all visitors.

16. Apart from the religious interest of this year there were certain political results, or potential political results, to be recorded. The ordinary visitor could not fail to be struck with the extraordinary universal appeal the Roman Catholic Church and the person of the Pontiff is still able to exercise. This was emphasised all the more by the Missionary Exhibition, opened in connection with the Holy Year in the Vatican Gardens, which provided a graphic picture of the all-pervading character of Catholic missions, and showed, in particular, the remarkably large share taken in those missions by the French. Then the Holy Year, coinciding as it did with the sixteenth hundredth anniversary of the Council of Nicaea, which was officially celebrated on the 15th November, also provided an opportunity of demonstrating the loyalty to the Holy See, which exists in large tracts of Eastern Europe where the Latin rite is not practised, and may well have done much to further the special aim of the present Pontiff, namely, of reclaiming the masses of schismatic orthodox to the Roman obedience.

17. Finally, the most striking immediate political result of the Holy Year was the way it furthered the ever-growing cordiality between the Italian Government and the Holy See. All the constant invasion of Rome by pilgrims of all nationalities and social conditions could not have been organised as efficiently as it was without the co-operation of the civic authorities, to whose help the Pope bore a grateful witness in his Allocution of the 14th December. Contrary to expectation the health of Rome was good during the year. Hotel prices were not unduly extravagant, and the special traffic arrangements made for carrying the pilgrims into and about Rome worked well. This contributed no little to an even greater friendliness of feeling between the Italian Government and the Holy See, and the former were probably shrewd enough to realise that many influential and devout Catholics on pilgrimage left Rome with a better impression of Signor Mussolini's Government than that with which they arrived. It is natural that towards the end of the year the ever-recurring talk about a solution of the Roman question should have revived. But that was still in the realm of rumour at the close of the year, and all that can be said with certainty of the Jubilee in relation to the Italian Government and people is that it amply demonstrated the spiritual dominance of the Catholic Church over the Italian people, and that it provided Signor Mussolini with one more, and that the most striking, opportunity of service to the Holy See, and that, so gratifying devout Catholic feeling, it perceptibly strengthened the international prestige of Italy at an important moment of her history.

18. To resume, the Holy Year was not only a success as a spectacle, a piece of organisation, a religious demonstration; it was also a political event of no little interest, with immediate results possible for anyone to estimate, and with less immediate results which have probably only entered into the calculations of the Holy See, accustomed as it is to think in terms of many years ahead and take the long view of historical progress.

IV.—RELATIONS WITH FOREIGN POWERS.

19. In the following section, devoted to relations between the Holy See and individual countries, certain nations will not be mentioned. This does not necessarily indicate that there was no link between them and the Holy See, but that their relations were uneventful or otherwise politically negligible. The number of countries in diplomatic relation with the Holy See at the close of 1925 was twenty-five, relations with Lithuania being in suspense and the appointment of a Minister for the Latvian Republic not having been given effect.

Great Britain.

20. When, in the course of my New Year's audience, I tendered my good wishes to Pius XI for 1925, His Holiness, in his turn, expressed the hope that the Jubilee Year, which had been proclaimed holy by the Church, would be one of exceptional prosperity for our King and Queen and the British Empire. These were not mere words. This same sentiment of goodwill, reiterated on various occasions to the British pilgrims who flocked to Rome throughout the year, was apparent in diplomatic as well as in other relations; while the Vatican, as in 1924, took no pains to conceal their view that Great Britain was the preponderating power for good in the councils of Europe. A typical instance of the Vatican tendency to assign a prominent rôle to British diplomacy occurred during a threatened rupture of relations with the Argentine Government. When it was thought that the Nuncio at Buenos Aires might be handed his passports at any moment, provision had to be made for the custody of the cyphers and archives. Instead of enlisting for this purpose the services of one of the great Catholic States represented at Buenos Aires, Cardinal Gasparri begged me hastily to appeal for the assistance of the British Minister. When the Secretary of State complied with this request by sending the necessary instructions to Sir B. Alston, Cardinal Gasparri, in expressing his thanks, showed clearly how much he preferred to be under an obligation to His Majesty's Government than to any other Government. At a subsequent period he again appealed, and not in vain, for British assistance in smoothing over further difficulties which had arisen between the Argentine Government and the Holy See. Nor were the Vatican, for their part, slow to render us service when the occasion arose. Early in March I was constrained to call the attention of Cardinal Gasparri to the fact that too much preference was being shown by propaganda to nationalities other than British in appointing prelates in South Africa. His Eminence, while explaining that the difficulty in our case consisted in the scarcity of priests—a statement which is unfortunately only too true—was quite ready to acknowledge the justice of the complaint, and promised to lay the matter before the congregation concerned. The result proved satisfactory, for shortly afterwards Mgr. O'Leary was ordained bishop and Vicar Apostolic of the Transvaal, and Father Bernard O'Riley was made Vicar Apostolic of the Western Vicariate of Cape Province. For this prompt response to my appeal I was instructed by the Secretary of State to convey to Cardinal Gasparri the appreciation of His Majesty's Government.

21. With Ireland the relations, which throughout the year ran smoothly, were marked by two outstanding events, the visit of President Cosgrave to Rome as a pilgrim, and the bestowal of the Cardinal's hat on Mgr. O'Donnell, the Archbishop of Armagh. In connection with these two events the Cardinal Secretary of State, anxious to display a correct attitude towards His Majesty's Government under the altered conditions, gave me early information as to the intentions of the Pope. Both as regards the high Papal Decoration which was conferred on President Cosgrave and the raising of Mgr. O'Donnell to the Cardinalate, I received intimation in time to inform His Majesty's Government before the news was published to the world.

22. Among the British visitors of note to the Pope during the past year I might specify Mr. Tim Healy, Mr. Collier, Premier of Western Australia, the Padikara Mudalivar of Ceylon and the Inter-parliamentary Commercial Conference.

23. I cannot close this paragraph on Great Britain's relations with the Holy See without recording the erection of a memorial tablet to Adrian IV, the only English Pope, near his tomb in St. Peter's by the Norwegian nation with the sanction and blessing of the reigning Pontiff.

24. *Palestine.*—In last year's report it will be seen that various causes of difference had been satisfactorily settled. The year under review showed a still

further improvement all round.   Though the departure of **Sir Herbert Samuel was** regretted in the Vatican, it was promptly acknowledged that no more acceptable High Commissioner could have been selected than Lord Plumer, whose previous administration of Malta had brought him into close and sympathetic contact with the Holy See.

25.   The situation was still further improved when the Pope, to whom it had been represented that the Latin Patriarch of Jerusalem had been creating fresh difficulties in Palestine for the Holy See among the different religious communities and rites, decided to end this unsatisfactory situation by the appointment of an Apostolic visitor.   The latter was to be the Pope's official representative, and on his arrival Mgr. Barlassina would have to confine himself exclusively to his regular episcopal functions.   The selection of His Holiness for this office could not have been better for all concerned, as it fell upon the Franciscan, Father Paschal Robinson, who enjoys the confidence of all parties in Palestine, who is a friend of this Legation, and whose work in the past has elicited the approval of His Majesty's Government.

26.   The question of the Holy Places was raised by Cardinal Gasparri on the occasion of a visit of the High Commissioner to Rome.   His Eminence enquired of Sir Herbert Samuel whether it would not be possible to make some arrangement with the Moslem authorities, in whose possession the building of the Coenaculum was vested, to transfer it to some Catholic authority in exchange for other properties. Sir Herbert explained that the Arab family in possession, who had been sounded, would under no circumstances entertain the proposal, no matter what properties were offered in exchange.   When this was reported home, His Majesty's Government laid it down that any discussion of the question on any other basis than that of settlement by the Holy Places Commission was dangerous, and that controversial claims of this nature, to a site in which Christian, Jew and Moslem have an interest, should be dealt with by that commission only.

27.   In June the Cardinal Secretary of State addressed a note to this Legation complaining of the action of the Governor of Jerusalem in sending a Government engineer to the shrine of the Holy Sepulchre to make a report on the repairs required by that edifice.   According to his Eminence this was contrary to all precedent. He was assured that His Majesty's Government had no intention of taking or allowing any action affecting the *status quo*, and that the vatican would do well to await the report of Father Paschal Robinson, who had just proceeded to Palestine as Apostolic visitor.

Italy.

28.   The excellent although, of course, always unofficial relations between the Holy See and the Italian Government, noted in the annual reports for 1923 and 1924, were maintained, and even made progress in 1925.   Whatever may be their view of the moral basis of Fascism, the chief personages of the Holy See have never, at least in private conversation, concealed their opinion that Signor Mussolini, who placed himself and his party between the country and the abyss of social revolution, was, in the circumstances, alone capable of maintaining law and order.   The coming of the Holy Year made it more desirable than ever that internal peace should be efficiently maintained; and if from no other motive, therefore, the Holy See began the year, if not supporting the Italian Prime Minister, at least seeing to it that any body of opinion which they could influence should not take part in subversive activities against him.   This prudent and correct attitude was particularly shown when the "Osservatore Romano" during May pronounced strongly against any collaboration between Catholics and Socialists, a reproof to those members of the Popular party who were making common cause with the Aventine Opposition. Previous to this Signor Mussolini had, by numerous measures calculated to win the favour of the Church, stolen the popular party thunder and entirely stultified their political activities in the country.   He now so directed his policy, not only so as to reciprocate the benevolent neutrality of the Holy See, but also to draw advantage for Italy's prestige abroad.

29.   The suppression of the masonic lodges, always hostile to the Church's policy, was warmly welcomed by the Vatican; the invitation of the Government in February to three ecclesiastics to take part in the deliberations of the commission which was to consider modifications in ecclesiastical legislation was a friendly gesture that was at once responded to, and Signor Mussolini's personal message to Italian missions abroad regarding the Franciscan celebrations to be held in 1926 met with much favourable comment in Catholic circles.   In the city of Rome the

civil authorities showed a goodwill towards the Church, which was a constant source of agreeable surprise to the hundreds of thousands of pilgrims, who must have carried into all parts of the world a much more favourable impression of Fascism than that with which the great majority arrived. The cross was restored to the Colosseum, the Governor of Rome, Signor Cremonesi, associated himself with various important Catholic celebrations, and the organisation of processions, the health and traffic measures incidental to the Holy Year found the fullest co-operation on the part of the civil powers, as was publicly acknowledged by the Pope in his Consistorial Allocution of the 14th December, delivered at the close of the Holy Year.

30. There were, nevertheless, a few discordant notes, and, in order not to exaggerate their importance, it is necessary to point out, first, that the Holy See distinguishes between the Government and the Fascist party, and, second, that it has never given up its principles regarding a just settlement of the Roman question. For Signor Mussolini, as head of the Government, the Vatican shows great regard; the warmth of the Pope's reference, in the allocution just cited, to the attempted assassination of the Italian Premier was undoubtedly sincere. But the excesses of which, sporadically during even the earlier part of the Holy Year, certain of Signor Mussolini's extremist followers were guilty met with no less hearty condemnation. In July the "Osservatore Romano" had a strong protest against Fascist violence, and drew upon itself in consequence a good deal of abuse from Signor Farinacci, secretary-general of the Fascist party. The exclusive Fascist claim to be the State met with similar firm opposition on the part of the Holy See, particularly in reference to social legislation. The Government's proposal to acknowledge as legal only the Fascist trade unions was answered by the Azione Cattolica, the chief Catholic lay organisation, working under the direct authority of the Vatican, who took a firm resolution to maintain the Catholic unions in existence, on the ground that liberty of association was a fundamental right of man and one of the basic principles of Catholic social philosophy as laid down by Pope Leo XIII. This refusal to contemplate the "Fascistification" of the Church and its various agencies was the cause of much irritation in certain sections of the Fascist party, but it does not appear to have stirred up any resentment on the part of the Government as a whole.

31. On the Roman question, the Holy See made only one public announcement during 1925, in the Consistorial Allocution of the 14th December, in which the Pope, after alluding to the co-operation of the civil authorities in the Holy Year, added that the faithful had, nevertheless, had an opportunity of seeing the anomalous condition of the Papacy. This was a mere repetition of an oft-stated point of view regarding the wrong done in 1870, and it aroused no particular comment. Except rumour, in fact, and the undoubted excellence of feeling between Vatican and Quirinal, there was nothing at the close of the year to suggest that any actual negotiations for a settlement were likely to be undertaken in the near future. In a word, the Holy See, during 1925, took up the attitude that, grateful as it was for all the assistance afforded the Church by Signor Mussolini's Government, it could not regard the Fascist régime as an absolutely and normal permanent feature of the country's political life; it could not withhold its protest when moral laws were flagrantly broken in the persecution of opponents; it could not allow that all the social activities with which it was identified should be absorbed into the Fascist ideal of the State; and, lastly, that, because the Italian Government was favourable in certain particulars to the Church, therefore the Roman question could be regarded as a closed book.

France.

32. French relations with the Vatican during the year under review passed through many vicissitudes, and it was only due to a change of Government that a complete, if not final, rupture was averted. M. Herriot, the head of the Socialist Government, had taken office pledged to suppress the French Embassy to the Holy See, and he lost no time in submitting this question to the Chamber. The debates which followed showed that the religious question was to be a real menace to the stability of his Government. His supporters wished him to withdraw the Ambassador, and he would willingly have complied with their demand had he not been hampered by the peculiar position of the Church in Alsace-Lorraine, which is free from the disabilities imposed on the French Church by the Law of Separation. The difficulties arising out of this disparity of status practically compelled the institution of some channel of negotiation with the Holy See, and M. Herriot endeavoured to effect a compromise on the basis of appointing a special envoy for the purpose. M. Briand and a large section of the Opposition continued to press for

full representation, and were ready to use the whole issue of the relations between Church and State as the basis of an attack on the Government. No political party, except the Extreme Right, cared much for the Church, but every party was ready to use the religious question as a weapon. In addition to the problem of Alsace-Lorraine, there was also the question of the French mandate in Syria, where the Church has extensive property and large establishments, for the protection of which France becomes responsible.

33. The debates were long and acrimonious, and the majority of votes, 314 to 250, which M. Herriot finally obtained left both the House and the Government in a somewhat anomalous position. As far as the Embassy to the Vatican was concerned, withdrawal was achieved, but the Government, holding itself bound by the decision of the Council of State in regard to Alsace and Lorraine (which was that the Concordat between France and the Vatican which existed up to 1904 still held good as far as the reannexed provinces were concerned), were virtually compelled to maintain a small mission in Rome representing the special interests of those provinces. This question provoked still further debates, during which the result was at one time doubtful. However, in the end the Socialists rallied round M. Herriot, and when the question of the supplementary credit to article 9 providing for the amount of 58,000 fr. for the maintenance of the Alsace-Lorraine mission was put to the vote it was approved by 317 votes to 248.

34. The Vatican during all this time were watching the proceedings with characteristic dignity, composure and vigilance. To certain allegations of the President of the Council affecting their actions, however, they felt compelled to reply, and the columns of the official "Osservatore Romano" were chosen for the purpose of stating their case.

35. To the first accusation, that Pope Benedict XV intervened with the United States in order to obtain a suspension of supplies to the Allied Powers, the Vatican organ opposed a categorical denial. It then went on to say that the charge that the Vatican had failed in its duty of protesting against German atrocities, proved to be untrue when it was considered that, after the Encyclical of the 22nd January, 1915, the Prussian Minister to the Holy See protested against the allusion to Germany contained therein, and that, in spite of this protest, the Cardinal Secretary of State informed the Belgian Minister that the Papal censure was directed solely against the invasion of Belgium. Pope Benedict XV had again protested against the German methods of warfare in Belgium in his allocution of the 4th December, 1916.

36. In defence of the Vatican's Near East Policy it was shown that, while each Power has its Capitulation rights, for the protection of Roman Catholics it orders such, irrespective of nationality, to refer themselves to the French agents for protection, and prohibits them from appealing to the agents of other Powers. From this it is argued that, but for this ordinance, France's protectorate (*i.e.*, protection of Catholic interests under the ægis of the Capitulation Powers) would have been speedily ended. The Capitulations gave France the right to protect and the Holy See gave France subjects to protect. After the Lausanne Treaty the French protectorate ceased; and the "Osservatore" takes exception to the manner in which the essential part that the Holy See had in it was treated in the discussions in the French Chamber.

37. In regard to liturgical honours the "Osservatore" asserted that the Holy See conceded these to France's representatives, not as a right, but in order, firstly, to elevate French prestige in Oriental eyes, and, secondly, to induce easier obedience of non-French communities; and, thirdly, as recompense for services rendered. Consequently, the extinction of the protection involved that of liturgical honours.

38. With regard to M. Herriot's charge against the Holy See, that, at Jerusalem, the question of the Holy Places remained hung up always; and that they refused to accede to the solution which was accepted by the British Government and had the almost unanimous consent of the interested Powers, the "Osservatore" merely said that this consent did not exist.

39. Turning to M. Herriot's criticisms with regard to Vatican policy in the Far East, the "Osservatore" pointed out that the 1858 Treaty of Tien-tsin conceded to France the right to protect throughout the whole Chinese Empire not only Roman Catholics, but also "schismatic and heretical" persons and institutions of whatever nationality. Belgium received a similar right, while other Powers only received limited privileges. The Holy See conferred on France an exclusive mandate for the protection of all Catholics and ordered such to render to the French agents the same honours as they enjoyed in the Near East.

40. M. Herriot's charge that these privileges were overridden by the creation in China in 1922 of an Apostolic delegate was answered by the assertion that the delegate's field was spiritual, while that of the French Minister was concerned with temporal affairs.

41. In discussing these articles in the Vatican organ with Cardinal Gasparri subsequently he admitted in reply to my enquiries that they had emanated from his own pen.

42. In the midst of these discussions further oil was poured on the flames by the action of the French cardinals. On the 10th March the six cardinals, together with the archbishops, issued a manifesto attacking the whole system of the " lois laïques " in the most violent terms. The prelates did not stop at condemnation of the republican laws, but suggested a definite means of action to oppose them, action on public opinion, action in Parliament and action on the Government. Laicism is described as fatal to the public and the private weal, and the manifesto insisted that the laws must be countered by persistent propaganda on public opinion, by demonstrations, by petitions to Parliament from all sections of the population, and, in general, by emulating the methods of political pressure employed by the Labour and Socialist and even Communist organisations in the country. The violence of the manifesto caused considerable dismay among the supporters of the Church, while the Socialists condemned it in no ambiguous terms. As the latter were contemplating an interpellation in the Chamber, the Finance Commission of the Senate took action which disturbed them even more than the proclamation of the cardinals. On the demand of a Senator, article 9 of the budget, which provides for the expenses of French diplomatic missions abroad, was rejected by one vote on the ground that it made no provision for the maintenance of the French Embassy to the Holy See. The relations between France and the Holy See were dealt with by the Pope on the occasion of the reading of the final decrees for the canonisations of St. Sophie Barat and St. John Eudes.

43. The Pope said he was unable to conceal his sorrow and pre-occupation at the recent developments in France, " the first-born of the great Catholic family." To try to break off relations which it had promised to maintain and which the Holy See had always faithfully observed, to travesty the facts of the case in public, and to do all this against a Power which had no other defence but justice, " was not fair, was not generous. was not French."

44. His Holiness praised the zealous organised campaign against this policy on the part of French Catholics, who, free from all political confusions and snares, worked for the greater good of the Church, society, religion and fatherland.

45. Such was the situation at Easter, when M. Herriot's Government was defeated in the Chamber over the budget, and was compelled to resign. In discussing the situation with me Cardinal Gasparri referred to M. Herriot's fall as " an Easter egg," for the Vatican could only profit by a change in the person of the Prime Minister whoever he might be. Both M. Painlevé and M. Briand have served as Presidents of the Council since then; the Ambassador to the Holy See remains at his post; the agitation over the cardinals' manifesto, especially when it was realised that it was not inspired by the Vatican, has died down; and public opinion, impressed and flattered no doubt by the preponderant rôle assigned to French martyrs in the Holy Year, has, for the moment at least, relinquished its struggle against the forces of the Church.

Belgium.

46. Belgian relations with the Vatican have on the whole been cordial and uneventful since the end of the war; and the Belgian Government acted wisely in selecting Baron Beyens as their first Ambassador. By his long diplomatic experience, by his conduct of Belgian foreign affairs during the war, and by his reputation as an historian and writer, he acquired a particularly distinguished position in Rome. With considerable tact and judgment he succeeded in removing such friction between Belgium and the Holy See as had been created under the Pontificate of Pope Benedict XV during the war; and, on more than one occasion, he has given moderating advice to the Cardinal Secretary of State, who has been accustomed to seek his views on questions of international policy. On the 1st March the Vatican organ, the " Osservatore Romano," quoted with evident approval from a book by Baron Beyens on the Second Empire, one chapter of which was devoted to a discussion of the Roman question. In carefully chosen language Baron Beyens, while considering that a solution of the question was only to be found in according

international Sovereignty to the Papacy, pointed out the difficulties connected with the national sentiments of the Italian people.

47.   It was a source of satisfaction to the Ambassador on the eve of his retirement from public life to learn that Pius XI had decided to send the Golden Rose to his Queen on the occasion of the twenty-fifth anniversary of their Belgian Majesties' marriage.   Though no special significance has been attached to this presentation, it may well be that, in honouring the Queen of a country which shows fidelity to the Holy See, the Pope may discern a substitute for the vanished Catholic sovereigns of the past.   France, Portugal and, finally, Austria, having renounced their Faithful Catholic and Apostolic Majesties, picturesque and puissant supporters of the Papacy, their mantles may not inconceivably in the future fall partially on the shoulders of the Belgian King.

Netherlands.

48.   The question of the continuance of diplomatic relations with the Vatican, which formed an annual subject of debate in the States-General, and which, in the first ten years of the existence of the Legation encountered no serious opposition, was destined to bring about a serious Ministerial crisis in November 1925.   During the discussion of the Budget for Foreign Affairs, M. Kersten, a fanatical Puritan member of the Second Chamber, introduced an amendment to the estimates of the Ministry for Foreign Affairs, proposing the suppression of the vote for the Legation to the Vatican.   The proposal was strongly opposed by the members of the Roman Catholic party, who received the support of the anti-revolutionary party, but it was carried by 52 votes to 42, the Christian Historical party also voting in favour.   After the result was known the four Catholic members of the Cabinet, M. Walter, M. Bougaerts, M. Lambooy, and M. Koolen, tendered their resignations.

49.   My Dutch colleague, to whom I hastened to express my regret, told me that the news from The Hague had greatly upset the Vatican, where the action of the Dutch Parliament was regarded as an unnecessary and gratuitous affront.   Jonkheer van Nispen, though an ardent Catholic, was broadminded enough to grasp the opposing points of view.   The anti-Catholic sentiment, he said, had been freely ventilated of late, aggravated perhaps by too visible an exhuberance on the part of his coreligionists.   The Eucharistic Congress at Amsterdam in the preceding year, the concourse of priests in elaborate vestments, and the religious processions in the streets has excited in the ultra-Protestant mind sentiments of suspicion, which had found their final expression in the recent vote of the Chamber.

50.   As the year closed the Ministerial crisis remained still unsolved, and with it the fate of the future relations of the Holy See with a State a third of whose inhabitants profess the Roman Catholic faith.   A reversal of the vote is hardly to be expected ; but in the Vatican they are not without hope that some compromise may be effected to avert a complete and final rupture.

Spain.

51.   When King Alfonso paid an official visit to the Pope in 1923 he asked that the number of Spanish cardinals should be increased, a request which, at the time, the Pope could not or would not take into consideration.   A year and a half was allowed to elapse, and in the Secret Consistory held on the 30th March the Pope created two new cardinals, his choice falling on two Spaniards, the Archbishops of Seville and Granada.   With these two new cardinals Spain will be represented in the Sacred College by five representatives, among these being Cardinal Merry del Val, ex-Secretary of State, and now Archpriest of St. Peter's.   The existing cordial relations were enhanced still further by this act, as well as by the numerous Spanish pilgrimages which appeared in Rome in the Holy Year.

Germany.

52.   The Holy Year was a particularly favourable one from the point of view of relations between the Holy See and the German Republic, the importance of which is fully recognised on both sides.   A message of condolence on the death of President Ebert was despatched by the Cardinal Secretary of State, and, subsequently, when during the Presidential election campaign there was a suggestion that the Holy See was exerting its no small potential influence on German politics in favour of the Catholic candidate, Dr. Marx, this was officially denied by the "Osservatore Romano," which declared that the Vatican had never pronounced either for or against any particular candidate, the election being a matter of German

domestic politics. On the other hand, it is clear that if, as some of the German parties of the Right hoped, the Vatican had let it be known that it disapproved of the collaboration between the Centre party and the Social Democrats, the effect might well have been considerable. The ultimate election of President Hindenburg caused no misgiving in Vatican circles, and tribute was paid to his patriotism in the official paper.

53. In a speech of the 19th May the German Foreign Minister testified to the understanding of Germany shown by His Holiness the Pope, and called attention to the enormous influx of German pilgrims into Rome. There is no doubt that the size and devotion of the German pilgrimage made a deep impression on all connected with the Holy See, and it was noted that, on several occasions, in giving audiences, the Pope paid a more than ordinary tribute to German Catholic devotion, and recalled the fact, speaking always in German, that he had studied in Germany, and was able to appreciate the qualities of the German people. The German Government is obviously always watchful for an opportunity of using, through its very active Ambassador at this post, this high regard; while the Holy See, as was proved by the action it took during the invasion of the Ruhr, is always willing to exert its influence in the direction of peace and good international relations in Central Europe. The Cardinal Secretary of State has on more than one occasion shown himself sceptical of the permanence of the present territorial settlement between Germany and Poland, and Catholic influence in both countries may yet prove a valuable adjunct to any mediation between them which may, in the course of years, become necessary.

Bavaria.

54. Bavaria continues to enjoy, as before the war, separate representation at the Holy See, and this distinction from the Reich was emphasised during 1925 by the ratification of a special concordat. Certain constitutional objections were raised in the rest of Germany and by the non-Catholics of Bavaria, but these were not effective; and on the 15th January the concordat was ratified by the Bavarian Landtag, the occasion being marked by the exchange of cordial messages between the Cardinal Secretary of State and the Bavarian Prime Minister. Considerable satisfaction was felt by the Vatican at the conclusion of the negotiations, not only because the concordat was the first to be negotiated since the end of the war, but because it gave the Church, in respect of its property, institutions and education, a degree of liberty from interference by the State such as it had never had before. It was also felt that the concordat would be the precursor of a similar agreement with the Reich. It is not out of place to add that the separate dealings of the Holy See with Bavaria in no way imply any encouragement to separatist political tendencies; the greatest care, in fact, has been shown to maintain absolutely correct relations with the Berlin Government.

Poland.

55. The present Pope has a special affection for Poland, and well remembers his mission to that country at the hour of its greatest tribulation. I do not think this has any undue influence on the policy of the Holy See, but there was more than ordinary courtesy in the presentation, at the beginning of the year, of a special autographed letter from His Holiness to the President of the Republic. The negotiations between the Holy See and the Polish Government for a concordat were in progress at the time, and when the terms became known it was alleged, particularly in Lithuanian circles, that the Pope's pro-Polish sentiments had weighed against the Cardinal Secretary of State's views, and that exceptional concessions had been made to the Warsaw Government. The actual text of the concordat, which was signed on the 10th February and ratified on the 3rd June, does not bear this out. Except for the inclusion of Vilna in the treaty, which is dealt with separately under the heading " Lithuania," the necessity for a Polish Government placet in questions of appointments, particularly of non-Polish ecclesiastics, and the oath of loyalty to the republic secured from the bishops of non-Polish race, the Polish Government obtained very little solid political benefit, and the Vatican concessions in the matter of emoluments to the clergy may well have been due to an anxiety, dictated by the Pope's close personal knowledge of the Polish political situation, to secure as full agreement in the Polish Diet as possible.

56. The concordat apart, relations between the Holy See and the Polish Republic have been uneventful. In the numerous questions affecting the Eastern Churches, which are dealt with in this report under the heading " Russia," Poland

seems now to be allowed little or no part, the Holy See apparently realising the unwisdom of employing Polish ecclesiastics in the great work of effecting a reconciliation between East and West. Certainly there has been no sign, rather the contrary, of any favouring of the Latinising tendency in Eastern Galicia with which Poland used to be so much identified. As regards Polish-German relations, the Holy See seems to have kept an absolutely even balance, neither side being able, with any show of justification, to claim exceptional favouritism. The special case of the Free City of Danzig is referred to separately below.

Free City of Danzig.

57. A little difficulty was caused during the Holy Year by the attempt of the German Ambassador to the Holy See to identify himself with the Danzig pilgrims, and the Polish Ambassador found himself compelled to make private representations to the Vatican on the subject. The Catholic citizens, for their part, felt much misgiving at article 3 of the Polish concordat, by which the powers of the Papal Nuncio in Warsaw were expressly extended to the Free City. It was explained that this provision was solely due to the clause of the Versailles Treaty under which the foreign relations of the Free City were confided to Poland, and the Danzigers were subsequently reassured that it meant no Polish infiltration in the matter of ecclesiastical appointments by the nomination of Mgr. O'Rourke, the Apostolic delegate to Danzig, to be the first bishop of the Free City, and directly responsible to Rome.

Lithuania.

58. Relations between the Holy See and Lithuania were not happy during 1925. The inclusion of the diocese of Vilna in the concordat with Poland met with strenuous opposition on the part of the Lithuanian Government, but the Vatican, holding that in such treaties it could only take account of the actual recognised status of the territory, held to its original point of view, though it was understood that in making the diocese subject directly to the Holy See it was making an endeavour to go as far in the direction of meeting the Lithuanian wishes as was possible in the circumstances. With the signing of the concordat the irritation of the Lithuanians with the Vatican and its representative at Kovno reached its height, resulting in demonstrations against the Apostolic delegate at Kovno and a communication to the press in Rome by the Lithuanian Chargé d'Affaires strongly criticising the action of the Holy See. This latter proceeding was so irregular that the Holy See gave the Kovno Government to understand that their representative was no longer *persona grata*, and in May he was withdrawn. Another representative of the Holy See was subsequently despatched to Kovno to see what arrangements could be made for a reconciliation and also to report on the general condition of the Lithuanian clergy, which is far from satisfactory, so many of them, as a highly-placed ecclesiastic at the Vatican remarked one day, caring more for politics than religion. There had been no new development by the end of 1925.

Russia.

59. During 1925 there were no official dealings between the Holy See and the Union of Socialist and Soviet Republics. It is said at the Vatican that feelers are still occasionally thrown out from Moscow regarding official recognition of the Soviet Government, on certain terms, by the Holy See; but, since in all cases, it appears, it has been stipulated that recognition must come first, the terms to be discussed afterwards, these approaches have come to nothing. The Moscow Government last October permitted a well-known Jesuit, Père d'Herbigny, who presides over the Pontifical Oriental Institute, to visit Moscow in a purely private capacity, in order to report on the religious conditions of the country. Père d'Herbigny's account, given on his return to Rome, was gloomy in the extreme; the Orthodox Church was hopelessly divided and the Roman Catholics of Russia suffering from a complete absence of bishops and acute shortage of priests. The Holy See nevertheless does not despair of an eventual opportunity for missionary work, and quiet but thorough preparations are continually being made in Rome. During the year the Pope himself acquired a large piece of land in Rome in which will be erected a Russian seminary for the training of priests, chosen from the exiled clergy. It is now realised that only by using native priests, trained in the Slav rite, is there any prospect of success, and numerous " Westerns," especially from the Dominican and

Benedictine orders, are adopting the Slav rite in the prospect of assisting, when the time comes, in the attempt to promote the adhesion of Russia to Rome.

Czechoslovakia.

60. The fundamental features of the relationship between the Holy See and the Czechoslovak Republic did not alter during 1925. These are the importance and growing political influence of Catholics in the Republic, despite the numerical losses to the "National Church," inaugurated on the 6th January, and the ineradicable hostility of the President and Foreign Minister to the Holy See and, indeed, the Catholic religion altogether. This contradictory state of affairs has produced trouble ever since the foundation of the Czechoslovak State, and the year under review was no exception; in fact, conditions were, for a good part of the year, exacerbated first by a conflict in which the Holy See was made to appear in the part it has frequently been accused of taking in the succession States generally, the part, that is, of opponent to the country's national aspirations and historical traditions; second, by an apparent intervention in the domestic affairs of the country, due to the superior fervour with which the Catholic cause is supported by the Slovaks as compared with the Czechs.

61. During January there was violent controversy, fanned by the Socialists, regarding the reading in the churches of a pastoral letter of the Slovak hierarchy forbidding the faithful to join anti-Catholic societies. The Papal Nuncio attempted, in the interests of domestic peace, to prevent the public reading of the letter, but this did not save him or his office from a flood of abusive propaganda. In the meantime, the movement for the separation of Church and State, to which the Slovak bishops' pastoral was regarded as a counter-blast, continued, but, as to have brought it to a head would have broken up the Government and caused a disastrous split in the country, it was allowed officially to slumber. The point of view of the Holy See on this question was that, if separation came, it would not only be the Church that would suffer; and that, in any case, a purely unilateral arrangement would be sheer spoliation. The right way to compose the differences which constantly arose, and remove a grievance of which the Czechoslovak Government often complained, namely, the appointment of bishops without their . previous consent, and the promotion of candidates who were said to be hostile to the policy of Prague, was to restore friendly official relations and come to a definite agreement, a concordat, in fact.

62. Along this path, however, Dr. Benes was absolutely disinclined to travel, and the result was a serious crisis later in the year over the observance of John Hus's day as a national holiday. The Bill ordering this was met with protests by the Papal Nuncio, but passed; and the first solemn celebration of Hus's day was preceded by a number of incidents which led up to a partial rupture of relations. The previous December, so it appeared from an account in the "Osservatore Romano" during August, Dr. Benes had had an interview with the Under-Secretary of State, who had remarked that if, as reported, the Czechoslovak Government celebrated Hus Day as a national holiday the Holy See, which could not dissociate the purely civil side of Hus from the anti-Catholic, would regard this in a serious light. The point of view of the Czech Government was that the matter was one of internal administration, and that in any case there were no juridical ties with the Holy See. The celebrations therefore took place amid, according to the organ of the Holy See, much manifestation of anti-Catholic feeling. The fact that these were attended by the President of the Republic brought the matter to a head; and on the 6th July the Nuncio was summoned to Rome, after protesting to the Minister for Foreign Affairs. The Pope himself, in greeting a number of German pilgrims from Czechoslovakia immediately after the recall of the Nuncio, made reference to the incident, saying that had the Holy See remained indifferent to the Hus celebrations "the whole world would have had the right to be astonished, at least in the name of history." The Prague Government's reply to the withdrawal of the Papal Nuncio was to recall their Minister to the Holy See, but as in both cases Chargés d'Affaires were left there was no actual rupture of relations; and there was an evident desire on both sides to avoid a bitter struggle over the question. One important effect the incident had was to bring the Czech clergy into line with the Slovak, a solidarity which had not been manifested over the dispute regarding the previous pastoral letter. Towards the end of the year there were preparations for the elections, and a speech of M. Benes in connection therewith was taken up by the "Osservatore Romano." Replying to his statement that he was in favour of

the separation of Church and State, and that where weaker States, such as Chile and the Argentine, had succeeded, there was no reason why Czechoslovakia should fail, the official organ of the Vatican reiterated the opinion that separation in this case meant spoliation and that there was no analogy with the two States mentioned. The crisis was unresolved at the end of the year; but a more conciliatory spirit seemed likely to prevail on the Vatican side owing to the influence of the Czech hierarchy, who have every interest in avoiding bad relations with the Government, and on the Government's side owing to the increased Catholic influence shown at the elections.

Jugoslavia.

63. During the year 1925 the Catholic Church in the Serbo-Croat-Slovene State made considerable progress, and seems almost entirely to have emancipated itself from the charge of being a mere agency of Austro-Hungarian domination. From owning only one church in Belgrade, that of the former Austro-Hungarian Embassy, the Catholics, who are said to number over 20,000 in the Jugoslav capital alone, have made remarkable progress, and now have their own Archbishop of Belgrade, Mgr. Rodic, who was consecrated by the Papal Nuncio and afterwards given an official welcome by the Government.

64. The increase of Catholic influence in Serbia proper seems to have excited the jealousy of the Orthodox, but it also confirmed the Belgrade Government in the wisdom of maintaining relations with the Holy See. These were not entirely satisfactory during the year. The conversations that took place, earlier in the year, with a view to the conclusion of the long-expected concordat, proved difficult, the question of liturgical language being one important stumbling-block, and the uneasy and indefinite situation was not relieved by the campaign of the Croat leader, M. Stefan Radic, whose quick-change propensities are not at all appreciated at the Vatican. In the course of July he was reported as having advocated the formation of an independent Croatian Church which would eventually unite with the Serb Orthodox Church, and although it seemed clear that this did not represent the bulk of Croat opinion, his utterances caused a distinct misgiving at the Holy See.

65. The following November another incident occurred which troubled relations between Belgrade and the Holy See and contributed to a further procrastination in the discussions regarding the concordat. This was the occupation of the Jugoslav Seminary of St. Jerome in Rome by the Vatican. This ecclesiastical seminary had been sequestered by the Jugoslav authorities on the settlement of the Fiume dispute. The Holy See, appealing to a Bull of Pope Leo XIII, under which the nomination of the Rector is within the exclusive right of the Pope, appointed an Italian cleric. The Jugoslav Minister insisted that a Jugoslav subject should be appointed, and in the subsequent dispute seized part of the seminary as offices for his Legation, behaving with such incorrectness that the Holy See preferred to make representations direct to the Belgrade Government through the Papal Nuncio. The Minister subsequently departed, and at the end of the year there seemed every likelihood of the dispute being ended by the Belgrade Government's acceptance of the Holy See's point of view and the withdrawal of the Minister. This, it was anticipated, would leave the way clear for the concordat negotiations to be recommenced, but matters had not progressed so far by the end of the year, and, in general, relations between the Holy See and Belgrade seemed to have entered on a period of uncertainty, the internal situation in Jugoslavia being viewed by the Vatican with no little anxiety.

United States.

66. Although no official relations exist between the Holy See and the Government of the United States, American influence in Rome increases in proportion to large and increasing numbers of American Catholics, their devotion to the Holy See —shown in the pilgrimages during the Holy Year—and their considerable share in the financial support of the Church. During the year there was a great deal of talk in the newspapers regarding a loan which the Holy See had secured from two important American banking houses, and, shorn of exaggeration, it is true that, on the security of its property, the Congregation of Propaganda had obtained a loan with which to finance the building of new premises. American support of Catholic foreign missions is also becoming very considerable, not in personnel, but in terms of money—a fact which has influenced the Holy See in removing more and more the administration of foreign missionary enterprise from France, which has long had a monopoly of it, to Rome, it being understood that American Catholics preferred to

have the funds they contributed under direct Vatican control. Towards the end of 1925 preparations were beginning, on a characteristic American scale, for the great Eucharistic Congress to be held in Chicago in the following June. The cardinal-archbishop of that city visited Rome with the object of securing the attendance of a number of Cardinals in Curia, but seemed unlikely to succeed in his object, the Vatican determining on only one cardinal *a latere*. So far no American Cardinal in Curia seems in prospect, and the cardinals in the United States do not make themselves prominent in the counsels of the Church, but the great importance of American Catholicism is certainly a latent factor in Vatican policy of which, particularly in regard to the Roman question and the League of Nations, account must be increasingly taken. If, for example, any solution of the Roman question involving the League were proposed, or any suggestion were mooted involving closer association of the Holy See with the League, it would, I think, be found that the Vatican would give due weight to and be influenced by the fact that the United States is not yet a member of that body.

China.

67. The unrest which prevailed in China throughout the year was watched with grave concern in the Vatican, where regular reports were received from Mgr. Constantini, the Apostolic delegate. In June the professors in Peking solicited the Pope's support in connection with the outbreak at Shanghai, and, in response, His Holiness empowered the Apostolic delegate to express the sympathy of the Catholic Church with the great Chinese people. At the same time, Mgr. Constantini, on behalf of the Pope, deplored the shedding of fraternal blood, and prayed that concord and order might soon be restored. These wishes of the Pope, made known throughout China, placed the missions outside the fray.

68. The Catholic missionaries had remained at their posts, with the exception of the fathers at Maryknoll, near Canton, who had had to take refuge at Hong Kong. At the beginning of the disturbances the Catholic schools had closed and the pupils were sent home. The line the Apostolic delegate took, the bishops being in agreement with him, was that the missions must not concern themselves in the slightest degree in political matters. Chinese Catholics are free to manifest their patriotism so long as they use lawful means. They thus weathered the storm without serious damage. Catholic students had taken part, here and there, in the demonstrations of their colleagues. To have prevented them would have been to raise a movement against the missions, because the Chinese regard these demonstrations as a legitimate manner of showing their nationalism.

69. China is regarded by the Vatican as an immense field for evangelisation, and they are well aware that missionary work can only flourish under conditions of peace and order. Here, as in other countries, they are filled with apprehension of Bolshevik activities, and if they view political developments from a different standpoint to that of the Powers, they can be no less anxious to see a peaceful and satisfactory solution.

Japan.

70. From reports received at the Vatican, it would appear that Japan is distinctly sympathetic to Catholicism. The reception of Mgr. Giardini, when he was appointed by Benedict XV in 1921, by the Catholic communities was most encouraging. The proposal, raised on various occasions since, to establish diplomatic relations, a scheme favoured by the Court and the Government, had to be dropped owing to the threats of the Bonzes, who stated that they would withdraw their votes at the elections. The question thus became political rather than religious.

71. The Council held at Tokyo last autumn was called, on the advice of Mgr. Giardini, to discuss the condition of the Roman Catholic Church in Japan, the means of evangelisation, religious instruction in schools and the construction of hospitals and other charitable institutions. In the past few years a marked increase in the number of converts to Catholicism was noticeable, especially in Tokyo and amongst the students in university towns. Jesuit missionaries are engaged by the State to hold courses in religion. The Japanese appreciate particularly the discipline and traditional principles of the Catholic Church, traits which are inherent in the Japanese race.

Argentina.

72. The tension in the relations between the Holy See and the Argentine Government, which prevailed during the whole of the year 1924, showed no signs of

diminishing until late in 1925. The various differences were then, to a certain extent, adjusted, but as long as the present Minister for Foreign Affairs retains office there is no real hope of a peaceful and abiding settlement, his policy throughout being coloured by rancorous dislike of the Cardinal Secretary of State and the Argentine Minister to the Holy See. It will be recalled that the main controversy raged round the nomination of Mgr. Andrea to the Archbishopric of Buenos Aires without reference to the Vatican. The appointment was naturally not confirmed by the Holy See, and their attitude was made the pretext for attacks in the Chamber, culminating in a demand for a complete rupture of relations. This was happily avoided, though at one moment, in the beginning of the year, the crisis was in so far imminent as to cause the Cardinal Secretary of State to approach me with a view to obtaining the consent of His Majesty's Government to send instructions to their representative at Buenos Aires to take charge of the archives of the Nunciature in the event of the recall of the Papal Nuncio. This consent was granted, but the occasion to profit by it fortunately did not occur, though pin-pricks from either side were not wanting to bring the crisis to a head. That the rupture should have been averted was in no small measure due to the attitude of His Majesty's Government, who, both at Buenos Aires and at the Vatican, caused it to be known that they would view with satisfaction an amiable adjustment of the prevailing differences. Their influence at both centres, their impartiality and disinterestedness exercised a sobering influence on the disputants, and the visit of the Prince of Wales to the Argentine facilitated an arrangement acceptable to both parties. The Nuncio, Mgr. Giovanni Beda Cardinale, for whose recall the Minister for Foreign Affairs was incessantly clamouring, remained at his post for the royal reception in his capacity as doyen, and then, in the midst of the subsequent festivities, steamed unostentatiously away from the Argentine, nominally on leave of absence, though in reality with the knowledge that his activities would be transferred to another sphere. With the disappearance of Mgr. Beda Cardinale, and the withdrawal of Mgr. Silvani, the unpopular Uditore to the Nunciature, and a tacit agreement that the Archbishopric of Buenos Aires, now vacant, would not be filled without the usual reference of three names to the Vatican, more peaceful dispositions prevailed towards the close of the year.

Chile.

73. The President of the Republic of Chile visited Rome in February and was received, with his family, in private audience by the Pope. The ceremonial accorded by the Holy See to heads of States was omitted on account of the short space of time Dr. Alessandri was able to remain in Rome, and the organ of the Vatican pointed out that the same absence of formality had marked his visit to the King of Italy. The same month a Chilean pilgrimage, which had also visited the Holy Land, was received by His Holiness, and to this, and to a similar pilgrimage which arrived later in the year, reference was made in the Papal Allocution of the 14th December, which called attention to the proposed new Chilean Constitution and separation of Church from State. This measure, although disapproved on principle by the Holy See, was recognised to be " of such a nature that it may be called a friendly living together in which . . . . the Catholic Church will be able to continue its beneficent work." In any case, it did little to disturb the usual friendly, if uneventful, relations which exist between the Holy See and the Government of Chile. The credit for this satisfactory state of affairs is largely due to the agreeable and charming personality of the Chilean Ambassador, M. Subercaseaux, who is *persona grata* at the Vatican.

Bolivia.

74. Relations between Bolivia and the Holy See showed no departure from their usual cordiality during the year. In January the Holy See appointed Mgr. Gaetano Cicognani Apostolic Internuncio to the Bolivian Government, and the following July he was definitely installed as Nuncio, the ceremony of presentation of his credentials to the President being carried out with elaborate ceremony. On the 31st October a similar ceremonial, expressive of the good relations between Bolivia and the Vatican, was carried out on the occasion of the presentation of his credentials to the Pope by the new Bolivian Minister to the Holy See, M. Jorge Saenz. In the speeches exchanged emphasis was laid on the profound loyalty of the Bolivian people to the Holy See, and His Holiness the Pope made special reference to the religious character given to the celebration of the centenary of Bolivian independence.

Mexico.

75. The anti-clerical character of the Mexican Government showed no modification during the year, a fact which His Holiness the Pope publicly deplored in his Allocution of the 14th December, 1925. Early in the year the Holy See had, it is true, been able to secure the admission of Mgr. Cimino as Apostolic delegate on the condition that he should enjoy freedom of communication with Rome, but for reasons of health Mgr. Cimino was apparently absent from his post for the greater part of the year, and the Vatican, unless they can secure the support of Catholics in the United States, has no means of bringing effective pressure to bear on the Mexican Government. The point of view of the Holy See is that 90 per cent. of the Mexican people are Catholics, and that the anti-Catholic basis of the 1917 Constitution does not represent the real sentiments of the population, who are, however, helpless to make their real views prevail.

V.—THE SACRED COLLEGE.

76. One vacancy occurred in the Sacred College in 1925 by the death of Cardinal Bégin, Archbishop of Quebec, which took place on the 18th July. In order to fill previous vacancies two Consistories were held during the year, the first on the 30th March, when two Spanish prelates, Mgr. Ilundain y Esteban, Archbishop of Seville, and Mgr. Casanova y Marzol, Archbishop of Granada, were raised to the Cardinalate, this being a deliberately tardy accession to the desire of the King of Spain, expressed two years previously, that more Spaniards should be included in the Sacred College; the second on the 14th December, when the Red Hat was formally conferred on the two Spanish cardinals just mentioned, and four more prelates were created cardinals, namely, Archbishop Cerretti, Papal Nuncio in Paris, Archbishop O'Donnell, Primate of Ireland and successor of Cardinal Logue in the See of Armagh, Mgr. Verde, secretary of the Congregation of Rites, and Mgr. Enrico Gasparri, Papal Nuncio in Brazil.

77. The elevation of Archbishop Cerretti to the Sacred College had been expected for some time, in recognition of the success with which he had carried out his difficult mission in Paris. As he was still engaged on this he was not present to receive the biretta, and a little difficulty was caused by the insistence of the French Government that this should be conferred by the President of the Republic. Since President Doumergue is a non-Catholic this was demurred to by the Holy See, and eventually a satisfactory compromise was arranged. The appointment of Cardinal Cerretti was accompanied by persistent rumours that he would return to Rome to succeed Cardinal Gasparri as Cardinal Secretary of State, but no development in this direction had occurred by the end of the year.

78. By the close of 1925 the Sacred College consisted of sixty-nine cardinals, of whom thirty-three were Cardinals in Curia.

VI.—THE PRESS.

79. The relations between the Holy See and the newspaper press are almost altogether indirect, and its machinery of communication largely decentralised. The only two papers—apart from the monthly " Acta Apostolicae Sedis," the official record of all decrees and so forth—that can be said to represent the Vatican, or of which it can be said that what they publish can be relied upon as more or less directly authorised, are the daily " Osservatore Romano " and the bi-monthly " Civiltà Cattolica." Neither is in any way showy or sensational, but both are, with few lapses, conducted on efficient journalistic lines, and cannot be neglected by anyone who wishes to follow the trend of the policy of the Holy See. During 1925 the former continued the progress referred to in the annual report for 1924. It was deservedly praised in the " Morning Post " of the 13th January for its reliability and independence, and this encomium became even more applicable later as the non-Fascist press in Italy became scarcer. This does not mean that, by reading the " Osservatore Romano " one could discover all that the Fascist papers suppressed; and, in fact, both in its comments and its news items, the paper touched comparatively little on the internal situation, except where the Holy See desired to make a protest or call attention to any specific event. What one could be sure of, however, was that the columns of the paper were free from any Italian Government influence; and that

its foreign correspondents, who are chiefly monsignori attached to the various nunciatures and Apostolic delegations throughout the world, and are therefore numerous and well informed, are free from any bias in favour of the existing régime The same remarks, *mutatis mutandis*, apply to the " Civiltà Cattolica." The official notices of the Cardinal Secretary of State in the " Osservatore Romano " are easily distinguished by being printed separately in a prominent position. When wide publicity is desired for them they are generally handed by an official of the Vatican, a certain Mgr. Pucci, to the Stefani and other agencies; the same official also acts, when required, as an intermediary for conveying to the press the semi-official Vatican view on any topic of public interest.

80. Most of the important Italian papers keep generally in touch with the Holy See, either through the official just mentioned or through personal contact with a cardinal or monsignore; but the degree of reliability of the various " Vatican correspondents " varies considerably. The ex-Popular party "·Corriere d'Italia " has long been a wholehearted supporter of the Fascist régime; but it is still Catholic, and its Vatican comment is practically always authoritative. The Milan " Corriere della Sera " has an assiduous Vatican correspondent who is often well informed, especially in regard to forthcoming appointments. The Rome " Tribuna," which it is necessary to mention particularly as its information being sensational, as, for example, the report in November that the Pope was going to leave the Vatican in connection with the Franciscan celebrations of 1926, is often quoted abroad, is often as unreliable as it is picturesque in its news.

81. During 1925, mainly, no doubt, because of the Holy Year, but also in consequence of other less transitory reasons, the English and American press showed greater regular interest in the doings of the Holy See. The accredited correspondents of the " Times " and " Morning Post " sent intelligent and well-informed messages when occasion offered, and the " Manchester Guardian's " representative. presumably in consequence of the considerable number of Catholic readers of that paper in Lancashire, received instructions to devote much more space to Vatican affairs, a concession of which he took regular advantage. This increased reporting of Vatican news in England is to be welcomed, as it tends to increase contact with officials of the Holy See and keep them better informed regarding aspects of British policy on which they are too often ignorant.

82. In the United States and America generally the Catholic Church is on the whole well served by the National Catholic Welfare Committee's press organisation, a body which was founded under the auspices of the American Catholic hierarchy and well supplied with funds, has correspondents in almost every capital. Its Rome correspondent is the same cleric, Mgr. Pucci, who acts as the semi-official intermediary with the press generally. The Rome correspondent of the English Catholic weekly, the " Tablet," also acts as occasional Rome correspondent for a considerable number of papers in the United States.

83. The influence of the Holy See, such as it is, on the press thus having been briefly dealt with, it remains to touch on the influence of the press on the Vatican. This may at once be said to be very small. The principal personalities in the Secretariate of State have very little time to do more than hastily read their own official paper and their favourite Italian daily. For the rest they rely to a certain extent on a service of newspaper cuttings from the most important papers in the world, but much more on the regular reports from Nuncios and Apostolic delegates, and on the direct verbal information they receive from their numerous callers. bishops making visits *ad limina*, missionaries and diplomats accredited to the Holy See. It is rather through these callers and their personal representations that they are kept in touch with affairs; in a word, although the " apostolate of the press " is by no means underrated by the Holy See, it is rather to the radiation of personal influence than to wireless and the cable that the headquarters of the Catholic Church look to, both for keeping themselves informed in regard to the world and the world informed in regard to themselves.

CONFIDENTIAL.

(13243)

HOLY SEE.

Annual Report, 1926.

[C 4935/4935/22]

Sir O. Russell to Sir Austen Chamberlain.—(Received June 7.)

(No. 85.)   *British Legation to the Holy See,*
Sir,   *Rome, May 31, 1927.*
    I HAVE the honour to transmit herewith the annual report on the Holy See for 1926, which has been drawn up on this occasion entirely by Mr. Randall, secretary to the Legation.

                             I have, &c.
                             ODO RUSSELL.

Enclosure.

Report on the Holy See for 1926.

CONTENTS.

I.—INTRODUCTION.

    IT is sometimes pointed out by Roman Catholic historians how mistaken is that view of the history of their Church which postulates an age of faith and practically unchallenged appeal or domination, against which came a revolt in the sixteenth century, since when the Church has been settling down to regain the position it lost or regularise its standing in countries which, once hostile even to its very existence, have now agreed to tolerate its activities. Contrary to this picture, they continue, the Church, from its very beginning, has been involved in a perpetual struggle against hostility by its enemies, misunderstanding by the well-intentioned and, in some ways most serious of all, insistent support by those friends who demanded too high a political price in return. Even in its most tranquil moments the Holy See, the centre of what is, from a worldly point of view, one of the greatest and most complicated organisations in the history of civilisation, has constantly been engaged in a never-ending and often intensely difficult adjustment of its relations with the civil power in every country. Day by day it has to watch over not only the dogmatic orthodoxy and spiritual welfare of its millions of adherents, but over all developments of Government policy which may help or hinder the practice of their religion. This tremendous task has perhaps been simplified since the end of the temporal power; the Pope stands out to-day as a spiritual sovereign, still claiming, it is true, a territorial basis for his sovereignty, but now with no thought of worldly dominion. As a spiritual, inter-national power the Papacy to-day probably enjoys far more respect from the non-Catholic world than at any time in its history. Yet the task of adjustment of its moral principles and religious interests to the modern world of politics cannot be taken lightly, and since civil Governments, largely as a result of the war, have tended to rate more highly the moral influence of the Holy See, every year brings its full record of activity, not only religious, with which this Legation has no direct concern, but political. Of this aspect of the Holy See a detailed account will be given in the chapter of this report dealing with relations with foreign Powers; only a few salient facts will be presented here.

2.   The number of nations in regular diplomatic relations with the Holy See is not altogether a trustworthy index to the international standing of the Vatican, since there are countries, the United States most obviously, which have no official relations but are yet a great source of strength to Catholic prestige. The precise figures, how-ever, are of interest. By the close of 1926 there were twenty-six Governments who maintained missions in Rome, or accepted Papal diplomatic representatives. Holland had withdrawn her Minister, but the Nuncio remained at The Hague. Latvia had cordially accepted an inter-Nuncio; Lithuania seemed to be getting ready to re-establish her Legation, vacant since 1925. San Marino had sent a Minister; Peru had established a regular Embassy, after long leaving the post to a Chargé d'Affaires. The chief exceptions to a consistent record of friendly relations with Governments and peoples, whether by official representation or not, were Mexico, where the Church had to sustain a bitter and disastrous conflict with the authorities, and France, where the Papal condemnation of the Royalist movement threatened to throw the Catholic ranks into confusion. On the non-diplomatic side the chief new developments to record are the establishment of a new diocese for the Free City of Danzig, the formation of a number of new dioceses in Chile, the creation of an entirely new ecclesiastical province for Lithuania, the establishment of a Delegacy Apostolic for the Antilles, the formation of new prefectures or mission provinces in Peru, at Kavirondo in the Upper Nile, Bondo (Belgian Congo), Meru (East Africa), Windhoek, Hudson's Bay territory and Suanwafu, and last, but perhaps most important of all, the establishment of a native Chinese hierarchy with the consecration of six Chinese bishops. Turning to matters of mainly religious interest it was not to be expected that 1926 would give the same impressive display of world-wide devotion to the Holy See as was afforded by the preceding jubilee year, but the celebra-tion of the seven hundredth anniversary of the death of Saint Francis brought an unusual number of pilgrims from all over the world, not only to Assisi, but to Rome, as did the celebration of the second centenary of the canonisation of the Jesuit saint Aloysius Gonzaga. Outside Italy the most remarkable religious event was the Inter-national Eucharistic Congress at Chicago, which demonstrated, on a characteristic-ally colossal American scale, the hold the Church possesses over the devotion of its followers, and the appeal it makes to the imagination or sentiment of those outside its communion.

3.   Among the many official pronouncements by the Pope during the year the following should be singled out :—

February 22.—Letter to the Cardinal Secretary of State on the ecclesiastical legislation proposed by the Italian Government (discussed under " Italy " in Chapter III below).

March 6.—Encyclical " Rerum ecclesiæ," which laid down certain principles to be followed in Catholic foreign missions. These are described in the following chapter of this report.

May 7.—Encyclical on Saint Francis of Assisi and the application of the saint's virtues to modern life.

June.—Letter on the celebration of Saint Aloysius Gonzaga, the patron of Catholic youth.

June 21.—Letter to the bishops in China on the native clergy, described in more detailed manner under " China " in Chapter III below.

September 5.—Letter to Cardinal Andrieu, Archbishop of Bordeaux, approving his attitude to the " Action française " (described under " France " in Chapter III).

November 15.—*Motu proprio* regarding the new Christian museum to be established in the Lateran Palace. It is intended that this museum, formed from the Missionary Exhibition held in Rome the previous year, shall develop into a museum of comparative religion, serving not only the religious interests of priests about to proceed to pagan countries, but also the scientific interests of students of ethnology and anthropology. It has been placed under the scientific direction of Father Schmidt, a well-known Austrian ethnologist.

November 18.—Encyclical on religious conditions in Mexico, bringing to the notice of the faithful all over the world the persecution of religion alleged against the Mexican Government (see " Mexico " in Chapter III below).

December 20.—Allocution at Secret Consistory, which dealt with affairs in Mexico, the " Action française " affair, and conditions in Italy (this last summarised under " Italy " in Chapter III below).

4. Attention should be called, in conclusion, to the prominence given in the foregoing list to documents dealing with Catholic missions in pagan countries. This side of the Holy See's activities is too often obscured. In journalism of a certain type it seems to have become once more the fashion to write in a mysterious, but now, as a rule, friendly way, of " Vatican policy " in regard to this or that question of the day. During the year Brazil's withdrawal from the League of Nations, the increased propaganda in Austria and Germany for the " Anschluss," and the Italo-Spanish Treaty, not to mention other examples even more sensational and inherently less probable, were all ascribed by reputable newspapers to the influence of the Holy See. It is obvious that Catholic opinion in this or that country does tend to take up on certain, but by no means all, current questions a more or less consistent attitude. But from this to deduce a regular Vatican interference with civil policy is a proceeding both illogical and unsupported by facts. Said Napoleon : " I regard religion not as a mystery of the Incarnation, but as the secret of social order." Against the implications of that conception the Papacy of his day fought and won; it fights against it equally to-day, condemning all who suggest that religion is no more than an instrument of Government, a powerful weapon for imposing authority or advancing policies. Such political effects as there may be, in the view of the Holy See, come as a result, they are not present as a motive. If comparison is possible, I should be inclined to say that the present Pope, more than any of his immediate predecessors, far from inspiring a uniform Catholic attitude to political questions, tends to withdraw Catholics as such from association with this or that political party and concentrate Catholic attention throughout the world on the tasks of the Church in the religious and missionary sphere. It would not be inappropriate to label the present Pontiff " the missionary Pope," and for this reason I have ventured to include in this report a separate chapter on the missionary organisation of the Holy See. Religious considerations apart—and I have already said that these in themselves are no concern of His Majesty's Legation; it is only their relation to secular policy that comes within its scope—it is in this light that we may best study the Roman Catholic Church in all its traditional tenacity of purpose and length of vision, resisting the disruptive influences of Bolshevism on the one hand, on the other moderating excessive nationalism while yet proclaiming that the day of European exclusiveness is over. One of the less hackneyed passages in Macaulay's famous essay on the Papacy comes to mind; it was written, of course, of the world after the French revolution, but, with a few changes of name, it seems perfectly applicable to a world which has been ravaged by a great war and stirred to its depths by an even greater revolution :—

" A new order of things rose out of the confusion, new dynasties, new laws, new titles; and amidst them emerged the ancient religion. The Arabs have a fable that the Great Pyramid was built by antediluvian kings, and alone, of all the works of men, bore the weight of the flood. Such as this was the fate of the Papacy. It had been buried under the great inundation; but its deep foundations had remained unshaken; and when the waters abated, it appeared alone amidst the ruins of a world which had passed away. The republic of Holland was gone, and the empire of Germany, and the great Council of Venice, and the old Helvetian League, and the House of Bourbon, and the parliaments and aristocracy of France. Europe was full of young creations, a French empire, a kingdom of Italy, a Confederation of the Rhine. Nor had the late events affected only territorial limits and political institutions. The distribution of property, the composition and spirit of society had, through great part of Catholic Europe, undergone a complete change. But the unchangeable Church was still there.''

II.—The Missionary Organisation of the Catholic Church.

5.   The missionary organisation of the Catholic Church, to which the present Pope has given such impetus, and in whose policy he has carried through such remarkable innovations, is of importance to most Governments, above all to Governments with responsibilities for backward peoples and a prestige to maintain among non-Christian races. The reasons for this importance are various and for the most part obvious, but they may be summed up as follows :—

(1.) In most non-Christian regions the Catholic missionary organisation is the oldest-established, largest, and, because most adaptable, most closely-intertwined with the life of the people.

(2.) Although in several areas inferior to the non-Catholic missions in charitable, educational and social work, for this it regards everywhere as secondary to its religious aims, it nevertheless represents, in the non-Christian world as a whole, the most important and often the only medium for higher education securing contact with the traditions of Western civilisation.

(3.) The international character of the Catholic missionary organisation affords an opportunity to Western nations, exploited by France throughout her history, for example, for the promotion of their cultural prestige.

(4.) Where the Catholic missionary organisation is effective and working in accordance with Roman tradition, a respect for authority is inculcated, with benefit to the Power in administrative control of Christian territory.

(5.) It is easily the largest Christian missionary organisation working under a unified direction and radiating its activity from a single centre, to which Governments can turn with requests for assistance or protests against abuses.

6.   Certain peculiar dangers are inherent in such a large, complex and cosmopolitan organisation, and by general consent it has been reckoned to the credit of Pope Pius XI that he has perceived these dangers more clearly, and has attempted to meet them more resolutely, than any of his predecessors. They may be summed up briefly by saying that there has always been a tendency on the part of certain Powers, not only to use within legitimate limits the advantages of the Catholic missionary organisation as just set forth, but to exploit its prestige and machinery for the purpose either of selfish political aggrandisement as against other Powers, or as a weapon in the suppression of native ambitions towards self-government.   In pursuance of this double design there had grown up the tendency, fostered chiefly by the French, who, in spite of their magnificent qualities as missionaries, were too often capable of making the Catholic Church in the East regarded as a "French Church"—the tendency, namely to assign particular areas of the non-Christian world rigidly to particular religious orders, and to resist any attempt to introduce the indigenous element into the life of the Church. With both these tendencies the Pope dealt emphatically during the past year, in particular by the encyclical "Rerum ecclesiæ." This document, published in February, first strongly recommended the formation of a native priesthood, recruited from the indigenous inhabitants of missionary countries, "who are not to be regarded as of inferior race," and then stated in emphatic terms the Pope's right and duty to assign missionaries to whatever regions seemed appropriate, a claim which could only be interpreted as meaning that the Holy See intended that its foreign missions should, so far as possible, be utilised less than had hitherto been the case for the extension of the political or cultural influence of this or that European nation. How, against no little opposition, effect was given to this principle by the creation of a native Chinese hierarchy, will be described in a later section of this report, but it may be said that in other regions, even India and Africa, there was a pronounced tendency during the

year to bring the national element into closer contact with the Church, due regard being paid to the qualifications of the candidates and the political or social considerations in each instance.

7.   In the light of such general considerations we may now study the missionary organisation of the Catholic Church in some detail, under two heads :—

(1.) At the centre.

(2.) Abroad, that is, among the pagan, Moslem or predominantly Orthodox peoples whom it aims at converting.

The Central Organisation.

8.   This is now divided into two parts, namely, the Sacred Congregation of Propaganda and the Sacred Congregation of the Eastern Church.

(a.) *The Sacred Congregation of Propaganda*, hereafter called Propaganda, is responsible for missionary organisation among Catholics of the Latin rite, in all so-called "missionary" countries, that is, those where there is either no Catholic hierarchy or where the hierarchy is in a more or less experimental and unsettled condition.   Thus not only are the pagan areas of Africa under Propaganda. but also Australia and Japan, for example.   Great Britain was once also under this Congregation, but was freed from its jurisdiction and came under the Consistorial Congregation, as did Canada a few years ago.   The Congregation was founded by Pope Gregory XV in 1622, and included until 1917 a section for the supervision of missionary organisation in Orthodox countries.   In order to meet Orthodox susceptibilities, Pope Benedict detached this section and founded the separate Congregation of the Eastern Church.   To-day Propaganda consists of a Prefect, who is always a Cardinal, a Secretary in control of a secretariat, twenty-three Cardinals, who meet regularly for the purpose of deliberating over and, subject to the Pope's final word, deciding questions of policy and organisation, and, finally, of a considerable body of "consultors," who may be called in to give their expert advice on any question where they are specially competent.   The function of Propaganda is to supervise generally all Catholic missions in the territories entrusted to it, fix the boundaries of new missions, select new missionaries, watch over their training and subsequent careers, wherever and of whatever nationality they may be, and, finally, control their intellectual, scientific and religious equipment and financial support. In practice, of course, there is a wide decentralisation of machinery, since the trained missionary personnel is drawn either from the great religious orders, who have their own discipline and rules, or from missionary communities in various countries living under simple vows or without vows, such as the Foreign Missionary Society of St. Joseph at Mill Hill, for England; the International Missionary College of the Consolata, of Turin, for Italy; or the Society for Foreign Missions, of Paris. But Propaganda, besides having its own training college and scientific missionary museum, forms, under the Pope, the final court of appeal, and is entitled to regular reports from all national missionary enterprises.   In finance, too, it holds final control, for the machinery for stimulating interest in and collecting money for the support of Catholic missions, which consists chiefly of the Association for the Propagation of the Faith, was founded and developed an enormous activity at Lyons, but was by the present Pope transferred to Rome, whence it branches out into almost as many national sub-organisations as there are countries.   Most of these are represented on an international committee of control, and France still plays by far the leading part in financing Catholic missions, but the political importance of the close- geographical association between Propaganda and the Association for the Propagation of the Faith is obvious, since it rules out undue French preponderance in missionary policy.

(b.) *The Sacred Congregation of the Eastern Church* had its origin in the Congregation for the Affairs of the Eastern Rite, founded by Pius IX in 1862. This body remained subject to the Cardinal Prefect of Propaganda until 1917, when Benedict XV formed it into an entirely independent organisation.   It consists to-day of a Prefect, who is the Pope himself, a Secretary, who is a Cardinal, a deliberative body of sixteen Cardinals, and the usual number of consultors and secretarial staff.   It controls the whole business of the Church in countries where there are Catholics of non-Latin rite, estimated at about seven and a half millions, or Orthodox.   For training its personnel it has a central Institute of Oriental Studies in Rome, and a number of colleges for the separate rites, such as the Greek,

Ruthenian, Armenian, Ethiopian and Maronite Colleges in Rome, and the Greek-Melkite College in Jerusalem. The three largest communities over which it has control are the Ruthenian, numbering nearly five millions and spread over Russia, Poland, the United States and Canada, the Roumanian, numbering over a million, and the Syro-Malabar, in India, numbering nearly 500,000. Many of the Catholics whose affairs are administered by this Congregation live in territories either lately subject or still subject to Turkish or Soviet rule, and political conditions in general make the work of the Congregation, in recruiting appropriate clergy, much more complicated and delicate than the corresponding work of Propaganda. The interest of the present Pope, however, in winning the allegiance of the Orthodox is even keener than that of his predecessors, and during the year there was a great increase in activity in this direction, of which the appointment of the first native Bulgarian bishop was one of the most notable signs.

The Missionary Organisation abroad.

9. A brief description may be given here of the organisation into which the missionaries are fitted when once established on foreign soil. In every large area the Holy See maintains a direct representative called a Delegate Apostolic, charged with the duty of general supervision. In the British Empire there are four of these representatives, in Canada, Australasia, South Africa and India. In its very beginning among non-Christian peoples a missionary centre constitutes a mission; after some degree of stability is obtained, the area is definitely marked out, approved by Propaganda and called a Prefecture Apostolic. Then, when further progress is made, the territory is given the higher status of a Vicariate Apostolic, containing within it a number of Prefectures, and ruled over by a priest of superior rank, generally a titular bishop. It has been pointed out above that the European or American personnel required for staffing all these stations is drawn either from the religious orders, or from other communities established for recruiting purposes in various countries. These number 68 for men (20 historical orders or congregations, such as Benedictines, Jesuits or Franciscans, 32 recently founded congregations, and 16 associations of secular clergy); for women, 190 institutions, including six of the historical orders and 39 congregations devoted entirely to missions. There are also a number of native congregations, both for men and women religious and for lay brothers and sisters.

10. The total number of Catholic missionaries employed in the whole world (figures for 1925) is as follows:—

> Foreign (*i.e.*, non-native) priests: **8,196.**
> Native priests: **4,516.**
> Foreign lay brothers: **3,187.**
> Native lay brothers: **732.**
> Foreign sisters: **12,944.**
> Native sisters: **11,158.**

In this table the native priests working in predominantly Orthodox countries, in number about 3,000, have not been included. Leaving these out of account, it is interesting to compare the proportions of native priests to foreign in three typical years, 1913, 1918 and 1925 (latest figures available, certainly increased since to the advantage of the indigenous clergy). It shows the following:

	1913.	1918.	1925.
Total number of priests	11,219	11,081	12,712
Native priests ...	3,118	3,581	4,516

The increase has been most striking in China, where to-day there are nearly 1,100 native priests, ministering, with the European or American priests, to nearly three million native Catholics, and in India, which has about 1,850 native priests, to about 1,200 Europeans, ministering to just over three million Catholics. Of the share taken by the various orders, congregations and institutes the most prominent is that of the Jesuits, which, in 1925, numbered 1,399 missionary priests in heathen or Moslem countries alone, and staffed eight university colleges (five in India, one in each Syria, Japan and China), and about 3,700 other educational establishments of a non-ecclesiastical type. Not very far behind come the Franciscans, with about 1,200 priests, and the Paris Society for Foreign Missions, with about 1,100. Not all of these last are of French nationality, but it is sufficiently clear how large a part ıs still played by France in the supply of missionaries. Material for judging the proportionate share taken by other nations is not easy to collect, but a general survey of the whole missionary organisation of the Catholic Church abroad would show the Italians, Germans, Spanish, Belgians Irish and Dutch very prominent, with the first two considerably on the increase, and the Dutch also growing in numbers and increasingly receiving their specialised training in Great Britain. If British education in Moslem and pagan countries is to be maintained and spread it seems very necessary that the number of English-speaking and English-trained missionaries shall be increased. This is a problem to which this Legation gives its constant attention. The difficulties, however, are considerable. The Roman Catholic population of Great Britain is small and such vocations as there are for the priesthood nearly always go to home-parishes, or to the Dominions. It also takes much longer to train a missionary for work in India, the colonies or mandated territories than for ordinary work in England, and until Cardinal Vaughan founded St. Joseph's Missionary College at Mill Hill in 1866, the French, Belgians, Spanish, Portuguese and Italians almost monopolised the field. It will take some time before it will be possible to ensure anything like an adequate supply of British personnel for Roman Catholic missions in the Empire, and in the meantime it is for His Majesty's Legation to exercise their vigilance and see that, in the distribution of missionaries determined by propaganda, there is adequate attention to British interests.

III.—RELATIONS WITH FOREIGN POWERS.

Great Britain.

11. Relations between Great Britain and the Holy See during 1926 were, as in the preceding year, of marked cordiality. In the various private audiences I have been privileged to have with the Pope, and in the audiences accorded to the numerous British pilgrims and visitors, collectively or individually, His Holiness seldom fails to give expression to his affection and regard for Great Britain and his confidence in the good sense and stability of the British character. This esteem, I find, has communicated itself to a great part of the Pope's entourage, and has produced a much keener appreciation than existed a few years ago of the importance of the British Empire as a whole as a factor in world peace and, indirectly, in the progress of many of the ideals for which the Roman Catholic Church stands. It was one of the chief tasks of this Legation during the past year to nourish this sentiment and see that it was translated, as frequently as possible, into practical effect by the nomination of British subjects to important ecclesiastical positions in the British Colonies and mandated territories. Some idea of the difficulty experienced by the Vatican in this connection, owing to the lack of sufficient qualified candidates has been given in the second chapter of this report; and it is hardly necessary to say that direct presentation of candidates would not be attempted by His Majesty's Government or welcomed by the Holy See, but I am convinced that all the Vatican authorities concerned are now familiar with the principle, not only of avoiding all ecclesiastical action calculated to make the task of British administration in the less-developed countries more difficult, but of actually assisting that administration to the utmost by the appointment of suitable vicars-apostolic and the like. One example in this connection will suffice. In conformity with the new Vatican policy of utilising native priests wherever possible, the scheme of establishing a native priesthood in Uganda was drawn up, but submitted first to the observations of His Majesty's Government. The progress towards a general recognition here of the religious tolerance and benevolence practised under British rule may have been somewhat slow, but I think it may be fairly said now to be firmly established.

12. It was with the object of taking advantage of this improved state of affairs that His Majesty's Minister was instructed to approach the Cardinal Secretary of State in response to a hint thrown out by the Under-Secretary of State with the suggestion that, not only should high ecclesiastical appointments in the British Empire be filled, so far as possible, with suitable British candidates, but that His Majesty's Government should be allowed some measure of supervision over candidates selected by the Pope, in particular those intended for service in the Colonies and Mandated Territories. The choice of an American prelate as Delegate Apostolic for India, noted below under " India," had been made, ratified by the Pope, and even published, before any notification was made to His Majesty's Legation, who only obtained prior knowledge of it from private sources. It was felt that some means should be devised to obviate His Majesty's Government being

taken by surprise in this way, since, although in the case of all but Nuncios, or in cases where special concordats or agreements exist, the Vatican's appointments are not regularly notified to civil authorities, the occupants of the higher posts come into contact with the local Governments, whose work they can frequently help or hinder, particularly among less advanced populations. The Holy See showed a friendly disposition, but was opposed to any participation in the Pope's unfettered choice, a point of view maintained in all post-war concordats, and even seemed disinclined to agree to any prior notification of appointments. They argued that an agreement of this kind would be innocuous so far as Great Britain was concerned, since British reluctance to interfere with the work of the Church was well known and appreciated. Such an agreement, however, would become known to other Governments not so modest in their demands on the Holy See and the Vatican might well find itself in difficulties with, say, France or Italy, or even China. Eventually, after much discussion, an understanding was reached in November by an exchange of notes, under which the Holy See, immediately the Pope has appointed a new Delegate Apostolic to any part of the British Empire (Australasia, Canada, India or South Africa), undertook that the passport of the delegate should be submitted to His Majesty's Minister, who would thus be enabled to make the notification to His Majesty's Government some time in advance of publication. It is obvious that this formality—for it would in practice probably be little more—has no apparent effect on the question His Majesty's Government had more in mind, namely, some measure of control over the Vatican's selections of Vicars-Apostolic and Prefects-Apostolic in backward regions in the Colonies and Mandated Territories. But experience has shown that, short of an actual concordat, which, of course, was never in question, relations with the Vatican are best regulated by verbal understandings and personal contact. The definite understanding reached, limited though it was, soon proved itself of much more than its superficial value, for after it was reached, no doubt on a general instruction from the Cardinal Secretary of State, the various high officials primarily concerned with appointments in the regions His Majesty's Government had principally in mind, showed themselves anxious to keep more closely in touch with His Majesty's Legation than hitherto. In other words, the agreement seemed likely to serve as a signpost to the Vatican that His Majesty's Government were not completely disinterested in its appointments, but expected these to be made in accordance with British interests and in recognition of the goodwill shown to Catholic missions in the British Empire generally.

13. Two events during the past year contributed especially to raise British prestige at the Vatican. The first was the general strike, the progress of which was followed with anxious attention by all important personages here; and the termination of which was greeted with relief and general admiration at the Government's handling of a grave situation. Particularly frank expression was given to this admiration in a leading article of the Vatican paper, the " Osservatore Romano," on the 15th May. The second event was the passing of the Bill for the Relief of Roman Catholic Disabilities. During the visit he paid to the Pope in December Cardinal Bourne reported to the Pope that the success of this measure had been due first to the goodwill of the Government in allowing the necessary time; and second, to the support given by a large majority of the Houses of Parliament, without distinction of party or religious belief. The Vatican, naturally, were under no misapprehension regarding the actual freedom which Roman Catholics in Great Britain enjoyed in the practice of their religion, but the friendliness of the gesture was none the less warmly appreciated, and contributed no little to the creation of an atmosphere of cordiality and co-operation.

14. It would not be fitting to conclude this general account of the regard in which Great Britain is held at the Vatican without a reference to the publication of the first volume of the definite text of the Vulgate, prepared for twelve years past by a commission working under Cardinal Gasquet, the only British representative in the Sacred College resident in Rome. In honour of the occasion, so important to the Church and to Biblical scholarship in general, the Pope commanded that a special medal should be struck and a new honour created, of which the venerable Cardinal was the first recipient.

Palestine and Iraq.

15. So far as this Legation is concerned the year 1926, in Palestine and Iraq, was comparatively uneventful. Early in the year there was a danger that, by the

absence of the Latin Patriarch and procrastination on the part of his substitute, certain urgent repairs necessary in the Church of the Holy Sepulchre might be postponed, with unfortunate results. Representations were made to the Holy See, whereupon suitable instructions were sent to the Visitor Apostolic in Jerusalem, Father Paschal Robinson, O.F.M., who continues to be held in high regard at the Vatican for the success with which he maintains an atmosphere of concord as between the local authorities and the Latin Patriarch. During October the Custos of the Holy Places, Father Marotta, O.F.M., visited Rome and publicly paid a tribute to the goodwill of Lord Plumer, the British High Commissioner. He also stated that the Latin Patriarch was now subject to the Delegate Apostolic in matters of religious discipline, an announcement which, with the definite nomination of Father Robinson earlier in the year to be the sole channel of communication between the High Commissioner and the Vatican, was understood to point to the establishment of a separate Delegacy Apostolic for Palestine, detached from Syria. No definite step in this direction had, however, been taken by the end of the year.

16. *Iraq.*—The year opened with the receipt by the Vatican of harrowing stories of atrocities perpetrated against the inhabitants of the Goyan district, on the borders of the mandated territory. In response to urgent enquiries by the Holy See, the Cardinal Secretary of State was informed of the great charitable effort already made by Great Britain and of the impossibility of British official action at this particular juncture, in view of the dispute with Turkey over Mosul. The cogent reasons for the reticence of His Majesty's Government were fully appreciated at the Vatican which, in its turn, circularised all Governments with which it was in diplomatic relations, urging them that the Turkish anti-Christian campaign should be raised at Geneva. This appeal, however, led to no useful practical result, but the incident served at least the purpose of showing the relief felt at the Vatican at the transference of considerable bodies of Christians in communion with Rome from Turkish to British rule. Later in the year the Holy See approached His Majesty's Government with a request that the rights of Catholics should be safeguarded in the projected legislation to be brought in under the Iraq Organic Law. The attitude of the local mandatory authority in this connection was favourably commented upon at the Vatican, and the matter was still under discussion at the end of the year.

Australia.

17. This Legation obtained audiences of the Pope for an exceptional number of visitors from Australia during the year, Catholic and non-Catholic alike. At the close of the Chicago Eucharistic Congress, it was announced that the next congress would be held at Sydney in 1928, and preparations were in progress for a worthy celebration of the event and the adequate attendance of high ecclesiastical personages from all parts of Europe.

Canada.

18. The Delegate Apostolic in Canada, Mgr. Pietro di Maria, was in November 1926 appointed Papal Nuncio in Berne, and was succeeded by Mgr. Cassulo, transferred from Cairo.

India.

19. A new Delegate Apostolic to India was appointed early in 1926 in the person of Mgr. Mooney, an American priest, spiritual director of the North American College and a prelate whose ability was highly esteemed in Rome. In the course of the year the Archbishop of Bombay, Mgr. Alban Goodier, who had been ill for some time, definitely resigned. In this connection there was renewed discussion in Rome of the long-standing difficulty of the Portuguese ecclesiastical patronage in the Bombay district, and at the Vatican a disposition showed itself to attempt to bring about a settlement of this question more in accordance with present-day conditions. The part played by Roman Catholic missionaries in educational and social enterprise in India continued to be prominent during the year, but, despite intense effort, a lack of sufficient British candidates was noticeable, and the question of the readmittance of the German Jesuits to help make good the deficiency was raised for the attention of His Majesty's Government.

Malta.

20. The Maltese are in general at once loyal subjects of the British crown and devoted adherents of the Roman Catholic Church. In the various places along the Mediterranean where they congregate, above all in Tunis and Egypt, they constitute vigorous centres of Catholicism, but their British sentiments are often in danger of being undermined by a failure to have religious ministrations afforded them in English or Maltese. Three examples of this fact were dealt with by this Legation during the year. The first was the attempt of the Salesian Order, established at Turin, to get the contract for a school run by them in Malta altered so as to allow for the predominance of a non-British element on the staff. Representations were duly made to the Holy See, and as a result the *status quo* was still being maintained at the end of the year. In Tunis the Maltese community complained that the archbishop was leaving them without priests of their own race. This was also brought to the attention of the Holy See. Finally, when it was learnt that the Holy See was about to create a new vicariate for the Suez Canal zone, where many Maltese workers reside, a request was made to the Vatican that adequate provision should be made for Maltese priests, and that Maltese Catholics should not be left to Italian ministrations under the impression, encouraged by interested parties and even prevalent in the highest quarters, that all Maltese were equally conversant with the Italian language as with their own. A favourable reply was received from the Vatican on this point, and it is hoped that the persistent representations regarding the true feelings of the Maltese Catholics which have been made by this Legation to the appropriate departments of the Vatican may result in a better appreciation of their wishes.

Egypt.

21. Relations between the Egyptian authorities and the Catholic Church in Egypt are satisfactory from the point of view of the Holy See, the King in particular being on good terms with the Delegate Apostolic. This circumstance revived the rumour in 1926 that the Delegacy would be raised to a Nunciature, and that an Egyptian Minister would be appointed to the Holy See. This Legation sought, and obtained, satisfactory assurances from the Cardinal Secretary of State that no step would be taken without due regard to British interests, and the remainder of the year, so far as Egypt came within the purview of His Majesty's Legation, was occupied with securing adequate attention, both educational and religious, for the British, mainly Maltese, Catholics, who reside in considerable numbers in Egypt. During the year the Holy See, looking forward to a great development of the Canal zone, formed a new vicariate, and, having received generous financial support from the Suez Canal Company and being faced with the necessity of providing for the religious needs of large numbers of French residents, appointed a French bishop, the Franciscan Mgr. Dreyer, as Vicar Apostolic, much to the annoyance of the Italian Government, who saw in the move a threat to their cultural interests. Their unofficial protests, however, were disregarded by the Vatican. Towards the end of the year it was learnt that the Delegate Apostolic for Egypt, Mgr. Cassulo, was being transferred to another post, a move which postponed the Nunciature discussion but raised the interesting question of a successor, on whom, to a great extent, will devolve the duty of seeing that the machinery and prestige of the Catholic Church in Egypt are not used to British detriment.

Italy.

22. There was no essential change to record in the relations between the Holy See and the Italian Government during the year 1926. Incidents, favourable and unfavourable, there were in plenty, and some of considerable interest and importance, but fundamentally both Church and State remained where they were in the previous year, the State maintaining a policy of respect for the Catholic religion and great regard for the Pope, the Holy See accepting this homage and all it implied with thankfulness, but reserving the right to criticise Fascist policy where necessary and, above all, refraining from any step which would link itself too closely with Signor Mussolini s régime. In the first part of the year the air was filled once more with rumours that the Roman question was about to be discussed. On New Year's Eve the Governor of Rome, Signor Cremonesi, whose brother is Almoner to the Pope, visited the Jesuit Church, the Gesù, and was officially received, a public association of the city of Rome with the Catholic religion which would have been unthinkable a

few years ago. The pointed comment which this caused was soon turned into another direction, however, by the announcement of the Holy See's attitude to the Italian Government's projected ecclesiastical legislation. For over a year a commission had been working on this, and three ecclesiastics had collaborated. The recommendations were favourable to the Church, comprising as they did a legal recognition of all public churches and religious houses, State pensions for the clergy and the suppression of the exequatur necessary to the appointment of bishops. The suggestion in certain quarters that this had formed the subject of consultation between the Holy See and the Italian Government was sharply denied by the "Osservatore Romano," and this led to a certain amount of bitter recrimination from Signor Farinacci, Secretary-General of the Fascist party, directed against the Cardinal Secretary of State, whose alleged connection with the Popular party was, in any case, a constant source of resentment in certain Fascist circles. Some time later in the year Signor Farinacci resigned his office, much to the relief of the Vatican, which, however, so far from changing its attitude to the ecclesiastical legislation which had been the immediate cause of the controversy, reaffirmed it in particularly solemn manner by a letter addressed by the Pope to his Cardinal Secretary of State. This document asserted that the ecclesiastics who had collaborated in the work of the commission were not authorised to commit the Vatican in any way, and that before there could be any co-operation by the Holy See it would first be necessary to repair the wrong done in 1870. This time, owing to a *mot d'ordre* from the Italian Government, there was nothing but a colourless comment in the Italian press, and the incident soon dropped into obscurity, leaving relations between the Government and the Holy See tranquil, but also leaving the Roman question in a state of complete suspense. There is no doubt that both sides continued to give much attention to the prospects of a solution, but the nearer they approached to a concrete consideration of all the issues involved, the more the difficulties increased and the less desirable appeared any disturbance of a situation which, although not ideal, worked out fairly well in practice. As things are at present, the Holy See, being in a condition of legal dispute with the Italian State, considers itself above all suspicion of favouring Italian interests. The Italian State, on its part, may well feel that this security in the Vatican's mind leads to a more favourable regard for Italian wishes than would be entertained if the Government, so to speak, put itself in the Vatican's debt by according a solution agreeable to the Holy See. So far as the Holy See is concerned, it is clear that the paramount necessity of maintaining its complete aloofness from and independence of the Italian Government outweighs all such detailed considerations as the acreage of the territory over which the Pope shall be accorded juridical sovereignty.

23. The Italian Government's endeavours during the year to bring about a uniformity of social and political organisation could not fail to raise a certain amount of friction. The suppression, for example, of all political papers but Fascist hit several Catholic papers, hitherto tinged with Popular party colour. For the most part these were withdrawn, to be reissued later under purely ecclesiastical authority and devoid of any political bias. Then the "freezing-out" process applied to all non-Fascist trade-unions meant the practical extinction of the Catholic unions, but these were eventually reorganised under the ægis of the Azione Cattolica, the chief Italian Catholic lay association, and received assurances that their purely social and religious work among professional and manual workers would not be interfered with. In the meantime the attitude of the Holy See towards Signor Mussolini remained entirely friendly. After the Prime Minister's escape from assassination at Bologna the "Osservatore Romano" had a warmly-worded note of congratulation, while the Franciscan celebrations at Assisi in October provided a remarkable opportunity for demonstrating the respectful attitude of the Government. For the first time since 1870 a Papal Legate, in the person of Cardinal Merry del Val, crossed former Papal territory in a Royal train and was received everywhere with Royal honours. His Eminence, who had been accounted one of the "intransigent party," made a notable reference in one of his speeches to the services Signor Mussolini had rendered to the nation and to religion. In spite of all this cordiality, however, the Holy See always makes a reservation in regard to what may be called the philosophy of Fascism, and also the manifestations of Fascism on the outskirts, where it should always be remembered, there are many anti-clerical elements. This was shown with the utmost clarity in the Pope's Allocution at the December Consistory, in which, after a reference to the attempt on Signor Mussolini's life, affirming that, "whoever puts his life in jeopardy jeopardises the

country itself," His Holiness delivered a long and energetic protest against the attacks which had been made by hot-headed local Fascists on Catholic associations, and asserted that there was prevalent a conception of the State which was opposed to the Catholic conception, since it made the State an end in itself, and the individual only a means to this end. Only colourless comment on this plain-spoken statement was permitted in the Italian press, and it seemed probable that the Pope's protest could only have the effect—it was credibly said to have had the intention—of strengthening the Prime Minister's hand in dealing with recalcitrant elements in his party.

France.

24. Towards the end of 1925 the Holy See had proposed Mgr. Maglione, Papal Nuncio in Berne, as the successor to Mgr. Cerretti, as Nuncio in Paris. After some resistance by the French Government, on the ground—unjustified, it would seem—that he had been pro-German and unfavourable to France over the question of the Holy Places, the objections were withdrawn in May and Mgr. Maglione, who is accounted one of the most distinguished members of the Papal Diplomatic service, proceeded to his post later in the year. Here he found the way well prepared for him by Mgr. Cerretti, so far as relations with the French Government were concerned. The threat to the Embassy to the Holy See seemed to have been entirely removed, and there existed in practically complete draft an agreement under which modified liturgical honours in the East were to be rendered to the French representatives, so long as the local authorities did not object, and so long as France maintained her Embassy to the Holy See. The former provisions made the agreement innocuous so far as His Majesty's Government were concerned, and the document was signed in Paris in December without protest from any quarter. In the meantime, however, the Nuncio had been confronted with a very difficult problem of internal policy, namely, the Papal condemnation of the "Action française." This Royalist body had for some time past had the support of many influential French Catholics, above all among the aristocracy and the young men, and, since it was a strong opponent of the Government in all anti-clerical proposals, it had received warm encouragement from the hierarchy and the priests. Nevertheless, its doctrine was not genuinely Catholic; its chiefs, above all Charles Maurras, Léon Daudet and Maurice Pujo, editor of the "Action française," professed a preference for pagan culture over Christian, and appeared to regard the Church merely as a useful and powerful instrument in maintaining authority and in furthering their particular propaganda. The Church, seeing a serious danger in the spread of such doctrines, had intended a condemnation on more than one occasion previously, notably under Pius X, but had refrained from promulgating the decision from reasons of expediency, above all because of the coming of the war. Now, however, since the essentially un-Catholic religious and moral propaganda persisted, and seemed to be increasing in effect, a drastic step was decided upon. In August 1926 Cardinal Andrieu, Archbishop of Bordeaux, issued a manifesto to French Catholics in which, while stating that the "Action française" were free to hold what political views they liked, he severely condemned their teachings in regard to faith and morals. A week or two later the Pope gave emphatic public approval to the Cardinal's manifesto, on which the "Action française" began an energetic propaganda, asserting their innocence and urging that the action of the Holy See was due to imperfect knowledge, or was the result of intrigue, either on the part of M. Briand or of German agents. These allegations, and others even more ridiculous, were consistently answered in the "Osservatore Romano," but the effect of the condemnation soon showed itself to be serious from the point of view of the Church in France, where it produced complete disunion among Catholics, almost open defiance of the Vatican on the part of many priests, and something like a desertion of their religion by a considerable body of the laity. To both the Vatican and the Nuncio the whole dispute was a cause of grave anxiety, which was not dissipated by the evident pleasure the strong stand by Rome had produced in French Government circles. There seems no reason to believe that the motives for the condemnation were any but what were given; the Pope's action was taken only after deep and careful personal study, and it seemed gratuitous to suggest, as some observers did, that a corresponding concession was hoped for from M. Briand. Favourable as was the general attitude of the Government after M. Herriot's fall in July, the minimum demands of the Church in France in regard to education and freedom from vexatious local restrictions were far from being met, and although an influential movement had for some time been growing up, even in Left circles, in favour of concessions to Catholic education in France, in the interests of French prestige abroad, this had produced no tangible result by the close of the year.

Netherlands.

25. The logical step consequent upon the refusal of the Dutch Senate to vote the necessary credits for the maintenance of the Legation to the Holy See was taken early in 1926, after one more vain attempt by the new Government to induce a change of view. In June the Minister, Jonkheer Van Nispen tot Sevenaer, much to the regret of the Vatican and all his colleagues of the Diplomatic Corps, presented his letters of recall to the Pope, and the Legation was wound up. For Holland the maintenance of the Legation had been only to a comparatively slight extent a concession to Dutch Catholic feeling; it had rather been due to a recognition of the importance of the Vatican as a factor in international relations, and it was realised in Rome that the withdrawal of the Minister, although effected in a manner which caused a certain resentment, had been mainly due to party bargaining. In spite of the suppression of the Legation, Holland remained in diplomatic relations with the Holy See by the maintenance of the inter-Nunciature at The Hague, but matters for negotiation seem extremely rare.

Portugal.

26. For some time it could be said that there was a marked decline in the anti-clerical policy of the Portuguese Government, but with the coming of the Carmona Government in July a positive partiality to the Vatican might be said to have become a reality. Not only was the activity against secret societies in Portugal favourable to the Church, but the colonial policy of the Government, though dictated by motives of self-interest and undertaken without consultation with Rome, nevertheless caused satisfaction at the Vatican by its tacit confession that Portugal had damaged herself by her attack on the religious and educational work of Catholic missions. Since the separation of Church and State, Catholic missions among the 8½ million inhabitants of Portuguese colonies have greatly declined, and foreign missionary agencies have tended to take their place, with unfortunate results for Portugal's cultural prestige. There were earlier efforts to remedy this state of affairs, but none so thoroughgoing as the Colonial Minister's decree of October, under which, with the avowed object of counteracting foreign infiltration and supporting Portuguese national interests, the Government decided to endow liberally the Portuguese missionaries and the missionary training colleges in Portugal, and to grant free land, exemption from taxation and other inducements to the Church in Portugal to extend its operations in the colonies. At the Vatican there was a certain reserve in regard to the text of the decree, as it implied a determination of the Portuguese to confide missions only to Portuguese nationals. As a sign of better feeling, however, the decree was heartily welcomed, and particular attention was paid to the National Catholic Congress which met a little later in Lisbon, attended not only by the Cardinal Patriarch, the Nuncio, and all the bishops, but also by the Foreign Minister and other members of the Government. There were signs towards the end of the year that Portugal, in this improved atmosphere, was desirous of making a general settlement of her relations with the Holy See, with particular regard to the Padroada in India. Nothing definite, however, emerged from the conversations which were then initiated.

Germany.

27. The re-emergence of Germany as a Great Power can hardly be seen so strikingly or so clearly as in Rome. So long as she was kept under strict control and ranked as an inferior in the comity of nations, her policy in regard to the Holy See was mainly directed to securing assistance in relieving her distress and enlisting the aid of the Vatican in contending with French disruptive propaganda among German Catholics. In both these negative aims she had no small success. But in 1926 a positive policy seemed to have supervened. The remarkably well-organised German Catholic community in Rome kept itself prominently before the public eye by all kinds of celebrations, frequently assisted by the German Ambassador, himself a convinced Lutheran. German religious proceeded once more to posts abroad, the Beuron Benedictines in Jerusalem, for example, from which they

had been excluded, and the discussion of a concordat with the Holy See, either with Prussia or with the Reich as a whole, came within the range of practical politics, without, however, leading to anything definite by the end of the year. Innocuous, or even valuable ,though all this activity may be, there seems to be no doubt that it formed part of a deliberate policy of furthering Germany's cause by means of the world-wide influence of the Holy See. Considerations of internal policy alone would dictate a certain respect for the Vatican, but foreign policy, even more, demands, in the German view, an association with Catholic missions and a share in Catholic cultural and educational enterprises generally. That this is likely to increase may be inferred from the religious statistics. At the end of 1925 there were in Germany 536 religious houses for men alone, with nearly 10,000 professed monks, friars, or Jesuit priests. As compared with 1913 the number of novices for the men's religious orders had advanced from 6,430 to 11,250, which means that Germany, sooner or later, will have available once more a considerable body of trained missionaries of the various orders to send abroad. Naturally, this state of affairs is favourably commented upon in Rome, but of undue pro-German feeling in the Vatican there is no trace. On the contrary, with more bitterness than justice, the German Ambassador more than once has referred to the pro-Polish sentiments of the Pope, and the alleged harsh treatment of the German Catholic minority in Poland is certainly one of the standing causes of embarrassment to relations between the Holy See and the German Government. In connection with a similar problem elsewhere, however, the Vatican during the year did good service to Germany. Acting on the consistent principle that Catholic children must receive their religious instruction in their mother-tongue, the Holy See, very discreetly, assisted to bring about a modification of the anti-German measures in Tyrol. The remaining problem of German foreign policy which closely affects the Vatican is the " Anschluss." It is often said that this is an aim of Vatican policy. But this is a superficial phrase which, on analysis, is found to mean nothing more than that, on the ground that a political change seems likely to benefit the Roman Catholic Church, the Vatican is immediately charged, with small logic, with furthering such a change. Nevertheless, seeing that in this matter the moral influence of the Holy See is so considerable, this Legation was instructed during the year to ascertain the precise view taken at the Vatican and found, as expected, that there was complete *désinteressement* regarding the political issues involved. On a superficial view the increase in the German Catholic population might be considered advantageous to the Church, but this could weigh very little against the disturbance to general European peace, which a forcing of the " Anschluss " would undoubtedly bring about. Peace, in other words, is a more insistent Vatican interest than the formation of a large compact Catholic *bloc* in Central and South-East Europe. It may therefore, I think, be taken for granted that although Germany will be active in prosecuting her cultural aims through her official association with the Holy See, she will not meet with encouragement in any attempt to enlist support over purely political questions.

Lithuania.

28. In April the Holy See placed the ecclesiastical organisation of Lithuania on a regular and permanent basis, in accordance with the geographical constitution of the State. The new province consists of the Archdiocese of Kovno, five dioceses and a prelatura for the Memel territory. Among the prelates appointed to bishoprics were one or two priest-politicians, of the type who have played a prominent and not always edifying part in Lithuanian public life. Earlier in the year there had been a move from the Vatican with the object of confining such prelates more strictly to their purely religious duties, and it was hoped in Rome that the new organisation would lead to a great increase in devotion and parochial efficiency on the part of the Catholic clergy. Among Catholics who, of course, form the overwhelming majority of the population, the settlement by the Vatican met with full approval, but the action of the Government, with its Christian Democrat majority, in acquiescing in the arrangement on the eve of the elections and without raising the question of Vilna, was widely criticised by the Opposition parties, who, having gained the victory at the polls, seemed likely to show their resentment by embarking on a more or less anti-Catholic policy. In their turn, however, they were swept away by the *coup d'État* of December 1926, and in the succeeding Government much more friendly feelings towards the Holy See prevailed, so much so that it looked at the end of the year as if the diplomatic relations, broken off over the Vilna question in May 1925, would shortly be resumed.

Soviet Russia.

29. With the recognition of Moscow by several of the most important Governments, the one-time anxiety of the Soviets to receive recognition from the Holy See practically disappeared. Events in Russia nevertheless continued to be carefully followed by the Vatican, which sent the President of the Pontifical Institute for Oriental Studies, Father Michel d'Herbigny, S.J., twice to Russia during the year for the primary purpose of ministering to the religious needs of French, Italian, German and other Catholics in Moscow, Leningrad, Kiev and Odessa. His first visit was in May, when he was left unmolested by the Soviet authorities, although he had considerable difficulty in obtaining permission to move outside Moscow. The second visit was in August, when he appeared as a titular bishop and publicly celebrated Pontifical High Mass in Moscow. Shortly after this he was requested to leave Soviet territory at short notice. Both visits formed the subject of sensational rumours in Rome, as that the bishop had gone on a secret mission to the Soviet Government, or alternatively had introduced himself into Russia on false pretences. Both were untrue. During his stay on both occasions Mgr. d'Herbigny, who obtained his passport in Paris in the normal way, carefully avoided any contact with the Soviet authorities, and fulfilled no mission but the carrying of the comforts of religion to the much-neglected foreign Catholic communities. At the same time, he could not have failed to bring back observations and impressions regarding the prospects of the Catholic Church in Russia. On the whole these were described as most unpromising. There was no sign of any modification of the Government's anti-religious policy, and it would seem that the Vatican, taking the long view, was resolved to concentrate its efforts on the training of native Russian priests among the exiles, and to use every opportunity of demonstrating its goodwill towards the Catholics of the Slavonic as of other Eastern rites. One sign of this was the solemn celebration in October of a Slavonic High Mass in Westminster Cathedral, at which Mgr. d'Herbigny assisted as a representative of the Pope; another was the progress made with the preparations for a new Russian seminary which will eventually be established in Rome.

Czechoslovakia.

30. The year brought no solution of the difference between the Holy See and the Prague Government caused by the John Hus celebrations, and both sides continued to be represented by Chargés d'Affaires. As John Hus day, the 6th July, approached, the Vatican showed much nervousness, since they had learnt that the Czechoslovak Government had made the celebration coincide with the Sokols festival, to which deputations from several countries had been invited. Anticipating a repetition of the occurrences of the previous year, a number of countries, foremost among them Italy, withdrew their acceptance of the invitations, and several diplomatic representatives in Prague abstained from the port of the proceedings, which it was thought would be offensive to the Vatican. The outcome, however, was not so serious as the previous year. Numerous inspired assurances appeared in the Czech press, stating that the Government had no intention of offending Catholic sentiment, and it was noted that the Hus flag was not flown from the palace of the President of the Republic. The atmosphere, in any case, had not been made worse, and feeling in favour of a settlement improved still further later with the prospect of the inclusion in the Government of two members of the Slovak Catholics People's party. The first stumbling-block, however, the recognition, which the Vatican seems determined to obtain, by the Government that the John Hus celebrations are not a confessional matter, had not been removed by the end of the year, and even should this occur, it is hardly necessary to say that several more difficulties in the way of complete reconciliation remain, above all the question of the Government's right, said by them to have been inherited from the Austro-Hungarian Monarchy, of presenting their own candidates for bishoprics.

Kingdom of Serbs, Croats and Slovenes.

31. Relations between the Holy See and the Jugoslav Government showed no marked improvement during the year, but in the circumstances this may be regarded as satisfactory. In February fresh difficulty was caused by M. Raditch, who made a public attack on the Nuncio for having made a journey to Southern Dalmatia without informing the Government, and for having carried on clerical propaganda.

The Nuncio protested to the Foreign Minister, who made a tactful statement which ended the incident. At about the same time it was announced that the vacant Legation to the Holy See would be filled by M. Simitch, Jugoslav Minister at Warsaw, and after his arrival at his post in August it was anticipated that negotiations for a settlement would begin. This, however, proved unduly optimistic, for by the close of the year the first difficulty, namely, the question of the rectorship and ownership of the Jugoslav College in Rome, had not been definitely settled, an Italian monsignore, nominated by the Vatican, still being in charge.

Bulgaria.

32.   Although not in diplomatic relations with the Holy See, Bulgaria has in recent years followed a policy of friendliness to the Catholic Church, which on its part does not obtrusively proselytise, and is, above all, not anxious to Latinise such Bulgarian Catholics of Oriental rite as there are, in number about 5,000 out of a total of 50,000. A notable concession to Bulgarian national sentiment was made during the year by the consecration, in Rome, of the first native Bulgarian Catholic bishop of the Oriental rite, Father Stefan Kurteff. Preceding this event, the Visitor Apostolic to Bulgaria, Mgr. Roncalli, visited Rome, and it was reported that his mission might shortly be raised to the higher status of Delegacy.

Roumania.

33.   The long-negotiated concordat took a considerable step forward to completion in September, when General Averescu visited Rome and was received by the Pope in private audience. It was he who, in 1920, established the Roumanian Legation to the Holy See and initiated the concordat discussions, and although no detailed negotiation took place on the occasion of his visit, it was clear that all the Premier's influence would be cast on the side of a speedy settlement. The importance of an agreement, when it comes, should be considerable. From having a negligible number of Catholics, Roumania, through the acquisition of new territory, above all Transylvania, brought within her borders about a million and a half Catholics of the Roumanian rite and an almost equal number of Latins. A satisfactory settlement of the educational and cultural condition of this body, a great proportion of it belonging to racial minorities, could not fail to be of political value to the Bucharest Government, and there seemed every prospect that the fervent opposition of the official Orthodox Church would be overcome.

United States.

34.   The Government of the United States, in relation to religion, is held in high esteem at the Vatican for precisely the same reasons as inspire respect for His Majesty's Government, namely, that it shows complete tolerance, affords perfect freedom and never interferes in ecclesiastical organisation, contrasting in this last respect with certain of the "Catholic Powers." A striking example of the freedom and prosperity of the Catholic Church in the United States was given in June by the Eucharistic Congress at Chicago. Cardinal Mundelein, Archbishop of Chicago, wishing to make this event a " record," applied to Rome for the visit of the Cardinal Secretary of State and several other Cardinals in Curia, but received only one Papal Legate in the person of Cardinal Bonzano, former Delegate Apostolic to the United States. His visit was heralded with a cordial message from the President, numerous and most imposing civic receptions, and a triumphal progress, in a " Cardinal's train " across America to Chicago, where the various functions were held on a stupendous scale, but did not, according to observers, lose in dignity and impressiveness. A certain reaction from Protestant circles to this somewhat lavish display of the power and splendour of the Church was anticipated, but, except for certain extremists, goodwill prevailed, a circumstance which made a most favourable impression on the Vatican. As the Mexican campaign against the Church became acute, a certain propaganda was made in favour of intervention by the Catholic Knights of Columbus, but the hierarchy showed its disapproval, considering that Catholics had no right to demand intervention unless the general interests of the United States demanded it. This view was apparently shared by the Holy See, where, in any case, there was never any anticipation that America would proceed against Mexico for religious reasons alone, when even Catholic Powers, such as Spain, had shown themselves indifferent.

China.

35. For some years the Holy See has had a particular interest in China, for not only do Chinese Catholics much outnumber all other Christian converts (about $2\frac{1}{4}$ millions to 600,000), but this vast country is considered as a most promising field for Catholic missions, who are more heavily staffed there than in any other country. In pursuing its work, however, the Vatican has had to meet many obstacles. Four years previously it encountered French opposition to the sending of a papal representative, and yielded so far as the establishment of diplomatic relations was concerned. It sent, nevertheless, an able prelate, Mgr. Costantini, as Delegate Apostolic, under whose guidance the policy was patiently pursued of associating the native Chinese more prominently with the work of the Church. In June the Pope addressed a letter to all the Vicars and Prefects Apostolic in China, reminding them that, although the Catholic missions had at first to be carried on by foreigners, the Church was universal and international, and therefore willing to use native priests when occasion served. This pronouncement heralded the establishment of a native Chinese hierarchy, which was effected by the consecration, in St. Peter's, in October, at the hands of the Pope himself, of six Chinese bishops. This step was taken against much opposition on the part of the European clergy, but it was held to be justified by the fact that out of all the turmoil of Chinese civil war a new, self-conscious nation was growing, anxious and in numerous instances quite able to fulfil the highest ecclesiastical offices. The Church, which in China had suffered from being called a " French religion," would henceforward be freed from this embarrassment, and the decline of European influence would not be allowed to damage its religious interests. According to the Vatican, this liberal policy had already begun to bear fruit before the end of the year, but Catholic missions, in common with all Christian enterprise, suffered not a little from the prevailing anarchy and brigandage.

Argentina.

36. Relations between the Holy See and the Argentine Republic, after a considerable period of tension, were restored to cordiality during the year. The origin of the trouble, the nomination to the Archbishopric of Buenos Aires, was overcome in October, when from the three names submitted to him by the Senate, the President selected Father Bottaro, Provincial of the Franciscan Order and a prelate of great distinction and popularity. He in his turn was submitted to the Pope, who confirmed the nomination with particular pleasure. After this happy solution of a long-standing difficulty the Holy See proposed Mgr. Cortesi, Papal Nuncio in Venezuela, as Nuncio in Buenos Aires, and the *agrément* having been obtained this prelate presented his credentials in November, amid profuse expressions of mutual esteem and cordial goodwill. Of the rumoured elevation of the Argentine Legation to the Holy See to the status of an Embassy, however, nothing more had been heard by the end of the year.

Mexico.

37. The story of the Catholic Church in Mexico during 1926 was one of great depression to the Vatican, unrelieved by any feature, except the heroism and determination of the great majority of Mexican Catholics. The anti-clerical campaign, always intermittent under President Calles's Government, broke out in February into a regular and well-sustained attack on the Church, the immediate ostensible cause being a protest by the Archbishop of Mexico against the anti-Catholic clauses of the 1917 Constitution. Religious houses began to be closed all over the country, and there was a fairly general expulsion of all priests of non-Mexican nationality. From this the authorities proceeded to the closing of certain churches, which produced a violent reaction on the part of the populace. At about this time relations between Mexico and the United States were becoming strained, and the Vatican took the step of sending an American citizen, Mgr. Caruana, as Delegate Apostolic, with the object of examining the situation and establishing contact with the bishops. This prelate entered the country in disguise and then made his mission known, but produced no effect, being shortly afterwards expelled by the authorities on the pretext that he had posed as a " Protestant professor," a charge for which apparently no evidence was offered. During his brief stay Mgr. Caruana managed to deliver a letter to the Mexican hierarchy from the Pope, which, although dated the 19th February, was not made public until two months

later. In this document the Pope reviewed at some length the previous course of Mexican policy against the Church, and ended with giving counsel to the bishops, to the effect that they should maintain the Catholic faith but refrain from identifying themselves with any political party. In the meantime, the anti-Catholic campaign showed no sign of abatement, rather the contrary. Religious instruction was completely prohibited, religious celebrations were forbidden, as was the wearing of a distinctive religious dress, priests were called upon to register themselves with the authorities, and refused permission to exercise any function of their calling except by special authorisation. There was also a general sequestration of church property and, with the approval of the Holy See, all religious ministrations, such as baptism and religious burial, were suspended by the hierarchy, thus placing the country under the equivalent of an interdict. In bringing these facts to the notice of all Governments in relations with the Holy See the Cardinal Secretary of State, in a note dated the 8th August, pointed out the fundamental contradiction between certain articles of the Constitution and the particular anti-Catholic regulations the Mexican Government was attempting to apply, dwelt on the brutal methods employed, denied that the Church was fomenting the sporadic violent resistance then being offered to the Government's measures, and concluded by asserting that with such a Government as that of M. Calles no accommodation was possible. This indictment received wide publicity throughout the world, but only served to excite the Government to further repression. From the beginning the Holy See, although appealing for some protest by Governments, had harboured no strong hope that there would be any outside intervention. Where even a Catholic Power such as Spain showed herself lukewarm there was little anticipation that other countries, for religious reasons alone, would move to defend the Church, and all along it was held that if American intervention came over the oil question, it would be highly impolitic for any such move to appear to be connected with Vatican instigation. This accounts for the fact that while non-ecclesiastical bodies in the United States, such as the Knights of Columbus, carried on a vigorous campaign against Mexico and attempted to put pressure on the United States Government, the Catholic hierarchy adopted a much more moderate tone and deprecated all interference in foreign politics. From various causes, in any case, no Government had made any move towards intervention on behalf of the persecuted Catholics, and as the petition of the Mexican hierarchy to be allowed to lay their case before the Government was in September declared out of order by the Chamber, after a debate which even the Mexican press described as farcical and unreal, physical resistance by Catholics was intensified towards the end of the year, thus still more complicating the already difficult internal situation. It may be added that, as an accompaniment to their campaign against the Catholic clergy in Mexico, the Government had made an attempt to create a "Mexican National Church," and had, so it was stated by the Holy See, offered inducements to priests to enter the new organisation. According to reports by the Vatican this move met with complete failure, the number of desertions being negligible.

Guatemala.

38. Early in 1926 the Holy See appointed Mgr. Giorgio Caruana, Bishop of Porto Rico, to be Administrator Apostolic of Guatemala. It seems to be this prelate's fate to be sent to troublesome countries, for just as a little later he was to proceed to Mexico, so, on taking up his duties in Guatemala, he found one of the regular anti-Catholic administrations in power, putting into force decrees aimed not only at keeping Jesuits out of the country altogether, but at seriously hampering the activities of priests and religions in general. The new President, General Chacon, owed his election to the support of the Conservative-Clerical elements in the country, and a decree was issued by the new Government rescinding the previous anti-Catholic measures, and in general restoring freedom to the Catholic Church in Guatemala. This favourable development was carefully noted in Rome, where, however, it was realised that the differing racial elements in Guatemala rendered accommodation between Church and State no easy matter to attain.

League of Nations.

39. In 1926 the Holy See made one of its rare direct approaches to the League of Nations by instructing the Papal Nuncio at Berne to bring to the knowledge of the

secretariat the Vatican's views regarding the projected anti-slavery convention, which was regarded as not sufficiently emphatic in its support of Christian missions in pagan countries. A similar memorandum was communicated at the same time to all Governments in diplomatic relations with the Holy See. For the rest the connection between the Vatican and the League was uneventful, there being no sign, in spite of constantly recurring rumours, of any attempt by the Holy See to secure admission to the Council. When Brazil withdrew her membership of the League, one or two English papers asserted that this had been due to pressure from the Vatican, which was irritated by continued exclusion. The Secretariat of State had little difficulty in showing the report to be entirely unfounded, but the incident served to show once more the precise attitude of the Holy See to Geneva. This, as stated to me at the time by the Cardinal Secretary of State, may be summed up by saying that the Holy See could only accept consideration of relations between itself and the League in the sense that it would place itself, when requested, at the service of the League to enlighten it on moral principles and support it in any initiative to assist suffering populations. In other words, the Holy See, despite initial resentment at the manner in which it considered itself to have been elbowed out of the League when first formed, had no desire to obstruct or discourage the League's beneficent work for peace and charity, but would only give its open official support when asked, and then, probably, only by consultative association through the Papal Nuncio at Berne. Later in the year even stronger denial was given to the allegation of hostility to the League. Just as Spain seemed likely to withdraw, the " Osservatore Romano," on the 20th August, published a long article commending the work of the League and asserting definitely that it would be against the spirit of the Church to deny its support to institutions which were endeavouring to hold aloft, amid the unceasing winds of national egoism, the white banner of peace.

IV.—THE SACRED COLLEGE.

40. In marked contrast to the preceding year, 1926 was a year of exceptional mortality among the cardinals. On the 24th January news was received of the death of Cardinal Mercier, Archbishop of Malines, and universal tribute was paid to his scholarship, saintly character and patriotic devotion and loyalty during the German occupation of his country. He was succeeded in March by Mgr. Roey, who was an obvious choice, since he had been for some time the cardinal's vicar-general, and was highly esteemed in his archdiocese and in Belgium generally. The anticipation that he would also be raised to the Sacred College was not fulfilled by the close of the year. In February, more than fulfilling the Roman saying that " Cardinals die in threes," four members of the Sacred College died, namely, Cardinal Dalbor, Archbishop of Gnesen and Primate of Poland, on the 13th; the Cardinal Archbishop of Burgos on the following day, and Cardinals Sili and Cagliero, both cardinals in Curia, on the 27th. The successors to the Polish and Spanish cardinals had not been raised to the Sacred College by the end of the year, but at a consistory held in June two more cardinals in Curia were appointed, namely, Mgr. Perosi, Assessor of the Congregation of the Holy Office, and Mgr. Capotosti, Secretary of the Congregation of the Sacraments. Both, from the important religious offices they filled, were marked out for promotion sooner or later, but there was no political interest in the event. In September Cardinal Touchet, Archbishop of Orleans, died, and again his successor was not created cardinal. At the consistory the following December two more vacancies were filled by the promotion of Mgr. Gamba, Archbishop of Turin, and Mgr. Lauri, Papal Nuncio in Warsaw since. Only the former arrived in Rome to receive the red hat, the conferment in Mgr. Lauri's case being made by the President of the Polish Republic, who claimed and was given the privilege formerly enjoyed by the kings of Poland. Thus all the appointments to the Sacred College made during 1926 went to Italians, who numbered thirty-seven by the end of the year, as compared with thirty non-Italian cardinals, a larger proportion than had existed since 1911. There were three cardinals short of the full complement of seventy, and it was considered inevitable that the appointments to be made during the following year would include one or two non-Italian archbishops. Of cardinals who appeared most prominently during the year, apart from the Cardinal Secretary of State, whose activities will be found described in the third chapter of this report, I would mention Cardinal Bonzano, who went to the Chicago Eucharistic Congress as Papal Legate, Cardinal Merry del Val, who went to the Franciscan celebrations at Assisi in the same capacity, and Cardinal

Vannuttelli, whose 90th birthday found him in remarkable vigour and was marked by universal congratulation, not least from the Italian Prime Minister. The usual rumours in Rome that this or that cardinal—it is chiefly Cardinal Cerretti, former Papal Nuncio in Paris, who is mentioned in this connection—was to replace Cardinal Gasparri as Secretary of State, were not substantiated, and beyond the customary appointment of newly or recently appointed cardinals to act as protectors of religious orders or to serve on various Congregations, Cardinal Cerretti, for example, to serve on the Congregations of Extraordinary Ecclesiastical Affairs and the Eastern Church respectively, there was no important change in the distribution of the work of the Sacred College to be chronicled during the year.

o

(13363)

HOLY SEE.

Annual Report, 1927.

[C 1769/1769/22]

Sir O. Russell to Sir Austen Chamberlain.—(Received March 5.)

(No. 32.)   British Legation to the Holy See,
Sir,   *Rome, February 27, 1928.*
    I HAVE the honour to transmit herewith my annual report on the Holy
See for the year 1927.

                              I have, &c.
                             ODO RUSSELL.

Enclosure.

Report on the Holy See for the Year 1927.

I.—INTRODUCTION.

    THE sixth year of his Pontificate was one of unremitting labour and no
little anxiety for Pius XI. Though he celebrated his 70th birthday, and his
Cardinal Secretary of State celebrated the golden jubilee of his ordination to
the priesthood, there was no sign of flagging—nay, rather an intensified
centralisation and an even firmer grasp of the countless threads which control
the interests of the Holy See were apparent to close observers. In the
allocution delivered by the Pope on the occasion of receiving the customary
Christmas greetings from the College of Cardinals, His Holiness recapitulated
the events of the year which had caused him joy or grief. Foremost among the
former were the inauguration of a permanent missionary exhibition in Rome;
the Eucharistic Congresses at Bologna, Einsiedeln, Lyons and other missionary
congresses held in France, Belgium and Germany; the great religious
manifestations in Peru at which the head of the Government had been present.
Further causes for rejoicing were the nomination of the first Japanese bishop,
and the preparation for a great Eucharistic Congress in Australia. These
rejoicings were, however, counterbalanced by several sad events. Mexico,
Russia and China revealed a page of history dark with persecution and
atrocities inconceivable in this 20th century in the open sight of all so-called
civilised nations without a word of protest from any of them. The allocution
did not explicitly call for the intervention of Christian Governments, but it
included some strong and searching words which might be subjected to that
interpretation. Turning then to France, Pius XI first took thankful note of
the multiple and fruitful Catholic activities in that land, especially " le denier
du culte." As to the " Action française," His Holiness said that the number of
Catholics misled by it was steadily dwindling, but that even a small remnant
of truants from Catholic loyalty was grievous to him. His Holiness, after
praising the Catholic publicists of France who have written books and articles
to rebut false charges aganst the Papacy, deplored the mischievous importation
into Italy of the " Action française " dispute. Finally, coming back to Italian

affairs, he thanked Almighty God for many blessings—such as the improved position of religious education—but disclosed his anxiety concerning other Catholic works. Of the Catholic Action, " Nostre carissime preziossime organizzazioni di Azione Cattolica," the Pope said that Catholic Action must be " the laity's share in the Hierarchy's apostolate."

2. The consistent policy of the present Pope to withdraw the Church as far as possible from the political arena so that Catholics should unite on a religious and moral basis was still further accentuated during the year. In this connexion I might mention that the Congregation of the Council, which is the authorised body for dealing with questions of ecclesiastical discipline, laid it down that the chief local ecclesiastical authority had the right and duty of forbidding political activity to ecclesiastics who did not conform to the instructions of the Holy See, and that those ecclesiastics who did not obey would be proceeded against in accordance with the provisions of the Canon Law of the Church. This decision was officially approved by the Pope. The Vatican formula is that the Church only comes into direct contact with politics when politics threaten the altar of the family; and the Pope is particularly desirous. that this rule shall be universally enforced.

3. Concordats were signed during the year with Lithuania and Roumania. though the terms of the concordat with the latter have not yet been ratified with the Parliament at Bucharest; and a *modus vivendi* was concluded with Czechoslovakia together with the renewal of diplomatic relations. At the present time the terms of a concordat are under consideration with the German Reich, with Prussia, Würtemburg, Jugoslavia and Albania. Diplomatic representation to the Holy See again showed an increase. The Argentine and Columbian Legations were raised to Embassies; and Hayti, Lithuania, Latvia and Liberia inaugurated diplomatic relations and appointed Ministers. There are now ten Embassies and eighteen Legations to the Holy See, twenty-eight representatives compared with sixteen before the war. There has naturally been a similar increase in the number of representatives sent by the Holy See to the various countries. Before the war the Holy See maintained five nunciatures and twelve other diplomatic missions. To-day there are twenty-one nunciatures and eleven internunciatures, more than double the number before the war. Over and above this the Holy See has numerous delegates who are not accredited to the Governments of the countries in which they reside, but have immediate relations only with the local episcopate. Such delegates number eighteen, of which five are under the Consistorial, eight are under Propaganda and five under the Congregation for the Oriental Rites.

II.—RELATIONS WITH FOREIGN POWERS.

Great Britain.

4. Two circumstances in 1927 served to enhance the cordiality of the relations existing between His Majesty's Government and the Holy See. The first was a pronouncement by the Secretary of State for Foreign Affairs on diplomatic representation in Rome; the second was an arrangement come to between His Majesty's Legation and the Vatican with regard to ecclesiastical appointments in the British Empire. In reply to a question in the House of Commons from Viscount Sandon on the maintenance of His Majesty's Legation to the Holy See, Sir Austen Chamberlain said :—

> "His Majesty's Government found it convenient to establish this Legation at a time of great international trouble and difficulty. To withdraw it now would, I think, be an almost offensive course which we should be slow to adopt. Apart from that, whatever views we may take individually about the Roman Church, there can be no doubt that the Head of that Church represents a great force in the world, and is venerated by many millions of His Majesty's subjects."

Great satisfaction was expressed at the Vatican at this definite statement by Sir Austen Chamberlain as to the permanency of the Legation. Coming so soon after the repeal of the anti-Catholic laws in England, a measure which the Pope described as one " worthy of a great nation," and the withdrawal of the Netherlands Mission to the Vatican, the gratification felt by the Pope was all the greater. The understanding with regard to ecclesiastical appointments constituted a further step in the direction of friendly discussion of matters which were of increasing interest to His Majesty's Government. The difficulties which had existed for so long in connexion with the appointments of Delegates Apostolic in the Dominions and Colonies were finally overcome by an agreement with the Vatican by which it was arranged that the Cardinal Secretary of State should, on the nomination of a Delegate Apostolic, at once inform His Majesty's Minister privately, at the same time submitting the nominee's passport to receive the visa for the Dominion or Colony in question. Thus, before the knowledge of the nomination became public property, it would be possible to inform the Government concerned of the impending appointment, and at least seven days' time (or, by tacit agreement with the Vatican, longer if necessary) would be given for consideration of the suitability of the appointment. Thus, too, while His Majesty's Governments would in no way interfere with the free choice of the Pope in his appointments of delegates, it reserves to them the right and possibility of discussing the appointment and, should such a contingency arise, to put forward their reasons for the non-acceptance of a particular candidate before the nomination has been made public knowledge. The Vatican, whilst binding themselves to no agreement on the matter, show every desire to fill vacancies in the Dominions and Colonies with delegates of British nationality; but, owing to a scarcity of British candidates, this is not always possible. Among the ecclesiastical appointments, three were made in the course of the year which were of especial interest to His Majesty's Government. Father Paschal Robinson, O.F.M., was consecrated Archbishop of Tyana and sent as Delegate Apostolic to Jerusalem; Father William Heard was appointed to be the English judge on the Court of the Roman Rota; and Bishop Hinsley, Rector of the English College in Rome, was appointed Visitor Apostolic in Africa for the purpose of inspecting all the chief Catholic missions in British territory and reporting on their efficiency. Among leading British personalities who were received in audience by the Pope were: The Right Hon. Winston Churchill, Chancellor of the Exchequer; Viscount Peel, First Commissioner of His Majesty's Office of Works; Mr. Arthur Samuel, M.P., Parliamentary Secretary of the Department of Overseas Trade; and Sir Rowland Blades, Lord Mayor of London. The most interesting pilgrimages which came to Rome were those of about forty officers and men of H.M.S. "Barham," which was stationed at Naples in September—the party was presented to His Holiness by Mgr. Redmond, Vice-Rector of the English College, and by Mr. Randall. of this Legation; and in October a party of Metropolitan Police, who came to Rome under the direction of the London Metropolitan and City Catholic Police Guild and who received a warm welcome from His Holiness.

5. Another matter which caused considerable satisfaction to the Vatican was the initiative displayed by His Majesty's Government in the rupture which occurred with the Soviet Government about the Arcos offices in London. The Vatican, in begging me to transmit their congratulations to His Majesty's Government, expressed the hope that the firm stand taken by His Majesty's Government would serve as an example to other Governments who were only too lax in their vigilance over Soviet propaganda.

Australia.

6. Cardinal Bonaventura Cerretti, who was Delegate Apostolic in Australia from 1915 to 1917, was appointed by the Pope to be his Cardinal Legate at the International Eucharistic Congress to be held at Sydney in September 1928. Since the congresses were instituted, none has been held in the Australasian continent, and it was thought that the time had come for that region to be chosen, more especially in view of the active development of the Catholic Church there in recent years. General satisfaction was expressed in Rome at the choice of Sydney.

Canada.

7. Mgr. Cassulo, titular Archbishop of Leontopoli and Delegate Apostolic in Egypt, was appointed Delegate Apostolic to Canada; and on proceeding thither to take up his duties in October was accorded an enthusiastic reception in Quebec. Mgr. Rouleau, who succeeded Cardinal Bégin as Archbishop of Quebec in 1926 on the death of that prelate, was raised to the cardinalate in the December consistory.

Ireland.

8. Ireland sustained a great loss by the death of Cardinal O'Donnel, Archbishop of Armagh, who had only so recently been raised to the purple. He was universally beloved, and the Pope paid a fitting tribute to his memory in an address to the Roman Catholic archbishops and bishops of Ireland collected in Rome in October to celebrate the third centenary of the Irish College.

India.

9. In the early part of the year the Bishop of Dacca, having reported to the Vatican that the missionary he had sent to work among the Lushai tribe at their own request had not been allowed to settle down by the local authorities, the Cardinal Secretary of State begged me to intercede on his behalf with the Government of India. In reply to this I was in due course instructed to inform His Eminence that it was not possible to grant permission for Catholic missionaries to enter the Lushai Hills, as that territory was inhabited by a semi-civilised and excitable people, and that the difficulties of dealing with the unrest that had lately been prevalent among them had been accentuated by the existing religious cleavage. If religious rivalry were allowed to develop, it would, in the opinion of the authorities, lead to serious disturbances. I was at the same time to disclaim any hostility on the part of His Majesty's Government to the admirable work done by Catholic missions in various parts of India. This explanation was perfectly understood and courteously acknowledged by the Vatican. In May the following changes in the Roman Catholic ecclesiastical organisation in India were approved by the Pope. A new diocese, Chittagong, was formed in the Diocese of Dacca, and Father Le Pailleur, a Canadian and the former secretary of the Bishop of Dacca, was appointed as the first bishop. Also in Krishnagar a new diocese was formed called Dinajpur, and from the Archdiocese of Calcutta a new diocese, Ranchi, was created. But of these two last named no bishops have so far been appointed. In July the Pope appointed Mgr. Doring, Vicar Apostolic of Hihoshima, to be Bishop of Poona. He had held this same position at the outbreak of the war, but had then to be transferred elsewhere. The Vatican authorities expressed much satisfaction at the attitude of His Majesty's Government in regard to this return of the Diocese of Poona to its former German Superior. (Negotiations concerning the Padroado and the Archbishopric of Bombay are reported under the heading of Portugal.)

Malta.

10. A delegation of the Pontifical Order of the Knights of Malta paid a visit to the Island of Malta on their way back from Jerusalem and Rhodes, and were accorded an official reception. The news of this gave great pleasure at the Vatican.

11. On his return to Malta in October the Governor, Sir John Du Cane, tarried for some days in Rome, which gave me an opportunity of introducing him to the Cardinal Secretary of State. In the course of this visit his Excellency explained that for years past the Maltese clergy had taken an active part in Maltese politics, but that a decree of the Bishop of Cozo now forbade this practice; and the Archbishop of Malta, while not actually forbidding it, had done his utmost to discourage it. In consequence, a campaign against the archbishop, Mgr. Caruana, had arisen, and it was generally feared that certain priests, in an excess of party zeal, might make representations against the archbishop in Rome. The Cardinal Secretary of State assured his Excellency that no such representations would be listened to or tolerated, and that no Italian politicians who were suspected of using the priesthood for furthering Italian political aims would ever influence the Vatican's policy. Later in the year I again mentioned this subject to the Under-Secretary of State, and he assured me that, since the abstention of the clergy from politics had been rigorously enjoined in Italy, he would try and enjoin the same abstention in Malta.

Egypt.

12. During the visit of the King of Egypt to Rome His Majesty was received in private audience by the Pope. The interview, which was marked by great cordiality, terminated with the bestowal by His Holiness of the Order

of the Golden Spur on King Fuad—an honour which has hitherto not been accorded to any sovereign. In connexion with the audience, the Vatican organ, the " Osservatore Romano," published an inspired article. King Fuad's visit, it said, was yet one more proof of the esteem which the sovereign of one of the oldest and also youngest of States, the first king of independent Egypt, manifested for the Catholic Church and its head. With a view to encouraging all that assisted the progress of his country, King Fuad and his Government had given full liberty to the Catholic Church in Egypt, and one could see what remarkable developments of Catholic institution were taking place, in schools, social organisations, and the ordinary religious work of the various dioceses. the Delegacy Apostolic at Cairo, in supreme control under the Pope, the three vicariates for Latin Catholics, the Coptic Patriarchate at Alexandria and the Bishopric for Catholics of the Armenian rite in Cairo. Not content with tolerating these activities, the King had given much personal encouragement and assistance to the congregations and religious authorities. In September Mgr. Valerio Valeri, Uditore of the Papal Nuncio in Paris, was appointed Delegate Apostolic at Cairo in succession to Mgr. Cassulo. Every effort had been made to secure the appointment of a British subject, but as this in the end proved impracticable, no better choice could have been made. During Mgr. Valeri's sojourn in Rome, when he was consecrated titular Archbishop of Ephesus, I had various opportunities of meeting him and was glad to perceive that he not only had a good knowledge of the English language, but also a real appreciation of the special British interests with which he will be brought in contact.

Italy.

13. The most trustworthy clue to an understanding of the Vatican view of Fascism lies in the fact that the Holy See, in its comments on the present Italian Government, consistently keeps theory and practice in separate compartments. What the Pope condemned twice, first in the allocution of December 1926, second in the letter of the 24th January to the Cardinal Secretary of State on the Catholic Scouts Organisations, was not the Fascist Government, but a conception of the State to which a certain number of theorising Fascists, such as Professor Gentile and Signor Rocco, have given their adherence. This conception, to quote the Pope's words, is that which " makes of the citizen the individual, a means and of the State an end, monopolising and absorbing him," whereas the Catholic conception, as authoritatively expounded by the Jesuit review, the " Civiltà Cattolica," is that the individual forms part of the State only as a member of another society, namely, the family; and that neither State nor individuals should be considered solely as means, but as interacting for the common good of society. Criticism of the evil results of the Fascist system has been unsparing as usual throughout the year, but all benefits to religion and morality which have come from that system have received unqualified commendation from the Pope himself and from those entitled to speak on behalf of the Holy See. Thus, the Italian Prime Minister's instructions to the prefects at the beginning of the year were commended in the " Osservatore Romano," as was the Government attitude to the " Azione Cattolica " in connexion with the coming into force of the Corporations Law, which was not allowed to interfere with the work of the " Azione Cattolica " in promoting associations aimed at permeating society with Catholic social, moral, and religous principles. In the summer there were two incidents which afforded fresh and striking illustration of the religious peace which prevailed in this country. The first was the restoration, in the presence of the Royal Family, of the Cross in the Colosseum, which had been torn down in 1870. This event gave great pleasure to the Vatican as symbolising yet again the complete break with the anti-clerical policy of pre-war Italian Governments. The second incident was the Eucharistic Congress at Ancona, which was attended by the Crown Prince; by an official representative of the Government; and by the Papal Legate, Cardinal La Fontaine, Patriarch of Venice. The last named, at the close of the function, expressed his gratitude to the " National Government, which with tenacity of will and effort had succeeded in re-establishing the faith in Italy." Two administrative provisions which gave emphasis to these words deserve to be mentioned. The first was the suppression of the decree of October 1886, under which, in order to obtain the necessary *placet*, religious orders had to make a declaration of secularisation; the second was the decree approved by the Chamber on the 25th March, under which the Fondo del

Culto, the body which administers the ecclesiastical patrimony of suppressed religious institutions and sees to the financial provision of churches, is detached from the Ministry of Justice and constituted an autonomous body. That this reform should have been granted is a sign that, although the juridical conditions for a concordat between the Holy See and the Italian Government are not present, the spirit which would inspire such an agreement was amply in evidence.

14. The anniversary of the fall of Papal Rome was observed without the slightest sign of anti-clerical feeling, though on the Vatican side the occasion was not allowed to pass without a reminder that full justice had not been done to the Holy See for the wrongs of 1870. In the newspaper controversy which ensued between the officially inspired "Osservatore Romano" on the one hand and the Fascist press, supplemented by a Fascist "foglio d'ordine" on the other, certain facts emerged which can be said to denote a classification of the situation. The first of these was the rejection by the Holy See of the theory of foreign intervention. Never before has there been such a solemn and emphatic repudiation by the Holy See of the idea of an international tribunal, sitting in judgment on Italy's action in 1870. The second was the adoption by the Holy See of the solution of a "miniature State," over which the Pope should be accorded juridical sovereignty. The third was the *non possumus* attitude of the Fascist party with regard to any territorial concession. The situation was still further clarified in the course of subsequent conversations between His Majesty's representatives and the leading protagonists in black and white Rome. Cardinal Gasparri cast no doubt on the good intentions of the Italian Prime Minister, but said there was a remnant of the anti-clerical masonic group which had established itself in the Fascist party and would fight to the last against any settlement or alteration of the present status. The Fascist party's pronouncement against any territorial settlement he regarded merely as an undiplomatic move calculated to give the impression to outsiders that the reasonable attitude of the Vatican had been misjudged. The head of the Government expressed his opinion that, beyond the production of a definite statement that no foreign intervention would be tolerated in the settlement of the Roman question, nothing really new or in any way decisive had arisen. The Holy See was, to all intents, already an independent State, for Italy would never violate the precincts of the Vatican. Moreover, the Pope received and nominated Ambassadors as any foreign Power. But, the President added, no question of territorial increase for the Vatican could ever be considered, unless it were a mere enlargement of the Vatican grounds or garden, which might be considered necessary for practical reasons of habitation but would never be meant or interpreted as a concession of territory to the Holy See. As to the idea of a "corridor" to the sea, it was unthinkable and would lead to endless trouble, even as the Danzig Corridor had caused unmitigated trouble in the north. The opinion of the Under-Secretary of State was that Italy should always follow "une politique concordataire, mais ne jamais faire un concordat." The Governor of Rome expressed the opinion that no solution of the question could be found. The Pope was bound by tradition to claim territorial sovereignty, but would be the loser should it ever be granted. At present the Papacy enjoyed Italian protection and a grievance that it is not independent. Also Italy, who would in any case be bound to protect the Vatican in the case of foreign invasion, would gain nothing by such a settlement. He further expressed his opinion that both parties were, *au fond*, content to continue in their present, not unsatisfactory, relations.

France.

15. At the annual reception of the Diplomatic Corps at the Elysée on the 1st January Mgr. Maglione delivered a speech, in his capacity of doyen, in the course of which he eulogised the peaceful policy pursued by the French Government and by M. Briand in particular, and assured the President that for the carrying out of such a policy the French Government could count upon the active and loyal collaboration of the other Powers, and especially of the Vatican. In uttering these words Mgr. Maglione was faithfully interpreting the instructions he had received, and the express intentions of the Pontiff, whose great ambition is to co-operate, within the moral and religious sphere, in the work of ending extreme nationalism in Europe. Although the condemnation of the "Action française" by the Holy See (see last year's annual report) was clearly due primarily to the anti-Christian attitude of its leaders, the moment

was chosen with the object of affording moral support to the French Government, in whose hands, it was considered, international peace was safer than it had been for some years. This clear indication of the Vatican attitude, though it met with condemnation, naturally enough, from the extreme Nationalist press, and, above all, from the " Action française," did much towards cementing the good relations subsisting between the Holy See and Government circles in France. A few days after this interchange of courtesies at the Elysée the " Action française " was definitely put on the Index *librorum prohibitorum*. This was a continuation of the prohibition to Catholics to read certain works of M. Charles Maurras and M. Léon Daudet. After the recent fresh series of condemnations of the Royalist newspaper and all its associations it was inevitable, in default of its submission, that it should be visited with one of the severest punishments which the discipline of the Church has in its power. In Rome this was taken as a sign of the extent to which the " Action française " had contrived to secure the support of the Catholic Church in France, clergy, high and low, as well as the laity, that so weighty a condemnation should have been laid upon it. Following the decree placing the " Action française " on the Index, a memorial enjoining submission to the decree was sent by the Vatican to France for the signature of the entire French hierarchy. Out of some seventy prelates only three declined to sign, and even these made their submission later in the year. In spite of this submission on the part of the hierarchy, the crisis within the Church continued throughout the year on account of the extraordinary ascendancy of the " Action française " over the minds of French Catholics; but, severe as this crisis was, the Vatican declined to modify their attitude. They were convinced that the agitation would subside in time—and time they were ready to allow. An address in which the Pope delivered to the French seminary in Rome on the topic of the " Action française " reveals better than anything else the attitude of the Holy See. His Holiness opened his address by expressing his pleasure in receiving the seminarists, a pleasure doubly appreciated at a moment when, he had to admit, many grievous and serious afflictions were coming to him from their native country, afflictions which were partly compensated for by the expressions of loyalty and consolation offered to him by so many members of the French episcopacy and clergy who had written to thank him for his decision and intervention in the question of the " Action française." He himself felt sorrow and pity for his misguided sons who had allowed themselves to be led astray by a strange form of Catholicism, half pagan sensuality and half vague philosophy, which he himself, permitting himself to speak as an old librarian, could assure them was by no means new or original, but was an entirely erroneous doctrine which preached revolt against the very head which it proclaimed as its authority. and which yet refused to distinguish between the words spoken by the Pope ex-Cathedra—a necessarily very rare occurrence—and those spoken in the every-day fulfilment of administrative duties. So-called theologians and authorities had been quoted and invoked, theologians who had forgotten their theology and authorities who had forgotten their supreme authority. In such a state of affairs it is better to face the truth, and the Pope could not let this occasion pass without expressing his profound sorrow for all that was occurring. He could see but two motives for consolation : that of being able to pardon whole-heartedly all those who had been led astray, and of being able to say, in the words of the Bible : " Forgive them, for they know not what they do." It was with the keenest sense of pity that he thought of the moment of their awakening to a sense of their errors and to a realisation of their delusions. His Holiness closed his address with an admonition to the students not to allow themselves to be dragged into such affairs, but to remember that in order to be with Christ it was before all necessary to be with Peter, one with the Pope.

16. It was not to be expected that men of the type of Maurras and Daudet would submit to condemnation without retaliating. They proceeded to bring the following charges against the Holy See : that in condemning the paper and movement, and in subjecting its adherents to severe ecclesiastical penalties, the Pope has interfered in internal French politics. Also that the whole motive of the Vatican condemnation was not religious but political, inspired by pro-Germanism. Lastly, that prior to the condemnation an abnoxious agreement was made between the Vatican and M. Briand. The accusation of pro-Germanism levelled at the Vatican by the " Action française " arises from the fact that the original condemnation of the " Action française " by Pope Pius X was signed by Mgr. Esser, a German prelate who held an important

post in the Congregation of the Holy Office, and was based on the propaganda of the pro-German Belgian, M. Passelecqs. The absurdity of such an accusation is apparent. Mgr. Esser, more Roman than German, acted under Vatican orders, and the latter's policy was none too acceptable to the German Government.

17. As to an agreement between the Holy See and M. Briand, should such an agreement exist it is clearly not to the advantage of the Holy See. The Pope, by his action, has weakened the political support of Catholicism in France, thus throwing French Catholics, already disunited, into greater confusion. Only later, when it is generally realised that the Pope's action was motivated by religious and not political reasons, can it be hoped that the supporters of the " Action française " will dissociate themselves with M. Daudet and M. Maurras and return once more to their spiritual head.

18. Though the dispute concerning the " Action française " is primarily one between the Church and individuals, it has had such a far-reaching effect on public opinion in France that the forthcoming elections cannot fail to feel the effect. For that reason and for its unavoidable influence on French politics and French relations with the Holy See an account of recent developments has been included in this report.

Germany.

19. The influence of Catholicism in Germany, which continued to show a striking increase during the year, produced, as was to be anticipated, a corresponding increase in the importance of diplomatic relations with the Holy See. The position of the Catholics in the Reich has undergone a complete change. Before the war they were practically excluded from public affairs in Prussia and the Empire; and in 1927 in all that matters Catholicism had more than its full share of influence and power. Since the revolution there have been three Catholic Chancellors, Fehrenbach, Wirth and Marx; the Cabinet has five Catholic members; practically all the officials in the Reichskanzlei; and a large proportion of the Prussian judiciary are Catholic; not to mention a number of Landräte. This change, which almost constitutes a revolution, is due to the position and influence which the Centre has acquired in the last few years as a political party. Though the political views within that party are widely divergent, there is one corporate tie and one common aim, membership of the Catholic Church and the furtherance of Catholic interests. In everything else compromise is permissible, and co-operation with any other party or parties can be effected whether to the Right or to the Left, as the situation of the moment may seem to demand. As an arbiter of political destiny the Centre party has never been more firmly established. The increase in the influence of the Catholic cause, which this party represents, can be ascribed mainly to the decrease in the authority of the Lutheran Church with the collapse of Prussianism, its staunch supporter; from the fact that the aspirations and desires of the Catholics of Germany are shared by millions of German-speaking men and women who do not owe allegiance to the German Commonwealth, but who have the sympathies of all within; and, above all, to the attitude of the Centre party during the war, which was known to favour a peace of under-standing by which Germany would have secured terms infinitely more favourable than those of the Treaty of Versailles. With the increase of the influence of the Catholic cause the demands for a concordat became more insistent. In the early part of the year the German Ambassador told me that little progress had been made with the negotiations, but in the course of a debate in the Reichstag in April Dr. Stresemann stated, in reply to a question, that the situation had changed materially since the Federal States were negotiating separate concordats, and that, in his opinion, a Reichsconcordat was desirable. In the meantime, I gathered at the Vatican that for Prussia a kind of provisional *ad hoc* arrangement had already been drawn up with a view to mutual consultation and agreement between the Holy See and the Prussian Government when any episcopal see falls vacant. This, however, was quite informal and will need to be replaced by a full concordat, the desirabilty of which is recognised by both sides.

Portugal.

20. Though the Portuguese Government were anxious to rid themselves as far as possible of the presence of foreign missionaries in the Portuguese

colonies, the decree they published relating to Catholic missions contained no definite threat in this sense, and the Vatican, on receiving the text officially, did not feel called upon to make any comment. In the meantime, the Portuguese Government had approached the Holy See with the request that the question of the concordat should be re-examined. The negotiations on this subject, which proceeded intermittently throughout the year, resulted in a draft agreement containing the following provisions :—

(1.) The Archdiocese of Goa, to which the patriarchal title remains annexed, is to be enlarged (*a*) by the addition of the Portuguese possession of Damaun to the north of Bombay, (*b*) by the addition of the Island of Diu off the Kathiavar coast. The archbishop to be called Archbishop of Goa and Damaun.

(2.) The portion of Diocese of Damaun not incorporated in the Archdiocese of Goa will be annexed to the Archdiocese of Bombay, which retains its present ecclesiatical organisation.

(3.) The Archbishop of Bombay shall be of Portuguese nationality, and shall have jurisdiction over all the territory of the archdiocese enlarged as above.

(4.) The Holy See and the Portuguese Government declare themselves in accordance for the modification of the composition and limits of the Diocese of St. Thomas of Meliapor, so as to assure in its best form the continuity of the respective episcopal jurisdictions.

(5.) The present protocol refers only to the episcopal jurisdiction and not to Portuguese property, &c. The clergy of the Portuguese parishes will continue to be Portuguese.

21. The Government of India, who had all along been freely consulted, objected not unnaturally to article 3, but wishing to be conciliatory put forward three alternative proposals. These were that :—

(*a*.) Appointment of British coadjutor to Portuguese Archbishop of Bombay with right of succession to the latter, *i.e.*, coadjutor archbishop or bishop *cum jure sucessionis*, but not an auxiliary bishop.

(*b*.) Appointment of Portuguese Archbishop of Bombay on this occasion only, on understanding that his successor will be a British subject, *i.e.*, Portuguese archbishop *pro hac vice*.

(*c*.) Appointment of a Portuguese archbishop should be accompanied by the appointment of a British coadjutor *cum jure successionis*, but it should be understood that on the succession of the British national to the archbishopric, his successor as coadjutor should be of Portuguese nationality, and so on alternately, thereby securing permanently both Portuguese and British representation in the diocese.

22. As the Portuguese Government declined to accept either of these proposals a deadlock ensued, and all further negotiation in Rome was suspended.

Spain.

23. More than once in the course of the year I ventured to suggest to Cardinal Gasparri, when he appealed for British intervention on behalf of Catholics undergoing persecution in Mexico and elsewhere, that he ought in the first instance to invoke the assistance of Spain, the most prominent of the Catholic Powers. His Eminence, though not saying so in so many words, gave me to understand that there was little to hope for in that direction, and that Spain could only be regarded as a broken reed when called upon for co-operation. Whether it is for commercial or other reasons that Spain is unwilling to come to the assistance of the Vatican on these occasions it is difficult to say; but it is obvious that the Spanish press is muzzled over Mexican affairs and seldom, if ever, permitted to give a true account of the barbarities perpetrated in that country. As an example of the official attitude, I might cite one of the Spanish Prime Minister's statements to the press in February last : General Primo de Rivera said that while Spain could not but feel grief at the religious dispute between the Mexican Government and Roman Catholics in Mexico, yet respect for Mexican independence and the ties of friendship

and interest between Spain and Mexico made any gesture a delicate matter unless it were simply an expression of the hope that Catholics in Mexico would have the benefit of proper guarantees of hospitality.

Jugoslavia.

24. M. Simitch, Jugoslav Minister at Warsaw, who was transferred to the Holy See more than a year ago for the express purpose of finding some solution of the dispute with regard to the ownership of the Institute of St. Jerome, told me in March that, in spite of the strained relations between his country and Italy, he was glad to find a propitious atmosphere at the Vatican which led him to hope for a settlement. The claim of the Serb-Croat-Slovene Government that the Rector of the Institute of St. Jerome should be of Serb-Croat-Slovene nationality was, he said, a modest one which might well be granted, as it was granted to every other country. Until the Vatican conceded this and other small points he could not even discuss with them the question of negotiations for a concordat. As the months rolled by and M. Simitch was unable to obtain the slightest concessions, his optimism waned, and he was more than once on the point of leaving Rome in despair. The Vatican declined even to discuss the question of the rectorship of the Jugoslav college, but the Minister remains at his post, and it may well be that the importance of concluding a concordat will in the end outweigh the importance of an agreement with regard to the Institute of St. Jerome.

Czechoslovakia.

25. In 1925 the official participation of the Czechoslovak Government in the anti-Catholic Huss celebrations at Prague led to the withdrawal of the Nuncio. In 1926 the official attitude was considerably modified, and in 1927, following the visit of Mgr. Ciriaci of the Secretariat of State, there was a still further improvement. Three Ministers were, in fact, present at the celebration, but, as was expressly stated, in an individual capacity, and the President took no part in them. Especially significant was this absence of the President, who, it was thought, in view of his anti-clerical past and his known intellectual convictions, showed a notable desire for conciliation with the Holy See by not attending the function in question, divested though it was of official anti-Catholic features. The road to an understanding being thus cleared, it was not long before the mission of Mgr. Ciriaci was followed by the return visit of Dr. Krofta, Czechoslovak Under-Secretary of State for Foreign Affairs, to Rome, where he found an atmosphere very different from that prevalent when Mgr. Marmaggi was recalled from Prague. At that time the Huss celebrations were treated by the Government as a question of principle. This was attenuated by the record of the subsequent years, and in the meantime the generous provision by the Pope of the ground for the Czechoslovak College and its solemn ceremony of foundation by the Cardinal Secretary of State had also contributed to produce more favourable conditions for negotiation. As the year closed an amicable *modus vivendi* was established by an exchange of notes between Cardinal Gasparri and Dr. Krofta, which will no doubt lead in due course to the re-establishment of regular diplomatic relations. With Dr. Krofta, as the Cardinal Secretary of State told me, they had a man with whom, at any rate, it was possible to negotiate. Unlike his predecessors, he was not always placing in the forefront the demand to be allowed to present candidates for bishoprics. This the Holy See absolutely refused, holding that the succession States do not inherit the privileges of the Habsburg Monarchy in this respect.

Hungary.

26. In April Count Bethlen, the Hungarian Prime Minister, came to Rome and was received in audience by the Pope. The dispute, which at that time was raging between Yugoslavia and the Italian Government, was causing the Holy See some alarm, and it is believed that the Hungarian statesman was able to render a reassuring account of his dealings with the Italian Government and the attitude of Hungary. In any case, his visit produced a good effect.

27. With the death of Cardinal Csernoch, Archbishop of Esztergom, on the 25th July, the difficulties connected with the appointment of his successor

were brought into prominence. After some delay these were solved by the Appointment of the Benedictine, Justinius Serédi, and his promotion to the dignity of cardinal took place at the last consistory. The Archbishop of Esztergom being, *ex officio*, Prince Primate of Hungary, the question of the succession to the primacy is now settled.

28. The nomination came as a surprise, and is generally interpreted as a "diplomatic defeat" of the Government. Under the Dual Monarchy the nomination of ecclesiastical dignitaries for appointment by the Pope was a prerogative of His Apostolic Majesty. After the downfall of the monarchy the provisional Constitution of 1920 made no provision for the transfer of the prerogative. It merely stated that it was not to be vested in the Governor, and it was understood that it was to be left in abeyance. Subsequent Governments have not attempted to conclude a concordat with the Holy See in this connexion, because it has always been understood that in the case of the restoration of the monarchy the rights of the King would automatically be revived. In the meantime, the Holy See exercises the right of appointing bishops as a matter of course. In Government circles it has been maintained that such questions have always been settled in perfect accord with the Holy See, but it is common knowledge that such appointments have been effected in complete disregard of the wishes and proposals of the Hungarian Government.

29. Whatever the political aspect of the matter may be, the appointment of the Primate has been well received by the press and by the public at large, and is generally considered as a satisfactory solution. Mgr. Serédi, it is pointed out, has been long absent from the country and is, therefore, unaffected by the political troubles of recent years. He is a learned man, and an acknowledged authority in the domain of Canon Law, the latest edition of which he compiled. The fact that Mgr. Serédi was at once to be created a cardinal made a very favourable impression in Hungary, since it had been feared that under the political status of the country the Holy See might not have been disposed to accord such a distinction to her Primate.

Soviet Russia.

30. The year 1927 brought no improvement in the conditions prevailing since the revolution, and the Soviets continued to attempt to disguise their internal weakness by concentrating political hatred and suspicion on the representatives of religion. The Vatican, while organising assistance outside for the distressed populations, took care that no direct campaign against the Soviets should be launched from Rome on account of the danger it would involve for Catholics in Russia. Cardinal Sincero, secretary of the Congregation of the Eastern Church, told me in this connexion that the Holy See were besieged by people who wanted it to lead a crusade against the Soviets. To these the same reply was always given, namely, that the Holy See had no concern with Russia's politics but only aimed at spreading the truths of Christianity in Russia and the world generally, this in itself a powerful agency against the evils of Bolshevism. Although the first concern of the Vatican was the condition of religion in the Soviet Union, it followed hardly less closely during the year the general development of Soviet policy, and I gathered that the active manifestation of Bolshevik activity abroad was regarded by them as a reflection of internal weakness, rather than strength. The firm stand taken by His Majesty's Government over the Arcos affair and subsequent rupture of relations with the Soviet Government was hailed with great satisfaction in the Vatican, where it was hoped that other States would soon follow suit. As it was difficult to cope with events in Russia in the normal manner, a separate commission was appointed by the Pope with instructions to study conditions, and above all, religious conditions in Russian territory, and to watch over the religious interests of Catholics living under the jurisdiction of the Soviet Union. Cardinal Sincero was named president of the commission, and Bishop D'Herbigny, the Jesuit priest who in 1925 and 1926 made a number of journeys into Russia, was appointed the "relator." The importance of this commission was enhanced by the addition of the two Under-Secretaries of State, an arrangement which facilitated the flow of news to the highest quarters.

Lithuania.

31. Early in the year the Holy See received a letter from the Foreign Minister of Lithuania requesting that diplomatic relations, broken off over

the Vilna question in May 1925, should be re-established.   The Vatican, who were anxious that the influence of the Church in Lithuania should be directed towards promoting an understanding with Poland, while themselves remaining aloof from political controversies, made haste to meet this overture in a friendly spirit.   Mgr. Schioppa, titular Bishop of Mocisso, was appointed as Inter-nuncio, and shortly afterwards M. Sanlys, former Governor of Memel, presented his credentials as Lithuanian Minister to the Holy See.   With the re-establish-ment of relations no time was lost in preparing the concordat which was signed on the 27th September by the Cardinal Secretary of State for the Pope and Professor Voldemaras, Prime Minister and Secretary of State for Foreign Affairs, for the Republic of Lithuania.   The concordat, which for the most part follows the Polish concordat, contains a number of additional clauses which make it more favourable to the Holy See :—

> Article 9.   The Lithuanian Government accepts absolutely the ecclesiastical delimitation of the country which was prescribed by the Holy See, thus agreeing formally to the Bull " Lithuanorum gente."
> Article 15 makes a religious marriage independent of the civil ceremony and equal in all respects to the latter.
> Article 21 lays down a principle to which the Holy See attaches the greatest importance, namely, that all Catholics living in Lithuania shall receive religious ministration in their own language.
> Article 25 obtains from the Lithuanian Government full liberty for such religious and social organisations as correspond to the " Azione Cattolica " in Italy and elsewhere.

Latvia.

32.   On the 27th December M. Germain Albat, the new Minister of the Republic of Latvia to the Holy See, presented his credentials to the Pope. He is the first permanent representative, though, from time to time, envoys have been sent on special missions.   The first of these was in 1919, shortly after the constitution of Latvia as an independent State, when the Bishop of Riga was sent to Rome to seek the recognition of the new State by the Holy See and to ask for a concordat.   At the same time, the present Pope, who, at that time, as Mgr. Ratti was Apostolic Nuncio to Poland, was nominated by Benedict XV as Apostolic Visitator to the various countries which had formerly formed part of the Russian Empire.   The result of his visit was the concordat which was signed soon after his accession to the Pontifical throne.   This concordat, although Catholics form only 25 per cent. of the population in Latvia, provided for the dignity and requirements of the Church in that country.   At first there was no exchange of diplomatic representatives, but, after the appointment of Mgr. Zecchini as Internuncio to the Baltic countries, the Latvian Government decided to send a representative to the Vatican.

Roumania.

33..   After protracted negotiations the Holy See concluded in the month of May a concordat with the Roumanian Government.   At the moment of writing the terms of this concordat still remain a secret, as they were not to be disclosed until after ratification, and ratification has been delayed by the death of the King and the subsequent death of the Prime Minister.   As these two were the most powerful supporters of the agreement, with their disappearance parliamentary and popular opposition may possibly become more formidable. The Vatican authorities appear on the whole to be satisfied with the outcome of the negotiations, which have been difficult and subject to much interruption by changes of Government in Bucharest, the extreme nationalism of the régime in the years immediately following the end of the war, and the hostility of the Roumanian Orthodox clergy.   I understand, in the meantime, that on all the questions involved it has been possible to arrive at a satisfactory conclusion. Among the points of special difficulty were the jurisdiction over and the division of the dioceses containing the Magyar and German Catholics, the relation between the Government and the Catholic schools, especially, of course, among the minority populations, and the question of the Catholics of Oriental rite.

Bulgaria.

34. The policy of friendliness adopted by Bulgaria towards the Catholic Church, described in the last report, was still further accentuated by a visit in October of King Boris to the Pope. The visit was devoid of official character and had no particular purpose beyond an act of courtesy towards the Head of the Church in which, had it not been for Russian pressure, His Majesty might well have been brought up. In view of his forced secession from the faith of his fathers, the King approached the Vatican with extreme nervousness; but was soon comforted by the very sympathetic welcome extended to him by the Pontiff. That his heart had remained Catholic transpired in the course of this visit, but eventual reconciliation with the Holy See, owing to constitutional reasons, is not anticipated. Though there were still no diplomatic relations, friendly intercourse prevailed through the channel of the Visitor Apostolic. Mgr. Roncalli. The latter, who, throughout the year, directed his energies to reorganising the Catholics of Thrace and Macedonia, was considered here to have been successful and to have met with favourable assistance on the part of the Bulgarian authorities.

United States.

35. The cordial relations existing between the Holy See and the United States Government, which were recorded in the previous annual report, were still further cemented during the year under review, and on this side no opportunity was omitted of extending a benevolent welcome to citizens of the republic, who sought audiences of the Pontiff The Mayor of New York was received in state; and the American legionaries, who came in great force, elicited an address of exceptional warmth from the Pope. The allusion made by His Holiness in the course of this address to the " decisive intervention " of the United States in the Great War threatened at one moment to rekindle the controversy in the European press with regard to Papal neutrality; but the " Osservatore Romano," with commendable promptitude, checked further outburst by issuing an official statement to the effect that the words contained not the slightest derogation from the determined impartiality of the Holy See. This official *démenti* was accepted and the matter was dropped. Considerable interest was taken during the year in Vatican circles in the projected candidature of the Roman Catholic Governor, Alfred Smith, for the presidency of the United States, though nothing was done to further that candidature. On the contrary, every effort was made to convince American public opinion of the aloofness of the Holy See from questions of party politics. During the Chicago Eucharistic Congress the Papal Legate, it is true, made a friendly reference to Governor Smith's political progress, but that was excluded from the published report of the cardinal's utterances, a proof that the Catholic authorities in the United States are very much alive to the danger of confusing their religion with politics. In this they had the whole-hearted support of the Holy See, who, under the present Pontiff, have shown themselves particularly anxious to disentangle the Church from political embarrassments.

Argentina.

36. The nomination of an archbishop to the vacant see of Buenos Aires at the end of 1926, after a long period of tension, gave the opportunity for a further act calculated to enhance the importance of the relations between the Holy See and the Argentine Government. This act, which was brought into operation towards the end of the year under review, was the elevation of the Argentine Legation to the Holy See to the status of an Embassy. This alteration was not effected without certain objections from both sides. When the Vatican heard that it was the intention of the Argentine Government to raise their Legation at Mexico City also to the status of an Embassy they objected strongly to the conjunction with that Government in view of the persecution they were waging against Catholics. The Holy See let it be known at Buenos Aires that under those circumstances they would prefer the Argentine Legation in Rome to maintain its existing status. No sooner were these Vatican objections overcome than the Socialists in the Argentine Parliament in their turn endeavoured to wreck the project, taking the line that the creation of an Embassy to the Holy See would be a step towards the subordination of the State to the Church. After the Acting Minister for

Foreign Affairs had replied that it was a simple act of courtesy in return for the Pope's action in sending a Nuncio to Buenos Aires, the measure, though opposed, was carried both in the Senate and in the Chamber of Deputies. In November Dr. Alberto Blancas, the Argentine Minister in Belgium, was selected for the post of Ambassador to the Holy Seé and will take up his duties early in the new year.

Mexico.

37.   Early in January Cardinal Gasparri told me that he was in the act of addressing instructions to the Papal Nuncios in the various European capitals with regard to the persecution of Catholics in Mexico with a view, if possible, to stimulating a joint protest. The situation was, he said, growing worse and was intolerable according to his most recent accounts. As there was no Nuncio in London he intended to address a note to me giving full details to be laid before His Majesty's Government. This note, containing a memorandum of the intensified religious persecution being carried on by the Mexican Government, and appealing to His Majesty's Government to remonstrate on the grounds of humanity, was forwarded by me a few days later to the Foreign Office. The two main points in the memorandum on which the Holy See considered that a protest could most effectively be made were the forbidding of religious observances, even in private houses, the most serious penalties being inflicted on those who might celebrate or assist at such functions; and the fact that women, having adopted mourning dress as a sign of protest against such fierce persecution, had their clothes torn from them in the public streets. To this, after careful enquiry, His Majesty's Government replied that, in regard to the first point, the position appeared to be that the Mexican Government now allowed priests to celebrate mass in private houses; and, in regard to the second point, His Majesty's Government had been able to obtain no confirmation of violence having been offered to women who may have protested, in the manner mentioned by the Holy See, against the Mexican Government's decrees. As the year progressed the condition of religious affairs in Mexico continued to cause the Holy See the greatest concern. On one occasion when I was at the Vatican the Cardinal Secretary of State, who had just come from the Pope, with whom he had been discussing this subject, was much stirred by indignation and grief. The conduct of the Mexican authorities, he said, according to a trustworthy report which the Holy See had just received, surpassed anything laid to the charge of the Bolsheviks in their campaign against religion. Merely for expressions of loyalty to their faith Catholics had been seized, tortured with extreme barbarity, and killed. In June the Committee of Exiled Bishops residing in Rome issued a statement recounting a number of alleged atrocities by the agents of the Mexican Government. At Toluca, they said, a young Catholic was nailed to a cross and then shot; at Guadalajera the priest Saba Reyes, who had disappeared, was found covered with petrol, having been burned alive. In Mexico City seventeen priests who had been imprisoned in the fortress of Tlalteloo were taken out to the cemetery of Dolores and there shot in front of an open grave, into which some fell and were buried while living. A general denial to this statement was subsequently issued by the Mexican Minister to the Quirinal, who stated that there was no religious persecution in his country. This is, I think, unlikely to count very much against the detailed statements of the bishops. Throughout the year the "Osservatore Romano" and the "Unità Cattolica" kept up a continuous day to day report of the details of President Calles's anti-religious campaign, but the press in general in Italy and elsewhere gave no real support to any policy of intervention. The situation, therefore, remained unchanged.

China.

38.   The establishment of a native Chinese hierarchy and the consecration of six Chinese bishops by the Pope in 1926 was followed by the despatch of two Belgian Benedictine monks to China in 1927. These were sent with the object of establishing a Chinese Benedictine congregation, to which it is hoped native novices will be attracted. For some years past there have been native Chinese religious settlements; the Trappists at Pekin are a notable example, but this will be the first regular settlement in China of the Benedictine Order, whose whole tradition is in favour of decentralisation and the establishment of

local, autonomous congregations aiming at the pursuit of the religious life and higher education. This may seem a somewhat bold undertaking at the present juncture, but the reports which the Delegate Apostolic in China regularly submits to the Congregation of Propaganda are not at all pessimistic. In spite of severe difficulties for all Christian missions, and in spite of sporadic persecution even of native Catholic congregations. Mgr. Costantini remains firm in the opinion he expressed last year that ultimately bolshevism will be found foreign to the genius of the Chinese people, and that the Catholic Church, purged of all suspicion of being an instrument of foreign penetration, has a great work before it in the new China which should emerge from the present chaos.

39. When, in the course of the autumn the Belgian and Spanish Governments, who were negotiating treaties with the Chinese Government, proposed to insert additional articles guaranteeing the liberty of Christian worship and institutions, the Cardinal Secretary of State told me, in reply to my enquiries, that there was no question of any protectorate for Catholic missions. The right of protection by any authority but that of the Chinese themselves had explicitly been renounced by the six Chinese bishops at the time of their consecration in Rome, and would not now, he thought, be revived. What was intended was rather a solemn recognition by the Chinese Government of the rights of Christian missionaries in China.

Japan.

40. The death of the Emperor of Japan was received at the Vatican with particular regret because the deceased monarch had always followed a benevolent policy towards the Roman Catholic Church in Japan. Even during the war, on his intervention, the German priests and religious who held posts in the Japanese educational service or were engaged in missionary work were permitted for a great part to remain unmolested, and when Spanish missionaries in certain instances were called to take the place of Germans, the Japanese Government bore the expenses of their journey. It may also be recalled that, when the Japanese Government took over the Marshall Islands, it sent an emissary to discuss with the Holy See questions affecting the status of the German missionaries employed there.

41. In the early part of the year the Holy See decided to make a beginning with the establishment of a native Japanese hierarchy, considering that this step was necessary, as it was in China, if any progress was to be made with the evangelisation of the people and the eradication of the prejudice against a so-called foreign religion. Modern Japan has never been such a promising field for Catholic missionary activity as China. From numbering more than a million members at the end of the 16th century the Catholic Church in Japan was in the course of time reduced to a mere handful, and progress, even after western missionaries were readmitted, has been very slow. There are little more than 100,000 Catholics, with not quite 600 hundred churches. There is only one Catholic missioner, clerical or lay, for every 86,000 inhabitants, and this scarcity of personnel, together with the prohibition to Catholic missions to organise elementary schools, has been a serious check on progress. Where the Catholic Church makes progress is rather among the educated class, and there are a considerable number of intellectual Japanese who, while not believing in Catholic dogmas, are ready to encourage the Church as a factor in civilisation and in maintaining the idea of authority. With this the Holy See, however, is not content; and the decision to appoint the first Japanese bishop has been taken in the hope that it may be increasingly possible to reach the common people who, according to reports received here, are a fairly easy prey to Bolshevik propaganda and subversive activities of all kinds.

42. On the 2nd August the Pope, in an imposing ceremony held in St. Peter's, consecrated Mgr. Hayasaka as Bishop of Nagasaki, he being the first native Japanese bishop to be appointed in the history of the Catholic Church.

IV.—THE SACRED COLLEGE.

43. No less than seven cardinals died in the course of the year. These were: Cardinal Ranuzzi, Camerlengo of the Sacred College; Cardinal Cagiano de Azevedo, Chancellor of the Holy Roman Church; Cardinal Bonzano, who represented the Pope at the Eucharistic Congress in America; Cardinal Lualdi,

Archbishop of Palermo; Cardinal O'Donnell, Archbishop of Armagh and Primate of Ireland; Cardinal Reig y Casanova, Primate of Spain; and Cardinal Czernoch, Primate of Hungary. A further vacancy was created by the resignation of Cardinal Billot, at the advanced age of eighty-one. A French Jesuit, he was one of the most distinguished theologians the Church has possessed in modern times. The strain of Nationalism in his character led to a difference of opinion with the Pope regarding the condemnation of the " Action française," and it was thought best to accede to his wish to be allowed to retire and to live the life of a simple Jesuit. In the consistory held on the 20th June the Pope raised the following prelates to the Sacred College : Mgr. Lauri, titular Archbishop of Ephesus, and Papal Nuncio in Warsaw; Mgr. van Rooy, Archbishop of Malines; and Mgr. August Hlond, Archbishop of Gnesen. As the predecessors of the two latter were both cardinals their own advancement was only to be anticipated sooner or later, while Mgr. Lauri received his hat in the ordinary course of events after a successful term as Nuncio. On the 20th December the Pope held a second consistory, at which he created five new cardinals, all of which, strange to say, were non-Italians. These were : Mgr. Lépicier, Archbishop of Tarsus; Mgr. Rouleau, Archbishop of Quebec; Mgr. Segura y Saenz, Archbishop of Burgos; Mgr. Binet, Archbishop of Besançon; and Father Szeredyi, a Benedictine, who was raised to the Sacred College as Archbishop of Strigonia and made Primate of Hungary. In the appointment of the Archbishops of Burgos and Quebec there is nothing that calls for special remark, as both Toledo and Quebec are places where the archbishop is, as a rule, raised to the Sacred College sooner or later. The promotion of the Archbishop of Besançon was unexpected, but his see is a large one, and reasons connected with the faithfulness of the diocese to the Holy See over the " Action française " may have influenced the Pope's choice. The appointment of Archbishop Lépicier filled the gap left among the French Cardinals by the retirement of Cardinal Billot; and Father Szeredyi, a distinguished figure in the Benedictine Order, and one of the chief authorities on Canon Law, was considered in Rome to be a happy selection for the somewhat difficult position of Primate of Hungary under the present régime. At the close of 1927 the Italian members of the Sacred College numbered thirty-three as against thirty-two non-Italian cardinals. There were various changes in the distribution of the work. Cardinal Sincero replaced Cardinal Tacci as Secretary of the Oriental Congregation of Extraordinary Ecclesiastical Affairs; Cardinal Cerretti was appointed a member of the Sacred Congregation of Rites and the Sacred Congregation of the Eastern Churches; Cardinal Boggiano to the Sacred Congregation of Religious; Cardinal Frühwirth to be Chancellor of the Holy Church; and Cardinal Bisleti to the Sacred Congregation of the Holy Office and the Pontifical Commission for Biblical Studies. I must also not fail to mention that a large silver medal, struck by special order of the Pope, was presented to Cardinal Gasquet, the English Cardinal in Curia, to commemorate the historic event of the presentation to the Sovereign Pontiff of the Book of Genesis, the first fruits of the Revision of the Vulgate.

o

CONFIDENTIAL.
_____

(13604)

HOLY SEE.

═══════

Annual Report. 1928.

─────────────

[C 3397/3397/22]

Mr. Chilton to Sir Austen Chamberlain.—(Received May 13.)

(No. 103.)   *British Legation to the Holy See,*
Sir,   *Rome, May 9, 1929.*
    I HAVE the honour to transmit herewith my annual report on the Holy See
for the year 1928.
    I am indebted to Mr. Randall, second secretary in this Legation, for the
compilation of the major portion of the report.

                     I have, &c.
                        H. G. CHILTON.

──────────────────

Enclosure.

Annual Report on the Holy See for 1928.

───────

CONTENTS.

─────────────

I.—Introduction.

FOR the Holy See the year 1928 was comparatively calm and uneventful. Outwardly it was marked by a quiet consolidation of good relations with certain States, where difficulties had previously arisen; internally the most noteworthy feature of the year was the progress in the building and formation of new educational institutions, the prosecution of a policy of expansion in the sphere of ecclesiastical training and scholarship, to which the Pope, whose interests in this direction are well known, set his hand soon after his election. With the first, the relations with foreign States, Chapter II of this report will deal in some detail. The second may conveniently be examined here. The chief institutions which were completed or brought much nearer completion during 1928 were the following :—

The Pontifical Gregorian University, whose buildings had become too small for the increasing number of ecclesiastical students of all nationalities who came to Rome to take their degrees in theology and canon law. The new building will accommodate 2,000 students, and, together with the Pontifical Biblical Institute, near by, and the Pontifical Oriental Institute, will provide a complete specialised training for priests who wish to proceed to post-graduate studies in ecclesiastical subjects, both of the Latin and the Eastern Churches.

The Pontifical Oriental Institute, now ready in an excellent site near the Church of Santa Maria Maggiore, with a staff of professors qualified to teach oriental languages and everything connected with oriental religions, from which, it may be remarked, Islam is not excluded, this department being presided over by a convert Turkish scholar. The rector of the institute is Mgr. Michael D'Herbigny, a well-known French Jesuit and authority on Slavonic subjects.

The Pontifical Institute of Christian Archæology, now completed, which will deal with Christian archæology in all its branches, particularly with the discoveries constantly being made in Rome.

The Museum of Missions and Comparative Religions, housed on a floor of the Lateran Palace.

The General House of the Company of Jesus, or headquarters of the General of the Jesuits and his Curia, housed in a large new building at the foot of the Janiculan Hill, near the Vatican.

The College of Propaganda, a new building in the same neighbourhood, for the training of missionaries to non-Christian countries.

The North American College, also in the same district, where nearly 200 ecclesiastical students from the United States will be in residence.

The Ethiopian College, a new building in the Vatican precincts.

The Bohemian College, a larger building to replace the inadequate present college.

2. In addition, plans were agreed to for a new Brazilian College for Brazilian students who hitherto have studied at the general Latin-American College. This, an example of the apparent settled policy of the Holy See to provide all Christian nations with their own national college in Rome, had not been begun by the end of the year, but the Brazilian Government was reported to have promised its co-operation in the work to be undertaken.

3. Few formal Papal utterances of general importance were delivered during the year. The most noteworthy were the following :—

Encyclical " Mortalium animo," published the 11th January, and dealing at length with the principles of religious unity, with an unmistakable reference to the "Malines Conversations," and various other suggestions regarding the unification of the Christian Church.

Encyclical " Miserentissimus Redemptor," published the 12th May, and of exclusively religious interest, to the confusion of certain newspaper-prophets, who had anticipated a pronouncement on the Holy See's attitude to nationalism.

Telegram of the 1st August to the Chinese Catholic Bishops, of which an account will be given in Chapter II under "China."

Encyclical "Rerum orientalium," of the 8th September, commending to the whole Catholic world the work of the Pontifical Oriental Institute, to which reference has just been made.

Motu proprio of the 30th September, by which the Pope decreed the unification of the Gregorian University, the Biblical Institute and the Oriental Institute.

Allocution of the 17th December, to the Secret Consistory, at which it had been anticipated the Pope would make a long speech with reference to Mexico, France, Russia, also possibly Italy. Instead the published text revealed nothing but a most cordial appreciation of the reception accorded by the authorities and people of Australia to the Papal delegation headed by Cardinal Cerretti, which had visited Sydney on the occasion of the Universal Eucharistic Congress the previous September. No new cardinals were created at this consistory, but a large number of episcopal appointments in all parts of the world were confirmed, among which the following are of particular interest :—

> Dr. Downey to be Archbishop of Liverpool.
> Mgr. Forbes to be Bishop of Ottawa.
> Mgr. Lima to be Archbishop of Bombay.
> Mgr. Rokossian to be Armenian Archbishop of Constantinople.

4. During December there were published two Papal letters, the first to the Catholic University of Washington, commending its activities, and the second to Cardinal Bertram, Archbishop of Breslau, urging the development in Germany, as in Italy and elsewhere, of Catholic action, or Catholic social and religious organisation entirely independent of all party politics. The same month the Pope said Mass in St. Peter's in inauguration of his jubilee year, or fiftieth anniversary of his ordination. It was anticipated that this event would be marked, in the succeeding twelve months, by an unusual number of pilgrimages from all over the world.

5. Audiences proceeded as usual all through the year, with the exception of several weeks' interruption during the exceptionally hot summer months, which it was reported had severely tried the Pope's strength. During September, however, His Holiness resumed his normal activities, with his customary energy. Among the audiences accorded during the year, special mention may be made of the following, taken in chronological order :—

January 16.—A Hungarian pilgrimage, in Rome, for the consecration of Dom Seredi, O.S.B., as Cardinal-Primate of Hungary.

March.—The Roman Diocesan Committee, of which the Pope took occasion to criticise the pro-Fascist Catholic party, the Centro Nazionale, for their alleged lack of regard for the Supreme Pontiff.

April.—General Nobile and his companions, before setting out on their ill-fated airship expedition to the Pole.

June 16.—The whole of the staff and students of the French Seminary in Rome, to whose expression of loyalty importance was attached in view of the agitation over the " Action française."

June 22.—To Sir Odo Russell, for the purpose of presenting his letters of recall.

October 18.—A pilgrimage of 250 Civic Guards of the Irish Free State.

November 24.—To myself, for the purpose of presenting my letters of credence from His Majesty the King; to this I return in Chapter II.

December 24.—To the Sacred College, to whose Christmas wishes the Pope replied by urging sympathy for the Christians of Russia and Mexico, and expressing sympathy at the better news of the health of His Majesty.

6. On the last day of the year the Pope received eighty teachers from the Dominions, who, at their request, were presented by the secretary of this Legation and to whom His Holiness addressed words of cordial welcome and encouragement.

II.—Relations with Foreign States.

7.   Immediately before the Great War there were fourteen diplomatic missions accredited to the Holy See, two Embassies and twelve Legations.   At the beginning of 1928 the number was twenty-eight (or twenty-nine, if Prussia be counted separately from the German Reich), namely, ten Embassies (Argentina, Belgium, Brazil, Chile, Colombia, France, Germany, Peru, Poland, Spain), and eighteen Legations (Austria, Bavaria, Bolivia, Czechoslovakia, Costa Rica, Great Britain, Hayti, Hungary, Latvia, Liberia, Lithuania, Monaco, Nicaragua, Portugal, Roumania, San Marino, Venezuela, Yugoslavia).   Of these, Bolivia was raised to an Embassy in the course of the year.   In addition, the Netherlands and Switzerland maintained diplomatic relations by the acceptance of an Inter-Nuncio, without corresponding Legations in Rome.

8.   Three deaths occurred in the Diplomatic Corps during the year: the French Ambassador, M. Doulcet, in February, the Austrian Minister, Baron Ludwig von Pastor, in September, and the Venezuelan Minister, M. Mata, in October.   The following presentations of credentials took place :—

   M. Blancas, Argentine Ambassador, on the 6th March.
   M. le Vicomte de Fontenay, French Ambassador, on the 2nd May.
   M. Vladimir Radimsky, Czechoslovak Minister, on the 10th June.
   M. Gustavo Guerrero, San Salvador Minister, the 11th November (after
      which he returned to Paris, where he resides).
   Myself, on the 24th November.
   M. Rudolf Kohlruss, Austrian Minister, on the 22nd December.

9.   In regard to its foreign relations in general, the Holy See, with the two usual exceptions of Mexico and Soviet Russia, had a fairly satisfactory if comparatively uneventful year.   The Prussian, Albanian, Yugoslav and Roumanian concordats did not reach the conclusion some observers had anticipated, but settlements, satisfactory even if in part provisional, were reached with Czechoslovakia, Portugal and Guatemala.   Details of these will be found below.

(a.) *The British Empire.*

Great Britain.

10.   The occasion of the presentation of my letters of credence from His Majesty the King to the Pope, which took place on the 24th November with all due ceremonial, was clouded by the bad news from England of His Majesty's health.   Both in his formal reply to my address, and in the less formal private audience which followed, His Holiness spoke with great solicitude and sympathy of the King, recalling the pleasure which the visit of their Majesties in 1923 had given him.   On several subsequent occasions the Pope, either in receiving me or at functions such as the New Year's reception of the Sacred College, made anxious enquiries or references of the deepest sympathy, and begged me to transmit these expressions to His Majesty, for whose recovery, His Holiness said, he prayed continually.   The same concern was shown by the Cardinal-Doyen, when I had my customary audience with him, and with all the members of the Papal Curia with whom I came into contact.   Naturally, too, there was constant enquiry from the various British ecclesiastical institutions in this city, such as the English and Scots Colleges, and many of my colleagues of the Diplomatic Corps to the Holy See called to make special enquiries and express sympathy, or, later, when a definite improvement was reported, to convey their gratification at the good news.

11.   It is impossible not to be struck with the universal esteem in which the British sovereigns are held here in Vatican circles, and I might venture to say that this is due, not only to a high personal regard, increased by the fact of their Majesties' visit and the deep impression which that caused, but also to a sincere recognition of the value of British civilisation to the ideals of peace and international understanding and educational progress, to which the Holy See, particularly under the present Pontiff, attaches such a capital importance.   The way in which the Papal Visitor Apostolic, Mgr. Hinsley, who continued his journey of inspection of Catholic mission schools in Africa all through the year without interruption, was received in

the Dominion of South Africa and in the various colonies was often commented on with pleasure by Vatican officials, and the reception of the Papal Legate, Cardinal Cerretti, in Australia, on the occasion of the Eucharistic Congress in Sydney in September, was mentioned with marked gratification by the Pope himself in a public statement.

12. During the year there were three particular instances of the goodwill existing between Great Britain and the Holy See. The first was the rescue of a number of Catholic missionaries in China by British sailors, for which a special message of gratitude was sent by the Cardinal Secretary of State for transmission to His Majesty's Government. Then, on the occasion of the Asiatic Congress in Oxford, the Legation was instructed to invite the Holy See to nominate a delegate. This was done at once, and the convert Turkish Professor of Islamic Studies at the Pontifical Oriental Institute, Mgr. Mulla, was sent. Finally, in connexion with the preparation of a stellar map by the Vatican Observatory, Professor Turner, of Oxford, was an active collaborator, and His Majesty's Government were asked to transmit to him and his assistants gold and silver medals from the Pope in recognition of their collaboration.

Australia.

13. The Pope was represented at the Eucharistic Congress at Sydney, which took place during the summer of 1928, by Cardinal Cerretti. His Eminence was accompanied by a staff of about ten persons, among whom were Mgr. Caccia-Dominioni, Papal Maestro di Camera, Mgr. Carlo Respighi, Prefect of the Pontifical Ceremonies, Canon of the Lateran; Mgr. Mella di Sant'Elia, Privy Chamberlain Participant of His Holiness, Canon of St. Peter's; Mgr. Grosso, Master of the Pontifical Ceremonies, and two Papal Chamberlains.

14. The Papal Legate arrived in Australia on the 30th August and left on the 16th October, after visiting Brisbane, where he laid the foundation-stone of the new cathedral, and Melbourne, where he opened a new college, and Canberra.

15. The Italian press published daily accounts of the congress, the Catholic press notices being especially detailed and devoting much attention to all developments, from the inauguration with the special message from the Pope to the Catholics of Australia, delivered by the Papal Legate, to the enthusiastic closing scenes. The proceedings seem to have been purely religious and devotional and devoid of political interest, but a certain amount of criticism was aroused in Rome owing to the absence from the congress of any Catholic bishops from Great Britain.

16. Cardinal Cerretti returned to Rome viâ the United States of America. He told me he was very much struck by the excellent organisation of the congress, and that he was glad to taste again of the unbounded hospitality of the Australians, which he had constantly enjoyed when he was Delegate Apostolic in Australia.

India.

17. The most important event of the year mutually concerning the Holy See and India, namely, the abolition of the Portuguese Padroado in Bombay, will be found described under the heading "Portugal." Otherwise there was little that calls for special remark. During the year the former Bishop of Poona, the German Jesuit, Dr. Döhring, who had had to leave India during the Great War, was permitted to return and again took possession of his former See.

Malta.

18. Malta was a frequent subject of discussion between His Majesty's Legation and the Holy See during the year. The fervent catholicism of the Maltese people, the position of the Church and the intermingling of religion and politics, with the fact that Malta is the one part of the British Empire in regard to which there is a definite concordat with the Vatican, these are the peculiar conditions which serve to bring Maltese problems frequently, and often insistently, before the attention of the Legation.

Relations between Ecclesiastics and Maltese Government.

19. His Majesty's Chargé d'Affaires reported in September that there had been recently a certain recrudescence of the anti-English propaganda in regard to Malta in certain Italian papers. The "Corriere d'Italia," for instance, repeated the familiar story that the present Prime Minister of Malta, Lord Strickland, was intent on destroying both the Italian culture and the religion of the Maltese people; an account of a meeting was also reported, at which the cry of "Down with the bishops, down with Christ the King, *viva* Calles!" was alleged to have been raised. It was insinuated that this was due to the anti-Catholic partisans of the present Government in Malta, and a letter of protest by the Bishop of Gozo was quoted.

20. The Papal Under-Secretary of State drew Mr. Randall's attention to this article. The latter pointed out that there was little doubt that certain priests in Malta had been carrying on party political propaganda, and this was courting trouble. Mr. Randall added that, as the Under-Secretary was aware, there was always a small but noisy element of pro-Italian propagandists in Malta, who misrepresented the real feelings of the Maltese people and in general seized upon any pretext to undermine British influence.

21. The Vatican point of view, however, appeared to be that it was unjust that the archbishop-bishop, whose loyalty to Great Britain was above all suspicion, should be attacked on account of a few clerics whose party zeal exceeded their discretion and caused them to disregard their bishop's injunctions against political activity.

22. It was even said that certain leaflets attacking the archbishop-bishop emanated from a printing-press under the control of the Prime Minister, and that endeavours had been made to press the two senatorial representatives of the archbishop into the service of the political party in office.

23. Lord Strickland, while admitting that Mgr. Caruana, the archbishop-bishop, was pro-British, maintained that he opposed the Government to the utmost of his power and encouraged the priests in the Senate to adopt a similar attitude. Lord Strickland felt that there must be some collusion between Signor Mussolini and the Vatican in this matter. He was anxious for a clear definition of the Papal policy of restraining priests from electioneering in Malta and, in general, from interfering in politics. It is well known that the Vatican are adverse to this, as is shown by provisions in certain concordats with foreign Governments.

Archbishop of Malta.

24. His Majesty's Government were informed that the Pope had decided that henceforth the Bishop of Malta, having lost his traditional title of Archbishop of Rhodes owing to the establishment of a separate archbishopric in that island, should hold the title of archbishop-bishop. His Majesty's Government caused their thanks to be conveyed to the Vatican for this action, which ensured that the Bishop of Malta could not be brought under any superior jurisdiction outside the island.

Visit of Lord Strickland to Rome.

25. Lord Strickland called at the Foreign Office in September and stated that it was his desire to visit Rome in order to discuss with certain cardinals the question of the relations between the ecclesiastics in Malta and the Maltese Government. He stated that he wished to see Cardinal Cerretti and Mgr. Caccia-Dominioni, who were absent in Australia at the time, and Cardinal Merry del Val, who, Lord Strickland was warned by His Majesty's Chargé d'Affaires, would, if he attempted to discuss foreign political matters, refer him to Cardinal Gasparri. This proved to be the case. Cardinal Gasparri, however, expressed his readiness to receive Lord Strickland.

26. Lord Strickland was also desirous of being received by the Pope, but the Cardinal Secretary of State, mindful of matters in dispute between the Maltese Government and the ecclesiastical authorities in the island, apparently fearing that Lord Strickland might attempt to discuss politics, considered it expedient to state that the audience would have to be postponed until some future date.

27. Lord Strickland and Professor Bartolo, Maltese Minister of Education and Emigration, arrived in Rome on the 9th November.

28. Lord Strickland had a frank and full discussion with Cardinal Gasparri of the questions at issue, which were, briefly :—

(1.) *The despatch of a Visitor Apostolic to Malta* (a Delegate Apostolic was subsequently sent).

(2.) *Local non-political difficulties with the Maltese clergy.*

(3.) *Domestic political difficulties with the Maltese clergy.*—The Vatican's view was that all cases should be treated on their merits and by negotiation with His Majesty's Government. Lord Strickland suggested that, pending the despatch of a Visitor Apostolic, priests should be inhibited from political activity and the two clerical members of the Senate restrained from voting. The Vatican point of view was that this would constitute direct interference on the part of the Holy See in Maltese domestic politics.

(4.) *International political difficulties with the Maltese clergy.*—Cardinal Gasparri succeeded in convincing Lord Strickland that Vatican policy was in no way dictated by considerations of Italian national interests. The heads of the religious orders represented in Malta were mostly non-Italians and did the best they could with the material at their disposal.

Endowment by Lady Strickland of a Boys' College in Malta.

29. Up to about 1904 there was in Malta a boys' college conducted by English Jesuits. Their departure was a serious blow to education and was deeply deplored by all those who took an interest in the higher education of young men; many of the best men in the Government service, legislature and commerce had been educated there. After the closing of the college the youth of Malta, who could not afford to go to England, were obliged to go to the College of the Italian Jesuits, started soon after the English Fathers left Malta, or finish their education in Sicily or Southern Italy.

30. Lady Strickland in 1928 offered the archbishop-bishop the sum of £5,000 a year and an endowment of £100,000 for a boys' college in Malta if his Grace would give his approval to such a college being carried on by an English religious order.

31. It was feared possible that those opposed to the spread of English ideas and the English language in Malta would bring influence to bear on the Vatican to defeat this project.

32. The Vatican, however, to whom the scheme was propounded by His Majesty's Chargé d'Affaires, expressed extreme readiness to assist. Cardinal Gasparri approached the General of the Jesuits, who, however, was unable to find anyone in his Order suitable for the post of headmaster; nor was there anyone available among the Benedictines. Lord Strickland thereupon applied to Cardinal Bourne, who was eventually able to find an ex-naval chaplain who was capable of undertaking the task.

The Case of Fathers Carta and Micallef.

33. In December Father Carta, a Sardinian and the superior of the Franciscans in Malta, ordered Father Micallef to leave Malta within a few days on account of an expression of politics in private conversation. The Government of Malta alleged that Father Carta was in the habit of indulging in pro-Italian propaganda. The archbishop agreed to Father Carta's appointment because the Franciscan friars were very undisciplined, and it was necessary to appoint a strict disciplinarian. Father Micallef was apparently truculent and had defied his superior, and he was said to have given scandal by his manner of life. The Government demanded the expulsion of Father Carta. The Governor replied that he could not take the action they recommended if such recommendation were based on this case, which seemed to be primarily one of internal discipline in the Order. If the Government wanted Father Carta expelled they must prove to the Governor beyond all possibility of doubt that he had taken part in political propaganda against them. The Vatican was approached unofficially on the subject, but no definite conclusion was arrived at before the end of the year.

Palestine.

34.   On the 5th January a dispute took place in the Grotto of the Nativity in Bethlehem between two Franciscan friars and two Orthodox sacristans.   They came to blows, and eventually the affair was brought before the courts, which sentenced the offenders to varying terms of exclusion from the Sanctuary, the Orthodox, as the original aggressors, for a longer term than the Catholics.   The decision formed the subject of a bitter article in the Florentine Catholic paper " Unitá Cattolica," of the 11th February, which accused the British administration of ignoring Latin rights and failing to understand the roots of the quarrel.   There were similar unfavourable comments in other Catholic papers, but the Cardinal Secretary of State, when questioned about the matter by Sir Odo Russell, pointed to the silence of the " Osservatore Romano," and indicated that he would discuss the matter again after receiving an official report.   Since, however, his Eminence did not take the question up again, it was inferred that the Holy See had not considered it of sufficiently serious importance for official representations, and later, when the Italian Government, through their Embassy in London, attempted to reopen the question, it was possible to point to the continued silence of the only authorities directly concerned, namely, the ecclesiastical.

35.   Two incidents more especially affecting Italy, but of possible interest also to the Vatican, were those attendant on the visit of His Royal Highness the Italian Crown Prince to the Church of the Holy Sepulchre and the Cenaculum, during Holy Week.   In the first, a misunderstanding was caused by the claim of the Italian consul-general that His Royal Highness should make a " solemn entrance," which has a special significance and is reserved only for the Patriarchs; in the second, there was a dispute regarding the Prince's right to make entry into the Cenaculum, which is in Moslem ownership and is a Moslem Holy Place, with boots on.   A compromise was eventually arranged in both cases, and the incidents passed without much comment in the Italian press and with no comment whatever, it should again be emphasised, from the Holy See.   Such comment on Palestine as was to be found during the year in the Italian press, in fact, was to be ascribed exclusively to Italian propaganda and not to specifically Vatican inspiration.   Leaving aside the question of the Holy Places, the reopening of which was not even remotely suggested by the Holy See, the only particular matter directly interesting the latter during the year was the proposed Palestine Education Ordinance.   Information was received that the Latin Patriarch had forwarded to the Holy See representations regarding the way in which he considered the draft ordinance would unfavourably affect Catholic schools.   Nothing on the subject, however, was communicated to His Majesty's Legation by the Papal Secretariate of State.

36.   The English bishop-auxiliary to the Latin Patriarch, Mgr. Codric Kean, who had retired to Cyprus, resigned during the year, and the question was mooted once more whether the Patriarch, Mgr. Barlassina, might not be promoted to the Sacred College; but no development in this direction took place.   In May Mgr. Paschal Robinson, O.F.M., the Visitor Apostolic in Palestine, returned to Rome, and did not proceed again to Palestine, being engaged in consultations with the Vatican authorities.

(b.) *Other Countries.*

Afghanistan.

37.   At the conclusion of his official visit to the King of Italy, the King of Afghanistan paid a visit to the Vatican, and was received by the Pope with the same honours as the King of Egypt the previous August.   The matter was a purely formal one, for there are no Catholics in Afghanistan, and no Catholic missionary seems able to establish himself there.   This does not appear to have changed in any way as a result of the Royal visit, although the Vatican seems to have cherished certain hopes in this direction.

Albania.

38.   In January it was announced that the negotiations for a concordat between the Holy See and Albania had been concluded, and optimistic reports of an early signature were given in the papers.   These received no confirmation, and, in fact,

the Albanian delegation returned, and the Delegate Apostolic, Mgr. Della Pietra, paid a visit to Rome without any further apparent progress towards a settlement. From private information, it appeared that the discussions had reached a deadlock, mainly owing to the Albanian Government's refusal to withdraw the divorce provisions, which it proposed to apply equally to Roman Catholics as to other religions, from its proposed Civil Code. There had also been a difficulty over the Albanian demand that only Albanians should occupy episcopal sees in the country. The question of signature was still in abeyance at the close of the year.

Austria.

39. At the end of September the death took place at Innsbruck of Baron Dr. Ludwig von Pastor, the distinguished historian of the Popes, who had served as Austrian Minister to the Holy See since the end of the war, and was widely esteemed both at the Vatican and in diplomatic and academic circles in Rome. He was replaced at the end of the year by Dr. Kohlruss, Austrian Minister at Sofia, and a diplomat *de carrière*.

40. Two matters affecting Austria seem to give the Holy See some concern. The first is the falling off in membership of the Catholic Church, which is attributed to Socialist propaganda, and also the fact that with many, under the old régime, such membership was a mere formality which can now be discarded. The extent of the loss, which for 1928 was estimated at over 28,000, led during the year to the promotion of a special mission in Vienna and other centres. The other matter is the liability of the Vatican to be involved in the agitation for the " Anschluss." It was partly to influence clerical opinion against this that in October Cardinal Dubois, Archbishop of Paris, visited Vienna, and took part in several functions arranged for him. The French Minister professed to be well satisfied with the result of this move. For its part, however, the Vatican continued to display a studious neutrality, and a statement by M. Briand in December, that the Holy See was opposed to the " Anschluss," was commented on privately at the Vatican, in the sense that the Vatican had made no official pronouncement which could be interpreted either in this way or the contrary. The allegation by a Paris newspaper that Cardinal Gasparri's views on the matter were the same as those of the German Government, received an immediate official denial. The truth seems to be that the Vatican is conscious of the delicate international factors in the situation, and is also under no illusion that, although the union of Austria and Germany might bring benefits to the Church, it might well bring disadvantages also, especially if such a change came about against the desire of the neighbouring countries or France. The fact that the Austrian Chancellor is a priest makes the situation all the more delicate, and, incidentally, there were signs that this fact, together with the favourable attitude taken up by Mgr. Seipel in regard to certain Catholic demands, above all regarding the proposed Catholic University of Salzburg, might mean disaffection among the pan-German components of the Chancellor's parliamentary majority.

Bolivia.

41. During the year it was announced that the Bolivian Government had raised their Legation to the Holy See to the status of an Embassy. No Ambassador, however, had been appointed by the end of the year. A Papal Nuncio, in the person of Mgr. Chiarlo, had been nominated, but had not reached his post when news was received of the outbreak of the conflict between Bolivia and Paraguay in December. As soon, therefore, as the Pope received the information that war seemed imminent, he directed the Cardinal Secretary of State to confer with the Bolivian Chargé d'Affaires in Rome, and the Papal Nuncio to Paraguay, who resides in Buenos Aires, to take up the matter with the Paraguayan Government, with a view to avoiding any outbreak or extension of hostilities. At the same time two identic telegrams were despatched from the Pope to the Bolivian and Paraguayan Presidents respectively, appealing to their Christian sentiments to endeavour to find a peaceful solution of the dispute. The *démarche*, which appears to have been made with discretion by all concerned, was welcomed by both sides, who sent appropriate assurances and expressions of gratitude to the Holy See.

China.

42.   The Catholic missions in China, although they did not suffer much loss of life, were disastrously affected in a material sense by the civil war, particularly in the Yangtze districts, and the Hupeh and Hunan Provinces.   One vicariate was completely destroyed, fourteen missions in another ruined, and there was a general expulsion of missionaries in Anhwei and Canton.   An estimate, published in Rome in February and based on reports from sixty Catholic ecclesiastics, put the probable loss in property at between 75 to 125 millions of francs.   With the return of better conditions, however, the missionaries, the majority of whom had, it was claimed, remained at their posts, resumed their work, and began to derive benefit from the Holy See's policy of utilising, as far as possible, the native priesthood and hierarchy, with the object of securing the Church against any anti-foreign agitation.   In August the Pope sent a long telegraphic message to the Chinese Catholics, expressing satisfaction at the end of the civil war and recalling that the Holy See, by the consecration of the six Chinese bishops in 1926, had been the first Power to treat the Chinese on a footing of equality.   The Pope proceeded to enjoin on the faithful obedience to legitimately constituted authority and to recommend the organisation of Chinese lay-Catholics along the lines of Catholic action for the furtherance of Catholic religious and social aims, so contributing to the general good and the greatness of the country.   The Chinese bishops sent a cordial reply and the Papal document seems also to have gratified the Chinese Nationalist authorities, for soon after the Foreign Minister, Dr. Wang, sent a letter of thanks to the Delegate Apostolic, Mgr. Costantini, and in a press interview commented with much satisfaction on the Pope's words regarding the treating with China on a footing of equality.   From this the Holy See hoped for favourable treatment for Catholic missions, and in December the delegate reported that the Government had decreed the evacuation within two months of all houses, schools and hospitals belonging to the missions, Catholic as well as non-Catholic.   Isolated cases of obstruction or hostility by local authorities were reported to the Vatican from time to time, but the intentions of the Government were regarded as generally favourable, a matter of no small importance to the Holy See, since Chinese Catholics form a majority of Chinese Christians in general, while the country is regarded as a most promising field for missionary effort, in which the Vatican is now practically unhampered by such political considerations as the French Protectorate.

Colombia.

43.   Towards the end of the year a summary was published in Rome of the new convention between the Holy See and Colombia, signed the previous May, and dealing with the supply of missionaries for the missionary territory of the republic, that is among the aboriginal inhabitants.   The territory in question was divided into three vicariates, seven prefectures and three missions, and provision was made on a liberal scale for the financial support of the priests, some of whom appeared to be British.   The Colombian Republic has always been bound by strong ties to the Holy See and the agreement was admittedly inspired by the belief that the Catholic missionaries could play a most important part in the work of civilising the backward inhabitants of the country.   It was subsequently explained that the agreement was renewal of a former convention, revised to meet new conditions.

Czechoslovakia.

44.   As a result of the conversations in Rome at the end of 1927 between M. Krofta, Under-Secretary of State, and Mgr. Ciriaci, of the Papal Secretariate of State, a *modus vivendi* was reached of which the terms were made known in February.   The document, which Dr. Benes subsequently explained as the result of a compromise between the opposing ideas of a separation between Church and State, and a full concordat with the Holy See, comprised six articles.   The first and most important laid it down that no part of the republic was to be subject to an ordinary resident outside the boundaries of Czechoslovakia, and that no diocese would extend beyond the frontiers of the country.   The Holy See and the Government would proceed, by means of two commissions to be nominated within two months, to a new delimitation and endowment of the dioceses of Czechoslovakia.   The religious orders and congregations in the country would not be subject to provincials outside

Czechoslovakia, except where a provincial house could not be established, when they would depend direct on the mother-house. Provincial superiors would be of Czechoslovak nationality. Article 3 laid down that before proceeding to the filling of episcopal sees the Vatican would communicate the name of the Pope's choice so as to make sure that there was no political objection to it. The prelates in question would be Czechoslovak citizens and would take an oath of loyalty to the republic.

45. The *modus vivendi* was characterised in Rome as extremely favourable to the Prague Government, but it was regarded as satisfactory in that it enabled normal relations to be resumed in the appointment of Mgr. Ciriaci to be Papal Nuncio in succession to Mgr. Marmaggi, and of M. Radimski to be Czechoslovakian Minister to the Holy See. The latter presented his credentials to the Pope in June, and then proceeded to discuss with the Secretariate of State the various difficult questions which still remained to be resolved. No definite report of any concrete result of these discussions was available at the end of the year, but the John Hus celebrations in July, which had previously been a cause of trouble, passed off without any untoward incident and seemed unlikely any more to disturb relations between the Holy See and Czechoslovakia. Moreover, on the occasion of Mgr. Marmaggi's withdrawal from the post of Nuncio in Prague, the Government conferred a decoration on him, thus effacing the controversies with which his original departure from his post had been associated. It also made a considerable financial contribution to the new Bohemian College for ecclesiastical students in the course of construction in Rome.

France.

46. On the 12th February the French Ambassador, M. Jean Doulcet, died, much regretted by the Holy See, between whom and the French Government, by his tact and unremitting personal effort, he had brought relations to a far more satisfactory condition than they had been at the commencement of his mission. He was succeeded by the Vicomte de Fontenay, who came out of retirement; and it must be said that the somewhat unfavourable prognostications among certain of the Diplomatic Body of the results of this appointment were not borne out by experience, although whether the credit for this happy result was not more due to the tact and charm of the Papal Nuncio in Paris, Mgr. Maglione, is open to legitimate question. Early in March a stir was caused by the publication in the " Croix " of a letter from Cardinal Gasparri, with an introductory note by the Cardinal Archbishop of Paris, containing instructions to French Catholics in regard to their political activities. This document laid down that Pius XI maintained the same point of view as Leo XIII, namely, that Catholics, although allowed liberty in purely political questions, should unreservedly accept the Third Republic, and recognise the constituted authority. Work to alter the bad laws against the Church was legitimate, and the Cardinal Secretary of State gave the opinion that it was regrettable that French Catholics had not united to defend their religion against such laws, adding, in a later paragraph, a warning against those parties who asked for Catholic support pretending to further the Church's interest, but really attempting to advance their own cause. This last, a plain hit at the " Action française," called forth a strong reply from that party, and in other circles there was a certain resentment over what seemed to be an attempt by the Vatican to influence the Catholic vote at the elections then just due. It appeared, however, that the Cardinal Secretary of State's letter was ten months old, having been sent for the private guidance of the Papal Nuncio; it contained a true and consistent account of the Holy See's attitude towards political parties, which was that religion was to be kept apart from politics, and so long as this was done Catholics were free to fight in elections for any good cause or for any party which would benefit the Church. Finally, Cardinal Gasparri denied, in conversation with Sir Odo Russell, that his letter could be interpreted as the expression of a desire on the part of the Holy See for the formation of a specifically Catholic party. Eventually, after some criticism in the press, one item in which, a leading article in the " Temps " for the 11th March, it was understood was due to M. Poincaré, the general excitement died down, except among the " Action française," which, throughout the year, was unremitting in its attacks on the Holy See, and on the Cardinal Secretary of State in particular. Not until later in the year was there a revival of excitement. This was caused by the Government's proposal, in articles 70 and 71 of the draft Budget Law, to restore certain property to a number of missionary congregations and authorise their re-establishment in France. The motive for this step was stated to

be the French Government's concern at the decline of French prestige abroad, which had been caused by the severe falling-off in the recruitment of French missionaries since the separation, and the consequent replacement of French schools, in the Near and Far East and in Africa, by Italians, Canadians, Belgians, Dutch, Swiss and Americans. The Vatican, from its statistics, confirmed this, but maintained a most reserved and discreet attitude over a question which, at the end of the year, threatened to lead to an acute political crisis, the Left parties holding that the Government's proposals, which were defended by both M. Poincaré and M. Briand, constituted a serious breach with the "lois laiques." The disturbance over the unveiling of a monument at Pons to M. Combes, by M. Herriot, was a further cause of agitation by the parties of the Left, and it was thought that the whole question of Church and State, raised in so conspicuous a manner, might result in the collapse of M. Poincaré's Government. This, however, has not occurred by the close of the year.

47. In December the "Osservatore Romano" printed a denial of the rumours that the Holy See was now not inclined to persist in extreme measures against the "Action française," and the official organ of the Vatican, the "Acta Apostolicæ Sedis," during the same month, gave point to the denial by issuing a decree under which priests who gave absolution to persons who persisted in supporting the "Action française" were held guilty of particularly grave sin. This very severe provision served to show the determination of the Vatican to carry out its disciplinary action in this respect to the uttermost, but it also indicated to a certain extent the persistence of the opposition to the decrees of the Holy See. It was not possible to say that the "Action française" crisis had been resolved.

48. The last question involving relations between French politics and the Vatican was the autonomist movement in Alsace. Here a difficulty was created by the fact that the movement is largely supported by priests, who are able to find arguments against the Paris Government in the words of certain politicians of the Left, who do not conceal their desire to extend the "lois laiques" to the regained province. Despite this, the policy of the Vatican appears to have been inspired by a wish to keep the priesthood out of political controversy as far as possible, and in particular discourage all identification of the Church with the extreme autonomists. To this end Mgr. Ruch, Bishop of Strasbourg, and Mgr. Polt, Bishop of Metz, addressed certain communications to their clergy, with the express authorisation of the Cardinal Secretary of State; whilst M. Poincaré, on his side, in the course of speeches made in Alsace-Lorraine during October, gave a solemn assurance that the confessional schools should be respected. Neither the one action nor the other, however, secured the Church from being involved to a certain extent in the autonomist agitation.

49. In regard to French colonies, the appointment may be chronicled of Mgr. Dreyer, a Frenchman, and former Vicar-Apostolic of the Suez Canal Zone, as Delegate Apostolic in Indo-China.

Germany.

50. Relations between the Holy See and Germany are cordial, but the concordat, or rather concordats, which have been discussed for some considerable time past make no apparent progress. The Vatican anticipates that eventually the concordat with Prussia will be concluded first, and that then, with this as a precedent, it will be comparatively simple to arrive at an agreement with the Reich as a whole. In October it was announced in the newspapers that the negotiations between the Nuncio and the Prussian Government were ended, and that the text was ready for signature. But this proved to be premature, or, as the Centre party paper, "Germania," suggested, a possible calculated indiscretion for the purpose of prejudicing the issue. However this may have been, the signature did not take place, and it was then reported—although no confirmation could be obtained at the Vatican—that the project had been wrecked on the demand of the Holy See to establish two new bishoprics, at Berlin and Essen respectively, which had been rejected. It was also suggested that Protestant and Liberal opposition to the proposals regarding religious education in the schools had made a successful conclusion impossible, although the Centre party members of the Prussian Diet had attempted to disarm criticism by announcing that they were in no way opposed to similar legislative agreements for the other chief religions.

51. In the meantime the Centre party had emerged from the Reich elections in a somewhat weaker position, and this was ascribed to various causes, such as the drift to the Communist or Nationalist parties on the part of electors discontented with the continued occupation of the Rhineland. To a certain extent, too, it seemed to be due to the indifference among former Centre party voters caused by the dissensions in the ranks of the party, and Dr. Marx, as president of the non-party Katholischer Volksverein, in a speech in October, lamented the large abstentions of Catholic voters. The following month the Pope, in a letter addressed to Cardinal Bertram, Archbishop of Breslau, encouraged the extension of Catholic Action, or the organisation of all Catholics in social and religious and educational work entirely independent of party politics. One paragraph of this document contained a clear hint that even the Centre party, which was not named, was not to be regarded as monopolising the adherence of German Catholics. This step was a logical continuation of the policy of the Holy See under the present Pope, namely, to intensify Catholic religious and social work and prevent the Church from being embarrassed by a too close association with any particular party. It seemed unjustifiable, however, to deduce from it that the Holy See intended to criticise the Centre party, which incidentally does not consist entirely of Catholics, or do anything to encourage its dissolution. Towards the end of the year a Catholic priest, Prälat Kaas, was elected leader of the Centre party, but it was not thought that this would bring about any alteration of Vatican policy. Matters like this, it was explained at the Vatican, are largely in the hands of the local bishops, on whose decision the participation of priests in politics depends. Appeal to Rome is always open, but in practice is comparatively rare.

Guatemala.

52. During the year relations between the Holy See and Guatemala showed a marked improvement, to such an extent that it was found possible to give effect to the Papal Bull of July 1921, under which a new diocese of Quezaltenango was created and the ecclesiastical delimitations settled. These proposed arrangements, which had been obstructed by a long-standing dispute caused by the anti-Clerical activities of the Government, were all carried into effect, and two important ecclesiastical appointments were made by the Pope, namely, of Father Louis Durou, a French missionary long resident in Guatemala, to be Archbishop of Guatemala City, and Mgr. Jorge Garcia, to be Bishop of Quezaltenango, his native city.

Hungary.

53. On the 8th January the Pope carried out, in the Sistine Chapel, the episcopal consecration of Cardinal Serodi, Archbishop of Strigenia and Primate of Hungary. A little later His Holiness received in special audience a pilgrimage of Hungarian Catholics, who had come to Rome for the occasion, and expressed his pleasure at the flourishing condition of Hungarian Catholic institutions. Both events were commented on with satisfaction in Hungary.

Italy.

54. During the year the relations between Italy and the Holy See continued on the same lines as before, that is, no official link was established, but much deference towards the Church continued to be shown by the former, while the Vatican, while showing due appreciation for the favourable attitude towards religion adopted by Signor Mussolini's Government, let no opportunity slip of reminding Italian Catholics, and the world at large, that there was still a fundamental difference between Church and State to be bridged. In February the "Osservatore Romano" published a very clearly but moderately worded statement to the effect that the Roman question, being one which concerned the spiritual independence of the Church, could not be treated on party lines, but could only be discussed between the Church and the State as a whole. This was merely a repetition of the Vatican's consistent thesis that fascism was only a party, and that a settlement could only come as a result of negotiation between two sovereign powers, the King and the Pope. There was no notable controversial consequence of this declaration, but in March the Pope publicly reproved the members of the National Centre party, or those Catholics who supported fascism, for having linked together in a resolution the names of the Pope and King, as if the differences arising from the events of 1870

D

were at an end.   The Pope acknowledged the services the Italian Government had rendered to religion, but called attention to the gravity of the situation in regard to education, where obstacles were being placed in the way of the "Azione Cattolica" and its work for Catholic youth, which fascism wished to monopolise.   The Pope also expressed his grief that a body of Catholics had presented themselves at the Capitol, but had not paid their respects to himself, the head of their religion.   A deferentially-worded reply was issued by the National Centre party, affirming their devotion to the Holy See, and stating that the fact that they were a political party had been the motive for their not making application to be received by the Holy Father. Thereupon the matter was dropped, but other incidents were not wanting to demonstrate the Vatican's determination to avoid being placed in a position of dependence on or subservience to the Fascist régime.   At about the same time as the Papal rebuke just described, it became known, through publication in the Austrian press, that the Cardinal Archbishop of Vienna had appealed to the Pope to do something for the Catholics of the Tyrol, who were not allowed, it was alleged, to receive religious instruction in their mother-tongue, a constant principle of Vatican policy, embodied in more than one concordat.   The Pope stated that he had done all that was possible to obtain this concession, and feared that further efforts would aggravate the situation rather than improve it.   There was a marked absence of the angry comment which might have been expected in certain sections of the Italian press on this, and later in the year it was reported that, under pressure from the Vatican, certain of the Tyrolese grievances in regard to religious instruction in German had been remedied.   In any case, the matter was not allowed to disturb general relations between the Holy See and the Italian Government, and the same can be said of the next incident, which was a circular to the Diplomatic Corps by the Cardinal Secretary of State, dated the 11th April, but not made public in Italy until the following June, when an inaccurate version in a provincial paper led the "Osservatore Romano" to give the correct text.   In this His Eminence stated that it had been noted that among certain members of the Diplomatic Corps to the Holy See the conviction had come about that it was no longer necessary to show the same reserve in regard to their colleagues accredited to the Quirinal and in regard to the Italian authorities.   For this change of attitude, the Cardinal said, there was no justification, and the diplomats were therefore requested to confine their relations with the other side to the purely personal.

55.   It was rather in the sphere of education and political philosophy that, at one time, open and serious controversy threatened between the Holy See and the Italian Government.   The complete disbandment of the Catholic boy scouts, who were merged into the Balilla organisation, was, it is true, in the last resort, commented on by the Vatican press, and in an official letter from Cardinal Gasparri, more in sorrow than in anger, but there was a more vigorous reaction, expressed, among other things, by a letter from the Pope to his Cardinal-Vicar, to the women's and girls' athletic competitions which in May were held in Rome under the auspices of the Fascist party.   The proposed public gymnastic exhibition, the Pope said, was an offence against feminine delicacy of which even Pagan Rome had not been guilty. His Holiness did not anticipate any of the excesses of immodesty which had occurred elsewhere, and disclaimed any intention of discouraging proper physical training for women and girls.   It was the vanity and violence of the display proposed which perturbed him, and this was understood to be an allusion to the semi-military drill which was to form part of the programme.   The display took place as arranged, however, and on the whole did not entirely justify the Pope's fears.   The "Osservatore Romano," in a subsequent article, did not bring any accusation of lack of modesty, but repeated, even more emphatically, with quotations from Fascist documents, the Vatican protest against the aggressive militaristic tone of the Fascist programme of physical education for women.   With this the matter dropped, and after, a few days later, a circular from Signor Mussolini had been published, addressed to the prefects and explaining that only the semi-military non-Fascist organisations were to be dissolved, thus by implication exempting several of the institutions managed by the Azione Cattolica, harmony reigned once more and was not disturbed when the "Osservatore Romano," in a comment on the Prime Minister's speech regarding the new electoral law, propounded the well-known Catholic thesis of the existence of the State for the individual and not the individual for the State. In all this one had the impression that the "Osservatore Romano," as the only really independent paper in Italy, was being allowed a freedom which the Government could not very well deny it without risking a quarrel with the Vatican, but that the

other side was being restrained from rejoinders in the interests of a reconciliation between State and Church to which the régime attached the highest importance.

56. The summer in Rome was exceptionally hot, and the Pope, unable to move from the Vatican, was admitted to have suffered severely from the heat. This formed the text of certain articles in the provincial press, to the effect that it had been decided that His Holiness, in order to avoid a similar distressing experience in the following summer, would leave the Vatican for the Papal Villa at Castel Gandolfo. It was suggested that this might be done without prejudice to the question of the non-acceptance by the Holy See of the Law of Guarantees, and that it would not be necessary first to reach a settlement of the Roman question. On this there was no comment whatever from the Vatican side, but when the usual 20th September article appeared in the "Osservatore Romano," on the anniversary of the entry of the Italian troops into Rome in 1870, it was couched in such moderate terms that a number of papers, most prominently the "Popolo d'Italia," whose editor, Signor Arnaldo Mussolini, is the Duce's brother, took it as the text for articles suggesting that a compromise was now coming within the range of practical politics and that there was now, by the new Electoral Law, a new arbitrator between Church and State, namely, the Grand Fascist Council. To this the Vatican organ replied that the point of view of the Holy See had not changed at all, and that while the Pope, as a sovereign, could appoint his plenipotentiaries, the Grand Council had no right to act in a similar fashion for the Italian Government. To this somewhat blunt observation the "Popolo d'Italia" made a colourless reply to the effect that, in any case, the position had been clarified and simplified, and the Roman question retired from the scene once more—as so often before—to be brought out again, however, in the following December. But this time, it was the German press which acted as introducer, and a number of articles in responsible German papers, for example, the "Frankfurter Zeitung," in a message of the 18th December from its Rome correspondent, reported that for some time past there had been negotiations between representatives of the Holy See and the Italian Government, and that a draft agreement had been reached which, if approved, would have the effect of bringing about a general agreement between the State and the Church and so ending the deadlock which had prevailed since 1870. This time there was complete silence in the Italian press, and when, at the very end of the year, it was ascertained by this Legation that this silence had been imposed on all Italian newspapers by strict and explicit orders from the Government, there were observers who felt that, at least, after so many unfounded rumours, something definite was really on foot.

57. In conclusion, three incidents in the relations between the Church and the Government should be recorded. The first is that at the end of February an attempt was made to murder Father Tacchi Venturi, a well-known Jesuit. The assailant was not caught, but it was suggested in the press that, if he was not merely a lunatic, he was in the service of some secret anti-Fascist organisation which hoped, by striking at the priest, who was well known to be on terms of friendship with the Prime Minister, to strike at the régime and put a stop to its policy of reconciliation. The second incident was the definite re-establishment of the Archdiocese of Rhodes, which took place in August, after long delay by the Vatican. The step had long been urged, it was said, by the Italian Government, in the interests of the greatly-increased Catholic population in the island, since it had come definitely under Italian rule. The last was the passing by the Senate in December of a measure designed to relieve the clergy from taxation, which had pressed heavily on their small stipends. Here was a sign that, in spite of the attitude of assertive independence on the part of the Holy See, of which there was, as has been shown, no lack of examples during the year, the importance of the ecclesiastical organisation was recognised in the highest and most responsible circles of the régime. Whether this would issue into a wider and more fundamental settlement with the Pope as the head of an international religious body, whether, in short, the main Vatican demand for complete and visible independence of the Papacy, would be possible of attainment, was still in doubt at the end of the year, but feeling was stronger than at any other time previously that full reconciliation would come soon or be postponed for years.

Liberia.

58. Diplomatic relations between the Holy See and Liberia, which had been established the previous year by the creation of a Liberian Legation in Rome, were completed in March by the definite appointment, and acceptance by the Liberian Government, of Mgr. Oge as Chargé d'Affaires of the Holy See in Monrovia.

Lithuania.

59. During 1927 Mgr. Schioppa, inter-Nuncio in the Netherlands, was also appointed in the same capacity to Lithuania.

60. In the spring of 1928 it was decided to appoint a separate inter-Nuncio in Lithuania and Mgr. Riccardo Bartoloni, totular Archbishop of Laodicea in Syria, was selected for the post. Mgr. Bartoloni had been at one time temporarily in charge of the Nunciature in Venezuela, and was subsequently employed in the Secretariate of State, where his ability attracted the notice of His Holiness.

Mexico.

61. From the point of view of the Vatican, the Mexican situation in 1928 showed no essential difference from the preceding year. It was a record of resistance by individual Catholics to those provisions of the law which prevented the free exercise of their religion; and where this agitation became mingled with political motives—and often it was impossible to disentangle it—this took place without any encouragement from the Vatican or even, so it appeared, from the Mexican hierarchy. The Vatican held that the Mexican Government's proceedings disclosed a firm intention of crushing the Catholic religion, or of making the ecclesiastical organisation so completely subservient to the State that all spiritual development would be made impossible. Now and then it was reported and confirmed by impartial authorities that priests were caught redhanded leading parties of rebels, but the Vatican held that such incidents were either exaggerated or falsified, or that, alternatively, they did not represent the attitude either of the Holy See or of the Church in Mexico as a whole, which desired nothing but freedom to teach and practise the religion of the bulk of the Mexican people. This thesis was illustrated by the constant reporting of incidents such as, in January, the closing of a seminary because the students wore cassocks, or, the same month, of two convents because the sisters wore religious habits. In a similar case a number of nuns were arrested for living in a religious community, and their library of religious books was confiscated, although the Mexican authorities admitted, according to a report from His Majesty's Minister in Mexico City, that there was no charge of sedition. Early in the year the Bishop of Tamaulipas was arrested for failing to report daily to the police. In the meantime the Mexican bishops, headed by Mgr. Diaz, Bishop of Tabasco, had presented an appeal asking that their reasoned demands for religious liberty, which had been submitted to the Mexican Congress, should be given an answer; but there was no reply.

62. In the meantime the United States Ambassador in Mexico, Mr. Morrow, in the belief that an ending of the religious dispute was in the interests of the general pacification of the country, had been attempting to use his influence with M. Calles, and secured a conciliatory attitude to such an extent that the President in May received two representatives of the American Catholic hierarchy and the Mexican Bishop Ruiz. A certain *détente* had been hoped for by the declaration in April of the Mexican Minister of Education that the régime did not wish to eradicate the traditional religion of the Mexican people, and Sir Odo Russell unofficially represented to the Cardinal Secretary of State the desirability of listening to any proposal which might be made and which might point to the possibility of a settlement. His Eminence replied that the Vatican was intensely desirous of seeing an end of the trouble and that the Pope would be only too glad to listen to any overtures likely to lead to an improvement in the unfortunate conditions prevailing in Mexico. Mgr. Ruiz duly arrived, and was received by the Pope. But in June the Cardinal Secretary of State informed His Majesty's Minister that although he had discussed the Mexican situation at length, he had not been able to show any definite mandate from the Mexican authorities, and had been unable to produce any definite suggestion. The visit, therefore, was unlikely to lead to any result, for earnestly desirous though the Vatican was to reach a settlement, it was useless to discuss matters when there were no guarantees suggested for the future and no sign of contrition for the wrongs of the past. Even had anything like such terms been forthcoming from the Mexican Government, however, the approach to any conciliation had been obstructed by public discussion in the press of the so-called " Ruiz–Calles " plan. This had had the effect of rousing the more intransigent section of the Mexican Catholics. Their influence would have been negligible in Rome had anything definite been put forward by M. Calles, but the absence of authorised Mexican proposals on which the Vatican

felt they could rely only increased the atmosphere of distrust. The same month the
" Osservatore Romano " published a solemn denial of the report that the Pope had
given any encouragement whatever to the rebel movement in Mexico.

63. On the 17th July the President-Elect Obregón was murdered. The
" Osservatore Romano " at once published a strong condemnation of the crime, but
M. Calles immediately ascribed it to religious fanaticism, and this was the signal
for a long polemic in the Catholic press, which continued throughout the trial of
Toral and the nun Concepcion. It was pointed out that M. Calles's hasty assertion,
made before any investigation whatever, was proof of his ineradicable bias, and that,
since President Obregón was commonly said to have been ready to offer conciliatory
terms to the Church, it was at least equally arguable that the enemies of the latter
were responsible for the deed. In any case, it was obvious that there could, for the
moment, be no more talk of conciliation, and matters were not improved when
M. Portes Gil, on his nomination to the vacant presidency, announced that he would
continue the religious policy of M. Calles. In the meantime the Mexican Catholics
had again presented a petition to Parliament, appealing for a modification in the
laws against their religion along the following lines : —

(1.) The recognition of the legal existence and personality of all denominations.
(2.) The separation of Church and State, and in consequence the non-
interference of the State in religious affairs.
(3.) Friendly co-operation between Church and State, each being supreme in its
own sphere, the State in matters temporal, the Church in matters
spiritual.

64. It is certain that a gesture of conciliation from the Mexican Government
in regard to these demands would have been most cordially welcomed by the Vatican,
but there was nothing except a persistent circulation of rumours of imminent settlement, for which, the Vatican stated, there was no warrant, and whose origin could
be traced to Mexican propaganda. At the end of October Bishop Ruíz returned to
the United States. Before leaving Rome he stated in an interview that he had simply
come to Rome to lay a report on the situation before the Holy See. In regard to the
possibility of a settlement, the bishop gave it as his opinion that there were only two
ways open, namely, the acceptance of the Mexican Catholics' petition by Congress,
or negotiations between the Pope and the Mexican Government. This last remark
the Vatican explained as meaning that they would be glad to see anyone from Mexico
who could show any mandate from M. Calles or bring any suggestions which had
authority from the Mexican Government; it was useless to discuss matters with
unofficial persons, who produced all kinds of proposals and, when asked whether
these represented the views of the Mexican Government, immediately disclaimed all
such authority. Towards the end of the year the Mexican press announced that
Cardinal Cerretti, who had gone to the United States on his way back from
Australia, was going to open unofficial negotiations for a *modus vivendi* between
Church and State. But this was emphatically denied by the Holy See, and the year
closed with the Vatican still waiting for some sign from the Mexican Government.

Poland.

65. Poland and the Holy See remained on the usual friendly terms during the
year. In February, on the occasion of the anniversary of the Pope, extremely cordial
messages were exchanged between His Holiness and the President, and it may again
be pointed out that the present Pope never forgets the time he spent in Poland as
Nuncio. In February the Nunciature in Warsaw was filled by the appointment of
Mgr. Marmaggi, former Nuncio in Prague. After the conclusion of the *modus
vivendi* with Czechoslovakia, the Vatican were desirous of sending Mgr. Marmaggi
back to his old post, but the Prague Government preferred a fresh nomination, and
this the Vatican conceded, at the same time, however, showing their approval of
Mgr. Marmaggi by sending him to the senior post of Nuncio in Warsaw, where he
presented his credentials in March, to the accompaniment of enthusiastic demonstrations of loyalty to the Holy See on the part of Polish Catholics. In April M. Zaleski,
the Polish Foreign Minister, visited Rome and was received in private audience by
the Pope. His reception was not quite so enthusiastic as might have been anticipated,
since he had neglected to ask for an early audience, and had plunged into negotiations with the Italian Government before seeking an opportunity of paying his

respects to the Pope. The actual audience, however, when finally arranged, passed off satisfactorily, except that M. Zaleski did not receive the customary high Papal decoration bestowed on Foreign Ministers of Catholic countries.

Portugal: The Padroado.

66. After protracted negotiations between His Majesty's Government, the Portuguese Government and the Vatican, an agreement with regard to the Portuguese Padroado in India was signed on the 15th April by the Cardinal Secretary of State and the Portuguese Minister to the Holy See, under article 3 of which the Archbishop of Bombay is to be alternately British and Portuguese. By suppressing the Padroado, by abolishing the Bishopric of Damaun, by making the ecclesiastical boundaries coterminous with the political, and by restoring the whole of the Bombay Archdiocese to the normal ecclesiastical jurisdiction common to the rest of India, the anomalies of the past were obliterated. The other provisions of the agreement were practically unaltered from those contained in the draft agreement of 1927. It appears that the assent of the Portuguese Government to article 3 was only obtained by an ultimatum on the part of the Holy See. The signature was celebrated by the exchange of orders and decorations. The agreement was ratified by the Portuguese Government on the 23rd April.

67. Father Cioacchino Lima, of the Society of Jesus, was selected as the new Archbishop of Bombay. He was consecrated by Cardinal Granito di Belmonte on the 2nd December in the Church of the Cesù in Rome.

68. The new archbishop came to call upon me, and told me that between his appointment and his consecration he had visited his archdiocese and had been well received by both British and Portuguese Catholics there, and that since the agreement between the Holy See and the Portuguese Government a much better spirit had prevailed. It may be assumed that this is so, since the Legation has ceased to be bombarded by protests on the subject of the Padroado.

Roumania.

69. The concordat between the Holy See and Roumania, which had been negotiated and signed the preceding year, went forward for ratification by the Roumanian Parliament, and the Foreign Minister, M. Titulescu, after being received in audience by the Pope in February, gave the Cardinal Secretary of State assurances that this would be duly accomplished. It was, however, realised in Rome that the matter was one of considerable delicacy and that some opposition was bound to show itself. Absolute reserve, therefore, was maintained as to the contents of the concordat, until later, when the Minister responsible, M. Goldisch, published the text in a pamphlet. In response to enquiries, the Vatican admitted that the text was accurate, but declined any further information pending ratification. This had not been effected by the end of the year, political changes in Roumania having caused delay.

Serb-Croat-Slovene Kingdom.

70. In January the Minister for Foreign Affairs, Dr. Marinkovitch, in a speech to the Skupshtina, referred to the advantages of having a concordat with the Holy See. But no apparent progress was made, although later in the year an earlier cause of dispute was definitely disposed of by the signature of an agreement regarding the Yugoslav Institute of St. Jerome in Rome. By this it was arranged that the appointment to the rectorship of the institute should be in the hands of the Pope, and that the administrative committee should be composed of Jugoslav Catholic religious. The first rector appointed under the new conditions was Mgr. Cuka, former assistant to the Bishop of Spalato. Unhappily, he died after only a short residence in Rome, and in November was succeeded by Mgr. Magjoreo.

Soviet Union.

71. No change occurred during 1928 in the condition of the Catholics in Soviet territory. Early in the year the Assistant Bishop of Kiev, Mgr. Skalsky, was sentenced to ten years' imprisonment by the Soviet Military Tribunal on the charge of counter-revolutionary activities, the charge of espionage having been dropped.

The statement that the prelate had conducted anti-Bolshevik activities in connexion with the Polish mission in Moscow was denied by the Vatican, and later in the year the " Osservatore Romano " published a number of articles aimed at proving that the anti-religious attitude of the Soviet Government had in no way diminished, but that hundreds of priests and nuns, Catholic and Orthodox, were still undergoing terrible imprisonment. In spite of the apparently hopeless outlook, the Pontifical Oriental Institute in Rome, under the presidency of Bishop Michel D'Herbigny, S.J., continued its work actively in preparing priests for work among Christians of the Slavonic rite, against the time when religious work was once more freely permitted in Soviet territory, and in this connexion it should be mentioned that during the year Father Abrantovicz was appointed Bishop for Slavonic Catholics living on the borders of China and the Soviet Far Eastern Republic. He was received in audience by the Pope in November, and then proceeded to Harbin, where he will reside.

Spain.

72. Relations between the Holy See and Spain were uneventful. The Cardinal Secretary of State, in more than one conversation with Sir Odo Russell, deplored the attitude of indifference taken up by the Spanish Government in regard to the treatment of Catholics by the Mexican Government, but the Vatican's disappointment on this score was never allowed to appear openly in any way. During the year there was considerable discontent among the Spanish clergy in regard to their economic condition and representations were made by the hierarchy regarding the distress which many of the lower clergy were suffering owing to the extreme smallness of their stipends. Later in the year a promise of alleviation was made; although it appeared that a number of the clergy, tired of waiting, and driven to desperation, had formed an organisation, independent of the bishops, with the object of promoting their claims.

Turkey.

73. The attitude of the Turkish Government to foreign schools and other institutions has been a serious obstacle to Catholic missionary work in Turkish territory, and when it was announced in February that Mgr. Rotta, the Delegate Apostolic, had gone to Angora and had been received by the Foreign Minister, it was freely assumed in the press that he had been charged to treat with the Government regarding the establishment or reopening of Catholic schools, in which, it was added, the French and Italian Embassies had a direct interest. The Cardinal Secretary of State, however, stated that Mgr. Rotta's mission was not so wide in scope; he had gone to secure the Government's permission for the Assumptionists to build a house at Angora, which, when finished, would also accommodate the delegate. There was no question of official relations between Turkey and the Holy See.

74. In the following May the Pope summoned to Rome a synod of the Church of the Armenian Rite in communion with Rome. It met under the presidency of the Patriarch, Mgr. Terzian, who for some years past, owing to Turkish obstruction, the Armenian persecution and the troublesome attitude of certain of his flock, had been resident in Rome, though his nominal headquarters were Constantinople. Only nine Armenian bishops and archbishops were present, as compared with twenty-five at the preceding synod in 1911, the difference being mainly due to the devastating effect of the war and massacres. The two chief results of the synod were to reinstate Mgr. Terzian in full jurisdiction over his Church and to transfer the seat of the patriarchate to Beirut from Constantinople, its original home. Mgr. Rokossian was appointed Armenian Bishop at Constantinople.

United States of America.

75. As a proof that the Holy See in no way desired to interfere in the presidential elections in the United States in favour of the Roman Catholic candidate, Governor Smith, Cardinal Sincero, who was in August visiting certain religious houses in Canada of which he is the protector, and who wished to proceed to the United States subsequently, was ordered to return to Europe direct from Quebec. This was done at the instigation of the Catholic bishops of the United States, and in particular of the Cardinal Archbishop of New York, who represented to the Holy See that the presence of a cardinal in Curia might give rise to the impression that the Vatican was attempting to influence the elections in favour of Governor Smith.

76. There was no doubt that the nomination of Governor Smith, while welcomed by the Vatican as evidence of American tolerance, was regarded as being fraught with embarrassing possibilities. In fact the Cardinal Archbishop of Boston told me in September, before I left the United States, that the Holy See did not wish to see Governor Smith elected because they thought that he was not the right sort of Catholic to be president, and because they felt that if he were elected all the mistakes made by the Administration would be blamed on the Church. In any case the Vatican cultivated an attitude of complete aloofness, feeling no doubt that although the position the Catholic Church holds in America is increasingly powerful, any endeavour to exert that strength along party lines would create a dangerous prejudice and threaten the facilities for religious and educational expansion at present enjoyed.

77. The attitude of reserve and caution taken up by the Vatican before the elections was, if possible, intensified after their result was made known. The religious motives urged against Governor Smith, and the immoderate language frequently used by persons of some standing were discreetly not reported in the "Osservatore Romano," but appreciation was expressed privately in Vatican circles at the testimony of several press correspondents, including those of the "Times" and the "Morning Post," to the fact that before and during the election the Catholic Church in the United States had not employed its organisation in the interest of one-sided party politics.

78. In general the Vatican appears to expect no great change from the new Administration, though it is possible to deduce a certain apprehension lest Mr. Hoover's victory may prove to be the triumph of a narrow and exaggerated nationalism, against which the present Pope has more than once protested as the greatest danger to peace and to the interests of the Church.

III.—THE SACRED COLLEGE AND VATICAN ADMINISTRATION.

79. During the year three cardinals died, namely, Cardinal Tacci, on the 30th June; Cardinal De Lai, on the 24th October and Cardinal Nava, Archbishop of Catania, on the 7th December. In place of Cardinal De Lai, who had been secretary of the Consistorial Congregation, Cardinal Perosi was appointed, having been pro-secretary during his predecessor's illness.

80. On the 8th January the Pope himself consecrated Cardinal Seredi, Primate-designate of Hungary, archbishop. There were no other functions of the kind during the year, which passed without any additions to the ranks of the cardinals. At the close of the year the Sacred College consisted of sixty-four cardinals, of which thirty-four were non-Italians.

81. In regard to Vatican administration, two changes during 1928 may be chronicled. First the Papal Major Domo, Mgr. Sanz de Samper, with whose name rumour, favourable and unfavourable, had been busy for a considerable time, was relieved of his office, and, receiving the title of Major Domo emeritus, left Rome. His important duties were taken over by the Maestro di Camera of His Holiness, Mgr. Signor Cascia Dominioni, who now combines both offices. In the Secretariate of State Mgr. Ciriaci, on his appointment as Papal Nuncio in Prague, was succeeded in the office of Assistant Secretary by Mgr. Ottaviani, former rector of the Bohemian College.

CONFIDENTIAL.

(13728)

HOLY SEE.

Annual Report, 1929.

[C 2470/2470/22]

Mr. Chilton to Mr. A. Henderson.—(Received March 31.)

(No. 69.)   *British Legation to the Holy See,*
Sir,   *Rome, March 27, 1930.*
   I HAVE the honour to transmit herewith my annual report on the Holy
See for the year 1929.

   2. I am indebted to Mr. Randall, first secretary in this Legation, for his
valuable assistance in the compilation of this report.
                        I have, &c.
                        H. G. CHILTON.

Enclosure.

Annual Report on the Holy See for 1929.

CONTENTS.

I.—INTRODUCTION.

THE year 1929 was one of the most important in the recent history of the Holy See. The year of celebration of the Pope's sacerdotal jubilee was marked by the reconciliation between the Holy See and the Italian Dynasty and State, formally at enmity since the Italian troops broke through the Porta Pia on the 20th September, 1870, and the Pope enclosed himself within the Vatican, imposing on himself and his successors a rigorous imprisonment so long as the Pope's claims to independence were not recognised. If it were possible to take a long view, it might be said that the ending of this long-drawn-out quarrel between the Pope and the Italian State marked the beginning of a new era in the history of the Papacy, as providing for a wider and more striking internationalisation of the central government of the Church. But even in its immediate effects and the dramatic manner of its conclusion, the Lateran Pact was of prime importance, first to Italy, then to the world at large. The scope and nature and immediate outcome of the Lateran Treaty and Concordat will be dealt with in detail in a later chapter; here it is only necessary to remark that it gave an exceptional solemnity and importance to the Pope's Jubilee, which in any event would have been celebrated with many pilgrimages and religious functions.

2. Actually the Pope opened the year of his jubilee, the fiftieth anniversary of his ordination to the priesthood, on the 21st December, 1928. In the New Year, the pilgrimages began, and increased in numbers in the spring, particularly after the signature of the Lateran agreements. Almost all nations were represented, the French, Spanish, Belgian and German pilgrimages being particularly numerous and frequent, while a considerable number of influential American Catholics, accompanied by American cardinals or bishops, came to Rome. Later, when the actual date of the jubilee approached, the congratulations of sovereigns, heads of States and Governments became more frequent, and in most instances these were accompanied by gifts of varying value and significance. On the 19th December the Pope received the whole Diplomatic Corps accredited to the Holy See in a special collective audience, and received their collective felicitations on the auspicious year which was then concluding. In this, as in many other previous similar receptions in the course of the year, the Pope made a reply that was much more than a mere perfunctory discourse, and it seemed to all close observers that the crowded and important events of the year, and the especially heavy responsibility which fell to the Pontiff in the conclusion of the Lateran Treaty, must have meant a serious strain on His Holiness's strength. Yet at the end of the year the Pope appeared almost as vigorous and energetic as at the beginning, giving the impression of complete command of the vast and intricate and lofty task to which he had been called.

3. Many of the numerous Papal pronouncements will be mentioned later in this report. Here a list of the more solemn utterances of general interest or importance will be given.

Apostolic Constitution, " Divini Cultus," of the 6th February. This was a pronouncement on the necessity for more general use, throughout the Church, of the Gregorian form of liturgical music.

Letter appointing the Cardinal Secretary of State Papal Legate at the celebration of the fourteen hundredth anniversary of the foundation of the Monastery of Montecassino by St. Benedict.

Allocution, delivered at the Consistory of the 16th December. This dealt briefly with the Lateran Treaties, and mentioned with satisfaction the agreements with Portugal, Roumania and Prussia.

Encyclical, " Mens nostra," of the 20th December, which was of purely religious interest, advocating more frequent religious retreats.

Encyclical, " Quinquagesimo ante anno," the 23rd December. This was a long review of the principal events of the year, with particular reference to the various concordats, the religious celebrations at Montecassino, in Czechoslovakia, in Sweden (of St. Ansgar), the beatification of the English and Scots martyrs, and the celebration in Great Britain and Ireland of the centenary of Catholic Emancipation—a celebration which, the Pope said, "had been carried through not for the purpose of recalling past injustice, but rather in order to study how to use the liberty so recovered . . . . for the more faithful observance of the law of Christ, or the public good, naturally with due submission to the civil power."

Encyclical, "Rappresentanti in terra," of the 31st December. This document, which was issued in Italian, English and other modern languages, and not in Latin, dealt with the Catholic principles of education, defining the limits of the prerogatives of the Church and State respectively in this sphere, and insisting on the importance of family life in the training of children and young people. There were suggestions that this long, detailed and precise summary of the views of the Church had been issued with a particular reference to the education controversy in Italy, but it was subsequently made clear, particularly when all the other versions in different languages were officially published by the Vatican, that the Pope was addressing the whole Church, and laying down principles of general application.

4. There were various beatification ceremonies in Rome in the course of the year, all attended, as usual, by vast crowds. In Italy the beatification, which gave rise to the greatest popular enthusiasm, was that of the Piedmontese priest, Don Bosco, founder of the new world-wide Salesian order, who, as both a devout Catholic and a fervent Italian patriot, had some significance in the history of Italy. The honour done to his memory shortly after the Lateran agreement had a peculiar interest. Three other Italians and one French candidate were also beatified, and at the close of the year 136 English, out of a possible total of about 250, with 1 Scots Jesuit of the 16th century, were given the title of the " Blessed."

5. The Pope granted an exceptionally large number of audiences during the year. Among the more noteworthy visitors were the King of Sweden, in February; the Dayang Muda of Sarawak, in May; Sir Eric Drummond, Secretary-General of the League of Nations, in October; their Majesties the King and Queen of Italy, on the 5th December; in July, on the introduction of the Legation, a party of Catholic sailors from H.M.S. " Resolution " were received by the Pope, also a party of teachers from Canada. On the 31st December a large party of teachers from the various Dominions were presented to His Holiness by Mr. Thynne.

6. In the sphere of general administration of the Church we may note the continued close attention given by the Pope to foreign missions, signified by new mission-foundations in China, Africa, Japan, Dutch East Indies and India. On the 24th June, by a " motu proprio " the Pope co-ordinated the work of all the Pontifical Mission organisations. Not less was the interest which continued to be shown by the Holy See in the Eastern Churches. On the 15th August the Constitution of the Pontifical Russian Seminary was issued, laying down rules for the admission of Russians who wished to be received into the Roman Communion, with retention of their rite. Towards the end of the year it was announced that the Pope had appointed a commission to study the codification of the Canon Law of the Eastern Church, and had entrusted the supervision of this task to Cardinal Gasparri, Secretary of State, who had been responsible for the codification of the Canon Law of the Western Church. This announcement was generally held to be the prelude to the definite news of Cardinal Gasparri's retirement from the office of Secretary of State.

II.—RELATIONS WITH FOREIGN STATES.

7. All the countries in diplomatic relations with the Holy See in 1928, to the number of twenty-eight—ten Embassies and eighteen Legations—maintained those relations during 1929. Three additions were made in the course of the year, namely, Panamá, whose Minister, M. Obarrio, presented his credentials to the Pope on the 11th June, Italy, whose Ambassador, Conte De Vecchi, presented his letters on the 25th June; Irish Free State, whose Minister, Mr. Charles Bewley, presented his letters on the 27th June.

8. In general the relations of the Holy See to foreign States were satisfactory. The action of the Vatican in regard to Malta was the cause of a serious difference of opinion with His Majesty's Government, and ecclesiastical affairs in Lithuania were not satisfactory, while the long-drawn-out negotiations regarding a definitive arrangement with Czechoslovakia had not reached a conclusion by the close of the year. Conditions in Yugoslavia were also not

entirely satisfactory from the point of view of the Holy See. Mexican religious affairs were still in a most unsatisfactory state early in the year, but later a decided improvement took place. Soviet Russia continued to be a source of grief and concern to the Holy See throughout the year. Against this must be set the marked improvement in relations with France, the ratification of the concordat with Roumania, the conclusion of the agreement with the Prussian Government and the continued improvement of relations with Portugal of which the ratification of the agreement in regard to the diocese of Portuguese jurisdiction in India was a sign. Details of all these are given below.

(a.) *British Empire and Mandated Territories.*

United Kingdom and Colonies.

9. With the important exception of the Vatican's attitude over Malta, which is dealt with in a separate chapter below, it may be said that British relations with the Holy See were tranquil. It is true that, when appealed to in connexion with the law for the stabilising of the date of Easter, the Vatican did not show any sign of wishing to comply with the wishes of His Majesty's Government, but in this respect it was merely confirming a view which it had more than once expressed to the League of Nations when that body was dealing with the subject. Otherwise there were a number of signs of goodwill. His Majesty's Minister received instructions, on the signing of the Lateran agreements, to convey the congratulations of His Majesty's Government, and the latter quickly followed up the recognition of the sovereignty of the Holy See by an invitation to the Secretariate of State to nominate a delegate to the Congress of the International Postal Union, which was then sitting in London. The Holy See appointed Professor Hewins, and conferred on him full powers to sign the various international agreements which were the outcome of the Congress. This step by His Majesty's Government was warmly appreciated at the Vatican.

10. Towards the end of the year the Papal visitor to Africa, the Right Reverend Mgr. Hinsley, Rector of the English College in Rome, returned from a two years' tour of practically the whole of British territory in Africa, where he had inspected the Catholic mission schools with a view to seeing how they could best co-operate with the different British colonial authorities in carrying out a programme of native education. On reaching Rome his Lordship expressed his warmest appreciation of the sympathy and assistance he had received from the various British authorities, and the Holy See officially expressed their gratitude to His Majesty's Government on the same account. At the end of the year the Vatican informed His Majesty's Legation that Mgr. Hinsley had been appointed to visit the Sudan, the only important part of Africa he had left untouched, and the request for similar facilities was acceded to by His Majesty's Government.

11. On the occasion of the celebration of the Pope's sacerdotal jubilee, His Majesty's Minister was commanded to present a letter of congratulation from His Majesty the King. This was received with much gratification, and was subsequently printed in the " Osservatore Romano " at the head of a large number of messages from the heads of States.

12. In December a large body of distinguished English Catholics, at their head Lord Fitzalan of Derwent, visited Rome for the purpose of conveying their congratulations to the Pope on the happy settlement of the Roman question, and of assisting at the beatification of a considerable number of English Roman Catholics who had died for their faith in the 16th and 17th centuries. This event, following on the celebration of the centenary of Catholic Emancipation, attracted much attention from all over the English-speaking world.

Canada.

13. The " Osservatore Romano " published some figures in January showing the increase in French-speaking Canadian missionaries, whose numbers amounted to 1,200. Canadian Catholic missions despatched missionaries during 1929 to India, Indo-China, China and Japan. France's quota of Catholic missionaries shows signs of falling off; French-speaking Canada is taking her place.

14. The Cardinal Archbishop of Quebec paid a visit to Rome in the spring of 1929, and a number of other Canadian bishops followed in the summer and autumn, for the purpose of making the usual *ad limina* visit to His Holiness.

Irish Free State.

15. On the 25th March the Irish Free State Minister for Foreign Affairs mentioned to the Secretary of State for Dominion Affairs the probability than in the near future the Government of the Irish Free State might wish to raise the question of appointing a Minister to the Holy See, and possibly also of receiving a Papal Nuncio at Dublin.

16. Mr. McGilligan expected to visit Rome to discuss the question. He did, in fact, arrive in Rome in April preceded by Mr. Walshe, the Secretary of the Department of External Affairs of the Irish Free State.

17. I was instructed, previous to their arrival, to sound the Vatican as to whether they would be prepared to receive a Minister from the Irish Free State, pointing out that His Majesty's Government in the United Kingdom were favourable to such an appointment.

18. On the arrival of Messrs. McGilligan and Walshe I took them to see Cardinal Gasparri, who, after several prolonged conversations, stated that the Pope was agreeable to the establishment of diplomatic relations between the Irish Free State and the Holy See, and it was eventually agreed that an Irish Free State Minister should be appointed as soon as possible, and that a Nuncio would be appointed to Dublin. A communiqué was issued in the Dublin and Vatican papers announcing this arrangement.

19. A Minister from the Irish Free State was duly appointed in the person of Mr. Charles Henry Bewley, who presented his letters to the Pope on the 27th June.

20. It was not until the 28th November that the appointment as Nuncio Apostolic to the Irish Free State was announced of Mgr. Paschal Robinson, O.F.M., titular Archbishop of Tiana. Mgr. Robinson, though born in Dublin and speaking with an Irish accent, has lived a great many years out of Ireland, particularly in the United States of America, where he was Professor of Mediæval History in the Catholic University of Washington, and in Palestine where he was Visitor Apostolic between 1925 and 1928. In 1929 he was appointed Apostolic Delegate to Malta, where he remained for about three months.

21. On the arrival of a Minister in Rome it is customary for the rectors of the various colleges interested to call first upon the Minister. For instance, when I arrived the rectors of the English, Scotch, Canadian and Beda Colleges called upon me, as well as certain priests from certain Irish institutions, such as the Augustinians and Irish Dominicans, but the rector of the Irish College did not call; nor had he called upon my predecessors. The new Irish Free State Minister, knowing full well that this ecclesiastic would not call upon him, called first at the Irish College, and was politely received; the visit was returned.

22. Early in December the Archbishop of Armagh, Mgr. MacRory, was created a cardinal and proceeded to Rome to receive his hat. According to custom I called upon his Eminence at the Irish College, where he was receiving, and was courteously received by the rector, who introduced me to the cardinal, who was most cordial and held me in conversation for some fifteen minutes.

Malta.

23. The relations between Malta and the Holy See, already somewhat strained, took a turn for the worse in 1929.

B 3

24. As I stated in my annual report for 1928 (paragraph 33) the Governor of Malta had refused Lord Strickland's request to deport Father Carta, the Franciscan sent by the Vatican to restore order among the Franciscans in Malta, on the grounds that there was not sufficient evidence that he was taking part in political propaganda against the Government. So Father Carta remained in Malta. In the summer it was reported that he had been offered a high appointment at Assisi. In the meantime the Government brought an action against him for sending letters privately by hand to Rome and not through the ordinary post. Although the Government were anxious for Father Carta to leave Malta, he could not do so with an action pending against him, and thus the Government defeated its own ends. The action was eventually dropped, but Father Carta was still in Malta at the end of the year.

25. Father Carta had, in the interests of discipline, ordered Father Micallef to leave Malta. Father Micallef, backed by Lord Strickland, had refused. The Vatican point of view was that the removal of Father Micallef was justified by the scandal he was causing by the excesses of his private life, and in the interests of the good name of the Franciscan Order. In any case, Micallef eventually did come to Rome at Lord Strickland's expense. He was well treated by his Order and by the Congregation of Religious. He was offered a post outside of Malta, and he was to be retained in the Order. He refused to go elsewhere than Malta, and only desired to return there as a secular priest. This, of course, could not be tolerated by the General of his Order.

26. In January 1929 the idea of an investigation of the Carta and Micallef affair by an Apostolic Visitor was first suggested by the Governor of Malta. The Vatican were sounded privately and expressed their disinclination to send a Visitor at that time, not being desirous of appearing to intervene in Maltese politics. They would prefer to wait for a calmer atmosphere before taking such a step, and held that the best solution lay in allowing the ordinary rules and regulations of the Franciscan Order to take their usual course.

27. However, shortly afterwards, I was instructed to inform the Cardinal Secretary of State that whilst His Majesty's Government had no wish to intervene in the internal disciplinary affairs of monastic orders, they desired to make their own the carefully considered request of the Governor of Malta that an Apostolic Visitor should be sent to investigate the whole question of the relations of the ecclesiastical authorities in Malta to the political Government having regard to the importance of avoiding friction in the future as a consequence of the intervention of priests in politics.

28. As a result of my representations the Vatican agreed to send not a Visitor Apostolic but a Delegate Apostolic, and for this purpose they selected Mgr. Paschal Robinson, late Visitor Apostolic in Palestine. This appointment met with the cordial approval of His Majesty's Government and the gratification of the Maltese Government. The Government offered Mgr. Robinson accommodation, and also suggested application to the Admiralty for a warship to convey him to Malta. Both these offers were politely refused on the ground that Mgr. Robinson was, as the direct envoy of the Pope, not committed to any party, either British or Italian, either to Lord Strickland or the Opposition. He would therefore prefer to travel privately to Malta and while there to stay at the house of the Blue Sisters, which would be neutral territory. Mgr. Robinson left for Malta on the 1st April.

29. Lord Strickland, at the end of 1928, addressed a letter to Sir Austen Chamberlain making certain suggestions as to the means of communication between the Government of Malta and the Vatican, to the effect that His Majesty's representative to the Holy See should be able to use his discretion, with reference to His Majesty's Government, as to what communication he would and would not forward from the Government of Malta to the Holy See. The Foreign Office pointed out that His Majesty's Legation were not prepared to accept full responsibility. The Vatican would certainly refuse (as they continually did) to take any action unless the notes were presented as coming with the authority of His Majesty's Government.

30. On the 3rd February I received a note from the Cardinal Secretary of State complaining that three Anglican bishops had held a solemn course of " propaganda lectures " in the throne room of the Governor's Palace, that Lord Strickland had suspended the sitting of Parliament for a day in order that he

and his colleagues might " do homage " to the illustrious guests, adding to the prestige of the speakers by their presence. The note pointed out that the Palace was for many years the seat of the Grand Master of the Order of Malta, " so gloriously connected with the Catholic religion," and that the meetings were offensive to the convictions and sentiments of the large majority of Maltese, who fervently profess the Catholic religion, since they constituted a solemn and official favouring of the Anglican creed.

31. The note concluded with an expression of confidence that His Majesty's Government would share in the displeasure of the Vatican at what had occurred, and would effectively show their disapproval.

32. His Majesty's Government naturally took serious exception to this note for the following reasons :—
   (1) Because it practically amounted to a demand that the Government of Malta should not extend to other religious communities official civilities which would, in similar circumstances, be extended to the Roman Catholic community.
   (2) Because the Vatican seemed to imply that the Roman Church had some special rights with regard to the Palace at Valetta.
   (3) Because the note definitely asked that His Majesty's Government should reprimand Lord Strickland for having attended the meeting at the Palace, and for having suspended the sitting of Parliament on that particular day.

33. The alternative courses which presented themselves to Sir Austen Chamberlain were either to ignore the note altogether unless the Vatican returned to the matter, or to instruct me to inform Cardinal Gasparri that the subject was not one which His Majesty's Government were prepared to discuss with the Vatican, or lastly to return the note to the Vatican. It was decided that the second course was the most expedient, and I was therefore instructed to inform the cardinal verbally that His Majesty's Government were not prepared to discuss these subjects with the Vatican. In making this communication to his Eminence, I was to impress upon him that although as an act of courtesy I had been instructed to use this informal method, it was to be clearly understood that if occasion arose His Majesty's Principal Secretary of State would be prepared to state the view of His Majesty's Government in this matter both officially and publicly.

34. Up to the end of the year nothing further was mentioned with regard to this matter.

35. On the 4th July I received a despatch from the Foreign Office stating that Lord Strickland had called there and had discussed a proposal made by the Apostolic Delegate to Malta that a series of " heads of agreement," the result of discussions between the Maltese Government and Mgr. Robinson regarding the relations between the ecclesiastical and civil authorities in Malta, should be embodied in a concordat between His Majesty's Government in Great Britain and Northern Ireland and the Holy See.

36. Lord Strickland proposed to visit Rome on his way back to Malta, and His Majesty's Government had no desire in any way to restrain him from discussing the matter informally with the Papal authorities provided it was made quite clear that such discussion was entirely provisional and in no way committed His Majesty's Government either as regards the substance of the " heads of agreement " or as regards the form in which they were eventually to be cast.

37. I was instructed to make this attitude clear both to Lord Strickland and to the Holy See, and to accord Lord Strickland all the facilities that I properly could for his discussions in Rome.

38. On the same day that I received the above-mentioned despatch from the Foreign Office I also received from the Cardinal Secretary of State a note enclosing a copy of a letter addressed by him to the Bishops of Malta and Gozo instructing them publicly to inform the Maltese people that Lord Strickland was not *persona grata* to the Holy See, as he pretended to be, and that the Holy See entirely supported the action of the Ordinaries of Malta and of Gozo in their disapproval of the activities of Lord Strickland, which were not in

accordance with the Catholic Church and the ecclesiastical authority of the island.

39.   The note also enclosed copy of a pro-memoriâ sent to the Holy See by eye-witnesses of the activities of Lord Strickland in Malta, and pretending that he had done considerable harm to the prestige and popularity of Great Britain in that island.

40.   The covering note suggested that His Majesty's Government would no doubt adopt such measures as they might consider necessary to prevent such subversive activities or at least divorce their responsibility from that of Lord Strickland.

41.   Lord Strickland arrived in Rome on the 5th July and requested an audience of Cardinal Gasparri.   Not only was this refused, but the cardinal would not permit any of his subordinates to see Lord Strickland.   I was obliged to tell the latter that he was *persona non grata* to the Holy See, and, after obtaining the concurrence of the Cardinal Secretary of State, I showed him the note which I had just received and its enclosures.   He immediately drafted a statement in defence against these accusations which he requested me to communicate.   I informed him I could not do so without the consent of His Majesty's Government, and he replied that he left it entirely to my discretion as to how and when the statement should be communicated to the Vatican.   As His Majesty's Government instructed me not to send to the Vatican any communication from Lord Strickland, the latter's statement still reposes in the archives of this Legation.

42.   I called upon the Cardinal Secretary of State and remonstrated with him for refusing to see Lord Strickland, who was a Prime Minister of one of the possessions of the British Empire, pointing out that the accusations were vague and anonymous.   But to no avail.

43.   His Majesty's Government naturally took a very serious view of this gross interference in the internal affairs of a British Colony.   Four offences had been committed by the Vatican :—

(1) The declaration by the Vatican that Lord Strickland, in his official capacity as an executive Minister of the Crown, was, in spite of the friendly diplomatic relations existing between the Vatican and the British Empire, a *persona non grata*.

(2) The communication of a highly improper note denouncing the Maltese Government and calling upon His Majesty's Government to dissociate themselves from Lord Strickland.

(3) The issue of a manifesto to the hierarchy of Malta denouncing the Maltese Government and calling upon the clergy to resist them.

(4) The breaking off, by the above action, of the negotiations initiated at the request of His Majesty's Government, and since carried on in Malta with conspicious success, for the settlement of the religious difficulties in Malta, and this without warning or explanation.

44.   I was instructed to deliver a memorandum to the Cardinal Secretary of State laying stress upon these points, and expressing surprise that the Holy See, before issuing its instructions of the 30th June to the Maltese hierarchy, and before requesting His Majesty's Government to condemn the policy of the Maltese Ministry, should not have availed themselves of the negotiations already initiated by Mgr. Robinson in order to explore with His Majesty's Government the possibility of a settlement of the difficulties existing between Church and State in Malta.   Instead of this the Vatican preferred to prejudge by its action the very questions which the Apostolic Delegate had, at the request of His Majesty's Government, been sent to Malta to investigate.

45.   While expressing themselves in this unequivocal language, His Majesty's Government desired at the same time to add an appeal to their remonstrance.   They sincerely hoped that nothing should mar their satisfaction at the conclusion of the Lateran agreements.   For this reason they would earnestly appeal to the Holy See to observe in relation to His Majesty's Government that moderation, consideration and restraint, which His Majesty's Government expected and were entitled to expect, to find in the policy of the Holy See wherever its activities were exercised.

46. I was instructed to proceed to England as soon as possible after delivering the memorandum to the Cardinal Secretary of State. To this note, which was firm but full of moderation and forbearance, the Vatican replied immediately in a memorandum giving a recital of the events which had led up to the present situation in Malta, expressing surprise that Lord Strickland should have published Cardinal Gasparri's note to me of the 2nd July without reference to His Majesty's Legation or to the Vatican, pointing out that before writing the letter to the bishops the Vatican had ascertained that Lord Strickland in no way represented the British Government in Malta, but was simply the head of a Maltese party, that the Holy See had no intention of interfering in the domestic politics of a British Colony, and still less of inciting the bishops to an illegal resistance to the constituted authority, but merely to an attitude of " firm and justified watchfulness," explaining the reasons for the " postponement " of Lord Strickland's audience of the Pope in November 1928, and declaring that the Holy See had at no time thought of showing a lack of the proper loyalty and courtesy towards His Majesty's Government. The memorandum also rejected with vigour the "false and malicious insinuation" made by Lord Strickland that the Holy See had acted in favour of an Italian party in the island. In writing the letter to the bishops it had had in mind nothing but the religious interests of catholicism, which were threatened by Lord Strickland's attitude.

47. His Majesty's Government on the 28th September instructed His Majesty's Chargé d'Affaires to deliver another statement to the Cardinal Secretary of State in reply to the above. In this statement His Majesty's Government regretted that the Holy See had in their last memorandum made no proposals for solving the present unsatisfactory situation, and suggested that the only way to do so was by initiating negotiations through the diplomatic channel. With regard to the accusations against Lord Strickland, His Majesty's Government must refuse to take into consideration allegations which had never been tested either by information furnished to His Majesty's Government or by proceedings in the Maltese courts. In reply to the suggestion by His Majesty's Government that negotiations should be initiated through the diplomatic channel, the Vatican agreed with His Majesty's Government in initiating negotiations through the diplomatic channel " with the object of putting an end to so painful a situation."

48. The pro-memoriâ from the Vatican went on to state, however, that at the outset of the discussions in question it would be as well to remember that the principal, if not the sole, cause of the disturbed religious conditions in Malta had been the anti-clerical attitude of Lord Strickland since he first arrived in Malta.

49. On receipt of this reply, in which the Vatican agreed to negotiate through the diplomatic channel, I was instructed to return to Rome, and on the 20th December I handed to Cardinal Gasparri a note calling the attention of the Vatican to my note of the 1st March, and emphasising the view of His Majesty's Government that the primary cause of the trouble was the political activity of the Maltese clergy and not the anti-clerical attitude of Lord Strickland.

50. It was true that in the same communication the fact was recognised that the forthcoming negotiations would afford an opportunity " to examine and dispose of the accusations made by the Holy See against the Maltese Administration last summer."

51. I was at the same time instructed to enquire of the Cardinal Secretary of State whether it was the intention of the Vatican to furnish His Majesty's Government with a copy of the report drawn up by Mgr. Robinson on his return from Malta. Cardinal Gasparri promised to communicate a copy to me, but this promise was never kept, since only that portion of it which dealt with the accusations against Lord Strickland was subsequently communicated to me.

52. The cardinal stated that he would be pleased to start conversations with me shortly, but begged that they might be postponed until the New Year.

Iraq.

53. The Latin Patriarch of Bagdad, Mgr. Berré, died in April. He had a long and deep knowledge of the country and its people, and a message

of sympathy from the High Commissioner was conveyed to the Vatican by the Legation. Later in the year he was succeeded by the French priest, Mgr. Drapier, who also became Delegate Apostolic. Before announcing the appointment the Holy See, through His Majesty's Legation, conveyed the knowledge of the proposed nomination of Mgr. Drapier to His Majesty's Government, and received the reply that His Majesty's Government had no objection to offer to the appointment.

54. In legislation under consideration by the Government of Iraq the question of the personal status of the Christian communities will be settled, and the Vatican has an interest in this so far as those communities in relation with the Holy See are concerned. This aspect of the matter was brought to the attention of His Majesty's Government and formed the subject of discussion between the Government and the Delegate Apostolic.

55. In the course of the summer the Chaldean Patriarch, Mgr. Emmanuel Thomas, who resides in Mosul, visited Rome in order to congratulate the Pope on his jubilee. Shortly after his arrival he visited His Majesty's Legation and spoke in terms of the warmest praise and gratitude for the assistance the British Government and people had given his nation.

56. The Iraq Minister of Finance, Josuf Chanina, who is a Catholic, visited Rome in August, and was received in special audience by the Pope. In an interview given to the press he emphasised the goodwill of his Government towards Christian communities.

Palestine.

57. In February the Holy See proposed to His Majesty's Government that the jurisdiction of Mgr. Valerio Valeri, Delegate Apostolic in Egypt, should be extended to cover Palestine, Transjordania and Cyprus. It was understood that the Vatican, in suggesting this change, had in mind the desirability of having, as supreme representative in Palestine, someone more tractable than the Latin Patriarch of Jerusalem, Mgr. Barlassina, who, although respected for his purely pastoral work, has often made difficulties for His Majesty's Government and the Holy See, in politico-religious matters. His Majesty's Government replied that they had no objection to raise to the proposed appointment, which was thereupon announced. It was anticipated that the new Delegate Apostolic would reside for a considerable part of the year at Jerusalem, where the Vatican had acquired a residence for him. It may be added that Mgr. Valeri, who had been auditor of the Papal Nunciature in Paris, speaks English well, and has always shown a friendly disposition to British institutions.

58. In March the appointment was announced of Mgr. Francis Fellinger to be Bishop-Auxiliary to the Latin Patriarch of Jerusalem, in succession to Bishop Godric Kean, who had resigned. Mgr. Fellinger, an Austrian by birth, had been in Palestine since 1913, and Vicar-General to the Patriarch since 1916.

59. For some considerable time past the proposed educational ordinance and regulations for Palestine had been under discussion, and, in their original form, had found objections from the Latin Patriarch, also from the French and Italian consuls in Jerusalem, who feared that the regulations proposed for the due inspection of schools by the Palestine Government would lead to excessive interference. In order to allay these fears the Government decided on certain amendments, and in April this Legation received instructions to explain these in detail to the Holy See with a view to showing that the power of inspection of schools maintained by religious authorities—one of the chief sources of the Patriarch's opposition—was to be restricted to what was absolutely necessary for the maintenance of good government in Palestine. No fresh developments in the matter were to be chronicled by the end of the year.

60. There was a curious and annoying incident in May. The " Daily Telegraph " ecclesiastical correspondent announced, with every appearance of authority, that the Archbishop of Canterbury, who was then touring the Mediterranean as the guest of Mr. Pierpont Morgan, would not carry out his project of visiting Jerusalem as representations had been made by the Holy See that his Grace's visit would be untimely. This statement was repeated by the " Daily Telegraph " in a subsequent issue with added telegraphic comment, alleged to have been obtained from Vatican circles. These rumours, in view of the

great assurance with which they were printed in London, were largely reproduced in the French and Italian press, and this Legation brought the matter to the attention of the Secretariat of State, which absolutely denied that the Holy See had taken any action of the kind described. The Apostolic Delegate, by a mistake, had reported that the archbishop had paid a short incognito visit to Jerusalem, but this was rectified, and it was made clear that no protest against the Archbishop's visit had been made by the Holy See or any responsible authority. His Grace had merely had to postpone his visit owing to Mr. Pierpont Morgan's hurried recall to Paris. With a public statement to this effect the incident ended, an example of the international confusion which a newspaper *canard* can produce.

61. When the conflict between the Jews and Arabs in Palestine reached a serious point in the summer the " Osservatore Romano " published an article strongly condemning the attacks made on the Jews, but stating that, although this could be no excuse for the attacks, it was the politics of Zionism and not the religion of Israel which lay at the root of the trouble. The Italian Catholic Union for the Holy Places took advantage of the occasion to pass a resolution calling for a definite settlement in Palestine, but this and other similar manifestations in the Italian press were disclaimed by the Vatican, which showed no sign of wishing to raise any question regarding the Christian Holy Places.

(b.) *Other Countries.*

Abyssinia.

62. Mgr. Marchetti-Selvaggiani, Secretary of the Congregation of Propaganda, left Rome in November as special envoy from the Holy See to return the visit paid to the Pope by Ras Taffari in 1924 and to bring gifts and a message from His Holiness.

63. His Majesty's Minister at Addis Ababa reported that the mission did not meet with any great enthusiasm, and the Abuna found it convenient to be absent from the capital during the visit of the mission.

64. Although it was affirmed that the mission had no political significance it appears that an attempt was made to obtain from the King Regent an assurance that freedom of action and protection would be accorded to Catholic missions in Abyssinia. Sir S. Barton stated that on this point the mission had to be content with polite expressions of goodwill, since, although the King Regent himself was favourably disposed towards mission work in the interests of progress, the Church of Abyssinia was averse to any proselytising by other churches.

65. The Vatican newspaper reported, on the return of the mission, that the reception accorded to the Envoy was entirely worthy of his work and mission.

Bolivia.

66. On the 7th March the new Papal Nuncio to Bolivia, Mgr. Carlo Chiarlo, who had been consecrated titular Archbishop of Amido in Rome in the previous December, presented his credentials to the President of the Republic. In his speech the Nuncio referred to the pacific interests of the Pope as shown during the year before in the dispute between Bolivia and Paraguay.

Chile.

67. His Majesty's Chargé d'Affaires at Santiago reported in July that the press had announced the opening of negotiations between the Chilean Government and the Holy See with a view to the conclusion of a concordat. It appears that the Chilean Government were desirous of securing recognition of the principle that the Church in Chile is a private institution. This principle was unlikely to be accepted by the Vatican. The Chilean Government were, however, anxious to see the relations between the Papacy and Chile placed upon a regular footing and having ascertained that the conclusion of an agreement would be welcomed in Rome a draft had been prepared and is, I believe, still under consideration.

68. The Chilean Ambassador to the Holy See left Rome in June, having given up his house. He has not yet returned, but it is understood that he will come back to Rome shortly for a few months before retiring altogether.

69. A Chilean pilgrimage visited Rome in December.

China.

70. The Holy See continued its policy of transferring mission work in China more and more to the native Catholic clergy, while two more Chinese Catholic bishoprics were created in December. The working out of this policy was followed attentively and critically by the French Embassy, which felt that the Vatican was going too fast and still has regrets for the vanished protectorate.

71. To illustrate the unremitting attention devoted to China by the Holy See, it is worth noting that the Pope in August addressed a letter to Father Stehle, the American Benedictine of the Abbey of St. Vincent in Pennsylvania, who acts as chancellor of the Catholic University in Peking, praising the work of the university and urging that more should be done to make it an illustrious seat of learning.

72. It was announced in the press in February that a Chinese Minister was shortly to be appointed to the Holy See, and a name actually appeared in certain Roman papers. The Vatican Secretariat of State denied this, however, and nothing more was heard of the matter.

Colombia.

73. The Colombian Ambassador to the Holy See, Señor Concha, died in Rome on the 8th December. As the representative of a country in which the Church plays an important part in politics and which is bound by close ties to the Holy See, he was highly esteemed by the Vatican.

Czechoslovakia.

74. On the occasion of the celebrations in honour of St. Wenceslas in Czechoslovakia, the Pope addressed a special letter to the bishops and laity of that country. The celebrations were originally planned as a counter-demonstration of the Roman Catholic elements in the country to the Hus demonstrations. Cardinal Bourne attended on behalf of English Catholics.

75. The *modus vivendi* concluded between the Czechoslovak Government and the Holy See in January 1928 seems to have engendered better relations between them. The Czechoslavak Minister to the Holy See informed me it is working satisfactorily.

76. A new Bohemian seminary in Rome was inaugurated in April to take the place of the old Bohemian college, which was inadequate for the number of students. The Archbishop of Prague performed the ceremony.

77. On the occasion of the Pope's sacerdotal jubilee the Czechoslovak Government presented His Holiness with a vase of Bohemian crystal.

Denmark.

78. In July the Cardinal-Prefect of the Congregation of Propaganda, Cardinal Van Rossum, visited Iceland and inaugurated a vicariate, to replace the prefecture which had until then existed. The Vicar-Apostolic, Mgr. Meulenberg, was consecrated a bishop, as is customary with Vicars-Apostolic, and the local Catholic church was raised to cathedral status. In view of the small number of Catholics in Iceland, not more than 250, there was some surprise at the creation of a Catholic bishopric, but it was pointed out that during the fishing season the number of Catholics increases considerably, and, moreover, an independent bishopric had not, in fact, been set up, but only a missionary vicariate, dependent on propaganda. The ceremonies connected with the event were carried through in an impressive manner, and were attended not only by the local political authorities, but also by the Lutheran clergy.

79. In Denmark itself Catholic propaganda continued to make a certain progress against the overwhelming numerical superiority of the Lutheran State Church. The latest statistics showed 22,137 Catholics in the country out of a total population of about 3½ millions.

Egypt.

80. His Majesty's High Commissioner in Egypt stated that it was reported that the Apostolic Delegate was to be raised to the rank of Nuncio. King Fuad disclaimed any intention of seeking any change in the status of the Papal representative. The Vatican also denied any idea of raising the rank of the Apostolic Delegate. Mgr. Valeri, the Apostolic Delegate, was subsequently appointed in the same capacity to Palestine, Transjordania and Cyprus as well as Egypt. The Egyptian Government continued to show goodwill towards the Catholic missions, an example being a particularly favourable cession of land for the new cathedral of Port Said.

France.

81. The official French attitude to the Lateran agreements was favourable, and the French Government was among the first to offer its congratulations to the Pope on the settlement of the Roman question. But in important circles in France there was undoubtedly serious misgiving and resentment—misgiving because it was felt that the settlement would increase Italian prestige at France's expense, resentment because in a matter in which France by historical tradition had so strong an interest, there had not been the slightest attempt by the Holy See at consulting France, not even to the extent of taking the French Catholic hierarchy into its confidence. Both the misgiving and the resentment, mingled with other criticisms of the Lateran Treaty, found their way into certain sections of the French press, and decided answers were given by the Vatican, so that eventually, especially when serious differences of view developed between the Pope and the Italian Prime Minister, it came to be realised that the Church had not allied itself with fascism, nor was it likely to underestimate the services it could receive from France. At the end of the year it could be said that loyal French Catholic opinion was favourable, and the remainder resigned to the inevitable with a determination to watch more closely than ever French interests as affected by the world-wide activities of the Vatican.

82. It was the pressing necessity of safeguarding French interests abroad that was emphasised from the Government side in the various parliamentary discussions at the beginning of the year on the proposal to readmit certain French missionary congregations, whose services to French cultural prestige abroad was gravely menaced by the necessity of recruiting and training their members outside of France. Against bitter anti-clerical opposition the proposals strongly supported by M. Briand were eventually carried in March, and the Minister of the Interior, M. Tardieu, excited much criticism from a section of the left by announcing that discussions had been taking place with the Vatican regarding the settlement of certain outstanding points. This was held, in some quarters, to indicate that negotiations for a new Concordat were being pursued, but there was no sign of these at the end of the year, and it seemed most improbable that any comprehensive treaty obligations would be entered into. Nevertheless, French relations with the Holy See had become decidedly cordial, and, apart from the frequent public expressions of friendship by the French Ambassador to the Holy See—which may have been less due to official instructions than to an exuberant temperament—two examples may be given. The first was the celebration of St. Joan of Arc at Orleans—the fifth centenary of that city's liberation—to which Cardinal Lépicier went as Papal Legate. The President of the French Republic, with various Cabinet Ministers, attended the official celebrations, and there were exchanges of messages of the most marked cordiality. The second was the friendly exchange of views which took place regarding the successor to Cardinal Dubois, Archbishop of Paris, whose funeral, incidentally like the deeply religious celebration of Marshal Foch's obsequies, showed the growth of a more favourable attitude to the Church. The Pope's choice for the Archbishopric of Paris fell on the Sulpician priest, Mgr. Verdier, with the full and cordial assent of the French Government, and it seemed as if, under his archipiscopate, an era of greater cordiality and stability in the relations between Church and State might begin.

83. The "Action française" agitation, although by no means at an end, was much less in evidence in 1929 than the previous year, and no important action by the Holy See in its regard is to be chronicled, except a sharp denial by the "Osservatore Romano" to its assertion that the French missions had formed a bargaining counter with Italy in the Lateran Treaty negotiations.

84. Politico-religious conditions in Alsace-Lorraine continued to receive close attention from the Holy See. Its policy of supporting Mgr. Ruch, Bishop of Strasbourg, in his action against the members of the clergy who took a prominent part in the autonomist movement, was strongly criticised in certain French Conservative circles, but was not modified.

85. French pilgrimages to Rome during the year in connexion with the Papal jubilee were particularly frequent and numerous.

Syria.

86. The Syrian Patriarch, Mgr. Efrem Rahmani, died in May. He was well known to this Legation, and was held in high consideration at the Vatican. His successor was appointed in July, in the person of Mgr. Tappuni, who came to Rome to receive the pallium from the hands of the Pope. Mgr. Tappuni is about 50 years of age; he had hitherto been Archbishop of Aleppo.

87. At the beginning of the year the Armenian Patriarch, Peter Paul XIII Terzian, who had been resident in Rome for some years owing to the difficulty of living in Constantinople, established himself near Beirut, which thus became the headquarters of those Armenians who are in communion with the Holy See.

Germany.

88. The Lateran agreements were very favourably received in Germany, both by the Government and by German Catholics. Influential though the latter are in German domestic politics, there is evidence that it is not only on that account that official Germany attaches considerable importance to the maintenance of cordial relations with the Holy See. The world-wide influence of the Church, the opportunities its missionary activities offered to cultural expansion, the steadying social influence exercised by its discipline—these seem to be appreciated by leading political authorities in Germany without any reference to personal religious views. And the Holy See in general maintains a discretion in regard to German domestic affairs, which is best calculated to allow this friendly and unprejudiced atmosphere to continue.

89. At the beginning of the year a favourable impression was created by the publication of the Pope's instructions to Cardinal Bertram, Archbishop of Breslau, in regard to the development in Germany of " Catholic Action," that is, lay Catholic organisation for moral and social purposes, strictly dissociated from party politics. One passage in the Pope's letter, which spoke of the necessity for Catholics, in these matters, to follow the lead of the hierarchy, even if opposed to the interests of particular political parties, was interpreted by certain German papers—the wish no doubt being farther to the thought—as aimed against the Centre party and as heralding an effort by the Holy See to discourage the continuance of that party in its present form. But it appeared that there was no such intention behind the Pope's letter, which was an affirmation, in regard to Germany, of the Vatican's principle, already affirmed in other countries, that the cause of the Church must not be exclusively identified with a particular political party.

90. The most important event in German-Vatican relations during 1929 was the conclusion of the convention or treaty (vertrag—convenzione)—the term " concordat " was placed in a secondary position—between Prussia and the Holy See. This agreement had been under negotiation for a considerable time previously, and it looked as if discussions might be protracted indefinitely. There was Protestant opposition to be contended with, it being argued that no agreement should be concluded with the Vatican without a similar and simultaneous arrangement with the Evangelical Churches. Another obstacle was the Vatican's desire to include the " school-question " in the settlement. Ultimately, as the correspondence between the Nuncio and the Prussian Premier, attached to the treaty, showed, this thorny subject was dropped for parliamentary reasons and Dr. Braun was able to secure parliamentary sanction against Nationalist and Communist opposition to the ratification of the treaty, which took place in Berlin on the 13th August.

91. The event caused much satisfaction at the Vatican, where the significance of an agreement with a predominantly Social Democratic Government, ruling a predominantly Protestant State, was emphasised. On the German

side, as several German non-Catholic papers pointed out, it was advantageous to settle, in accordance with present day conditions, such relations between State and Church as had been governed by the out-of-date 1821 Concordat. The State secured a method of appointing bishops—by voting of the cathedral chapter from a list approved by the Pope—and a power of veto, which was agreeable to its interests; it also ensured that all ecclesiastical instruction should be in the hands of well-qualified priests of German nationality. The Church, for its part, obtained authorisation for an increase in archbishoprics and diocesan seminaries; the State contribution to clergy stipends was increased to 28 million marks, and, most important of all, permission, which had always been withheld under the Hohenzollern régime, was obtained to establish a bishopric in Berlin, where about half a million Catholics reside.

92. Towards the end of the year, Mgr. Eugenio Pacelli, the Papal Nuncio, who had been serving in Germany continuously since 1916, was recalled to Rome, and raised to the rank of cardinal. His departure from Berlin was the occasion of great cordiality on the part of President Hindenburg and the German Government, and the former, at about the same time, gave expression to German official regard for the Pope by addressing an autograph letter to His Holiness, congratulating him on his jubilee, and accompanying it with a remarkable gift of fine porcelain, which was presented by the German Ambassador in a special audience.

Greece.

93. During 1929 a certain uneasiness was caused at the Vatican by the report that the Orthodox opposition to the work of Mgr. Calavassy, the leader of those Greeks who were in communion with the Roman See, had been intensified, to the extent that it was hoped to secure from the courts a declaration that Mgr. Calavassy's activities were illegal. There was a protest against this campaign in the " Osservatore Romano," but the matter was not taken up again, the measures proposed against the Greek Uniates apparently not having been carried into practice.

94. In June a Greek pilgrimage—the first of its kind, it was said—led by Mgr. Filippucci, Catholic Archbishop of Athens, was received by the Pope. It included two relations of the President of the Republic, a Deputy and a university professor.

Italy.

The End of the Roman Question.

95. The settlement of the Roman question, which took place in February, was much more than an event in Italian domestic politics. Outside participation was absolutely excluded by the two parties to the negotiations; even during the war Cardinal Gasparri, in an interview, had expressly laid it down that a settlement was solely to be expected from the Italian sense of justice. Nevertheless, as the decisive moment appeared to be drawing near, the whole world felt that a question of universal interest and importance was about to be resolved. Seldom has an event of such importance and dramatic significance been allowed to grow to fruition in such complete secrecy. In January, it is true, newspapers all over the world were printing confident accounts of the impending settlement. Some of these were afterwards proved inaccurate, such as the statement that the new Papal territory was to be enlarged by the addition of the park of Prince Doria, on the Janiculan Hill near the Vatican; less responsible papers spoke of the Pope's " corridor to the sea," while the estimates of the amount of financial indemnity to be paid to the Holy See, which had never touched the compensation grant accorded under the Law of Guarantees, also varied widely. There was however, unanimity, that some fundamental settlement was on the way.

96. In the face of this universal chorus the Italian and Vatican press, under orders, kept complete silence—in itself an indication that serious and definite discussions were being held. The Vatican, in response to requests for enlightenment, presented Ambassadors and Ministers—not to speak of the press correspondents and film operators and expert photographers who had hurried

thither from all over Europe—with a blank wall of non-committal statements, from which, so it was rumoured, even certain heads of missions, in reports to their Governments, deduced that no settlement was probable or imminent. And this was within about a fortnight of the actual signature. There were other diplomats, less inured to the cry of " Wolf ! Wolf !" who felt that perhaps for this once the cry might prove true. But no one could say with the certainty of official or semi-official information that the Roman question was approaching its end.

97. Eventually, particularly when it was known that one of the experts on the Italian side, Signor Barone, had died, with a special blessing from the Pope, the Vatican admitted that all their terms had been made known to the Italian Government, that the fundamental condition was the recognition of the Pope's territorial sovereignty, and that if the Government agreed there could be a settlement the next day. As soon. however, it was added, as anything definite could be said, the Cardinal Secretary of State would summon the whole Diplomatic Corps. This Cardinal Gasparri did on the morning of the 7th February, when he read to the assembled Ambassadors and Ministers a statement to the effect that an agreement had been reached between the Holy See and the Italian Government, consisting of a treaty, securing full liberty and real visible independence in the government of the Universal Church, and a concordat adequately providing for the state of religion in Italy. No details were vouch-safed by his Eminence; his audience had no choice but to wait for the signature which it was understood would be effected within a few days.

Course of the Negotiations.

98. Before proceeding to describe the contents of the agreements between the Holy See and the Italian Government it may be well to give a brief account of the course of the negotiations and discussions which had been carried on since 1926. After the signature, Signor Pacelli, one of the experts on the Vatican side, gave an interview in which he revealed the fact that the initiative had been taken by Signor Mussolini in August 1926, and no objection being raised by the Vatican to preliminary, non-committal discussions, a considerable number of meetings took place between Signor Barone and Signor Pacelli. In the following October, on the day of St. Francis, written authorisation was given by the Italian Prime Minister to Signor Barone to carry on the conversations on his behalf, and Cardinal Gasparri similarly authorised Signor Pacelli, and there were many meetings between the representatives of the Italian Government and the Holy See, held at the residence of Cardinal Belmonte on the outskirts of Rome. At certain of these meetings other Italian Government representatives, such as the Minister of Justice, Signor Rocco, and actual members of the Secretariat of State, such as Mgr. Borgongini-Duca, were present. Signor Pacelli also had numerous audiences with the Pope. Thus the *grandes lignes* of a settlement were elaborated. These were, in brief, the recognition of the sovereignty and indepen-dence of the Holy See by the Italian State, and the recognition by the Papacy of the House of Savoy as the lawful rulers of a united Italy with Rome as her capital. Another main condition insisted upon by the Pope was the conclusion, at the same time as a treaty embodying this mutual recognition, of a concordat regularising the position of the Church in Italy, and giving a legal status to marriage as. laid down in Canon law. In May 1928 definitive drafts of both treaty and covenant were made. There were difficult moments, as when, for example, the whole discussion was held up in 1928 by the action of the Italian Government in suppressing the Catholic boy scouts, but discussions were resumed in November, and when at the beginning of 1929 Signor Barone died and a final draft of treaty and concordat was ready, Signor Mussolini, with the authority of the King, took the negotiations into his own hands, and Cardinal Gasparri received authorisation from the Pope to carry the matter to a conclusion.

The Signature of the Lateran Agreements.

99. On the 11th February, in the historic Palace of the Lateran, once chief palace of the Popes and adjoining the celebrated Church of St. John Lateran, which has associations with great men and stirring events going back to the reign of Constantine the Great, the Lateran Treaty and concordat, with an additional financial agreement, were signed. The signatories were Cardinal

Gasparri, Secretary of State, for the Holy See, and Signor Mussolini for the Italian Government. An ample official summary was at once issued. The main provisions of all three documents will be given below. The news of the signature was the sign for a great outburst of popular enthusiasm, and soon a great part of the city was beflagged, the Italian and Papal flags flying side by side from all the chief public buildings and many private houses. On the 12th the Pope descended into the basilica of St. Peter's to preside over the Solemn High Mass sung in honour of the anniversary of His Holiness's coronation, and this was an opportunity for a most imposing demonstration of popular joy and devotion, both inside the Church and in the great square outside, where it is estimated about 200,000 people were gathered, refusing to leave until, at the conclusion of the ceremony, the Pope, against his original intention, appeared on the balcony and gave his blessing to the crowd. Immediately after the signature telegrams and messages of congratulation had poured into the Vatican from all over the world, and I was charged by His Majesty's Government to express to the Holy See their felicitations at the auspicious event.

Purport of the Agreements.

100. It had been understood that the full text of the Lateran agreements would not be published until after the ratification, but publication acually took place on the 19th March. The provisions may be summarised as follows :—

(a) *The Treaty* (twenty-seven articles).

The preamble refers to the settlement of the " Roman question," that state of affairs brought about by the annexation in 1870 of Rome by the Kingdom of Italy under the House of Savoy. Article 1 reaffirms the statute of 1848 under which the Catholic, Apostolic and Roman religion is the religion of the State. By articles 2 and 3 Italy recognises the sovereignty of the Holy See in the international domain, and also the full proprietorship and sovereign power and jurisdiction of the Holy See over the Vatican as at present constituted, with its dependencies, thus creating a State of the City of the Vatican. The Square of St. Peter's is to be Papal territory, but provisionally policed by Italy, and left open to the public. By articles 5 to 7, Italy frees the Vatican territory from all servitudes, agrees to give it adequate water supply, postal, telegraphic and wireless communications, and an independent railway station, with communication with the State lines. Article 8 declares that the person of the Pontiff being sacred and inviolable, all offences against his person shall be treated as offences against the person of the King. Articles 9 and 10 deal with the status of persons in the service of the Vatican, all those having stable residence in the City-State being recognised as subjects of the Pope in accordance with international law. Full and untrammelled communication between the Vatican and all other States is accorded by article 12, and diplomatic relations between Italy and the Holy See are established. By the two following articles Italy recognises the full ownership by the Holy See of a number of buildings in Rome devoted to ecclesiastical purposes, in particular the patriarchal basilicas, with their annexes. The Papal Villa, at Castel Gandolfo, with the addition of the adjoining Villa Barberini, is also made over to the Pope. By article 16 certain ecclesiastical buildings, although remaining in Italian territory, are declared free from taxation and expropriation. There follow certain agreements in regard to passports and customs dues. By article 21 Italy agrees to treat all cardinals as princes of Royal blood; those living in Rome, even if outside Vatican territory, are to be recognised as Vatican citizens. Articles 22 and 23 deal with offences committed inside Vatican territory, which are, on demand, to be punished by Italy, while the Vatican undertakes to deliver up anyone accused of offences committed on Italian territory who shall take refuge in the Vatican State. In article 24 the Holy See declares that it wishes to remain apart from conflicts of a temporal nature between other States, and from international congresses called to settle them, unless the parties concerned make an appeal to its mission of peace. By article 28 the Holy See and Italy give a mutual recognition of their respective sovereignties, and the Holy See declares the Roman question definitely settled and eliminated.

c

(b) *The Concordat* (forty-five articles).

The preamble declares the concordat to be the necessary complement of the treaty. The first two articles assure to the Catholic Church full freedom in the exercise of its spiritual power, and the Government undertakes to treat Rome as its sacred character demands, and to give freedom of communication between the Holy See and the bishops, and between the latter and the clergy and the faithful. Articles 3 and 4 confer certain exemptions on the priest-hood and students therefor notably from military service except in case of general mobilisation, and from juries. Succeeding articles deal with the position of priests in the Italian public service and inviolability of priests property, and provide for an understanding with the bishop in the case of accusations before a magistrate against an ecclesiastic. The privileges of religious edifices are dealt with in articles 9 and 10, and the succeeding article provides for the recognition of certain of the most important festivals of the Church. The Church agrees to include a prayer in the sacred liturgy for the prosperity of the Italian King and State. Articles 13 to 15 settle the question of religious ministrations in the armed forces of the State. The three succeeding articles deal with the delimitation of dioceses and parishes. Articles 19 and 20 lay down that the choice of archbishops and bishops belongs to the Holy See, but that before a decision, enquiry will be made whether there are political objections to the proposed nomination; bishops shall swear an oath of allegiance to the Italian State. Articles 21 and 22 deal with benefices generally. By articles 24 and 25 the Royal placet and exequatur are abolished, also the State right of patronage in certain cases. Article 27 returns to the Holy See the basilicas of the Holy House at Loreto, of St. Francis of Assisi, and of St. Anthony of Padua. The lengthy article 29 deals with the juridical recognition of ecclesiastical establishments, religious orders and the like, and succeeding articles settle the question of the adminis-tration of the property of such establishments. Article 33 gives the Holy See a right to the catacombs discovered or to be discovered. Article 34 lays it down that the Italian State shall confer civil effects on the sacrament of marriage as regulated by Canon Law. Articles 35 to 40 deal with education, and foreshadow the extension of religious instruction, at present given in the elementary schools, to secondary schools. Schools maintained by religious establishments are placed on an equality with State schools. Articles 41 and 42 give recognition to Papal orders and decorations, this being retrospec-tive to 1870. Article 43 assures the recognition of the Catholic Action, a non-party organisation for the development of Catholic principles. Articles 44 and 45 provide for the friendly settlement of any differences of interpreta-tion, and for the setting up of a commission to apply the concordat.

(c) *Financial Convention* (three articles).

This document, which is really annex IV of the treaty, provides that Italy, in compensation for the serious losses caused to the Church by the annexation of 1870, shall, on ratification, pay to the Holy See 750 millions of lire in cash, and Italian 5 per cent. bonds to the nominal value of 1 milliard lire—very much less than the Italian State would have had to pay had the financial clauses of the Law of Guarantees of the 13th May, 1871, been executed.

First Criticism of the Agreements.

101. It was not to be expected that both the Pope and the Italian Government would be free from criticism, the former from Catholics both inside and outside Italy, the latter from "Liberals" or anti-Clerical politicians or from sincere supporters of a policy of reconciliation, who yet felt that Signor Mussolini had gone too far in his attempt to meet the wishes of the Holy See. In general, it may be said that the Pope was criticised on account of the treaty, and Signor Mussolini on account of the concordat, since by the very insignificance of the Pope's territorial acquisition it was hardly possible for any Italian to raise the once-popular cry of "sacred Italian soil" and inveigh against the recognition of the temporal sovereignty of the Papacy.

102. Very shortly after the signature of the agreements the Pope, in public utterances, dealt with some of the objections that had been raised, and these replies were elaborated and explained by the semi-official organ of the Holy See.

The first class of critics, a very small and dwindling number of those clerics or intensely devout Catholic laymen for whom the annexation of Rome was a " peccato nazionale " to be expiated, one would assume, only by large territorial restoration, were entirely disregarded by the Pope. Apart from these, however, there were some who thought the Pope should have accepted a small addition to the actual Vatican territory—and it was reported that this might have been possible. But the Pope, in an address shortly after the signature, stated that he had been anxious to receive the least amount of territory which was compatible with the full and evident recognition of his sovereignty, only so much of the material as was necessary to the spiritual. Then there were critics who complained that the Pope had given away all and in return had received no guarantees. This objection was voiced with particular emphasis by certain French papers, and received equally emphatic rejoinders from the Pope himself, in more than one utterance, and from the " Osservatore Romano." The most solemn pronouncement by the Pope on this aspect was made when His Holiness, on the 9th March, accorded a collective audience to the entire Diplomatic Corps and in reply to an address of congratulation from the doyen, gave a carefully prepared statement. This drew a clear distinction between a juridical and a moral guarantee. The first, the Pope said, implied either defence or tutelage and why should the Papacy accept either, for it was the enemy of none, and could not put on others the responsibility of its tutelage. There were, however, moral guarantees, first in the presence of the Diplomatic Corps, second in the world-wide approval of the Lateran Treaty and concordat. In this same speech the Pope referred to one of the principal justifications of the momentous step he had taken; it had led to a notable revival of religion in Italy. In other words the old contradiction for Italian Catholics between their patriotism and their loyalty to the Papacy, which did not trouble the conscience of Catholics in other countries, had been abolished, and all Italians could now unite the two loyalties. It is, in short, from this point of view that all criticisms of the Lateran agreements directed against the Papacy should primarily be judged.

103. The criticisms directed against the Italian Prime Minister were of a different order, and it was no doubt in order to placate these that Signor Mussolini, in his speech on the agreements to the Chamber of the 13th May and in certain utterances subsequently, adopted a tone which was by no means pleasing to many Catholics and emphasised first the crucial importance of Rome in the development of the Christian religion, secondly the monopoly of education by the State, and thirdly the nationalist gains to Italy brought about by the settlement—as if the Risorgimento had entirely triumphed over the Papacy.

104. The Holy See did not allow these debatable points to pass without repeated challenge, and between the signature and the ratification of the Lateran agreements there was a distinct tension in the relations between the Vatican and the Italian Government. For example, the Pope, the day after Signor Mussolini's speech just mentioned, receiving a number of Italian students, insisted that in education the tasks of the State was to assist the individual and the family, not to absorb or swallow them up. Later, after a not very successful attempt by the Italian Prime Minister to meet the Vatican criticisms of his first speech, the Pope, almost on the eve of ratification, issued, in the form of a letter to his Cardinal Secretary of State, a moderately worded but clear and determined answer to what he regarded as the questionable parts of the Prime Minister's case. His Holiness, referring to Signor Mussolini's statement that but for Rome Christianity would have remained an obscure Palestinian sect, said that Christianity was a vaster thing than the Roman Empire. He also asserted that the remark that the State had not given anything up to the Church implied, wrongly, an enmity between them. In the concordat as well as the treaty two sovereignties, each perfect in its own order, had come to an agreement. The Pope also, among other points, insisted that the Church had the right to impart religious instruction without interference on the part of the State. Finally, His Holiness asserted that the treaty and the concordat were inseparable and indivisible.

105. Notwithstanding these open differences of opinion the treaty and concordat, having passed both Chamber and Senate, were duly ratified on the 7th June at the Vatican. The polemics which had preceded this event were regarded in Catholic circles as not to be taken too seriously; the Italian Prime

Minister had had to conciliate the anti-clerical element in his party in order to secure wide agreement with his policy. The Pope had been under the imperative necessity of allowing no false interpretation to get a start. In one respect the dispute, which had revealed once more that at least theoretical and doctrinal incompatibility of Catholic philosophy and the extreme Fascist conception of the State had been at an advantage; it had quickly confounded those critics who had said that by making the agreement (of) the Holy See had surrendered itself to fascism and placed itself at the disposal of Italian nationalism. The Holy See stood out as supra-national, and from the practical assertion of this principle it was hoped that the way would be smoother for co-operation with those countries which had at first felt the Lateran accords to be a threat to their national interests, to the undue advantage of Italy.

After the Ratification.

106. The ratification of the Lateran agreements was followed by the accrediting of the first Papal Nuncio to the King of Italy, in the person of Mgr. Borgongini Duca, Papal Under-Secretary of State. The first Italian Ambassador to the Holy See to be appointed was Count Cesare Maria de Vecchi di Val Cismon, one of the members of the original Fascist quadrumvirate and later Governor of Italian Somaliland. He presented his credentials to the Pope on the 25th June, and speeches of a remarkably cordial character were exchanged. On the 25th July the Pope made his first exit from the Vatican, in a procession of the Blessed Sacrement round the Square of St. Peter's. This was witnessed by an enormous crowd in impressive silence, and although the Pope did not actually leave his own territory the event was taken as a seal to the reconciliation. The Pope, incidentally, actually left Papal territory on the 20th December, when, quietly, he took possession of his Cathedral Church of St. John Lateran. Instances of friction between the Holy See and the Italian Government, however, continued from time to time; for example, the Jesuit review the " Civilta cattolica " was sequestrated in July for an article comparing Signor Mussolini's ecclesiastical policy with Napoleon's, and the Pope immediately conferred his jubilee medal on the editor. Again, in September the Pope, receiving a large pilgrimage of young Italian Catholics, complained that they were being unfairly treated by the authorities, and that obstacles were being put in the way of the Catholic Action. The practical significance of such incidents, however, was not to be exaggerated; they did not interfere with the regular carrying out of the Lateran agreements, and they did not appear to diminish the cordiality which had grown up between the Pope and the House of Savoy. This cordiality was shown in the messages exchanged between the Pope and the King on the occasion of the Crown Prince's betrothal, and again on the 6th December, when the State visit to the Pope of their Majesties the King and Queen of Italy initiated a long series of such visits on the part of all the chief members of the Royal Family and the principal officers of State, with the exception of the Prime Minister himself, who had not been received by the close of the year. This notwithstanding, there were signs that the earlier friction had much diminished and that both the Holy See—completely reconciled with the Savoy dynasty if not with extreme fascism—and the Italian Government were prepared to settle down to the normal application of all the terms of both treaty and concordat.

Lithuania.

107. The Papal Inter-Nuncio was raised to the rank of Nuncio in November 1928.

108. In January at an assembly of the Christian Democrat party at Kovno the policy of the Lithuanian Government was severely criticised by those members of the clergy who were present. Another anti-Government movement was discovered in the organisation known as the " Centre of Catholic Activities," which was stated to have the support of the Vatican.

109. In February Professor Voldemaras attempted to discuss with the bishops certain questions arising out of the concordat of 1927. This plan proved abortive. He then wrote to the Vatican complaining of the action of Mgr. Staugaitis in embarking, without permission from Rome or from the Lithuanian Government, upon the construction of a seminary, which action

Voldemaras asserted contravened the concordat. Staugaitis, however, seemed to have the official blessing of the Vatican, who, in their reply to Voldemaras's note, upheld his action and denied that it was in any way contrary to the terms of the concordat.

110. Voldemaras then informed the Holy See that the Nuncio, Mgr. Bartoloni, was no longer *persona grata* to the Lithuanian Government, owing, it was said, to his interference in local Church affairs and to his alleged support of the Christian Democratic organisation which to some extent formed the stronghold of catholicism in Lithuania. The Lithuanian Minister to the Holy See was also absent for some time from Rome, but both subsequently returned to their posts. Professor Voldemaras then attempted to reduce from twenty-two to ten the chairs of the theological-philosophical faculty at the University of Kovno. But the President of the Republic refused to sanction the reduction, beng backed by the Vatican, who contended that the reduction would contravene the concordat. The general question of education is also causing differences of opinion between the Government and the Catholic Church, just as it is between the Italian Government and the Vatican.

111. Relations between the Vatican and the Lithuanian Government were not made easier by the instructions sent to the Nuncio that he was not to meet socially the wife of Dr. Zanius, the Minister for Foreign Affairs, owing to the fact that Dr. Zanius had divorced his first wife and married a singer, with whom he had had a liaison for some time. Dr. Zanius had responded by saying that if the Nuncio refused to meet Mme. Zanius, he (M. Zanius) would refuse officially to receive the Nuncio. It was hoped that a way out of this *impasse* might be found.

Mexico.

112. From the point of view of the Holy See, the year opened with no sign of any improvement in the Mexican religious situation. In February, in fact, there was much depression over the news that another Jesuit priest had been shot. The Vatican, however, declared itself ready to discuss a settlement with any representative of the Mexican Government who had power to formulate proposals which, if accepted, would be binding on the Government. No one with such powers arrived in Rome, and the *impasse* continued until the end of May, when the Holy See nominated Archbishop Ruiz, who had been in Rome, Delegate Apostolic, and authorised him to proceed to Mexico to treat on its behalf with the Mexican President with the object of finding a *modus vivendi*. After a consultation with those members of the Mexican hierarchy who were in the United States, Mgr. Ruiz, accompanied by another bishop, was received in Mexico by President Portes Gil, and shortly after a decree was issued giving exiled priests the right to return and permission to say Mass. In the discussion between the President and the two Mexican prelates, assisted by the American Ambassador, who had played an important part in the preliminary negotiations, an agreement was reached, and, approved by the Holy See, came into force towards the end of June. It represented a modification, by interpretation, of the Mexican law against which the Church had protested. Thus the priests to be registered in accordance with the Constitution were to be designated by their bishops; religious instruction was not to be allowed in the schools, but might be given in the churches; and full liberty was given to Mexican Catholic citizens to apply for any desired modifications in the Constitution. The Government honoured the agreement by beginning the handing back of the confiscated churches, amid scenes of popular rejoicing, and by releasing all women religious, except the nun imprisoned for her share in General Obregón's murder. The Pope appointed the Jesuit Bishop of Tabasco, Mgr. Díaz, who had taken a share in the negotiations, to be Archbishop of Mexico City and Primate of Mexico, and it was hoped in Rome that the settlement which was welcomed as an instalment would lead to the removal, and not the mere " re-interpretation," of all those regulations against the free exercise of the Catholic religion which were still left on the Mexican statute book. For the Mexican Government and all those with material interests in Mexican stability and prosperity the advantage of the settlement lay in the immediate surrender of most of the Catholic insurrectionists, the " Cristeros," and a general improvement in the prestige of the Central Government.

The Netherlands.

113.   The Netherlands Government, although still having no representative to the Holy See, maintained diplomatic relations, as the year before, by continuing to receive a Nuncio at The Hague.   In May a Dutch college for the special ecclesiastical studies of students for the priesthood from Holland was established in Rome.   The Netherlands Minister to the King of Italy, with representatives of the Pope and several Dutch ecclesiastics living in or visiting Rome, was present at the inauguration ceremony.

Portugal.

114.   On the 11th April the Cardinal Secretary of State and the Portuguese Minister to the Holy See signed an agreement relating to the delimitation of the Diocese of Meliapor.   A copy was at once communicated to His Majesty's Government, and the instrument was ratified by the Vatican and Portuguese Government on the 29th June.   The agreement was negotiated in order to give effect to article 4 of the Padroado agreement concluded on the 15th April the previous year, and it laid down that the Diocese of St. Thomas of Meliapor should henceforward consist only of two distinct adjoining territories, namely, San Romé and Tanjore, enlarged or modified as described in detail in succeeding articles.   One of the clauses provided for an exchange of ecclesiastical territory between the Diocese of Meliapor and the Archdiocese of Madras.   Isolated protests from British Indian Catholics against this provision reached the Legation, but no action was taken on them, and they were disregarded by the Holy See.

115.   In July the Portuguese Minister for Foreign Affairs, M. Trindade Coelho, gave an interview, speaking in cordial terms of the Vatican and saying that he would work for the friendly settlement of such matters as might still be in suspense; Portugal, he said, must regain her traditional position at the Vatican.   Oh the 12th October the same Foreign Minister presented his letters to the Pope as new Portuguese Minister to the Holy See, and in doing so dwelt, in his speech to His Holiness, on the services Portugal in past centuries had rendered to Catholic missions

Roumania.

116.   The concordat between Roumania and the Holy See, which had been under negotiation since 1920, was finally ratified on the 7th July in Rome, having previously received the assent of the Roumanian House of Deputies and the Senate, the Magyars and certain of the Orthodox clergy being alone in opposition. The agreement was regarded as of particular importance in Rome, since, with the exception of the unratified pre-war concordat with Serbia, it was the only treaty concluded with a non-Catholic and predominantly Orthodox country.   The terms of the concordat were of considerable political interest, since they brought the Catholic ecclesiastical organisation of Roumania into line with the political boundaries—this, of course, being the principal grievance of the Magyar Catholics, who are now to be subject to the spiritual authority of Roumanian bishops.   This political advantage to the unified Roumanian State was emphasised in speeches in the Roumanian Chamber.   Any exceptions to the rule that Roumanian Catholic dioceses shall be subject to non-Roumanian superiors is to be the subject of special agreement between the Bucharest Government and the Holy See.

117.   In return for this notable concession the Vatican secured a complete recognition of the juridical status of the Catholic Church of whatever rite— Latin, Greek, Armenian or Roumanian—while the Latin Archbishop of Bucharest and the Catholic Roumanian bishops are to be *ex officio* members of the Senate.   Catholic religious congregations and seminaries are also recognised by the State, and the Church obtains the right to establish and maintain at its own expense both primary and secondary schools, as well as imparting religious instruction in the mother-tongue of the children, the teachers selected to be subject to the approval of the local Catholic bishops.   This last was a concession in favour of the national minorities, the majority of whom are Catholics, which was to be set against the concession by the Holy See in the matter of boundaries of dioceses, against which the Magyars raised their chief complaint.   The total effect of the concordat, however, was to deprive Magyar propaganda of the

religious weapon, and, in return, to give the Catholic Church, of all rites, a settled position in the Roumanian State. From the point of view of the Orthodox, the importance of the agreement lay in the recognition of the Catholics of the Roumanian rite—a denial of the position hitherto taken up that Roumanian citizenship and nationality was bound up exclusively with the Roumanian Orthodox profession of faith.

118. The new Roumanian Minister to the Holy See, Dr. Caio Brediceanu, presented his credentials to the Pope in July, and the subsequent ratification of the concordat was attended by an exchange of high decorations between the principals on both sides.

Russia.

119. The religious situation in Soviet Russia and the reintensification of the anti-religious campaign of the Soviet Government caused growing apprehension at the Vatican during 1929. In the early months of the year there was a rumour, spread in certain German papers, that negotiations were to be begun between the Holy See and the Moscow Government, with a view to the establishment of relations and the settlement of the religious situation. These reports, to which no one in Rome gave any credence, became, however, so persistent, that in April the " Osservatore Romano " felt obliged to issue an official communiqué to the effect that much as it was to be desired that the Soviet Government should show some sign of desisting from its anti-Christian campaign and should be willing to advance the cause of religious pacification, it gave no indication of any readiness to do so. Only within recent weeks, the Vatican organ added, it had exiled the aged Catholic Bishop of Vladivostok, Mgr. Slivovski, one of the two Catholic priests left in Moscow, had been arrested and imprisoned without cause or trial, and in Podolia fourteen others had been arrested. And all the time large numbers of priests and nuns, Orthodox and Catholic, were suffering tortures of imprisonment in the horrible prisons of the Solovetski Islands. Later in the year Mgr. d'Herbigny, the rector of the Papal Oriental Institute, gave a lecture in Rome, in which he showed, on the basis of numerous quotations from the Soviet press, the way in which the anti-Christian policy of the Moscow Government, in closing churches, in the total prohibition of religious instruction, in the positive encouragement of " anti-God " propaganda, had made progress in recent months.

120. In the meantime, the " Russicum," the Russian section of the Papal Institute just named, received its definite constitution during the year, while precise instructions were issued from the Holy See regarding the reception and instruction of Russian would-be converts to catholicism.

Yugoslavia.

121. In spite of a statement by several newspapers during August that the proposed Yugoslav concordat with the Holy See was again under discussion between Rome and Belgrade, there was no apparent sign of progress in this direction. On the contrary, it was clear that certain administrative reforms proposed in Belgrade would arouse the opposition of the Holy See. In particular, the idea of passing a law for the administration of the Catholic Church in Yugoslavia, counterpart of the law proposed for the Orthodox Church, against the wishes of that body, could not expect to meet with favour at the Vatican, unless such changes were brought about as the result of a general settlement by negotiation. In regard to education, too, the action of the Yugoslav Government was decidedly unsatisfactory from the point of view of the Holy See, and the Papal Nuncio protested against certain of the terms of the Schools Act which came into force in December, in particular, against the lack of provision for the " missio canonica " for those deputed to give religious instruction, and against clauses which attacked the rights of private schools, which, established for Catholics, are particularly numerous in the Catholic region of Slovenia. Representations on these and certain other grievances were made by the Catholic bishops as well as the Nuncio.

III.—Constitution of the Vatican State.

122. With the ratification of the Lateran Treaty the Holy See became established and recognised as an independent sovereign State, the State of the Vatican City (lo Stato della Citta Vaticana). Obviously, in several respects it is a unique political phenomenon. Apart from its various annexes, scattered in the City of Rome, of which, of course, the Pope remains bishop, it has an area of only forty-four hectares, about a hundred acres, and the temporal subjects of the Pope number only 523. The majority of these are ecclesiastics and the Swiss Guard; the contrast between the actual political sway of the Pope and his tremendous, world-wide religious jurisdiction, over about 300 millions, could not be more strikingly suggested. The Pope has become, faithful to the age-long claims of the Papacy, a real sovereign, subject to no one else, but, safeguarding this principle, he has accepted the absolute minimum of material dominion consonant with those claims.

123. Within the very narrow material limits established and recognised by the Lateran Treaty, however, the Vatican secured most of the outward signs of sovereignty. Vatican authorities, supported by some leading international lawyers, always contended since 1870 that the unimpeded reception and despatch of diplomatic representatives by His Holiness demonstrated a sovereignty which was never lost, but the Papacy, apart from the fact that by the unilateral Italian Law of Guarantees, it could only "enjoy" the use of the Vatican palaces at the will of the Italian King or Parliament, was under many servitudes. All its communications, for example, were in Italian hands. Now they are no longer. Telegraphic stations, post office, with a regular stamp-issue, an independent wireless station and railways, these were all provided by the terms of the Lateran Treaty. Voluntarily the new State undertook not to take part in international conferences unless called upon—this was interpreted as indicating the wish of the Holy See to remain aloof from the League of Nations—but there seemed to be nothing to prevent it from adhering to international conventions, such as the Universal Postal Union, which affected the material side of its existence.

124. In June the first laws of the new State were issued in the "Official Gazette," the "Acta Apostolicæ Sedis." These were six in number, and may be summarised as follows :—

The Fundamental Law of the Vatican City.

(1) This proclaims the Supreme Pontiff as Sovereign of the State, with full powers, legislative, executive and judicial, the first and second of which His Holiness can in part delegate to the Governing Body of the State. The Governor is responsible only to the Pope. The delegation of the judicial power is only duly provided for, and the law concludes with a description of the flag, arms and seal of the State.

(2) This law lays it down that the sources of the State's law are chiefly the Code of Canon Law and the laws issued from time to time by the Pope or his delegates. For criminal offences the Italian Penal Code is adopted more or less completely, which is comprehensible if one considers that, by the treaty (article 22), the Italian State will punish those convicted of crime committed within the Vatican State. The remainder of this section deals with the Civil Code, much of which is also based on the corresponding Italian Code.

The Law of Citizenship and Sojourn.

(3) This defines the citizenship of the new State, which belongs to the cardinals resident in the State or in Rome, to those who have permanent residence in the Vatican City for reasons of dignity, duty, office or employment, when such residence is prescribed by law or regulation, and, finally, to those who are authorised by the Sovereign Pontiff to reside in the Vatican City. Citizenship is extended also to the husbands or wives, the children, the parents, brothers or sisters of the foregoing if authorised to reside in the Vatican City. Vatican State citizens lose this quality if they cease permanently to reside there.

Law of Administration.

(4) This determines the functions and attributes of the Governor of the State of the Vatican City, and other officers.

Law of Economic, Commercial and Professional Regulation.

(5) This establishes that the Vatican City shall have its own coinage, and that until it is issued Italian currency shall circulate. It also prescribes that the acquisition of goods for the purpose of resale is reserved to a State monopoly, according to regulations to be determined. The Vatican State shall maintain a pharmaceutical service. Here it may be remarked that the Vatican pharmacy has been established for some years, and that both this and the preceding regulation seem designed to free the citizens of the State as much as possible from the ordinary business of competitive buying and selling prevalent in other States. Private citizens of the State may, on payment of such dues as may be levied, introduce goods for their own use, but their requirements must be so limited that trading is excluded.

Law of Public Security.

(6) The Governor is made responsible for the maintenance of public order and the security of the citizens of the State and their property. No association may be formed without the Governor's permission, but this does not apply to religious orders or congregations. The keeping of arms and the exercise of printing, lithography and photography is forbidden without licence; this latter, presumably, because it is desired to maintain the monopoly of the celebrated Vatican press.

125. The general impression one would derive from a perusal of these first laws of the Vatican State is that they are in keeping with the fundamental principle already mentioned, namely, that the State, being the barest minimum of territory necessary to support the visible independence of the Pope, has similarly attempted to reduce as far as possible the material responsibilities of its citizens. A kind of co-operative commonwealth, which the size and character of the State should render comparatively easy of achievement, seems to be foreshadowed, under an autocratic but paternal Government, directed mainly to the carrying out of its religious aims and spiritual functions, a " city of souls rather than of things and men," to use Signor Mussolini's phrase. From 1870 until now this has been on the whole the characteristic of Vatican organisation, and the laws to a great extent translate into actual legal fact the practice of the Holy See, within its confines, of many years past. It is on this exceptional, tiny and materially insignificant political basis that the Holy See will continue to exercise its immense spiritual authority and moral and intellectual influence. Pope Leo XIII, in the face of a threat, once said that, if necessary, he would continue to govern the Church from the prison-cell. Pope Pius XI undertakes the task from a regularly constituted State, whose smallness, both in area and population, makes it incapable of offending Italian national sentiment or any national loyalties, and whose utter material powerlessness and declared neutrality free it from the risk of being drawn into international rivalries.

IV.—SACRED COLLEGE.

126. The following cardinals died in the course of 1929 :—

Cardinal Tosi, Archbishop of Milan, the 7th January.
Cardinal Vico, Prefect of the Congregation of Rites, the 25th February.
Cardinal Lucidi, the 1st April.
Cardinal Gasquet, the 6th April. His Eminence, although of advanced age, was a prominent and active figure in Rome, and universally respected for his charm of manner and his wide scholarship. His death was a serious loss to the English colony in Rome, by whom his character and staunch patriotism were appreciated. A message of sympathy was received from His Majesty the King.
Cardinal Dubois, Archbishop of Paris, the 25th September.
Cardinal Gamba, Archbishop of Turin, the 26th December.

D

127.   To replace Cardinal Tosi in the Archdiocese of Milan, the Pope in July appointed Mgr. Ildefonso Schuster, O.S.B., Abbot of St. Paul's without the Walls, Rome, a well-known authority on liturgy.   As librarian of the Roman Church, in succession to Cardinal Gasquet, the well-known German Jesuit scholar, Cardinal Ehrle, was nominated.   On the 28th October the Pope held a consistory, at which His Holiness conferred the Red Hat on Cardinal Pedro Seguia y Sáenz, Archbishop of Toledo, who had been raised to the Sacred College at the end of 1927, but had not attended the customary ceremony in Rome.

128.   On the 16th December the Pope held another consistory, at which six more cardinals were created, namely :—

Mgr. Manuel Cerejeira, the Patriarch of Lisbon, who had been bishop-auxiliary to the late Patriarch, and before that Professor of Literature in the University of Coimbra.

Mgr. Luigi Lavitrano, Archbishop of Palermo, to which dignity he was raised the previous year.

Mgr. Carlo Minoretti, Archbishop of Genoa, to which dignity he was raised in 1925, having previously taken a prominent part in Italian Catholic social work.

Mgr. Joseph MacRory, Archbishop of Armagh and Primate of Ireland, in which See he succeeded the late Cardinal O'Donnell the previous year.

Mgr. Jean Verdier, Archbishop of Paris, in succession to the late Cardinal Dubois.   He had had a long and distinguished career as Professor of Theology in Paris, and in 1928 became Superior of the important French ecclesiastical institute of St. Sulpice.

Mgr. Eugenio Pacelli, Papal Nuncio in Bavaria during the war, and then Nuncio to the whole Reich.   In both capacities he had won universal esteem, both on account of his good priestly character, and his diplomatic abilities.   At the end of the year it was generally taken for granted that he would succeed Cardinal Gasparri as Papal Secretary of State.

129.   With these appointments the Sacred College was raised to the number of fifty-nine, of which thirty-one were non-Italian.

130.   In consequence of the sovereign status accorded to the Holy See by the Treaty of the Lateran, a number of important administrative changes were made after the ratification.   The former Director of the Vatican Galleries and Museums, Commendatore Serafini, became Governor of the Vatican City State, Marchese Pacelli, the lay ecclesiastical lawyer who had played a prominent part in the discussions leading up to the treaty, became counsellor;   Commendatore Nogara became State Treasurer.   The former Secretary of the Congregation of Extraordinary Ecclesiastical Affairs, Mgr. Borgongini-Duca, whose office is more or less equivalent to Under-Secretary of State, was appointed first Papal Nuncio to the Italian Court, and was succeeded by the Secretary for Ordinary Ecclesiastical Affairs, Mgr. Pizzardo, who in his turn was replaced by Mgr. Ottaviani. The assistant to Mgr. Pizzardo was Mgr. Tardini.   Several other minor appointments, both lay and ecclesiastical, were made, giving to the Vatican State, of course on a small scale suited to its tiny territorial extent, a regular civil and judicial administration.

V.—The Press.

131.   One or two changes in regard to the Catholic press in Italy have to be chronicled.   The specifically Catholic press, during the year, had peculiar difficulties to contend with, owing to the special conditions of the press generally in Italy.   No paper in Italy can hope to succeed if it does not enjoy the favour of the régime, which, if it does not actually suppress it, can exercise such influence in regard to advertisement revenue as practically to ensure the extinction of any paper of which it disapproves.   More than once the Holy See had occasion to protest against the harsh treatment of Catholic papers, which, if they were not wholehearted supporters of the régime, were treated as clandestine supporters of the hated Popular party and doomed to extinction in consequence.

132.   In Rome the former Popular party organ, the " Corriere d'Italia," became a strong Fascist partisan, although it still maintained its distinctive Catholic colour, and often printed documents and news of the Holy See, which

were dismissed with brief summaries in the other papers. This paper, which the Vatican disowned as in any way representative of its views, got into financial difficulties and ceased publication in September.

133. Scarcely more fortunate was the Florence "Unitá cattolica," which was understood to be independent of the Fascist régime, but in receipt of support from the Vatican. Certainly it reproduced regularly all the official news from the semi-official Vatican paper, the "Osservatore Romano," and often reprinted unofficial articles from the same source. After the Lateran Treaty it announced that it would cease publication as a daily, but would appear weekly. This arrangement, which was clearly due to motives of economy, did not last very long, for the paper shortly came to a complete stop and it was understood that its equipment had been transferred to the new Vatican State.

134. It was merely as a logical consequence of the recognition of the new State of the Vatican that the semi-official Vatican organ, the "Osservatore Romano," on the ratification of the Lateran agreements, transferred itself entirely to within the Vatican walls, and began to appear as the one daily authorised paper of the new Papal State. In consequence of the change the paper, although continuing to appear in Italian, began to devote more attention to international news, especially any news from all over the world which affected the Catholic Church. It became the one absolutely sure vehicle of news in Italy for Papal announcements, and during the period of controversy between the Pope and Signor Mussolini, it enjoyed a marked popularity, since it gave in full the Papal pronouncements which the rest of the press, doubtless on a *mot d'ordre*, declined to print.

135. The Jesuit review, the "Civilita Cattolica," continued to appear as an Italian organ, and in consequence of a frank article on the controversy between the Pope and Signor Mussolini its number for July was sequestrated, not, however, before a great part of the issue intended for subscribers had been sent out. The Pope, with characteristic determination after the sequestration, immediately presented the editor with a complimentary letter and a gold medal, but the incident was sufficient to show the difficulties which might arise for the purely Catholic press after the ratification of the Lateran treaties and in the present condition of things in Italy. It is, however, only fair to add that such incidents during the year were rare.

CONFIDENTIAL.

(13880)

HOLY SEE.

Annual Report, 1930.

[C 1077/1077/22]

Mr. Ogilvie Forbes to Mr. A. Henderson.—(Received February 17.)

(No. 33.)   *British Legation to the Holy See,*
Sir,   *Rome, February 13, 1931.*
     I HAVE the honour to transmit my annual report on the Holy See for the
year 1930.

     2.   While it is my own work, the willing and conscientious help afforded
by the members of the staff, Mr. Roger Thynne and Miss A. A. Johnson, have
considerably lightened the task.   I desire to place on record my appreciation.
                                                       I have, &c.
                                                       G. OGILVIE FORBES.

Enclosure.

Annual Report on the Holy See for 1930.

CONTENTS.

5787   [5111]   B

I.—INTRODUCTION.

THE story of the year 1930, when compared with that of 1929, which saw such an epoch-making event as the settlement of the Roman question, makes comparatively dull reading. Yet 1930 had interesting developments. The experiment of an independent Vatican State, little more than a Basilica with palace and grounds attached, was continued with success. Such success necessarily implied mutual co-operation and a genuine spirit of goodwill as between the Holy See and the Italian Government. This reciprocal goodwill was exemplified on the part of His Holiness the Pope by his praise of the Lateran Treaty on more than one public occasion, and on the part of the Italian Government by the support which they accorded to the infant Vatican State in temporal matters—for, indeed, a hostile Italy would make life unbearable—and by their solicitude in granting to the Holy See special marks of consideration and facilities as occasion arose. Harmony and friendship with Italy was, therefore, a prominent feature of the past year.

2. Free, therefore, from anxiety and care at his doorstep, the Pope was able to devote himself with all his accustomed vigour to the development of Catholic Action, a subject which is treated in a special section of this report. On looking back at the events of the year 1930, Catholic Action would seem to have been the most prominent feature, being constantly preached by the Pope not only for Italy, but also in increasing measure for all other countries, and to be adapted to every form of activity. Its main object is to counteract the ever spreading spirit of irreligion and of Bolshevik communism. The main interest of Catholic Action to secular Governments and especially to His Majesty's Governments in the British Commonwealth is the danger that, if it is rashly or imprudently pressed, it may overstep the limits of religion into the region of politics, especially as it necessarily covers many subjects connected with moral conduct on which the spiritual and the temporal powers are in conflict.

3. Another important feature was His Holiness's vigorous protest against recent events in Russia and his determination to leave no stone unturned for the restoration of Christianity in that great conglomerate of nationalities, in view of the apparent collapse of the Russian Orthodox Church. The quiet spadework of the Oriental Institute and the newly-formed Commission " Pro Russia " is a subject of ever-increasing interest.

4. As regards His Majesty's Government in the United Kingdom, the Malta dispute has clouded the good relations which hitherto existed between London and the Vatican. His Holiness would not give way on what he considered to be a question of principle, which ought never to have arisen as such. Fundamental and regrettable though the difference was, the Malta dispute did not in any way impede the despatch of public business in other matters as between His Majesty's Government in the United Kingdom and the Holy See.

II.—HIS MAJESTY'S LEGATION.

5. On the 26th May Mr. Henry Chilton, His Majesty's Minister, presented his letter of recall on promotion to be His Majesty's Ambassador in Chile. He was, on the occasion of His Majesty's birthday, appointed K.C.M.G. On Mr. Chilton's departure Mr. G. Ogilvie-Forbes, first secretary, who had arrived a few days before, assumed charge of the Legation, no Minister being appointed during the rest of the year.

III.—RELATIONS WITH THE BRITISH EMPIRE.

United Kingdom.

6. On the retirement of Cardinal Pietro Gasparri from the office of Secretary of State on the 7th February, His Majesty's Minister expressed to his Eminence his regret and confidence that the pleasant personal relations which had hitherto existed would be continued in the future. His Eminence

Cardinal Eugenio Pacelli, who succeeded Cardinal Gasparri, took the first opportunity of requesting His Majesty's Minister to convey his Eminence's respects to His Majesty the King, stating that he recalled with pleasure his visit to London in the suite of Cardinal Granito di Belmonte, Papal representative at His Majesty's coronation.

7. The Lords of the Admiralty in Fleet Orders No. 195, the 24th January, 1930, laid down that the Pope was to be regarded as a Chief of a State and to be received with the honours accorded to Presidents of Republics, and that the diplomatic representatives of the Pope were entitled to the honours due to their diplomatic status.

8. Cardinal Merry del Val, formerly Secretary of State to Pius X, born and educated in Great Britain, died suddenly on the 26th February. He was ordained for the Westminster diocese, but was retained in the Roman Curia. He was a member of the Papal Mission to Queen Victoria in 1887, secretary of the Commission on Anglican Orders 1896, and Papal Legate at the coronation of King Edward VII. He was cardinal protector of the English, Scots and Beda Colleges. His death was a loss to British prestige in Curia, in which the United Kingdom has no ecclesiastic of any effective influence.

9. On the 23rd June the Cardinal Secretary of State informed His Majesty's Chargé d'Affaires of the ratification by the Holy See of seven International Acts signed in London on the 28th June, 1929, in connexion with the Postal Union Convention.

10. On the 29th June Cardinal Robert Bellarmine, famous for his controversy with James I on the question of the deposing power, was canonised. This act was considered in certain circles in the United Kingdom to have been specially directed against His Majesty's Government in view of the dispute over Malta. It is, however, much more likely that it was a coincidence, as the canonisation of Cardinal Bellarmine had been under consideration for the last two and a half centuries.

11. On the 9th July Cardinal Vincenzo Vanutelli, dean of the College of Cardinals, died, aged 94. His Majesty's Government in the United Kingdom sent to the Vatican a message of condolence.

12. The question having arisen, in connexion with liability to United Kingdom income tax, whether as a result of the Lateran Treaty His Majesty's Government in the United Kingdom recognised the Holy See as a sovereign State and the Pope as a monarch distinct from a temporary head of a State, it was decided that the Lateran Treaty made no difference to the nature of the recognition accorded by His Majesty's Government to the Pope, who was regarded as a Spiritual Monarch.

13. In the absence of diplomatic relations between the Holy See and the United States Government, His Majesty's Government in the United Kingdom, on request of the Vatican, acted as intermediary for obtaining the adhesion of the Holy See to the Washington International Radio-Telegraphic Convention of 1927.

14. On the 7th October rather a delicate question arose, not for the first time in recent years. His Holiness caused a telegram to be sent to Cardinal Bourne requesting him to convey to His Majesty the King and to his Government in the United Kingdom an expression of His Holiness's condolences for the disaster to the airship " R. 101." This use of the Cardinal Archbishop of Westminster as an official channel of communication was most probably due to an oversight on the part of the Secretariat of State during the holiday season. His Majesty's Government, through His Majesty's Chargé d'Affaires, conveyed to His Holiness a warm expression of thanks and did not, in the circumstances, repeat their objection to the use made by the Vatican of the channel of Cardinal Bourne.

15. The Rev. Herbert Dunnico, M.P., Deputy Speaker of the House of Commons, was in October cordially received by His Holiness the Pope, once His Holiness had satisfied himself that he was in no way an emissary of Lord Strickland's, nor had taken a prominent part in the Malta dispute.

B 2

16. Mr. Walter Newbold, formerly Communist M.P. for Motherwell, in which there is a large Roman Catholic electorate, and ex-member of the Communist International, visited the Vatican towards the end of the year. Although His Holiness was not able to receive him, even in semi-private audience, Mr. Newbold had some quite successful interviews with the Cardinal Secretary of State and other prelates, which, it is hoped, may in time be of benefit to relations between the United Kingdom and the Holy See.

17. The dispute over Malta, one of the results of which was the decision not to appoint, for the time being at least, a Minister in succession to Sir Henry Chilton, is described elsewhere in this report.

Canada.

18. While His Majesty's Government in Canada have no official relations with the Holy See, the Pope is represented for ecclesiastical purposes by a Delegate Apostolic, Mgr. Andrea Cassulo. His duties are no sinecure, as the Roman Catholic community are torn in two rival factions, the French and the Irish. The struggle between French and Irish Canadians is one of language and orientation. There consequently exists in Rome a constant state of friction between the two races, which manifests itself particularly in the appointment of bishops in the Middle West, into which the French Canadians seem to be rapidly spreading. On the whole, the Irish have hitherto gained the upper hand in Rome and succeeded in securing the appointment of an Irish archbishop for Regina in succession to a French Canadian, although a French Canadian suffragan bishop was appointed for the Diocese of Gravelbourg.

19. The policy of His Majesty's Legation, whose intervention has more than once been invoked by the losing side, was, in the absence of any instructions from the Canadian Government, one of strict abstention and neutrality, coupled, nevertheless, with an indication that such neutrality did not necessarily imply either hostility or want of sympathy—an attitude which was understood and appreciated by the French Canadians in Rome.

20. The canonisation on the 29th June of six French Jesuit missionaries martyred by Indians in what is now Canadian territory provided some measure of consolation for the French Canadians. A pilgrimage of about 200, headed by Cardinal Rouleau, Archbishop of Quebec, came to Rome for the event. About fifty of this party and two bishops were of English speech. The Province of Quebec sent a special representative in the person of Mr. Honoré Mercier, Minister of Posts and Telegraphs.

21. Unfortunately another quarrel broke out, this time over a college which the Irish have founded in Ottawa, where there is already a Catholic university providing bi-lingual instruction. A special lay emissary, a Senator Murphy, came to Rome in the autumn to further the project.

22. M. Arsène Henry, appointed in August as French Minister in Ottawa, was formerly counsellor at the French Embassy to the Holy See, where he is said to have acquired experience of French Canadian questions.

23. The Roman Catholic community as a whole in Canada appear also to have had trouble in connexion with the Saskatchewan schools question. So far as is known, the Vatican have not yet intervened, nor does the problem seem to have developed beyond the stage of Canadian internal politics.

Commonwealth of Australia.

24. There is nothing of special interest to record other than the visit to the Vatican in December of Mr. Scullin, the Prime Minister, and Mr. Brennan, Attorney-General, who, as of Irish race, were presented to the Pope and the Cardinal Secretary of State by the Irish Free State Minister.

25. Mr. Scullin also gave an interview to the " Osservatore Romano," in which he illustrated the progress made by Roman Catholicism in Australia, and paid a tribute to the spirit of tolerance shown by his non-Catholic fellow-Australians.

Union of South Africa.

26.   There was a certain amount of friction with the Government over the schools question, especially in cases where poor missions are unable to meet the expense of superior accommodation and higher standards of instruction.   The alleged intention of the Union Government to abolish denominational schools also caused certain resentment.

Irish Free State.

27.   On the 15th January Mgr. Paschal Robinson, O.F.M., Archbishop of Tyana, presented his credentials to the Governor-General.   At the speech of welcome made at the State banquet held later on in the day, Mr. Cosgrave is reported to have expressed the pleasure of his Government at the action of His Holiness in establishing a Nunciature in Ireland.

28.   Mr. Bewley, the Irish Free State Minister at the Vatican, established more friendly relations with the Irish College, of which Mgr. Curran, the former vice-rector, was appointed rector.

29.   In the month of July the Papal Nuncio in the Irish Free State was welcomed to the City of Cork, of which he received the freedom.

30.   Towards the end of the year the Irish Free State was given considerable publicity in the " Osservatore Romano " in view of the forthcoming Eucharistic Congress to be held in 1932, to which a complimentary allusion was made by the Pope in his Christmas Allocution.

31.   On the 12th December Mr. Scullin, Prime Minister of Australia, was presented to His Holiness the Pope by the Minister of the Irish Free State.

India.

32.   Archbishop Mooney, the Apostolic Delegate, a citizen of the United States, and formerly on the staff of the North American College, visited Rome during the year.   He informed His Majesty's Chargé d'Affaires that the relations between the ecclesiastical authorities and the Government of India were satisfactory.   All the problems connected with the 1929 treaty with Portugal, abolishing the Padroado régime, were not yet settled, as in certain districts the natives resented transference to the jurisdiction of Portuguese ecclesiastics.   From time to time the Legation receives copies of resolutions and complaints on this subject.

33.   At the end of October Mar Ivanios, Jacobite Archbishop of Betania, together with the Bishop of Tiruvella, and a number of clergy and nuns were received into the Roman Catholic Church, the bishop and clergy being allowed to retain their rank, privileges and customs.

34.   The following are the latest available statistics of Roman Catholicism in India and Ceylon :—

Total number of Roman Catholics, about 3 million.
Schools—

Primary	...	...	...	...	3,800
Secondary	...	...	...	...	164
Arts colleges	...	...	...	...	33
Seminaries	...	...	...	...	32

Twenty-five per cent. of the clergy, including several bishops, are natives; the remainder European or American.

35.   The proceedings of the Round Table Conference were followed with considerable interest.   While no opinion was expressed, the general impression was one of sympathy for His Majesty's Government in the United Kingdom and the Government of India in the problems confronting them.

Southern Rhodesia.

36. The mission at Bulawayo, Southern Rhodesia, was in December detached from the Prefecture Apostolic of Salisbury and entrusted to the Trappist Fathers of Mariannhill.

East Africa and the Sudan.

37. Archbishop Hinsley, late rector of the English college in Rome, was appointed Delegate Apostolic for all missions in British Africa, excluding those under the superintendence of the Delegates Apostolic in South Africa, the Congo and Egypt. On the 9th May the archbishop expressed to His Majesty's Minister his warm appreciation of the facilities afforded to him during a recent visit by the Governor-General and other officials of the Sudan.

38. Some apprehension was expressed in the Congregation of Propaganda at a statement alleged to have been made by the Director of Education of Kenya Colony in his 1929 report, in which it is said that the following statement appears : " The native has indicated in no uncertain terms that he no longer wishes to be educated in institutions which are controlled by missionaries." The correspondent of the Press Agency of Propaganda reported that the natives warmly repudiated that statement.

Malta: The Negotiations for a Concordat.

39. The position at the beginning of the year was that Sir Henry Chilton was awaiting—

(1) The opening of the negotiations promised by the Vatican on the 13th October, 1929, for the discussion and settlement of the questions at issue over Malta, and

(2) A copy of Mgr. Robinson's report, which Cardinal Gasparri had also undertaken to supply.

40. Neither event took place. Moreover, notwithstanding Sir Henry Chilton's frequent reminders to the Secretariat of State on the subject, a pro-memoriâ, dated the 29th January, was communicated to him instead, which contained a long recital of the complaints of the ecclesiastical authorities against Lord Strickland, based on Mgr. Robinson's and other reports.

41. Briefly summarised, this pro-memoriâ was to the following effect :—

Lord Strickland, a Catholic, shows hostility to the Church and to the clergy—

(1) By allying himself with dissident priests in Gozo.

(2) By having proposed the omission of the word " Roman " from the official designation of the Roman Catholic Church in Malta.

(3) By speeches insulting to the Holy See in the Parliamentary debates on the recognition of Papal titles.

(4) By making a freemason president of his club, and by the action of his followers in shouting in the streets " Viva Calles."

(5) By a general campaign of slandering the clergy in the press and Parliament.

(6) By permitting at the same time three Protestant bishops to hold lectures in the Governor's palace.

(7) By his intervention in the case of Friar Micallef.

42. On the 7th February His Majesty's Minister again reminded the Cardinal Secretary of State that he was still awaiting the suggestions promised for finding a basis for settling the Malta question, adding that three months had now passed and nothing had happened. Cardinal Gasparri undertook to furnish a reply soon.

43. On the 10th February His Majesty's Minister was informed that the Vatican's pro-memoriâ of the 29th January would not be allowed by His Majesty's Government in the United Kingdom to pass without protest and must not be used as a basis for negotiations, and that it was the intention to link His Majesty's Government's criticism of the pro-memoriâ with a request that, for the time being, the Maltese clergy should be prohibited from taking part in local politics.

44. Cardinal Gasparri having retired from office, His Majesty's Minister, on the 14th February, recapitulated the situation to his successor, Cardinal Pacelli.

45. Between the 26th February and the 7th March His Majesty's Government expressed to the Vatican the hope that in return for an undertaking by Lord Strickland not to attack the clergy, the latter should be instructed—

(1) To refrain from active participation in politics and not to stand as condidates for the Legislative Assembly.
(2) To refrain from controversial and provocative pronouncements.
(3) To discourage unfriendly criticisms of a possible concordat between Malta and the Vatican.

46. The Cardinal Secretary of State replied on the 14th March that as the Vatican could not rely on a verbal undertaking by Lord Strickland the necessary undertaking could not be given. He added that His Holiness the Pope most emphatically did not believe in Lord Strickland's promises.

47. Negotiations for a concordat were not possible so long as Lord Strickland was in power. His Majesty's Minister then enquired why the Vatican had agreed last October to initiate these negotiations, and the cardinal replied he was not in office at the time.

48. Sir Henry Chilton handed in an aide-mémoire dated the 13th March giving the considered views of His Majesty's Government on the Vatican's pro-memoriâ of the 29th January. Its substance was as follows: After recapitulating the history of the dispute His Majesty's Government desired to emphasise that the real cause of the trouble was the participation of the clergy in politics and not the anti-clerical attitude of Lord Strickland. The accusations against Lord Strickland made in the Vatican's pro-memoriâ were no answer to His Majesty's Government's major thesis, *i.e.*, the undue political activities of the clergy. The pro-memoriâ of the Vatican only confused the main issue of the forthcoming negotiations, which was the exclusion of the Maltese priesthood from local politics, and not the examination of accusations against Lord Strickland, which were only an incidental matter.

49. As indicated above during the conversation, which was held on Sir Henry Chilton's handing in this aide-mémoire, it transpired that no negotiations whatever were possible so long as Lord Strickland was in power.

50. His Majesty's Government accordingly on the 26th March instructed His Majesty's Minister to inform the Cardinal Secretary of State that the refusal of the Vatican to commence negotiations would be communicated to Lord Strickland, who would also be considered as no longer bound by his undertaking.

51. On the 11th April His Majesty's Minister also handed to the Cardinal Secretary of State a statement protesting against the action of the Vatican in refusing to enter into negotiations, and in expressing distrust of the undertaking given by the head of the Maltese Ministry and sponsored by themselves. He also informed the cardinal of the desire of His Majesty's Government to publish the official correspondence on the subject.

52. Then ensued a discussion with the Vatican, lasting over a month, as to what papers they would consent to publish. In order to avoid unnecessary delay His Majesty's Government offered that, in cases where reports of conversations were published, the Vatican's version, if it differed from His Majesty's Government's, should be embodied in the form of footnotes. The cardinal, while agreeing to the publication of certain notes and pro-memoriâ suggested by His Majesty's Government, objected to the publication of records of conversations on the ground that they might lead to private polemics, and that they contained certain inexactitudes. His Majesty's Government on the 22nd May then offered to cut out all records of conversations, with the exception of three which were considered essential for the proper presentation of the case, provided the Cardinal Secretary of State would definitely agree thereto. In the event of the Vatican refusing such a compromise His Majesty's Minister was instructed to retain for His Majesty's Government a free hand to publish the

documents in the form originally proposed. The Vatican on the 25th May replied that they would very reluctantly consent to publication only if the text of the despatches was altered in a certain sense. His Majesty's Government decided they could not consent to this proposal as His Majesty's Minister definitely disagreed with the accuracy of the Vatican's version, and accordingly His Majesty's Chargé d'Affaires (Sir Henry Chilton having left) was instructed to inform the Vatican that His Majesty's Government intended to publish forthwith the documents as originally proposed, placing on record in their proper context the points which the Cardinal Secretary of State wished to bring out. The correspondence was published early in June in the form of a Blue Book, Cmd. 3588, 1930.

53.   It is now necessary to return to an event which burst like a bombshell on a situation already tense and overcharged. The Archbishop of Malta in the middle of April paid a brief visit to Rome. He returned to his post and on the 1st May conjointly with his colleague the Bishop of Gozo published a pastoral letter, which culminated in the following passage :—

   " And to come to the concrete, and in order not to leave in your souls any indecision. Know therefore as Catholics :

   " (1) You may not, without committing a grave sin, vote for Lord Strickland and his candidates, or for all those, even of other parties, who in the past have helped and supported him in his fight against the rights and the discipline of the Church, or who propose to help and support him in the coming elections.
   " (2) For even stronger reasons you may not present yourselves as candidates in the electoral lists proposed by Lord Strickland or by other parties who propose to support him in the coming elections.
   " (3) You are also solemnly bound in conscience in the present circumstances to take part in the elections and to vote for those persons who, by their attitude in the past, offer great guarantee both for religious welfare and for social welfare.

   " In order, then, to prevent abuses in the administration and reception of the Sacraments, we remind our priests that they are strictly forbidden to administer the Sacrament to the obstinate who refuse to obey these our instructions. It pains us greatly to see Catholics guilty of public and grave violation of Catholic discipline, continue freely to approach the Sacraments to the greatest wonder of the good.   It is time that those responsible performed their duty with firmness and without human respect, if they do not wish to draw down the wrath of the Divine Judge."

54.   The archbishop, also on his own responsibility, so to speak, rubbed this pastoral in by means of a personal letter to the Governor of Malta also, under date of the 1st May.   The Governor of Malta, on instructions from His Majesty's Government, issued a proclamation suspending the forthcoming elections and prohibiting further meetings.   On the 9th May His Majesty's Minister lodged with the Vatican a note protesting against the pastoral, and on the 16th May informed the Vatican that they could not resume negotiations until orders had been given by the Holy See to the Bishops of Malta and Gozo, with the object of restoring to the electorate complete freedom to exercise their political judgment. This, in a pro-memoriâ dated the 20th May, the Vatican declined to do.   On the 23rd May an attempt was made to assassinate Lord Strickland.   It was unsuccessful.   The following day the " Osservatore Romano " published a paragraph expressing condemnation of this outrage.   Finally, on the 30th May, His Majesty's Chargé d'Affaires, on instructions from His Majesty's Government, handed to the Cardinal Secretary of State the last word of His Majesty's Government previous to publication of the papers. which was to the effect that—

   (1) The action of the Maltese clergy obliged them to make the resumption of negotiations conditional on restoration to the electors by the ecclesiastical authorities of complete freedom to exercise their political judgment.
   (2) That the Vatican had neglected to take steps necessary for the restoration of normal political life in Malta.

(3) That the long-promised negotiations for defining the relations between Church and State had not only been delayed, but had been rendered impossible by attaching a condition as to the personality of the head of the Maltese Administration, which constituted nothing less than a claim to interfere in the domestic politics of a British Colony.

55. To this the Vatican replied on the 8th June—

(1) Repudiating responsibility for delay in the concordat negotiations, but declining to negotiate so long as Lord Strickland was in office.
(2) Denying the accusation of interference in Maltese internal politics, declaring that the bishops were only doing their duty in defending the Catholic religion attacked by Lord Strickland.
(3) Reminding His Majesty's Government of their guarantee, since Malta became a British possession, to protect and defend the Catholic religion.
(4) Appealing that either Lord Strickland's activities be curbed or that His Majesty's Government dissociate themselves from him.

56. On the 19th June Lord Strickland's reply to the accusations made against him, communicated to the Vatican " as a personal statement in regard to which His Majesty's Government were not consulted," and His Majesty's Chargé d'Affaires, on instructions, also reminded the Cardinal Secretary of State that His Majesty's Government could not pass over without comment the complaint made by the Vatican regarding the reception of the three Protestant bishops (see paragraph 41 above). As it could not be denied that the Bishop of Gozo had made a mistake in confusing the Governor with the head of the Ministry in Malta, the Cardinal Secretary of State offered to make a correction in the Vatican's White Book, then on the eve of publication. The only form in which it could be done was that of a footnote, which was added, at the last moment. Although it was not entirely satisfactory to His Majesty's Government the matter was then allowed to drop.

57. On the 21st June the Vatican published their White Book on this dispute, which, in general, contained nothing new, except the text of Mgr. Robinson's report, so far as it concerned Lord Strickland, and which had hitherto been withheld from His Majesty's Government. This took the form of a crushing indictment of the head of the Maltese Ministry, in which he was held up as totally unfit for his office.

58. On the 24th June His Majesty's Government announced their decision, owing to the urgency of the local situation, temporarily to suspend the Constitution of Malta, and to place full legislative and executive authority in the hands of the Governor, retaining the existing Ministry in office in a consultative capacity in so far as the Governor chose to make use of their services.

59. On the 30th June His Holiness the Pope, in his Allocution to the Cardinals in Secret Consistory, after expressing the hope that his relations with His Majesty's Government would become more cordial, drew attention to the Vatican's White Book, and also declared (1) that neither the Holy See nor the Maltese Episcopate were responsible for the trouble; (2) that return to peace had been made impossible by certain " persons, actions and facts . . . . contrary to the interests of the Catholic religion . . . . all the more serious when they concern a people so profoundly Catholic as the Maltese "; (3) that his intervention was not intended to transgress upon the political field, and was always limited to inculcating principles and moral laws guiding the action of Catholics.

60. On the 23rd August His Holiness received in audience a pilgrimage of 200 Maltese, under the leadership of the Bishop of Gozo. In an address which he made to them he urged them to beware of false prophets and to stand by their bishops. His words were punctuated with applause. On the 6th September another Maltese pilgrimage of about 100 persons was received in audience and was addressed to the same effect.

61. In the month of October there was a rumour current that the Archbishop of Malta would be transferred elsewhere, and that a certain Maltese prelate, Mgr. Dandria, was to be appointed in his stead. The question of the desirability of this appointment arose. On His Majesty's Chargé d'Affaires ascertaining from the Vatican that there was no intention of creating a vacancy in the See, the matter dropped.

62. In November the archbishop visited Rome for a few weeks. Although obviously suffering from nervous strain he showed no signs of modifying his attitude, and after two audiences with the Pope, returned to Malta apparently fortified and encouraged to hold out.

63. The above record is drawn from a mass of correspondence which in many instances deals at great length with comparatively trivial matters argued with prolixity and subtlety. Summed up in a few sentences, the respective arguments of His Majesty's Government and the Vatican, as developed in 1930, can be put as follows : His Majesty's Government contended that the recent troubles in Malta were due to the excessive interference of the clergy in politics, and they accordingly invited the Vatican to enter into negotiations for the settlement of these dfficulties. The Vatican, on their side, denied that the trouble was due to excessive clerical interference, and cast the responsibility on Lord Strickland, who, as a Roman Catholic, had caused great scandal and harm to religion by attacking the Church. They accordingly declined to enter into negotiations so long as Lord Strickland was in power. While these conversations were going on, the bishops of Malta pressed home the Vatican's point of view by forbidding the electors of Malta, under pain of grave sin, to vote for Lord Strickland at the impending general elections, an action which probably originated in and certainly received the full approval of the Vatican. His Majesty's Government protested and declined to proceed with the negotiations until the bishops restored to the electors their freedom of choice. This the Vatican refused to do on the grounds that the bishops were only doing their duty as pastors of their flocks, and that it was for the ecclesiastical authorities alone and not for any outside Power to decide what was or was not sinful.

64. During the year there was no indication whatever that His Holiness the Pope, who personally handled the negotiations, would recede in the slightest from the position he had, through his Secretariat of State, taken up, and His Majesty's Government in the United Kingdom took no further steps towards appointing a Minister to the Holy See.

Palestine.

65. There was practically no event during the past year of special interest to record. His Majesty's Minister on the 10th April informed the Cardinal Secretary of State that pending the result of enquiries as to the liability of Roman Catholic communities and parish priests in Palestine to pay land tax, demands for payments of this tax already served in the above-mentioned cases would not be pressed.

66. The *status quo* with regard to the Holy Places was strictly maintained during the year, and although the Vatican are far from satisfied with the position no representations were made to His Majesty's Legation on the subject.

67. Mgr. Barlassina continued to be Latin Patriarch, a report of his impending transfer being denied at the Vatican.

68. Towards the end of the year the vice-rector of the Latin Patriarchs' Seminary in a public address protested against the increase of Protestant propangada, especially amongst the Christian Churches not in union with Rome.

69. The Jerusalem correspondent of the " Giornale d'Italia " also reported the intervention of the Governor of Jerusalem at the Grotto of the Nativity at Bethlehem with a view to commencing certain restorations. He added that a formal complaint by the Delegate Apostolic would be lodged, and that the policy of the mandatory Power was considered by Roman Catholics in Jerusalem as a studied attempt to diminish the prestige of the Latins in the Holy Land.

70. To neither of these incidents, however, did the Vatican draw the attention of His Majesty's Legation in the year under review.

71. The Vatican maintained during the year an attitude of strict reserve regarding the Zionist and Arab questions.

Iraq.

72. The Vatican were concerned for the future of the Christian minority, said to be about 100,000 in number, on the expiry of the British mandate in 1932. The Apostolic Delegate, Mgr. Drapier, a French Dominican, came to Rome during the autumn. He called on His Majesty's Chargé d'Affaires and expressed embarrassment at the possible effect of certain highly coloured and partly inaccurate articles, which in September and October appeared in the British Roman Catholic press, regarding the ill-treatment of Christians. He said that those articles were written neither with his authority nor with that of the Chaldean Patriarch. He, nevertheless, did not minimise his apprehensions as to the future, and frankly expressed the opinion that both France and Great Britain were pursuing a mistaken policy in the Near and Middle East, by sacrificing the interests of the Christians for those of the Moslems who would in the end display no feelings of gratitude. Towards the end of the year the Secretariat of State at the Vatican in corroborating the views of the Apostolic Delegate suggested that inasmuch as the delegate's negotiations with the Iraq Government were making no progress, a possible solution of the problem might be found either in the conclusion of some form of minorities treaty on the Central European model or in a treaty between Iraq and the Holy See negotiated with the support of His Majesty's Government in the United Kingdom and providing effective guarantees for its observance.

IV.—RELATIONS WITH OTHER COUNTRIES.

Abyssinia.

73. It will be remembered that in 1929 a special mission was sent to Abyssinia under Mgr., now Cardinal, Marchetti Selvaggiani.

74. Early in 1930 the Coptic Patriarch paid a visit to Addis Ababa with a view, so it was understood, to counteracting the effect of the Papal Mission.

75. Bishop Jarosseau, Vicar Apostolic of the Galla, represented His Holiness the Pope at the coronation of the Emperor Haile Silassie I. His Majesty was presented with an autograph letter of congratulation and good wishes, together with various presents, the Pope's representative receiving in return the Grand Cordon of the Order of Menelik.

76. The Congregation of Propaganda, under whose jurisdiction the missions in Abyssinia lie, when referring to the coronation, publicly expressed appreciation of the attitude of the Emperor towards the Roman Catholic Christians in Abyssinia, who are said to number about 16,000 as compared with 7 million Copts and 3 million Moslems.

77. The first Ethiopian bishop, Bishop Cassa, was consecrated in Rome on the 3rd August, 1930.

Austria.

78. On the 7th February Herr Schober, the then Austrian Chancellor, was received by the Pope.

79. The nomination, on the 3rd April, of Mgr. Geisler, a German, as Bishop of Brixen, with the concurrence of the Italian Government, created a favourable impression in Vienna, as regards Austrian relations with both the Holy See and Italy.

80. A short time before the Austrian elections the Cardinal Archbishop of Vienna visited Rome, and on his return to Austria the bishops issued a joint

pastoral enjoining on Catholics to support their associations, pay heed to the counsel of the clergy and not to vote for any candidate or party professing anti-Christian maxims. The "Osservatore Romano," in commending this pastoral, denied that the Church was unlawfully interfering in politics, and affirmed that it was her duty to work for the restoration of Christian society.

81.   Dr. Otto Ender, the new Chancellor, who is a Knight Commander of the Order of St. Gregory the Great, is a *persona grata* at the Vatican, who welcomed his appointment.

Brazil.

82.   Brazil is the favoured, if not the favourite, daughter of the Church in South America. Cardinal Arcoverde having died, his coadjutor, Mgr. Leme, was raised to the purple with unusual celerity after but a few weeks of office as archbishop. He is highly thought of by the Pope, and acted as the doyen of the five cardinals created last June.

83.   The Brazilian Ambassador informed His Majesty's Chargé d'Affaires that in Brazil there was no religious question as in many other Latin American countries. The Church was not by law established, and her relations with the State were good.

84.   The Vatican adopted an entirely neutral attitude during the revolution of 1930.

Bulgaria.

85.   During the past year the Vatican came into intimate contact with the Bulgarian Church and nation over the marriage of King Boris to Princess Giovanna of Savoy. It is understood that for some time past both the King of Bulgaria and the Italian Government had been desirous of bringing off this match, but that the difference of religion and the insistence of the Pope on the fulfilment of the necessary conditions for a dispensation to contract a mixed marriage had always stood in the way. These conditions take the form of promises—

(1) Not to prevent the Catholic party from exercising his or her religion.
(2) To bring up all the children as Catholics.
(3) Not to have a religious ceremony in any other but a Catholic church, except in cases where the local law insists that non-Catholic services are necessary for the completion of the civil act.
(4) In the case of the Catholic party, to do everything in prudence to secure the conversion of the non-Catholic party.

86.   On the 5th October the Italian press announced the engagement of King Boris to Princess Giovanna, adding that the Pope had granted the necessary dispensation. This was, on the following day, categorically denied by the Vatican in a statement to the effect that the dispensation had neither been requested nor granted.

87.   A fortnight later the Vatican announced that the Princess Giovanna asked for a dispensation and made the necessary undertakings and her request was granted. The Under-Secretary of State further informed His Majesty's Chargé d'Affaires that the King of Bulgaria had added a postscript to the Princess's letter to the Pope endorsing her request and promises. The marriage was duly celebrated in the Papal Basilica of St. Francis at Assisi on the 25th October.

88.   Immediately on their arrival in Sofia the King and Queen proceeded to the Orthodox cathedral and took part in a religious service. It is not known for certain in Rome whether this was a second marriage ceremony or not. It nevertheless evoked a thinly-veiled remonstrance from His Holiness the Pope in his Christmas Allocution to the College of Cardinals.

89. The question has arisen: Why did His Holiness agree to grant a dispensation for a mixed marriage in the circumstances? Was it from motives of subservience to, and under pressure from, the Fascist Government or for any other reason? The general impression at the Vatican, in a case, the details of which are treated with great privacy, is that the weighty considerations which impelled His Holiness to do so were (1) the hope or prospect that, as King Boris himself is understood to be sympathetic to the Catholic religion, the Bulgarian law compelling the heir to the throne to be brought up in the Orthodox religion might not eventually be enforced; and (2) the necessity of avoiding what would probably be considered a greater evil, namely, the marriage taking place in defiance of the Church.

China.

90. In 1930 there were approximately 2,486,841 Catholics, and 99 ecclesiastical divisions manned by 27,624 priests, nuns and lay helpers.

91. In the North the missionaries do not appear to have been seriously affected by the institutes. The new Catholic University of Peking had 268 students, the secondary school 431.

92. In the South, however, owing to banditry and communism engendered by privation and suffering caused by the civil war, Catholic missions have in places, especially in the valley of the Blue River, suffered seriously. Five priests and one bishop (Mgr. Soggiu) were killed and on the 31st December five kidnapped priests, including the Irish Father Tierney, were still in captivity.

Czechoslovakia.

93. The Holy See has not been satisfied with the execution of the *modus vivendi* during the past year. It is said that the Czechoslovak Government have not inserted this instrument in their list of international treaties. This omission seems to have engendered uncertainty as to whether the Czechoslovak Government desire to bind their successors to the terms of the *modus vivendi*. With regard to the establishment of dioceses wholly within Czechoslovak territory it is also complained that while the Holy See is expected to bring pressure to bear on the Hungarian and German Governments to that end, the Czechoslovak State has neglected the financing of the newly-constituted dioceses. Finally, the preference alleged to be shown to the Sub-Carpathian Orthodox clergy is contrasted with the difficulties put in the way of the Roman Catholics.

France.

94. The year was uneventful. The new Cardinal Archbishop of Paris is considered to be doing well, and to have the confidence of the Pope. He came to Rome towards the end of the year to be installed in his titular Church. His visit entailed such a round of functions and entertainments that, accustomed as he was to a life of austerity his health was quite undermined. He was taken ill in the streets and hurried off to a public hospital before his identity became known. Amongst the entertainments offered was a luncheon by the Canadian College to which I was invited.

95. France is determined not to be ousted by Italy from the *beaux yeux* of the Vatican. Of this the multifarious activities of the French Ambassador to the Holy See provide ample evidence. M. de Fontenay never misses a chance either of entertaining or of placing himself in the public eye. No mission to the Holy See even approaches the French Embassy in their lavish scale of entertainment, nor is there any function whatever, be it funeral, charity tea-party, lecture, French pilgrimage, or collective audience in which the Ambassador is not to the fore. He seems to take under his wing the whole French colony in Rome, and in the public print it is generally speaking the case of M. de Fontenay taking the lead rather than M. de Beaumarchais, his colleague at the Quirinal. The French Ambassador certainly serves his country well so far as outward representation is concerned. Whether such a policy really pays with the Curia, and especially with the present Pope, is open to question. For the few prelates at

the Vatican who can claim to have any influence with the Pope, regard entertainments and social functions as an unpleasant duty to be performed as rarely as possible compatible with ordinary courtesy.   So when one sees the French Ambassador and his Staff organising receptions to hundreds at a time in which the guests when not French, are Italian lay folk and diplomatic colleagues, and obtaining in return only about 15 minutes worth of two or three cardinals and Under-Secretaries, it would seem that France is paying a high price for her external prestige.

96.   His Holiness honoured France last May by appointing the French Cardinal Lépicier to be his Legate at the Carthage Eucharistic Congress.

97.   He also created a new French Cardinal in the person of Mgr. Liénart, Bishop of Lille, a young man who is held in high esteem at the Vatican as an expert in labour questions, and as a conciliator.

98.   Of the " Action Française " almost nothing was heard.

99.   The course of the Malta dispute was followed with close and not unsympathetic interest by the French Embassy.

Germany.

100.   Mgr. Cesare Orsenigo, a former Milanese collaborator of the Pope, was appointed Nuncio in succession to Cardinal Pacelli.

101.   The sudden rise and sweeping electoral victories of the National Socialist (Nazi) party impelled the Bishop of Mainz, through his Vicar-General, to forbid the Sacraments to any of his flock who should join the movement, the bishop objecting to certain items in the Nazi programme.   The Cardinal Secretary of State was careful to point out to His Majesty's Chargé d'Affaires that the bishop was acting on his own initiative.   It was also obvious that embarrassment had been caused, and nothing further was allowed to be published on the matter during the rest of the year.

Greece.

102.   Propaganda by the Uniates, *i.e.*, those who are Roman Catholic in allegiance but use the Greek rite, dress and other concessions such as clerical marriage, have been a source of friction.   To counter such propaganda the Greek Government prohibited the attendance of Greek children in the primary classes of foreign schools.   An Order was also issued requiring Uniate priests to alter their dress so as to distinguish them from the Orthodox Clergy.   The Latin archbishop protested to M. Veniselos in a telegram addressed to him in Geneva during the Assembly of the League.

103.   The possible influence of the Lambeth Conference and the Greek Orthodox Church as exemplified by the statements in favour of Anglican Orthodox co-operation made by the Orthodox Patriarch of Alexandria when returning through Greece on his homeward journey, did not pass unnoticed at the Vatican.

Hungary.

104.   On the 26th March the Archduke and Archduchess Joseph of Hungary were received in private audience by His Holiness the Pope with the honours due to their rank.

105.   In Augu.t the Pope sent Cardinal Sincero as his Legate to preside over the religious festivities in honour of the 900th anniversary of the death of St. Emery, the only son of St. Stephen, King of Hungary.   The celebrations were a great success, and the messages contained in the Papal Bull appointing the Legate and Cardinal Sincero's own utterances appear to have been enthusiastically received by the Hungarian nation, but not, so it later transpired, by the Little *Entente*.   In addition to the Papal Legate, five cardinals were present, including his Eminence Cardinal Bourne.   There were also eighteen foreign archbishops and bishops.

Italy.

106. As was to be expected, relations with Italy were good throughout the year, but in no way was the Vatican subservient to the Fascist Government, as was sometimes the impression.

107. In January the Prince of Piedmont and his bride paid a State visit to His Holiness the Pope. On the 10th February Signor Turati, then secretary of the Fascist party, was also received by the Pope, and on the 11th February, the first anniversary of the signing of the Lateran Treaty, the Italian Government presented His Holiness with a fine lace surplice. The late Cardinal Secretary of State, Cardinal Pietro Gasparri, was also decorated with the Collar of the Order of the Annunziata, and the Grand Cordon of St. Maurice and St. Lazarus was conferred on the Nuncio at the Quirinal. A special Order of the Day of the Fascist party was also published, commenting on the happy significance of the Lateran anniversary.

108. In the month of March the Fascist authorities, in a circular, made it known that there was no incompatibility between simultaneous membership of the party and of the " Catholic Action " movement. In September, the Italian Government issued a decree abolishing the National Festival of the 20th September, the anniversary of the capture of Rome in 1870, substituting in its place a public holiday to be observed on the 11th February, the anniversary of the signing of the Lateran Treaty.

109. In his allocutions on the 30th June and on the 24th December, when speaking of Protestant Proselytism in Italy, the Pope called for a more careful observance of the relevant provisions of the Lateran Treaty. He praised the Italian Government for giving legal recognition to the Institute for the Preservation of the Faith. In his Encyclical " Casti Connubi," on Marriage, he specially held up the Lateran Treaty as an example of the happy co-operation of Church and State for the ends His Holiness desired. The Papal authorities enjoyed the support and co-operation of the Italian Government for the carrying out of Vatican legislation, especially as regards customs and police matters. No clash occurred over the delicate question of education.

110. There were also a few points of friction. For example, Signor Mussolini was not received by the Pope. His continued absence from the Vatican, notwithstanding the reception accorded to other members of his party and to the Royal House, is noteworthy. Many months passed before agreement was reached filling the vacant Archbishopric of Turin. The Pope allowed his annoyance to be shown at the publication of the engagement of Princess Giovanna to King Boris of Bulgaria, before the necessary dispensation had been sought and obtained.

Japan.

111. According to latest information, the Roman Catholics number about 93,000 out of a total population of about 60 million.

112. On the 7th December, Prince Takamatsu of Japan, brother of the Emperor, was received in audience by the Pope. The Japanese Chargé d'Affaires at the Quirinal was present in the capacity only of a member of the Prince's suite. The visit did not have any special political significance. The question of establishing diplomatic relations with Japan was still under consideration.

Yugoslavia.

113. Some slight progress was made during the year towards opening negotiations for the conclusion of the concordat intended to replace the Serbian concordat of 1914, which was never brought into force.

114. There were certain serious preliminary obstacles, some of which were overcome. Those falling under the category of education are the most important. The Education Act of the 6th December, 1929, provided for religious instruction

by lay teachers, not necessarily approved by the Church, forbade the formation of religious associations in the schools, and the existence of private schools which would not adapt themselves to the provisions of the law.

115. As a result of representations made by the Vatican authorities, the Government, on the 15th January, in their regulations for the carrying out of the Education Act, agreed to submit the religious curriculum and the names of teachers of religion to the prior approval of the Church, and permitted the formation of religious associations outside the schools (in this connexion, see the section on Lithuania).

116. The dissolution of the Catholic " Orao " societies nevertheless caused discontent.

117. In July, however, King Alexander issued a decree which had the effect of handing over religious instruction in Catholic schools to the ecclesiastical authorities. This concession so improved relations as to lead to the appointment by the Yugoslav Government of two negotiators to proceed to Rome to start conversations for a concordat. Towards the end of October, His Majesty's Chargé d'Affaires was informed at the Vatican that the Holy See were ready to commence these negotiations. By the close of the year the Yugoslav negotiators had not arrived, and it was understood that the hostility of the Minister of Religion, the recurrence of difficulties over education, disagreements regarding the appointments of bishops, and the expropriation of Church property, under the Agrarian Law, had all contributed to the delay.

League of Nations.

118. During the year the Vatican maintained their usual attitude of sympathetic interest in the League, which, in spite of certain blemishes, is considered in many spheres to be actuated by Christian and Catholic principles advocated for many years past by the Holy See.

Liberia.

119. The President of Liberia decorated, on the 7th December, the Papal Chargé d'Affaires, Mgr. Ogé, with the insignia of Grand Commander of the Order of the Star of Africa, on the occasion of the fortieth anniversary of his arrival in Africa.

120. No opinion was expressed on the slavery question, to which the attention of the public was drawn at the end of the year.

Lithuania.

121. Relations with Lithuania were troubled. They afford an illuminating example (1) of the disadvantages of a Church party in the State; (2) of the pitfalls to which an injudicious use of Catholic Action can lead. The Lithuanian Government having already, in 1929, antagonised the Opposition and Church party (the Christian Democrats) by reducing their numbers and influence in the university, turned to the schools and decreed the suppression of " Catholic Youth " organisations, " Ateitininkai,'' part and parcel of the Catholic Action movement, which His Holiness the Pope has so much at heart. The Lithuanian Government alleged that the reason for this measure was that the Catholic Youth Associations were nothing else but party organisations of the Christian Democrat party organised for political purposes and consequently were neither suitable for the State schools nor covered by the concordat. Both the Nuncio and the Christian Democrat party vigorously protested alleging that the suppression of these associations was a violation of the concordat, article 25 of which safeguarded the rights of associations organised under the auspices of the Catholic Action Movement. It was further alleged that there had also been a breach of article 13 of the concordat which recognised the rights of the bishops to control Catholic education. The situation was also aggravated by the conduct of the Nuncio, Mgr. Bartoloni, who not only had antagonised the Lithuanian Minister for Foreign Affairs, for reasons connected with the latter's private life, but also had apparently openly associated himself with the Opposition party.

122.   Early in November the Lithuanian bishops issued a joint pastoral, which was publicly answered by the Lithuanian Government.   In short, the bishops contended that the action of the Government is suppressing these Catholic Youth Associations (1) infringed the rights of the Church over religious education of youth, which were superior to those of parents, (2) was a breach of the concordat.

123.   The Government replied to the effect that :—

(1) The Minister of Education had an equal, if not greater, responsibility than the Church for the education of children.
(2) The Church being granted the right to teach religion in the schools should be satisfied with that.
(3) That the associations in question were not only religious, but also political, which conducted an active propaganda in favour of the Christian Democratic party.
(4) That consequently such associations were not covered by the concordat.
(5) That the bishops in promulgating their pastoral laid themselves open to the charge of infringing article 12 of the concordat which required them to take an oath of loyalty to the Lithuanian Government.

124.   Towards the end of the year the conversations on the subject were transferred to Rome, where the Lithuanian Minister to the Holy See informed His Majesty's Chargé d'Affaires that the settlement of this dispute would take a considerable time.

Mexico.

125.   While the Vatican cannot and will never be satisfied with the 1929 religious settlement, even at its best, there was a feeling of relief that conditions were as favourable as could be expected.   When, however, there came in the autumn the news of the burning of a church in Tobasco with some eighty worshippers, a wave of depression supervened and His Holiness spoke sadly to His Majesty's Chargé d'Affaires about the situation in Mexico.   Moreover, owing to the insistence of the Governor of Tobasco in maintaining the law providing for the compulsory marriage of priests, no steps could be taken towards manning the parish churches in that State.

126.   By the end of the year, however, the clouds seem to have somewhat lifted, and the general impression here was that President Ortiz Rubio was at least not showing himself as hostile as was feared.

127.   Archbishop Ruiz, the Delegate Apostolic, is considered to be performing a difficult task to the satisfaction of both Church and State.

Norway.

128.   In July, on the occasion of the ninth centenary of the death of St. Olaf, the Pope addressed to Mgr. Offerdahl, the Vicar Apostolic of Norway, a letter in which he expressed his pleasure at the action of the Norwegians in honouring the Sovereign who brought them into the Christian fold.   His Holiness sent his blessing to Norway.

Poland.

129.   Since the resurrection of Poland there always has existed an under-current of sympathy between the Holy See and that country, which might be called the eldest Slav daughter of the Church.   During the past year the concordat appears to have worked smoothly.   In November, however, an otherwise uneventful and placid relationship was slightly ruffled when it became known at the Vatican that the Polish Government had censored a certain section in a pastoral of the Uniate bishop, Mgr. Szeptycki, in which his Lordship criticised certain acts of repression against Uniates in Eastern Galicia.   It is understood that the Pope, at first, remonstrated rather strongly with the Polish Ambassador,

but towards the end of the audience removed much of the sting from his remarks. In this connexion it is also understood that the Latin bishops in Poland supported the action of the Polish Government.

130.   The question of the formation of Uniate dioceses in the Kresy was also responsible for a difference of opinion.   The Vatican desired to do so, the Polish Government, in order not to alienate the Orthodox Church, demurred.   As the concordat prohibits the appointment of diocesan bishops if the Polish Government have political objections thereto, the only course open to the Vatican would be to appoint suffragan bishops in the existing Latin dioceses to take charge of the Uniates, a step which would be equally objectionable to the Polish Government. By the end of the year no action in that direction had been taken.

Russia.

131.   On the 2nd February the Pope addressed a letter to the Cardinal Vicar expressing horror and emotion over the acts of persecution and sacrilege that were being perpetrated in Russia, adding that he had tried unsuccessfully at the Genoa Conference to induce the Powers to make freedom of conscience, religious liberty and respect for Church property a *sine quâ non* for the recognition of the Soviet Government.   He had, however, succeeded in saving the life of the Patriarch Tikhon, and the Papal mission in Moscow had for some time been feeding more than 150,000 starving children a day.   He protested against the ill-treatment and imprisonment of the Catholic clergy, including three bishops, two of Latin and one of Byzantine Rite, and against the activities of the anti-God League.   He announced his intention of forming a special commission for Russia, and commended the work of the Oriental Institute.   He protested against the masquerading of sacred objects during the past Christmas season.   He accordingly announced his intention of celebrating a Mass of Reparation and Intercession in St. Peters on St. Joseph's day, the 19th March, expressing the hope that the Christian world would associate themselves with him on that or on another suitable occasion.

132.   Enquiry having been made whether the above letter was in any way intended to be a special message from the Pope to His Majesty's Government, His Majesty's Minister replied in the negative.

133.   The Mass on the 19th March was attended by a large congregation. Official invitations were not issued to the Diplomatic Corps, and representatives of countries in diplomatic relations with the Soviet Government did not attend.

134.   On the 9th April the Commission " Pro Russia " was formed under the chairmanship of Mgr. d'Herbigny, S.J., titular Bishop of Ilion.   It is housed in the Vatican near the Secretariat of State.   Its main object is to collect information regarding Russia and to consider and advise what steps can be taken for the restoration of religion in that country.

135.   At the secret consistory held on the 30th June the Pope expressed his appreciation of the response made all over the world to his appeal for intercession for Russia, and his conviction that his prayers would not be unheard. He ordered that the prayers said after Low Mass in all Catholic churches be applied for the intention of religious toleration in Russia.

136.   The Soviet Government in reply to the Pope's letter of the 2nd February denied that there was religious persecution in Russia and published a statement to that effect from the Metropolitan Sergius.   The " Osservatore Romano " in a series of articles in reply pointed out that, while the Soviet Government possibly were neutral about religion they allowed atheism under the guise of the Ecclesiastical Department of the G.P.U. to extirpate religion. Atheism was not only tolerated but given full liberty to persecute.   The Metropolitan had made his statement under compulsion.   The Soviet Government boasted that atheism had in July 17 million adult and 18 million child adherents, as compared with some 6,000 in July 1929.

137.   In October it was reported that Mgr. Roth Vicar Apostolic of the Kuban and a Father Wolff had been shot at Krassnodar.

138. Throughout the year the "Osservatore Romano" published in a prominent position under the heading: "Under the Bolshevik Yoke" all available press reports of the religious and other troubles in Russia, special attention being drawn to the correspondence and discussion on forced labour in the timber yards.

139. A Russian seminary for the training of priests in the Byzantine Rite for service in Russia was formed early in the year. It has about thirty students.

140. The library of the Papal Institute for Oriental Studies, the gift of a Spanish lady, was inaugurated in November. It is planned to accommodate 80,000 volumes.

141. The institute itself, which is directed by Jesuit Fathers, continued its courses of instruction in Eastern theology, languages and history, to about forty post-graduate students, of whom at least half were studying Russian. This institute whose main object, as regards Russia, is the restoration of religion and reunion with the Russian Orthodox Church did much unobtrusive work during the past year, the results of which will only be evident after the passage of some three or four years.

Sovereign Military Order of Malta.

142. The year 1930 saw the establishment of diplomatic relations with the Sovereign Military Order of Malta. This order, in view of the prominent part it played in the past as the champion of Christianity against the infidel, has always enjoyed the favour and protection of the Papacy, and not the least of the present Pope, who has been at pains to demonstrate his regard and sympathy. The first Minister, Don Luigi Pignatelli della Leonessa, Prince de Monteroduni, died during the year, at the end of which the appointment of his successor was imminent.

Spain.

143. Spain is very independent, perhaps naturally, in view of the special privileges enjoyed by the Church. She is entirely unrepresented on the personnel of the Papal Court. Her Ambassador is a pleasant, but retiring, personality who entertains rarely and is seen only at Vatican functions. The Secretariat of State are, nevertheless, concerned over the unsettled state of the country and fear an outbreak of anti-clericalism.

United States of America.

144. As in Spain, the 19 million Catholics in the United States are inclined to be independent of Rome. To quote an example, His Majesty's Chargé d'Affaires, on asking a well-known American Jesuit friend what Catholics would have said to a "mortal sin" ban laid on a candidate for the presidency, was met with the reply: "Why, of course, they would go and vote for him straight away."

145. During the past year there was a considerable diminution in American visitors, and the United States had a share in the work of the curia even more meagre than the United Kingdom. Though personal contact may have been slight, American interest in the affairs of the Holy See was sufficiently great to cause the International Telephone and Telegraph Company to present an entire telephone system, free of charge, to pay for a special press agent at the Secretariat of State, and to require the telegraphing, within twenty-four hours, of the 20,000 words of the "Encyclical on Marriage," at a cost of over £550.

146. As the Holy See is not in diplomatic relations with the United States Government, the good offices of His Majesty's Government in the United Kingdom were invoked in December for obtaining the adhesion of the Vatican State to the International Radio Convention of Washington, 1927, a request which was readily granted.

[5111] . **E**

V.—His Holiness the Pope.

147. His Holiness throughout the year showed great energy, personally controlling the conduct of affairs even of lesser importance, so much so that his Secretary of State was in practice reduced to the position of a clerk. In the early summer alarming rumours were current as to the state of his health. These were categorically and officially denied. His Holiness's general appearance and his mental and physical activity certainly did not give the impression that he, in his 74th year, was either sick or failing.

VI.—The Vatican.

Building Operations.

148. On the 31st December the following was the position of the construction work in the Vatican State :—

(1) New residence for the Cardinal Archpriest of St. Peter's, completed.
(2) Court and Government, building half-finished.
(3) Railway station, building nearly finished.
(4) Railway line, embankment tunnel under wall and entrance gate complete; rails not yet laid.
(5) Ethiopian College, completed.
(6) Wireless station, almost ready.
(7) Motor garages, complete.
(8) New officers' quarters, building of " Osservatore Romano " and Polyglot Press, completed and in use.
(9) Residence for Governor, in course of construction.

Catholic Action.

149. One of the principal features of Vatican policy, in every field of activity, during the past year has been the constant advocacy of what is known as " Catholic Action." " Catholic Action " is the co-ordinated organisation and dedication of lay activity under the control of the Church authorities for the diffusion of Roman Catholic principles amongst all classes of society in every walk of life. In other words, it is a weapon which the Pope is fashioning for combating the prevalent state of, what His Holiness has described as, " neo-paganism," in the world, and for establishing in its place the principles and practices of Roman Catholicism. " Catholic Action " is intended to be elastic and adaptable to the local circumstances of each country, making use of existing institutions, if necessary, or starting new ones where none exist. The Catholic Action Movement has been making considerable progress in Italy, where it is organised in an elaborate system of central and local committees. It has also been introduced into Spain, Mexico and certain Latin American countries, where it is making rapid strides. It also exists, at present in a less developed form , in France, Germany, Poland, Czechoslovakia and Austria. In Great Britain it does not bear that name, as bodies such as the Catholic Truth Society, the Catholic Evidence Guild, the Catholic Union, the Westminster Federation and the Knights of Columba already cover the ground within the scope of " Catholic Action." " Catholic Action," as the inspirer and co-ordinating force for Catholic ideals, has received from the Pope a great impetus during the past year, in the course of which there were few Papal utterances which did not make allusion thereto, urging lay folk to co-operate. More will be heard of " Catholic Action " in 1931.

The College of Cardinals.

150. The College of Cardinals, on the 31st December, consisted of 59 cardinals, of whom 29 were Italian and 30 non-Italian. Twenty-six are cardinals in curia, *i.e.*, employed in the government of the Church, and resident in Rome, of whom 22 are Italian and 4 non-Italian. The great preponderance of the Italian cardinals in curia is worthy of note.

151. The following is the list of the cardinals, in order of seniority, showing date of creation, appointment and nationality :—

Cardinal Bishops.

(1) G. Pignatelli di Belmonte (1911). Bishop of Ostia. Dean of College of Cardinals. (Italian.)
(2) Basil Pompilj (1911). Vicar-General of Rome. Bishop of Velletri. (Italian.)
(3) Michael Lega (1914). Bishop of Frascati. (Italian.)
(4) Donato Sbarretti (1916). Bishop of Sabina. (Italian.)
(5) Thomas Boggiani (1916). Bishop of Porto. (Italian.)

Cardinal Priests.

(6) Leo Skrbensky (1901). (Czech.)
(7) Pietro Maffi (1907). Archbishop of Pisa. (Italian.)
(8) Pietro Gasparri (1907). Cardinal Chamberlain. (Italian.)
(9) Paulinus Andrieu (1907). Archbishop of Bordeaux. (French.)
(10) Francis Bourne (1911). Archbishop of Westminster. (British.)
(11) William O'Connell (1911). Archbishop of Boston. (United States.)
(12) Gaetano Bisleti (1911). Curia. (Italian.)
(13) William van Rossum (1911). Curia. (Dutch.)
(14) Gustavus Piffl (1914). Archbishop of Vienna. (Austrian.)
(15) Andrew Frühwirth, O.P. (1915). Chancellor of the Holy Roman Church. (Austrian.)
(16) Raphael Scapinelli (1915). Curia. (Italian.)
(17) Pietro La Fontaine (1916). Patriarch of Venice. (Italian.)
(18) Alexius Ascalesi (1916). Archbishop of Naples. (Italian.)
(19) Louis Maurin (1916). Archbishop of Lyons. (French.)
(20) Adolf Bertram (1916). Archbishop of Breslau. (German.)
(21) Alexander Kakowski (1919). Archbishop of Warsaw. (Polish.)
(22) Francis Ragonesi (1921). In Curia. (Italian.)
(23) Michael de Faulhaber (1921). Archbishop of Munich. (German.)
(24) Dionysius Dougherty (1921). Archbishop of Philadelphia. (United States.)
(25) Francis Vidal y Barraquer (1921). Archbishop of Tarragona. (Spanish.)
(26) Carl Schulte (1921). Archbishop of Cologne. (German.)
(27) Achille Locatelli (1922). Chamberlain of the College of Cardinals. (Italian.)
(28) John Baptist Nasalli-Rocca (1923). Archbishop of Bologne. (Italian.)
(29) Luigi Sincero (1923). In Curia. (Italian.)
(30) George Mundelein (1924). Archbishop of Chicago. (United States.)
(31) Patrick Hayes (1924). Archbishop of New York. (United States.)
(32) Eustace Ilundain (1925). Archbishop of Seville. (Spanish.)
(33) Bonaventura Cerretti. In Curia. (Italian.)
(34) Enrico Gasparri (1925). In Curia. (Italian.)
(35) Luigi Capotosti (1926). In Curia. (Italian.)
(36) Lorenzo Lauri (1926). In Curia. (Italian.)
(37) Joseph van Roey (1927). Archbishop of Malines. (Belgian.)
(38) Augustus Hlond (1927). Archbishop of Gnesen and Posen. (Polish.)
(39) Alexius Lépicier (1927). In Curia. (French.)
(40) Raymond Rouleau (1927). Archbishop of Quebec. (Canadian.)
(41) Pedro Segura y Saenz (1927). Archbishop of Toledo. (Spanish.)
(42) Charles Binet (1927). Archbishop of Besançon. (French.)
(43) Justinian Sérédi, O.S.B. (1927). Archbishop of Esztergoni. (Hungarian.)
(44) Alfred Schuster, O.S.B. (1929). Archbishop of Milan. (Italian.)
(45) Emanuel Cerejeira (1929). Patriarch of Lisbon. (Portuguese.)
(46) Eugenio Pacelli (1929). Secretary of State. (Italian.)
(47) Luigi Lavitrano (1929). In Curia. (Italian.)

(48) Carlo Minoretti (1929).   Archbishop of Genoa.   (Italian.)
(49) Joseph MacRory (1929).   Archbishop of Armagh.   (Irish.)
(50) John Verdier (1929).   Archbishop of Paris.   (French.)
(51) Sebastiano Leme da Silveira Cintra (1930).   Archbishop of Rio de
      Janeiro.   (Brazilian.)
(52) Francesco Marchetti-Selvaggiani (1930).   In Curia.   (Italian.)
(53) Raphael Rossi (1930).   In Curia.   (Italian.)
(54) Giulio Serafini.   In Curia.   (Italian.)
(55) Achille Liénart (1930).   Bishop of Lille.   (French.)
(56) Camillo Laurenti (1921).   In Curia.   (Italian.)
(57) Giuseppe Mori (1922).   In Curia.   (Italian.)
(58) Francis Ehrle (1922).   In Curia.   (German.)
(59) Alessandro Verde (1925).   In Curia.   (Italian.)

152.   Of the thirty non-Italians, it will therefore be seen that the nationality
distribution is as follows :—

> Austrian 2, Belgian 1, Brazilian 1, British 1, Canadian 1, Czechoslovak 1,
> Dutch 1, French 6, German 4, Hungarian 1, Irish 1, Polish 2,
> Portuguese 1, Spanish 3, United States of America 4.

153.   The following cardinals died during the year : Cardinal Merry del
Val, Archpriest of St. Peter's; Cardinal Perosi, Secretary of the Consistorial
Congregation; Cardinal Arcoverde, Archbishop of Rio de Janeiro; Cardinal
Charost, Archbishop of Rennes; Cardinal Vanutelli, Dean of the College of
Cardinals; Cardinal Mistrangelo, Archbishop of Florence; Cardinal Casanova,
Archbishop of Grenada; *i.e.*, Italians 3, non-Italians 5.

Legislation.

154.   The following laws have been promulgated since the coming into
existence of the Vatican State, by the ratification of the Lateran Treaty and
Concordat on the 7th June, 1929 :—

No.   I.   June 7, 1929.   Fundamental Law.
No.   II.   June 7, 1929.   Law on the Sources of the Law.
No.   III.   June 7, 1929.   Law on Citizenship and Residence.
No.   IV.   June 7, 1929.   Law on the Administration.
No.   V.   June 7, 1929.   Law regulating economic, commercial and
                                  professional matters.
No.   VI.   June 7, 1929.   Law of Public Security.
No.   VII.   June 8, 1929.   Ordinance *re* access to the Vatican City.
No.   VIII.   June 30, 1929.   Postal Ordinance.
No.   IX.   September 28, 1929.   Ordinance *re* Health Services.
No.   X.   November 23, 1929.   Ordinance *re* Telegraph and Telephone
                                  Services.
No.   XI.   December 31, 1929.   Ordinance prolonging Ordinance
                                  No. VII.
No.   XII.   January 31, 1930.   Regulations *re* circulation of Motor
                                  Vehicles.
No.   XIII.   May 31, 1930.   Law granting legislative power to the
                                  Governor over Monopolies.
No.   XIV.   June 2, 1930.   Law on the Salt and Tobacco Monopoly.
No.   XV.   June 2, 1930.   Decree approving Salt and Tobacco regu-
                                  lations.
No.   XVI.   June 30, 1930.   Ordinance prolonging Ordinance No. XI.
No.   XVII.   July 31, 1930.   Decree approving regulations for importation
                                  and exportation of merchandise.
No.   XVIII.   August 1, 1930.   Ordinance amending Postal Tariffs.
No.   XIX.   December 22, 1930.   Ordinance *re* postal subscriptions to
                                  newspapers and periodicals.
No.   XX.   December 22, 1930.   Ordinance prolonging Ordinance No. XI.
No.   XXI.   December 31, 1930.   Coinage Law.

Constitutional Progress.

155. From the above list of legislation, it will be seen that in 1930 there were no innovations of principle, and such laws as were passed were in execution of principles already established in the first six laws of 1929. The policy of the Vatican was to go slow and only to make new laws as and when necessity arose.

Foreign Missions.

156. The following is a brief summary of missionary activity during the year 1930.

Progress.

157. New mission centres have been established in China at Wuchow and Tali; in India two new dioceses have been created in Vitayapuram and Kottar; in British Africa Archbishop Hinsley was appointed Delegate Apostolic to the African missions not under the superintendence of the Delegates Apostolic in South Africa, the Congo, Egypt, French Africa, Eritrea and Abyssinia.

158. While the number of conversions was stationary in China and Japan, considerable progress was made in the Congo and in South India, where two Jacobite bishops joined the Roman Catholic Church.

159. The new Catholic University in Peking (268 students) and the colleges in India are reported to be progressing satisfactorily.

Problems.

160. Banditry, communism, and general disorder in China, unrest in India, communist propaganda in South Africa, anti-religious educational laws in China and Japan, financial burdens on Catholic schools in British Africa, and the general loss of income, the result of the world economic crisis, formed the principal obstacles and setbacks to missionary work in 1930.

Papal Institute of Oriental Studies.

161. Another activity of the past year of no less importance than the Catholic Action movement, has been the further development of the Papal Institute for Oriental Studies. Started soon after the war by Benedict XV in order to provide advanced intellectual training for work amongst the Churches of the East not in union with Rome, it was installed in a special extra-territorial building in the centre of Rome. The Institute has been entrusted to the Jesuits, the superior being the French Bishop d'Herbigny, S.J., who has collected a staff of seventeen Jesuit Professors and experts of various nationalities. Twenty-two subjects are taught, and during the past year lectures were given in Oriental Dogma, History, Patrology, Liturgy, Canon Law, Archæology, Palæography, Islamic Institutions and Modern Judaism. Amongst the Oriental languages taught were Arabic, Armenian, Coptic, Greek, Palæo-Slav, Russian, Syriac and Turkish. The courses last two years, at the end of which the students are examined for the Degrees of Bachelor, Licentiate, and Doctor of Oriental Ecclesiastical Studies. In October the Library and Reading Room organised and equipped according to the latest American ideas, were formally opened by Cardinal Sincero, the President of the Oriental Congregation. The Commission " Pro-Russia," which formed part of the institute, has been transferred to new quarters in the Vatican (see section on Russia).

Papal Pronouncements.

162. The following are the more important encyclicals and other pronouncements issued during the year :—

    (1) Letter to the Cardinal Vicar, the 2nd February, on the situation in Soviet Russia.

    (2) Encyclical *Ad salutem humani*, the 20th April, in commemoration of St. Augustine of Hippo on the fifteen hundredth anniversary of his death.

(3) Allocution at the consistory of the 30th June, making reference to relations with Great Britain, Malta, Russia, the Carthage Eucharistic Congress, Protestant propaganda (see relevant sections of this report).

(4) Christmas allocution, the 24th December, referring to the St. Augustine and St. Emmerich of Hungary Celebrations. Dublin Eucharistic Congress to be held in 1932, the economic crisis, the Russian persecution, Protestant propaganda in Italy, Catholic Action, the need for real peace and disarmament, the Bulgarian Royal marriage, all of which are treated in their respective sections.

(5) Encyclical *Casti connubii* of the 31st December, 1930, on Christian marriage, giving the Roman Catholic teaching on every aspect of marriage and especially of present day problem in connexion therewith. A document of great importance, the detailed discussion of which lies more appropriately within the scope of the annual report for 1931.

Peace and Disarmament.

163. In his Christmas allocution to the College of Cardinals, His Holiness made an appeal for the development in the world of a genuine spirit of Christianity, without which no true peace amongst peoples was possible. One of the principal obstacles in the way of such a peace was the selfishness amongst nations and the various classes of society, which was reflected in exaggerated nationalism and the inequitable distribution of the good things of this world.

164. Peace was also not attainable so long as the nations were threatened with disorder internal and external with no protection against such evils, as anti-religious and anti-social propaganda. So far as concerned the threat of war it was incredible that a civilised State would nowadays take such a " monstrously homicidal and almost certainly suicidal step."

Press and News Services.

165. There are two Vatican newspapers, the daily "Osservatore Romano" and the fortnightly " Illustrazione Vaticana," an illustrated paper started in December, which publishes articles descriptive of the Vatican and its dependencies. It is also the intention to print articles on historical subjects.

166. Although not, strictly speaking, a Vatican, but an Italian paper, the fortnightly Jesuit review "Civilta Cattolica" publishes articles of a higher intellectual standard and written always with the concurrence or approval of the Pope. It can therefore be considered in practice, if not in theory, an official organ.

167. The Congregation di Propaganda Fide has a newsagency of its own called the "Fides" Agency, organised on American principles and directed by an American priest. This agency circulates to the press and to any others interested a series of communiqués in Italian, English, French, German and Spanish on subjects mainly concerned with the foreign missions.

168. A prelate is attached to the Secretariat of State charged with the duty of communicating to the press, Italian and foreign, any information passed for publication. He receives a retaining fee of not inconsiderable amount from the United Press for their American services, with the result that the United States have a better service of Catholic news than Great Britain. This press agent is the principal Vatican source from whom the correspondents of the Times," "Morning Post," "Daily Telegraph," "Manchester Guardian," "Daily Herald" and Reuter's receive their information, for which, it is understood, he receives a fee. The British Roman Catholic press, strange to say, is badly served, there being no organisation or proper co-ordination, and the correspondents obtain their information by hand to mouth methods.

Protestant Propaganda.

169. His Holiness publicly protested on two occasions against the Protestant propaganda which was being carried on in Rome and Italy, and he called on the Italian authorities to see that the relevant provisions of the Lateran Treaty were properly observed. He drew attention to the fact that

the toleration accorded to other religions did not imply freedom to indulge in proselytism against the Roman Catholic religion, which was the religion of the State.

170. His Majesty's Chargé d'Affaires was informed, on good authority, that His Holiness's complaints were directed not against the Church of England or the Church of Scotland in Rome, but against the American Methodists.

Telephone System.

171. A new automatic telephone system embodying the latest improvements has been installed and was inaugurated on the 19th November. It was presented by the International Telegraph and Telephone Company of New York, free of charge, who also gave His Holiness a golden telephone instrument for his personal use. The system is of the "International Rotary" type, controlling 800 lines within the Vatican. Thirty lines communicate with the City of Rome system instead of two as formerly.

VII.—Economic.

172. Previous to the Lateran Treaty there was no place, in an annual report on the Vatican, for an economic section. Now, however, the recognition by the Quirinal of the Pope's territorial sovereignty, and the consequent withdrawal of the Vatican State from the Italian economic system—in theory at least—justifies attention being paid to a minute, but not uninteresting feature. It is by a very slow, tentative and gradual process that the Vatican is developing a separate economic existence. The Holy See, being essentially a spiritual power, has no interest in commercial development. All it requires is the supply of such commodities as are necessary for the maintenance of a State of some 400 inhabitants, and for the upkeep and reconstruction of its buildings. Apart from these buildings and the areas specified in the Lateran Treaty the Vatican State, as such, has no other property except the funds used for religious purposes which are invested in various countries all over the world and are administered in accordance with the laws of those countries. The temporal requirements of this, territorially speaking, minute State are therefore comparatively insignificant. Once extra-territoriality was recognised, the policy of the Vatican with regard to setting up an independent economic régime has been to go very slow and to pass legislation only as and when necessity arose. In the year 1929, apart from the fundamental laws establishing the principle, few steps were taken to carry out the details. It was not till June and July 1930 that regulations were made governing the importation of merchandise in general, and tobacco and salt in particular. The chief tendency of these regulations was not indeed so much to control imports, but to ensure that no abuse or fraud was practised on the Italian Government through exportation into Italy. The best illustration of the position of the Vatican in these matters is to visualise it as one large Diplomatic Mission, established in Italy, for which the necessaries of life are on requisition from the Governor free of all Italian restrictions. With regard to these necessaries no legislation has been passed for such commodities as food-stuffs, which are free from Italian taxes or duties. Those commodities which are liable to tax are either imported on requisition, as occasion arises, or are the object of special legislation. Amongst the latter are tobacco and salt, concerning which certain regulations, intended mainly to prevent fraud or abuse of privilege, were passed during the year under review. The Italian Government, who were previously consulted, are apparently satisfied with the steps taken and have so far taken no overt action, either in the form of police or customs barriers, to control any commodities conveyed back into Italy over the imaginary frontier line. They have relied hitherto on the vigilance of the Papal gendarmerie or the Swiss Guards to check any abuses.

173. Apart from the service of spare parts for the postal telegraph, telephone and radio installations, the only import during the past year of possible interest to British industry was that of tobacco and cigarettes. His Majesty's

Chargé d'Affaires drew the attention of the European manager of the British-American Tobacco Company to this matter as, in view of the inferior quality of Italian cigars and cigarettes, there is a possibility of some orders being booked for British firms.

174.   The Vatican has also established a private bank for the convenience of its inhabitants in the purchase of the necessaries of daily life.   This bank is still in an embryonic stage, and it has been so far impossible to obtain precise information as to its activities.

175.   A representative of the Anglo-French Banking Corporation requested in October introductions to the competent Vatican authorities, with a view to providing banking facilities for the investments of the Holy See.   While no business was actually done, satisfactory contacts were made for which the bank were so good as to express their appreciation to His Majesty's Chargé d'Affaires.

176.   The Vatican investments are controlled by the Administration of the Goods of the Holy See, whose chief, a prelate, is directly responsible to the Pope, and who is assisted by at least two lay experts, one of whom is a Signor Bernardino Nogara, a director of the Banco Commerciale Italiano.

177.   The question arose during the year as to whether the dividends and interest on the Vatican's investments in the United Kingdom were exempt from British income tax.   This was decided in the affirmative and in the course of correspondence the nature of His Majesty's Government's recognition of Papal Sovereignty was set forth (see section on relations with Great Britain).

178.   A further commercial matter, affecting Great Britain more than the Vatican, was the question of the supply of building material for the new Roman Catholic cathedral in Liverpool.   As this is to be the second largest church in the world, costing upwards of £1 million, and as there was some question of utilising Roman bricks, His Majesty's Chargé d'Affaires expressed to the prelate in charge of the design the hope that British material would, as far as possible, be used.   Mr. Ogilvie-Forbes, at the same time, drew the attention of His Majesty's Government to the subject.   Sir E. Lutyens, the architect, was duly communicated with, and the reply was satisfactory.

179.   It is understood that most of the cables and tubing of the new telephone system inaugurated on the 19th November are of British manufacture.

CONFIDENTIAL.

(14044)

HOLY SEE.

Annual Report, 1931.

[C 1550/1550/22]

Mr. Ogilvie Forbes to Sir John Simon.—(Received February 25.)

(No. 27.)   *British Legation to the Holy See,*
Sir,   *Rome, February 19, 1932.*
    I HAVE the honour to transmit my annual report on the Holy See for the
year 1931.
    I am much indebted to my staff for their assistance in the compilation.
                                                            I have, &c.
                                                    G. OGILVIE FORBES.

─────────────────────

Enclosure.

Annual Report on the Holy See, 1931.

CONTENTS.

6337   [6801]   B

I.—Introduction.

THE principal events in the history of the Vatican during the year 1931 were the publication of encyclicals on a variety of important subjects common both to Church and State, such as matrimony, birth control, education, socialism, poor law, disarmament.

2. These documents enjoin what is the teaching of the Church on those matters, and consequently shape the general lines of policy to be followed by ꞌRoman Catholics all over the world. The significance of the Catholic Action movement was stressed in last year's report, in which it was prophesied that more of that subject would be heard of in 1931. This forecast has been entirely justified. Second only to the above-mentioned encyclicals, whose effects will be lasting, came the Pope's call to Catholic Action which provoked a memorable struggle with the Italian Fascist State.

3. The disagreement over Malta still continued, but its existence did not in any way hamper the excellent relations existing between the Legation and the Vatican. Unlike his Spanish and Lithuanian colleagues, His Majesty's Chargé d'Affaires not only suffered no embarrassment, but was always given the fullest measure of courtesy, friendship and understanding. Every facility was granted to him and to those citizens of the British Commonwealth of Nations who had recourse to the good offices of the Legation.

II.—Relations with the British Empire.

United Kingdom.

4. Despite the deadlock over Malta, the Holy See gave no sign to His Majesty's Legation that relations were anything but cordial. The Pope has never discussed Malta with His Majesty's representatives. He leaves that delicate subject to his Secretariat of State. At the end of the year His Majesty's Chargé d'Affaires heard, on good authority, that His Holiness, while he would not give way on the subject of Lord Strickland, for whom he seems to have the same antipathy as for M. Daudet, was equally unwilling to say or do anything further to embarrass His Majesty's Government in the United Kingdom, and is content to let the situation remain as it is.

5. On the 27th March the Pope received in public audience a party of some 150 citizens of English cities of Roman foundation under the leadership of the Mayor of Bath. He gave a learned address on early Roman associations with England. Special arrangements were made to show the visitors the Vatican Library and museums. They expressed great pleasure at the reception accorded to them.

6. On the 15th May three Roman Catholic members of the Labour movement formed the British delegation at the international celebration of Leo XIII's Labour Encyclical " Rerum Novarum."

7. Cardinal Bourne represented the Pope as Legate at the celebration in Rouen of the fifth centenary of Joan of Arc, the 29th May to the 1st June, 1931.

8. The changes of Government and the general election in Great Britain were followed with interest, the fluctuations in sterling with apprehension. The Vatican in various forms and under different names have large holdings in sterling securities. So far as is known they did not betray any signs of panic or of a desire to sell out on the depreciation of the pound. They willingly gave every facility for the publication of the Chancellor of the Exchequer's statement of the 10th December.

9. The cause of Margaret Sinclair, an Edinburgh working girl who died in 1925, was introduced towards the end of the year for possible eventual beatification.

10. His Majesty the King's expression of sympathy for the disaster to the Vatican Library was highly appreciated by the Pope, as also the messages of other learned bodies and authorities in Great Britain. Some of the books concerning England were damaged in the collapse.

11.   While the resolution of the Lambeth Conference on Birth Control came in for some criticism in the Vatican press, relations with the Church of England authorities in Rome improved.   His Majesty's Chargé d'Affaires was able to arrange a very friendly interview beween the Bishop of Gibraltar and the Cardinal Vicar, at the end of the year.

12.   During the year an unfortunate dispute arose between a British-owned concern and the Vatican, with reference to contracts for the rebuilding of churches in the south of Italy destroyed by the earthquake of 1908.   The total sum involved is said to amount to 17 million lire.   The circumstances were briefly as follows :—

13.   The Anonima Costruzione Edilizie, a subsidiary company of the Società Finanziaria Italo-Britannica was formed by Lloyds, National Provincial and Westminster Banks and the Bank of England, to realise the assets of the defunct Italo-Britannica Bank.   The A.C.E. is occupied in carrying out contracts for the building of churches in Reggio Calabria, Bovio, and Oppido Mamertino. The contracts concluded between the company, the Italian Government and the bishops of the three Calabrian dioceses concerned provided that two-thirds of the price was payable by the Italian Government and one-third by the ecclesiastical authorities out of the realisation of Messina Earthquake Bonds. The latter found that they were not able to make the necessary payments, and wished to repudiate the contracts on the ground that signatories on behalf of the Church had no authority, and in one case had not been in a state of health good enough to realise what was being signed.   The result was that while the Italian Government were apparently paying their share, no payment whatever was forthcoming from the ecclesiastical authorities.   Recourse to law being out. of the question as none of the parties was willing to incur the expense of registering the contracts, the A.C.E. requested the good offices of His Majesty's Chargé d'Affaires.

14.   After considerable difficulty and delay and a personal visit to the churches under construction, His Majesty's Chargé d'Affaires succeeded in bringing the parties together in an amicable atmosphere, and the year closed with some hope of an eventual friendly settlement.

15.   It is, perhaps, unnecessary to add that throughout the year His Majesty's Chargé d'Affaires met with every kindness and consideration in all his dealings with the Vatican.

Canada, Dominion of,

16.   The Hon. Howard Ferguson, High Commissioner of Canada in London, was, on the 2nd April, received in private audience by the Pope.   He afterwards called on the Cardinal Secretary of State.

17.   A party of thirty-five Canadian school-teachers, under the auspices of the Overseas Education League, Winnipeg, visited Rome in July, and were also received by the Pope.

18.   The appointment of Mgr. Rodrigue Villeneuve Bishop of Gravelbourg to be Archbishop of Quebec was greeted with satisfaction by Canadians connected with the Vatican.

19.   The Right Hon. F. Anglin, P.C., Chief Justice of Canada, visited Rome at the end of the year and had a private audience of the Pope.

20.   The majority of the annual party of school-teachers, organised by the League of the Empire, who, at the end of December, had an audience of the Pope, were this year of Canadian nationality.

Irish Free State.

21.   On the 27th February the Minister of the Irish Free State, in the name. of his Government, presented to the Pope a carpet of Irish manufacture. Measuring 10 yards by 5, it is mainly crimson in colour and decorated with the Papal Arms and the Arms of Ireland and her provinces.   His Holiness had it placed in his private study.

22. On the 29th March Mr. James MacNeill, Governor-General of the Irish Free State, was, with Mrs. MacNeill, received in audience by the Pope. As Mr. MacNeill's visit was of a private nature there was no guard of honour in the courtyard. In other respects the protocol observed was that of the reception of a Roman Catholic Ambassador, the usual visits to the Cardinal Secretary of State and to St. Peter's being made.

23. The Minister of the Irish Free State gave a reception in honour of Mr. MacNeill, to which the Cardinal Secretary of State and His Majesty's Chargé d'Affaires with other members of the Diplomatic Corps were invited.

24. On the 19th September the Pope received in audience an Irish pilgrimage numbering about 240. His Holiness, in his address, paid a tribute to the devotion of Irish Catholics to the Holy See, and expressed fervent wishes for the success of the forthcoming International Eucharistic Congress to be held in Ireland.

25. During the year intensive preparation was made for this congress, which will take place in Dublin in June 1932. Articles frequently appeared in the " Osservatore Romano " drawing attention to the matter.

India.

26. On the 7th February the Pope received in private audience Rao Bahadur Pannir Selvam, president of the All-India Catholic Conference, and representative at the Round-Table Conference of the 3 million Roman Catholics of India.

27. During the audience, at which His Majesty's Chargé d'Affaires was present, His Holiness expressed interest in and sympathy with the work of the Round-Table Conference.

28. The Very Rev. Leo P. Kierkels, a Dutchman by nationality and General of the Passionist Order, was consecrated archbishop in April, and appointed Delegate Apostolic in the East Indies. Before announcing the appointment, the Vatican took steps to ascertain whether His Majesty's Government would grant the necessary visa which was, in due course, authorised, and Mgr. Kierkels proceeded to his post in June. He replaced an American, Mgr. Edward Mooney, who was transferred to Japan.

29. Mr. Gandhi arrived in Rome on the 12th December, having applied, through His Majesty's Legation, for an audience with the Pope. Owing to previous engagements His Holiness was not able to receive him. Mr. Gandhi was accordingly politely informed. Not satisfied with the position he made more than one attempt, through private channels, to obtain an audience, but in vain.

Kenya.

30. Additional schools have been started, including a high school for natives. Some friction exists with the Director of Education, who is stated to consider the mission schools as below standard, and to desire to entrust control of education to native councils.

Malta.

31. The deadlock, the circumstances of which were described in paragraphs 39 to 64 of the 1930 report, continued throughout the year. The Vatican showed no inclination to cause the ecclesiastical authorities in Malta to alter their policy of spiritual intervention in secular politics. His Majesty's Government in the United Kingdom in February decided to appoint a Royal Commission to visit Malta, to consider the existing political situation and to make such recommendations as might seem desirable as to the steps to be taken to deal with the situation with special reference to the possibility of re-establishing constitutional Government. The commission consisted of Lord Askwith, president; and of Sir Walter Egerton and Count de Salis, members. While the Vatican would have preferred a commission with a membership equally divided between Protestants and Roman Catholics, it was evident that the inclusion of Count de Salis was welcomed and nothing was done to render the work of the commission more difficult. When the commission had completed their visit, the

Cardinal Secretary of State in conversation with His Majesty's Chargé d'Affaires, commented informally on the correct attitude adopted by them towards the local ecclesiastical authorities.

32. The Archbishop of Malta visited Rome several times during the year.

Nyasaland.

33. Nyasaland is divided into two Vicariates Apostolic, Shiré and Nyasa. The Education Ordinance of 1930 has apparently given satisfaction to the Roman Catholic missionaries in that Protectorate.

Northern Rhodesia.

34. The missions have made progress during the past year, especially at Banguelo, in the Kasempa copper belt, and in the centres linked by the Cape to Cairo Railway. New missions have also been opened in Barotseland. The Roman Catholic missions in Northern Rhodesia are manned mainly by French White Fathers, Polish Jesuits, Italian Franciscans (Conventuals) and Irish Franciscans (Capuchins), under a British Jesuit Vicar-Apostolic.

Sudan.

35. This is considered a difficult mission field. Moslem fanaticism, the wild Shilluk tribes on the one hand, and competition from other Christian bodies, Protestant, Greek Orthodox and Coptic, on the other, are stated to hamper the activities of Roman Catholic missions. In the Southern Sudan especially, the system of zones, where Catholic and Protestant missionaries are, by law, excluded from working in the same area, has been a subject of grievance to the Vatican, who in the past year made friendly informal representations to His Majesty's Chargé d'Affaires, with a view to securing the abolition of these restrictions. The Sudan Government did not see their way to accede to this request.

Uganda.

36. The authorities at the Vatican considered this country from the missionary point of view to be the most flourishing of those on the eastern side of the African continent. Not only are there seminaries for native clergy, but there are also an Intermediate School for natives and several convents of native nuns.

Mandated Territory.

37. *Palestine.*—The Archbishop of Canterbury, having expressed his intention of visiting the Holy Places, the Vatican in March displayed apprehensions lest the *status quo* be altered, and drew the attention of His Majesty's Legation to the matter. His Grace completed his journey according to plan, and there was, of course, no infringement of the *status quo*, a fact which was subsequently admitted by the Vatican in the same form as the original representation.

38. The alleged levying of land tax and tithe on certain institutions under the Latin Patriarchate gave rise to certain complaints to be dealt with in the year 1932.

39. *Tanganyika Territory.*—Missionary work is reported to be flourishing in this territory. An Irish bishop from Tanganyika has commented favourably to His Majesty's Chargé d'Affaires on the good relations existing between the Governor and the Roman Catholic ecclesiastical authorities.

III.—RELATIONS WITH OTHER COUNTRIES.

Afghanistan.

40. The news came to hand in 1931 that a Roman Catholic priest, in the person of the Rev. George J. Blatter, of Chicago, visited Afghanistan in 1930 for the first time since the second Afghan war. Father Blatter expressed appreciation of hospitality and facilities provided by His Majesty's Legation. He met, and was well received by, King Nadir Shah and several of the Ministers. Through illness he was forced to leave the country in October 1930. He did

not officiate in public, and he failed to obtained permission to re-enter the country in order to minister to the spiritual needs of Roman Catholics in Afghanistan, where the law apparently excludes all Ministers of religion other than Mahometan.   Afghanistan is, therefore, still a closed country to the Roman Catholic missionary.

Austria.

41.   The question of a concordat in substitution for the concordat of 1855, which the Holy See declared to have lapsed with the dissolution of the Austrian Empire, was under consideration during the year.   Progress was slow, in view of the well known reluctance of certain of the Pope's present advisers, often of the Pope himself, to conclude such instruments except on certain conditions insisted on by His Holiness, as a *sine qua non*.   With regard to Austria, the terms required by the Vatican would appear to be the waiving by the State of all former rights of interference in the internal economy of the Church, and particularly with regard to the appointment of bishops ("Josephism"), reform of the marriage laws, safeguards for religious instruction, and recognition of the Catholic Action movement.

Brazil.

42.   Two imposing religious ceremonies took place during the past year, in which the Papal Nuncio played a prominent part.   One was the dedication of Brazil to the Virgin of Apparecida as the Patron Saint of the nation, and the other was the inauguration of a monument of Christ on the Corcovada.   The Cardinal Archbishop of Rio de Janeiro was appointed Papal Legate for the latter occasion.

43.   During the trouble with the Italian Government over Catholic Action, the Pope was reported to have received an offer of asylum in Brazil.

Bulgaria.

44.   Early in November the Vatican raised the status of the Pope's representative in Bulgaria, who, it is understood, is not a member of the Diplomatic Body, to the rank of Delegate Apostolic.

China.

45.   Mgr. Costantini, Apostolic Delegate to China, visited Rome during the past year, in order to report on the position of the Roman Catholic Church in that country.   The number of Roman Catholics in China is estimated at about 2,500,000, in the spiritual charge of 27,700 clergy and nuns.

46.   The Roman Catholic missions in China in many places suffered severely at the hands of brigands and bandits.   One Irish priest, the Rev. Cornelius Tierney, was murdered by bandits in the month of March.   The Pope, in pursuance of his policy for the encouragement of native clergy, authorised the consecration of another Chinese bishop during the past year, making a total of ten native Roman Catholic bishops.   His Holiness was also specially interested in the translation into Chinese of books on theology.   Six volumes of the works of St. Thomas Aquinas, on which the theology of the Roman Catholic Church is based, have already been translated into that language.

47.   In January the Pope addressed an open letter to a Chinese Benedictine, Dom Peter Lou Tseng Tsing, formerly representative of China at the Versailles Conference, commending the activities of the National Anti-Opium Association of China, condemning the traffic and use of opium, and expressing the hope that with the re-establishment of law and order in China, the Government will be successful in suppressing the cultivation of the poppy and the opium trade.

48.   The Apostolic Delegate in China, in drawing attention to the matter, issued instructions to the Roman Catholic missions, enjoining, under penalties, the observance of the anti-narcotic decrees.

Czechoslovakia.

49.   The *modus vivendi* appears to be working satisfactorily.   Delimitation of dioceses in conformity with the national frontier line and the consequent

redistribution of episcopal revenues were the principal problems to be faced. The fact that they were being solved in a manner agreeable to the Czech Government was confirmed by two hasty visits to Rome of the Cardinal Primate of Hungary, in an endeavour to defend the interests of Hungarian bishops who were the parties principally affected by the *modus vivendi* with Prague.

50.   Considerable comment was caused by the action of the Pope in removing the Archbishop of Prague and causing another to be appointed in his stead.   The exact reasons are still obscure, but they are believed to be based mainly on personal antipathy between the aged archbishop and the comparatively young and energetic Nuncio.   Prague is usually a Cardinalitial See.

France.
51.   There is nothing of outstanding interest to record.   Relations with the French Embassy were as cordial as ever.

52.   Early in May the Comte de Paris was married to Princess Isabella of Orleans-Braganza at Palermo.   The Pope gave permission for the marriage to be celebrated by the Cardinal Archbishop.   M. Maurras and other prominent members of the Action française were present, and the public demonstrations, in which they are reported to have indulged, caused considerable annoyance at the Vatican.

53.   France was represented by some 1,600 pilgrims at the celebration in May of the fortieth anniversary of Pope Leo XIII's Encyclical on Labour Questions.

54.   Serious exception was taken to an article in the "Europe Nouvelle" attacking the centralising policy of the Vatican for Catholic Action, and commending Signor Mussolini for breaking in Italy the incipient organisation of "Pontifical fascism."   A semi-official reply was prepared for publication in 1932.   The identity of the author of this article, who wrote under the pseudonym "Noel Abrieu," was not known to the Vatican.   He is the adviser on ecclesiastical affairs to the Quai d'Orsay.

Germany.
55.   The ecclesiastical divisions in Prussia were reorganised.   Provision was made for three provinces, Cologne, Breslau and Paderborn.

56.   The bishops of the Prussian provinces and of Bavaria had, by the end of March, issued joint Pastorals in condemnation of the National Socialist party, declaring that Catholics were not allowed to join the party so long as it held principles contrary to Catholic doctrine.   The principal grounds of objection were : —

   (1) Article 24 of the party programme, which declared that all creeds were subordinated to racial considerations.
   (2) The exaltation of nationalism over religion.
   (3) The recognition of violence as a legitimate political weapon.
   (4) The desire to denounce the concordat.
   (5) The agitation for undenominational education.
   (6) The tolerance of artificial birth control.
   (7) The anti-clerical activities of certain leaders of the party.

57.   It is understood that many Roman Catholics, if they are not actually members, are, nevertheless, supporters of the greater part of the National Socialist programme.   If the above objections could be removed, there is reason to suppose that the ecclesiastical ban would be withdrawn.   Except in the Mainz case, in 1930, no spiritual penalties appear to have been threatened until September, when the same Mainz authorities denied Christian burial to a National Socialist Deputy.   Responsibility for this action is ascribed rather to the local ecclesiastical authorities, than to the Vatican.

58.   Dr. Kaas, the leader of the Centre party and a prelate, visited Rome in December, mainly, so it is stated, for reasons other than political.

59.   The developments in the German political situation during the year were watched with some anxiety by the Vatican, a certain apprehension being

felt at the prospect of Germany going Communist and thus opening the flood-gates of bolshevism in Central Europe. This consideration, no doubt, influenced the Vatican not to go too far towards the condemnation of the Nazi party.

Greece.

60.   Early in the year the Pope appointed as Delegate Apostolic in Greece a prelate well known in Rome as an authority on questions connected with Eastern Churches.   The Vatican were desirous of preparing the ground for the conclusion of a concordat with Greece.   A difficulty arose, in that the Delegate Apostolic, who is an Italian, has, by reason of his position as representative of the Pope, jurisdiction over Catholics of Greek nationality, and the Greek Government demurred to the idea of accepting a diplomatic representative armed with such authority.   Little progress was made with the negotiations during the year.

Hayti.

61.   A Nuncio having been appointed in 1930, a M. Louis Barom came to Rome in November on a special mission in order to thank the Pope, on behalf of his Government, for this nomination.

62.   His Majesty's representative in Hayti has commented on the allusion by the Archbishop of Port-au-Prince, in his speech of welcome to the Nuncio, to the Vatican's interest in the Haytian national revival.

Hungary.

63.   The Empress Zita, early in June, was received in private audience by the Pope, a visit which provoked considerable comment and rumours in Vatican circles.

64.   The French Ambassador assured His Majesty's Chargé d'Affaires on more than one occasion that he had good authority for believing that the objects of the visit were to discuss a possible marriage between Prince Otto and Princess Maria of Savoy, and to hint at a possible *coup d'Etat* in Hungary with a view to placing Prince Otto on the throne.   The Pope was understood to have taken a non-committal attitude.

Iraq.

65.   The Vatican expressed some concern for the future of the Christian minorities in Iraq and particularly for those Christians owing spiritual allegiance to the Pope, in the event of His Majesty's Government resigning the mandate over Iraq and that country attaining a full measure of independence. The suggestion was made that, as a condition for admission to the League of Nations, Iraq should enter into some form of engagement safeguarding the rights of the Christians and should provide some effective guarantee for its observance. His Majesty's Government decided that it was for the Assembly and Council to decide what assurances in regard to the minorities Iraq should be invited to give before her admission to the League.

66.   The Permanent Mandates Commission of the Council of the League of Nations, which reported in favour of the release of Iraq from the mandatory régime, recommended, *inter alia*, that Iraq should make a declaration on the lines of undertakings given by certain European States and should accept any special provisions which the Council of the League, in agreement with the Iraq Government, may consider necessary as a temporary or a permanent measure. This proposal is in general agreement with the suggestion made by the Vatican.

67.   The Rev. Edmund Walsh, S.J., of Georgetown University, U.S.A., formerly head of the Papal Mission to Russia, 1923, and who played a prominent part in the negotiations of the *modus vivendi* between Church and State in Mexico, 1929, was in the spring sent by the Pope on a private journey of observation to Iraq.   His opinion as to the possibility of that country, after the grant of independence, maintaining herself in peace and contentment was somewhat pessimistic, as was his view of the future of Christianity in Meso-potamia, unless assistance was forthcoming from without.

Italy.

68.   The year 1931 proved to be eventful in the relations between the Holy See and Italy. Opening calmly, there came a storm of hurricane violence over Catholic Action which well-nigh shattered the whole Lateran settlement.   It suddenly subsided, and the year closed quiet and peaceful once more.

69.   On New Year's Day was published the Encyclical on Marriage, in which the Pope held up to the world the convention with Italy on matrimony as an example of the harmony and friendly co-operation worthy· of " the glorious history and of the sacred traditions of the Italian people," declaring it to be an agreement between two sovereign authorities without detriment to the prerogatives of either party.

70.   In February the Archbishop of Zagreb in Yugoslavia issued a pastoral letter appealing for prayers for the persecuted Yugoslav fellow-countrymen over the border.   Other Yugoslav bishops followed suit.   There arose a wave of indignation in Italy against this alleged reflection on the Italian treatment of the Slav minority. The Italian Government demanded not only satisfaction from Belgrade, but also that the Vatican should reprove the offending bishops.   The Pope refused to take any action, at least in public, the Vatican maintaining that, subject to faith and morals, the drafting of a pastoral was the private affair of the bishop.   The Vatican were also strengthened in their attitude by the fact that a Visitor Apostolic, sent a few months before to the Slav districts of the Near East, furnished a report which gave some justification for the archbishop's language.   The refusal of the Vatican to act created a grievance to be nursed for the future.

71.   Very shortly afterwards the great controversy over Catholic Action broke out.   Trouble had long been brewing.   Ever since the Lateran Treaty the Fascist party had eyed with jealousy the prospect of the Italian Catholic Action movement taking advantage of its privileged position, under article 43 of the concordat, to encroach upon spheres reserved to the State, and even to set up rival organisations, especially of working men.

72.   Article 43 provided that the Italian State should recognise the organisations depending on Catholic Action so long as they developed their activities outside party politics and under the immediate control of the hierarchy, for the diffusion and realisation of Catholic principles.   An explosion was caused by an indiscreet circular from the president of the local centre of the Italian Catholic Federation of Youth, regarding the creation of " professional groups."   The Vatican, realising that a mistake had been made, quickly suppressed the offender, but it was too late.   In the storm of protest which arose against interference with the powers of the State, Mgr. Pizzardo, Under-Secretary of State at the Vatican, and chief ecclesiastical adviser of Italian Catholic Action, became involved.   He was attacked for a speech he had made some months before, claiming for Catholic Action certain functions which were considered to belong solely to the State.   Mgr. Pizzardo had argued in favour of the thesis that in economic and social matters it was the duty of Catholic Action to promote the well-being of the workers, a task enjoined by Divine Law.   His Holiness lost no time in supporting his Under-Secretary, declaring publicly that Catholic Action knew no limits and was legitimate, necessary and irreplaceable.   A lengthy polemic in the Vatican and Fascist press was then launched forth.   The Pope returned to the charge by addressing an open letter to the Cardinal Archbishop of Milan, rebuking by name Signor Giuriati, then secretary of the Fascist party, for certain expressions made in a public speech which His Holiness considered disrespectful to himself.   He reiterated his vindication of Catholic Action and of its beneficent influence over the education of youth.   He declared that it did not indulge in party politics.

73.   A fortnight later the international celebration of the fortieth anniversary of Leo XIII's Labour Encyclical, " Rerum Novarum," was held. Twenty thousand working men from various countries of Europe came to Rome. The Italian contingent was organised by Italian Catholic Action, who held meetings and expressed opinions considered heretical to fascism.   In the universities Fascist students commenced to " rag " the Catholics.   To console the latter, the Pope, in a public audience, protested against those attacks,

mentioning by name the head of the Young Fascist Combatants. Further raids on Papal property and attacks on Catholic students were made. The Apostolic Chancery, a building enjoying diplomatic immunity under the Lateran Treaty, was involved. A Vatican mail van was overturned. The recent Encyclical on Labour was burned. The premises of the Jesuit organ, " Civilta Cattolica," were raided. Even Mgr. Pizzardo and the editor of the " Osservatore Romano " were threatened with personal violence if they set foot outside the Vatican. The Fascist Government ordered the closing of all Catholic clubs and the dissolution of Catholic associations, even of children. The Pope summoned a meeting of cardinals, who passed a vote of sympathy. By means both of his Nuncio at the Quirinal and by his own speeches at public audiences, His Holiness continued to protest against the action of the Italian Government. He also forbade all public religious processions and suspended the despatch of his Legate to the St. Anthony festivities at Padua, action which in the former case involved some rioting in the south of Italy, and in the latter case caused disappointment and financial loss to the caterers for the pilgrimages. On the other hand, a meeting of the Fascist Directorate was held on the 3rd June. A resolution was passed taking note of the hostile attitude of certain sections of Catholic Action, and, while affirming profound respect for the Catholic religion and its head, declared in the most explicit manner that it would not tolerate anti-fascism taking protection under any flag, old or new.

74. The Pope continued to protest in public against the attacks made on Catholic students and on Vatican property, the closing of the clubs and the above-mentioned resolutions. Telegrams of sympathy and of criticism of the policy of the Fascist Government poured in from all over the world, notably from the United States of America, and were published in the " Osservatore Romano." On the 29th June, St. Peter's Day, an encyclical to the Catholic world, " Non abbiamo bisogno," written in Italian, and not the customary Latin, was signed, conveyed surreptitiously out of Italy for fear of suppression by the Fascist Government, and communicated to the press in Paris and London.

75. This encyclical, after giving thanks for the expressions of sympathy and solidarity with the Holy See, protested against the violent anti-clerical measures taken by the Fascist Government, as if Catholic Action were a conspiracy dangerous to the State. Serious exception was also taken to a radio message broadcast by the Fascist Government which contended that the Church was not only not being persecuted, but was guilty of grave ingratitude.

76. The Pope repeated his affirmation that Catholic Action was above and beyond all party politics. He further declared that the Fascist Government had contended that the leaders of the Partito Popolare had been given prominent positions in Catholic Action. The Pope had asked for their names and they were not forthcoming. He also protested against the Vatican being styled a " foreign " Power, especially by Italian Catholics. He denied the right of the Fascist Government to claim the entire monopoly of youth in order, so he stated, to propagate pagan ideas of State government in direct conflict with the rights of the family and of the Church. He declared that the Church had never opposed the rights and duties of the State in education, provided those rights and duties remained within the limits allowed to the State. The Church was the authority on all matters concerning Christian education, and the salvation of souls, and it was wrong and incompatible with the profession of the Catholic faith to presume to teach the Church and Pope what was sufficient for that form of education. Catholic Action was essential in the interests of religion. The Fascist aim that youth, from earliest years, should belong entirely to the State was reconcilable neither with Catholic doctrine nor with Divine Law.

77. The Pope then protested against the oath which he said was imposed on members of the Fascist party, not excluding children, to serve the régime with might and main, even to the effusion of blood. Such an oath, he said, was not lawful, but the consciences of those called upon to take it could be relieved by a clause " saving the laws of God and of the Church."

78. His Holiness denied that the Italian people were anti-clerical. Anti-clericalism was the product of freemasonry and liberalism, and formerly used to be rampant. The Fascist party had it in their power to switch on or off

the anti-clerical current as they pleased and since the Lateran Treaty anti-clericalism had undoubtedly been the order of the day.

79. One of the results of this encyclical was a further stream of telegrams, all duly published in the "Osservatore Romano." The Fascist Directorate published a reply, which, however, did not deal with the main points of the encyclical, *i.e.*, the defence of Catholic Action, the condemnation of the Fascist theory of State worship, and the vindication of the claim of the Church to a share in the education of youth.· The fact that it was drafted in a non-provocative manner was noted with some relief at the Vatican, and showed that counsels of moderation were prevailing in the Fascist party.

80. On the 17th July a bomb was found in St. Peter's and removed to a place of safety where it exploded a few hours later, doing no damage.

81. As time passed it became clear that the Pope, by the vigorous action he had taken in protesting to the whole Catholic world on what was an entirely local controversy, had shot his bolt, and short of excommunicating Signor Mussolini or placing Italy under an interdict, there was little else that he could do. Moreover, the expressions of sympathy and support from abroad could not continue to flow in indefinitely. In other words the law of diminishing returns was beginning to operate. It was also clear that the head of the Italian Government did not desire a final and definite breach. Unofficial conversations were begun, and thanks largely to the intermediary of the Jesuit Father Tacchi Venturi, *persona grata* to both parties, and who played a very important rôle in the negotiations for the Lateran Treaty, a settlement of the controversy was reached on the 1st September.

82. The agreement provided that Italian Catholic Action should depend directly from the bishops who would not select any directors from parties in opposition to the Fasci st régime. Catholic Action was to refrain from associating itself with party politics and from adopting outward forms associated with political parties. It would use the Italian flag. It was not to form professional associations or syndicates, and such professional branches as already existed must have an exclusively religious object. Juvenile associations of Catholic Action must also fly the national flag, refrain from activities of a sporting or athletic nature, and restrict themselves solely to "educational recreations with a religious aim." On the conclusion of this agreement the Fascist Government reversed their ruling as to the incompatibility of membership of the Fascist party with membership of Catholic Action, and permitted the reopening of the Catholic clubs and associations.⁺⁺

83. In short the Pope, while retaining in principle the right of the Church to provide for religious education as she pleased, gave way on the other points at issue, regarding which there seems no doubt he had in many cases been badly advised. It was, moreover, quietly admitted in Vatican circles that Catholic Action, by reason of its privileged position under the Lateran Treaty, had become the refuge of anti-Fascist elements.

84. As the year drew to a close, relations with Italy improved still further. In facing the problems presented by the economic crisis, and by the reparations and disarmament questions there seems to be considerable agreement between the Vatican and fascism, and both parties realise the undoubted advantages of mutual co-operation.

85. On the 21st December Signor Arnaldo Mussolini, brother of the Duce and editor of the important Fascist newspaper "Popolo d'Italia," died. As Signor Arnaldo was known to have been a devout Catholic and to have exerted a moderating influence in the counsels of the party his death evoked from the Vatican a genuine expression of sorrow and of sympathy.

League of Nations.

86. The attitude of the Vatican towards the League was one of support and sympathy tempered with reservations concerning certain features such as an alleged anti-Christian spirit and masonic interference, both of which were considered to be on the wane. The "Osservatore Romano," in a leading article on the 26th January, paid a compliment to Mr. Arthur Henderson especially for

his declaration, at the 62nd session of the Council, that His Majesty's Government sought no alliances other than the world alliance provided by the League; and declared that his pronouncement against military alliances was a repetition of the teaching of Leo XIII and Benedict XV, which had been ignored.

87.   On the 22nd April Sir Eric Drummond was received in private audience by the Pope.

Liberia.

88.   In the month of April the Pope received a special mission from the Republic of Liberia, which was sent to express thanks for the establishment of a Nunciature in that State.   The head of the mission was Mr. Grimes, Minister of Justice of Liberia.   He was accompanied by the delegate of the Liberian Republic at the League of Nations.

Lithuania.

89.   Relations with Lithuania became still further strained almost to breaking-point.   The causes of trouble, *i.e.*, the political activities of Lithuanian Catholic Action, the anti-clerical reprisals of the Government. the personal antipathy between the Nuncio and the Minister for Foreign Affairs, were summarised in last year's report.   Early in the year the Pope's letter to the Lithuanian bishops, dated the 27th December, became generally known.   His Holiness urged the bishops not to falter in the encouragement of Catholic Action, and to invite the co-operation of laymen. despite obstacles being placed in the way.   He indicated the various forms that Catholic Action could take, as for example the maintenance of religion and the protection of moral standards. He pointed out how, in present conditions, a layman could penetrate to persons and places from which priests were debarred, and he added that Catholic Action must not be connected with political affiliations or parties.

90.   In April the antagonism between the Nuncio and the Lithuanian Minister for Foreign Affairs, who apparently for over a year had not been on speaking terms, came to a head.   The Nuncio, who earlier in the year had been called to Rome for purposes of consultation, returned to his post.   The Lithuanian Government were incensed at his Excellency's return, as their Minister at the Vatican had been given to understand that Mgr. Bartoloni would not be sent back, and, indeed, he had left Rome for Kovno unbeknown to him.   The result was that when the Nuncio desired an audience with the President, to present, on behalf of the Pope, the gift of a set of the new Vatican coinage, he was informed that he was *persona non grata*, and the Lithuanian Government declined to have any further dealings with him.   They also recalled their Minister at the Vatican, on the ground that the Holy See had disregarded the Lithuanian request for the removal of the Nuncio.   The latter, for some weeks, stuck to an impossible position until, on the 5th June, he was informed by the Lithuanian Government that inasmuch as he continued to act as Nuncio in Lithuania against the formally expressed wish of the Lithuanian Government, and as such participated in certain congresses, and since no notice was taken of the Lithuanian Government's request for his recall, he must leave the city without delay.   On the following day the Nuncio departed under police escort.

91.   The Vatican denied the reports which were current that Mgr. Bartoloni had been expelled, stating that he departed in compliance with instructions to to come to Rome to report.   A note of protest was also addressed to the Lithuanian Government against the treatment meted out to the Nuncio, and complaining that the Lithuanian Government had, notwithstanding the requests made by the Holy See, failed to specify the reasons why the Nuncio was *persona non grata*, such an explanation being in conformity with international comity (*cf.* Pradier Fodéré: " Cours de droit diplomatique." vol. I, p. 393, and vol. II, p. 571).

92.   The Lithuanian Minister at the Holy See did not return to his post and was eventually withdrawn.   Neither side. however, broke off relations, their respective missions being entrusted to Chargés d'Affaires.   The Lithuanian authorities continued their anti-clerical policy abolishing eighteen professorships

held by Christian Democrats in the University of Kovno, and not hesitating to take strong action against clergy who attacked the Government.

Mexico.

93. As the year advanced there were signs that the better relations, created by the *modus vivendi* of 1929, were suffering a set-back. Certain State Governors, and particularly the Governor of Vera Cruz, refused to comply with the letter or spirit of the *modus vivendi.* The Governor of Tabasco, for instance, was unwilling to allow priests to function, unless they were married, and the Governor of Vera Cruz, a notorious and avowed enemy of the Church, promulgated a law limiting the number of priests in his State to one per 100,000 inhabitants.

94. On the 24th July an attempt was made by a young Catholic to assassinate the Governor. It was unsuccessful, and it brought in its train the destruction, by anti-clerical mobs, of churches in the State capital, and a raid on the parish church of the City of Vera Cruz, where two priests conducting a children's service were attacked, one being killed and the other severely wounded. The Federal Government, too, not only failed to protect the Church in the States, but themselves gave proof of anti-clerical feeling. A law was passed limiting to 25 the number of churches, and of priests, whose services could be utilised in the Federal District by a population which numbered more than 1,300,000, and those 25 priests might only function in the churches assigned to them by the Government. The Archbishop of Mexico protested against this measure in an open letter to the President of the Republic, and on the 31st December, while instructing his clergy not to interfere in party politics, ordered them to remain at their posts and to carry on their duties.

Persia.

95. A new Delegate Apostolic was appointed to Persia in the person of Mgr. Egidio Lari, formerly auditor of the Nunciature in Brazil. It was also decided to entrust the personal supervision of Christians of Latin rites in that country to the English Dominicans.

Roumania.

96. On the 11th March the Pope received a special mission bringing gifts from King Carol in commemoration of the Sacerdotal Jubilee of His Holiness.

97. It is understood that the delimitation of dioceses, in accordance with the terms of the concordat of the 10th May, 1927, has been finally and satisfactorily accomplished.

Russia.

98. The condition of religion in Russia, and particularly the anti-God movement, occupied the close attention of the Vatican during the past year. According to Mgr. D'Herbigny, S.J., the head of the Department dealing with Russian affairs, the work of the restoration of Christianity would have to be started from the very beginning, as if in a country which had always been pagan. The preparation of priests for such mission work was one of the principal objects of the Oriental Institute over which he presided. It was pointed out that a generation was arising which knew nothing of Christianity. The Holy See also considered that the moral and physical condition of this rising generation, owing to disease and promiscuity, left much to be desired.

99. According to information received at the Vatican the following Administrators Apostolic of Latins and Roman Catholic Uniates in the Soviet Union are in prison. The names of the districts over which they preside are given in brackets :—

Mgr. Sloskan (Mohilev), Mgr. Maleski (Leningrad), Mgr. Bacaratian (Tiflis), the Rev. Vincent Ilgin (Kharkov), the Rev. Michel Jodokas (Kazan, Samara, and Simbirsk), the Exarch Leonidas Feodoroff (for the Uniates in Moscow), Mgr. Augustin Baumtrog (Volga), Mgr. John Roth (Caucasus), Mgr. Theophilus Skalski (Zytomir), Mgr. Casimir Naskreski, deputy to the above.

100. During the year the journals of the Vatican frequently published articles depicting conditions of misery in the Soviet Union and criticising the anti-religious policy of the Bolsheviks and the tyranny of the Communist party in Russia. '

Sovereign Military Order of Malta.

101. Prince Ruffo della Scaletta, on the 5th February, presented his credentials to the Pope as Minister of the Sovereign Military Order of Malta in succession to Prince de Monteroduni, deceased.

102. On the 26th March Prince Thun and Hohenstein, Grand Master of the Order, died. Prince Ludovici Chigi Albani, Hereditary Marshal of the Conclave, was elected in succession to Prince Thun, the nomination being approved by the Pope, who received the new Grand Master in solemn audience shortly afterwards.

103. A dispute arose between the Sovereign Military Order of Malta and the Order of the Holy Sepulchre on certain matters of privilege. Amongst other things the Order of Malta objected to the Order of the Holy Sepulchre using the adjective '' sacred '' or '' military '' and to the Patriarch of Jerusalem describing himself as '' Grand Master.'' A special commission of cardinals was appointed to enquire into the matter and recommend a settlement. The Pope, on the 26th December, in endorsing the report of the commission, decreed that the Order of the Holy Sepulchre should in future bear the title '' Equestrian Order of the Holy Sepulchre of Jerusalem,'' and that the Latin Patriarch of Jerusalem should be styled '' Rector and Perpetual Administrator '' of the Order. In this decree it was also laid down that the Latin Patriarch of Jerusalem had authority to confer decorations in the Order of the Holy Sepulchre '' not merely by Papal authority, but *ex officio* and by his own authority.''

Spain.

104. The Vatican had for some time foreseen that the fall of the monarchy, the establishment of a Republican form of Government, and the consequent loss by the Church of her privileged position, were inevitable. Accordingly when these events came to pass they were at first received with calm, especially as the new Government did not immediately attack the Church. Nevertheless, the accession to power of a Provisional Government, in which the Socialist party was strongly represented, and the lack of organisation of the elements in the electorate sympathetic to the Church, caused considerable anxiety as to the future. The question was being asked, would Señor Zamora, practising Catholic though he might be, prove to be a second Kerensky ?

105. Apprehensions were justified by the anti-clerical outbreaks of the 11th May, in which many churches and ecclesiastical buildings were burned and their occupants expelled, the principal victims being the teaching orders, such as the Jesuits, Salesians, Christian Brothers, and the Nuns of the Sacred Heart. In Madrid the Jesuits suffered particularly severely by the destruction of their professed house and technical school. The Carmelite Church and Library was also destroyed. The Vatican protested through the Nuncio, pointing out that the rights of the Church had not been respected, and demanding compensation and an assurance of protection in the future. To this the Spanish Government, so far as is known, did not reply. Shortly afterwards the Spanish Government proposed the name of Señor Luis de Zulueta, as Ambassador to the Holy See, in succession to Señor de Palacios, who had been withdrawn. The Pope declined to grant an *agrément* on the ground, it is understood, of Señor de Zulueta's anti-clerical opinions.

106. In the meanwhile a pastoral letter of Cardinal Segura, Primate of Spain, together with certain pro-monarchical utterances attributed to him, had given umbrage to the Spanish Government, and it was hinted to His Eminence that it would be better for him to leave the country, as his personal safety could not be guaranteed. Cardinal Segura accordingly left Spain and came to Rome. After a sojourn of about three weeks he returned secretly to Spain, was almost immediately discovered in Guadalajara, and on the following day was placed under arrest and expelled from the country. The Holy See instructed the Nuncio to lodge a protest against the Primate's expulsion.

107. On the 12th June, in view of the forthcoming elections to the Constituent Assembly the Archbishops of Spain published an appeal to the country in which, while expressing confidence that the rights of the Church and of social order would be respected, they called upon the Catholics of Spain to rally in defence of those rights. A list of grievances suffered by the Church in Spain, drawn up in Rome by the Cardinal Primate, was transmitted to the Provisional President.

108. On the 2nd October it was announced that Cardinal Segura had resigned the Primacy. The Pope, both by letter and in his Christmas Allocution to the College of Cardinals, paid a tribute to what he described as a noble act of self-sacrifice. It is, however, an open secret that the cardinal was not by temperament fitted for the leadership of the Church in Spain in her hour of crisis.

109. Shortly afterwards article 24 of the new Spanish Constitution, concerning relations between Church and State, came under consideration by the Cortes. Any hopes engendered, as the result of the conciliatory gesture of the Vatican in accepting the resignation of the Cardinal Primate, were speedily dispelled when this article was passed. It provided for the disestablishment of the Church and special control of the Religious Orders, including the dissolution of any Order whose members took a special vow of obedience to others than the lawful authorities of the State. This latter provision was aimed at the Jesuits.

110. Immediately on hearing of this the Pope instructed the Nuncio in Madrid to inform the Catholic body of his sympathy, of his protest against the invasion of the rights of the Church, and of his intention specially to associate the needs of the Church in Spain with a Mass of Intercession he was personally to celebrate in St. Peter's in connexion with the world economic crisis. He furthermore addressed an open letter of sympathy to the General of the Jesuits, and also proclaimed the Jesuit Cardinal Robert Bellarmine, famous in history for his controversy with James I and for his advocacy of Papal prerogative, to be a Doctor of the Church. The Nuncio was not withdrawn. The resignation of Señor Zamora, on the passage through Cortes of article 24, was noted with a modicum of appreciation.

111. The year closed with the election of Señor Zamora as President of the Republic, and the formation of a Ministry regarded by the Vatican as strongly anti-clerical with the very person whom the Pope had refused as Ambassador, Minister for Foreign Affairs.

United States of America.

112. According to the latest available statistics, the Roman Catholic population of the United States is believed to number over 20 million. The Church in that country is represented in the Sacred College by four cardinals. In the missionary field the Roman Catholic Church in the United States is represented by twenty-seven different religious orders in Alaska, Japan, China, India, Africa and the Pacific Islands. The Catholic University of Peking is in the charge of American Benedictines.

113. During the controversy with the Italian Government over Catholic Action, the number of telegrams of loyalty and adhesion received by the Pope from American Roman Catholic dioceses and associations was noteworthy.

Yugoslavia.

114. The long-expected negotiations for a concordat still hang fire. As indicated in last year's report, the principal problems at issue between the Vatican and Yugoslavia are—
(1) The appointment of bishops;
(2) The expropriation of Church property under the Agrarian Law; and
(3) The law prohibiting the foundation of new church schools.

115. Some progress has been made towards a settlement of the first two, but the schools question is apparently still in an unsatisfactory state.

116. The Archbishop of Zagreb in February issued a pastoral depicting the plight of the Yugoslavs under Italian rule, and calling for prayers for the

alleviation of those conditions. Certain other Yugoslav bishops associated themselves with the Croat Archbishop.

117. The Vatican were quite unmoved by the vigorous protests of the Italian Government and declined to censure the offending archbishop, taking the view that, subject to considerations of ordinary prudence, of faith and of morals, the drafting of a pastoral was a matter in which a bishop had complete freedom. The Vatican were also stiffened in their attitude by the report, of a Visitor Apostolic, on conditions in the Julian provinces, which to some extent appeared to justify the complaints of the Yugoslav bishops. The refusal of the Holy See to give way to Italian pressure was undoubtedly one of the immediate causes of the conflict with the Fascist Government over Catholic Action, which broke out shortly afterwards.

IV.—THE VATICAN.

Coinage.
118. After considerable delay, the first Papal coinage since the restoration of the Temporal Power was issued in April. The monetary system is decimal, the unit being the gold lira of 0·07919 grains of fine gold. The following categories of coins were struck : A gold 100-lire piece, 10 lire and 5 lire in silver, 2 lire and 1 lire, 50 centesimi and 20 centesimi in nickel, 10 centesimi and 5 centesimi in copper. Ten thousand sets, bearing the commemorative date 1929, were sold specially at a profit of 100 lire over face value. Issues bearing the dates 1930 and 1931 were also put into circulation. The total value of coinage minted during the year was : Gold, 129,500 lire; silver, 1,510,000 lire; nickel, 482,000 lire; copper, 38,000 lire.

119. The design of these coins is artistic. All bear on the obverse either a bust of the Pope or the Papal Arms. The 100-lire gold-piece has on the reverse a figure of Christ the King; the 10-lire, a figure of the Madonna and Child blessing, with an olive branch in the left hand; the 5-lire, a figure of St. Peter seated at the helm of his bark; the 2-lire, a figure of the Good Shepherd with the Lamb on his shoulders; the 1-lira, the Blessed Virgin; the 50-centesimi, St. Michael the Archangel sheathing his sword; the 10- and 5- centesimi, a bust of St. Peter.

120. His Holiness the Pope presented, through this Legation, a set of the 1929 coinage to His Majesty the King. A similar gift was made to other heads of States in diplomatic relations with the Holy See.

College of Cardinals.
121. A complete list was given in the 1930 report, paragraphs 150–153.

122. The following cardinals died during the past year : Maffi, Archbishop of Pisa; Pompilj, Cardinal Vicar; Rouleau, Archbishop of Quebec; and Ragonesi, in Curia; *i.e.*, one Canadian and three Italians.

123. By the death of Cardinal Rouleau the British Commonwealth of Nations was left with but two cardinals—Bourne, Archbishop of Westminster, and MacRory, Archbishop of Armagh.

124. At the close of the year the Sacred College numbered 55 cardinals, of whom 26 were Italians and 29 non-Italians, composed as follows : Austrian, 2; Belgian, 1; Brazilian, 1; United Kingdom, 1; Czechoslovak, 1; Dutch, 1; French, 6; German, 4; Hungarian, 1; Irish, 1; Polish, 2; Portuguese, 1; Spanish, 3; United States of America, 4.

125. Of the cardinals in Curia, *i.e.*, employed in the Government of the Church and resident in Rome, 20 were Italian, and 4 non-Italian (1 Austrian, 1 Dutch, 1 French, 1 German).

126. Father Louis Billot, S.J., who was created cardinal in 1911 by Pius X and relinquished his rank in 1927, died on the 18th December.

College of Propaganda.
127. On the 24th April the Pope inaugurated the new buildings on the Janiculum Hill of the College of Propaganda, which is the institution for

training students of all nationalities for the foreign missions. In so doing and in order to reach the college, he went outside Vatican territory for the second time since the signature of the Lateran Treaty.

The Ethiopian College.

128. The Ethiopian College, of which the foundation-stone was laid in 1928. is now complete and is in occupation.

129. The ancient Church of St. Stephen of the Abyssinians, which lies a few yards from the apse of St. Peter's. is being completely restored.

The Governor's Palace.

130. The Governor's Palace is an entirely new building planned by Signor Momo, the Pope's architect. It was formerly inaugurated by His Holiness early in November. It contains the residence of the Governor, the Administrative Offices, and suites of apartments sumptuously decorated, for visiting Royalties and heads of States.

The Law Courts.

131. The tribunals of the Vatican will shortly be installed in a building which is being adapted for law courts, and will also contain police offices and two punishment cells.

Legislation.

132. In continuation of the list given in paragraph 154 of last year's report, the legislation for 1931 was as follows :—

No. XXII. July 15, 1931 : Decree approving Regulations of Law XXI Coinage Law.
No. XXIII. September 15, 1931 : Ordinance *re* surcharging of postage stamps.
No. XXIV. December 14, 1931 : Law authorising issue of coinage in accordance with Italo-Vatican Coinage Convention.
No. XXV. December 15, 1931 : Ordinance *re* coinage for 1931.

Library.

133. On the suggestion of His Majesty's Chargé d'Affaires, a set of the publications of the Scottish History Society was subscribed for privately and presented to the Vatican Library. A French prelate, Mgr. Tisserant, was appointed pro-prefect and executive head of the library, which is being extended on a large scale, embodying all the latest improvements and devices. During the year Dr. Anne Cameron, of Glasgow University, was occupied in transcribing episcopal documents relative to Scotland in the 15th century for His Majesty's Register House in Edinburgh.

134. On the 22nd December a portion of the Sixtus Vth wing of the Vatican Library collapsed, killing five persons, destroying several works of art, and damaging, more or less seriously, about 15,000 books and nearly all the catalogues of the library. Only one manuscript was slightly injured. The part of the library affected forms the north side of the Cortile Belvedere. The exact cause of the accident has not yet been ascertained, but it was probably due either to a defect in the roof of the Sala Sistina, which collapsed, involving the reference library beneath it and the store rooms on the ground floor, or to a weakening of the foundations due to minor alterations in the basement of a building which between 1586 and 1588 had been hastily constructed with inferior material. The principal works of art destroyed were the font used for the baptism of the Prince Imperial and two large vases of malachite and of pink granite, one of which was a present from the Czar Nicholas I to the Pope. A certain number of books affected were in the English section. His Majesty the King immediately sent his condolences to the Pope. Messages of sympathy were also transmitted from the Master of the Rolls and the Deputy Keeper of the Public Records.

135. His Holiness, who expressed deep appreciation for the King's message, informed His Majesty's Chargé d'Affaires that, while the loss of life

deeply affected him, he did not consider that any irreplaceable books had been destroyed. A committee was appointed to enquire into the accident, but had not reported by the end of the year.

Mosaic Studio.

136. Near the railway station a building has been constructed for the mosaic studio, which is now once more in use. It comprises the artists' work rooms and a gallery for the finished mosaics exposed for sale. The store rooms were planned, according to the latest ideas, to hold sufficient stocks of the 28,500 different coloured pieces in use. .

Picture Gallery.

137. The new picture gallery, situated north of the Vatican Gardens, is about three-quarters complete. It is hoped that it will be ready for inauguration in May 1932. An entrance to this building is being constructed through the Leonine Wall on to the Piazza del Risorgimento.

Population.

138. According to the latest figures, the population of the Vatican City was approximately 639, of whom 550 were residents. The remainder consisted of the Cardinals in Curia, the prelates and the employees in buildings reserved to Papal sovereignty under the Lateran Treaty.

Post Office.

139. The Vatican, having joined the Universal Postal Union, is now one of the States which regularly receive the information sent to all members. In the month of October a further set of postage stamps was issued for parcels and express parcels post. These stamps are similar in design and in denomination to the other postage stamps, but are surcharged.

Power Station.

140. A new electric power station for the supply of light and power to the Vatican City, consisting of four Diesel motors, each of 200 h.p., driving four Marelli dynamos, providing direct current of 135 kilowatts each, the whole plant with a capacity of about 8,000 ampères, was formally inaugurated by the Pope on the 10th February.

Press and News Services.

141. The illustrated fortnightly, "Illustrazione Vaticana," founded at the end of 1930, was regularly published, and its articles and illustrations maintained a high standard during the year.

142. The "Manchester Guardian" correspondent having left Rome, the principal British newspapers whose correspondents frequent the Vatican are the "Times," "Daily Telegraph," "Morning Post," "Glasgow Herald" and "Daily Herald." Most of the correspondents obtain their information from the Press Prelate, whose duties are described in paragraph 168 of last year's report, quantity and quality depending on the amount of fee paid; and in this respect complaint is made of American competition. The representative of the "Daily Telegraph" has channels of his own and is perhaps the best informed. The "Morning Post" representative is a Scotsman of ability and culture, and, although a thorough Protestant, receives frequent invitations and is always welcome to the National College. The "Daily Herald" is represented by a Maltese, and "Reuter's" by a lady, both of whom are inclined to send inaccurate reports. All the above frequently have recourse to His Majesty's Chargé d'Affaires, who is always ready to furnish every help. Friendly contact was maintained with the staffs of the "Osservatore Romano" and "Civiltà Cattolica," with the result that, on one occasion, the cessation of certain public attacks on the Church of England was obtained.

Protestant Propaganda.

143.   Some apprehensions having been caused in Church of England circles by the Pope's outspoken denunciation of Protestant propaganda at the close of 1930, His Majesty's Chargé d'Affaires, after making enquiry of the competent authorities, was able to assure His Majesty's Ambassador at the Quirinal that the Pope's remarks were directed, not at the Anglican community, but at the American Methodists, who were conducting an active propaganda, both in Rome and in the Abruzzi.   In Rome "no-Popery" leaflets were distributed in certain churches, and proselytism was being conducted by unfrocked priests, and in the Abruzzi the activities of Methodist preachers provoked riots.   By request of the Bishop of Gibraltar, His Majesty's Chargé d'Affaires let it be known in the proper quarter that the responsible authorities of the Church of England in Italy repudiated all connexion with the proselytism against which the Pope protested.

Radio.

144.   The Vatican radio station, erected under the supervision of Marchese Marconi, was opened by the Pope on the 16th February, His Holiness broadcasting an address to the world.   The wave-length used was 19·84 metres, call sign HVJ, and reception was, on the whole, satisfactory all over the world.

145.   In October a telephoto apparatus, the invention of a M. Bélin, was presented to the Pope and installed at the radio station.

146.   Through the good offices of His Majesty's Government in the United Kingdom, the Vatican State acceded to the Washington Radio Convention of the 25th November, 1927, and to the General and Supplementary Regulations pertaining thereto, and was placed in the sixth class for purposes of contributions to the expenses of the International Bureau of the Telegraphic Union in Berne.

The Railway Station.

147.   The external building, the tunnel through the Leonine Wall, and the necessary embankment were completed, but the internal fittings of the railway station had not been installed, nor were the rails laid.

V.—PAPAL PRONOUNCEMENTS.

148.   The following is a list of the more important public documents issued during the year 1931 :—

(1) Encyclical "Casti Connubii," the 31st December, 1930, on Marriage and various moral, economic and social questions connected therewith. (Published in 1931.)

(2) Broadcast.   "Qui arcano Dei," the 12th February, broadcast to the Roman Catholic world.

(3) Autograph letter to the Cardinal Archbishop of Milan, "Dobbiamo intrattenerla," the 26th April, *re* Catholic Action.

(4) Letter.   "Felix faustumque," the 10th May, to the German Episcopate, *re* the seventh centenary of St. Elizabeth, Queen of Hungary.

(5) Encyclical "Quadragesimo Anno," the 15th May, on reconstructing the Social Order.

(6) Encyclical "Non abbiamo bisogno," the 29th June, concerning Catholic Action.

(7) Apostolic Constitution "Deus Scientiarum," the 29th June, on universities and ecclesiastical studies.

(8) Letter.   "Monumentum insigne," the 14th September, to the Cardinal Primate of Brazil.

(9) Apostolic letter "Providentissimus Deus," the 17th September, declaring Cardinal Bellarmine to be a Doctor of the Church.

(10) Encyclical "Nova impendet," the 2nd October, on the Economic Crisis, Unemployment and Armaments.

(11) Official letter "Mi gode l'animo," the 29th October, from the Cardinal Secretary of State by direction of the Pope, to the General of the Jesuits regarding the situation in Spain.

(12) Encyclical "Lux veritatis," the 25th December, on the fifteenth centenary of the Council of Ephesus.

VI.—QUESTIONS OF THE DAY.

149.   The Pope during the past year issued three encyclicals, dealing with various problems of the day, namely, the Encyclical on Marriage, dated the 31st December, 1930, but published after the New Year, the Encyclical on the Labour and Social Question on the 15th May, the 40th Anniversary of Leo XIII's "Labour" Encyclical "Rerum Novarum," and the Encyclical "Nova Impendet" of the 2nd October, on the Economic Crisis, Unemployment and Armaments.   As these documents set forth, in detail, the doctrine of the Roman Catholic Church on important questions of the day which are also of not a little interest to the secular State, a brief summary is given below quoting salient extracts from the official texts.

Birth Control.

150.   In the Encyclical on Marriage of the 31st December, 1930, the practice of birth control other than by voluntary abstention was condemned in the following words :—

"First consideration is due to the offspring; which many have the boldness to call the disagreeable burden of matrimony and which they say is to be carefully avoided by married people not through virtuous continence (which Christian law permits in matrimony when both parties consent), but by frustrating the marriage act.   Some justify this criminal abuse on the ground that they are weary of children and wish to gratify their desires without their consequent burden.   Others say that they cannot on the one hand remain continent nor on the other can they have children because of the difficulties, whether on the part of the mother or on the part of family circumstances.

"But no reason, however grave, may be put forward by which anything intrinsically against nature may become conformable to nature and morally good.   Since, therefore, the conjugal act is destined primarily by nature for the begetting of children, those who in exercising it deliberately frustrate its natural power and purpose, sin against nature and commit a deed which is shameful and intrinsically vicious."

Disarmament.

151.   The Vatican were cautious in their attitude towards the forthcoming Disarmament Conference.   The Pope was reluctant to make a public pronouncement on the subject too early in the year, in order to avoid being associated with individual parties and movements in the outside world with the same objects in view.   He did not take action until the 2nd October, when, in his Encyclical " Nova Impendet " he referred to the subject in the following words :—

"The acute crisis, which we lament, is at one and the same time the effect of the rivalry among nations, and the cause of the enormous squandering of public moneys, and these two evils are, to no small extent, due to the excessive and ever-increasing competition in the output of military stores and implements of war.   Hence we cannot refrain from renewing on this occasion the timely warning given in our Allocution of the 24th December, 1930, and in our autograph letter of the 7th April, 1922, ' Con vivo piacere,' as well as that of our predecessor in his exhortation of the 1st August, 1917, ' Dès le début,' a warning which we regret has not so far been successfully put into practice.   At the same time we exhort you, venerable brethen, to strive, by every means in your power, in the pulpit and in the press, to enlighten men's minds and to shape their hearts in conformity with the saner dictates of right reason and Christian law."

152.   About the same time His Holiness granted an audience to Viscount Cecil of Chelwood.   The following is an extract from Lord Cecil's report on that interview :—

" I then referred to disarmament as a partial remedy.   The Pope agreed, but had difficulties.   In the first place what did disarmament mean ! He was not in favour of unilateral disarmament ?   I explained I meant general disarmament.   Then what about unemployment ?   I said that undoubtedly transitional measures would be necessary, but in the end the world would be the richer by transferring effort from unproductive to productive industry. He agreed with this, saying with great conviction that the manufacture of armaments was loss and worse than loss. He enlarged on the horrors of war and warmly agreed that air-bombing and submarines were thoroughly inhuman, speaking with great horror of both, and warmly agreeing that to abolish them would be a great step forward. I asked if he thought of issuing any message on the subject, and he said one was actually on its way, dealing first with the poverty caused by the economic crisis and secondly with disarmament (since issued). His Holiness then more than once expressed full agreement with my point of view."

153.   In his Christmas Allocution to the College of Cardinals the Pope declared that he had not intended to say anything about disarmament because all that was to be said had so often been repeated, and it was not possible for him to enlarge on that topic without being misinterpreted, with the result that discord would only be increased. Since mankind could not listen to counsels of peace and mutual charity, and since the present disorders of the world are due to human selfishness, distrust and intimidation, with competition in armaments leading nowhere, and open war in the Far East, he had no alternative but to sound the call for prayer for Divine assistance in the present troubles.

Easter : Stabilisation of.

154.   While the Vatican were not again approached on the subject, His Majesty's Chargé d'Affaires ascertained that there was no present prospect of the Roman Catholic Church agreeing to the declaration regarding the stabilisation of movable feasts, particularly Easter, passed by the Fourth General Conference on Communications and Transit at Geneva on the 19th October, 1931.

Economic Crisis, 1931.

155.   In the Encyclical "Nova Impendet" of the 2nd October the Pope made an appeal to the charity of the world for the unemployed workers reduced to destitution by the economic crisis, and also for starving children.

The Fair Wage.

156.   In the Encyclical on Marriage, the 31st December, 1930, it is laid down that every father of a family should be enabled to earn a sufficient wage for the proper support of himself and of his family, according to his station in life. It is unlawful " to fix such a scanty wage as would be insufficient for the upkeep of the family in the circumstances in which it is placed." Parties who desire to marry should try to dispose of material obstacles in the way.

Feminism.

157.   The Pope on more than one occasion was outspoken in his views on woman and the feminist movement, holding that woman was not by Providence intended to be the equal of man. His Holiness embodied his rulings on the married women in his Encyclical on Marriage of the 31st December, 1930, from which the following is a representative quotation :—

"The primacy of the husband with regard to the wife and children, the ready subjection of the wife and her willing obedience, which the Apostle commends in these words : ' Let women be subject to their husbands as to the Lord, because the husband is the head of the wife, as Christ is the head of the Church.'

" This subjection, however, does not deny or take away the liberty which fully belongs to the woman both in view of her dignity as a human person, and in view of her most noble office as wife and mother and companion; nor does it bid her obey her husband's every request if not in harmony with right reason or with the dignity due to wife; nor, in fine, does it imply that the wife should be put on a level with those persons who in law are called minors, to whom it is not customary to allow free exercise of their rights on account of their lack of mature judgment, or of their ignorance of human affairs. But it forbids that exaggerated liberty which cares not for the good of the family; it forbids that in this body which is the family, the heart be separated from the head to the great detriment of the whole body and the proximate danger of ruin. For if the man is the head, the woman is the heart, and as he occupies the chief place in ruling, so she may and ought to claim for herself the chief place in love.

"Again, this subjection of wife to husband in its degree and manner may vary according to the different conditions of persons, place and time In fact, if the husband neglect his duty, it falls to the wife to take his place in directing the family. But the structure of the family and its fundamental law, established and confirmed by God, must always and everywhere be maintained intact."

Property.

158. The right to own private property has been given to man by nature. The right to property must be distinguished from its use. The right to property belongs " to commutative justice, faithfully to respect the possessions of others, not encroaching on the rights of another, and thus exceeding one's right of ownership. The putting of one's own possessions to proper use, however, does not fall under this form of justice, but under certain other virtues, and therefore it is a duty not enforced by courts of justice. Hence it is idle to contend that the right of ownership and its proper use are bounded by the same limits, and it is even less true that the very misuse, or even the non-use, of ownership destroys or forfeits the right itself. . . . . It follows from the twofold character of owner-ship, which we have termed individual and social, that men must take into account in this matter not only their own advantage, but also the common good. To define in detail these duties, when the need occurs and when the natural law does not do so, is the function of the Government. Provided that the natural and Divine Law be observed, the public authority, in view of the common good, may specify more accurately what is licit and what is illicit for property owners in the use of their possessions. Moreover, Leo XIII has wisely taught that the defining of private possession has been left by God to man's own industry and to the laws of the individual peoples. History proves that the right of ownership, like other elements of social life, is not absolutely rigid, and this doctrine we ourselves have given utterance to on a previous occasion in the following terms : ' How varied are the forms which the right of property has assumed ! First, the primitive form in use among rude and savage peoples, which still exists in certain localities even in our own day; then that of the patriarchal age; later came various tyrannical types (we use the word in its classical meaning); finally, the feudal and monarchic systems down to the varieties of more recent times.' It is plain, however, that the State may not discharge this duty in an arbitrary manner. Man's natural right of possessing and transmitting property by inheritance must remain intact and cannot be taken away by the State, ' for man precedes the State,' and ' the domestic household is antecedent as well in idea as in fact to the gathering of men into a community.' Hence the prudent Pontiff has already declared it unlawful for the State to exhaust the means of individuals by crushing taxes and tributes. The right to possess private property is derived from nature, not from man; and the State has, by no means, the right to abolish it, but only to control its use and bring it into harmony with the interests of the public good. However, when civil authority adjusts ownership to meet the needs of the public good, it acts not as an enemy, but as the friend of private owners; for thus it effectively prevents the possessions of private property, intended by nature's Author in His Wisdom for the sustaining of human life, from creating intolerable burdens, and so rushing to its own destruction. It does not, therefore, abolish but protects private ownership, and, far from weakening the right of private property, it gives it new strength. . . . . A man's superfluous income is not left entirely to his own discretion. We speak of that portion of his income which he does not need in order to live as becomes his station. On the contrary, the grave obligations of charity, beneficence and liberality which rest upon the wealthy are constantly insisted upon in telling words by Holy Scriptures and the Fathers of the Church.

"However, the investment of superfluous income in securing favourable opportunities for employment, provided the labour employed produces results which are really useful, is to be considered, according to the teaching of the-

Angelic Doctor, an act of real liberality, particularly appropriate to the needs of our time.

" The original acquisition of property takes place by first occupation and by industry, or, as it is called, specification. This is the universal teaching of tradition and the doctrine of our predecessor. Despite unreasonable assertions to the contrary, no wrong is done to any man by the occupation of goods unclaimed and which belong to nobody. The only form of labour, however, which gives the working man a title to its fruits is that which a man exercises as his own master, and by which some new form or new value is produced." (Encyclical on the Social and Labour Question, the 15th May, 1931.)

Public Assistance.

159. " Provision must be made, also, in the case of those who are not self-supporting for joint aid by private or public guilds." When these resources are inadequate it is incumbent on the rich to help the poor. If private assistance is not sufficient, it is the duty of the public authorities to supply what is lacking. " They must do their utmost to relieve the needs of the poor." (Encyclical on Marriage, the 31st December, 1930.)

Relations between Capital and Labour.

160. " Capital cannot do without labour, nor labour without capital." In the past there has been an excessive and unjust disproportion of the commodities of life between capital and labour. The whole economic system must be reconstructed so as to ensure a more equitable distribution of the united proceeds of capital and labour. Differences in social conditions cannot be abolished, " but the condition of the proletarian worker cannot for ever be the normal condition of the bulk of mankind." In the present order this can only be accomplished by a fair and just wage, which must really be such as to satisfy " the legitimate requirements of an honest working man, not only for his person but also for his family, and to make it possible for him to improve his condition within the limits above described."

161. Trade unionism is approved as rendering the working classes more conscious of their dignity as men and Christians. " fitting them to protect the moral and economic interests of their class with knowledge and prudence . . . . asserting the right possessed by working men to form associations for mutual aid and legitimate defence of their common interests, a right which liberalism was endeavouring to impede by unjust use of power." (The quotations are taken from the official summary of the Encyclical on the Social and Labour Question, the 15th May, 1931.)

Socialism.

162. Socialism, which had for its object the remedying of the evils caused by " the exaggerated concentration in the hands of a few of the whole economic power, not only of single nations but of the entire world," has produced a remedy worse than the disease itself. It has split into two divisions, (1) communism, whose " teachings can in no wise be reconciled with the doctrines of the Church," and (2) " the other, which continues to be known as socialism, has frequently and notably mitigated its programme; in many points it has approached, now more, now less, so close to Catholic social principles, that some are asking themselves whether now the divergence is not one of mere name. The Holy Father, however, does not hesitate to declare solemnly that this socialism (provided, of course, it really remains socialism), even in mitigated form, and even though many points of its teachings are in themselves conformable to justice and admitted by the Church, has, nevertheless, a fundamental concept of human society so different from the true concept given to us by the gospel, that any agreement in doctrine remains always absolutely impossible. It is not possible to be at once a good Catholic and a true Socialist." (Quotation from the official summary of the Encyclical on the Social and Labour Question, the 15th May, 1931.)

VII.—ECONOMIC.

163. During the year His Majesty's Chargé d'Affaires examined the possibilities of openings for British trade with the Vatican State. The results

were disappointing. Apart from the necessarily small size of orders, there would appear to be in existence too many vested interests impossible to oust. For instance, all building contracts and repairs are entrusted to a Milanese firm. The new and up-to-date library, electrical, telephonic and radio installations are provided by companies quite capable of supplying all necessary spare parts. Insurance, too, is also a close preserve. Railway material is provided by the Italian Government. The only possible opening for British enterprise would be a share in the handling of the Vatican's funds. Some start was made in that direction in 1930, but the subsequent depreciation and uncertain value of the pound sterling put a stop to such operations. There may also be openings for tobacco and cigarettes when stores and selling agencies are established in the Vatican State. The position is being watched on behalf of a certain British company.

164.   VIII.—TREATY.

With (Country)—	Date of Signature.	Subject.	Date of Exchange of Ratifications.	Date of Entry into Force.	Remarks.
San Marino..	Dec. 30, 1931	Monetary Convention	--	The day after exchange of ratifications	Reciprocal recognition of Vatican and San Marino currencies.

o

CONFIDENTIAL.
_____
(14208)

HOLY SEE.
▬

Annual Report, 1932.
_____

[C 1850/1850/22]

Mr. Kirkpatrick to Sir John Simon.—(Received February 28.)

(No. 18.)   *British Legation to the Holy See,*
Sir,   *Rome, February 20, 1933.*
    I HAVE the honour to transmit my annual report on the Holy See for the
year 1932.
    I am much indebted to Mr. Thynne for his assistance in the compilation.
                             I have, &c.
                                 I. KIRKPATRICK.

▬▬▬▬▬▬▬

Enclosure.

Annual Report on the Holy See for 1932.
_____

CONTENTS.

▬▬▬▬▬▬▬

I.—INTRODUCTION.

THE year 1932 was a difficult and harassing period for the Vatican. The aggravation of the world crisis, with the attendant spread of social discontent, brought many anxieties. Of these the most serious is the menace of communism, which the Holy See regards with undisguised alarm as having declared open war on religion in general. The doctrines of communism were strongly condemned in the Papal encyclical *Caritate Christi*, and have been denounced by Catholic bishops all over the world, including English bishops. In the face of these pronouncements it is impossible for any practising Catholic to be a Communist. Less dangerous than communism in the eyes of the Vatican, but nevertheless a peril to society and to religion, is the growing materialism of the age. Scepticism, the worship of pleasure, luxury, ostentation are said to pervade present day manners, and the Church is exhorting its members to return to a simpler and less ease-loving life. Largely with a view to stimulating the enthusiasm of the faithful in the fight against the twin enemies, communism and materialism, the Pope decided in the last days of December to hold a Jubilee or Holy Year beginning on the 2nd April, 1933.

2. Another grave anxiety has been the fall in revenue, caused partly by the depreciation of the pound and partly by the fact that subscriptions are no longer flowing in on the old scale. This has been felt particularly by the missionaries, most of whom have no resources other than the mission funds. At the end of the year it was announced that owing to lack of money there was no immediate prospect of any substantial extension in the mission field. The problem is engaging the personal attention of the Pope, who may be said to attach more importance to the development of the missions than to any other activity of the Church.

3. In the realm of foreign affairs also there was much to preoccupy the Vatican. The clouds hung heavy over the international horizon. The problem of disarmament, war debts and reparations remained unsettled; there were hostilities in China and South America; in Europe signs of growing tension. On all of these questions the Pope was careful to maintain an attitude of strict neutrality.

4. In Russia and Lithuania there was no amelioration in the situation of the Catholic Church. In Mexico it deteriorated at the beginning of the year, with the result that the Pope was moved to denounce the Mexican Government in an encyclical, but his precipitate action does not seem to have had the unfortunate consequences which were generally anticipated at the time. In Spain the threatened confiscation of the properties of the religious congregations was a heavy, if not unexpected, blow, but it did not arouse much articulate hostility here, possibly because the Vatican do not wish to embarrass the Spanish Government in their struggle against anarchy. Relations with His Majesty's Government in the United Kingdom were improved by the acceptance of Lord Strickland's apology and the consequent holding of elections in Malta. This and the quite extraordinary improvement in the relations with the Italian Government were, from the Vatican point of view, perhaps the only satisfactory feature of the year. Between two autocratic characters, such as the Pope and Signor Mussolini, there is always the latent danger of a serious difference of opinion, but for the moment there is no sign of any rift and both parties seem determined that the present situation shall continue. In Yugoslavia no progress was made towards the conclusion of a concordat, a fact which seems to indicate that the outlook is not entirely settled. Relations with other countries remained friendly and call for no special comment.

5. In the Vatican City considerable progress was made both in the organisation of the civil Government and in the erection of the many buildings which are disfiguring the Papal gardens. Of the latter the most important to be completed were the new picture gallery, called the Pinacoteca, and the new entrance to the Vatican museums, both of which were formally opened at the end of the year.

6. The year has seen no falling off in the Pope's energy or capacity for work. In the opinion of those closest to him his health has actually improved. Despite

his 75 years and a complaint of the kidneys, he looks more alert and vigorous than any of the cardinals in Curia, and there seems no reason why his iron constitution should not enable him to survive them all.

II.—RELATIONS WITH THE BRITISH EMPIRE.
United Kingdom.

7. With the acceptance of Lord Strickland's apology by the Pope, the Malta question was regarded as settled by the Vatican. Quite apart from the satisfaction felt at the humiliation of the enemy, this consummation was hailed with relief, for the Vatican are anxious on general grounds to be on good terms with His Majesty's Government. The Pope regards the spread of communism as a mortal peril, and he looks on Great Britain as one of the principal bulwarks against the subversive doctrines of the day. Moreover, his recognition of the fact that the practice of the Catholic religion is allowed a complete measure of freedom throughout the British dominions, in contrast to the position in Catholic Spain and Mexico for example, predisposes him favourably towards Great Britain.

8. During the year His Majesty's Government showed the greatest goodwill in meeting the Vatican in regard to difficulties over the Sudan mission fields, and, whilst they were unable to give complete satisfaction to the request of the Catholic missionaries for the abolition of the zone system, their conciliatory attitude was appreciated by the Secretariat of State. In Palestine the only serious dispute was settled in favour of the Latins.

9. The friendliest personal relations exist between His Majesty's Legation and the various departments of the Vatican, who spare no trouble to satisfy the various demands for facilities, &c., which have to be made on behalf of British subjects.

10. In February His Majesty's Chargé d'Affaires received instructions to convey to the Pope the King's cordial congratulations on the tenth anniversary of his coronation. The message was personally delivered and was received with particular satisfaction by the Pope.

11. At the request of the Anti-Slavery and Aborigines Protection Society, the Vatican were asked to collect from their own sources information on slavery for eventual transmission to the Expert Slavery Committee of the League of Nations.

12. On the 30th July the Pope received in audience Mr. Taylor the representative in Italy of Imperial Airways (Limited). Mr. Taylor presented to His Holiness an album of photographs taken from the air of the Holy Land. The Pope showed himself most interested in the development of the air lines operated by the company.

13. In the autumn the fall in the value of the pound, coupled with exaggerated accounts in the Italian press of the activities of the hunger marchers, caused some apprehension at the Vatican, and I received anxious enquiries on the subject from the Pope and the Cardinal Secretary of State. I was able to reassure them, and the subsequent recovery of the pound, despite the strain of the payment of the debt instalment to the United States, was regarded as impressive evidence of the financial strength of Great Britain.

14. The year 1932 was the year allotted to the bishops of the United Kingdom for the performance of their *ad limina* visit, which must be made every five years. Consequently, every member of the British hierarchy came to Rome. The Pope, I am told, showed particular interest in eliciting information as to the economic conditions in the various dioceses. During his visit Cardinal Bourne fell seriously ill, but made a somewhat unexpected recovery. The King's enquiry after his health made a most favourable impression in Rome.

15. The Anonima Costruzione Edilizie Company continued during the year to make every effort to reach an amicable settlement of their claim arising from the repudiation of their contract for the construction of churches in three

Calabrian dioceses. His Majesty's Chargé d'Affaires brought the circumstances of the case unofficially to the knowledge of the Cardinal Secretary of State and asked him to use his influence in favour of a settlement. He also arranged a number of interviews between representatives of the company and various prelates including the cardinal in charge of the congregation concerned. Unfortunately, the negotiations proved fruitless and in June the company reluctantly reached the conclusion that conversations on these lines would lead to no result. They are, I believe, now considering what further action to take in defence of their rights.

Canada.

16. In December the Pope received in special audience a party of Canadian school-teachers, travelling under the auspices of the League of Empire.

17. The Archbishop of Quebec, the coadjutor Archbishop of Montreal and the Bishop of Gravelbourg visited Rome during the year. All of them took pains to establish friendly relations with His Majesty's Legation and to emphasise their loyalty to the Empire.

Irish Free State.

18. A Eucharistic Congress was held in Dublin in June and July. The Pope was represented by a papal legate, Cardinal Lauri, who was accompanied by a small suite selected from the personnel at the Vatican.

19. Towards the end of the year the Free State Minister presented Cardinal Lauri with a chalice, the gift of the members of the Free State Government.

India.

20. His Majesty's Chargé d'Affaires transmitted to the Pope a reply from the Maharajah of Travancore to a cordial letter which His Holiness had addressed to him on the occasion of his accession.

21. Mar Ivanios, the Archbishop of the converted Jacobites of Malabar, visited Rome on his way to the Eucharistic Congress at Dublin and received the pallium from the hands of the Pope himself on the 2nd May.

Malta.

22. The report of the Malta Royal Commission was published on the 11th February. The attitude of the Vatican was one of satisfaction and almost unqualified approval. In particular the criticisms of Lord Strickland, and even of His Majesty's late Government, and the recommendations for the dismissal of the Ministry were read as a justification of the attitude adopted by the Holy See in the controversy. The fly in the ointment was Lord Strickland's continued presence in the island and the possibility that he might be returned to power when the elections were held. Another point of friction was the commissioners' description of the 1930 pastoral as obsolete. The Archbishop of Malta at once informed the Governor that the pastoral was not obsolete, and that the issue of any new pastoral before the election would be dependent on the behaviour of the Constitutionalists in the interval.

23. On the 2nd March the Secretary of State for the Colonies announced in the House of Commons that His Majesty's Government had decided to give effect to the proposals set out by the Royal Commission in chapter 14 of the report. The Constitution would be restored to the island in accordance with the commission's main recommendation, and steps would be taken to give effect to the various other proposals in appropriate ways. On two points, however, His Majesty's Government decided to depart from the terms of the recommendations contained in the report. In the first place, they resolved to suppress forthwith the teaching of Italian in the elementary schools. Secondly, they decided not to accept the suggestion of the commissioners that judicial appointments should not in future be confined to Maltese.

24. Lord Strickland, faced with the prospect of an election and using the good offices of the Governor, made a determined effort towards reconciliation with the Church by forwarding a renewed apology to the Pope through the Archbishop of Malta. The apology was sent on the 10th March and was couched in the fullest terms, but it was not until the 30th April that the Archbishop of Malta told the Governor that he had been instructed by the Vatican to inform Lord Strickland that his apology was unacceptable. He added that the bishops intended shortly to issue a new pastoral, which would, however, not be so favourable as it would have been had Lord Strickland's apology been so worded as to be acceptable.

25. On the 20th May the Governor was shown a circular letter which was issued by the bishops on the 22nd May. The circular in effect confirmed the pastoral of 1930, and in consequence His Majesty's Government decided, on the 26th May, to cancel the forthcoming elections and to leave the Constitution suspended. On the following day the Constitutional and Labour parties, who must have got wind of the Cabinet decision, forwarded a message to the Secretary of State for the Colonies urging that the elections should be held notwithstanding the circular. On the 28th May Miss Strickland informed the Governor that an apology, drawn up by Mgr. de Piro and signed by Lord Strickland, had been sent to the archbishop and apparently accepted. This was confirmed the next day by Mgr. de Piro, who personally informed the Governor that the archbishop had accepted the apology, and that the Bishop of Gozo was taking it to Rome that evening with a strong recommendation in favour of its acceptance. This rapid and unexpected succession of events, which it is not within the scope of this report to explain, caused His Majesty's Government to decide to suspend action until it was known whether the bishops would issue a new pastoral. In the meantime, they informed the Governor that, failing the withdrawal of the 1930 pastoral, they were determined to maintain their decision to cancel the elections.

26. On the 1st June the Archbishop of Malta informed the Governor that the Pope had accepted Lord Strickland's apology, and that as soon as possible after the return of the Bishop of Gozo a new circular or pastoral would be issued. On the 3rd June the new pastoral was published. Its terms were considered satisfactory by His Majesty's Government, who, the same day, authorised the Governor to fix the elections for the date he considered most convenient and to issue the necessary proclamation when he thought fit. The elections duly took place in June, and resulted in a decisive victory of the Nationalist party. The result was due partly to the fact that the acceptance of Lord Strickland's apology and the new pastoral came too late to have much influence with the electorate, and partly to the fact that the clergy, despite the terms of the pastoral, in many cases used their influence improperly in favour of the Nationalist party.

27. The attitude of the Vatican from the outset was that, once Lord Strickland's apology had been accepted by the Pope, the Malta problem was settled. The Cardinal Secretary of State on more than one occasion voiced this opinion, and expressed his satisfaction that the relations between Great Britain and the Holy See were now unclouded by any difference.

28. As regards the language question, the Vatican have declared throughout that no religious issue is involved, and that in consequence they are not concerned. The Archbishop of Malta has taken the same line, but, unfortunately, he has not always been willing or able to compel his clergy to follow him. In particular, Mgr. Dandria, an ex-Minister, who has since died, made a speech in March, in the course of which he said that the language question could not be separated from the religious question, and that the war against the Italian language was a war against the position of the Catholic religion in the islands. In September the Archbishop informed the Governor that, in the course of an interview with the Cardinal Secretary of State, the latter had said that the Pope was most anxious that the clergy should keep quite clear of any controversy regarding the Italian language in Malta. The Archbishop intimated that this instruction from Rome would be of great assistance to him. So far as His Majesty's Legation are aware, there have not

been since that date any flagrant cases of clerical intervention in the language controversy.

29.   In October Lord Strickland, in a personal letter to the Secretary of State, said that the Vatican were considering the appointment of a bishop coadjutor to the Archbishop of Malta, with the reversion of the archbishopric, and that the two candidates discussed for the post were Mgr. de Piro and Mgr. Farrugia.   His Majesty's Chargé d'Affaires made discreet enquiries in authoritative quarters, and was informed that there was at present no intention of appointing a Coadjutor Bishop of Malta with the right of succession, but that the appointment of an auxiliary bishop without the right of succession was under consideration.   The Governor of Malta has asked that the position should be carefully watched, so that His Majesty's Government may have every opportunity of exercising their rights under the Rampolla–Simmons Agreement.

30.   In November the Under-Secretary of State enquired whether His Majesty's Government still adhered to the desire, said to have been expressed by His Majesty's representative in 1928, that the diocese of Malta should be an archbishopric.   He made it clear that, if His Majesty's Government still showed any interest in the matter, the Vatican would like to meet their wishes as a gesture of friendship.   His Majesty's Chargé d'Affaires replied that he would seek instructions on the point.

Straits Settlements.

31.   The Vatican " Fides " news service reported in April, with some satisfaction, that a Bill was to be introduced freeing missionaries from the obligation to obtain a special entry permit.   Nothing more has been heard of this proposal.

Sudan.

32.   At the beginning of the year His Majesty's Chargé d'Affaires was instructed to inform the Vatican, in reply to their representations, that the Sudan Government had considered the possibility of abolishing the system of missionary zones, but that they regretted that, for administrative reasons, they could not contemplate any change in the existing order for many years to come.

33.   In May the Vatican took up the case of the Catholic missionaries who had been ordered to cease work in Chief Iriwo's territory, on the ground that it was within the zone allocated to the Church Missionary Society.   The Vatican contended that the Catholic missionaries had entered the country in good faith and with the knowledge and tacit approval of the local authorities.   The Government of the Sudan, whilst not admitting in full these contentions, recognised that they had some weight, and eventually a solution was reached with the consent of the Church Missionary Society, whereby the territory of Chief Iriwo was included in the Catholic zone, on the understanding that this settlement was final, and that no further encroachments by the Catholic missionaries would be allowed.   In taking note of this decision, the Under-Secretary of State said unofficially that he did not think that the Roman Catholic missions could enter into any formal undertaking to confine their activities to a limited area, since such a limitation was contrary to the first precepts of Catholic missionary work.   Where, however, it was imperative that the work should conform to necessary measures of Government administration, it should not be difficult to reach some understanding.

Mandated Territory.

34.   *Palestine.*—In January the Vatican made representations on the subject of the alleged levy of land tax and tithe on certain Latin religious communities and parishes in Palestine.   It was contended that under the existing *status quo* these bodies should be exempt from such taxation.   His Majesty's Legation was in due course instructed to reply that investigations showed that in no case had land tax or tithe been collected from any Latin religious community or parish priest who could prove, or who claimed, enjoyment of immunity from taxation under the Ottoman régime.   The Vatican were assured that it was the intention of the Palestine Government to maintain all existing rights and privileges which were enjoyed by foreign religious communities under the

Ottoman régime; and that as regards land tax, this intention would shortly be given statutory force. The Vatican were at the same time invited to give particulars of any case in which taxes had been paid on Latin properties in respect of which exemption was claimed. The Cardinal Secretary of State appears to have been fully satisfied with the terms of the reply, for he made no attempt to substantiate his original complaint, and merely took note with satisfaction of the assurances contained in the note from His Majesty's Legation.

35. In April the Vatican addressed a complaint to His Majesty's Legation in regard to damage done to a tapestry in the crypt of the Sanctuary of the Nativity at Bethlehem. It was alleged that the Greeks, by filing away its supports, had caused it to fall to the ground in a damaged condition. The authorities had removed it by force, and it had not yet been restored to its place. In August His Majesty's Legation was instructed to reply that His Majesty's High Commissioner for Palestine had carefully investigated the case and was satisfied that the charges regarding the causes of the damage could not be substantiated, for there was no reason to doubt that the tapestry had fallen through its own weight owing to the fraying of the loops by which it had been suspended for sixty years. The Government of Palestine were examining the question of the ownership of the tapestry and were giving urgent consideration to the question of its eventual repair and replacement. In November I was instructed to inform the Vatican that the High Commissioner for Palestine was satisfied that the tapestry had been made by, and at the expense of, the Latins, and that therefore the Latins were properly entitled to carry out the repairs thereto. Steps were being taken with the concurrence of the Apostolic delegate for the authorities to carry out the work of repair at the expense of the Franciscans. As regards the replacement of the tapestry, it appeared that the wall of the crypt was in a bad condition, and investigations were therefore being made as to the best means to be adopted to support the tapestry in future. The Cardinal Secretary of State subsequently took an opportunity of expressing to me his satisfaction at the steps taken by His Majesty's Government to meet the wishes of the Holy See.

III.—RELATIONS WITH OTHER COUNTRIES.

Abyssinia.

36. On the 20th January the Pope received in audience the Crown Prince of Abyssinia. The Grand Cross of the Ordine Piano was conferred on the Prince and lesser decorations on the members of his suite.

Albania.

37. A party of 350 Albanian pilgrims visited Padua, Venice and Rome during the summer. They were received in audience by the Pope, who greeted them individually and addressed them. The pilgrimage was made under the auspices of the Italian authorities, and the party were accompanied by a secretary from the Italian Legation at Tirana and by a representative of the Italian press.

Bolivia.

38. The Vatican press has followed with pained interest the progress of the dispute between Bolivia and Paraguay. In response to a request put forward by the Pope through the Nuncios, the two Governments agreed to a suspension of hostilities between the night of the 24th December and the night of the following day.

China.

39. Mr. Yen, head of the Chinese delegation at Geneva, telegraphed in February to the Pope appealing in the name of the Chinese people for an expression of sympathy in their conflict with Japan. The Pope caused a somewhat non-committal reply to be sent by Cardinal Pacelli, stating that His Holiness expressed his good wishes to the Chinese people, and prayed that peace might return as soon as possible to the two great peoples whom Divine Providence had designed to live as neighbours. On the 28th February the Pope

referred to the Sino-Japanese dispute in the course of a broadcast address, and prayed that the blessings of peace and prosperity might fall on the two great Powers on whom was directed the attention of the world.

40. Throughout the course of the dispute the Vatican has been careful to maintain an attitude of strict neutrality. Thus for several days after the publication of the reply to Mr. Yen the *Osservatore Romano* gave unusual prominence to the communiqués from the Japanese Press Bureau.

Egypt.

41. During his visit to Rome Sïdky Pasha was received in private audience by the Pope.

France.

42. The relations between France and the Holy See remained on an extremely cordial basis. According to the French Embassy, one of their principal subjects of dispute with the Holy See arises from the desire of the Vatican to transfer from France to Rome the headquarters of certain religious orders founded by Frenchmen. The French Government apparently take little interest normally in the internal organisation of the Church, but the threatened Italianisation of the essentially French orders rouses them to passionate protests.

43. In May the French Ambassador, M. de Fontenay, retired and was succeeded by M. Charles-Roux, formerly French Minister in Prague.

Germany.

44. Relations between Germany and the Holy See have remained correct. The disappearance of Dr. Brüning was naturally regretted at the Vatican, who regard the progress of the Nazis with misgiving, principally because of the party's anti-Catholic bias.

45. On the 12th October a concordat was signed between the Holy See and the Republic of Baden. It was approved on the 9th December by the Landtag of Baden, but only after the President had given his casting vote in favour of the measure. On this occasion the Nazis and the Communists joined forces in order to oppose the concordat, a fact which aroused angry comment in Rome. By the end of the year the treaty had not yet been ratified, and it is therefore not yet in force.

46. By decree dated the 31st December, 1931, the Pope placed in the Calendar of Saints the name of Albertus Magnus, a German Dominican, who was at the same time declared a Doctor of the Church.

Hayti.

47. The Pope conferred on the President of the Republic the Grand Cross of the Order of St, Gregory the Great.

Iraq.

48. The Delegate Apostolic in Iraq informed His Majesty's Chargé d'Affaires privately that the Vatican would like Iraq, before she was admitted to the League, to agree in principle to conclude a convention with the Holy See regulating the status of Catholics. By the end of the year nothing more had been heard of this idea.

Italy.

49. Since the settlement last year of the dispute over the activities of Catholic Action, the relations between Church and State have been of the friendliest. There is every indication that the Vatican are satisfied with the existing state of affairs, and will do their best to avoid any further occasion of conflict with the Italian Government.

50. On the 5th January the Pope conferred the Order of Christ on the King of Italy and on the Prince of Piedmont. Ten days later His Holiness conferred on Signor Mussolini the Order of the Golden Spur, and on Signor

Grandi and Count de Vecchi, Italian Ambassador at the Holy See, the Grand Cross of the Ordine Piano. In March the same order was given to the Minister of the Royal Household, the Prefect of the Palace, and the King's first Aide-de-Camp General, as well as to the Minister of Education, the Minister of Public Works, the Minister of Communications, and the Prime Minister's Under-Secretary, in recognition of the part taken by him in the Lateran Treaty negotiations. At the same time the King of Italy conferred upon the Cardinal Secretary of State the Collar of the Annunziata, and other decorations on the Pope's Master of the Household, the Under-Secretary of State, the Assistant Under-Secretary, the Counsellor-General, and on Father Tacchi Venturi, S.J., who played a prominent part in the settlement of the Catholic Action dispute. This liberal exchange of decorations marked in a public manner the reconciliation between the Church and State.

51. On the 11th February, the third anniversary of the signature of the Lateran Treaty, the Pope received Signor Mussolini in private audience. It had been generally known for some time that the audience was in the air, but as time passed it was feared that some hitch had occurred. However, when it did take place the meeting was apparently a success, and Signor Mussolini declared himself highly pleased with his reception.

52. A convention was signed on the 7th September between the Holy See and Italy for the execution of article 10 of the Lateran Treaty, which deals with the exemption from military service of dignitaries and functionaries of the Holy See. At the same time a further convention was signed for the extension of the term of three years laid down in article 29, paragraph F, of the concordat, which deals with the recognition of Acts passed by religious and ecclesiastical bodies. A third convention was also signed, dealing with the notification of Acts relating to civil and commercial affairs.

53. On the 18th September Signor Mussolini unveiled at the Porta Pia a monument to the bersaglieri, which depicts a soldier of the corps sounding the advance on Rome. The 20th September would have been the obvious day for the ceremony, but it was held two days earlier, doubtless out of deference to the feelings of the Vatican. Nevertheless, the *Osservatore Romano* published an article complaining that some other exploit had not been selected as the subject of the monument. The Italian press did not take up the question, which was then allowed to drop.

54. The Fascist celebrations of the tenth anniversary of the establishment of the Fascist régime were sympathetically followed by the *Osservatore Romano*. The army bishop and a number of army chaplains took part in the review held in Rome by Signor Mussolini on the 28th October.

Japan.

55. There are few Catholics in Japan, and consequently the interests of the Holy See in the country are relatively unimportant. At the beginning of the year the total number of Catholics in Japan was estimated at 96,323, which represented an increase of about 3,000 over the preceding year. There is only one native bishop, and, with the exception of sixty-three native Japanese priests, the clergy are all missionaries of foreign nationality. There appears to be little prospect for the present of any substantial progress in the Catholic mission field.

League of Nations.

56. The activities of the League of Nations have been followed with sympathetic interest by the Vatican. In particular, considerable prominence has been given by the *Osservatore Romano* to the proceedings of the Disarmament Conference and to the efforts of the League to restore peace in China and in South America.

Liberia.

57. The appointment of a Papal Nuncio in Liberia was followed by the appointment of a Liberian Minister to the Holy See, a Dutchman, who presented his letters on the 1st February.

Lithuania.

58. No progress seems to have been made during the year towards a settlement of the dispute between Church and State.   In the meantime, Lithuania continues to be represented at the Holy See by a Chargé d'Affaires.

Mexico.

59. Towards the end of 1931 a violent anti-clerical campaign was initiated in Congress, which culminated in the passage of a law regulating article 130 of the Constitution in respect of the Federal district and territories.   The law provided that there should be only one priest for every 50,000 inhabitants, and, furthermore, that priests desiring to officiate must be Mexican nationals and must apply for permission to do so.   Provision was made separately for the numerous churches necessarily left without priests to remain open for private worship under the care of a member of the congregation.   At about the same time a decree was issued in the State of Vera Cruz limiting the number of priests to one for every 100,000 inhabitants.   Other States in the Union were invited to follow this example.

60. The archbishop answered the Federal law by withdrawing from their functions all priests in the Federal district and territories, so that for a time at the beginning of 1932 there were no services.   This attitude was subsequently reconsidered on instructions from Rome, and in February an official statement was published in the *Osservatore* to the effect that, whilst the Mexican ecclesiastical authorities might tolerate the conduct of public worship under the restrictions imposed by the law, this must not be taken to mean that the Holy See had sent instructions for the acceptance of the Government's decrees for the limitation of priests.   Any temporary compliance would be due entirely to *force majeure* and to avoid a greater evil, namely, the cessation of public worship.

61. The acceptance, though under strong protest, of the law by the Church brought a temporary appeasement to the tension between Church and State.   The number of licensed priests being inadequate for the needs of the population, illegal masses were celebrated with the approval of the hierarchy, but the Government refrained from taking rigorous measures to put a stop to the practice. Nevertheless, there was no sign that the authorities intended to recede from the position which they had taken up.   In May the State of Mexico passed a law fixing at thirty-four the number of priests authorised to function within the State.   The armed truce continued through the spring and summer, with only an occasional incident, such as the forcible removal by the Government of the Archbishop of Guadalajara.

62. On the 30th September the Pope sprung a surprise by the publication of the encyclical *Acerba animi*, addressed to the Mexican bishops.   After denouncing before the world the violence of the Mexican Government and recording his own protests, the Pope terminated the encyclical with instructions to the Mexican clergy.   Whilst in no way abandoning the claims of the Church, he ordered them to submit under protest to the law so as to prevent as far as possible the complete cessation of Catholic worship in Mexico.   The encyclical drew a retort from the President in the form of a declaration which he handed to the press.   He complained that the clergy were being openly incited to break the law and to provoke social upheaval; and he concluded by saying that, if the haughty and defiant attitude exemplified in the encyclical continued, the churches would be converted into schools and workshops for the benefit of the proletariat. This, in turn, drew a response from Mgr. Ruiz y Flores, the Apostolic Delegate in Mexico, who denied that the clergy were being incited to break the law, and invited the President to read the encyclical with greater attention.   In consequence of his intervention, the Apostolic Delegate was immediately expelled from the country.

63. On the 31st October the local congress of the State of Jalisco passed a Bill limiting the number of priests to fifty.   In consequence, the ecclesiastical authorities ordered the suspension of all religious services throughout the State till further notice.   This state of affairs must probably have given rise to expressions of popular dissatisfaction, for His Majesty's representative at Mexico City reported that, shortly afterwards, the State was put under martial law and the local garrisons were considerably reinforced.

64. During the course of the year the *Osservatore Romano* has continued to publish telegrams from every quarter of the globe, assuring the Pope of support and sympathy in his struggle against the persecutors of the Church in Mexico. It is a subject on which he feels strongly, and unless there is a change in the situation the encyclical *A cerba animi* is not likely to prove his last word on the controversy.

Persia.

65. The new Delegate Apostolic, Mgr. Lari, presented his letters to the Shah of Persia on the 21st March.

Roumania.

66. In May a mission arrived in Rome under the Roumanian Minister of Justice, M. Valer Pop, to discuss difficulties which had arisen from the activities of the so-called " Status Catolic," a Catholic organisation dating from the days of the Hungarian régime. The negotiations were successful, and on the 30th May an agreement was signed between the Holy See and Roumania which settled the question to the satisfaction of both parties.

Russia.

67. The activities of the Soviet Government have continued to engage the attention of the special department dealing with Russian affairs. Particular regard has been paid to the anti-religious campaign waged by the Communists, to such an extent that it is possible that this aspect of the question has dwarfed all others and has assumed exaggerated importance in the eyes of the Vatican authorities. However that may be, there is no doubt that the Vatican, from the Pope downwards, are deeply impressed with the Communist peril.

68. The Vatican press have lost no opportunity of attacking communism and of depicting in the blackest colours the policy of the Soviet Government and conditions in the Soviet Union.

San Marino.

69. The exchange of ratifications of the Monetary Convention of the 30th December, 1931, with the Holy See took place on the 25th May, 1932.

Spain.

70. On the 23rd January the Spanish Government published a decree dissolving the Jesuit Order in Spain. The next day the Pope took the opportunity afforded by a public ceremony to make a protest against the decree. The *Osservatore Romano* also protested in trenchant terms. In October anxiety was caused by the publication of a draft law, providing for the confiscation by the State of the properties of the religious congregations, forbidding them to teach and enabling them to be dissolved by decree of the Cortes.

71. During the year the attitude of the Vatican towards the Spanish Government has been one of quiet but undisguised hostility, only tempered by the knowledge that if there is to be a change in Spain it will only be a change for the worse.

72. Since the Vatican refused an *agrément* to the present Spanish Minister for Foreign Affairs, Spain has been represented by a Chargé d'Affaires. The Pope has not withdrawn the Nuncio from Madrid for the reason that he considers that his presence there is likely to be useful.

IV.—THE VATICAN.

College of Cardinals.

73. The following cardinals died during the year: Van Rossum, Prefect of the Congregation of Propaganda, and Piffl, Archbishop of Vienna; *i.e.*, one Dutchman and one Austrian.

74. At the end of the year the Sacred College numbered 53 cardinals, of whom 26 were Italians and 27 non-Italians. These were distributed as follows: In Curia: 20 Italians, 1 Austrian, 1 French and 1 German. Outside Rome:

6 Italians, 5 French, 4 United States of America, 3 German, 3 Spanish, 2 Polish, 1 Great Britain, 1 Irish, 1 Austrian, 1 Brazilian, 1 Czechoslovak, 1 Hungarian, 1 Portuguese.

75.   The Sacred College is now seventeen short of its full number, and some inconvenience is being caused by the lack of new blood since no consistory has been held for over two years.   Not only is there a shortage of cardinals to fill the major offices in Curia, but many of the surviving members of the college are becoming so old that they are scarcely up to their work.   Rumours of a new consistory are constantly in circulation, but the Pope keeps his counsel and no one has the slightest inkling of his intentions.   The coming year is certain to take its toll of the older cardinals, but it is possible that there will be no consistory, and that a still more attenuated and antiquated college will be left to take up the burdens of 1934.

Legislation.

76.   In continuation of the list given in paragraph 154 of last year's report, the following are the laws promulgated in 1932 :—

No. XXVII.   January 24, 1932.   Appointment of special commission to determine responsibility for the Vatican Library disaster.
No. XXVIII.   May 10, 1932.   Ordinance regarding traffic in the Vatican City.
No. XXIX.   May 14, 1932.   Decree regarding nomenclature of streets and squares.
No. XXX.   May 25, 1932.   Monetary Convention with San Marino.
No. XXXI.   June 24, 1932.   Prolongation of period laid down in Law VII of June 8, 1929.
No. XXXII.   December 1, 1932.   Organisation of the Governor's department.
No. XXXIII.   December 5, 1932.   Regulations for the various offices and services in the Governor's department.
No. XXXIV.   December 5, 1932.   Regulation for the administration of the Papal property at Castel Gandolfo.

Holy Year.

77.   To the surprise of all present the Pope announced during his Christmas allocution to the College of Cardinals that 1933 would see the beginning of a Jubilee or Holy Year.   The reasons given for this decision were first that it was right that the Church should fittingly celebrate the nineteenth centenary of the death of Jesus Christ, and secondly, that it was desirable to turn the thoughts of men from the material troubles afflicting the whole world.   The Holy Year is to begin on the 2nd April, 1933, and to end on the 2nd April of the following year.

78.   The Pope's pronouncement was given a generally favourable reception in Italy and abroad.

Picture Gallery.

79.   The new picture gallery, called the Pinacoteca, was opened by the Pope in October.   It contains pictures taken from various Papal collections.

Vatican Galleries.

80.   The new entrance to the Vatican Galleries from the Piazza del Risorgimento was opened by the Pope in December.

Vatican Passports.

81.   In reply to an enquiry from His Majesty's Legation, the Governor of the Vatican State supplied the following information : Holders of British passports are not required to obtain a visa for entry into the Vatican.   Vatican passports are issued only ·to citizens of the Vatican State, whose citizenship, owing to its particular nature, precludes permanent residence abroad.   In the majority of cases citizens of the Vatican State retain their nationality of birth by reason of the dispositions of their State of origin and can therefore hold not only a Vatican passport, but also a passport of their original nationality.   The

question of special regulations for the issue of Vatican passports is still under consideration, and meanwhile the system adopted follows the regulations in force in Italy.

Vatican Radio Station.

82.   On two occasions, in February and in December, the Pope used the station in order to broadcast a message to the whole world.

Vatican Library.

83.   The special commission appointed by the Pope to enquire into the responsibility for the disaster to the Vatican Library submitted its report in May. The Director of Works and the foreman mason was acquitted of civil and penal responsibility. Both were, however, found guilty of negligence, and the commission recommended that they should be dismissed. It also recommended that the contracts with the firm of builders hitherto employed should be annulled.

84.   The work of restoration is being done more quickly than was originally thought possible, and it is hoped that the library may be opened once more in time for the inauguration of the Holy Year on the 1st April.

Law Courts.

85.   In October the Pope nominated a commission to draw up proposals for the organisation of the civil law courts of the Vatican City. In the meantime civil cases are to be heard by a special commission invested with full powers, even in the matter of procedure.   No modification of the organisation of the ecclesiastical courts is involved.

V.—PAPAL PRONOUNCEMENTS.

86.   The following were the two encyclicals issued during the year 1932 :—

Caritate Christi of the 3rd May, 1932, on social discontent and anti-religious activities.
Acerba Animi of the 29th September, 1932, on the dispute between Church and State in Mexico.

87.   There were no other Papal pronouncements of any particular importance, in contrast to the practice of previous years, which saw a spate of edicts on every kind of moral and social question.

VI.—QUESTIONS OF THE DAY.

88.   The encyclical *Caritate Christi* was a general appeal for the application of the principles of Christianity to the economic crisis, which the Pope described as a scourge only exceeded in its universality by the Flood. It also contained an emphatic denunciation of communism on the ground that it was a declared enemy of religion and of the social order.

89.   The efforts of the Powers to reach agreement on disarmament, the Sino-Japanese dispute and war debts and reparations have been followed with sympathetic interest, and the Pope has emphasised the importance to the world of an early solution of these problems. But he has expressed no opinion on the issues involved, doubtless because of their controversial character.   The *Osservatore Romano* has declared itself in favour of general cancellation of war debts and reparations, but, in conversation with me, the Pope would not commit himself even so far, and confined himself to saying that there was a conflict of legitimate interests, which it would be difficult to reconcile.

Easter: Stabilisation of.

90.   Semi-official enquiries showed that, whilst the proposal presents no difficulties from the point of view of dogma, the Vatican maintain their view that there is not sufficient reason to make an immediate change. In any event, the

Holy See would not be prepared to consider the question, except on the advice of an Œcumenical Council, a body which is not likely to be convened in the near future.

Marriage.

91. The Pope has continued his efforts to propagate his views on marriage. He has taken advantage of a scheme whereby the Italian Government grant a railway reduction of 80 per cent. to all newly-married couples visiting Rome, to grant a special daily audience to these people. He speaks to each couple individually, gives them a memento of the occasion, and delivers a long address to the assembly on the duties of the married state. Many thousands of persons of all nationalities have availed themselves of this opportunity.

92. ## VII.—TREATIES.

With (Country)—	Date of Signature.	Subject.	Date of Exchange of Ratifications.	Date of Entry into Force.	Remarks.
Roumania ..	May 30, 1932	Interpretation of article 9 of Concordat	No ratification clause	On signature..	Settlement of the question of the Status Romano-Catholicus Transylvaniensis.
Baden ..	Oct. 12, 1932..	Concordat ..	Not yet ratified	On exchange of ratifications.	

o

CONFIDENTIAL.
_____

(14364)

HOLY SEE.
———

Annual Report, 1933.
———

[R 153/153/22]

Sir R. Clive to Sir John Simon.—(Received January 9.)

(No. 1.)   British Legation to the Holy See,
Sir,   Rome, January 1, 1934.

I HAVE the honour to enclose herein the annual report for 1933.

2. I am indebted to Mr. Montgomery, second secretary at this Legation, for his assistance.

I have, &c.
R. H. CLIVE.

_____

Enclosure.

Annual Report on the Holy See for 1933.
———

CONTENTS.

_____

I.—INTRODUCTION.

THE year 1933 has been a memorable one for the Vatican, and the Holy Year, which began on the 2nd April, has exceeded the most sanguine expectations in attracting to Rome many thousands of pilgrims. From England alone there have been some fifty pilgrimages, varying in numbers from 30 to 500. Every pilgrimage has been received in audience and addressed by the Pope. In many cases His Holiness delivered an allocution of twenty to thirty minutes, the French and German pilgrims being addressed in their own language. Complete

7219 [9552]   B

harmony has existed between the Vatican and the Italian Government. The great inrush of visitors to Rome has been of mutual benefit, the 70 per cent. reduction in railway tickets contributing both to increase the numbers of pilgrims to the Vatican and to swell the general tourist traffic, to the advantage of the Italian revenue.

2. In the foreign relations of the Vatican the most notable events have been the resumption of normal relations with Great Britain, by the appointment of a Minister after a lapse of two and a half years; a perpetual state of friction with the German Reich, in spite of the signature and ratification of a concordat; the conclusion of a concordat and increased friendliness with the present Government of Austria; the publication in the summer—more in sorrow than in anger—of an encyclical on the subject of Spain, and the oppressive measures taken against the Church and religious education in that country; considerable friction with Czechoslovakia; and increased friendliness with the Italian Government, who for the first time have sent official representatives to attend the great Church ceremonies in the Basilicas.

II.—Relations with the British Empire.

United Kingdom.

3. Early in the year His Majesty's Government in the United Kingdom decided again to appoint a Minister to the Vatican after an interval of more than two and a half years. During this period the Legation had not been closed, and correct and friendly relations had been maintained by Mr. Ogilvie-Forbes, and, later, by Mr. Kirkpatrick, as His Majesty's Chargé d'Affaires, and it is a pleasure to pay a tribute to the work of both these gentlemen. The dispute in connexion with Malta had been settled, in the view of the Vatican, by the acceptance, more than a year previously, of Lord Strickland's apology. The delay in reappointing a Minister was not understood, and hints had been dropped that it would be agreeable to the Holy See if official relations were again placed on a completely normal footing. His Majesty's Government were not, however, disposed to hurry matters, and it was not until the 30th March that I presented my letters to the Pope as His Majesty's Minister. There is no doubt that the Vatican was much gratified by the decision of His Majesty's Government, and nothing could have exceeded the friendliness with which I was received by the Pope and the Cardinal Secretary of State. In the course of a long conversation which I had after the formal presentation of my letters, His Holiness, in referring to the recent reception of the Prime Minister and Foreign Secretary, remarked that the rôle of England in the world was very great. Like the Catholic Church, England's influence was world-wide and her responsibility was enormous. For their Majesties the King and Queen His Holiness has on every occasion on which I have seen him expressed his regard and affection. That His Holiness extends that regard to the British people has been repeatedly evinced throughout the year both in public and in private utterances which have come to my knowledge. The orderliness, the freedom, the tolerance of England appeal to the precise and orderly, yet autocratic, temperament of the Pope. He looks upon England not merely as a bulwark against communism and subversive ideas, but as a beacon-light which shines forth in a sea of economic and financial chaos.

4. In March, before my arrival, the Pope had received in private audience the Prime Minister and Foreign Secretary on the occasion of their visit to Rome to see the head of the Government. The visit, the first ever paid by a Prime Minister of the United Kingdom to the Pope, was much appreciated. It certainly creates a precedent, and I feel that in future, when a distinguished member of His Majesty's Government pays an official visit to Rome, the Vatican will expect him to apply for an audience or, in case his time is too limited, to make his excuses through His Majesty's representative for not doing so. I did this, with his consent and approval, when Mr. Arthur Henderson, president of the Disarmament Conference, paid a fleeting visit to Rome in July.

5. Still earlier in the year Lord Baden-Powell was received in private audience by the Pope. His Lordship wished to induce the Holy See to appoint a clerical adviser to the Boy Scout movement. At the audience the Pope warmly welcomed Lord Baden-Powell, as a man of whom he had heard so much. His

Holiness, while praising the Boy Scout movement as a magnificent work which had his fullest approval, declined, however, to appoint a clerical adviser to the movement.   The Nuncios and Apostolic delegates by whom the Holy See were represented in almost every country were, with the bishops, His Holiness said, the proper people to whom to apply for advice.   Lord Baden-Powell did not demur and said to His Majesty's Chargé d'Affaires that the Pope's expression of approval would, in itself, be a great help in extending the movement in Catholic countries.

6.   In April some twenty-five English M.P.'s, who had come to Rome to attend the Inter-Parliamentary Commercial Conference, were received in audience, when the Pope, addressing them in French, expressed his gratification at receiving them and referred to " L'Angleterre la bien-aimée."

7.   In addition to these private or special audiences, there have been to date some fifty pilgrimages from England in connexion with the Holy Year, the largest one being a pilgrimage of over 500 British unemployed in September, promoted by Sir Martin Melvin, proprietor of the Catholic newspaper, the *Universe*.

8.   The age and indifferent health of Cardinal Bourne are a source of anxiety to English Catholics.   Since the death of Cardinal Gasquet there has been no English cardinal in Curia, and the appointment of a second English cardinal would be welcomed by many.

Malta.

9.   Already a year ago it was clear that the patience of His Majesty's Government must in the end be exhausted if the Nationalist Ministry in Malta continued to encourage Italian propaganda and play with the language question. This Legation was only concerned with the possible repercussions in the Vatican, and the desirability of enlisting their sympathy to proposals for strengthening the English element in the religious (teaching) orders in Malta.

10.   In this connexion it may not be out of place to enumerate briefly which are the religious orders established in Malta.   They may be divided into two categories.   The first consists of—

> Augustinians (Mendicant).
> Minor Conventuals.
> Carmelites.
> Dominicans.
> Minor Observants.
> Capucins.

These have each three convents in the islands and, therefore, a right to a provincial of their own.   Their personnel is exclusively Maltese and, with the exception of the Augustinians, they keep no schools.
The second category consists of—

> Jesuits.
> Salesians.
> Christian Brothers.
> Discalced Carmelites.

The Salesians have two institutions in Malta, one under the English province of the order, the other under Italy.   The Jesuits, who come under the Italian province of the order, conduct the largest college in Malta and the environment is almost entirely Italian.   Some thirty years ago the English Jesuits sold this property in Malta and were replaced by Italians.

11.   On the 14th July I received instructions to submit to the Vatican a proposal—

> (1) That the Italian Jesuits in Malta should gradually be replaced by Englishmen.
> (2) That the opening in Malta of the English province of another teaching order, such as the Benedictines, would be viewed with satisfaction by His Majesty's Government.

12.   I called on the Cardinal Secretary of State the following day and spoke to his Eminence of the difficulties which had arisen in Malta and of the embarrassment caused to the British authorities by the intensive propaganda in favour of the Italian language at a time when the very friendliest relations existed with the Italian Government.   His Majesty's Government had no wish to interfere in the internal administration of the Church, and the proposals I had been instructed to put forward were only intended to strengthen the English element in Catholic schools in what was after all a British Colony.

13.   His Eminence, whose attitude was most friendly, did not demur to what I said and promised to consul the Father-General of the Jesuits and the Abbot-Primate of the Benedictines.

14.   A difficulty, however, arose which had not been foreseen and which consisted in the lack of available Englishmen for the purpose.   Father Welsby, an influential English Jesuit, who works in close touch with the Father-General in Rome, told me that there was work to be done in many parts of the world for which English Jesuits would be especially suitable, but, unfortunately, there were not nearly enough to go round.   As regards the Benedictines, the same difficulty existed, as the English Benedictines were fully occupied with their own educational programme in extending the number of Benedictine schools in England.

15.   At the same time it is of interest to know that the Vatican do not appear to oppose these suggestions.   There is, in fact, no reason why they should, for they are in no way derogatory to the Church.

16.   On the 20th September the Governor of Malta enacted an ordinance whereby *inter alia* all foreign institutions in Malta would in future be subject to licence.   As the Maltese Nationalists were putting it about that this action was aimed at the Catholic religion, His Majesty's Chargé d'Affaires was instructed to explain the details of the ordinance at the Vatican, and to state that he felt sure that the Vatican would lend no countenance to these false reports.   He was informed, in reply, that no complaints had been received at the Vatican from Malta and that he could rest assured that the Holy See would listen to no claim which could not be fully established.

17.   A few weeks later, in the course of an interview with the Cardinal on my return from leave of absence, his Eminence handed me a pro-memoriâ enquiring whether in the recent ordinance were included those members of religious orders who were not concerned with teaching, but whose activities lay within the sacred ministry, and also such religious as might be sent by their legitimate superiors for purposes concerned with the internal affairs of such orders.   Hope was expressed that a favourable reply would be given.

18.   The Governor of Malta wrote, in a despatch to the Colonial Office with reference to this point, that he anticipated no difficulty in administering the Aliens Ordinance as regards members of religious orders not engaged in teaching in such a way as to meet the wishes of the Vatican.   I so informed the cardinal on the 10th November, who expressed his gratification and said that this would be very welcome to the Holy Father.

19.   It is satisfactory to be able to record that the Vatican press has abstained from unfriendly criticism of recent events in Malta, and I have reason to believe that the *Osservatore Romano* received a hint to adopt a completely neutral attitude.

India.

20.   In a private letter early in the year His Majesty's Chargé d'Affaires reported that " as regards India the Vatican are definitely pro-British because they get their information from sources which are anti-Gandhi."   I received confirmation of the correctness of this view in two conversations I had in the summer and autumn with Mgr. Kierkels (a Dutchman), who is Apostolic Delegate in India.   Mgr. Kierkels spoke in the highest terms of the Government of India and of their fair and impartial attitude towards missionaries of any faith.

21.   It was perhaps natural that the Pope and the Cardinal Secretary of State should have received with every mark of sympathy and friendship the

Maharajah of Travancore during his visit to Rome in August, in view of the large number of Catholics in that State—about 600,000. But it was very satisfactory that on the vexed question of the appointment of native bishops the cardinal agreed without demur to my leaving with him a memorandum pointing out that it would be greatly appreciated if, before nominating natives of the State to the Episcopacy, the Holy See would agree to make confidential enquiries in the first instance as to whether there was any objection to the candidate on political grounds. His Eminence promised to refer the matter to the Propaganda Fide and to speak to His Holiness, and I propose, when an opportunity occurs, to mention the matter to Cardinal Fumasoni-Biondi, who is head of the Congregation of Propaganda Fide.

22. Maharajahs and Rajahs have a liking for audiences with the Pope, and when they are officially recommended these are invariably granted. In June the Maharajah of Alwar, G.C.S.I., asked the Vatican direct for an audience. The latter referred to me, and, as I had received no instructions in the matter, and no application from the Maharajah, I replied that I could not support his application or accept any responsibility in the matter. The audience was not granted and the Maharajah left Rome without calling at this Legation.

23. A Mr. Basil Gomes, claiming to represent the British Indian Catholics of Bombay, or at least a large section of them, has continued to bombard this Legation throughout the year with letters enclosing petitions for the removal of the Portuguese Archbishop Lima of Bombay. No action is taken on these letters. In accordance with the agreement come to in 1928, the Archbishop of Bombay is alternately a Portuguese or an Englishman.

24. On the 26th December I called on Cardinal Fumasoni-Biondi, the head of the Congregation of Propaganda Fide, and himself a former Apostolic Delegate in India, with Dr. Ambedkar who wished to speak to his Eminence about the many thousands of " Untouchables " who had become Catholics. Dr. Ambedkar pointed out that the social disabilities of these " Untouchables " had in no way been removed by their conversion to Christianity, as either a part of the church was railed off for them to prevent any contact with the " Caste " Hindu Catholics, or, as more often happened, " Caste " Hindu Catholic and " Untouchable " Catholics did not attend Mass at the same time. This, said Dr. Ambedkar, appeared to be contrary to the teaching of Christ that all men were equal in the sight of God.

25. The cardinal, in reply, explained that the Catholic Church moved very slowly and was indifferent to time. Great changes could not be brought about suddenly, and the Church were careful not to embarrass the civil authorities when complicated and vexed questions like " caste " were in question. At the same time the point raised by Dr. Ambedkar was appreciated by the Church and had his full sympathy and that of the Catholic missionaries in India. Patience was needed. Time and teaching would in the end smooth out the difficulties.

26. I cannot say that Dr. Ambedkar found much satisfaction in this reply, but it is very typical of the extreme conservatism and cautious wisdom of the Vatican. I remember Dr. W. W. Yen saying to me, when I left China ten years ago in a welter of chaos and civil war, that these things would pass away. What were a few years, even a few centuries in the life of a nation? And so the Vatican with some of this wisdom of the East appears to view the caste system in its relations to Christianity.

Canada.
27. At the consistory, held on the 13th March, Mgr. Villeneuve, Archbishop of Quebec, was among the six prelates elevated to the Sacred College. Before the consistory Mgr. Villeneuve called at His Majesty's Legation and was at pains to emphasise to His Majesty's Chargé d'Affaires his loyalty to the Empire.

28.   Father Bastien, the head of the Canadian College in Rome, called on me shortly after my arrival and, though speaking no English, was no less emphatic in his expressions of loyalty and devotion.

29.   The complete liberty of language and religion of the French Canadians, combined with their loyalty, is an outstanding example in the eyes of the Vatican of the tolerance of British rule.

30.   On the last day of the year, although it was a Sunday, the Pope received in audience fourteen school teachers from Canada. These teachers, none of whom were Catholic, were members of the League of the Empire at whose instance the audience was arranged. His Holiness welcomed them in a speech praising the profession of teaching, and gave them his benediction.

Australia and New Zealand.

31.   Mgr. Filippo Bernardini, a nephew of Cardinal Gasparri for many years Secretary of State, was appointed in March Apostolic Delegate to Australia and New Zealand. A slight misunderstanding occurred at the time of the appointment, as the Vatican neglected, before publishing the appointment, to forward to this Legation Mgr. Bernardini's passport with a request for a visa, in accordance with the agreement come to in 1926, whereby no publication was to be made before the passport had been returned to the Vatican duly visé. When the attention of the cardinal was drawn to this his Eminence expressed his sincere regret and promised to see that such a mistake should never occur again. Mgr. Bernardini is a hearty prelate, speaking excellent English, who had been eighteen years in Washington as Professor of Canon Law.

Irish Free State.

32.   So far as relations between the Irish Free State and the Holy See are concerned, while these have been friendly and correct, extreme care has been taken by the Vatican to let nothing occur which might in any way give offence to His Majesty's Government in the United Kingdom.

33.   Mr. de Valera visited Rome at the end of May. He was received with the respect due to his office, and a high Papal decoration was conferred upon him.

34.   Mr. Bewley, the first Irish Free State Minister to be appointed to the Holy See, was transferred to Berlin. He had been here four years. No new Minister has been sent and the Legation is under a Chargé d'Affaires, Mr. McCauley.

Mandated Territory.

35.   *Palestine.*—It is pleasant to be able to record that since the liquidation of the tapestry incident in the Grotto of the Nativity at Bethlehem at the end of 1932 there has been no serious discord between the Latin and Orthodox communities. It is true that the Under-Secretary of State drew the attention of His Majesty's Chargé d'Affaires in February to two quite minor subjects of controversy, but the latter declined to take them up and his action was approved. At the same time the Holy See officially conveyed their thanks for the satisfactory (to the Latins) settlement of the tapestry incident.

36.   On the 5th April His Majesty's Legation were notified of the proposed appointment as Apostolic Delegate in Palestine, Egypt, Transjordania, Arabia, Ethiopia, Eritrea and Cyprus of Mgr. Bartoloni, in succession to Mgr. Valeri, who had been nominated as Nuncio in Roumania. A few days later authority was received to viser his passport, and in July Mgr. Bartoloni left for Palestine. Early in October he died of appendicitis, to the universal regret. He was a man of tact with great personal charm.

37.   A month later Mgr. Dini, Rector of the Propaganda College, was appointed to succeed him. He expects to leave first for Egypt in January after his consecration as titular Archbishop of Dara on the 6th January.

III.—RELATIONS WITH OTHER COUNTRIES.

Argentine Republic.

38. In view of the insufficient number of dioceses in Argentina, the Apostolic Nuncio (Mgr. Cortesi) has long been urging upon the Government of the Republic the desirability of erecting a large number of new bishoprics. His efforts have now been crowned with success, as, urged on, no doubt, by the approach of the Eucharistic Congress, which is to be held in Buenos Aires in October 1934, and which will be a great international occasion, the National Assembly has approved a law whereby the number of the archbishops will be raised from one to seven, and that of the bishops from ten to fourteen. Henceforth, there will be one archbishop or bishop to each department of the republic; and an imposing array of Argentine prelates will be available to greet the Papal Legate and the numerous foreign cardinals who are expected at Buenos Aires next autumn.

Austria.

39. The long-drawn-out negotiations between Austria and the Holy See were brought to a successful issue in June, and on the 19th of that month a concordat was signed at the Vatican by Cardinal Pacelli for the Pope and by Chancellor Dollfuss (who was on a visit to Rome) for the Austrian Government. The text of the concordat has not yet been published, and will probably not be until it comes before the Vienna Parliament for ratification.

40. The Pope appointed Cardinal La Fontaine, Patriarch of Venice, to be his Legate for the celebrations in September, the 250th anniversary of the liberation of Vienna from the Turks. Cardinal Pacelli told the French Ambassador that the Austrian Government had wished to have him as Legate and that he would gladly have gone. The Holy Father had, however, decided otherwise.

41. The Vienna celebrations, which lasted four days, were attended by the Cardinal Prince Primates of Hungary and Poland, and by the Cardinal Archbishop of Paris, as well as by the Papal Legate. The great German prelates were remarkable by their absence, and Germans in the mass were precluded from attendance by the 1,000 mark visa.

42. On the occasion of the anniversary His Holiness conferred the Sovereign Order of Christ on Dr. Miklas, President of the Austrian Republic, and the Order of the Golden Spur on Dr. Dollfuss, the Austrian Chancellor. The *Osservatore Romano*, in announcing these distinctions, added that they were conferred in recognition of the share taken by the two recipients in the recent celebrations, as also of their well-known devotion to the Catholic Church.

Brazil.

43. The first national Eucharistic Congress ever to be held in Brazil took place during September at Bahia, the seat of the Primate. The Cardinal Archbishop of Rio de Janeiro, the Papal representative, and fifty-three archbishops and bishops, as well as many thousands of priests and laymen from all parts of the country took part.

Bulgaria.

44. On the 13th January the Queen of Bulgaria (*née* Princess Giovanna of Savoy) gave birth at Sofia to her first child, a daughter, and on the 16th the infant princess was baptised according to the Orthodox rite by the Metropolitan of Sofia.

45. On hearing what had occurred, the Pope, through the Apostolic Delegate at Sofia (Mgr. Roncalli), protested energetically against the princess's baptism by a non-Catholic prelate, on the ground that it constituted a breach of the solemn engagements taken by King Boris on his marriage. A few days later the *Osservatore Romano* published a statement from which it was clear that the King

and Queen had accepted all the conditions, including that of the Catholic upbringing of their future offspring, on which the grant of a dispensation in the case of mixed marriages is made dependent.

46. The Papal protest was not reproduced in the Italian papers, which confined themselves to reporting the fact of the baptism, and the Italian Royal Family was fortunately not involved in the controversy, for the Queen of Italy, who set out to visit her daughter soon after she received the news of the princess's birth, did not arrive at Sofia until the ceremony was over. Indeed, her train is said to have been purposely delayed by the Bulgarian authorities.

47. The Vatican were, and are, inclined to take a severe view of the King's conduct, and argue that what is described by them as his " breach of faith " was all the more indefensible, in view of the fact that the infant is a girl and therefore not in the line of succession to the Bulgarian Throne. King Boris's own brother and sister are Roman Catholics, and he was certainly under no necessity to have his daughter baptised into the Orthodox Church. Political expediency may, however, have suggested the desirability of allaying, by means of this baptism, the disappointment of the general public at the sex of the child.

48. However this may be, the Italian Royal Family would appear to have been taken completely by surprise, and the Queen of Bulgaria does not seem herself to have had any inkling of the King's intention. Enquiries made by the Vatican into the extent, if any, of her responsibility, resulted in her complete exoneration from blame, and in the allocution delivered by the Pope at the consistory of the 13th March, his Holiness said that he could not and should not inflict " any canonical sanctions upon, or even deny his paternal apostolic blessing to, an already afflicted mother, who protested her innocence in all that occurred, all having been done without her expressed or tacit consent." In the same allocution the Holy Father very strongly condemned King Boris's action. His Holiness had had complete confidence, he said, that the promises given would be observed with that perfect loyalty which is to be expected from sovereign persons. He had been disappointed, and as the matter had been noised abroad, to the surprise and scandal of many, he felt obliged in conscience to acquit his responsibility before that solemn gathering in the sight of God and man. To pretend, as had been done, that the action in question was inspired by high motives of public weal, was but to remind him of the Divine phrase, now too often forgotten, that " Justice exalteth a nation: but sin maketh nations miserable." (*Proverbs* xiv, 34.)

49. Having set this precedent in the case of his first-born daughter, King Boris is presumably committed to the Orthodox upbringing of any future issue; and Mgr. Roncalli stated privately to a member of His Majesty's Legation, that each future baptism will count as a separate breach of faith and will call for a renewed protest on the part of the Holy See.

Czechoslovakia.

50. The complicated question of squaring the ancient ecclesiastical divisions with the new frontiers set up in 1919 was left unsolved by the *modus vivendi* of 1927, which simply laid down that no part of Czechoslovakia should be subjected to foreign ecclesiastical rule. A final solution of the various problems had been hoped for as a result of the deliberations of two commissions, one purely Czechoslovak and one " mixed," under the presidency of the Nuncio, which were appointed some years ago. The recommendations of the two commissions have, however, found scant favour in the eyes of various prelates, Hungarian and otherwise, who would stand to lose heavily thereby; and the important question of an archbishopric for Slovakia, also raised by the commissions, will have to stand over until the territorial difficulty has been overcome.

51. The settlement of questions of this kind is made no easier by the fact that the Papal Nuncio to Czechoslovakia, Mgr. Ciriaci, is a man of decidedly impulsive temperament. It is true that he has had serious difficulties to contend with. In the autumn of this year a newspaper, *Venkev*, the organ of one of the Government parties, published a violent attack both on his Excellency and on the Holy See, who, it was alleged, had consistently slighted Czechoslovakia.

The failure of the Pope to create a Czechoslovak cardinal was cited as an instance of the Pontifical want of tenderness to the young republic. The Nuncio demanded and received half-hearted excuses from the Government, but the offending article was not withdrawn. A little later, in reply to a letter from Father Hlinka (leader of the Slovak Popular party) expressing the devotion of the Slovaks to the Holy See, Mgr. Ciriaci, in a communication subsequently given to the public, complained of the manner in which he was " insulted " at Prague and compared the Czechs, much to their disadvantage, with the " generous-hearted Slovak race."

52. This tactless outburst drew down a torrent of Czech indignation on Mgr. Ciriaci's head. There was even question of the Government's demanding his Excellency's withdrawal. Milder counsels, however, prevailed, and the Czech representative at Rome was merely instructed to express the wish that the Nuncio should be invited to furnish explanations. He left Prague for Rome in October, after explaining that he had anyhow been intending to take his leave about then. The Czechoslovak Minister informed His Majesty's Minister in November that Mgr. Ciriaci was unlikely to return to Prague. However this may be, there seems no reason to suppose that the prelate's stock has gone down at the Vatican.

Estonia.

53. In the autumn negotiations, which had for some time been in progress between the Holy See and Estonia with a view to the establishment of diplomatic relations, were brought to a successful conclusion; and on the 30th September Dr. Otto Strandman, a former Minister for Foreign Affairs, who also represents his country in Paris, delivered his credentials to the Pope as Estonian Minister. In October an Apostolic Nunciature was established in Estonia, and Mgr. Arata, resident at Kovno, was appointed to take charge also of the Tallinn post until such time as a Nuncio should be appointed.

54. The decision to establish relations between Tallinn and the Holy See might appear surprising, in view of the smallness of the Catholic population of Estonia; but, according to His Majesty's representative, both the Tallinn Government and the Pope are anxious that the waning influence of the Orthodox Church in the Baltic States should wane yet further. The Estonian Government care but little what influence takes its place, provided it be an influence which will draw their people westwards and away from Russia; and the Holy See is interested to have another outpost from which to observe conditions in Russia.

France.

55. The French Embassy have an obsession that the Pope is as much an Italian Nationalist as Mussolini, that, in spite of all that has happened this year, he is at heart pro-German, that he has the same antipathy to Yugoslavia as any other Italian, and that his attitude towards France is inevitably tinged by all these factors.

56. It cannot be said that the behaviour of Frenchmen in Rome this year has been calculated to gain the sympathy of the Vatican. At the Canonisation of St. Bernadette, which was attended by several thousand Frenchmen, the behaviour of many of them in St. Peter's was hardly decent, and it has been reported to me by eyewitnesses that they loudly criticised everything in the ceremony from the Pope downwards. Of twenty French Deputies who were received in special audience in April, I was told that more than half declined to kneel and kiss the Pope's ring.

57. The French Ambassador to the Holy See has not the reputation of being a friend of Italy. Catholicism to him is merely a part of the political game, and he loses no opportunity to press French claims on the Vatican, always with a political aim in view.

58. Relations, however, between the Holy See and the French Republic were disturbed by no untoward incident. The French, it is true, were irritated at the appointment of the Italian, Mgr. Lari, as Apostolic Delegate in Persia, as they still cling to their ancient claim to protect Catholics in the Near and Middle East.

59. Large numbers of French pilgrims flocked to Rome during 1933, attracted, no doubt, by the fact that both Saints canonised during the year, and two of the new Beati were of French nationality. Two parties of French parliamentary Deputies were received by the Pope, one in May and the other in December. While the first delegation had come to Rome primarily to attend the Economic Inter-Parliamentary Conference, the second was present expressly to attend the Canonisation of St. Bernadette of Lourdes. Twenty French bishops, including those of Lourdes and Nevers, the towns with which the new Saint is most closely connected, were present on this latter occasion.

Germany.

60. In spite of the conclusion, for the first time in history, of a concordat between the Holy See and the German Reich, it must be admitted that, far from improving, relations between these two Powers have deteriorated during the year. This was due largely to the lack of goodwill shown by the Nazi Government in carrying out the stipulations of the concordat. Moreover, the condition which renders the working of a concordat with the Fascist State comparatively easy, viz., the almost universal catholicism of the Italian people, is absent in a State with a large non-Catholic majority. A concordat, be it remembered, does not imply mutual respect, still less affection. An eminent English Jesuit recently wrote : " A concordat represents the compromise, outside matters of principle, which the Church enters into with a Government which does not, fully or freely, recognise her entire claims to independence and autonomy."

61. The record of the National Socialist party, where the Catholic Church was concerned, had rendered it suspect at the Vatican, and it was with considerable misgivings that ecclesiastical circles in Rome heard in February the news of Herr Hitler's accession to power. With customary caution, however, the Vatican avoided any public expression of opinion ; the *Osservatore Romano* was non-committal ; and when at Easter Captain (now General) Göring visited Rome, the Vatican organ merely mentioned that he had fought energetically against bolshevism, and had taken strong measures against corruption and immorality.

62. Herr von Papen, the German Vice-Chancellor, visited Rome at the same time as General Göring. It was an open secret that he had come to prepare the way, if possible, for a concordat between the Holy See and the Reich. His overtures were coolly received, and the Under-Secretary of State remarked at about this time to His Majesty's Minister, that it hardly seemed worth while to conclude a new concordat when 18 of the 20 million German Catholics were already covered by the three existing concordats (with Prussia, Bavaria and Baden).

63. Two months later, however, the Vatican executed a *volte-face;* and when, at the end of June, the Vice-Chancellor came again to Rome, he met with a different reception. The position had, indeed, changed considerably since April ; and it seems that recent outrages on Catholics in Bavaria and elsewhere, combined with the dissolution of the Centre and Bavarian People's parties and the issue of decrees which were likely to result in the suppression of Catholic societies, had at last convinced the Holy See that a continued refusal to discuss a concordat would seriously prejudice the position of Catholics in Germany. The Pope, though he had watched, without many tears, the Centre party go the way of the Partito Popolare, was determined to save the Catholic youth associations in Germany as he had saved the " Azione Cattolica " ; and in order to obtain the greatest possible religious, educational and administrative freedom for Catholics in Germany, was prepared to give up political rights, so far as these still existed, and to fall in with the Nazi wish for a divorce (in so far as Catholic principles would allow) of religion from politics.

64. Herr von Papen had come with clear instructions; he had been told how much he might offer; and the answer " yes or no " had to be given within a week. The generous nature of the German Government's concessions, and the urgent desire of the Holy See to safeguard the essential liberties of German Catholics, made it possible for the negotiations to be quickly concluded, and, by the 8th July, the concordat had been initialled. At about this time the Cardinal Secretary of State told His Majesty's Minister that the Church had no reason to be dissatisfied

with the new concordat, provided the Reich Government were true to their undertakings. It is to the uncertainty on this point that the Vatican's anxiety is due. In a statement issued to the press, Herr von Papen assured the world that the clear delimitation of their respective spheres assigned in the concordat to Church and State would for the future eliminate every source of disagreement between them. The German Government was also satisfied with the concordat, which appeared, said Herr Hitler, to offer " a sufficient guarantee that German Catholics would henceforth be able to devote themselves unreservedly to the service of the National Socialist State."

65. The concordat was signed on the 20th July by Cardinal Pacelli and Herr von Papen, and from the text, published that evening, it was clear enough what sacrifices and what advantages it imposed on Church and State alike. On the one hand the Reich now officially guaranteed the religious education of its Catholic subjects, and made such teaching a part of the regular curriculum in every school while undertaking to protect Catholic associations and conceding to the Catholic clergy many of the privileges of State officials.

66. On the other hand, the Church renounced, once and for all, the last remnant of her purely political power in Germany. Thus before the Bills appointing any archbishop or bishop are issued, the civil authority in the person of the local Reichsstatthalter must be informed of the name of the chosen person in order that he may ascertain that there are no objections of a general political character to the appointment. It is true that the final protocol adds : " Right of veto on the part of the State is not to be construed out of this," but though this is doubtless the fact legally the concession on the part of the Church is great, and in practice no one obnoxious to the civil authorities can be appointed. Again, it is laid down that parish priests and religious superiors, resident in Germany, must be German, and, most significant of all, the Holy See undertakes to issue orders excluding the clergy from political activity of every kind.

67. In order to gain an idea of the general character of the concordat, it may be well to run briefly through the main provisions of the document, which consists of thirty-four clauses and a final protocol.

68. Article 1 recognises the right of the Catholic Church, " according to the general laws in force, to regulate and administer her own affairs, and, within the field of her own competence, to decree laws and ordinances which are binding." Article 2 deals with the three already existing concordats which are not abrogated by the new one, though the latter is valid on questions untouched by the former documents. Article 3 confirms the position of the Nuncio, who is to remain doyen of the Diplomatic Corps, while article 4, which guarantees freedom of communication between the Holy See and German Catholics, also exempts from censorship the pastorals and other official utterances of the hierarchy. .

69. Articles 5 to 10 are concerned chiefly with the rights and privileges of the clergy, who are to enjoy the protection of the State, and are exempted from distraint to the same extent as Government officials. Their right to preserve secrets acquired during the exercise of their sacred ministry is also recognised.

70. Articles 11 to 14 deal with questions of diocesan and parish boundaries, also with appointments to high ecclesiastical office, and lay down that priests entrusted with the cure of souls must be German citizens with German educational qualifications. Article 14 also lays down the rule mentioned above that bishops' names must be submitted, before appointment, to the Reichsstatthalter for approval. Article 15 recognises the rights of religious congregations to live and multiply on German soil, but imposes conditions, including one already mentioned, to the effect that the superiors must, if resident in Germany, themselves be Germans. Article 16 imposes on the bishops an oath of loyalty to the German State; articles 19 to 25 deal with questions of education and contain the concessions regarding religious instruction in schools, which, as mentioned above, are so valued by the Holy See.

71. Article 26 allows the Church marriage, in special cases, before the civil ceremony; article 27 provides for religious teaching in the army on a more generous scale than hitherto and also for the appointment of an army bishop; article 28 deals with religious ministrations in hospitals; article 29 grants

facilities, in language, &c., to ethnical Catholic minorities in Germany (who would be chiefly Poles); article 30 prescribes public prayers for the Reich.

72. Articles 31 and 32 are the most important from the point of view of the State. The first of these articles stipulates that, while Catholic organisations which serve purely religious, charitable and cultural purposes and, as such, are under the control of the ecclesiastical authorities, will be allowed to continue their own work, Catholic associations " which serve other. purposes " will be incorporated in an association under inter-State protection, " where they will be able to pursue their objects only in so far as these are not connected with party politics or trade union activities."

73. Article 32 contains the undertaking already mentioned whereby the Holy See engages to forbid the Catholic clergy in Germany to belong to political parties or take part in political activities. Article 33 concedes to the Church that matters relating to religious affairs, which are not dealt with in the concordat, shall be regulated on the ecclesiastical side in accordance with Canon Law. Article 34 states that the concordat will enter into force on the day on which ratifications are exchanged.

74. That the conclusion of the concordat (which was ratified on the 10th September) implied very little sympathy on the part of the Vatican for the Nazi régime in Germany was proved, if proof were needed, by the tone of Cardinal Pacelli's remarks on the subject to His Majesty's Chargé d'Affaires in August. His Eminence deplored the anti-Semitism of the German Government, their treatment of political opponents and the reign of terror to which they had subjected the whole nation. The Holy See had only consented to the concordat because it had appeared to be a choice between that and the virtual elimination of the Catholic Church in the Reich. The Church had no political axe to grind and her only object in concluding this agreement had been to further the spiritual welfare of the 20 million German Catholics.

75. At about this time the French Ambassador informed Mr. Kirkpatrick in confidence that Cardinal Pacelli had admitted to him the truth of the rumours, which had been long rife, and had found their way into the *Temps*, that the concordat contained a secret clause providing that, should compulsory service be restored in Germany, the clergy should be exempted. M. Charles-Roux bitterly criticised the Vatican for weakness in giving what he described as " tacit consent " to German rearmament..

76. Despite the ratification of the concordat in September, reports from Germany indicated more and more clearly that the German Government had no intention of faithfully executing their part of the concordat. Nevertheless, Cardinal Pacelli told His Majesty's Minister in November that he was glad the agreement had been signed and ratified. Whatever excesses the Germans could and did commit, and however much they infringed both the letter and spirit of the concordat, it was, at any rate henceforth, clear that they were in the wrong and that the Church had nothing with which to reproach herself.

77. By the late autumn it. had become common knowledge that the execution of the concordat was causing friction between the Vatican and the Reich. The arrests of priests, on flimsy grounds, the threats to arrest Cardinal Faulhaber, the methods adopted to prevent episcopal letters from being made public, these and other real or apparent breaches of the concordat caused much anxiety to Catholics throughout Germany and at Rome. According to the German Ambassador to the Holy See, however, the chief cause of friction lay in the application of article 31, of which mention is made above. He said in November that the task of drawing up a list of Catholic organisations which have other aims besides religious, philanthropic and cultural, was a difficult one, and that so far it had not been possible to come to an agreement. The Government were not, however, being deliberately unreasonable. The concordat had been drawn up in a great hurry and the issue was a very contentious one. Herr Buttmann (the Hitler Government's chief go-between with the Vatican) would, however, be returning to Rome before the end of the year to resume negotiations.

78. Another source of conflict between the Vatican and the Nazis is provided by the law for the sterilisation of the unfit, which is to come into force next year. As the Catholic Church is fundamentally opposed to sterilisation, an awkward situation might arise if Catholic doctors employed in State hospitals were ordered to carry out the operation in question. It is possible that the Church might waive its objection to the operation where this could definitely be regarded as a punishment inflicted on certain types of criminal, but in no other case.

79. The end of the year thus leaves relations between Germany and the Holy See in a state of uncertainty. In October, when addressing a group of German pilgrims, the Pope said that affairs in their country were causing him the gravest disquiet, and nothing can have happened since to lessen his anxiety. The Pope will not, however, wish to deprive German Catholics of the many safeguards which the concordat secures to them; and Herr Hitler, with such difficult problems confronting him at home and so much hostility to face abroad, can hardly desire to bring upon himself the scandal which an open breach with the Holy See would involve. It may be therefore that some compromise will be found, though the question of Catholic associations, which appears to be the chief source of friction, is not one on which either party is anxious to give way further than it need.

Greece.

80. A three days' holiday visit paid by the Cardinal Secretary of State to Athens in September gave rise to a rumour, which annoyed his Eminence, that the Greek Government were about to conclude a concordat with the Holy See. There was, of course, no truth in the report; indeed, the somewhat strained relations between the Greek Government and the local Catholic authorities, and their resentment at the activity of the Uniates, preclude the possibility of any such development at present.

Italy.

81. Though the Italian Ambassador to the Holy See continues to take up at least an hour of the Cardinal Secretary of State's time at the latter's weekly reception, no serious incident disturbed the even tenor of relations between the Vatican and the Quirinal, which, since the settlement of the " Azione Cattolica " dispute in 1931, have remained close and cordial. Princes of the Royal House were present at several of the great religious ceremonies held in connexion with the Holy Year, as well as official representatives of the Italian Government, and it is rumoured that the King and Queen will themselves attend the Canonisation next Easter of Don Bosco, the founder of the Salesian Order, who died only about fifty years ago and whom the present Pope knew as a young man.

82. The Railway Convention between the Vatican State and the Italian Government was signed on the 20th December by Cardinal Pacelli and the Italian Ambassador. It will be remembered that, according to article 6 of the Lateran Treaty, the Italian Government undertook to construct a railway station, with the necessary accompaniment of lines and signals, in the Vatican State. Although it is said that the station only provides room for a short train and that a long one will be half in Italy, this work has now been accomplished to the satisfaction of the Holy See. The railway will only be used on rare occasions, such as for a possible journey by His Holiness and for the arrival and departure of special missions to the Pope.

83. It may be of interest to mention that, departing from his customary reserve on such occasions, the Holy Father, in January, condescended to discuss Signor Mussolini with a British visitor. The Pope said he had been criticised for going too far both in the Lateran Treaty and the " Catholic Action " compromise. It must be remembered, however, that Mussolini had also made concessions, notably by restoring religion to the schools, whence it had been banished for forty years and more. As for the Duce's profession of faith, as given in Ludwig's book, it was indeed defective, but it must be remembered that Mussolini had never received a religious education or, indeed, any education at all. What he knew he had taught himself. The archbishop, added His Holiness, must not imagine that, as many people supposed,

he was afraid of Mussolini. When the Duce had applied for an audience, the Pope had said that he would grant one only on condition that the visit was regarded as one of reparation for Mussolini's attitude over the "Azione Cattolica," but the great man had come all the same.

Roumania.

84. During the summer the Roumanian Government complained to the Vatican about the alleged political activities of Mgr. Stefan Fiedler, Bishop of Satu-Mare and Oradea Mare, a diocese near the Hungarian border. The Roumanian authorities had originally approved of the appointment of this prelate, as they thought that, being of German origin, he would take little interest in the political unrest of the Catholics of Hungarian race, who formed the majority of his flock. The diocese under Bishop Fiedler's rule had, however, become a focus of revisionist agitation, and something, it was felt, must be done.

85. In response to the urgent appeals of Bucharest, Mgr. Fiedler was eventually summoned to Rome to justify his conduct. After careful examination it was decided that the Bishop's faults were, at worst, faults of omission. He had not himself taken any part in revisionist propaganda, and if he had been to blame, it had been merely by omitting to restrain, at least with sufficient vigour, the political activities of certain of the Magyar clergy under his charge. In return for a promise to exert more efficient discipline for the future over his clergy, who were to be restrained from engaging in politics, Mgr. Fiedler was allowed to return to his diocese, and the Roumanian Government expressed themselves satisfied.

86. Mgr. Valerio Valeri, a former Apostolic Delegate to Egypt and Palestine, was appointed in the autumn to succeed Mgr. (now Cardinal) Dolci as Nuncio to Roumania.

Russia.

87. A Riga paper published in September a rumour, which subsequently found its way into the British press, that there was some possibility of an agreement being reached between the Vatican and the Soviet Government whereby the Roman Catholic Church, "on condition that it did not interfere in politics," would be given certain liberties in Russia as a reward for recognising the Moscow régime.

88. The rumour, which was speedily denied by the *Morning Post*, was promptly discredited in Rome, where it is thought that it may possibly have been put forward with a view to hastening the American recognition of Soviet Russia, which followed soon afterwards.

89. Actually no change was observable in the uncompromising attitude of the Holy See towards Moscow, and it was with a wry smile that the Cardinal Secretary of State commented to His Majesty's Minister on the warmth of the welcome extended to M. Litvinov on his visit to Rome in December. His Eminence categorically denied that any contact had been established during his stay between the Russian statesman and the Vatican; and the *Osservatore Romano* vigorously repudiated the rumours published in the *Daily Telegraph* at this time to the effect that a *modus vivendi* was about to be established between Moscow and the Holy See. It had also been suggested that Signor Mussolini had asked M. Litvinov for concessions in favour of Italian ecclesiastics similar to those reported to have been made by the Soviet Government for American clergy to hold services in Russia. There appears to have been no foundation for the suggestion.

Spain.

90. The passing by the Cortes, in the early summer, of the Law on Religious Congregations, whereby Church property is secularised, and monks and nuns are forbidden to teach, caused a most painful impression at the Vatican. On the 3rd June, the day after the law had received President Zamora's assent, a manifesto was issued by the Spanish hierarchy denouncing the new measure and declaring those responsible for it to be excommunicated; and on the 4th June the Pope followed up the bishops' pronouncement by an encyclical, addressed to

the Spanish bishops, clergy and people. In this pronouncement His Holiness roundly condemned the attitude and conduct of the Republican Government towards the Catholic Church, and exhorted the faithful to use all legitimate means to obtain the repeal of a law so opposed to the rights of every citizen and so hostile to religion. Opening with the words *Dilectissima Nobis*, from which, accordingly, the encyclical takes its name, the Holy Father begins by recalling that, on account of her Catholic traditions, Spain is especially dear to him, and mentions the benefits that she has conferred in the past upon religion and civilisation. The Pope adds that he has frequently pointed out to the Spanish Government the danger of the path they have been pursuing, and adds that it is impossible to remain silent in face of this law, which constitutes " a new and more serious offence, not only to the Church and religion, but also to the asserted principles of civil liberty declared to be the basis of the Spanish régime."

91. The encyclical goes on to demonstrate the absurdity of the charge that the Holy See is moved by antipathy to the new form of government, and points out that concordats have been concluded with several republics. The Government cannot therefore maintain, with any show of logic, that their anti-religious attitude is dictated by a wish, at all costs, to defend the republic; only hatred of God and the religious and social order established by Him can explain this attitude. The Pope proceeds to condemn the principle of a separate Church and State, and points out how disastrous such a separation must be in a country with an entirely Catholic population, disastrous not only to the youth of the country and to family life, but also to the civil authority, which loses in the Church its most powerful ally in the maintenance of order.

92. The " odious exception " to the guarantee of property, which has led to the Church's being despoiled of her goods, is bitterly attacked, and complaint is made that the Church is now compelled to pay taxes for the use of buildings of which she has been despoiled for all purposes but those of public worship. The encyclical goes on to complain that religious orders, falsely accused of political activities against the State, and no longer allowed to teach or practice any form of charitable work which would provide them with the means of subsistence, are now so heavily taxed as to render their very existence impossible.

93. In the suppression of the Jesuits the Pope sees a deliberate blow at his own authority, as Vicar of Christ, which is actually described as " foreign to the Spanish nation."

94. After recounting other offences to the Church, the encyclical denounces a law " so at variance with the Divine Constitution of the Church," and declares that " it can never be appealed to against the imprescriptible rights of the Church." An appeal is finally made to all the faithful to join the " Catholic Action," which, while not being a political body, is invaluable as a means of forming a Catholic national conscience which can unite to defend the faith against oppression.

95. The swing to the Right in the elections of November was naturally noted with pleasure at the Vatican, who also welcomed the inclusion in the Government formed in December of members of the moderate parties. On the whole, despite the Communist disturbances which followed the elections, the close of the year brought with it, from the Vatican point of view, the promise of better things, and a report has been published in the press that it is the intention of the Spanish Government again to appoint an Ambassador to the Holy See.

Yugoslavia.

96. Relations between Yugoslavia and the Holy See remain somewhat cool. The year began badly with the issue by the Catholic hierarchy in that country of a joint pastoral attacking the " Sokol " or national youth movement on account of its non-religious character. The pastoral gave rise to a storm of resentment in Government and Serbian circles, and the Italian press made the most of the " growing tension " between the Catholic Church and the Yugoslav State. One result of the bishops' action was the introduction into the Skupshtina of anti-clerical legislation, including a Bill for the suppression of the Jesuits. Though the Bills were not sponsored by the Government and it soon became clear that they would be allowed to drop, they were largely supported by Serbian

Deputies and provided the occasion for bitter speeches, which aroused the Pope's resentment.

97. In February the Under-Secretary of State at the Vatican discussed the Sokol question with His Majesty's Chargé d'Affaires. The organisation was, he said, an undenominational one, and an attitude of religious neutrality was too apt in these days, especially where adolescents were concerned, to develop into one of hostility to all institutional religion. The action of the bishops was consequently approved by the Holy Father, whose strong views on the crucial importance of a Catholic education for the young were well known.

98. Proof that the Holy Father's wrath had not subsided, despite conciliatory speeches by Yugoslav politicians, was furnished in April by his flat refusal to receive a delegation of four Yugoslav Senators and eight Deputies who had come to Rome to attend the inter-parliamentary Economic Conference and had applied for an audience on King Alexander's express instructions. It is difficult to understand the Pope's motives for refusing to give an audience on this occasion, for not only had the anti-clerical legislation already been withdrawn, but the delegation had been instructed to inform the Vatican that the Yugoslav Government wished for nothing but the friendliest relations with the Holy See. Moreover, only a few days previously, the new Yugoslav draft for a concordat, which conceded several points to the Vatican, had been forwarded by the Yugoslav Minister to Cardinal Pacelli.

99. Although news of the snub administered by the Pope to the delegation must have caused much irritation in Government circles in Yugoslavia, it fortunately never appears to have reached the general public; and later in the year His Holiness to some extent corrected the painful impression which he had made by saying to a group of Yugoslav pilgrims that he dearly loved their country, and that they must never believe anyone, " even an angel," who tried to persuade them to the contrary.

100. In December the King and Queen of Yugoslavia made a bid for the popularity of their Croat subjects by spending the 45th anniversary of His Majesty's birthday in Zagreb, where they even attended, at the Catholic Cathedral, a High Mass at which the Archbishop (Mgr. Bauer) preached the sermon.

101. It may be mentioned in conclusion that Mr. Kirkpatrick, under instructions from His Majesty's Principal Secretary of State for Foreign Affairs, informally mentioned to Cardinal Pacelli in February the anxiety felt by His Majesty's Government in the United Kingdom at the unsatisfactory state of Italo-Yugoslav relations and their hope that these would soon improve. His Eminence said that, although the question did not directly concern the Vatican, he fully shared this feeling of anxiety; he thought indeed that the tension between Italy and Yugoslavia constituted the most immediate of all the dangers which beset contemporary Europe. His Eminence was careful to express no opinion on the rights and wrongs of the controversy.

IV.—The Vatican.

(i) *College of Cardinals.*

102. During 1933 the Sacred College lost three members, viz. :—

(1) Cardinal Frühwirth, Chancellor of the Holy Roman Church, who died on the 9th February, aged 88. He was an Austrian and a Dominican, and from 1891 to 1904 he had been Master-General of his Order. He then represented the Holy See at Munich, and became a cardinal in 1915, under Benedict XV. He was well known for his learning and piety.

(2) Cardinal Cerretti, who died on the 8th May, aged 61. During the war he was Apostolic Delegate in Australia, where in 1928 he also presided as Papal Legate over the Sydney Eucharistic Congress. He was extremely popular in Australia. From 1921 and 1926 he was Papal Nuncio in Paris. His British sympathies were well known, and the Pope had been in the habit of consulting him in matters concerning the Empire. His premature death is therefore to be deplored from the point of view of Great Britain, as well as for other reasons.

(3) Cardinal Scapinelli, who died on the 16th November, at the age of 75. He was Nuncio at Vienna from 1912 to 1915, when Benedict XV created him cardinal. In 1931 he succeeded the late Cardinal Vannutelli as Papal datary (in which office he, in his turn, has been succeeded by Cardinal Capotosti).

103. The Pope held a secret consistory on the 13th March at which he announced the elevation to the Sacred College of six prelates, viz. :—

> Mgr. Fumasoni Biondi, Apostolic Delegate to the United States of America.
> Mgr. Dolci, Nuncio at Bucharest.
> Mgr. Fossati, Archbishop of Turin.
> Mgr. Villeneuve, Archbishop of Quebec.
> Mgr. dalla Costa, Archbishop of Florence.
> Mgr. Innitzer, Archbishop of Vienna.

104. His Holiness also announced the creation of two cardinals *in pectore*. Such announcements sometimes precede by several months, or even years, the publication of the prelates' names, though precedence is given to them according to the date of creation. It is thought that Mgr. Caccia Dominioni, the Master of the Pope's household, may be one of the cardinals *in petto*.

105. Other promotions and changes announced by His Holiness at this consistory were the following :—

> Cardinal Sincero was promoted (together with Cardinal Cerretti, whose death occurred soon afterwards) from the rank of cardinal priest to that of cardinal bishop; Cardinal Boggiani became Chancellor of the Roman Church in succession to the late Cardinal Frühwirth; and Cardinal Mori was promoted from the rank of cardinal deacon to that of cardinal priest.

106. At the close of 1932 the Sacred College numbered fifty-three cardinals; at the end of this year the total number (not including cardinals *in petto*) amounts to fifty-six, of whom twenty-six are Italians. The Curia is poorer by one cardinal than it was at the new year, and the Sacred College is fourteen short of its full quota.

107. Though it is to be regretted that there is still no English cardinal in Curia, both of the Roman cardinals created during the year, Fumasoni Biondi and Dolci, are well disposed towards England. The former, who speaks English, was for some years Apostolic Delegate in the United States of America, while the latter, who fulfilled a like office at Constantinople during and after the war, received a C.B.E., for his services to British prisoners, and retains happy memories of his relations with the British authorities after the armistice.

108. Of the four new cardinal archbishops the most interesting, from the British point of view, is naturally his Eminence of Quebec. His Majesty's Chargé d'Affaires was present at the ceremony of the delivery of the letter of creation (which immediately followed the secret consistory) to Cardinal Villeneuve. On this occasion his Eminence, in the course of the usual speech of thanks, gave graceful expression to his loyalty to the British Empire, and noted with satisfaction that he had been the recipient of warm congratulations not only from his co-religionists in Canada, but also from members of the Government. He certainly won universal esteem during his stay in Rome, and both his youthful bearing and the charm of his personality won well-deserved tributes on every hand.

(ii) *Holy Year*.

109. In his Christmas allocution the Pope, as stated in last year's report, had announced his intention of proclaiming, in honour of the 19th centenary of the Redemption, an extraordinary Holy Year to last from Passion Sunday (the 2nd April) 1933 to Easter Monday (the 2nd April) 1934.

110. The Papal Bull promulgating the Holy Year was published on the 15th January, and in a speech which accompanied the publication of the Bull, his Holiness said that he wished this Holy Year to be regarded as extraordinary (or,

perhaps better, '' significant'') in the fullest sense of the word. He wished the year to be one of spiritual peace and progress, and hoped that it would result also in material progress, and would help to bring about an improvement in the depressed conditions of the world.

111.   In the Bull itself there was nothing of special interest except that the Pope exhorted the faithful to make pilgrimages, where possible, not to only Rome, but to Jerusalem. The usual conditions were laid down for gaining the Jubilee Indulgence, these involving visits to the four patriarchal basilicas of Rome and the recital of prescribed prayers.

112.   On the 1st April the Pope formally inaugurated the Holy Year by opening the Holy Door at St. Peter's, while specially appointed Cardinal Legates performed a similar function at the Lateran, St. Paul's without the Walls, and St. Mary Major. These doors are normally walled-up, but were last closed as recently as 1925, Pius XI having created a record by proclaiming two Holy Years in the course of his Pontificate.

113.   On Easter Sunday the Holy Father sang High Mass at St. Peter's. It was the first time since 1870 that a Pope had performed this rite. His Holiness created further precedents by appearing at St. John Lateran on Ascension Day, at St. Paul's without the Walls on the 30th June, and at Santa Maria Maggiore on the 11th October. On each occasion he was received with great enthusiasm when, from the balcony of the basilica, he imparted the benediction *urbi et orbi* to the vast waiting crowd. '' Just as good as the welcome they give Mussolini,'' was the comment of an Italian State official who witnessed the scene at St. John's.

114.   Pilgrimages are the chief outward sign of a Holy Year, and since Easter a continuous stream of pilgrims of almost all nations and languages has been flowing Romewards. The more prominent English pilgrimages are mentioned elsewhere in this report (see paragraph 1), but it may here be mentioned that Great Britain has sent a larger number of pilgrimages (though not of pilgrims) to Rome than any other country. At the end of the year the total of British pilgrimages amounted to forty-eight. It was doubtless the sight of so many Englishmen thronging the Vatican that inspired the Pope on one of these occasions to speak of the '' nostalgia for Rome which seems to fill so many English hearts.''

115.   Mr. Kirkpatrick, who was transferred to Berlin in the late summer, was received by the Pope in farewell audience on the 28th August. In reply to a question, his Holiness said that he was more than satisfied with the results of the Holy Year, and was particularly touched and consoled at the number of English pilgrimages. England, in his opinion, occupied the place of honour, not only on account of the quantity and quality of her pilgrims, but also on account of the special manner in which the underlying idea of the Holy Year had been grasped in England. His remarks applied not only to Catholics, but also to Protestants. He had only recently received a cleric and a layman of the Church of England, whose visits had told him of the sympathy felt by Anglicans for the idea of a Holy Year.

116.   Two canonisations and five beatifications took place in 1933 (since 1930 no one had been canonised), and several more of these ceremonies are expected to occur before the close of the Holy Year. The two newest Saints were both of French nationality, namely, Blessed André Fournet, founder of the Daughters of the Cross, who died in 1820, and Blessed Bernadette, the Visionary of Lourdes, who died at Nevers in 1879. Among the Beati were Catherine Labouré, a French 19th century nun, whose story is connected with that of the Miraculous Medal, popular among Catholics; and Father Joseph Pignatelli, a valiant Jesuit of the late 18th and early 19th centuries, who refused to be discouraged when his order was suppressed by Clement XIV in 1773, and did more than any one man to prepare the way for its triumphant restoration in 1814.

(iii) *The Pope's Visits to Castel Gandolfo.*

117.   Under article 14 of the Lateran Treaty the Italian Government recognised the rights of the Holy See to the pontifical palace of Castel Gandolfo in the Alban Hills, about 20 miles from Rome, as also to the Villa Barberini in the same neighbourhood. Hitherto the Pope has continued, as heretofore, to pass

the whole summer at Rome, and until this year his Holiness had not even visited his new property, which has been greatly improved and altered since it came into his possession in 1929.

118.   On the 10th July, and again on the 24th August, his Holiness paid a short visit to Castel Gandolfo to inspect the building and the estate, and to take' stock of the alterations which have been carried 'out by his orders and which included the reconstruction of the gardens and the embellishment of the private chapel.   On each occasion the Pope, who was accompanied by a small suite, drove to Castel Gandolfo in a closed car with the blinds drawn.   As these are the first occasions since 1870 in which a Pope has left the City of Rome they are perhaps worthy of record, especially as the precedent may encourage his Holiness to spend the hottest weeks of future summers in the coolness and seclusion of his mountain retreat.

(iv) *Bomb Outrage at St. Peter's.*

119.   On the 25th June, at about midday, a small bomb, which had been concealed in a suit-case left in a corner of the main portico of St. Peter's, exploded, slightly wounding four people, but otherwise doing no material damage.

120.   The individual who had left the case was subsequently arrested by the Italian police and is still awaiting trial.   He appears to be a Levantine Greek, born at Alexandria, who was travelling on a Spanish passport.

121.   Three Italians, known to be anti-Fascist agitators, were arrested later in the year by the Italian authorities on suspicion of complicity in the crime.

(v) *Reduction of Vatican Salaries.*

122.   A revision of salaries of Vatican officials has been made and will come into force on the 1st January, 1934.   According to this revision, a 10 per cent. reduction will be made on salaries of over 1,000 lire a month, but not exceeding 2,000 lire, while 15 per cent. reduction will be made on all salaries exceeding 2,000 lire a month.

123.   The reductions will, however, be less in the case of Vatican officials non-resident in the Vatican City, since these latter do not enjoy the special fiscal and housing advantages conceded to subjects of the Vatican State.

124.   This revision had been decided on at the time of the reorganisation of the Vatican Government offices, and was originally to have come into force on the 1st July of this year, but its application was again postponed for six months, *i.e.*, until the 1st January of the coming year.

125.   It is understood the reduction applies to every member of the Pontifical Court from cardinals to the humblest menial.

(vi) *Legislation.*

126.   The following are the laws promulgated by the Government of the Vatican State during 1933 :—

> XXXVII (the 10th January, 1933).—Ordinance regarding the use of machines for franking postal correspondence.
> XXXVIII (the 1st April, 1933).—Ordinance regarding the issue of commemorative stamps for the Holy Year.
> XXXIX (the 8th May, 1933).—Regulations for Sanitation Corps and for sanitary and hygienic services.
> XL (the 8th May, 1933).—Disciplinary regulations for the Papal gendarmerie.
> XLI (the 20th May, 1933).—Ordinance for the issue of a new series of postage stamps.
> XLII (the 29th August, 1933).—Agreement between the Holy See and Italy regarding postal dues.
> XLIII (the 25th November, 1933).—Law regarding the issue of coinage for 1933.
> XLIV (the 27th November, 1933).—Ordinance concerning striking and issue of coin for 1933.

127. Mention should also be made at this point of Laws No. **XXXV**, of the 15th December, 1932 (being an ordinance regarding the striking and issue of coin for 1932), and No. **XXXVI**, of the 27th December, 1932, which is in the nature of a list of regulations governing the right of entry to the Vatican City. (By an oversight these two measures did not appear in paragraph 76, concerning Legislation, of last year's annual report.) The regulations governing access to the Vatican State, which came into force on the 1st January, 1933, had the effect of completing the ordinance of the 7th June, 1929, on the same subject. They provide for the issue of permits of access to the Vatican City, but, in practice, no obstacle is placed in the way of members of the general public who desire to enter the Basilica of St. Peter, the museums or the picture galleries. The principal object of the regulations is doubtless to control admission to the private part of the Pontifical Palace and to the Vatican Gardens.

128. The Secretariat of State has, incidentally, assured His Majesty's Legation that holders of British passports, wherever issued, are exempt from the necessity of obtaining a Vatican visa before entering the city precincts.

V.—PAPAL PRONOUNCEMENTS.

129. (i) The bull *Quod nuper*, proclaiming a Holy Year from the 2nd April, 1933, to the 2nd April, 1934, in commemoration of the nineteenth anniversary of the Redemption of the Human Race (see also paragraph 110).

130. (ii) The allocution of the 13th March, *Iterum vos*, on the occasion of the Secret Consistory.

131. In this allocution His Holiness, after announcing the elevation to the Sacred College of the six prelates referred to in paragraph 103, and the creation of two other cardinals *in petto*, dealt with certain administrative matters, including the appointment of some hundreds of archbishops and bishops throughout the world, after which he went on to review events since the last consistory, which was held in June 1930. Among these events, the Holy Father said, he gave pride of place to his encyclicals, *Casti Connubii, Quadragesimo Anno* and *Deus Scientiarium Dominus*, which dealt respectively with the all-important problems of the family, fair conditions of labour and the development of theological studies. His Holiness also mentioned the memorable Eucharistic Congress at Dublin and the recent celebrations at Lourdes on the occasion of the seventy-fifth anniversary of the apparitions.

132. The Pope then turned to international affairs and pointed out that the critical situation of the world was rendered more critical still by mutual distrust, by opposing interests, by the inadequate and often contradictory measures of alleviation adopted by those in power, and by that exaggerated and unjust nationalism than which nothing could be more opposed to the true ideal of Christian brotherhood.

133. The Pope next turned to the problem of unemployment, the distress that it caused, the dangers it involved. There were always men, he said, who were ready to exploit human misery for their own sinister ends. The activities of such men, who were at war with civil and with religious authority, were plainly to be seen in countries like Russia, Mexico and Spain.

134. His had, till recently, been the only voice to warn mankind of the grave dangers which threatened Christian civilisation, he alone had indicated the one remedy for the ills that beset the modern world, namely, a return to the belief and the practice of that religion, which finds perfect expression in the teachings and life of the Roman Catholic Church. He would not cease to raise his voice in the name of truth and justice, or to point out what terrible harm was done (especially among the younger generation) by open or secret opposition or hostility to the Church.

135. His Holiness then went on to speak of the Orthodox baptism of Princess Marie Louise of Bulgaria (see paragraph 44 of this report).

136. (iii) The encyclical *Dilectissima Nobis*, addressed to the bishops, clergy and people of Spain (see paragraph 90 of this report).

137. (iv) Allocution on the 23rd December to the cardinals resident in Rome.

138. Replying to the Christmas greetings offered in the name of the Sacred College by its Dean, Cardinal Pignatelli di Belmonte, the Pope expressed his heartfelt satisfaction at the gratifying response which had been made to his appeal for a devout observance of the Holy Year, and added an expression of homage to the new Saints and Beati proclaimed during the year.

139. His Holiness said that he did not wish to make a formal speech, but that, in response to "filial enquiries" as to his views on the subject, he felt bound to make some reference to that unpleasant word "sterilisation," which had now crept into legislative dispositions. On this subject, however, it was only necessary for him to refer the faithful to the encyclical *Casti Connubii* of 1930, which contained all the guidance needed by the faithful and their pastors.

140. With regard to the grave international situation, the Pope said that, when he looked at humanity in the midst of so many disputes, negotiations and refusals to negotiate, he could only find one word to utter. Just as Napoleon, when asked what was the one thing necessary for a successful war, had said : "Money, money, and again money," so he could only reply, to those who asked him by what means peace could be brought upon earth, with the words : " Prayer, prayer, and again prayer."

o

CONFIDENTIAL.

(14534)

HOLY SEE.

Annual Report, 1934.

[R 402/402/22]

Sir C. Wingfield to Sir John Simon.—(Received January 18.)

(No. 9.)   *British Legation to the Holy See,*
Sir,   *Rome, January 12, 1935.*

I HAVE the honour to transmit to you herewith the annual report of this Legation for the year 1934.   Owing to the short time I have been here, and to the novelty of the problems and outlook that confront a newly appointed Minister to the Holy See, I have entrusted the task of reporting on the past year to Mr. Hugh Montgomery, secretary to His Majesty's Legation, and I venture to think that his report furnishes an interesting and accurate picture of the course of events in the year under review.

I have, &c.
CHARLES WINGFIELD.

Enclosure.

Annual Report on the Holy See for 1934.

CONTENTS.

7790   [11170]

I.—INTRODUCTION.

THE year 1934 gave to the Vatican about equal cause for satisfaction and concern. The successful close of the Extraordinary Holy Year and the enthusiasm and number of the pilgrims from all countries, and not least from Great Britain, must have gratified the Sovereign Pontiff, who had declared this jubilee on his own initiative. A fresh sign of the excellent relations between the Holy See and Italy was given this year by the presence of the Italian Crown Prince at the Easter ceremonies in St. Peter's; the ratification of the Concordat with Austria in May sealed the close relations of the Holy See with that Catholic country; in Yugoslavia no more was heard of the proposed anti-clerical legislation which had so agitated the Pope in 1933; in France, the Stavisky scandals tended to increase public sympathy with the Catholics; in South America, the Pope's Legate to the Eucharistic Congress was received with boundless enthusiasm and Royal honours; in Spain, the position of the Church began, slowly but steadily, to improve, and a distinguished Ambassador, in the person of Sr. Pita Romero, was sent to the Vatican with a view to securing some *modus vivendi* between Church and State.

2. On the other hand, the situation in Germany continued to cause the Pope the gravest anxiety; no sign of any serious intention to fulfil their neglected obligations was given by the Reich Government; Nordic neo-pagan doctrines of the most pernicious type continued to be disseminated with the blessing of the Nazi authorities; the persecution and even the murder of leading Catholics took place with the expressed approval of Herr Hitler; the Austrian Chancellor, a devoted Catholic, was assassinated by National Socialist fanatics; and the only restraining influence in the Third Reich was removed when the veteran President von Hindenburg died and was replaced as Chief of State by the *fons et origo mali* himself. Events in Mexico, where the bishops were threatened with expulsion and the position of the Catholic schools was made impossible, were hardly less disturbing; and the admission of Soviet Russia to the League of Nations caused indignation at the Vatican, where it is felt that an impassable gulf should divide the nations of ancient Christian culture from the chief protagonist of atheistic communism.

3. Another cause of concern to the Pope has been the considerable reduction in his revenues. This reduction, which is due to losses in investments and also to the falling off of remittances from North and South America, has necessitated a diminution of the Church's missionary activity in the Near and Far East. It also perhaps accounts in some measure for the Pope's reluctance to create new cardinals, who are a heavy charge upon the papal purse.

4. On the 1st January, 1935, the Sacred College numbered only fifty-two members out of a possible total of seventy. In November it had lost its most distinguished Italian member in the person of the former Secretary of State, Cardinal Gasparri, and the one English Prince of the Church, the venerated Cardinal Bourne, who had been in failing health for two years, survived the entry of 1935 by only half an hour.

5. Relations between the Holy See and the British Empire remained excellent throughout the year. Cardinal Pacelli, on more than one occasion, expressed his desire to do all in his power to meet the wishes of His Majesty's Government in the United Kingdom, and a correct attitude was observed by the Vatican in regard to the language question in Malta. The new Minister, Sir Charles Wingfield, moreover, received a cordial welcome from the Sovereign Pontiff, who expressed once again his affection for the British monarchy and people and his interest in their welfare.

II.—RELATIONS WITH THE BRITISH EMPIRE.

United Kingdom.

Change of Ministers.

6. The appointment of His Majesty's Minister as Ambassador to Tokyo was announced in February, and shortly afterwards, the usual formalities as to an *agrément* having been gone through, Sir Charles Wingfield was appointed to succeed his Excellency as Minister to the Holy See.

7. Sir Robert Clive, whose tenure of this post had almost exactly coincided with the period of the Extraordinary Holy Year, did not leave Rome until the 22nd April. Prior to his departure, Sir Robert had, on the 17th April, delivered his letters of recall in the course of a private audience with the Holy Father, at which Lady Clive and Miss Clive were also present.

8. Shortly after Sir Robert's departure, the Cardinal Secretary of State expressed to His Majesty's Chargé d'Affaires his sincere regret at the loss of a Minister whose tact, charm and courtesy had endeared him to all with whom he had been brought into touch during his time in Rome. The *Osservatore Romano* paid a similar tribute to his Excellency, and added that he was followed to his new post by the good wishes of the many who had learned to appreciate his fine qualities during his all too short stay in the Eternal City.

9. Sir Charles Wingfield arrived in Rome on the 17th June, and was on the 25th June received in solemn audience by the Pope, to whom he presented his letters of credence. Signor Pio Manzia and two other members of the Papal Household came to the Legation with three motor cars flying Papal flags and the Union Jack, in which they escorted His Majesty's Minister and the Legation staff to the Vatican. Sir Charles Wingfield was met at the entrance of the Pontifical Palace by further officials, who escorted him and his staff in procession to the Papal apartments, where the Holy Father, seated on the Throne and surrounded by his Court, awaited the visitors. Before delivering the King's letter, Sir Charles Wingfield addressed to His Holiness, in French, a brief speech conveying an assurance of His Majesty's sincere friendship and asking for the Pope's assistance in the task of developing yet further the excellent relations existing between Great Britain and the Holy See.

10. In his reply, which was also spoken in French, the Pope expressed his best wishes for the health of their Majesties the King and Queen, whose visit to Rome he remembered with so much pleasure, and added a cordial reference to His Royal Highness the Prince of Wales, whose 40th birthday had been celebrated two days previously. The Holy Father went on to express his particular goodwill for the British Empire, and dilated upon the marks of affection for the Papacy evinced during the Holy Year by the British people, especially in the matter of pilgrimages to Rome. The Pope also made some friendly remarks of a more personal nature, and assured Sir Charles Wingfield that he could count on his own unlimited confidence and co-operation.

11. On the termination of the above speech, which was delivered without notes and somewhat haltingly, the Pontiff conducted the Minister to his study, there detaining him in conversation for some twenty minutes, during which he spoke freely on a wide range of subjects, and expatiated on the gravity of the times and on the importance of the part Great Britain was called upon to play in the solution of the problems with which the world is faced.

12. In describing Sir Charles Wingfield's reception, the *Osservatore Romano* stated that, on presenting his letters, His Majesty's Minister uttered words of "devoted homage" on the part of Great Britain. This was scarcely an accurate description of the speech actually delivered, but there is no reason perhaps to regret that words which were intentionally guarded should have given an unexpected amount of satisfaction. In accordance with a practice which had now become usual, the texts of the two speeches were not published, an omission which may perhaps be due to a fear on the part of the Pope lest the wording of such pronouncements by him in the French language may at times be open to criticism. *A propos* of the above it may here be mentioned that an article which appeared in the *Churchman's Magazine* during the summer alleged, on the authority of an unspecified press correspondent, that His Majesty's Minister had presented his letters to the Pope "on bended knee." Needless to say, the allegation was entirely devoid of foundation, the only difference between this and an audience with a secular Sovereign being that, in accordance with the ceremonial prescribed for non-Catholic "chefs de mission," while Sir Charles Wingfield stood, the Holy Father remained seated.

13. In July His Majesty's Principal Secretary of State for Foreign Affairs learnt with some surprise that a letter addressed by the Pope to the King in reply to His Majesty's letter accrediting Sir Charles Wingfield as Minister to the

Holy See had been delivered at Buckingham Palace by Cardinal Bourne's private secretary. His Majesty's Minister was instructed to point out at the Secretariat of State that the channel adopted by the Vatican authorities for the transmission of this letter represented a departure from that previously and properly employed, and was directed to request that henceforth the existing diplomatic channel might always be used. Mgr. Ottaviani, with whom Sir Charles Wingfield raised the question, fully assented to the view of His Majesty's Government that the procedure adopted on this occasion had been quite irregular, and promised that the mistake, which was due to the ignorance of some minor official, should not be repeated in the future.

Naval Salutes.

14. In March, acting under instructions from His Majesty's Principal Secretary of State for Foreign Affairs, Sir Robert Clive informed Cardinal Pacelli in an official note that the question of the firing of naval gun salutes in honour of ecclesiastical authorities had been under consideration by His Majesty's Government in the United Kingdom, and that it had been decided that the only ecclesiastical dignitaries henceforth to be so saluted were His Holiness the Pope, as Sovereign Head of a State, and his representatives abroad, by reason of their diplomatic, as distinct from their ecclesiastical, status. The note went on to state that the Pope, as Chief of a State, would accordingly, should occasion arise, be given the regulation salute of twenty-one guns. Nuncios and Internuncios, who are diplomatic agents of His Holiness and rank, the former as Ambassadors and the latter as Ministers, would receive salutes of nineteen guns and seventeen guns respectively. Papal Legates possessing diplomatic status would be given "the salutes appropriate to their diplomatic rank," while representatives of His Holiness without diplomatic rank would, though not entitled to salutes or military honours, be accorded such marks of respect as their position demanded.

15. From the reply addressed to Sir Robert Clive by the Cardinal Secretary of State, in which mention was made of the Pope's gratitude to the competent authorities, who, by their action, had "given a fresh mark of their deferent sympathy to the Holy See," it was clear that the decision of His Majesty's Government had given real pleasure in the highest quarters at the Vatican.

Army Bishop.

16. Early in the year the question arose of replacing the Catholic Bishop-in-Ordinary for the Army and Air Forces, Mgr. Keatinge, who had been suffering from a bad nervous breakdown, and who, it was clear, would have to resign his position. The War Office were anxious that the Holy See should appoint another army bishop, as the arrangement, which dated only from 1917, when Mgr. Keatinge was appointed, had proved to work very well and was considered much preferable to the previous system, whereby the administration of chaplains was nominally in the hands of the Archbishop of Westminster. On the 3rd February, with the concurrence of Mgr. Keatinge's Vicar-General, Mgr. Mullins, who was in Rome at the time, a memorandum was handed to the Under-Secretary of State pointing out, unofficially, that His Majesty's Government would be pleased if the Holy See saw fit to appoint a successor to Mgr. Keatinge on his resignation.

17. Mgr. Pizzardo said he thought there would be no difficulty about the appointment of the new army bishop, and it was therefore a disappointment when, on the death of Mgr. Keatinge, which occurred a few weeks later, the Vatican appointed Mgr. Myers, one of the auxiliary bishops of the Westminster archdiocese, to carry on the work of the late bishop pending a decision as to his successor. Mgr. Pizzardo assured His Majesty's Minister in March that, as touching the army, Mgr. Myers was in a position completely independent of the See of Westminster. The present position is, accordingly, not a return to that which existed before 1917, but is rather in the nature of a compromise, doubtless due, though Mgr. Pizzardo said nothing of this, to the unwillingness of the Vatican to offend the late Cardinal Bourne, who was believed to persist in the objections which he had always entertained to the appointment of an army bishop.

18. In order that the importance attached to this question by the army authorities might be fully realised at the Vatican, Sir Robert Clive, before leaving Rome for good, handed a note to the Cardinal Secretary of State requesting that, before a permanent arrangement was made, full consideration should be given to the wishes of His Majesty's Government. In November Sir Charles Wingfield, at the instance of the War Office, raised the question once more, and Cardinal Pacelli said he thought that everything was proceeding in the direction desired by His Majesty's Government.

19. It was perhaps too much to hope that any progress would be made in this matter during Cardinal Bourne's lifetime. Now, however, the Vatican will probably comply with the wishes of the War Office, and it is satisfactory to note in the meantime that the appointment of Mgr. Myers as Administrator of Chaplains is only " temporary " and that the way is thus left open for the eventual appointment of an army bishop or bishop for all His Majesty's forces, who will be entirely unconnected with the Archbishopric of Westminster.

Audiences.

20. The Lord Privy Seal was received in audience of the Pope during his visit to Rome in February. His Holiness retained Mr. Eden in conversation for half an hour and expressed his lively interest in the question of disarmament. After the audience, Mr. Eden, whose visit to the Vatican is believed to have been much appreciated, was received by Cardinal Pacelli.

21. In March Colonel Etherton, organising secretary of the Mount Everest Flight (1933), who had come to Rome to lecture on the flight, was privately received by the Pope. Among other distinguished visitors to whom special audiences were granted during the year were Lady Chilston, wife of His Majesty's Ambassador at Moscow, and Lady Phipps, wife of His Majesty's Ambassador at Berlin. On the 5th April the Holy Father received a group of a hundred British schoolteachers, mostly Protestant, to whom he made a cordial speech, in which he thanked them for their kind thought in coming to visit " an old Father."

22. During August the alumni of the English and of the Scots colleges, both of which have summer residences near Castel Gandolfo, were received in audience at the Papal Villa. To the English students the Holy Father recalled the memory of their heroic predecessors of the 16th century, no less than forty of whom suffered as " seminary priests " under Elizabeth. The Pope's speech to the Scottish students was cast in a lighter vein, for, after pointing out that the scenery of the Alban Hills, in which he and they were neighbours, must remind them with its lakes and hills of their native Caledonia, he added that, so far as he knew, no " monster " lay concealed beneath the placid surface of the Alban Lake.

English Bishops.

23. Among members of the English hierarchy who visited Rome during the year were Archbishop Mostyn of Cardiff and Bishop Amigo of Southwark, while Archbishop MacDonald of Edinburgh was also in Rome. The improvement in the health of his Eminence Cardinal Bourne which had seemed, during the early part of the year, to justify hopes of complete recovery was unfortunately not maintained, though he was well enough to take part in various functions connected with his sacerdotal golden Jubilee in June. On this occasion the Pope sent him a message of praise and congratulation, singling out for special mention his Eminence's " zeal and energy in promoting the sound education of the young and, in particular, those destined for the priesthood."

24. It became known in May that Mgr. Hinsley, Titular Archbishop of Sardis, had been appointed to a Canonry at St. Peter's and had resigned on grounds of old age and increasing ill health the post of Apostolic Delegate for Missions in Africa which he had held since 1930, being the first prelate to occupy this position. During the period 1928–30 he had been Apostolic Visitor to the same gigantic area, comprising as it does the greater part of the African continent, and, during the whole six years of his time of office, he showed immense

energy, travelling far and wide, reorganising schools and setting up new missionary districts. In an article of the most cordial nature, the *Osservatore Romano* stated that the memory of the first delegate to Africa, his zeal and faithfulness, would never be forgotten in the continent where he had deserved so well of the Church and of Christendom. It had been hoped in some English quarters at Rome that his Grace's services would receive a higher reward than they actually did, but even if the archbishop is not destined to wear " the Sacred Purple," his presence in Rome will be a useful asset to his country in general and to British Roman Catholics in particular. His Majesty's Government in the United Kingdom had hoped that an Englishman would be appointed to succeed him. Some efforts would, indeed, appear to have been made by the Vatican in this direction, but they clearly failed, for in September it was announced that Mgr. Riberi, " Uditore " to the Nunciature at Dublin, had been appointed to the vacant post. The new Apostolic Delegate has a good command of the English language and is intelligent, young and tactful. It may therefore be presumed that his Grace is better fitted than would be most foreign prelates for the arduous task that lies before him.

Canada.

25. Two large groups of Canadians were received in audience during the year by His Holiness. The first party, which came to Rome early in August under the auspices of the Canadian Council of Education, consisted chiefly of lady schoolteachers; the second group came in September, under the leadership of Professor Morrison of St. Andrews, and contained representatives, mostly undergraduate, of all the leading Canadian universities. The Canadian visitors on each occasion were clearly much impressed by the Pope's kindness and simplicity, as also by the warmth of his greeting.

26. It was officially announced in December that Archbishop McGuigan of Regina had been translated to the Metropolitan See of Toronto, left vacant by the death of Mgr. McNeil.

Commonwealth of Australia.

27. Cardinal McRory, Roman Catholic Primate of All Ireland, represented the Sovereign Pontiff as Papal Legate at the National Eucharistic Congress which was held at Melbourne from the 2nd to 9th December, in connexion with the Victoria centenary celebrations. The English hierarchy was represented by Archbishop Downey of Liverpool.

28. On the 6th December the Holy Father, speaking from his private library, imparted the Apostolic Benediction by Vatican wireless to those participating in the congress, as also to Australia as a whole. Before pronouncing the words of the Blessing, His Holiness expressed sympathy for the sufferers from the floods which had recently devastated Melbourne. On behalf of His Holiness the Cardinal Legate subsequently gave £1,000 towards the relief of the victims.

29. It appears from information given by the Secretariat of State to His Majesty's Minister in October that Mgr. Mannix, Archbishop of Melbourne, had originally hoped that the Cardinal Legate would take part in the civil festivities connected with the centenary. It was found best, however, to abandon this idea and to decide that his Eminence, unless specially invited, should only attend the purely religious functions at Melbourne. The ostensible reason for this decision was that difficulties might arise over precedence, but it seems likely, though nothing of this was said at the Secretariat of State, that it may also have been feared lest too many public appearances by the cardinal at secular functions would cause resentment among the Protestant population. In any case, the Vatican, who quite understood the situation, ended by providing the cardinal with letters of introduction to the ecclesiastical authorities only. They hoped it would be clear, and asked His Majesty's Legation's assistance in ensuring this, that no disrespect was intended to the civil authorities, and that the Vatican only desired to spare them embarrassment.

Irish Free State.

30. Since the transfer to Berlin of Mr. Bewley, first Irish Free State Minister to the Vatican, which occurred early in 1933, the Legation had been conducted by a Chargé d'Affaires, Mr. Leo McCauley. In April, however, the Irish Free State consul-general in New York, Mr. James Macaulay, was appointed to the vacant post, being replaced in New York by Mr. McCauley. The new Minister presented his credentials to the Pope on the 2nd May, being received with the usual ceremonial. The speeches delivered on this occasion were not made public.

31. Shortly before Easter a large Irish pilgrimage, one of the largest of the Holy Year, came to Rome by sea under the leadership of Cardinal MacRory. The pilgrims were received in audience on St. Patrick's Day.

India.

32. The Vatican, as is well known, claims that its attitude in purely political matters and questions of race is one of complete neutrality. The attitude of the *Osservatore Romano* in regard to India would certainly seem to bear out this contention, for it seldom comments favourably or otherwise on Indian affairs, and leaves Indian news, which duly figures in its pages, to speak for itself. At the same time there can be no doubt that the Holy See, with its love of law and order, its respect for the British attitude towards missionaries and its fear and hatred of bolshevism in all its forms, is in truth a warm partisan of British rule in India.

33. In April the Pope and Cardinal Secretary of State received in audience the Maharajah and Maharani Gaekwar of Baroda, their daughter, the Maharani, and their grandson, the Maharajah, of Cooch Behar. The Holy Father, who remarked how much he had always wished to visit India, said he was sure it was superfluous for him to commend the Catholic inhabitants of Baroda to the Gaekwar's special care. His Highness, after assuring the Pope that the Catholics of Baroda had the same rights and privileges as all other good citizens of the principality, went on to say that, of all his Roman memories, the one he would cherish most would be the Papal audience.

34. The following appointments were made to Indian Sees during the year: Father Ansgar Sevrin, a Belgian Jesuit, was appointed in April to succeed Father van Hoeck, of the same nationality and order, as Bishop of Ranchi, in the ecclesiastical Province of Calcutta; in July Mgr. Mathias, a Frenchman, who was Prefect Apostolic of Assam, and Father Fernando, an Italian, who was also employed in the mission field of Assam, were appointed to be Bishop of Shillong and Bishop of Kashnagar respectively.

Malta.

35. True to their oft-expressed intention to remain henceforth on the best of terms with His Majesty's Government in the United Kingdom, the Vatican throughout the year maintained a correct and impartial attitude towards British policy in Malta, and the *Osservatore Romano* took no part in the heated polemics of the Italian press on the language question. The fact that, as stated in paragraph 143, the Pope, in his address to the Knights of Malta on the occasion of their pilgrimage to Rome in March, made no allusion to recent troubles is a further proof that the Vatican desires to avoid all possible occasions of friction with His Majesty's Government.

36. As stated in the annual report for 1933, paragraphs 17 and 18, the Cardinal Secretary of State had shown some anxiety during the autumn of that year lest the Aliens Ordinance of the 20th September, 1933, might unfavourably affect alien members of religious orders who were not engaged in teaching and other clerical persons whom the Vatican desired to see unmolested. Sir Robert Clive had been able to assure the cardinal in December that the ordinance would be interpreted in accordance with the desire of the Holy See, and early in January His Majesty's Legation was authorised to confirm this assurance in a

memorandum which gave full satisfaction to the Vatican. It was at this time that Cardinal Pacelli said how much the Vatican appreciated the broad-minded tolerance of His Majesty's Government in religious matters.

37. A certain amount of propaganda continued, however, to be diffused in Nationalist circles in Malta to the effect that the Aliens Ordinance and other recent steps taken by the Governor, above all the suspension of responsible government, had been inspired in some unexplained manner by a wish on the part of His Majesty's Government in the United Kingdom to harm the Catholic Church and faith. The Governor, in a speech delivered on Candlemas Day (the 2nd February) to the parish priests of Malta, after saying that he had the archbishop's full concurrence in rebutting these charges, pointed out that they were not only false, but absurd, for, after 130 years of British rule, the Catholic Church was more safely and strongly established in Malta than probably anywhere else in the world. He added that it was even owing to British protection that the Church had escaped in Malta the buffetings which it had had to undergo during the last seventy years in other European countries.

38. In June the Cardinal Secretary of State informed His Majesty's Chargé d'Affaires that it was urgently desired by the Holy See that certain reforms should be carried out in the theological faculty of the University of Malta. As things stood at present, the conditions laid down in the encyclical *Deus Scientiarum Dominus* were not being complied with, a state of affairs which, if it continued, would automatically deprive the faculty of its right to confer theological degrees. The Vatican suggested entering into negotiations with His Majesty's Government with a view to regularising the position of the faculty, and undertook, if this suggestion were well received, to draw up a concrete plan for discussion between the two high contracting parties. The competent Department of His Majesty's Government decided to accept the proposal and enter into negotiations, merely pointing out that they might themselves wish to put forward "certain proposals affecting the education of the clergy generally and designed to preserve and strengthen the good relations existing between Church and State in Malta." The friendly reception of the Vatican suggestions by His Majesty's Government gave pleasure to the Cardinal Secretary of State, who expressed his gratification to His Majesty's Chargé d'Affaires, and said the Vatican proposals would be sent as soon as possible. These were duly received and forwarded to the Foreign Office in December. No doubt the most important section, from the point of view of His Majesty's Government, is that which suggests an increase in the number of professors to be employed.

39. In August, shortly before the publication of the decision of His Majesty's Government in the United Kingdom to replace Italian by Maltese as the official language of the Courts of Justice in Malta, His Majesty's Chargé d'Affaires, whose task was lightened by the fact that he at the same time had an agreeable communication to make, *i.e.*, that about the Malta University, was instructed to inform the Cardinal Secretary of State of the decision, to explain the reasons which made it necessary and to express the hope that the Vatican would instruct the ecclesiastical authorities in the island to restrain any tendency on the part of the local bishops and clergy to intervene in the matter. Cardinal Pacelli, who said that it was his desire to do all in his power to satisfy His Majesty's Government, but that in so important a matter he must first consult the Holy Father, sent for Mr. Montgomery two days later and informed him that a message had been sent in the Pope's name to Archbishop Caruana, to the effect that, should the measures about to be adopted give rise to political controversy, the bishops and clergy were to adopt "a moderate, correct and dignified attitude, consistent with their sacred ministry and such as not to involve them in disputes of a party-political character." This message clearly had its effect, for in the storm of controversy which followed on the publication of the decision in question, the Maltese clergy, though the private feelings of the majority of them are not in doubt, have adopted an attitude of reserve sufficiently marked to bring down upon them (see below) the unfavourable criticism of a section of the Italian press.

40. In last year's annual report (paragraph 14) Sir Robert Clive, when mentioning a scheme for increasing the number of Englishmen among members of teaching orders in Malta, pointed out that the great difficulty lay in dearth of

men.   The question was raised again in September by His Majesty's Chargé d'Affaires, who spoke on the subject both to Mgr. Pizzardo and to the English assistant to the General of the Jesuits, but although both expressed goodwill, neither was able to hold out any hope of the wishes of His Majesty's Government in this matter being realised for the present.   Mgr. Pizzardo said that, while both the General of the Jesuits and the Benedictine Abbot Primate protested they had not enough men to spare, the matter would be borne in mind, and he thought an effort might be made later to increase, little by little, the proportion of English priests in Malta.   Father Welsby, on the subject of the Jesuits, only said that at the moment there was such a shortage of priests that it was out of the question to send any to Malta.

41.   For the time being the prospects of obtaining a satisfactory number of British priests in Malta are clearly bad.   Even if it were not for the difficulties explained above, which are doubtless to a large extent genuine, the Holy See would clearly be unwilling at present to embark on any policy of replacing Italian priests and teachers in Malta by British ones.   It must be remembered that not only do the principal authorities of the Vatican, who are Italians, naturally share to some extent the prejudices of their fellow-countrymen on the Maltese question, but also that they are unwilling at this juncture to take any step which would create trouble for them with the Italian people.   It is not unreasonable to hope, however, that when the present agitation is over, the Vatican will be prepared to lend their support to the Governor's idea of gradually altering, in Great Britain's favour, the present state of affairs whereby Italian priests are predominant among the non-Maltese teaching clergy.

42.   The strength of Italian feeling in regard to the language reforms in Malta was shown by the fact that the question on this subject tabled at the end of October by Count de Vecchi, Italian Ambassador to the Holy See, acting in his capacity of a Senator, was supported by 320 members of the Upper House, and there can be little doubt that his Excellency has made it clear to the Vatican that considerable ill-will would be provoked in Italy by any sign of willingness on the part of the Catholic Church to help His Majesty's Government in the United Kingdom in a policy of displacing Italy from the unduly favoured position it has hitherto enjoyed.   It is of interest to observe that the Italian press, at about this time, endeavoured to draw the Vatican into the dispute; and a statement issued by the news agency " La Corrispondenza " referred to the attitude of the Maltese clergy towards the language reforms and underlined their non-participation   in   the   protests   in   defence   of   " Italianità."   The " Corrispondenza " attributed this abstention to the direct influence of Archbishop Caruana, whose English training and sympathies it emphasised, and went on to say that it was felt in Malta that His Majesty's Government would not have dared to go so far as they had without receiving in advance some assurance that the clergy would abstain from any protest.   Finally, the communiqué referred to the existence of " insistent rumours " to the effect that the Italian language was to be attacked in the ecclesiastical domain also, and expressed the hope that the Vatican would tenaciously resist any attempt to diminish the status of the Italian language in the churches and ecclesiastical institutions of Malta and Gozo.

43.   In consequence of these rumours His Majesty's Minister was instructed (16th November) to inform the Cardinal Secretary of State that His Majesty's Government were not contemplating any attack on the Italian language in the ecclesiastical domain; an assurance of which his Eminence gladly took note. The Cardinal had, incidentally, told Sir Charles Wingfield a few days previously that " the Maltese question was now closed," so far as the Vatican was concerned, and he could be assured that the Church had no intention of allowing it to trouble once more their good relations with His Majesty's Government, to which they attached the utmost importance.

44.   It was in November also that the Minister had an opportunity of talking over the Maltese situation with the Archbishop-Bishop of Malta, who said that his relations with the Governor were very friendly and that Sir David Campbell had made it most evident that, the last thing he desired was to weaken in any way the position or influence of the Catholic Church in Malta.

45.   With the approval of His Majesty's Government in the United Kingdom and at the instance of the Governor of Malta, whose views in the matter

are shared by Archbishop Caruana, His Majesty's Legation in October informally drew the attention of the Vatican to the question of the spiritual needs of the important colony of Maltese settled in Queensland. The Legation suggested that the Father-General of the Augustinians should be approached with a view to Fathers Mizzi and Gatt, priests of that order, whose candidature is favoured alike by the Governor and the archbishop, being sent to Queensland for this purpose.

Mandated Territories.

Palestine.

46. His Majesty's Minister attended the consecration on the 6th January of Mgr. Dini, the deservedly popular Rector of the Propaganda College, who, as reported in the annual report for 1933, had been appointed Apostolic Delegate to Palestine and Egypt on the premature death of Mgr. Bartoloni. It would almost seem as though some evil fate pursued the Pope's emissaries to the Holy Land. At any rate Mgr. Dini was granted an even shorter span of life than his predecessor, for, to the deep regret of all who knew him, he died suddenly at Cairo on the 26th March at the age of 41. He had a good knowledge of, as well as a special sympathy for, the British character and mode of life, and would, it was hoped, have exercised a particularly beneficent influence in Palestine. This was not to be, however, and the task which would have been his to perform will devolve on Mgr. Gustavo Testa, who was appointed Apostolic Delegate in May (the third appointment within a year), though he was not consecrated as titular Archbishop of Anasea until November and did not proceed to his post until the following month. Before the appointment was announced, the Vatican duly submitted Mgr. Testa's passport to His Majesty's Legation who obtained permission from the Foreign Office to affix a visa. The same procedure was observed in the case of Mgr. Riberi, the new Apostolic Delegate for Missions in Africa (see paragraph 24 and 49) and in neither case was the name of the prelate concerned made public until the passport had been returned complete with visa to the Vatican. It would thus seem that the agreement come to in 1926 is by now well established and that the mistake made in the case of Mgr. Bernardini is unlikely to recur (see annual report for 1933, paragraph 31).

47. Mgr. Testa, though recently employed as Apostolic Visitor in the Saar, has, since 1929, held the position of counsellor to the Nunciature to the Quirinal. He served for some years at the Nunciature in Vienna and at the Secretariat of State and, having also been on special missions to the Ruhr and the Palatinate, as well as to the Saar, he is clearly a diplomatist of experience and reputation. He would thus appear likely to prove an admirable choice for what is admittedly a difficult appointment, and it is to be hoped that, as a result of his moderating counsels, the sense of tension between the Government and the Catholic authorities which has persisted, thanks to the difficult temperament of Mgr. Barlassina (Patriarch of Jerusalem), may again disappear as it did for a time under the good influence of Mgr. Bartoloni. His Majesty's Minister received a visit in November from Mgr. Testa and took the opportunity of warning him that the Patriarch always appeared to be suspicious of British intentions and motives, and would need careful handling. Sir Charles Wingfield added that he knew Mgr. Testa would always find the Governor ready and willing to smooth away whatever difficulties might arise. He also informed the delegate of a recent conversation he had had with the Bishop of Gibraltar, who had assured him that the Church of England had no desire to encroach on the rights of others in the Holy Places or to establish there any claims of their own. Mgr. Testa, who seemed well aware of the hyper-sensitiveness of religious communities in Palestine about the Holy Places, said it was his earnest desire to maintain the best of relations with the British authorities at Jerusalem.

Transjordan.

48. In July a rumour was brought to Sir Charles Wingfield's notice by the Under-Secretary of State at the Vatican to the effect that the Amir Abdullah hoped, with the consent of the mandatory Power, soon to be able to add Palestine to his realm of Transjordan. His Majesty's Minister who referred that matter to London was, however, authorised to inform Mgr. Pizzardo categorically that no political change of the nature indicated was under contemplation. It subse-

quently transpired indirectly that the rumour had reached the Secretariat of State through Mgr. Barlassina. In December, Archbishop Salman of Transjordan, on his return from a visit to Rome, presented to the Amir Abdullah a gold medal which the Pope had awarded to His Highness as a token of appreciation for the latter's benevolent attitude towards his Christian subjects. The Amir expressed himself much gratified with the gift.

Missions in Africa.

49. As stated in paragraph 24, Mgr. Hinsley was succeeded during the year as Apostolic Delegate for Missions in Africa by Mgr. Antonio Riberi, who, at the end of the year, had not yet left Italy for his new sphere of activities. His Majesty's Minister was present at the archiepiscopal consecration of the delegate, which was performed on the 28th October by the Cardinal Prefect of Propaganda, Mgr. Riberi's titular see being that of Dara. The headquarters of the Apostolic Delegate are at Mombasa and the very extensive regions which he will be called upon to visit are mostly under British rule or protection. These include : Kenya, Tanganyika, Uganda, Nyasaland, Northern Rhodesia, the Sudan, Seychelles, Mauritius, Nigeria, and the British Cameroons, the Gold Coast and British Togoland, Sierra Leone and Gambia. When it is remembered that as Apostolic Delegate Mgr. Riberi will have under his supervision over forty vicars apostolic, archbishops and bishops, who reside within this wide area, it will be realised that the position to which he had been appointed is one of no small responsibility for a man of 37.

50. By a decree of the Sacred Congregation *de Propaganda Fide*, issued on the 10th December, the Apostolic Prefecture of the Equatorial Nile (Uganda) was raised to the rank of a Vicariate Apostolic.

III.—Relations with Other Countries.

Argentina.

51. As elsewhere stated, the 32nd International Eucharistic Congress was held at Buenos Aires in the autumn. In addition to the Papal Legate, four cardinals (to wit, the Archbishops of Paris, Posen, Lisbon and Rio de Janeiro) were present at the congress, which lasted from the 9th until the 16th October. The main religious function occurred on the 14th October, when the Legate bore the Host in procession through the streets and the Pope transmitted his benediction to the congress by wireless. In spite of fears that disturbances might be created by the unruly elements in Buenos Aires, perfect order prevailed throughout the congress, and a wave of religious fervour seems to have swept the city. The Pope was delighted by the accounts he received from his Legate of the success of the congress, and, in his Christmas allocution, His Holiness referred to it as a *beata pacis visio*, and " a reflex of Heaven on this miserable earth." As a reward for his fervent participation in the congress, the Holy Father, in December, conferred on General Justo, President of the Argentine Republic, the Supreme Order of Christ, the highest Papal decoration.

Austria.

52. There is probably no country in Europe which is run on lines so entirely congenial to the Vatican as is the Austrian Republic, and the tragic events of July, which cost the Chancellor his life and jeopardised Austrian independence, only served to knit more closely the ties which unite Vienna to the Holy See.

53. A certain amount of misunderstanding had been caused in December 1933 by the action of the Austrian bishops in eliminating the clergy from political life. The episcopal decision had been interpreted in some quarters as indicating a cooling of relations between the Vatican and the Dollfuss régime, and a special episcopal communiqué had had to be issued to allay such suspicions. Actually, they were entirely groundless, for the Austrian bishops, who do not seem to have consulted the Vatican beforehand, had acted in this matter with the full approval of Dr. Dollfuss.

54. If proof were needed of the good relations between Church and Government, it was supplied by the joint pastoral letter issued at the end of 1933,

in which the Austrian hierarchy reiterated their firm and unambiguous support of the Dollfuss Government and sternly condemned national socialism.

55. As stated in last year's report (paragraph 39), the concordat with Austria was signed on the 19th June, 1933, but the text, which had been kept secret, was only published after ratification at Vienna on the 1st May, 1934. The concordat, which in most respects follows those concluded with other countries since the war, is more favourable to the Church than any of them, and is clearly the work of a Government which has Catholic interests very much at heart.

56. The concordat consists of twenty-three articles, and of a protocol, the existence of which had been unsuspected, and which has the effect of strengthening the Church's position. The following clauses of the concordat are, perhaps, the most interesting :—

(i) The right of the Holy See to choose bishops is admitted, but, before appointment, the Austrian Government are to be asked (article 4) if they have any objections of a political character to the proposed candidate. Should there be any such objections, and should agreement regarding an alternative candidate fail to be reached, the protocol states explicity that the Holy See shall have a right to insist on its own candidate being appointed.

(ii) The right of the Church to the complete control of Catholic religious instruction in all schools is admitted (article 6), as also (article 10) the right of any religious congregation to establish itself in Austria, with this one proviso, that the superiors shall be of Austrian nationality.

(iii) The legal validity of marriages contracted in accordance with canon law is admitted, and also the validity of decrees of nullity pronounced by the Holy See. Here the concordat resembles that concluded with Italy, and constitutes an advance on that with Germany, which insists on civil, as well as religious, marriage.

(iv) In the matter of Catholic associations (the most vexed of all the questions at issue between the Holy See and Germany), Austria makes great concessions, for the protocol (referring to article 14 of the concordat) binds the Federal Government to give full liberty to all associations " which form part of ' Catholic Action ' and thus fall under episcopal control."

(v) The freedom of the press is admitted in all matters connected with the defence of the Catholic faith. This proviso is peculiar to the Austrian concordat.

57. The concordat was justly described by President Miklas as " a guarantee of Catholic Austria's future within the strong rock of the Holy Catholic and Roman Church," and, such being the case, its ratification naturally caused great satisfaction at the Vatican. Cardinal Pacelli telegraphed congratulating Herr Dollfuss on finding time, amid his many burdens and difficulties, to place the work of reconstruction in Austria on " the traditional basis of loyalty to Christ and his Church."

58. It was in May that the concordat was signed, and before the summer was past the intrepid little Chancellor had laid down his burden for ever. The tragedy of the 25th July produced a profound movement of horror, not unmixed with anxiety, in Vatican circles, where the murdered statesman had not only been esteemed as a most devout Catholic, but also regarded as the principal champion of a weak but Catholic Austria against a powerful and pagan Germany. The *Osservatore Romano* described Dr. Dollfuss as a " Knight of God," and wrote that his murder was an act of defiance to Europe and the civilised world. A requiem was sung for him at the church of Santa Maria dell'Anima, and Cardinal Pacelli gave the absolutions.

59. In August His Majesty's Chargé d'Affaires drew the attention of the Cardinal Secretary of State to a report which had appeared in the Italian press to the effect that the Austrian bishops had expressed disapproval of

Herr von Papen's appointment as Minister to Vienna. His Eminence said that the bishops could hardly be expected to feel much enthusiasm for a Minister who had publicly attacked them for the views expressed in their Christmas pastoral.

60. The Italo-Franco-British agreement signed at Geneva on the 27th September was criticised by the *Osservatore Romano* on the grounds that it contained no fresh guarantee of Austrian independence, and was scarcely an advance on the declaration of the 17th February, which had been proved by events to have but little value.

61. On the 20th November, Herr von Schuschnigg, the Austrian Chancellor, and Herr von Berger-Waldenegg, the Foreign Minister, who had come to Rome on a visit to Signor Mussolini, were received in audience by the Pope, with whom they remained for nearly an hour. After the audience His Holiness conferred high Papal decorations on the two Ministers.

Belgium.

62. King Albert's untimely death on the 17th February caused much grief at the Vatican, and, on receiving the tragic news, the Pope at once sent a telegram of sympathy to the widowed Queen, and, a few days later, publicly referred to the deceased Sovereign as "a model of Catholic faith and virtue." The Cardinal Secretary of State gave the Absolutions at a Requiem Mass at the Gesù on the 22nd February, the day of the funeral at Brussels. The Diplomatic Corps accredited to the Holy See attended both this ceremony and also a further Requiem held at the Vatican on the 28th February in the presence of the Pope (see also paragraph 137).

63. A special mission appointed to announce to the Pope the accession of King Leopold III and led by Baron Maurice Houtart was received by His Holiness in solemn audience on the 19th May. In welcoming this mission the Sovereign Pontiff said that its presence brought two visions clearly before him : one, a vision of past life, a life made up of faith, determination, benevolence, courage, glory and also sorrow; the other a vision of the present, a vision of youth with all its magnificent promise, combined in the present instance with every assurance of fulfilment. This allusion to the new King is understood to have been much appreciated in Belgium.

Brazil.

64. The Papal Legate and various other cardinals called at Rio de Janeiro on their way back from the Eucharistic Congress at Buenos Aires and were given a magnificent reception. All the cardinals were treated as guests of the Government and the Legate received a Royal welcome. At an official banquet given by the President in the Cardinal's honour, his Excellency pointed out that the Church had recently come closer to the State in that, while the two Powers were to remain separated, the new Brazilian Constitution, unlike the old, admitted the necessity of their mutual collaboration in defence of the collective interest. On the 20th October Cardinal Pacelli, from the top of the Corcovado Hill, blessed the Brazilian people in the Pope's name, and, before re-embarking on the *Conte Grande*, bestowed a high decoration on the President, who conferred on him in return the Star of the Order of the Southern Cross.

Czechoslovakia.

65. Proof that Mgr. Ciriaci, in spite of the unpopularity he had earned among the Czechs (see annual report for 1933, paragraph 51), was still *persona gratissima* with the Pope was furnished, if such were needed, by his transfer as Nuncio to Lisbon in January. No successor has yet been appointed.

Negotiations for a concordat or *modus vivendi* are still being carried on by the Czechoslovak Minister.

Finland.

66. In January the Pope received in solemn audience a special delegation from the Finnish Government consisting of Dr. Rolf Witting, a member of the Finnish Government, and Dr. Carl Dahlström, a prominent Catholic Finn. Dr. Witting explained that the object of the mission was to express

(*a*) President Svinhufvud's thanks for the Pope's congratulations on his 70th birthday, (*b*) Finland's gratitude to the Holy See for having been among the first to recognise the young republic, and (*c*) appreciation of the manner in which the Holy See has facilitated access by Finnish students to the Vatican Library. The Pope, in a cordial reply, promised to pray for Finland, and said that naturally he would include petitions for the conservation and spread of the Catholic faith in "that magnificent country." It is interesting and perhaps not without significance that, so soon after the establishment of diplomatic relations between the Vatican and Protestant Estonia (see annual report for 1933, paragraph 53), the latter's even more Protestant neighbour should have made a gratuitous advance of this kind to the Holy See.

France.

67.   Relations between France and the Holy See were undisturbed by any untoward incident. In his New Year speech to the French colony, the Ambassador to the Holy See referred with gratification to the canonisation of St. Bernadette of Lourdes, and to the steady increase in the number of French saints. M. Charles-Roux said that, in her enthusiasm for civilisation and peace, France was glad to be on such cordial terms with "the highest moral authority." Indeed, the acute problems of the post-war period could only be solved by the application of "the essentially Latin and Christian ideals of Right and Justice."

68.   In June an article in the *Vie Intellectuelle* (a Catholic review) alleged that the "Action française" had recently changed its tactics, and, abandoning its attitude of open hostility to the Papacy, had taken the line that the quarrel with Rome had been exaggerated; that Rome had never formally anathematised the movement; and that bygones should be bygones. The *Vie Intellectuelle* violently disputed these premises and found no difficulty in proving that the condemnation of the "Action française" had been, and was, both formal and complete. The *Osservatore Romano* a few days later expressed entire agreement with the *Vie Intellectuelle;* and it is clear that, at least under the present Pope, there is no likelihood of the Church's weakening in its attitude to the "Action française."

69.   French foreign policy during the early summer caused considerable anxiety at the Vatican, and the *Osservatore Romano* expressed the view that the late M. Barthou's visits to Bucharest and Belgrade had been undertaken with the object of buttressing up the two causes of non-revision and Slav solidarity—for neither of which the Vatican feels the very slightest enthusiasm.

70.   During the latter part of the year, though intense irritation was felt at the strong support given by France to Soviet Russia's admission to the League, pleasure was felt at the conciliatory attitude adopted by that country in regard to the Saar, at the growing rapprochement with Italy, and at the moderating influence which the Quai d'Orsay was able to exercise at Belgrade in the troubled period following on the Marseilles murder.

Germany.

71.   A state of tension between the Reich and the Holy See continued throughout 1934, but, in spite of Vatican indignation at the numerous breaches of faith committed by the German Government, at the murder of leading Catholics in the "clean-up" of the 30th June, and at Nationalist Socialist participation in the Vienna "Putsch," the Concordat of 1933 has not been denounced. This is regretted in some quarters, where it is felt to be inconsistent for the Church to remain in relations with a régime which is such an offence to Christianity.

72.   At the same time, the policy pursued, which is one of official silence, combined with strong private encouragement to Cardinal Faulhaber, and the other German bishops, is probably the wisest for the moment. Whether it will be possible to postpone an open breach indefinitely is a matter of doubt; certainly things look very black for catholicism in Germany. Events in Russia and Mexico show what can be done by a ruthless Government, and the greatest anxiety is felt at the Vatican lest the youth of Germany should be removed from clerical influence and lost to the Church.

73. The chief cause of friction between the Church and the Reich in the matter of the concordat resulted from the Government's delay in fulfilling one of its cardinal points, namely, the drafting of a list of "recognised Catholic associations" as laid down in article 31.   Conversations on this subject took place at intervals throughout the year between representatives of the hierarchy and representatives of the Government, and an agreement was somewhat prematurely announced on the 29th June on the basis that the Catholic associations agreed to give up certain of their activities, such as drilling and gymnastics, and consented to be organised by dioceses and not in large centralised bodies. The agreement was not ratified by the German bishops or the Vatican, partly because the concessions demanded by the Government were considered too great, and partly no doubt because, on the following day, a number of important Catholic laymen, including Herr von Klausener, the leader of "Catholic Action" in Berlin, were murdered in cold blood by General Göring's S.S. men.   Conversations with a view to the interpretation of article 31 began afresh in the autumn, but had not reached any conclusion by the end of the year; indeed, it looked as though the Nazi Government were inclined to concede even less than before, and to take the line that the associations should be reduced to the status of sodalities or friendly societies with a purely religious character.

74. Another cause of friction between the Reich and the Holy See lay in the tendency of the former to resent and punish any expression of opinion by the Catholic clergy on affirmations of doctrine and law laid down by the National Socialist State in such matters as sterilisation and the alleged superiority of the Nordic race over others.   The numerous arrests of priests which took place in 1934, especially during the earlier part of the year, were considered by the Vatican to have been carried out in contravention to article 32 of the concordat, which, while forbidding priests to engage in politics, explicitly admits their right to teach and explain in public the faith and morals of the Church.

75. How bitterly the Vatican is opposed to the Nazi doctrines of "blood and race," to their exaggerated anti-semitism and to the fantastic doctrines of the German Christians was to be seen almost daily in the columns of the *Osservatore Romano*.   The placing on the index as heretical of Herr Rosenberg's book *Der Mythus des XX Jahrhunderts* was also a clear indication of the view taken by the Pope of Nazi ideology.   Constant signs like the continued, though largely unsuccessful, attempt of Herr Hitler to tie the Protestant Church to the party chariot made the Pope aware of the innate hostility of the National Socialist party to all forms of traditional Christianity.   On several occasions during the year the Pope expressed his apprehensions in regard to the growth of paganism in Germany.   Perhaps the most remarkable of those pronouncements was the message which His Holiness sent at Easter to the Catholic Youth of Germany.   In this he praised their constancy and devotion in spite of propaganda "working with alluring appeals for a new view of life leading back to heathenism."   In an audience given at about the same time to members of German youth associations, His Holiness said that these had given proof of a heroic courage recalling that of the early Christians, and reminded them that the Apostles had been glad " pro nomine Christi contumeliam pati."   The Pope promised, in conclusion, to do all in his power to protect and defend them.

76. In May the windows of the Bishop of Würzburg having been broken by an infuriated mob, the Cardinal Secretary of State telegraphed expressing the Pope's concern at what His Holiness regarded as an insult to himself as well as to the bishop.   An attempt made by the National Socialist Government to describe Herr von Klausener's death on the 30th June as due to suicide was foiled by the *Osservatore Romano*, which denied the tale flatly and clearly took the view that he had been murdered.   The Vatican paper pointed out how illogical this murder was, seeing that the victim's very unpopularity with the Nazis was due to his opposition to the elements which they were now attacking as "unhealthy."   In addition to the consternation inspired by the murder of innocent men, the Vatican felt particular disgust at the endeavours confessedly made by the German authorities to persuade their victims to commit suicide.   The fact that the bodies were cremated, unknown to the relations and contrary to Catholic usage, also caused much indignation.

77. The July Vienna " Putsch " and the murder of Chancellor Dollfuss caused much angry criticism of Germany in Vatican circles, and the *Osservatore Romano* said that the Nazis, within a month of the 30th June, were transferring to Vienna the methods of savagery which they had adopted in Munich and Berlin. The accession to power after the death of President Hindenburg on the 1st August of the chief author of the National Socialist tyranny only served to increase the apprehensions of the Vatican in regard to the future of religion in Germany.

78. A full translation of the pastoral of the German bishops (reunited at Fulda in June), the text of which had been withheld from the German press, was published by the *Osservatore Romano* in August, and the Vatican paper, in its comment, said that this document was alone sufficient to disprove the assertion that the Church had meddled in politics, making it clear that her only concern had all the time been with the religious interests of the people.

79. A bad impression was made in Rome in September by the report of a speech at Hanover by Reich Bishop Müller, who was alleged to have said that " one Church separate from Rome " was what he desired to see in Germany. He also said something upon a later occasion about the necessity of abolishing the use of Latin in German churches. Although, at least on the first occasion, the bishop endeavoured to explain away his words, the Vatican does not forget that the idea of a United German Church figures largely in the Nazi programme, and fears that, after the Saar has been safely gathered in, Dr. Müller or some other interpreter of Nazi religious thought may return to the charge on similar lines.

80. During the last few months of the year there was a decrease in the chronic friction between Church and Reich. Less was heard of clashes between Catholics and Nazis, of arrests of priests, and of censored sermons; indeed, several outspoken addresses against the new paganism were given by German prelates and reproduced in the *Osservatore Romano*, if not in the German press. Here again, it is feared, however, that the apparent improvement in the position of Catholics is merely due to a desire to encourage Catholic voters in the Saar to throw in their lot with Nazi Germany. At the end of November the Bishop of Berlin (Dr. Bares) was received by the Pope and is believed to have given him an exhaustive account of the situation in Germany.

81. The Bavarian Legation to the Holy See, which, as a result of the centralisation of the Reich, had become somewhat of an anomaly, was abolished in the course of the year and, though the former Papal Nuncio, Mgr. Vassalo Torregrossa, still resides in Munich, he no longer has any diplomatic status.

Hungary.

82. The Yugoslav memorandum sent to the League of Nations in November regarding alleged Hungarian responsibility for the Marseilles crime of the 9th October was commented on by the *Osservatore Romano* in a manner which clearly, though cautiously, indicated the Vatican's sympathy for Hungary. A generous offering was sent by the Sovereign Pontiff, through his Nuncio in Budapest, to assist the Hungarian people expelled from Yugoslavia in December.

Italy.

83. In spite of a series of incidents in Venezia Giulia, which might have given rise to difficulties, relations between Vatican and Quirinal remained excellent throughout the year.

84. The incidents which occurred in the early part of the year were due to the conduct of the Bishop of Trieste, Mgr. Fogar, whose offences consisted in an indiscreet speech to Italian seminarists; in alleged relations with a financier who turned out to be a Yugoslav agent; and in a flat refusal to bless the tomb of Oberdan (an Italian " martyr " executed by the Austrians some sixty years ago on the grounds that he had wished to assassinate the Emperor Francis Joseph).

85. The bishop's attitude caused much resentment in Trieste and throughout Italy. At the Vatican it was felt that, though his attitude in the matter of Oberdan's tomb may have been justifiable, he had been imprudent and tactless in regard to other matters. Mgr. Fogar, who had been summoned to Rome to

explain his conduct, was allowed, nevertheless, to return to his diocese, and the excitement seemed to die down. Further developments occurred, however, at the end of May, when two professors of the Gorizia Seminary (both priests of Slovene origin) were arrested and condemned to five years' " confino " each, on the ground that they had been actively engaging in Yugoslav propaganda. No evidence was offered, and the true explanation of their fate is probably that the Fascist Government, not desiring to embarrass the Vatican by arresting a bishop, endeavoured to appease the popular wrath by treating two prominent Slav ecclesiastics as his scapegoats. The condemnation of the two priests, though it must have annoyed the Vatican, did not, as a matter of fact, produce any official or unofficial protest on the part of the Pope, who will doubtless endeavour in due course to get the period of " confino " shortened.

86. During the summer all the works of the well-known philosophers, Benedetto Croce and Giovanni Gentile, were placed on the Index. This affront to the latter, who, as first Fascist Minister of Education, replaced the crucifixes in the schools, might possibly have led to dissatisfaction among Catholic Fascists, had it not been shrewdly balanced by the simultaneous condemnation of Croce, whom the Fascists heartily detest.

87. Signor Mussolini's action in sending troops to the Austrian frontier after the tragic events at Vienna in July was approved at the Vatican, and the *Osservatore Romano* said that Austria owed her continued independence largely to the Duce's promptitude and energy. As mentioned elsewhere in this report, the Prince of Piedmont attended the Easter ceremonies at St. Peter's. No member of the House of Savoy had been officially present at a Papal ceremony since Prince Umberto's grandfather wrested Rome from the Popes in 1870; and this event brought home vividly the completeness of the reconciliation of 1929. His Royal Highness is known to be a pious Catholic, and almost his first action on the birth of his eldest child in September was to send a respectfully worded telegram to the Sovereign Pontiff. Incidentally, the choice of the Princess's name, " Maria Pia," was probably due, in part at least, to a desire to compliment the Holy Father.

Japan.

88. In January Mgr. Paolo Marella, titular Archbishop of Doclea, who was for some time employed in the Apostolic Delegature at Washington, took up his position at Tokyo as Apostolic Delegate. He succeeded Mgr. Mooney, who had left Japan a year before on being appointed to the episcopal See of Rochester (U.S.A.).

Mexico.

89. The position of the Church in Mexico is one of the Vatican's chief anxieties at the moment. Recent legislation, if enforced, is likely to result in the disappearance of Catholic schools; and if, as seems probable, all the bishops are expelled, the Church in Mexico will before long be reduced to the status of the Orthodox Church in Russia. An indication of the gravity with which the Vatican view the situation is to be seen in the youthfulness of the ecclesiastical students brought from Mexico to Rome. Boys of 14 and 15 are being admitted to the colleges here, as their education in their own country has become impossible.

Persia.

90. Two British Dominicans, Father Blencowe and Father Rice, who had started a mission at Shiraz at the end of 1933, were recalled to England in October by the Father Provincial, their position having become intolerable as a result of the unfriendly attitude of the local authorities. Their insuccess seems to have been due to anti-British sentiment rather than to Mussulman opposition to Christian proselytising, and the Apostolic Delegate, Mgr. Lari, does not seem to have shown much goodwill towards them.

The Saar.

91. The Holy See was represented in the Saar during the past year first by Mgr. Testa (now Apostolic Delegate for Egypt and Palestine) and later by Mgr. Panico. A member of the French Embassy to the Holy See told His

Majesty's Chargé d'Affaires in September that his Government attached great importance to the presence of an Apostolic Visitor in the Saar. It was unfortunate, he added, that no provision had been made in the peace treaties for the separate ecclesiastical administration of the Saar district, but, as it was, the only person who, without giving offence, could exercise a moderating influence on the authorities of the two German dioceses between which the district was divided was the Papal Representative.

92. It is not improbable, in view of the attitude of Nazi Germany towards the Church, that the Vatican would prefer to see a continuance of the *status quo* in the Saar. The Vatican authorities were, however, careful to avoid any open expression of opinion on the subject, and when, in December, rumours appeared in certain papers to the effect that German influences had been brought to bear upon the Holy See in regard to the future of the Saar, the *Osservatore Romano* characterised the reports as groundless and said that the Holy See would continue to observe " a completely neutral and impartial attitude." The Bishops of Speyer and Trèves, however, between whose dioceses the Saar is divided, both showed by their pronouncements that they were not prepared to do anything to discourage reunion with Germany.

Siam.

93. The King and Queen of Siam were received by the Pope with Royal honours in May. Their Majesties profited by their stay in Rome to visit various monuments and sites of Christian interest, and were also present at the Canonisation and Papal Mass on Easter Sunday.

Soviet Union.

94. The " Commissio pro Russia " was deprived at the end of 1933—to the regret of many—of the experienced guidance of Mgr. d'Herbigny who, although ostensibly retired on grounds of ill-health, is generally believed to have fallen a victim to Polish ecclesiastical intrigue. Like the Oriental Institute, the commission, under an Italian cleric, continues its work of collecting information about the Soviet Union and in advising on the steps which should be taken with a view to the restoration of religion in that country. These two bodies are not what they were however (it is said, indeed, that the commission is almost moribund), and more important work is at present being done by the Jesuits, who are devoting very close attention to affairs in Russia with the evident desire that, whenever a religious renewal becomes possible in that country, it may take a Catholic form, possibly with Eastern rites, rather than lead to an Orthodox revival or a Protestant invasion.

95. The admission of the Soviet Union to the League of Nations in September caused much annoyance at the Vatican, where hostility to the Soviets is as uncompromising as ever. The suggestion that the Soviet Union's membership of the League might have a " humanising " effect on her and might improve the position of Catholics was brushed aside, and the view was taken that there should be no compromise with the evil thing and no truckling on the part of Western peoples to what the *Osservatore Romano* described as " this megalomaniac, this Imperialist, this anti-democratic tyranny."

96. Though opposed "tooth and nail" to the Soviet's candidature, the Vatican paper drew some comfort from the fact that ten States at Geneva either opposed Russia's entry or abstained from voting. Strong approval was expressed by the same organ for the speeches made by M. Motta and Mr. de Valera, " those two faithful interpreters of Christian thought," special stress being laid on the former's statement that " a minimum of moral and political conformity between States must not be sacrificed on the alter of universality."

97. In December the *Osservatore Romano* attacked M. Litvinov (whom it described as an " ex-bandit ") for what it called the " unheard-of effrontery " of his attitude in condemning political terrorism abroad when, at the very time when he was speaking, sixty-seven persons were being executed at Moscow, not because they had any part in Kirov's murder, but confessedly merely as potential dangers to the Soviet régime.

Spain.

98. Relations between the Vatican and Spain may be said to have improved somewhat since 1933.

99. In June Sr. Pita Romero, the Spanish Minister for Foreign Affairs, took over the post of Ambassador to the Holy See, which had been vacant since the latter refused its *agrément* to Sr. de Zulueta in 1931. He remained Foreign Minister until October, when the Spanish Government was reconstructed and he became Minister without portfolio in the new Cabinet.

100. During the summer Sr. Pita Romero had a series of conversations with the Cardinal Secretary of State, but these led to no satisfactory result, and though some said that the Vatican were purposely spinning out the negotiations in the hope that a Government further to the Right might shortly come into power, the *impasse* is more likely to have been due to incompatibility of views in the matter of civil marriage. The Vatican had not in any case hoped for more than a temporary settlement, being of the opinion that a Concordat is excluded by the nature of the present Constitution.

101. The Constitution is unwelcome to the Vatican on account of its anti-clerical, not its republican, character. In the matter of the monarchy, the Vatican, unlike a section of the Spanish clergy, would seem, indeed, to have no axe to grind. The Sovereign Pontiff made it clear in his encyclical *Dilectissima Nobis* (see annual report for 1933, paragraph 90) that it was only the question of religious liberty and not that of the form of government in Spain which he had at heart. As a matter of fact, Pius XI, who is not supposed to have any particular admiration for Alfonso XIII, would probably much prefer a "safe" republic, which would concede a reasonable amount of liberty to the Church to a precarious if clerical monarchy. There is therefore no question, and never has been, of the Holy See placing itself in opposition to the republic as such.

102. Although the year ended more or less happily, relations, nevertheless, suffered a slight set-back in February. This was due to the nature of the addresses delivered by the chairman of Catholic Action in Spain (Sr. Herrera) and by Mgr. Tedeschini, the Papal Nuncio, at a religious ceremony in Madrid in honour of the anniversary of the Pope's coronation. Sr. Herrera violently protested against the law suppressing the religious orders, and the Nuncio lamented that the unhappy Spanish nation, "the favourite daughter of the Papacy" should have been lured into courses bound to end in disaster. These rhetorical flights were resented in Spanish official circles, which described them as political allusions misplaced in church, especially as churches were now State property and only lent to the faithful for purposes of worship. After a long interview between the Nuncio and the Prime Minister, at which presumably explanations were offered, the agitation caused by the incident was gradually allowed to subside. There was, however, no outward sign of weakening on the Vatican side, the *Osservatore Romano* affirming that the addresses gave no ground for criticism, except of a purely partisan kind.

103. One concession, which the Vatican doubtless hopes will be the first of many, was offered by the Spanish Government in the autumn in the shape of a decree rescinding a clause of the 1932 Law on Congregations, whereby Jesuit property held by third persons was to be expropriated. As the property held in this manner is believed to be considerable, the Catholics had every reason to be satisfied by the decree, which did not, however, as had been hoped, bring Sr. Gil Robles to the rescue of the tottering Government.

104. The rebellion in the Asturias with its terrible toll of anti-clerical outrages led to a Catholic reaction in Spain, and the Government which came into power in the autumn is more favourable to the Church than any since the republic started. Sr. Romero's hand is thereby considerably strengthened, and it seems not unlikely that some *modus vivendi* between Church and State in Spain will be found during 1935.

Turkey.

105. Mgr. Roncalli, Apostolic Delegate to Bulgaria, was appointed in the autumn to succeed Mgr. Margotti, now Archbishop of Gorizia, as delegate to Turkey and Greece. His Excellency, when visiting Rome in December, seemed

somewhat perturbed by the recent Turkish legislation concerning clerical dress, and was doubtful whether an exception would be made in his own favour. According to the Italian press, the Turkish Government intend to deny official status to the Apostolic Delegate and also forbid his describing himself as the Pope's representative. Although the Catholic clergy do not cling to their cassocks quite so pertinaciously as the Greeks do to theirs, this new manifestation of Mustapha Kemal's anti-clerical feelings has naturally made the worst of impressions at the Vatican, which is inclined to wonder what the Gazi's next move will be.

Yugoslavia.

106.   On receiving the news of the assassination of the King of Yugoslavia, the Pope sent a telegram of condolence to Queen Marie, assuring her of his prayers and " paternal affection." A memorial service for the murdered King, arranged by the Yugoslav Minister to the Holy See, was held at the Church of San Girolamo degli Schiavi and attended by the Diplomatic Corps accredited to the Vatican. The funeral ceremonies at Belgrade were attended by the Papal Nuncio, Mgr. Pellegrinetti.

107.   Thanks, it is believed, to the late King's influence, there has been no further move towards the exclusion of the Jesuits, which Pius XI would inevitably regard as a blow at himself.

IV.—THE VATICAN.

Holy Year Ceremonies.

108.   The Extraordinary Holy Year (or Jubilee) of the Redemption proclaimed by Pius XI at Christmas 1932 did not, as will be remembered, actually begin until Passion Sunday 1933, which was also the 2nd April. It accordingly overlapped into the year now past and was not brought to a close until the 2nd April, 1934, which happened to be an Easter Monday. The year thus included two Good Fridays and Easters, an arrangement which had particularly appealed to the Pope in view of the fact that scholars are uncertain as to the exact date of the event (*i.e.*, the Crucifixion) which it was principally desired to commemorate.

109.   The Sovereign Pontiff was clearly determined to include as many canonisations as possible within the last three months of the Jubilee, for while only two of these ceremonies had occurred during 1933, no less than seven—a quite unprecedented number—were fitted into the period between New Year's Day and Easter 1934. This decision involved a considerable break with tradition. For instance, no canonisation had ever before been held on a Sunday in Lent, the penitential character of those six Sundays being considered to render them unsuitable for the purpose. Nor had Easter Sunday ever been chosen for the purpose, perhaps for fear lest the honours paid to the new Saint might seem to detract in some degree from the unique importance of the great Christian festival. Such objections were swept aside, however, by Pius XI, who cares little for precedents and less for the opinions of others. A Sunday in January, two Lenten Sundays and Easter Sunday were selected for the canonisations, together with the Feast of St. Joseph, the 19th March. The latter date, although it fell within the last fortnight of Lent, the period of the Church's deepest mourning, was singled out for the very unusual honour of a triple canonisation (that of three Italian Saints). The canonisation of a German Saint, nevertheless, " remained over " and was not performed until Whit-Sunday.

110.   The eight canonisations of 1934 were those of—

  (1) Blessed Jeanne Thouret, foundress of the Congregation of Sisters of Charity, who set up the Mother House of that order at Besançon in the face of great difficulties resulting from the French Revolution (the 14th January).
  (2) Blessed Maria Michaela of the Holy Sacrament, a Spanish nun who died in 1865 and founded various works of compassion (the 4th March).
  (3) Blessed Louise de Marillac, friend of St. Vincent de Paul and co-foundress with him of the Society of Daughters of Charity, who died in 1660 (the 11th March).

(4) Blessed Pompilio Perrotti, an Italian priest of much repute for sanctity, who died in 1767 (the 19th March).

(5) Blessed Margareta Redi, a Carmelite nun from Florence, who lived in the 19th century (the 19th March).

(6) Blessed Giuseppe Cottolengo, a Turin priest, great benefactor of the poor and founder of the " Little House of Divine Providence," who also lived in the last century (the 19th March).

(7) Blessed John Bosco, the Piedmontese founder of the Salesian (teaching order), which, since his death in 1888, has taken root in five continents (the 1st April, Easter Sunday).

(8) Blessed Conrad of Parzham, a lay brother of the Capuchin Friary of Altoetting, who died in 1894 (the 20th May, Whit-Sunday).

111. Of these canonisations, the most popular in Rome, both in clerical and lay circles, was undoubtedly that of " Don Bosco," as he is still affectionately called. The present Pope, as a young man, knew the Saint personally, and is believed to have a special devotion towards him, which is doubtless why he arranged for this canonisation to form, as it were, the culminating point of the Holy Year. As well as a fervent priest, Don Bosco was a patriotic Italian, which helps to explain the great popular enthusiasm which the ceremony of Easter Day evoked.

112. The beatifications of 1934 were fewer in number than the canonisations. There were, indeed, only two ceremonies of this kind, that of the 28th January, when three Argentine martyrs were proclaimed Beati, and that of the 10th May (Ascension Day), when the same honour was paid to Père René Rogue (guillotined at Vannes in 1796) and Soeur Jeanne Bichier des Ages (who died in 1838 after a long life of good works in which she was chiefly known as the collaboratrix of St. André Fournet, canonised last year).

113. Of the above Saints and *Beati*, thirteen in number, it may be noted that twelve belonged to the Latin countries (Italy, France, Spain and Argentina), whilst one was a German.

Closure of Holy Year.

114. The last weeks of the Holy Year, marred though they were by continuous bad weather, gave rise to remarkable scenes in Rome. Throughout Lent, pilgrimages, large and small, had continued to pour into the city and, as Easter approached, the multitude of visitors thronging daily into Rome from all parts of the world increased by thousands a day. The great churches were filled from dawn to dusk with the sound of tramping feet and with the voices of pilgrims reciting prayers and singing hymns in a score of different languages. Those who were present will not forget the scene in the Coliseum on Friday in Passion Week, when a thousand Spanish pilgrims made the Stations of the Cross to the light of flaring torches; while the procession of a famous Crucifix through reverent crowds from a church in the Corso to St. Peter's and back was scarcely less impressive.

115. During the last fortnight of the year the Holy Father, who showed really remarkable powers of endurance for a man of 77, received deputations and pilgrimages at almost all hours of the day; and this, although the ordinary audiences given to dignitaries of the Church and other important persons increased rather than diminished, and numerous fatiguing church ceremonies required His Holiness's active participation.

116. On Easter Sunday the Papal Mass at St. Peter's was preceded by the canonisation of St. John Bosco, which has been recorded above, and the Prince of Piedmont, representing his Royal father, set a notable precedent by attending the ceremony in State. His Royal Highness, who was greeted outside the Basilica by the strains of the Italian National Anthem, was escorted up the nave by a special Papal bodyguard, accompanied by the Italian Ambassador to the Holy See and his staff. The Prince sat in a special box some few feet in advance of that reserved for the other Royalties present, who included the King and Queen of Siam. The storm of cheers with which His Royal Highness was greeted on his entry evoked some criticism among certain of the foreigners present, but he himself clearly appreciated fully the solemnity of the occasion.

117. At the conclusion of the Papal Mass, to the dramatic accompaniment of crashes of thunder and flashes of lightning, the Holy Father gave the Apostolic Benediction "Urbi et Orbi" from the loggia overlooking the Piazza di San Pietro, which was filled with a crowd estimated to number at least 300,000 persons.

118. The final ceremony of the Holy Year, that of closing the Porta Santa, took place at the four patriarchal basilicas on Easter Monday, the 2nd April. The door at St. Peter's was closed by the Pope in person, while at the three other basilicas, St. John Lateran, St. Paul's without the Walls, and Santa Maria Maggiore, His Holiness was represented by Cardinals Marchetti, Granito di Belmonte and Dolci, each of whom had been appointed Papal Legate for the occasion.

119. Before proceeding to the closure of the Door, the Pope, in pontifical robes and tiara, was borne round St. Peter's on the Sedia Gestatoria, preceded by some three score mitred prelates and countless other dignitaries. His Holiness was greeted with indescribable enthusiasm by the immense concourse of people which filled the Basilica. On returning to the Atrium, where the Royal guests, the Diplomatic Corps and other privileged persons were accommodated in stands erected for the occasion, the Holy Father was the last to pass through the Sacred Doorway. He proceeded to bless the bricks and mortar, the aperture was filled up and the ceremony ended with the *Te Deum.* Pius XI, who has been the first Pope to include two Holy Years in his pontificate, is scarcely likely to see a third, but it may be that one of the fifteen cardinals who assisted at the closing of the door on Easter Monday is destined to preside at its reopening in 1950.

120. Meanwhile, if the Holy Father has not had the satisfaction of witnessing any great improvement in the world situation during the Holy Year, the devotion of Catholics from all countries to the See of Rome and the Sovereign Pontiff must have encouraged and touched Pope Pius XI. The number of pilgrimages, despite far less favourable monetary conditions, much exceeded that recorded in 1925, and the enthusiasm of the pilgrims, as well as the number and magnificence of the canonisations and other ceremonies which marked the Holy Year, made it, as the Pope had desired, indeed an extraordinary one.

College of Cardinals.

121. During 1934, as during 1933, the Sacred College lost three members. These were :—

(1) Cardinal Franz Ehrle, S.J., who died in Rome on the 31st March, aged 87. He was a Bavarian by birth, but had spent part of his early career as a Jesuit in England and never lost the strong affection for things British which he then acquired and which made him proud to be Protector of the Scots College in Rome (a position in which he has been succeeded by Cardinal Marchetti-Salveggiani). In 1895 Father Ehrle, who will be known chiefly for his writings on mediæval history, was summoned to the Vatican Library by Leo XIII, whose attention had been drawn to the brilliance of the young Jesuit's research work. In 1905, as Mgr. Ehrle, he became Prefect of the Library, a position which he retained until 1905 when he was succeeded by the present Pope. His Holiness raised Mgr. Ehrle to the Cardinalate as Cardinal Deacon at his first consistory (1922) and in 1929, on the death of Cardinal Gasquet, appointed him to the vacant office of Librarian and Archivist of the Holy Roman Church. During his time at the Vatican Library the late cardinal was responsible for the acquisition of many priceless books from the most famous private libraries of Rome, including those of the Barberini and Borghese families.

(2) Cardinal Giuseppe Mori, who died at Loro Piceno (Romagna) on the 30th September at the age of 84. After receiving his ecclesiastical training first at Fermo, and afterwards in Rome, where he was to spend almost the whole of his subsequent career, Mgr. Mori became in 1903 secretary of the Sacred Congregation of the Council, with which his principal activities were connected, though he was also later

an active member of the Congregations of the Sacraments and of the Apostolic Signatura. He was raised to the Purple in 1922 as Cardinal Deacon.

(3) Cardinal Pietro Gasparri, Camerlengo of the Holy Roman Church, Secretary of State from 1914 to 1929, who died in Rome on the 19th November (see separate paragraphs below).

122. At the end of 1934 the total number of cardinals is 53, of whom 27 are non-Italian and 8 are Archbishops of large Italian towns. Actually resident at Rome there are 20 cardinals, of whom only 2, Cardinal Lépicier and Cardinal Segura y Saenz, are non-Italians. In spite of the almost unprecedented number of 17 vacancies in the Sacred College and the persistent rumours that a consistory would be held in December, the Holy Father, who keeps his entourage very much in the dark in all such matters, had at the end of the year given no indication as to when or whether he would create any further cardinals. His Holiness has also as yet taken no steps to fill two important offices in the Church, those of Librarian and Camerlengo, which fell vacant during the year as a result of the deaths of Cardinal Ehrle and Cardinal Pietro Gasparri.

Cardinal Pacelli.

123. The fact that, as mentioned elsewhere in this report, Cardinal Pacelli was selected to represent the Pope at the International Eucharistic Congress held at Buenos Aires in October caused considerable comment in ecclesiastical circles. No Cardinal Secretary of State had ever before been sent as Papal Legate to preside at a ceremony outside Italy, and the unusual nature of the Pope's choice, combined with the general belief that the cardinal dislikes his present political work, resulted in the spread of rumours that the trip to Buenos Aires would prove a prelude to his Eminence's retirement to an archiepiscopal see. Though these rumours proved entirely devoid of foundation, it is probably true that Cardinal Pacelli's present duties are uncongenial to him and that he would prefer work of a more pastoral kind. His modesty and readiness to efface himself make him admirably suited, however, to the needs of the Pope, and it is quite unthinkable that, with the strong sense of duty which is one of his leading characteristics, Cardinal Pacelli would suggest resigning while he believed that the Holy Father had need of him.

124. In a comment inspired by the choice of his Eminence as Legate, the Paris *Temps* of the 30th July suggested that he was at present among the most " papabili " of the cardinals. This is probably true, in spite of the fact that Secretaries of State, for reasons not unconnected with the love of change common to all men, are but seldom elected to the Papal Throne. Save Pacelli, the Italian cardinals are not, so far as it is possible to judge in existent circumstances, very remarkable men; and Cardinal Marchetti, the most obvious exception to this statement, is probably himself too much of an autocrat to be chosen to succeed the present Pope by cardinals who have had experience of autocratic rule.

125. The suite of the Cardinal Legate, who sailed from Genoa on the 24th September on the *Conte Grande*, included the Master of the Pope's Household, Mgr. Caccia Dominioni, and several other distinguished Vatican officials. His Eminence was given an enthusiastic send-off at Genoa, where the streets were lined with Italian troops and the civic authorities assembled at the quay to do him honour. The *Conte Grande* flew the Papal flag on the principal mast, and in South America the Pope's representative was received with the honour usually reserved for the heads of States (for Cardinal Pacelli's visit to South America, see also the sections devoted to Argentine and Brazil). His Eminence reached Rome on his return journey on the 2nd November, and was met by all the heads of diplomatic missions, by numerous Vatican officials and by a representative of the Palazzo Chigi. There was also a guard of honour at the station.

The Late Cardinal Pietro Gasparri.

126. With the death of Cardinal Gasparri the Church lost one of her greatest men and one who will live in history, both as Benedict XV's principal collaborator during the war and as the chief adviser of Pius XI in the negotiations which led to the reconciliation of 1929 between Church and State. His Eminence was also probably the greatest authority living on Canon Law.

127.   The son of a shepherd in the Apennines, the future cardinal received his ecclesiastical education in Rome.   After a period as professor in Rome, Gasparri, in 1879, became professor of canon law to the Catholic Institute of Paris, a position which he filled with great distinction for twelve years, during which he acquired a profound knowledge, which was to prove useful later, of contemporary currents of political thought in France.

128.   In 1898 Leo XIII sent him as Apostolic Delegate to Peru, Bolivia and Ecuador, with the title of Archbishop of Cæsarea.   In 1902 he was recalled to Rome for several years and acted as Under-Secretary at the Secretariat of State, where he was called upon in particular to deal with the strained relations with France resulting from the anti-clerical policy of successive Governments.   In addition to these diplomatic labours, he was entrusted in 1904 with the congenial but heavy task of organising and directing the labours of the commission set up by Pius X for the codification of Canon Law, first in the capacity of secretary of the commission and later, after he had been created cardinal in 1907, as its president.

129.   In October 1914, Benedict XV appointed Cardinal Gasparri to be Secretary of State in succession to Cardinal Ferrata, who died after holding that position for six weeks only.   More fortunate than his predecessor, not only did Gasparri hold this position throughout the reign of Benedict, but on that Pontiff's premature death in January 1922, Pius XI took the almost unprecedented step of confirming him in office, and he thus remained Secretary of State until 1929, when, on the conclusion of the Lateran Treaty, he retired in order to dedicate his remaining years to the work of codifying the Canon Law of the Oriental Church.

130.   The first four of Cardinal Gasparri's years as Secretary of State were of unparalleled difficulty.   The wish to improve relations with France and Italy on the one hand, and, on the other, the necessity of remaining on good terms with the Central Powers, alike called for the exercise of the highest statesmanship and in Gasparri Benedict XV found a statesman equal to the task.   In addition to a brilliant intellect, Gasparri displayed the tenacity, caution and capacity for hard work which he inherited from generations of mountain peasants.

131.   The cardinal was considered by the Allies to have favoured the Central Powers during the war, not from any belief in the justice of their cause, but principally from the conviction that the victory of a Catholic Austria and a partly Catholic Germany would be of more advantage to the Holy See than the triumph of Orthodox Russia, Protestant England and anti-clerical Italy and France.   It is often said that, both during the war and also during the negotiations for the Lateran Treaty, his Eminence showed a certain lack of candour in his official relations with the diplomatic representatives to the Holy See, and he was certainly lacking in the courtesy and charm of his successor.

132.   Not content with the exacting labours of his high office, Cardinal Gasparri found time to continue the work of codification of the Canon Law, which he completed in 1917; and in the post-war period he was able to crown his many successes by signing, in 1929, the Lateran Treaty, which put an end to the quarrel between the Italian State and Church, which had lasted since 1870, and restored to the Pope the rank, though scarcely the dominion, of a temporal Sovereign.

133.   In view of Pius XI's masterful temperament, it seems probable that rumour is right in attributing to His Holiness the principal decisions eventually taken; but there is no doubt that in the preliminary conversation which began under Benedict XV the cardinal played an all-important part.   It was, never-theless, a cause of surprise to many that Cardinal Gasparri, who is believed to have had his own way to a large extent under the accommodating Benedict, was able to adapt himself as well as he did to the autocratic ways of his new master. It may very well be, however, that Pius XI in the early years of his pontificate was less unwilling to take advice than he is now and that, with his long diplomatic experience, Gasparri was invaluable to one who, until five years before the com-mencement of his pontificate, had been a librarian without much personal experience of the world and its ways.

134.   In 1929, after the signature of the treaty, Cardinal Gasparri, loaded with honours, which included the Collar of the Annunciata and membership of

the Italian Academy, as well as valuable gifts from the Pope, retired from the office of the Secretary of State to devote the rest of his life to the labours in connexion with Canon Law, which had so great an attraction for him.

135.   Cardinal Gasparri died in harness, and his end was probably just what the brave, tenacious, hard-working old man would have wished it to be.   As reported elsewhere, he met his death as the result of a cold caught when returning from one of the sessions of the Juridical Congress held at Rome in December. The funeral service at the Church of Sant' Ignazio was attended by His Royal Highness the Duke of Spoleto, representing the King of Italy, by the Minister of Justice, representing Signor Mussolini, by all the cardinals present in Rome, by the Diplomatic Corps accredited to the Holy See and by many other official and unofficial persons.

136.   In the name of himself and his colleagues, the German Ambassador sent a message of condolence, referring to the late cardinal as "that brilliant jurist, able diplomat, and Prince of the Church who had no other aim but the triumph of justice and the fulfilment of peace among the nations."   To the Belgian Ambassador, this message, in view of the cardinal's war-time reputation among the Allies, caused cynical amusement; but there seems no reason to doubt that the cardinal, whatever his faults, consistently did what he believed to be his duty and strove hard, in accordance with his lights, to bring peace and concord to a distracted world.

Cappella Papale for King Albert.

137.   As stated in paragraph 62 ("Belgium") a Requiem Mass *coram Pontefice* was celebrated in the Sistine Chapel on the 28th February for the late King Albert.   Although it is an old tradition at the Vatican to hold what is known as a "Cappella Papale" on the death of a reigning Roman Catholic Prince, this was the first ceremony of the kind at which the present Pontiff has presided.   Indeed, the last similar service was held so long ago as 1913, when Pius X assisted at a requiem for the Prince Regent Luitpold of Bavaria. (Doubtless, owing to the circumstances of the time, the ceremony was omitted when the Emperor Frances Joseph died in 1916.)   As is also prescribed by tradition, a Latin funeral oration was delivered during the Requiem Mass by the Secretary for Papal epistles *ad Principes* (Mgr. Bacci), in whose panegyric special stress was laid on the Christian virtues of the monarch's public and private life.

The Pope's Visit to Castel Gandolfo.

138.   Although there had been much speculation regarding the Pope's plans for the summer, no one at the Vatican seemed to know, until the last moment, whether His Holiness would after all be able to make up his mind to a prolonged absence from the Vatican, which he had not left for more than a few hours on end, and that only on rare occasions, since his election in 1922.

139.   All doubts were set at rest, however, when on the 1st August, the feast appropriately enough being that of St. Peter in Chains, the Pope, accompanied by the Master of his Household and a small staff, took up residence in the Castel Gandolfo Palace, where he remained for seven weeks.   It was sixty-four years since a Roman Pontiff had spent a night away from Rome, and on the 1st August, 1934, the Pope ceased in every sense to be the prisoner of the Vatican.

140.   The Holy Father's daily life while at his summer villa was scarcely different from that which he habitually leads when in Rome.   Papal chamberlains were on duty, though in smaller numbers than at the Vatican, and the Holy Father's person was protected, as in Rome, by Pontifical gendarmerie and Swiss guards.   Daily audiences were held, both public and private, and large numbers of pilgrims and other visitors, foreign and Italian, were driven out each morning to Castel Gandolfo by car and charabanc.   The Cardinal Secretary of State visited His Holiness weekly, and other cardinals and important church dignitaries laid their reports before him on the usual days.   In short, the Pope's so-called holiday was not what anybody else would be likely to describe as such, and amounted in reality to little more than a change of scene and air.   As all who know Rome will, however, admit, the change from the stifling heat of the

city in August to the comparatively cool atmosphere of the Alban Hills can alone be of incalculable benefit to a tired man; and the Pope, who had looked worn out as a result of the fatigues of the Holy Year, seemed to have regained much of his former health and vigour when he returned to Rome on the 22nd September. He is said to have been delighted with his stay in the country, and it is hoped and expected that a first experiment which proved so successful will now be repeated each year.

Pilgrimage of the Knights of Malta.

141. The Sovereign Military Order of St. John of Jerusalem and of Malta, better know as the Order of the Knights of Malta, and one of the most famous of Roman Catholic organisations, decided, at the suggestion of the Grand Master, Prince Chigi Albani, to celebrate the Holy Year, shortly before its close, by meeting in Rome for the first time since they were driven by Napoleon from their island stronghold. The primary object of this meeting was devotional, the three "languages" of Italy, Germany and Spain, together with the many associated bodies from other lands, wishing to join in making a pilgrimage to the tomb of St. Peter, in paying homage to his successor and in gaining the Jubilee Indulgence. As Cardinal Bisleti pointed out, in a circular addressed to the Italian branch of which he is Grand Prior, the gathering was also intended to strengthen the spirit of Christian brotherhood and co-operation, which is needed "more than ever in the asperity of our times."

142. Some 650 members of the order, Knights as well as Dames, including representatives from England, Ireland, Spain, France, Germany, Austria, Hungary, Holland, Belgium and Portugal, arrived in Rome in time for the inaugural ceremony held on the 14th March at St. Paul's without the Walls. The ten British Knights present in Rome did not include Lord FitzAlan, who had intended to come, but was prevented at the last moment from doing so. At the opening ceremony His Highness the Grand Master was supported by Cardinals Granito di Belmonte, Sincero and Bisleti, all three being members of the order, and other distinguished persons present at this and the other functions of the congress were Prince George of Bavaria, who is a Canon of St. Peter's, Prince and Princess Friedrich Victor of Hohenzollern, the Archduke Joseph of Austria, the Princess of Lichtenstein and the Duchesse de Montpensier.

143. On the 16th March, the Knights and Dames were received in audience by the Pope after paying the Jubilee visit to St. Peter's and hearing Mass there. The Holy Father replied to the Grand Master's address with an affectionate discourse of a religious character, completely devoid of any allusion to the Island of Malta and its recent political history.

144. On the evening of the 16th March the King and Queen of Italy gave a reception at the Quirinal in honour of the Knights, and on the 18th Signor Mussolini, who himself holds high rank in the order, received them at the Palazzo Venezia. On the 18th March the Grand Master gave a reception, at which members of the order were presented with special medals bearing his likeness. The proceedings ended on the 19th with the attendance of the Knights and Dames in full-dress uniform at the canonisation of three Italian saints in St. Peter's.

Diplomatic Dinner at the Vatican.

145. The Cardinal Secretary of State gave a dinner on the 16th April to the heads of missions accredited to the Holy See, at which Sir Robert Clive was present. It is but rarely that the Holy See entertains foreign representatives, and there was much speculation as to the reason for this dinner, the invitations to which were not sent out "by order of His Holiness the Pope," as was done in 1929, the last occasion on which an official party of this kind was given at the Vatican. The initiative for this function would appear to have come from the Cardinal Secretary of State, who represented to His Holiness that it might be fitting for him to return in some such manner the hospitality he had received from so many foreign representatives. The Pope seems to have fallen in willingly with the suggestion, and the occasion was one of much pomp and splendour, dinner being served in the Sala dei Paramenti, with its gorgeous ceiling and Gobelin tapestries. Besides the foreign Ambassadors, Ministers and

Chargé d'Affaires, the guests included Cardinals Lega, Gasparri and Laurenti, representing the orders of Cardinal Bishops, Priests and Deacons; the two Princes Assistant at the Throne, Colonna and Orsini; Prince Massimo and Marchese Sacchetti, both holding hereditary offices, and Count Ratti, nephew of the Pope and administrator of the Pontifical estate at Castel Gandolfo.

Fourth Centenary of the Society of Jesus.

146.   On the occasion of the fourth centenary of the first vows pronounced by the pioneers of Jesuitism, the Holy Father, who was at Castel Gandolfo, received in special audience Father Vladimir Ledochowski, General of the Society of Jesus, who was accompanied by all seven members of his curia, or staff (these including the " English assistant," Father Welsby), by the superiors of all the Roman houses of the society, and by representatives of all its different grades. About 300 members of the order were present in all.

147.   The general read an address of devoted homage to the Pope, in which he recalled the vows of special obedience which all Jesuits make to the Holy See, and the Pontiff, in a particularly cordial reply, spoke of the marvellous work of the society during its 400 years of life.

148.   The main official celebrations for the fourth centenary will not, it should be added, take place for six years, as it was only with the issue in 1540 of Paul III's Bull, *Regimini militantis Ecclesiæ*, that the Society of Jesus received full recognition as a religious order. At the same time, the event commemorated on the 15th August, when St. Ignatius de Loyola and his first companions dedicated themselves at St. Denys de Montmarte in 1534 to their special apostolate, is usually regarded as the real birthday of the order.

Congresses.

149.—(i) International Eucharistic Congress at Buenos Aires (see paragraph 51).

150.—(ii) Eucharistic Congress, Melbourne (see paragraph 27).

151.—(iii) International Juridical Congress, Rome.—The above congress was held under the auspices of the Vatican from the 12th to the 17th November. Such significance as this congress may have had will probably be overshadowed in modern Papal history by the fact that it was on returning from one of its meetings that Cardinal Gasparri literally caught his death of cold (see paragraph 135). The congress was inaugurated at the Pontifical Institute of S. Apollinaris by Cardinal Bisleti, who, in a Latin speech, referred to the fact that two centenaries were being commemorated, the seventh of the Decretals of Gregory IX and the fourteenth of the publication of the Code of Justinian. The labours of the congress concerned the history, development and present state of Canon Law, in which connexion the work of codification of Cardinal Gasparri was referred to by Cardinal Pacelli amid loud applause. Cardinal Gasparri himself addressed the congress on the 16th. He was too ill, however, to attend the closing session at the Vatican on the 17th November, at which the Pope presided.

Papal Pronouncements.

152.   No encyclical appeared during the year, and there were few Papal pronouncements of any importance. Mention should, however, be made of—

(a) The Bull *Quod superiori anno*, whereby the indulgences, which it had only been possible to gain during the Holy Year by means of visits to Rome, were made applicable on certain conditions to Catholics all over the world. These conditions included the recital of certain prayers and visits to churches prescribed by the various ordinaries.

(b) The Pope's Christmas Allocution to the Cardinals. This address was chiefly connected with four events of purely ecclesiastical interest, namely: (i) The above-mentioned Bull; (ii) the Eucharistic congresses; (iii) the reconstitution of the Holy House of Loreto, which has now returned to the tutelage of the Holy See in accordance with the provisions of the Lateran Treaty; and (iv) the Juridical Congress. The Pope also alluded to the spread of neo-paganism, which fills him with alarm, and, at greater length, to the rumours of war which are so prevalent to-day. As regards the latter, he said he trusted that the armed nations were sincere in protesting that their only desire was peace. He himself desired, invoked and prayed for peace, but, should some inconceivable access of suicidal mania lead the nations again into war, it would be his duty to formulate a different prayer, and this would be : " Lord, scatter the nations which delight in war." In the confident hope that such a calamity would be averted, he closed his address with the words : " Glory to God in the Highest and Peace on Earth, Peace, Peace, Peace."

V.—LEGISLATION.

153. The following are the laws, decrees, &c., promulgated by the Vatican State since mid-December 1933 :—

XLV (December 20, 1933).—Decree establishing registration dues for the admission of goods and merchandise.

XLVI (December 29, 1933).—Decree reducing salaries, pensions, &c., of Vatican officials.

XLVII (March 23, 1934).—Ordinance extending the period of validity for Holy Year commemorative postage stamps until the 31st December, 1934

XLVIII (June 12, 1934).—Ordinance regarding postmarks.

XLIX (December 21, 1934).—Ordinance regarding the striking and issue of coins for 1934.

L (December 21, 1934).—Ordinance reducing dues for insufficient postage.

LI (December 24, 1934).—Law delegating to the Governor of the Vatican State legislative power for the establishment, suppression and ordering of the Governor's Department.

LII (December 28, 1934).—Law passed by the Governor in virtue of immediately preceding law in respect of the establishment and ordering of the Governor's Department.

LIII (December 28, 1934).—Law introducing modifications into the law (No. XXXIII) of the 5th December, 1932, concerning various offices and services in the Governor's Department.

154.   VI.—TREATIES, 1934.

With (Country).	Date of Signature.	Subject.	Date of Exchange of Ratification.	Date of Entry into Force.	Remarks.
Austria	June 19, 1933	Concordat	May 1, 1934	On exchange of ratifications	See paragraphs 55 to 57 (inclusive) of present report.
Italy	Dec. 20, 1933	Railway Convention	Sept. 12, 1934	15 days after exchange of ratification	Concerns the Vatican Station; its use and upkeep; and also the circulation of Vatican rolling-stock on Italian railways.
Italy	Oct. 4, 1934	Hospital Convention	..	(Retrospective) Oct. 1, 1934	Concerns reception of Vatican citizens in Italian hospitals.

CONFIDENTIAL.

(14823)

HOLY SEE.

Annual Report, 1935.

[R 217/217/22]

Mr. H. Montgomery to Mr. Eden.—(Received January 13.)

(No. 9.)   *British Legation to the Holy See,*
Sir,   *Rome, January* 9, 1936.
    I HAVE the honour to transmit herewith the annual report of this Legation
for the year 1935.
    2. I am indebted to the members of the Legation staff, Mr. Thynne and
Miss Johnson, for their useful assistance.
                       I have, &c.
                       HUGH MONTGOMERY.

Enclosure.

Annual Report on the Holy See for 1935.

CONTENTS.

I.—General Introduction.

RELATIONS between the United Kingdom and the Vatican remain correct.

2. The canonisation of Bishop Fisher and Sir Thomas More in May, apart from its religious significance, was probably intended by the Pope as a sign of his esteem and admiration for England, and he took the opportunity which it provided of making several extremely cordial references to His Majesty The King and to the Empire over which he rules.

3. Since the spring there has been a certain diminution in His Holiness's cordiality towards England, corresponding to a definite sense of disappointment on the part of His Majesty's Government in the United Kingdom at the attitude of the Holy See. The coolness on the Pope's side, which probably deprived the new Archbishop of Westminster of a cardinal's hat, was due to a variety of causes, great and small, among which the following may be mentioned : The comparative lack of interest displayed in England about the canonisation from which the Pope had hoped great things; the inability of His Majesty The King to send a special mission to this function in accordance with His Holiness's desire; the unfortunate wording of the sermon delivered by the Archbishop of Westminster in October; the apparent unwillingness of His Majesty's Government to negotiate on the basis of overtures made by Signor Mussolini through His Holiness; the failure of British opinion to appreciate the latter's desire for a peace of compromise.

4. On the side of His Majesty's Government the disappointment felt was due to the attitude of the Vatican towards the Ethiopian dispute. Not since the reconciliation between Church and State in 1929 had Italy been involved in a serious international quarrel, and the attitude of the Vatican, who persisted in regarding the conflict as an Anglo-Italian one rather than as one between Italy and the League, went far to justify those who had seen in the Lateran Treaty chiefly a device to render the Papacy subservient to fascism. Thus, although the Pope was known to have disapproved beforehand of Signor Mussolini's war, and although Vatican officials have privately admitted that Italy is without a legal case, no clear utterance defending the sanctity of treaties or condemning unprovoked aggression has come from His Holiness since the fateful 3rd October.

5. As a result of these and similar facts and of the use of Vatican influence to secure British and other support for a settlement so favourable to Italy as to be acceptable neither to Ethiopia nor to the League of Nations, His Majesty's Principal Secretary of State, who pointed out that the voice of the Vatican had come to be scarcely distinguishable from that of the Italian Government, took steps in November to find out to what extent, if at all, the Vatican had endeavoured through their own machinery to sway world opinion against League action and in favour of Italy. The result seemed to show that, whatever their private views, the Nuncios of His Holiness had had the wisdom to refrain from any attempts at spreading Italian propaganda in the countries to which they were accredited.

6.   The only moment at which the Vatican clearly approved British policy on the Ethiopian issue was when Sir Samuel Hoare in December gave his approval to peace proposals which were subsequently disavowed by His Majesty's Government because they were considered by British public opinion to be unduly favourable to the aggressor.   The Vatican did not conceal their bitter disappointment at the shipwreck of these proposals, and although they blamed Signor Mussolini for not having at once accepted them as a basis of discussion they also undoubtedly disapproved of the resumption by His Majesty's Government of its former firm attitude which seems to them rigid and legalistic.

7.   Apart from their differences upon the Italo-Ethiopian question and the few Papal grievances alluded to above, relations between the Holy See and the British Empire have been harmonious.   The visit of the Papal Legate to Malta, which threatened for a time to be an occasion of friction between the Vatican and the Government of the island, passed off most successfully, thanks to the tact and the pains of His Majesty's Minister and of the Acting Governor of Malta. Some credit in this connexion is also perhaps due to the Cardinal Secretary of State who seems to have calmed the excited Legate (Cardinal Lépicier) and persuaded his Eminence that the British authorities were animated by nothing but goodwill even if they could not give him a Royal salute.   Some progress has been made with the negotiations for the reform of the Theological Faculty of Malta University which is being discussed between His Majesty's Government in the United Kingdom and the Vatican.   Authorisation was, at the request of His Majesty's Government, somewhat reluctantly given for the withdrawal of Maltese religious from posts of danger in Abyssinia.   The question of the Archbishopric of Bombay and its division for all practical purposes into three parts in contradiction to the letter and spirit of the Padroado Agreement, occasioned some discussion between His Majesty's Government, the Portuguese Minister to the Holy See and the Vatican; a suggestion mentioned by Cardinal Fumasoni Biondi and perhaps emanating from the Portuguese Government that the present archbishop should resign and be succeeded by another Portuguese, was not encouraged.

8.   Turning to foreign countries, the principal preoccupations of His Holiness, apart from those directly occasioned by the Italo-Abyssinian conflict, were connected with Soviet Russia, Mexico, and, to quote the Pope's own words, " to some extent " Germany.   As far as Soviet Russia is concerned these anxieties were closely connected with those caused by the conflict, for His Holiness, whose chief obsession is always " the Red Peril," thought he saw a great danger for the world in the fact that Moscow was enabled to pose as the champion of international peace and world security, thereby (for, in his opinion, her true motives could never be anything but bad) throwing dust into the eyes of the other members of the League.   It is indeed probable that the fact of Soviet Russia's making common cause with the other League Powers against Italian aggression was what influenced him more than anything else in an anti-League direction.

9.   Events in Mexico, including the passing of a law to put into effect the most anti-clerical provisions of the Constitution, have not been of a nature to cheer His Holiness.   As for Germany, his policy still seems to be based on the idea that it is best to ignore as far as possible the constant breaches and evasions of the concordat, lest, should the latter be denounced, the lot of Catholics in the fatherland might become even worse than it is at present.   Perhaps, for this reason, less outcry than might have been expected was raised at the arrest of various prominent German ecclesiastics.

10.   Relations with France remained particularly cordial throughout the year, and those with Spain improved so much that the Spanish Primate received the Red Hat in December.   The amelioration of relations with Czechoslovakia was also marked by the elevation to the purple of its leading archbishop. Yugoslavia, in spite of the signature, on the 25th July, of a much-needed concordat which it had taken fourteen years to negotiate, was not given a similar reward. As regards the Holy See's relations with other countries, which have been correct, nothing would appear to require particular emphasis.

11.   The replacement of Mgr. Ottaviani by Mgr. Tardini at the Secretariat of State gives cause for satisfaction, as, although the former was personally friendly, he probably has a less cosmopolitan outlook than his successor.

Mgr. Caccia Dominioni, who relinquished the appointment of Master of the Pope's Household, which he had held for fifteen years, on his elevation to the cardinalate in December, will be greatly missed.

II.—RELATIONS WITH THE BRITISH EMPIRE.
United Kingdom.
The King and the Silver Jubilee.

12. In March the Assistant Under-Secretary of State at the Vatican enquired unofficially of His Majesty's Legation what action was being taken by foreign Governments with regard to the Silver Jubilee. The Legation replied that no special missions were being sent, whereupon Mgr. Ottaviani explained that, while the Vatican did not wish to be behindhand in doing honour to King George on this auspicious occasion, they desired to conform to the action taken by other Powers. A report which appeared in the Italian press a little later, to the effect that the Pope wished to send a special mission, was characterised by the Vatican as " a pure invention of the journalists."

13. On Silver Jubilee Day His Holiness sent the following telegram to His Majesty :—

" On this auspicious day, when Your Majesty is celebrating with the Queen the Silver Jubilee of your reign over the peoples of the British Commonwealth, among whom you count millions of loyal Catholic subjects, we offer you our heartfelt felicitations on these twenty-five years of enlightened and beneficent rule, and we pray that God may bless you and Her Majesty The Queen with length of days and happiness, and with consolation and success in your labours for the peace and prosperity of your realm."

His Majesty replied as follows :—

" The Queen and I are deeply touched by the extreme kindness with which your Holiness has expressed yourself towards us on the Silver Jubilee of my accession, and we thank you wholeheartedly for your prayers and good wishes."

14. His Majesty's Minister was told at the Vatican that this gracious reply had given much pleasure to His Holiness.

15. In addition to the Papal telegram, which was printed in its original English, the official *Osservatore Romano* of the 6th May contained an article on the subject of the Jubilee, which reflected the sincere admiration which the Pope is known to feel for His Majesty's character, and took due note of the great and deserved affection with which the British throne is surrounded. One passage from the article deserves quotation : " Wise and austere," it runs, " brought up in the school of duty and self-sacrifice, The King . . . . gave proof, amidst the cares and anxieties of government, of the qualities of one who, while respectful indeed of traditions, is prepared to face with an open mind new and unsolved problems." The accounts from London, bearing witness to the sentiments of fervent loyalty of the people of England towards the monarchy, undoubtedly much impressed the Vatican, where they were looked upon as welcome evidence of the fundamental unity and strength at the heart of the Empire.

16. The celebrations at Rome, apart from the official service at the British Embassy Church, which was attended by His Majesty's Minister and the staff of the Legation, included two Roman Catholic functions, which were held respectively on the 5th and the 6th May, and were also attended by His Majesty's Minister and the staff. These last-named services took the form of masses of thanksgiving, the first being held at S. Silvestro in Capite (the English " national " church), while the second took place in the chapel of the Venerable English College. On the first occasion, Father Leeming, S.J., preached a sermon in praise of the British monarchy, while the proceeds of the collection were devoted to King George's Jubilee Trust. At the English College no sermon was preached or collection taken; the mass was, however, attended not only by the leading English Catholics in Rome, but also by his Eminence the Cardinal Secretary of State and by Mgr. Pizzardo, the Under-Secretary of State.

17. On the 18th May His Majesty's Minister and Lady Wingfield gave an afternoon reception in honour of the Jubilee. This date had been chosen in order

that Sir Charles and Lady Wingfield might include among their guests the English Roman Catholic bishops and a certain number of the other pilgrims who were then visiting Rome in connexion with the canonisation ceremony held on the 19th May. Many members of the " Black " society of Rome were also invited, and did not fail to take the opportunity of paying a mark of respect to His Majesty by being present. Cardinal Pacelli told His Majesty's Minister that it had been particularly agreeable to him to come, as he had been present at the coronation as a member of the special mission sent by Pius X. Cardinal Sbaretti, who told the Minister that he had met His Majesty in Canada; Cardinal Dolci, who received the C.B.E. for services to British prisoners in Turkey; Cardinal Fumasoni-Biondi, Prefect of the Congregation de Propaganda Fide, which sends out so many missionaries to British territory; and Cardinal Lépicier, Protector of the English College, were present in person, as were nearly all the English Catholic bishops and all the British monsignori resident in Rome. Prince Chigi, the Grand Master of the Sovereign Order of Malta, Marchese Serafini, Governor of the Vatican City, and other Papal dignitaries were also present, while the guests included nearly all the Ambassadors and Ministers accredited to the Holy See.

18. One episode in connexion with the Jubilee, which gave very great pleasure, was the gracious presentation by The King to the Venerable English College, the oldest English establishment in the Eternal City, of a signed portrait of His Majesty, which, beautifully framed, now hangs in the principal reception room of the college between the portraits of Benedict XV and Pius XI.

19. The vexed question as to how the Pope should be honoured at Catholic banquets in England was tactfully settled during the year by the Pope himself, who had doubtless learned of the grave objections felt in England to the custom which had crept in of drinking the health of the Pope and The King together and in that order. Cardinal Pacelli had told Sir Charles Wingfield in December 1934, when he raised the question, that Cardinal Gasparri had said there was no need for the Pope's health to be drunk, but some doubt remained as to whether His Eminence had meant that in this case The King's health should also be omitted. The matter was cleared up on the 14th May, when His Holiness declared to the Archbishop of Westminster his desire that, for the future, the toast be replaced by a prayer which would be offered at the conclusion of the grace before meat. The toast of The King would then be drunk by itself at the usual time.

Archbishopric of Westminster.

20. As stated elsewhere in this report, Cardinal Bourne died on the 1st January. His Eminence had never completely recovered from the serious illness which struck him down on his last visit to Rome (December 1932), and although as a result of his enfeebled state of health his influence during the last two years of his life was not what it had been, his loss has been greatly felt and the gap left by his disappearance has not been completely filled.

21. Cardinal Bourne, though in virtue of his office only *primus inter pares* among the bishops of England, was regarded by his Catholic compatriots as their undisputed leader, while his many statesmanlike qualities, his tact and patriotism and unfailing common sense had won him the respect of his Protestant fellow-countrymen.

22. Francis Bourne was born in 1861 at Clapham, the son of a Post Office official (a convert to Catholicism) by an Irish mother. He spent the earlier part of his priestly career chiefly in teaching, and was for some years rector of the Southwark diocesan seminary at Wonersh. In 1895 he became coadjutor to the then Bishop of Southwark, whom he succeeded two years later. On the death of Cardinal Vaughan in 1903, Mgr. Bourne, somewhat to the general surprise, was appointed by Pius X to the See of Westminster. It would have been easy to find an archbishop with greater intellectual attainments or of superior social status (among the names mentioned at the time were those of Mgr. Merry del Val and Abbott Gasquet), but it would probably not have been possible to find anyone so discreet, so reliable and so essentially English, alike in his modesty, his pertinacity and his shrewdness. Even the external faults due to the somewhat narrow surroundings of his youth were corrected as a result of his increasing knowledge of men and affairs, and, as an old man, he possessed both charm and dignity.

23.   Archbishop Bourne had to wait eight years for his Red Hat, which was conferred in 1911.   As cardinal he assisted at the conclaves of 1914 and 1922. During the Great War he visited the front more than once, and did all in his power to provide for the spiritual needs of the Catholic soldiers.   During the general strike of 1926 his words were regarded by all sides as significant and important.   The cardinal always had a special regard for France, where he had undergone part of his priestly training, and in 1931 he was enabled by the Holy Father to make a kind of *amende honorable* for England's share in the burning of the Maid of Orleans by attending at Rouen, as Papal Legate, the fifth centenary of her death.   Though an adequate theologian and a competent speaker and preacher, Cardinal Bourne was no scholar, and his published works consist of little beyond a volume or two of sermons.

24.   On hearing the news of the cardinal's death, the Pope sent to the Vicar-General of Westminster a telegram of condolence, in which His Eminence was described as having been " a noble son and leader of the English nation."   The *Osservatore Romano* in its obituary notice stressed the fact that his last thought had been for the Holy Father, to whom he had sent his dying homage and a request for the Apostolic Benediction.   Special requiems for the cardinal were sung at S. Silvestro and in the Chapel of the English College, and the second of these ceremonies was attended by His Majesty's Minister.   Sir Charles Wingfield was also present at a " Month's Mind " requiem which was celebrated by Archbishop Hinsley and attended by a representative of the Vatican and by the French, Belgian and Polish Ambassadors to the Holy See.

25.   Great uncertainty was felt both in England and in Rome as to the succession to the Archbishopric of Westminster, as there seemed to be no obvious candidate for this very important post.   The general view taken was, however, that an English diocesan bishop, such as Mgr. Williams of Birmingham, would be appointed to the vacant see.   The name of Mgr. Arthur Hinsley, Canon of St. Peter's and former Apostolic Delegate for Missions in Africa, was scarcely mentioned; indeed, two other English prelates resident in Rome (both much younger men) were considered to have better prospects than he.   However, on the 25th March Mgr. Hinsley informed Sir Charles Wingfield of his appointment, which duly appeared in that evening's *Osservatore Romano*.   Three weeks later, having received the pallium from the Pope's own hands, an unusual favour, His Grace proceeded to London for his enthronement, returning a few days afterwards for the ceremonies in connexion with the canonisation of the 19th May.

26.   It appears that Archbishop Hinsley, who is not an ambitious man and feels the weight of his years, made a strenuous attempt to decline preferment.   His objections were, however, overruled by the Holy Father, who appears in his masterful fashion to have practically commanded acceptance. Mgr. Hinsley's name would not appear to have been proposed by the English bishops or to have been on the list which, in accordance with custom, was sent in by the Chapter of Westminster; it may thus be assumed that his appointment was due to the personal initiative of the Holy Father, who is said to have wanted someone who was at the same time as English and as " Roman " as possible.   The new archbishop appeared to fulfil both these qualifications, for he is of pure English birth and upbringing, and has spent a considerable part of his life in Rome, including thirteen years as rector of the English College.   Archbishop Hinsley has a special devotion to the Papacy and to the present Pope, with whose centralising tendencies, in matters purely spiritual, he is in sympathy, and there is reason to suppose that he would welcome the appointment of an Apostolic Delegate to England.

27.   Arthur Hinsley was born near Selby in 1865, the son of a village carpenter.   He was educated at Ushaw and at the English College in Rome, of which, after being a headmaster at St. Bede's School, Bradford, and parish priest of Sydenham, he in 1917 became rector.   In 1928 he became Apostolic Visitor to African Missions in British Territory, and in 1930 was made first Apostolic Delegate for Missions in Africa and titular Archbishop of Sardis.   He devoted himself to his arduous task with great energy and zeal, winning the golden opinions alike of the Holy See, of the British authorities and of the missionaries under his jurisdiction, and it was not until, in 1934, his health showed signs of giving way under the strain that he was recalled to Rome and made a Canon of

St. Peter's. His Grace was under the impression that his active career was finished, and little anticipated that within the year he would be appointed to one of the most important sees in the Catholic world.

28.   In July, in a footnote to an article which he wrote for the *Dublin Review*, the archbishop committed himself, on the authority of the late Cardinal Gasparri, to the false statement that Pope Benedict's peace note of August 1917 was never even acknowledged by His Majesty's Government. This statement having been brought to the attention of the Foreign Office, the latter pointed out to the archbishop that he had seriously misrepresented the action of His Majesty's Government, who, in accordance with the wishes of the Pope, had transmitted copies of the note to the heads of Allied States not represented at the Vatican, while Count de Salis had expressed to Benedict XV the King's appreciation of the lofty and benevolent intentions which had inspired the proposals and had assured His Holiness, on behalf of the Government, that they would be given "the closest and most serious attention." Archbishop Hinsley replied expressing regret that misapprehension should have been caused by his footnote, and expressed himself at a loss to understand how such an unfortunate misunderstanding could have arisen. He made ample amends by causing the letter to be published, together with his reply, in all the English Catholic papers and in the *Dublin Review*.

29.   In August, the Pope having sent to the archbishop a message which he wished delivered personally to The King and which seems to have had to do with the Italo-Abyssinian conflict, his Grace enquired through a Roman Catholic member of His Majesty's Household whether he could be received in audience. As His Majesty was on the point of leaving London, it would not have been possible to arrange an audience, and this was the reason given to Mgr. Hinsley for transmission to the Vatican. At the same time, Sir Charles Wingfield, who was in London, was instructed to explain to the archbishop that it would in any case have been difficult for The King to receive the archbishop for such a purpose in view of the importance which His Majesty's Government attach to the rule that all official communications from the Holy See must be conveyed through the diplomatic channel. Sir Charles Wingfield, while frankly explaining the position, emphasised the importance attached by His Majesty and his Government to good relations with the Vatican and their desire to avoid even the appearance of discourtesy to the archbishop or to the Pope. His Majesty's Chargé d'Affaires was instructed to speak on the same lines to the Cardinal Secretary of State, which he did on the 2nd August. His Eminence seemed to understand, when it was explained to him, how awkward a precedent might be established if His Majesty's Government once admitted the right of persons who, however eminent, were without diplomatic status to perform diplomatic functions, and expressed appreciation of the assurance given to him by Mr. Montgomery of the value attached by The King and Government to the friendly sentiments so often expressed in regard to them by the Sovereign Pontiff. The cardinal assured Mr. Montgomery a few days later that he had explained matters to the Holy Father, who had not seemed offended. No suggestion was made, however, of conveying the message through the diplomatic channel.

30.   On the 13th October the archbishop preached a sermon at Golders Green on the Italo-Abyssinian conflict which, as His Majesty's Chargé d'Affaires shortly afterwards learned, caused considerable annoyance in Vatican circles, both because of the manner in which his Grace referred to the Pope and because of his hostile references to fascism. "What," asked the archbishop, "can the Pope do to prevent this or any other war? He is a poor helpless old man with a small police force to guard himself, to guard the priceless treasures of the Vatican, and to protect the diminutive State which ensures his due independence in the exercise of his universal right and duty to teach and guide his followers of all races." Later on, he described the Fascist rule as in many respects unjust. "It is one example," he said, "of the present day deification of Cæsarism and of the tyranny which makes the individual a pawn on the chess-board of absolutism."

31.   Of the two statements just quoted it was probably the second which upset the Vatican most. For reasons connected with their panic fear of bolshevism the Vatican are at the moment anxious above all thing to see a strong and anti-masonic Government in Italy and they were doubtless afraid that the

Italian Government might think that Archbishop Hinsley, whose sermon was welcomed in anti-Fascist circles in France and elsewhere, had been approved beforehand by the Pope. The reference to His Holiness, who is certainly anything but weak, must also have caused much annoyance.

32. It is to be feared that Mgr. Hinsley's well-meant sermon had the effect of depriving him of the hat which might otherwise have been his at Christmas. In informing His Majesty's Chargé d'Affaires somewhat shamefacedly that among the twenty cardinals who were to be created in December there would be fourteen Italians, but not one Englishman, Mgr. Ottaviani went out of his way to state that no reflexion was intended on Great Britain or on her policy towards Italy by the omission from the list of Archbishop Hinsley, which was due merely to the fact that it was unusual to give the Sacred Purple to occupants of even the most important sees so soon after their appointment. This may, of course, be the true reason, but it is not a very convincing one, for, although Cardinal Bourne had to wait eight years for his hat, Cardinal Vaughan was given his at once, as were, *inter alios*, the present Primates of Ireland and Hungary, and it is difficult to believe that had Mgr. Hinsley been in November as high in the Pope's favour as he was in April, when he received the pallium from His Holiness, he would, despite the Bourne precedent, have been given his hat. *A propos* of Mgr. Hinsley's relations with Rome, Cardinal Caccia-Dominioni in a conversation with His Majesty's Chargé d'Affaires implied that the sermon had made a bad impression, but said he felt sure that Mgr. Hinsley had spoken with the intention of making it clear that English Roman Catholics were thoroughly English.

Army Bishop.

33. In April the newly appointed Archbishop of Westminster told a member of His Majesty's Legation that he was not satisfied with the arrangement reported in last year's report (paragraph 17) where one of the auxiliary bishops of the Westminster archdiocese had charge of Roman Catholic spiritual interests in the army. Mgr. Hinsley said that the present arrangement meant either that the auxiliary bishop did not devote enough time to the army or neglected his other duties.

34. A few days later, Mgr. Pizzardo informed the secretary to His Majesty's Legation that Mgr. James Dey, D.S.O., rector of Oscott College, Birmingham, had been appointed to succeed Mgr. Keatinge, who had died early in 1934, as *episcopus castrensis.*

35. On the 16th May the Vatican informed His Majesty's Legation officially of the appointment, and a few days later sent a further official communication to the effect that Mgr. Dey would have spiritual charge over the naval and air forces as well as over the army. This arrangement was in accordance with the wishes of the Archbishop of Westminster, who did not want to have the chaplains to any of His Majesty's forces under his control.

36. It is unfortunate, however, that more pains had not been taken to ascertain the wishes of all concerned for, while the new arrangement suited the War Office and no objection was raised to it by the Air Ministry, it soon transpired that the Admiralty did not at all welcome the idea. The latter pointed out that they would much prefer that the new arrangement should be one under which the Archbishop of Westminster would ordinarily delegate to Mgr. Dey the control of naval chaplains, but would himself be still in ultimate charge and would be available for advice on matters of importance. In such matters the Admiralty expressed the view that an *episcopus castrensis* would be unable to give such valuable help as the archbishop, and they mentioned occasions on which Cardinal Bourne had been able effectively to solve problems which would have exceeded the competence of a less influential ecclesiastic.

37. His Majesty's Chargé d'Affaires was instructed in August to place these considerations before the Cardinal Secretary of State and to beg that the arrangements made might be modified in the sense desired by the Admiralty. His Eminence said that he would do his best to secure that the wishes of His Majesty's Government should be met, and in October the Secretariat of State informed the Legation that the Holy See had taken into favourable consideration the desire expressed by the Admiralty that the traditional relations between that Department

and the Archbishopric of Westminister should remain unchanged. The Holy See had therefore laid down that Mgr. Dey, in his capacity as Ordinary to the Fleet, should act in conjunction ("d'accordo") with the Archbishop of Westminster and should be his representative.

38. This reply would appear to have been considered satisfactory.

Change of Ministers.

39. It was announced in July that His Majesty's Minister had been appointed to succeed Sir Claud Russell as His Majesty's Ambassador at Lisbon, and shortly afterwards the usual formalities as to an *agrément* having been gone through, Mr. Francis D'Arcy Osborne's appointment as successor to Sir Charles Wingfield was announced by the British press and the *Osservatore Romano.* When applying for the *agrément* for his successor, Sir Charles Wingfield had been instructed to explain to the officials of the Secretariat of State that, owing to the exigencies of His Majesty's service, Mr. Osborne might be unable to take up his new duties for some considerable time. It turned out, indeed, that his services could not be dispensed with at Washington, where he held the rank of Minister, until the New Year, and from the time of Sir Charles Wingfield's departure until the end of the year under review the post was left in charge of the first secretary to the Legation.

40. On the 20th July Sir Charles Wingfield left Rome for London, prior to proceeding to his new post. Both his Excellency and Lady Wingfield are much missed in Rome, where they have many friends. The Cardinal Secretary of State told Mr. Montgomery soon after Sir Charles's departure how much he had liked and esteemed his Excellency and how greatly he regretted the shortness of his time as Minister to the Holy See.

Disturbances at Belfast and Edinburgh.

41. The occurrence during the summer in Belfast, and also to some extent in Edinburgh, of violent clashes between Catholics and Protestants were believed at the Vatican to have been provoked by the latter. His Holiness made anxious reference to the July troubles at Belfast in the course of his farewell interview with Sir Charles Wingfield.

42. The far less serious disturbances at Edinburgh were much exaggerated abroad, and the *Osservatore Romano, à propos* of a Protestant demonstration held on the occasion of a Eucharistic Congress in the Scots capital, published on the 29th June a violent article of protest from the pen of its editor.

Dominion of Canada.

43. His Eminence Cardinal Villeneuve paid a fortnight's visit to Rome in November. On his arrival and departure he was greeted at the station by His Majesty's Chargé d'Affaires as well as by representatives of the French Embassy to the Holy See and by many Canadian and French ecclesiastics. As his Eminence had decided, in view of the shortness of his stay and the amount of business he had to transact, not to accept any invitations, Mr. Montgomery was unable to entertain the cardinal to luncheon as he had desired. His Eminence was good enough, however, to express his gratification at being invited, and did Mr. Montgomery the honour of returning his call in person.

44. In the course of conversation with Mr. Montgomery, Cardinal Villeneuve, who was extremely friendly, said how much he had appreciated the honour of being received by The King recently, as also the kindness which His Majesty had shown him. His Eminence said that the French Canadians constituted a real "forteresse" for the protection of British interests in North America. He laid stress on their conservatism, which, together with their catholicism, made them a formidable bulwark against communism and other subversive movements.

45. The cardinal also paid a tribute to the far-sighted wisdom and what he described as the "souplesse" of British rule. Such wisdom was only, he said, to be found in an old country, and the respect shown by Great Britain for foreign traditions and languages contrasted most favourably with the methods of a

" new " country like the United States of America, which, for the sake of
outward conformity, sacrificed the separate traditions of which she had not
learned to appreciate the value. It was thus natural that the French Canadians
should find English ideals more congenial than those of the United States. As
for France, although bound to her by ties of language and sentiment, there was
much in modern French life of which French Canadians heartily disapproved
and which made them realise how fortunate they were to be under British rule.

46.   During this summer the place of Mgr. Bastien, who had been for some
years rector of the Canadian College, was taken by Father Garrouteigt, a genial
and friendly ecclesiastic of French birth, who has lived many years in Canada.

Commonwealth of Australia.

47.   The Hon. Joseph Lyons, Prime Minister of Australia, and Mrs. Lyons,
who were passing through Rome, were received in private audience by the
Sovereign Pontiff on the 29th June. His Majesty's Minister was present, with
the Prime Minister and Mrs. Lyons, both at the audience and at an interview
which they subsequently had with the Cardinal Secretary of State. After some
conversation on personal matters, in the course of which Mr. Lyons explained
that he was the second Catholic to hold office as Prime Minister of Australia, he
went on to ask whether His Holiness would have any objection to his requesting
his opinion in regard to the question of trade barriers and the resulting
phenomenon of the malnutrition of masses of people at a time when the world
could supply a superabundance of suitable food.

48.   His Holiness said he thought it best that such questions should always
be formulated in memoranda, since the exact ideas of the enquirer could thus be
more clearly expressed, whilst there was also an opportunity for consideration
before a reply was given. In talking afterwards to Cardinal Pacelli, Mr. Lyons
explained that he hoped that His Holiness might eventually consider the issue of
some further pronouncement as a sequel to his encyclical *Quadragesimo Anno*, in
which attention would be drawn to the disastrous effects of trade barriers. In
Italy, England and other countries large numbers of people were suffering from
the effects of insufficient and unsuitable food, while there was actually over-
production in the world of all that they required. It was useless for any
politician to draw attention to this, as he would be said to have an axe to grind;
but if the Holy Father would speak to the world, those in power might grapple
with the evil. Cardinal Pacelli endorsed the Pope's suggestion that Mr. Lyons's
views should be submitted in the form of memoranda, adding that the problem
of want in the midst of plenty was admittedly a most pressing one, the difficulty
being to find a satisfactory solution.

49.   In August His Majesty's Chargé d'Affaires received from Mr. Lyons
a letter enclosing a memorandum on the subject of " Agriculture and Health "
for presentation to the Pope. In the course of a conversation with Cardinal
Pacelli, Mr. Montgomery handed his Eminence copies both of the memorandum
and of the covering letter, in which Mr. Lyons succinctly summarised his views
regarding the urgent need of securing greater social justice by using the huge
increase in world production which has made itself felt of late years to improve
the standard of living among the underfed millions in all parts of the globe. In
speaking to the cardinal, Mr. Montgomery drew special attention to the Prime
Minister's hope that the Holy See would add the weight of its authority to the
endeavours being made at Geneva and elsewhere to secure a more generous
distribution of the new-found plenty.

50.   Cardinal Pacelli assured the Chargé d'Affaires that the memorandum,
together with the contents of Mr. Lyons's letter, would be brought to the Holy
Father's attention, and on the 9th September his Eminence addressed a letter to
Mr. Montgomery saying that the Sovereign Pontiff had perused the memorandum
with interest and had declared to him (the cardinal) that he could not but share
the opinions of Mr. Lyons, the wisdom and aptness of which deserved his paternal
praises. The Holy Father had also expressed the hope—if only for the sake of
the people's health—that efficacious measures might be taken in order to solve, if
possible, the distressing crisis which troubles the world.

51. His Majesty's Chargé d'Affaires duly sent a copy and translation of his Eminence's letter to the Prime Minister. Since these events the Pope has not had occasion to make any public reference to the economic crisis from which the world is suffering, and it is thus too early to judge of the effect which Mr. Lyons's representations may have had upon His Holiness.

52. In October it was announced that Mgr. Bernardini, who had only been Apostolic Delegate for Australia and New Zealand for a little over two years, had been appointed Papal Nuncio at Berne. It appears that the Australian climate did not suit Mgr. Bernardini, who won golden opinions during his comparatively short sojourn, and to whose tact and amiability the Prime Minister of Australia paid tribute in his conversation with the Cardinal Secretary of State.

53. In November Mgr. Giovanni Panico, Uditore to the Nunciature at Prague, who had done well as Apostolic Visitor to the Saar at the time of the plebiscite, was appointed to succeed Mgr. Bernardini. A visa was duly obtained from His Majesty's Legation, who had time to consult the proper authorities before the appointment was announced.

Dominion of New Zealand.

54. On the death in January of Archbishop Redwood, His Majesty's Minister transmitted to the Cardinal Secretary of State for communication to the Pope the following message on behalf of the Governor-General of New Zealand :—

"Permit me to express to your Holiness the sorrow and sympathy of Christians of all denominations in New Zealand on the passing of their deeply revered fellow-countryman, Archbishop Redwood, the oldest and most senior bishop of your Church in the world. He was powerful in promoting righteousness in this dominion throughout the seventy years of his priesthood and sixty years of his episcopacy and his invaluable work will live after him in the lives of our New Zealand people."

55. On the 5th February His Majesty's Legation received and transmitted to Lord Bledisloe a letter from Cardinal Pacelli, conveying the Pope's thanks to his Excellency.

56. As stated under Section II, paragraph 52, Mgr. Bernardini, Apostolic Delegate to Australia and New Zealand, was transferred to Berne and Mgr. Panico appointed in his place.

Irish Free State.

57. In November the rector of the Irish College in Rome sent a letter to the *Irish Press* attacking the sanctions policy of the Irish Free State Government. The letter gave rise to considerable criticism among Mgr. Curran's clerical colleagues, chiefly because he rashly claimed to speak on behalf of all his fellow-countrymen in Rome, many of whom are entirely in sympathy with the League policy of the Free State Government. The *Irish Press* commenting on the letter, pointed out that, as a loyal member of the League of Nations, the Government had had no choice but to join with other members in their action against Italy.

India.

58. In April the Maharaja of Patiala, who was passing through Rome, was received in private audience by the Pope who conferred upon him the Order of St. Gregory the Great. It seems that the Archbishop of Simla had pressed for the bestowal of a Pontifical decoration upon the Maharaja, and as it transpired, after His Majesty's Legation had been consulted in the matter, that the Pope felt obliged to comply with the archbishop's wishes, His Majesty's Government decided, in spite of the fact that it is unusual for Indian princes to receive foreign orders, to waive all objections and to authorise His Majesty's Minister to be present at the audience.

59. Petitions and letters continued, as in previous years, to reach the Legation from Catholics of the Bombay Archdiocese, who expressed their dissatisfaction with the Portuguese archbishop and their desire to see him

replaced by an Englishman. In accordance with the procedure approved by the Foreign Office, these petitions are now returned to the senders with the suggestion that, if they wish the matter taken up officially, they should address themselves in the first place to the Government of Bombay who will inform His Majesty's Government in the United Kingdom. The fact that many of the signatories of these documents have Portuguese names, and that so many such letters are written to the Legation, to the Congregation de Propaganda Fide, and to other authorities seems difficult to reconcile with the opinion of the Portuguese Minister to the Holy See, who alleges that the archbishop is supported and loved by his flock, and that the Portuguese "Padroado," wherever found, is and has been an unmixed blessing.

60.   Towards the end of 1934 His Majesty's Government in the United Kingdom learned with some concern from the Government of India that a scheme was on foot, originating from Rome, to split the Bombay Archdiocese (the only one in India which has the legal right, alternatively, to a British head) for all practical purposes into three parts, the far-flung missions of Ahmedabad and Karachi being detached from the archbishop's jurisdiction and placed under vicars-general to be appointed by the Holy See with practically independent powers.

61.   In view of the fact that any such arrangement appeared to be contrary to the provisions of the Padroado Agreement of 1928 between the Holy See and Portugal, His Majesty's Minister was instructed in January to make enquiries as to the nature of the reported changes and the extent to which they would affect the control of the Archbishop of Bombay over the whole of his diocese. In making these enquiries Sir Charles Wingfield explained that His Majesty's Government had no desire, as the Holy See were aware, to interfere with internal Church matters, their only concern being with the agreement of 1928, with which they had been closely connected and which they had hoped would settle once and for all the differences of opinion that had arisen with regard to the Bombay Archbishopric and Portuguese claims. Now, however, it seemed that new arrangements were being made which were calculated to change the whole situation. Cardinal Pacelli did not appear to be well-informed about the question, which had also, he said, been raised by the Portuguese Minister, but he promised to obtain further particulars from the Congregation de Propaganda Fide.

62.   Sir Charles Wingfield had himself seen the Portuguese Minister before his interview with the cardinal, and Sr. d'Oliveira, after confirming the report received by His Majesty's Government in the United Kingdom to the effect that about two-thirds of the archdiocese was to be placed under the effective control of vicars-general, went on to say that he suspected the whole business to have originated in the jealousy doubtless felt by the Spanish Jesuits of Ahmedabad for the Portuguese Jesuit (Mgr. Lima) who occupied the Archiepiscopal See. Sr. d'Oliveira thought that the Spaniards had prevailed upon Cardinal Fumasoni Biondi, the Prefect of Propaganda, who is a weak man, to consent both to their own desires and to those of the Dutch Franciscans in regard to the Karachi Mission. Sr. d'Oliveira thought that the Congregation de Propaganda Fide had probably made the new arrangement without consulting the Secretariat of State. He said that Mgr. Pizzardo had admitted to him that it was clean contrary to the agreement of 1928 but had said it would be difficult to reverse the decision once taken, as the Congregation could not be humiliated by its prompt cancellation.

63.   At the end of March His Majesty's Minister received from the Secretariat of State a memorandum in reply to his enquiries respecting the changes in the Archdiocese of Bombay. The Secretariat of State abstained from offering any observations with regard to this document which appeared both to Sir Charles Wingfield and to his Portuguese colleague, whom he consulted without delay, to be exceedingly disingenuous.

64.   It began by stating that, with a view to providing for the evangelisation of the huge Archdiocese of Bombay, the Congregation de Propaganda Fide had decided, after long consideration, that it was necessary to set apart the districts of Karachi and Ahmedabad and entrust them to the care of the Dutch

Franciscans and the Aragonese Jesuits respectively, two religious of the said congregation being set over the two regions as vicars-general with all the necessary faculties. The memorandum went on to state that this decision had been communicated to Archbishop Lima at the beginning of December 1933, but that as his Grace "did not appear to grasp the usefulness of these provisions" the Congregation (in order to provide, as was its duty, for "the welfare of souls") had decided itself to appoint the vicars-general and to communicate their names to the archbishop, giving him two letters conferring faculties to hand to them. It was thus made clear that the faculties, and, for all practical purposes, the nominations also, should enter into effect from the moment at which the Archbishop of Bombay had made formal notifications thereof to the parties concerned. It was accordingly obvious, continued the memorandum, that the Congregation de Propaganda Fide had not the slightest intention of altering the juridical status of the Archdiocese of Bombay and that the Archbishop of Bombay still remained the archbishop of the whole archdiocese. "None other than he had, indeed, the right of setting up his pontifical throne in the two districts concerned," concluded the memorandum, "and it is from him that the faculties of the heads of districts proceed."

65. This memorandum could not be regarded as in any sense satisfactory; what was worse, it was disingenuous. However, this was nothing new, for, as Sr. d'Oliveira pointed out, all the steps taken during centuries by the Holy See to diminish the rights formally secured to Portugal had always been justified on the ground that they were for the "good of souls." In any case, the pretence that the new arrangement is not contrary to articles 2 and 3 of the 1928 agreement is quite untenable. Article 2 laid down that the Archdiocese of Bombay would "maintain its present ecclesiastical organisation," while article 3 stipulated that the archbishop would "have jurisdiction over the entire territory of the archdiocese"; yet the Congregation had now removed from Mgr. Lima's control two huge zones, one including Sind and Baluchistan and the other Gujerat, Cutch and Kathiawar. The archbishop, as the Portuguese Minister justly remarked, would henceforth, in so far as these two districts were concerned, act merely as a post office for the transmission of the orders of Propaganda to persons who would be entirely independent of him; and the statement that he would retain the right of setting up "a pontifical throne" would be really comic, were it not that this represented all that would remain of his rights in these large fractions of his archdiocese.

66. The Portuguese Minister told His Majesty's Minister a few days after the receipt of this memorandum that he had frankly informed Mgr. Pizzardo of his disappointment, adding that no amount of dialectical skill would conceal the fact that the rights promised to Portugal had been diminished without previous consultation. He said that the Portuguese Government would expect the Secretariat of State to find some means of righting the manifest wrong done to Portugal by propaganda. Sir Charles Wingfield obtained the impression that Sr. d'Oliveira, while anticipating long delays before any settlement could be found, contemplated the possibility of eventually arriving at some arrangement under which the archbishop would himself nominate two vicars-general, who would be his subordinates in fact and would only have such powers as he should choose to delegate to them. It is to be hoped, at any rate, that the arrangement come to will not in any way diminish the reversionary rights of the British subject who is to succeed the present Portugues archbishop.

67. His Majesty's Principal Secretary of State, replying on the 10th May to the despatch transmitting the Vatican memorandum, said it was clear that, under the new arrangements effective control of Gujerat and Sind (with Baluchistan) would, in fact, pass from the Archbishopric of Bombay, and that the Prelate's position in relation to those areas would be confined to a primacy of honour and to the issue of faculties to ecclesiastical superiors, who, in practice would be entirely independent of him. The Secretary of State added that the Government of India would not wish to press the matter further if they could feel certain that the present arrangements had been dictated by doubts as to the capacity of the present incumbent, and that matters would later revert to the normal. Sir Charles Wingfield was instructed, therefore, to mention the subject again to Cardinal Pacelli in order to ascertain more precisely what were the

intentions of the Vatican in this matter. He was to indicate that an arrangement under which the effective control of the two important provinces in question was removed from the Archbishop of Bombay, who was left in a merely titular position in regard to them, would be one which His Majesty's Government could not regard with indifference, closely associated as they were with the arrangements laid down in the Padroado agreement and adverse to any changes that would result in a diminution of the authority of the one archbishop in India, who, by international agreement, is alternately, a British subject.

68. After consultation with the Portuguese Minister, who begged him not to suggest that Mgr. Lima was incompetent lest he should be made to resign by the Holy See, Sir Charles Wingfield carried out the above instructions in an interview with the Cardinal Secretary of State on the 10th May, and asked his Eminence to try and persuade Propaganda to restore the archbishop's effective control over the whole diocese. Cardinal Pacelli promised to enquire into the matter and let Sir Charles Wingfield know what could be done. By the end of the year, however, His Majesty's Legation had heard nothing more on the subject from Cardinal Pacelli.

69. Before leaving Rome in July His Majesty's Minister did, however, have some conversation on the subject of the Padroado with Cardinal Fumasoni Biondi, the Prefect of Propaganda. His Eminence said that the " Padroado " had arisen at a time when Portugal exercised civil power in all parts of Asia, so that she was able to afford protection to the Church in return for the rights conceded. Now, however, power had passed from the Portuguese to the British, and the Portuguese could not even find men capable of filling the few posts they still had a claim to. The present Archbishop of Bombay, regarding whose complete sanity his Eminence clearly had doubts, could not even speak English properly and was therefore quite unable to deal with the local officials or with most Christians in his diocese. His appointments were not satisfactory, and it had therefore been necessary to recomend to him persons capable of dealing with the huge districts outside Bombay and its neighbourhood, where there were but few Christians. Nearly all the Christian community was concentrated in the part left under the archbishop's direct control, so that his complaint that his rights were being reduced was without real substance, since he had in any case no power over the non-Christian inhabitants of these outlying districts which would, moreover, remain nominally under his jurisdiction. Sir Charles Wingfield said that it was difficult for him to discuss the capacities of the Portuguese archbishop with his Eminence. He trusted, however, that some " combinazione" would be found permitting the next archbishop, who would be British, to enjoy full jurisdiction over all the archdiocese. The cardinal only observed that perhaps, if the present archbishop were removed and thus did not remain in office for a normal term, His Majesty's Government in the United Kingdom might agree to another Portuguese taking his place. This idea Sir Charles Wingfield did not, however, encourage.

70. In December the Portuguese Minister told His Majesty's Chargé d'Affaires that the Vatican had in the course of the summer made one small concession (which had not come to the knowledge of the Legation). It seems that the Superior appointed by Propaganda to take charge of the Karachi district after all never proceeded to his post, but was replaced by another ecclesiastic. The latter was appointed last summer, and Sr. d'Oliveira said that the archbishop had himself received orders to nominate him and transmit the faculties to him, instead of being simply ordered, as had happened before, to send on official papers and faculties issued in the name of Propaganda. What was more, the new superior only had the title of " pro-superior " instead of " vicar-general " or " superior."

71. The Portuguese Minister did not attach much importance to these concessions as, in spite of them, all control over the districts of Karachi and Ahmedabad was still denied to the archbishop. He was afraid to press his objections, however, lest Propaganda should remove the archbishop on grounds of incompetence, a remedy which, from the Portuguese point-of-view, would be worse than the disease.

72. It may be pointed out that, *pace* Cardinal Fumasoni Biondi, the archbishop's complaint of reduction of rights is perfectly well-founded, for not only

do the churches and schools in the outlying districts, of which there are quite a considerable number, pass out of his effective jurisdiction, but also he loses the right to supervise methods for the conversion of non-Christians in districts which may at present be almost without the Catholic faith, but need not necessarily remain so.

Malta.

Teaching Orders in Malta.

73.   Mention was made in last year's report of the desirability of increasing the number of Englishmen in Malta and also of the difficulty of attaining this end, owing both to the shortage of suitable British religious and to the reluctance of the Roman Curia to remove any of the Italian priests who are already there. Events in the year under review have not been such as to lighten the problem. However, the opportunity was taken in January by Sir Charles Wingfield of mentioning to the Abbot Primate of the Benedictine Order, Father von Stotzingen, who was about to visit Malta, the desire of His Majesty's Government in the United Kingdom that British Benedictines should, if possible, be sent to Malta to teach.   The suggestions were well received by the Abbot, who is of German nationality, and, during a conversation which he had while in Malta with Sir Harry Luke, he promised to discuss the matter with the English Provincial of the Order.   Nothing has, however, as yet come of this move.

74.   Towards the end of the year it was brought to the knowledge of His Majesty's Legation that the arrangement whereby the Maltese province of the Dominican Order is placed under the jurisdiction of the Italian assistant is unpopular with certain of the Maltese Dominicans, who would much prefer to be under the English assistant.   His Majesty's Government are considering whether any steps could usefully be taken to persuade the Master-General of the Order to consent to a change of the kind contemplated, which would seem, if practicable, to be in the British interest.

Cardinal Lépicier's Mission.

75.   In May it was announced that His Holiness had appointed Cardinal Lépicier to be Pontifical Legate at the Maltese Provincial Council to be held in June.   Cardinal Lépicier, who is a member of the Servite Order and the only French cardinal in Rome, has spent much of his life in Great Britain, speaks English well, and is the Protector of two out of the three British colleges in Rome, for which reason, no doubt, he was selected for this mission, Mgr. Godfrey, rector of the English college, being appointed as one of his suite.   On the 23rd May the latter came to His Majesty's Legation and stated that his Eminence, who was due in Malta on the 8th June, would be very grateful if His Majesty's Government would place a British ship at the disposal of the party, which would otherwise have to make the sea voyage in an Italian vessel.   The Vatican, Mgr. Godfrey added, did not like to put forward the request officially, but would highly appreciate the offer of a ship.   Sir Charles Wingfield, while warning the rector that it might not be possible, especially at such short notice, to entertain the suggestion, consented to telegraph to the Governor of Malta, who replied on the 25th May that the Naval Commander-in-chief would be happy to send a destroyer to Syracuse to bring the cardinal to Malta.

76.   His Eminence, who did not feel able, in view of his age and delicate health, to face the additional train journey, but attached great importance to being conveyed in a British vessel, thereupon enquired if a ship could not be sent to Naples for him.   Sir Charles Wingfield having represented the cardinal's views to the Governor of Malta, the Admiralty thereupon authorised the Commander-in-chief's yacht, H.M.S. *Bryony*, to proceed to Naples and embark his Eminence.   The Governor pointed out that there would only be room for four persons on board as well as his Eminence, explaining that, owing to the departure of the fleet for the Silver Jubilee Review on the 11th June, it was impossible to place a larger ship at the cardinal's disposal.   His Majesty's Minister having conveyed this offer to Cardinal Lépicier, the latter replied in a brief note that, as the mission which consisted of nine persons would naturally have to travel together, other arrangements had been made for the journey.   The idea of sending H.M.S. *Bryony* to Naples was accordingly abandoned, and the cardinal made the

voyage both ways on board the Italian steamship *Firenze*. His Majesty's Minister, when expressing at the Vatican his surprise at the curtness of Cardinal Lépicier's note, pointed out to the Cardinal Secretary of State that even if Cardinal Lépicier did not wish to accept the Admiralty's offer, the latter had done their best to meet wishes which had been communicated to His Majesty's Legation unofficially and very late in the day. Mgr. Pizzardo said that the Vatican appreciated the difficulties and regretted that the Admiralty's offer, for which they were grateful, could not be accepted.

77. Unfortunately the question of transport was not the only source of embarrassment to His Majesty's Government in connexion with Cardinal Lépicier's mission. It had come to the knowledge of the Vatican that the Legate would not be received with a naval salute on his arrival at Malta, nor met on his arrival by the Acting Governor, on whom he would be expected to pay the first call. On the 30th May, referring to these facts, the Under-Secretary of State at the Vatican asked His Majesty's Minister to point out to the competent British authority that either the cardinal must be received with the honours due to a personal representative of the Pope or else must refrain from all official inter-course with the authorities, as had been done by Cardinal MacRory on the occasion of his visit as Legate to Melbourne in 1934. As an example of the honours which the Vatican consider to be due to a Papal Legate, Mgr. Pizzardo instanced the facts that Cardinal Pacelli, when he went to Lourdes in April (see section III, paragraph 104, of this report), was welcomed at the frontier by a Cabinet Minister, while, when Cardinal Lépicier himself went to Tunis in 1930, as Legate to the Carthage Eucharistic Congress, he was received by the Resident and given a naval salute. As an argument against following the Melbourne precedent the Under-Secretary of State pointed out that, unlike Australia, Malta was a 100 per cent. Catholic country where the Church was established by law, and the bishop took precedence after the Governor. It seemed, indeed, rather a case for following the French precedents, and he feared that, if the Papal Legate were obliged to abstain from official visits, a bad impression would undoubtedly be created on the island. This would be a pity, as the political atmosphere had improved of late; the clergy had joined whole-heartedly in the Jubilee festivities; and the religious differences of the past were being forgotten.

78. His Majesty's Minister having referred these representations to London, His Majesty's Principal Secretary of State for Foreign Affairs replied on the 3rd June to the following effect : It would not be possible for the Acting Governor to meet the cardinal in person, as the representative of the King is debarred by precedent from paying this honour to any one below the rank of a head of State. The cardinal would, however, be received by a high officer representing the Governor (a guard of honour was also provided). As for the naval salute, this was also impossible as, according to recent naval regulations, of which the Vatican had expressed appreciation, these were to be given only to representatives of the Pope possessing diplomatic status. In view of the fact that His Majesty's Government desired to do the Legate all the honour possible, it had been arranged that he should be met and escorted into port by two destroyers. Sir Charles Wingfield was instructed, in conveying the above information, to state that His Majesty's Government deplored the threat to refrain from official intercourse with the authorities, and would think it a matter for deep regret if the Legate failed to call upon The King's representative and to accept the latter's hospitality. The Minister was instructed to emphasise the desire of His Majesty's Govern-ment that the Legate should be received with every possible honour, while, at the same time pointing out that, with the best will in the world, they could not comply with requests which were either materially impossible or contrary to established precedent.

79. His Majesty's Minister on the 4th June explained the British point of view to the Cardinal Secretary of State in the light of the above instructions. His Eminence, after explaining that, from the standpoint of the Vatican, any cardinal, and still more a cardinal legate, had more than diplomatic status, agreed that in this case the omission of the salute and the absence of the Acting Governor from the pier could be overlooked; it would, however, be entirely out of the question for the cardinal to call first on the Acting Governor and, unless some way out of this difficulty could be found, the two would not be able to meet.

The following day, through the Under-Secretary of State, his Eminence suggested to Sir Charles Wingfield that the following arrangements might be made to solve the problem :—

(i) The cardinal will, as suggested, be received on landing by some high official representing the Governor.

(ii) After arriving at his residence, his Eminence will send a prelate of his suite to call on and thank the Acting Governor.

(iii) The cardinal and Acting Governor will subsequently meet as guests at some reception given in honour of the cardinal.

(iv) His Eminence will then be prepared to accept the hospitality of the Acting Governor.

These arrangements were accepted by the British authorities and duly carried out during the cardinal's visit to Malta.

80. His Eminence, who, before his departure, had, doubtless as the result of promptings from the Secretariat of State, atoned for his previous curt note by a friendly letter to Sir Charles Wingfield thanking for the offer of H.M.S. *Bryony*, left Rome on the 7th June in high good humour. The steamship *Firenze*, flying the papal flag at the foremast, arrived at Malta on the 8th and was met outside the port by two destroyers, which escorted her in as arranged. As the ship entered the harbour, which was gaily decorated with flags, a great shout of welcome went up from every side, and the Acting Governor's representatives came on board with the ecclesiastical and civic dignitaries to welcome his Eminence. The guard of honour drawn up on the quay was composed entirely of Catholic soldiers, and after inspecting and blessing the men his Eminence entered his car and surrounded by a mounted escort proceeded to the cathedral through decorated streets crowded with people. After the inaugural service at which the papal brief was read, Mgr. Godfrey paid an official call on the Deputy-Governor. The enthusiasm which had been shown in the Cardinal Legate's arrival, was maintained throughout his fortnight's stay, which passed off without friction and according to plan. The cardinal himself seemed delighted with the reception which was given to him, not only by the Maltese people, whose attachment to the Catholic faith and devotion to the Holy See he afterwards extolled in no measured terms, but also by the Government. He much appreciated the destroyer escort, the guard of honour, the mounted police and the other attentions shown to him, and when he met the Acting Governor on neutral ground on the day following his arrival, his manner to him was cordial in the extreme. Everything went according to plan except that his Eminence was prevented by a sudden indisposition from attending either the luncheon given in his honour at the palace, or a function at the cathedral, which had been arranged for the 17th June. On the following day he called personally on Sir Harry Luke and, in cordial and explicit terms, thanked him for the arrangements made by the Government for his visit, which had, he said, given him great satisfaction and would form the subject of an early report to the Vatican on his return to Rome. His Eminence, who left Malta on the 22nd June, arriving on the 24th in the Eternal City, spoke in similar terms to Sir Charles Wingfield, who met him at the station and to whom he expressed his satisfaction at having been received with so much honour. The reports of the *Osservatore Romano* on the mission were entirely satisfactory and contained no allusion to any supposed slights or omissions on the part of the Government. Acting on instructions from London, His Majesty's Chargé d'Affaires on the 2nd August expressed to Cardinal Pacelli the thanks of His Majesty's Government in the United Kingdom for the steps taken by his Eminence and by the members of Cardinal Lépicier's mission to ensure that the visit to Malta should pass off without friction. His Eminence, who seemed pleased, said that the Holy See attached particular importance to the existing good relations with Great Britain and that he was glad to be able to contribute in any way to their maintenance.

81. It has seemed best to report the incidents connected with Cardinal Lépicier's mission in some detail, as the decisions reached in the matter may provide a useful precedent for similar complications at some future date.

University Theological Faculty.

82. As stated in last year's report, proposals, made by the Vatican for the reform of the theological faculty of Malta University, were forwarded by His

Majesty's Legation to the Foreign Office in December (1934). Among these were included proposals that the Bishop of Malta should be Grand Chancellor of the University, that he should confer the canonical licence upon professors after having obtained the *nulla osta* from the Holy See, and that he should withdraw such licences in case of necessity. Other proposed reforms included :—

(*a*) An increase in the quota of professors, who must number at least eight.

(*b*) The provision of students with testimonial letters from their ordinary.

(*c*) The institution of the licentiate and the conferment of all degrees in the name of the Sovereign Pontiff.

(*d*) Practical recognition of the necessity for students to take a whole-time two years' course in scholastic philosophy.

(*e*) A change in the present arrangements for the baccalaureate in Canon Law.

83. As the result of exchanges of views between His Majesty's Government and the Vatican, which continued at intervals throughout the year, through the intermediary of His Majesty's Legation, a certain amount of progress was made and it seems probable that agreement will eventually be reached. In the counter-proposals of the Government of Malta, as endorsed by His Majesty's Government in the United Kingdom, it was made clear that the proposal that the bishop should be Grand Chancellor of the Faculty was unwelcome as being incompatible with the character of the university as a Government Department. The Vatican did not return to this point, which it seems that they will not press. On the other hand, His Majesty's Government in the United Kingdom agreed that there would be no objection to the bishop's conferring and withdrawing the canonical licence, provided that he did so on strictly canonical grounds. To this condition the Vatican consented.

84. As regards the desired increase in the number of professors, His Majesty's Government promised to make every effort to meet the wishes of the Holy See, and stated that in their view this matter, as well as that of the baccalaureate of Canon Law, was mainly financial and could better be examined after an agreement in principle had been reached. The Vatican would not seem, however, to share this view, for in a memorandum drawn up by the Congregation of Seminaries in September they reiterated the necessity of at least eight professors and insisted that, if the baccalaureate of Canon Law was to be retained, a special course of juridical and canonical studies would have to be initiated, which would alone require the services of three professors.

85. As regards the proposed arrangements for the licentiate, the provision of students with testimonial letters, and certain other minor proposals, including an increased use of Latin and the making of a profession of faith by the dean, His Majesty's Government fell in with the suggestions of the Vatican.

86. Apart from the question of the number of courses of study and of professors, which the Government of Malta have not yet begun to consider in detail, but which should not prove impossible of solution, the only point likely to prove at all difficult would seem to be that of the conferment of academic degrees, in regard to which a formula acceptable to both parties has yet to be found, the Holy See claiming that Roman Catholic theological degrees can, by their nature, never be conferred by the civil power except on delegated authority, while His Majesty's Government find it hard to admit that the Sovereign Pontiff can in any circumstances actually confer degrees gained in the State university of a British possession. It is to be hoped, however, that some compromise formula may be discovered.

87. A point conceded by the Holy See to His Majesty's Government is that the Theological Faculty shall be recognised as a " Pontifical Athenæum."

General.

88. In February the Rome correspondent of the Milan *Resto del Carlino* sent his paper a tendencious communiqué regarding the alleged desire of His Majesty's Government to conclude a concordat with the Vatican in respect of Malta. The correspondent suggested that the rumour, which was not confirmed in Vatican circles, originated with those persons who wished that the Italian language should be displaced in the ecclesiastical courts and in religious houses as it had

been in the law courts. He hinted that it was all part of a deep-laid plot to protestantise Malta, but expressed the view that the Vatican would be too prudent ever to lend itself to such schemes.

89. On the 17th October the Assistant Under-Secretary of State at the Vatican asked His Majesty's Chargé d'Affaires to ascertain whether there was any truth in the rumours which had been appearing in the Italian press to the effect that Father Carta, superior of the Conventual Friars Minor, had been arrested (presumably on account of anti-British activities). His Majesty's Chargé d'Affaires, on telegraphing to the Governor of Malta, was assured that there was no word of truth in the report, and that the arrest of the priest in question had never even been considered.

90. Speaking of certain deportations of undesirables from Malta, in the early autumn, the Bishop of Malta, who was in Rome in November, told His Majesty's Chargé d'Affaires that these had given rise to some criticism owing chiefly to the fact that of the persons deported several were well-known on the island. His Grace added that he felt no doubt that the Government of Malta had had very good grounds for their action.

Mandated Territory: Palestine.

91. In May His Majesty's Legation received from the Secretariat of State a memorandum concerning the threat to the safety of the hospital of St. Louis at Jerusalem, which was alleged to be caused by certain public works being carried out by the municipal council near the hospital. His Majesty's Government in the United Kingdom were also approached in this matter by the French Government. As a result of enquiries from the High Commissioner, it transpired that, while the works in question had involved exposing in part the foundations of the building, measures had been taken to secure the stability of the structure. The hospital authorities not being prepared, however, to admit the adequacy of these measures, it was decided by the municipal council that the question of the damage, if any, sustained by the building and of the possible compensation to be paid in consequence should be submitted to a mixed arbitration board. In communicating this information to the Secretariat of State in July, His Majesty's Chargé d'Affaires was instructed to express the hope that the decision to submit the whole matter to arbitration would result in the discovery of a solution satisfactory to all concerned.

92. In January a protest against the behaviour of the Latins in connexion with the annual cleaning of the Church of the Nativity at Bethlehem was lodged by the *locum tenens* of the Orthodox Patriarchate with the High Commissioner for Palestine. It appears that, in spite of the proposed compromise whereby the outside of the northern windows should be cleaned by the Government, the Franciscans profited by the accessibility of these windows to their premises to clean them ostentatiously before the official cleaning began and again after it was finished. No actual breach of the peace or of decorum occurred on this occasion (the 28th December, 1934). As a result of enquiries, the High Commissioner decided, with the approval of the competent department of His Majesty's Government, that in view of the doubt existing as to the *status quo* in regard to the northern windows, of the fact that the windows are in any case surreptitiously cleaned by the Latins, and of the impossibility of enforcing a decision in favour of cleaning by Government without a serious dispute with the Latins, it would be best for the British authorities to refrain from any interference in connexion with the cleaning of these windows. The established custom whereby necessary repairs to the northern windows are done by Government has, however, been maintained, and a broken window over the north transept was repaired in the autumn by and at the expense of the Government, the Custos of the Holy Land having given to the representatives of the Office of Works the necessary permit enabling them to have access via the Latin convent to the aisle roof. As for the annual cleaning, it has been arranged, to prevent disorder for the future, that both a British and Palestinian district commissioner shall be present henceforth.

93. At the end of 1932 it had been decided by the Governor of Palestine, with the concurrence of the Latin, Orthodox and Armenian Patriarchates of

Jerusalem, that complete structural surveys of the Churches of the Holy Sepulchre and of the Nativity should be carried out by the architect, Mr. William Harvey. The surveys having now been completed, Mr. Harvey has issued his reports in the form of two bound and illustrated volumes, of which copies were given in December by His Majesty's Government to the Pope. The reports indicate that extensive work, involving considerable expenditure, is required to secure the safety of both buildings. The condition of the Church of the Holy Sepulchre is particularly grave, and emergency measures have had to be taken to secure the building from collapse, pending the execution of permanent works of consolidation. The architect's recommendations are being considered by the Government in consultation with the representatives of the Latin Patriarchate and of the other two Patriarchates concerned.

III.—RELATIONS WITH OTHER COUNTRIES.

Baltic States.

94. Mgr. Zecchini, the Nuncio to Latvia, having died in the course of the summer, it was announced in August that Mgr. Arata, the Chargé d'Affaires of the Holy See to Lithuania and Estonia, had been appointed Nuncio to Latvia and Estonia, with residence at Riga. The Lithuanian Chargé d'Affaires informed His Majesty's Chargé d'Affaires that this new arrangement would not affect the status of Mgr. Arata in Lithuania, where, in spite of his high status in the other two republics, he would remain plain Chargé d'Affaires. This state of things, which is somewhat incongruous in view of the fact that Lithuania is the only one of the three countries that has a Catholic population, is of course due to the fact that, until the disagreements between the Holy See and Lithuania, which led to the withdrawal of the Nuncio, have been settled, the Vatican does not wish to re-establish full diplomatic relations with Kovno. Negotiations are, however, in progress with a view to a settlement.

Belgium.

95. The tragic death of the Queen of the Belgians on the 29th August caused a most painful impression at the Vatican, and the Pope addressed to King Leopold at Lucerne an affectionately worded telegram, assuring him of his sympathy and of his prayers for "the pious Queen who has entered into the eternal kingdom of the righteous." His Holiness ordered a special Mass of Requiem to be said for the late Queen at the Church of St. Martha in the Vatican City. The Diplomatic Corps were present at this mass, and the Cardinal Secretary of State himself gave the absolutions.

96. In October M. van Ypersele de Strihou was succeeded as Ambassador by Baron de Borchgrave. When the latter presented his credentials early in November, Pius XI asked him to convey to the King of the Belgians renewed assurances of his sympathy and a special blessing.

Colombia.

97. In November the draft project for a new Constitution was published, in which, while the Catholic Church is recognised as that of the vast majority of the population, the separation of Church and State is clearly insisted upon, and the point of view of the former is not accepted in matters relating to education and marriage laws. The draft project has evidently been drawn up with the purpose of giving effect to a policy which, while liberal, is not in any way anti-clerical. In this it corresponds to the policy inaugurated by Dr. Olaya Herrera, who in December took up his position as Colombian Ambassador to the Holy See. At least several months will elapse before the Bill can emerge from the Legislature in its final form.

Czechoslovakia.

98. The progress made with the negotiations for a *modus vivendi*, the success of the Eucharistic Congress held at Prague at the end of June, the appointment, after a long interval, of a Nuncio to succeed Mgr. Ciriaci, and, finally, the elevation to the purple in December of the Archbishop of Prague (Mgr. Kaspar), were so many milestones on the road towards better relations between the Czechoslovak Republic and the Holy See.

99. The Eucharistic Congress, to which crowds flocked from every part of Czechoslovakia, was attended by Cardinal Verdier (Archbishop of Paris), who had been appointed Papal legate for the occasion, as well as by the Cardinal Archbishops of Vienna and Posen. The principal functions, ecclesiastical and lay, were attended by Dr. Benes and other members of the Government.

100. The appointment of Mgr. Ritter to the post of Apostolic Nuncio, which had been vacant for a year and a half, was announced in August. His appointment was well received, as he was credited with having done much to smooth relations between the Vatican and the Czechoslovak State during the period 1927–30, when he had served as " Uditore " at the Prague Nunciature. Despite his name, the new Nuncio, who has been known to the Pope since the days of his youth, is an Italian from **Lombardy.**

101. Mgr. Ritter took with him to Prague in October a Bull which alters the boundaries of ecclesiastical provinces and dioceses so as to conform with political frontiers. As a result of this arrangement, the Czechoslovak portion of the Archdiocese of Esztergom, which, since the war, has been administered by the Bishop of Nyitra, will become part of the latter's diocese, while the Dioceses of Rozsnyo and Kassa, losing each a southern strip, will become purely Czechoslovak units. The remnants left to Hungary of the two last-named dioceses will then be joined on to the remnant of Esztergom, and the unit formed thereby—a long strip stretching across the north of Hungary—will be ruled by the Cardinal Prince Primate of Hungary (the Archbishop of Esztergom).

102. The Hungarian Chargé d'Affaires told Mr. Montgomery in August that the above arrangements, which are in accordance with the expressed wishes of the Czechoslovak Government, were accepted by the Holy See in return for concessions made during the summer by Prague in the matter of the Esztergom estates, which have again been put under ecclesiastical control, thereby making the 1928 *modus vivendi* for the first time truly operative. As a *quid pro quo* for these concessions the Cardinal Prince Primate was advised by the Vatican to withdraw the complaint lodged by his predecessor with The Hague Court regarding the confiscation of his archiepiscopal estates.

103. The appointment of Archbishop Kaspar to be cardinal in December caused much pleasure in Czechoslovakia, both on account of the honour done to Czechoslovakia and also because the unaffected simplicity and quiet dignity of the archbishop have made his Eminence deservedly popular among his countrymen.

France.

104. The Vatican is at present on better terms with secularist France than with any other Great Power, except perhaps Fascist Italy. The Vatican's approval of France, due in part to the peace-making trend of French policy in 1934 and to the rapprochement between France and Italy, as well as to discontent with the German Government, was increased by the visit of M. Laval to the Pope in January and by the official welcome accorded to Cardinal Pacelli when he visited Lourdes in April.

105. Tangible expression was given to the friendly feelings existing on both sides by a generous bestowal of decorations. Thus,. in March, the Legion of Honour was conferred on Mgr. Pizzardo and two other high Vatican officials, while in July President Lebrun received from the Pope the Supreme Order of Christ, while the French Ambassador to the Holy See was given the Order of Pius IX. In the autumn relations grew yet friendlier as a result of the approximation to each other of the attitudes adopted by the Holy See and the French Government respectively towards the Abyssinian conflict. Indeed, the French Ambassador, M. Charles-Roux, was never tired of informing whoever cared to listen that the views of M. Laval and His Holiness as to the conflict and the best means of settling it were practically identical. There is no doubt that the Holy Father felt the keenest sympathy with M. Laval's endeavours to find a compromise solution, and the wreck of the Paris peace proposals in December was undoubtedly a great blow to the Vatican (see also section on the Italo-Abyssinian conflict).

106. M. Laval's visit to the Pope on the 7th January was not without historical interest, as this was the first time since the foundation of the Third Republic that a French Foreign Minister had set foot in the Vatican. From 1871 until 1920 the Popes had refused on principle to receive guests of the King of Italy or his Government, and since 1920 (when Benedict XV withdrew the prohibition) no such personage had paid an official visit to Rome. M. Laval, on this occasion, not only visited the Pope, but also, in accordance with the protocol for distinguished Catholic visitors, venerated St. Peter's Tomb, a proceeding which would have seemed incredible not so many years ago. On the 9th January His Holiness received the journalists, clerical and anti-clerical, who had accompanied the French delegation to Rome. After reminding them of their responsibility as the chief agents in the formation of " what is known as public opinion," and exhorting them, in the words of his favourite Manzoni, " never to applaud vice or deride virtue," the Pope gave his benediction alike to the journalists and to that country which was " to him and them alike so dear."

107. On the 19th March His Holiness received 2,000 French ex-combatants who were visiting Rome, and also 400 youthful members of the " Jeunesse patriotique." To the former he recalled France's ancient title of " Eldest Daughter of the Church," while he reminded the latter that the noblest form of French patriotism combined love of country with devotion to the Catholic religion.

108. Cardinal Pacelli's visit to Lourdes in April for the great Triduum of Masses, which closed the extended Holy Year (see paragraph 104), was definitely a success from the Vatican point of view. The cardinal legate was met at the frontier by an important official representing the Government of the Republic by whom he was subsequently entertained to an official dinner in the wagon-restaurant, an unprecedented honour for a prince of the Church. Throughout the cardinal's mission the civil authorities vied with the ecclesiastical in showing every honour to his Eminence.

109. In the latter part of the year the Papal Nuncio in Paris paid frequent visits to the President of the Council, doubtless with a view to the settlement of the Italo-Abyssinian dispute. The elevation of the Nuncio to the Purple in December was no doubt in part a tribute to his skill in helping to establish good relations; and the conferment of the Red Hat on no less than three French subjects (these including the Syrian patriarch, Mgr. Tappouni) was yet another indication of the present Pope's benevolence towards the republic.

Germany.

110. So far as the interests of Catholic Christianity in Germany are concerned, matters went from bad to worse during the year under review. The licence permitted to the neo-pagan movement under such leaders as Rosenberg and Hauer grew steadily, while even narrower limits were set to Catholic freedom of speech and action. The campaign against denominational schools has proceeded apace, and the right of Catholics to retain their own press, their own associations, even their own principles (in such matters as that of sterilisation) has been denied by the Reich Minister of the Interior in a public speech. General Göring has given orders that " political Catholics " shall be proceeded against with energy and deliberation; and many ecclesiastics have been imprisoned for offences against the currency laws or for criticising the Führer and the régime. Nevertheless, the Vatican attitude, correctly reflected by the Apostolic Nuncio in Berlin, would appear to be one of half-despairing resignation. There seems to be no intention of denouncing the concordat presumably for fear lest any such act should render the already difficult position of practising Catholics throughout the Reich more difficult still. It is interesting, however, to note from an article published in the *Osservatore Romano* in reply to General Göring's circular that the Vatican consider that " the Kulturkampf is not a danger for the future; it is a living reality."

111. Towards the problem of the Saar district the Holy See has consistently adopted a completely impartial attitude, and no surprise or annoyance was manifested when, as a result of the plebiscite, it was reunited with the Reich. It was considered, however, that the loyalty of the Saar Catholics should have been rewarded by a change in the attitude of the Reich Government towards

Catholics in Germany as a whole, and disappointment was expressed by the *Osservatore Romano* at the speech made at this time by the Führer-Chancellor which, though conciliatory in regard to foreign policy, contained no mention of Church problems.

112. Indeed, far from improving, the attitude of the Government towards Catholic associations and denominational schools became so hostile that Cardinal Faulhaber of Munich was moved to make a strong public protest in the course of a sermon on the essential liberties of the Church, which he preached before the ex-Crown Prince Rupprecht on the 10th February. His Eminence received a great ovation after the sermon; two days later, however, cries of " Hang the cardinal ! " were raised at a mass-meeting held in Munich by Herr Bauer, president of the Nazi " Deutsche Schulgemeinde," who alleged that his Eminence was endeavouring to revive the educational policy of the defunct Centre party. In April, as a result of adverse votes to the Church in a plebiscite of parents, about a third of the Catholic schools in Munich were replaced by secular ones.

113. In March, while expressing appreciation of the respectful references made by the Nazi press to Bishop Bares of Berlin, whose premature death occurred at this time, the clerical *Avvenire d'Italia* drew attention to the increase of neo-paganism, and took particularly strong exception to Herr Julius Streicher's hostile attitude towards converted Jews, pointing out that Christianity has absolutely no use for Nazi doctrines of " purity of race," and regards all Christians as equal.

114. The news of the reintroduction into the Reich of military conscription and of the formation of an air force was philosophically accepted at the Vatican, where some such step had perhaps been anticipated, and where, in any case, the provisions of the Treaty of Versailles had never been regarded as final.

115. Indignation was aroused in April by the infliction of a sentence of one and a half years' imprisonment on Mgr. Leffers, the highly respected parish priest of Rostock, who was convicted of having spoken insultingly of the Führer, on the sole evidence of three young *agents provocateurs*, students in the town, who had visited the priest and asked his opinion of Herr Rosenberg's farrago of nonsense. Later on in the year the said author's defence against his critics (" Die Dunkelmänner unserer Zeit ") fitly joined the " Mythus des XX Jahrhunderts " on the index.

116. Reference to the religious situation in the Reich was made by the Pope on Easter Monday, when he received 2,400 German boys belonging to various Catholic organisations in Germany who were paying a visit to Rome. These boys had shown great enthusiasm for the Pope at the Easter High Mass in St. Peters, greeting His Holiness with loud and long continued shouts of " Heil ! " Whether for this or for some other reason, the ire of the Nazi authorities was aroused, and when the youths arrived at the frontier on their return journey they were set upon by the local officials and robbed of the pious objects they were bringing back from Rome, as well as of their provisions for the journey; while the emblems, badges and coloured shirts which some of them were wearing were torn off and confiscated.

117. In the comment made by the *Osservatore Romano*, it was pertinently pointed out that, far from having committed a crime, these boys had been spending a few days in the territory of a Sovereign with whom the Government of the Reich is on friendly terms. A few days later, the Holy Father took the occasion of an audience which he granted to a pilgrimage from the Rhineland to refer in scathing terms to the ill-treatment of the young pilgrims. " We hope," His Holiness said, " that you will be better treated on your return to Germany than the pious splendid youths, loyal alike to their Church and their country, who came but a short time ago to visit us, their Common Father. We recall them to mind; we name them with honour in the sight of the whole Catholic and civilised world."

118. Much sympathy was expressed at the Vatican in July with the Bishop of Münster, Mgr. von Gallen, who protested to the Governor of Westphalia against the proposed delivery in his cathedral city of a lecture by Herr Rosenberg,

on the ground that the latter's views were offensive to a large majority of the townsfolk, and that disorder might result. The lecture was given despite the bishop, but, if there was no disorder, this must be attributed largely to his Lordship's exhortations to his flock to keep the peace. Nevertheless, a few days later, on the occasion of the Nazi Party Congress for Westphalia, the Reich Minister of the Interior, Dr. Frick, in the course of a long diatribe against the Catholic Church, said it was intolerable that a bishop in the National Socialist State should dare to address himself to the authorities in the manner of Mgr. von Galen. That intrepid prelate remained unmoved, and when, a few days later, the municipality threatened to forbid a traditional procession through the town, he induced them to revoke the ban by threatening otherwise to proceed alone along the whole route, vested in full pontificals.

119. Dr. Frick's definition of the attitude of the State to the Church, as given in the speech just mentioned, was of a nature to cause lively disquiet to German Catholics. The Minister declared that Catholics had no right to oppose the sterilisation law, seeing that the concordat itself laid down that the laws of the State were binding to all. He also said that the Government desired the complete disappearance of religious denominations from public life; that they desired no Catholic or Protestant, but only a German press; that Catholic associations were out of date, because they encroached on a sphere allotted to the State.

120. Replying to this speech, the *Osservatore Romano* pointed out that many of Dr. Frick's contentions were in flat contradiction to the letter and spirit of the concordat, and regretfully noted that the enmity of ruling circles in Germany to the Church must henceforth be admitted to be an official enmity. The article went on to ridicule the suggestion that Catholics could ever be called upon to obey human laws which, according to the Church's teaching, violated the Divine law; recalled that the existence of the associations which Dr. Frick described as "out of date" was solemnly guaranteed by the concordat; pointed out that the complete religious liberty guaranteed to Catholics by the same instrument inevitably covered freedom to issue publications; and ended by quoting the official communiqué issued in September 1933 on the occasion of the ratification of the concordat, according to which the German Reich would do its best to secure a reciprocal undertaking in respect of the very matters, *i.e.*, liberty of speech and freedom of association, about which the Minister of the Interior had been so unreasonable. This article probably originated in the Secretariat of State, and may have represented the substance of a note of protest to the Reich Government. A translation of the article was read in all the churches of Berlin.

121. Soon after the Münster episode, General Göring, in his capacity as Prime Minister, issued to all Prussian administrative authorities an offensively worded circular against "political catholicism," the exponents of which were to be proceeded against "with energy and determination and without respect of persons." An acid reply to this circular, which was published in the *Osservatore Romano* on the 5th August, may, like the above-mentioned article, have reproduced the substance of an official Vatican note of protest. The Vatican paper ridiculed the general's suggestion that Christians are better off under the Third Reich than they were under previous régimes, and drew attention to the anomaly whereby, in a country in full diplomatic relations with the Holy See, persons like Herr Rosenberg are encouraged to insult the Papacy. General Göring's pious hopes that a Kulturkampf might yet be avoided were laughed at on the ground that one was already in being. The article ended by pleading for a loyal observance of the concordat on the German side as constituting the only way out of an impossible situation. Receiving a group of pilgrims at about this time, the Pope said that he was saddened by the campaign against God and Christianity which had been launched in Germany by "the protagonists of a new paganism." He also referred to the bishops and priests of that country "who were passing through such great tribulation."

122. In the end of August the *Osservatore Romano* protested against the publication by the *Brunnen Verlag*, under the title "Sie wer'n lachen," of a series of salacious anecdotes, some of which, so far as can be gathered from the guarded language of the Vatican organ, had reference to the Papacy.

123. The German bishops met at Fulda as usual during the course of the summer, and at its conclusion issued a pastoral, read in all churches on the 1st September, which, although moderate in tone, reaffirmed the hostility of the Church to neo-paganism and sterilisation, while making the Catholic attitude clear in regard to schools and associations. The bishops also said that the accusation of "political catholicism" was no more than a stick with which to beat any Catholic disliked by the authorities. Hopes had been held in certain quarters that the comparative moderation of the bishops would lead to concessions by the State, and the speech with which Herr Kerrl, the Reich Minister for Church Affairs, replied to the new Bishop of Berlin (Count Preysing), when the latter took his oath on the 30th August, gave rise to a certain optimism, as the Minister said that, if the bishop would see that the new State was respected by his flock, he might be sure that the Government would allow the free exercise of religious rights and show full understanding for the Church's needs. All such hopes were to prove delusory, as is sufficiently indicated by the fact that before the end of the year Count Preysing's own financial adviser, Canon Bannasch, was in prison awaiting trial on some trumped-up charge.

124. It was, indeed, clear as early as September that no change of attitude by the Government was seriously to be expected, for no less a personage than Herr Hitler himself, in the course of a discourse delivered at the Nuremberg Party Congress, said that the enemies of the Reich included, along with "Jewish Marxism" and "parliamentary democracy," their "ally," the Catholic Centre, which, he said, was pernicious, both from the moral and the political standpoint.

125. During the year a number of serious offences against German foreign exchange regulations were imputed to Catholic ecclesiastics and institutions and severely punished. The persons and bodies concerned had borrowed money abroad, and, being prevented from paying their debts by the regulations, attempted to smuggle money to their creditors. Much capital was made out of these offences by the Nazi authorities, and matters were not improved by the issue of a statement from the Archbishop's Court at Breslau, seeking to mitigate the gravity of the offence. In the end of October the Bishop of Meissen, Mgr. Legge, was arrested on a charge of violating the currency laws, together with his vicar-general, Canon Soppa, and his brother, also a priest. After some weeks in prison all three were tried and found guilty, but, while the other two received savage sentences of imprisonment, the bishop, who was clearly entirely ignorant of financial affairs and had acted on the advice of the others, escaped with a fine. The Vatican, though greatly distressed by this incident, was apparently unable to protest, as the law did seem to have been broken. Immediately after his release Mgr. Legge was summoned to Rome to report, but the state of his health did not permit him to obey the summons. Late in November Dr. Bannasch, financial adviser to the Bishop of Berlin, was arrested and his offices ransacked by the police. Other arrests were those of Father Clemens of Düsseldorf, general secretary of a large Catholic youth organisation, and Father Ansgar Sinnigen, O.P., of Berlin, general secretary of the Council of Superiors of Orders. None of these priests have yet been tried, nor has any reason been given for their arrest. It seems to be feared in Germany that the action against these priests represents the beginning of an undisguised onslaught on the Church, and that the first assaults are to be on the centres of ecclesiastical organisation.

126. Much annoyance was caused in Germany by a reference in the *Osservatore Romano* of the 7th December to Christmas trees as "pagan and Protestant." The Vatican paper tried, not very successfully, to explain away its remarks on the ground that they were only meant to apply to Italy, in which country Christmas trees were unknown to Catholics. German opinion was only partially mollified by these explanations.

127. Much publicity was given by the Nazi press to the administration of the Church oath by Dr. Kerrl to the bishop of the old Catholics, Dr. Kreuzer, who, in a sycophantic address, expressed the complete devotion of the old Catholics to Herr Hitler and his régime, partly on the ground that the Third Reich was likely to be more receptive than its predecessors to their message of a national Church. Dr. Kerrl replied in terms flattering to the Old Catholics, and it does not seem impossible that special State encouragement may now be given to this body in order that it may provide a succulent enough bait to lure Nazi-minded

Catholics away from the Roman obedience. In this connexion it may be of interest to mention that well-informed ecclesiastical circles in Rome do not exclude the possibility of Herr Hitler's making a determined attempt as soon as the time seems ripe, to detach German Catholics completely from Rome and incorporate them in a Church which would at first (like the Old Catholics) teach most Catholic doctrines, save that of the Papacy, but would gradually become less and less Catholic and would eventually be united with the (meanwhile somewhat catholicised) evangelical confessions in one National Church. It is widely feared that a beginning may be made with this attempt the moment the Vatican give the Government any excuse for an anti-Roman outburst; and the bishops are said, for this reason, to be anxious to dissuade the Pope from any strong denunciation of the Third Reich. Such action on His Holiness's part would give the Nazi leaders a chance of emphasising Italian and other foreign influence in the counsels of the Church, and of raising the cry of nationalism against the foreigner. In such circumstances, given the amount of intensive Nazi and neo-pagan propaganda to which the Catholic youth have been subjected, especially in districts with mixed populations, it is to be feared that defections among the younger generation might be very serious. It seems to be a fact that many of the Catholic bishops have been extremely weak, and it may now be too late for them to counteract the hold that the Nazis have obtained over a large proportion of the Catholic youth.

Greece.

128. Roman Catholic institutions are viewed with much suspicion in Greece because they are believed to be directly connected with political propaganda and especially with designs upon Greek territory. In view of this fact and of the traditional dislike of the Orthodox for their Western rivals, outbursts of anger against the Catholic Church are not unusual in Greece, and one such occurred during 1935 in connexion with the preparation of official measures to combat foreign religious propaganda. A committee was appointed to study the question, and among the measures it proposed was one according to which, if any foreign priest should die or leave his post, the post must be filled, if at all possible, by a Greek subject. It was also decided to make every possible difficulty about the granting of visas to foreign priests. Trouble was also made about the status and title of the Archbishop of Athens, neither of which had before been questioned. Feeling indeed ran so high that it seemed more than doubtful at one time whether the newly appointed Apostolic Delegate for Turkey and Greece, Mgr. Roncalli, would be allowed to visit the later country. It appears, however, that he was eventually allowed to do so, though receiving little or no official recognition. In May the Holy Synod took a hand in the anti-Catholic game and sent to the Ministry of the Interior a manifesto in which alarm was expressed lest the recent Turkish law prohibiting clerical dress might result in the transfer of Catholic religious orders from Turkey to Greece. It seems there is some question of transferring to Greece the Constantinople house of the Assumptionists, who are paid by the Holy Synod the compliment of being considered "the most dangerous of all the Catholic orders from the propagandist point of view."

Italy (see also Section IV of this report, concerning "The Vatican and the Italo-Abyssinian Conflict").

129. Relations between the Holy See and Italy remained on the whole good. When Cardinals Pacelli, Lépicier and Fumasoni-Biondi went as Papal Legates to various religious gatherings, &c., held during the year, their Eminences were speeded on their way and welcomed on their return with semi-royal honours provided by the Italian Government. The National Eucharistic Congress at Teramo in August was celebrated with great pomp in the presence of the Papal Legate and the local Fascist authorities.

130. On the 14th October Count Pignatti Morano di Custoza, who, after six months' delay had been appointed to succeed Count de Vecchi as Italian Ambassador to the Vatican, presented his credentials to the Pope. In his speech he asked for the Papal blessing on the King of Italy and the head of the Government, but the Holy Father in his reply, while making much of the special blessing he was sending the King, did not refer by name to Signor Mussolini. The only

tension occurred at the end of August when the Pope made his speech to the nurses (see Section VI (C)) in which he condemned wars of conquest in the strongest terms, and said that it ought to be possible to find a solution of the Italo-Abyssinian quarrel without fighting. The Italian Embassy are said to have endeavoured to prevent the speech from appearing in the *Osservatore Romano* and to have complained bitterly of the Pope's remarks. They did not have much cause to complain during the rest of the year. Indeed the Abyssinian war and sanctions had the effect of knitting more closely than ever the bonds of Church and State, for though most of the cardinals, his Eminence of Milan being a regrettable exception, showed proper discretion, the diocesan bishops and clergy rallied enthusiastically to the national cause by word and deed and set the example of unquestioning obedience and fanatical loyalty to the Fascist State.

131. The extent of the Vatican's own sympathy for fascism is hard to gauge. It is true that fascism and popular catholicism rest upon principles which are to some extent similar. Both admit no questioning of their creed; both insist upon the submission of the individual to the system, encourage large families, attach importance to external ceremonies, and to mass psychology. Granted the extremely close relations established between Vatican and Quirinal by the Lateran Treaty, it may, moreover, appear to be to the interest of the Vatican that a Catholic Power like Italy should increase its prestige by expansion, especially when it is opposed by other Powers where Protestant influence is predomiant, *e.g.*, the Scandinavian countries, Holland, Great Britain, or by an atheistic Power like Soviet Russia.

132. Too much should not, however, be built upon the above argument. The Fascists do not themselves dare to claim that the Pope favours their enterprise in Abyssinia, and their silence is significant. Moreover, the Vatican are under no illusions as to the reasons which make the Dictator patronise the Church, and a position of part-dependence on an earthly potentate must be irksome to a Pope who has not the submissive character of a Pius VII. In addition, it is by no means clear that the Fascists will come well out of the present struggle, and if they do not, the Sovereign Pontiff will be involved in their ruin exactly to the extent to which he has identified himself with them. Hence a policy of careful and strict neutrality seems to be dictated alike by religious and by prudential reasons.

133. In June the Fascist Government yielding to representations by the Pope, left Sunday free for religious observance and arranged for the gymnastic exercises, &c., of the Fascist youth to take place on Saturday instead. In November again, as a result of Vatican protests, the authorities cancelled an ordinance whereby (on account of the Italian Armistice Day falling on a Monday) the previous Sunday was to have been treated as a week-day.

Mexico.

134. Affairs in Mexico, where the campaign against the Church continued, were one of the Vatican's principal preoccupations throughout the year. In January the Apostolic Delegate for that country issued from his place of exile a pastoral forbidding all Catholics to co-operate in any way in the Government's scheme of Socialist education, and excommunicating Catholics belonging to the National Revolutionary party.

135. On the 23rd January a clash between the police and the populace took place outside the shrine of Our Lady of Guadalupe. Shots were fired and several persons wounded. Other disturbances of this kind took place at various places throughout the year, not without some loss of life.

136. On the 30th January Senator Borah introduced a resolution into the United States Senate, providing for an investigation of religious persecution in Mexico by the Senate Committee on Foreign Relations. At the same time a vigorous agitation was conducted by American Catholics against the Mexican Government. At a mass meeting at Philadelphia on the 24th February, Cardinal O'Dougherty addressed 17,000 persons, and alleged that 300 priests and 5,000 laymen had been done to death in Mexico during the last decade, and that the Soviet Government had spent 18 million dollars on Mexican propaganda.

137.   In March the Archbishop of Mexico (Mgr. Díaz) was arrested, detained for twenty-nine hours, and fined before release, on the pretext that his Excellency had taken up a collection at a confirmation service without first obtaining Government permission.   During the summer the religious question was in abeyance and less was heard in the press and elsewhere of religious persecution.   In July, however, President Roosevelt received a delegation of Congressmen, who handed him a petition in which it was stated that something should be done to " evidence an affirmative interest in the religious rights (in Mexico) of American citizens of all faiths and creeds."   The President replied expressing his belief in freedom of religious worship, not only in the United States but also in all other nations.

138.   In September a law was promulgated by the Mexican Government giving effect to the provisions for the expropriation of Church property contained in the Constitution.   The new law confirms the far-reaching and vindictive provisions of the Constitution, including those which place a premium on malicious denunciation by informers.   The Mexican bishops immediately appealed to President Cárdenas to repeal the law and amend the Constitution.   They must have known that the appeal would be (as indeed it was) unsuccessful; but they thought perhaps that the moment was opportune to stimulate reaction against a policy which is growing more and more unpopular, especially in the middle and professional classes.   On the 31st October priests were arrested for attending a religious function in a private house, and heavily fined.   In November an abortive rising took place in Sonora and it was believed in some quarters that arms and money had reached the rebels from Catholics in the United States.

139.   At about this time the Knights of Columbus addressed to President Roosevelt a petition demanding action on behalf of the Catholics in Mexico, in reply to which he said that no case in which freedom of worship had been denied to an American citizen in that country had come to his attention and that it was the policy of the United States Government to refrain from intervening in respect of rights enjoyed by Mexican citizens.   The President's letter was hailed with as much relief by the Mexican Government as with disappointment by Mexican Catholics.

The Netherlands.

140.   The Apostolic Internuncio at The Hague, Mgr. Schioppa, died in Holland in April and was accorded a State funeral at which the Queen was represented.   He was succeeded by Mgr. Giobbe, formerly Nuncio in Colombia, who took up his new duties in October, and who retains the personal rank of Nuncio during his appointment to a lower-grade post, his full title in Vatican parlance being now " Nuncio-Internuncio."

141.   The clerical *Avvenire d'Italia* published in March a message from its Rotterdam correspondent which dealt with the absence of a Dutch representative at the Vatican.   The correspondent quoted a series of articles which had recently appeared in the *Maasbode* and which set out to prove that the re-establishment of the Legation was desirable not only in the Catholic, but, even more, in the national, interest.   Sir Odo Russell was, moreover, quoted as having said at the time of the withdrawal of the Dutch mission in 1925, that Great Britain was retaining her own Legation to the Vatican because it was in the interests of the Empire for her to do so.

Peru.

142.   A national Eucharistic Congress was held at Lima from the 23rd to the 27th October.   It was well organised and well attended, and in a broadcast address delivered at the end of the congress the Pope, after certain exhortations of a purely religious character, said he prayed that the Christian peace which prevailed in Peru might spread throughout the world and above all through Europe and Africa.

Poland.

143.   As is well known, a divergence of view exists between the Vatican and the Polish Government regarding the rite to which converts to Catholicism from the Orthodox parts of Poland should belong.   In the eyes of the Polish Government and, though less openly, of the Polish bishops also, the Eastern rite

is identified with Russia and Russian traditions. Regarding Polish culture as essentially Western, the Government and Hierarchy desire that the religion of their people should be Western too, and consider it eminently desirable that those who abjure the Orthodox religion should also abandon the Eastern rite. The Vatican attitude on the other hand is based on the apposite decree of the Council of Florence (1437) which lays down that persons of the Eastern obedience should, on becoming Catholics, be allowed to retain their own rite. The Vatican also realise that the abandonment of the Eastern rite by Ruthene, White Russian and Ukrainian Christians would be regarded by their brothers in race as tantamount to a renunciation of nationality, a sacrifice which the Church has no right or desire to demand. A member of the Pontifical Oriental Institute told the first secretary to His Majesty's Legation in March that converts to the Uniate rite are not considered by the Orthodox population to have "lost caste" as they would by becoming "Latins," and he instanced the case of three young priests who were ordained in that rite at Easter 1934 and whose services as parish priests had since been invited by no less than fifty Orthodox parishes. It is true that in spite of his sympathy for the "Easternisers" the Pope was induced as a result of the pressure of the Polish bishops, added to Mgr. d'Herbigny's own lack of discretion, to consent to the latter's removal and to the dissolution of the "Commissio pro Russia" (see section on "Soviet Union"). Despite this concession, however, the Pope does not appear to have altered his view that, unless good reason exists to the contrary, converts from the Eastern Church to catholicism shall be allowed to retain their own rites. The Pope was, indeed, much irritated when a high Polish ecclesiastic alleged that he had expressed approval of the conversion of certain Orthodox to the Latin rite, and he indignantly denied the rumour. It can hardly be denied that the policy of encouragement to different rites is a liberalising influence in the Roman Catholic Church and forms somewhat of a counterpoise to the narrow Italianising policy of certain clerics of the Curia. Indeed, the policy of identifying catholicism with nationalism, be it in Poland or in Italy, is bound, though it may seem for a time to help the Holy See, to end by doing it harm.

144. When Mgr. Marmaggi, the Apostolic Nuncio, was raised to the cardinalate at the end of the year, he did not proceed to Rome for the Consistory, but, in accordance with the tradition usual in Catholic States, received the red biretta from the hands of the President of the Republic. His Eminence is a strong opponent of the Polish Government's point of view regarding the Uniate rite, which he thinks is the one best suited to converts from Orthodoxy.

Soviet Union.

145. A *motu proprio* issued by the Pope in March had practically the effect of putting an end to the "Commissio pro Russia," which, founded in 1925 as a department of the Sacred Congregation for the Oriental Church, enjoyed from 1930 onwards an independent existence under the leadership of Mgr. d'Herbigny. Since the resignation in 1933 of this learned prelate the commission had been more or less moribund, and its final dissolution will have come as a surprise to no one. As a result of the new *motu proprio* the affairs of all Catholics of the Eastern rite, whether following the Byzantine-Slav or other liturgies, and whether dwelling in Russia or elsewhere, will be conducted by the Sacred Congregation for the Eastern Church, to which a special Byzantine section is added. Such Catholics of the Latin rite as are to be found in Russia will, however, be placed under a special section "pro Russia" of the Congregation for Extraordinary Ecclesiastical Affairs, presided over by Mgr. Pizzardo. The general effect of the above developments will be to strengthen the hand of the "Latinisers" as against those who, like Mgr. d'Herbigny, think that the best hope of securing conversions in Russia and its confines is to encourage the Eastern rite.

146. As mentioned elsewhere, the present Pope is obsessed by a fear of bolshevism which colours his whole policy and outlook and it is probable that the adherence of Soviet Russia to the "sanctionist" front may have influenced the Vatican unfavourably towards the League Powers. It is clearly inconceivable to the Vatican that the rulers of the Soviet Union can ever be inspired by any but the worst motives; and so convinced are they that Moscow is "the enemy" that they are comparatively indulgent to the other foes of the Church.

Thus in November an article in the *Civiltà Cattolica* which was afterwards quoted with approval by the *Osservatore Romano* did not hesitate to cite Dr. Goebbels in support of the thesis that, under the cloak of an attack on tyranny and aggression, the Third International is trying to unite the parties of the Left in all countries against the forces of law and order. The spectacle of an Italian Jesuit attacking the Red Terror with weapons borrowed from the Brown House was both curious and distressing.

147. An article which appeared in the *Osservatore Romano* at about the same time illustrated the resentment felt by the Vatican at Moscow's attitude towards the Abyssinian conflict, which was said to be dictated by the desire to set the capitalistic nations by the ears, thereby paving the way for the triumph of communism. The article went so far as to state that the main reasons for the present unrest must be sought in "the subtle and poisonous intrigues of Communist propaganda."

Spain.

148. With the naming in January of six bishops to occupy vacant sees in Spain, relations between the Holy See and that country took another step forward, and a further mark of esteem was given to Spain when the Archbishop-Primate of Toledo was raised to the Purple at the end of the year. It is true that the *modus vivendi* for which the Ambassador to the Holy See, Sr. Pita Romero, is known to be working, has not yet been brought within sight, and that Cardinal Pacelli said to Sir Charles Wingfield in February, *à propos* of the six new bishops, that it was difficult to negotiate with a Government which was bound by so objectionable a Constitution and that the only comfort was that it had no right of veto on appointments. At the same time, it is difficult to believe that these appointments and the Hat of Cardinal Goma y Thomás are not the outward and visible sign of some unofficial understanding. Certainly relations with Spain are better than they have been for several years and she is no longer numbered, together with Mexico, Russia and Germany, among those sources of sorrow which the Pope is in the habit of enumerating in the speeches with which he celebrates the passing of the old year. Perhaps next year Spain may even figure among the sources of joy.

149. In the meantime His Holiness seems, wisely enough, to be very anxious to avoid doing anything which might offend the Catholic Republicans. This being so, the visit of numerous Spanish monarchists to Rome in January to attend the marriage of King Alfonso's eldest daughter, the Infanta Beatrice, to Don Alessandro Torlonia, was the cause of no little embarrassment to the Holy Father, as it was of annoyance to the Spanish Government. Immediately after the wedding, which was celebrated with great pomp in the Gesù in the presence of the King and Queen of Italy, Cardinal Segura y Sáenz, ex-Primate of Spain, being the officiant, Sr. Pita Romero is understood to have made strong representations at the Vatican, objecting to his Eminence's address to the young people, which seems to have contained allusions to the monarchy; insisting that a group audience would be awkward for His Holiness, as cries might be raised for Pope and King; and pointing out that the group was not primarily a Catholic but a political one, whose main purpose in coming to Rome was to demonstrate its loyalty to Alfonso XIII. The Ambassador seems to have urged in conclusion that any courtesy extended by His Holiness to this group would tend to confirm the thesis which the Catholic Republicans made a point of denying, viz., that the cause of the Church is identical with that of the monarchy.

150. The Pope's fear of offending the Spanish Government having doubtless been increased by these representations, His Holiness was placed in a dilemma from which he was only able to extract himself at the cost of giving considerable offence and causing much disappointment to the Royalist visitors, some 3,000 in number, whom he had already consented to receive in audience. Actually, when they arrived at the Vatican they were kept waiting for over an hour in a cold court-yard and, after their long wait, instead of being admitted to the audience-chamber, were rewarded only by a fleeting glimpse of the Holy Father, who appeared for a moment on a balcony and gave the blessing without adding any words of welcome.

151. Though it cannot be denied that the audience, which should never perhaps have been promised, was badly mismanaged, the wait in the cold being particularly regrettable, it is yet generally felt at the Vatican that the Pope was justified, in the circumstances, in avoiding any close contact with his visitors. Though all, no doubt, good Catholics, it was *quâ* Royalists, as their badges indicated, that they were in Rome, and there was no doubt some danger that, if His Holiness came among them and spoke to them, he would be made the centre of a Royalist demonstration which would be bound to react most unfavourably on the Vatican's relations with Spain and might even furnish the pretext for a renewed anti-clerical outbreak. The disadvantage of the solution chosen by the Pope was that many excellent Spanish Catholics, including grandees of Spain and their wives, felt deeply hurt and slighted at the treatment they had received. The whole incident, which could hardly have occurred under Benedict XV, only goes to prove that the present Pope is lacking in that inestimable gift which enables some people to extricate themselves from a delicate situation involving two other parties without giving offence to either.

152. It may be noted that the Infanta and her bridegroom were themselves most kindly received by His Holiness and that no outward incident of any kind marred the marriage of the Prince of the Asturias to Princess Maria Mercedes of Bourbon-Orleans, which took place, also in Rome, in the autumn, Cardinal Dalla Costa of Florence performing the ceremony.

Turkey.

153. The position of the Apostolic Delegate, Mgr. Roncalli, is not recognised by the present régime in Turkey, as he is not only a foreigner himself, but represents a foreign hierarch of whom that lay State has no official cognisance. His name was accordingly not included among those of the privileged ecclesiastics, some eight in number, who are exempted from obeying the regulations regarding clerical dress which came into force in June. As a result of this law all Catholic priests in Turkey are now wearing ordinary civil attire, except when actually officiating in church. It seems that they have received orders from Rome to show willing acceptance of the regulations. These also, of course, apply to the nuns, who have accepted with a less good grace the enforced and unwelcome change in their traditional attire.

United States of America.

154. The Seventh National Eucharistic Congress of the United States was successfully held at Cleveland in September, and on the closing day (the 26th September) His Holiness broadcast an address from Castel Gandolfo in the course of which he said that, although already, as it were, present in the person of his Legate, Cardinal Hayes, he desired to make that presence still more closely felt by letting the congress hear the sound of his voice. He then asked all his hearers to join with him in prayer that the threatened war might be averted, and ended by giving his benediction to " the great American nation and its rulers."

Yugoslavia.

155. Some annoyance was shown by the Orthodox authorities in Yugoslavia at the attitude of the Archbishop of Zagreb towards the national celebrations in honour of St. Sava. The main celebrations were held at the end of January, and early in the month Mgr. Bauer issued a circular to all the churches within his jurisdiction forbidding Catholics to take any part in the festivities. Bishop Nikolaj Velimirovic of Ohrid replied to this circular in an article that appeared early in February in all the Belgrade newspapers. He pointed out that the Serbian bishops in announcing the celebrations had never suggested that any but Orthodox Yugoslavs should participate so that Mgr. Bauer's intervention was most uncalled for. In order to prove the broadmindedness of his own co-religionists, the bishop added that the Orthodox Church had never attempted to minimise the importance of Bishop Strossmayer's services to the cause of national unity.

156. During the summer, after many hesitations, the Yugoslav Government at last decided to accept the Vatican's minimum conditions and to sign the concordat for which negotiations had been dragging on for over fourteen years. The

instrument, which at the end of the year had not yet been ratified or published, was signed at the Vatican on the 25th July by the Cardinal Secretary of State, for the Pope, and by M. Auer, Minister of Justice, for King Peter II.

157.　The concordat which has thus at last been signed will, it is to be hoped, bring order into the relations between the Catholic Church and the Yugoslav State which have hitherto been regulated, to the confusion of all concerned, by means of a number of separate arrangements concluded before the war between the Holy See and the Governments then responsible for the component parts of the present Kingdom.

158.　According to a statement given to the Italian press, the following are among the provisions of the concordat.　The boundaries of various dioceses are redrawn in order to conform to the administrative districts of the present Kingdom, while certain new dioceses are formed.　The Bishoprics of Split and Ljubljana are raised to the rank of archbishoprics and the procedure for the nomination of bishops by the Holy See is subjected to the condition contained in other recent concordats, viz., that the Vatican shall first enquire if there are any political objections to the proposed candidate.　The right of the Catholic Church to enjoy autonomy in the possession and management of property is recognised, subject to State supervision, in the same manner as that of other religious bodies in Yugoslavia.　The concordat also provides for religious instruction in the schools and regularises the position of the theological faculties at the Universities of Zagreb and Belgrade.　Ecclesiastical marriages are recognised as valid by the State; Catholic associations authorised by the bishops are given complete freedom of action; and the parish clergy are forbidden to belong to parties or to engage in politics.　As to the vexed question of the use of the Slav language in the liturgy a solution has been reached (according to this communiqué) which takes into account both national sentiment, the requirements of ecclesiastical discipline and the wishes of the various sections of the population concerned.

159.　In a speech delivered at an official dinner given at the Yugoslav Legation to the Holy See in honour of Cardinal Pacelli, M. Auer said that the conclusion of a concordat was largely due to the efforts of the late King Alexander, who had approved its main lines before his tragic death in October 1934.　In conversation with His Majesty's Chargé d'Affaires a little later the General of the Jesuits said that he also had heard that much credit was due to the late King, who had insisted on negotiations being speeded up in the teeth of strong opposition from the Orthodox bishops.

160.　From the 28th June to the 3rd July a National Eucharistic Congress was held at Ljubljana and presided over by Cardinal Hlond, the Primate of Poland, who had been chosen because as a Slav he would be welcome in Yugoslavia. Cardinal Hlond, in a sermon delivered on this occasion, spoke of "the mission of Catholic Slavdom," and said that the riches of the Slav soul, still largely asleep and inactive, constituted a magnificent reserve of moral strength for Europe which the Catholic Slavs must endeavour to save from Western materialism, "raciste" paganism and Soviet atheism.

IV.—THE VATICAN AND THE ITALO-ABYSSINIAN CONFLICT.

(A) *General Summary.*

(i) *Estimate of the Pope's Attitude.*

161.　It cannot be doubted that the Pope strongly disapproved of the initiation of war in Abyssinia.　Nevertheless, once the adventure was started, the Vatican attitude became non-committal, in so far as it was not pro-Italian. This might at first sight appear to indicate a change of view.　Actually it properly does not, the explanation being that the Pope consistently desired peace above all things, being afraid that the fall of fascism might result from an unsuccessful war, and that a Communist or anti-clerical régime might seize power, with disastrous results for the Papacy.　Thus having attacked the war so long as he thought there might be a chance of preventing it, once it had begun, he advocated the only peace which he thought Italy might be induced to accept immediately, *i.e.*, one which made large concessions to the aggressor.

162.   While, however, the Pope is not superhumanly detached from practical considerations, and especially those which affect his position in Italy, it would be a mistake to regard him as being completely in the hands of the Fascists.   The truth is perhaps midway.   His Holiness is conscious of the injustice of Signor Mussolini's attack upon Abyssinia, and conscious of his own responsibilities as head of an international Church which must take world opinion into account; but, at the same time, he is aware of the influence exercised by the Duce over Italian Catholics and extremely fearful of a possible world war and of an increase of the influence of the Third International.   On these fears the Italians have played unscrupulously and with considerable success.   To what extent Pius XI is influenced by Italian sentiment as an Italian it is difficult to state.

163.   On the whole the Pope's position may most fitly be compared with that of M. Laval.   Drawn in two ways between regret at Italian aggression and fear of the consequences should the Duce fall, he grasps, like the French statesmen, at any suggestion which seems to promise a speedy settlement.

164.   There is no evidence that His Holiness has manifested any strong or direct disapproval of the attitude of the Italian bishops and clergy, who, with some notable exceptions, have rallied enthusiastically to the Fascist cause.   It is permissible, however, to deduce from the silence of the *Osservatore Romano* on the subject of these utterances, and from other indications which have reached His Majesty's Legation, that the Pope regrets them.   It is not clear, however, to what extent His Holiness could restrain a national hierarchy from violent partisanship of a national cause.   It should be remembered that in addition to being head of the Catholic Church, His Holiness is Primate of Italy, and that these two positions involve him in almost contradictory sets of obligations. Probably he is willing to leave the Italian bishops free to follow their own judgments in such matters.   It may be doubted, indeed, whether he would be obeyed should he act otherwise.

(ii) *Grounds for Estimate.*

165.   The above conclusions are really in the nature of inferences drawn from a series of facts.   Since the invasion of Abyssinia the Pope has himself made no statement on the subject beyond the oracular one that he desires a peace based on truth, justice and charity; and the only means by which it is possible to arrive at a correct estimate of his views is by examining and correlating expressions of opinion deriving from such sources as the Secretariat of State, the *Osservatore Romano*, and the French Embassy to the Holy See.   Cardinal Pacelli is too discreet to have gone beyond vague expressions of the desirability of peace all round.   Mgr. Pizzardo, who was Acting Secretary of State during an important six weeks, and his principal subordinate, Mgr. Ottaviani, in the course of repeated conversations with His Majesty's Chargé d'Affaires which they themselves initiated, presented the Italian case with an interest which seemed more than academic.   In general, they did not defend or deny the illegality of Italy's act of aggression; but they maintained that a realistic policy must be adopted.   Italy had need of expansion; Abyssinia was barbarous and needed civilising; Moscow was supporting Geneva for her own sinister ends; Great Britain's attitude was rigid and legalistic; Italy must have terms which would save her honour; there was danger of world cataclysm, Signor Mussolini driving Italy into desperate courses, &c.

166.   The *Osservatore Romano*, though technically it has been correct in its attitude, has, nevertheless, given no moral support to the League Powers apart from France, while, in indirect ways, it has been of service to the Italian cause. For instance, its estimate of the effect of sanctions was that they would be ineffective; and its quotations from foreign papers were more generally from those hostile to the League.   Mgr. Pizzardo himself, moreover, indicated regretfully to His Majesty's Chargé d'Affaires that the editors of the paper were afraid of the Duce.

167.   The French Ambassador to the Holy See and his counsellor took pains to impress upon His Majesty's Chargé d'Affaires, especially during November and early December, that the Pope had considerable personal influence with the Duce, and had induced his Excellency in October to initiate somewhat more moderate proposals than any to which he had hitherto consented.   They added

that the Holy Father was by no means pro-Italian and did not believe in
" civilisation à coups de canon "; said that Mgr. Pizzardo argued the League's
case against the Italian Ambassador to the Vatican, &c. From these indications
taken together it would seem fair to assume that His Holiness's attitude really
was as stated. Nevertheless it is hard to be sure to what extent the members
of the Secretariat of State are in his confidence, and whether the French were not
more interested in the success of M. Laval's schemes for a peace of compromise,
than correct in their diagnosis of the Pope's mind. The general attitude of the
Vatican newspaper, however, confirms for the most part the indications drawn
from Mgr. Pizzardo and the French diplomats. It is, indeed, inconceivable that
the *Osservatore Romano* should ever consistently follow a line that was not
approved by the Pontiff himself.

168. It has seemed worth while to indicate the grounds from which this
Legation's estimate of the Holy Father's attitude has been deduced; and, making
due allowance for the secretiveness of his nature and for the fact that he often
surprises his entourage by taking some action for which they were completely
unprepared, it seems on the whole reasonable to assume that His Holiness will
continue to adopt an attitude of official neutrality which, in effect, helps Italy
more than the League Powers.

(iii) *Foreign Views on the Pope's Attitude.*

169. These general observations may fitly end with some reference to foreign
views on the Vatican attitude, though these are only of interest here in so far
as they may be thought to influence Vatican policy. Undoubtedly, among Roman
Catholics who are not Italian, uneasiness exists lest the Church allow herself
to be too closely identified with fascism or even with Italy. This uneasiness has
been increased by the Pope's silence; by the nomination of the surprisingly large
number of Italian cardinals in December; by the pro-Italian attitude of many
members of the Curia; by the wildly patriotic attitude of the Italian clergy, &c.
Such unlikely rumours have been current as that Mgr. Baudrillart was chosen
for a hat because he had signed the manifesto of French intellectuals against
sanctions, and hot-heads have remarked that the Fascist captivity of the Church
is worse than that of Avignon. This is, of course, an exaggeration, but even the
most pious of Catholics have found defence of the Pope's attitude somewhat
difficult. His own explanation, given in a secret memorandum, shown by the
French Ambassador to His Majesty's Chargé d'Affaires in November, viz., that
he preferred to incur the charge of blameworthy inactivity rather than imperil
the chances of peace by means of secret negotiation, did not carry conviction to
all. Of this His Holiness was clearly aware, for he declared in the above-
mentioned allocution that he had been unjustly blamed, adding simply that he
had done all that could properly be required of him. In private conversation he
is reported to have said that he had received many letters of disapproval from
abroad, including one from an English military man. It is probable, however,
that foreign opinion makes itself felt but little at the Vatican, and, such is the
awe inspired by His present Holiness that none of his entourage would ever
venture to tell him any unpleasant home-truths. In clerical circles the rumour
is being industriously spread that " international freemasonry " has vowed to
make use of the present situation to ruin Fascist Italy. To what extent this is
believed by Pius XI, it is hard to say; he was, however, brought up in an Italy
in which masonic influence was undoubtedly anti-clerical, and such suggestions
may have a powerful effect on his imagination. Indeed, such tales as these,
combined with the thought of the advantage which his *bête noire*, Soviet Russia
is drawing from the imbroglio, probably more than offset his disapproval of the
Abyssinian campaign and his fear of losing the good opinion and support of
Liberal Catholics outside Italy.

(B) *Course of Events.*

(i) *Early Stages.*

170. At the Consistory of the 1st April (see Section V of this report) the
Pope, who no doubt had already some inkling of the Fascist Government's
war-like intentions, spoke of the dark clouds which were gathering on the horizon,
and said that if the worst occurred he would feel bound to pray for the scattering
of " the nations which delight in war."

171. In July, when the clouds had become much more threatening as a result of the intransigent attitude of Signor Mussolini and his refusal to consider the proposals brought to Rome by Mr. Eden, the impression gained by Sir Charles Wingfield from the Cardinal Secretary of State, was that the Pope disapproved of an Abyssinian adventure, but felt powerless to do anything to prevent it. One chief reason for the Pope's disapproval, apart from his general dislike of war, was his fear of the deplorable effects of the adventure on Catholic missions in Africa. It became known to the Legation at about this time that the Holy See had asked for and obtained from Africa reports on the probable effect of Italy's policy on missionary work. The universal view taken by the missionaries has been that, if the Vatican appeared to approve, even tacitly, of Signor Mussolini's policy, the effect on the work of the Church among the black peoples would be disastrous. They further urged that the Holy See should make a public declaration in condemnation of Italy's East African policy and in favour of justice to the coloured races. The problem before His Holiness was thus how, when and to what extent he should dissociate himself from the Duce's Abyssinian gamble. The *Osservatore Romano* at this time was disapproving but pessimistic. " Italy," it wrote on the 24th July, " does not believe in the feasibility of arbitration; she hopes for nothing from Geneva, but concentrates on her military preparations."

172. On the 28th the Holy Father made his first public allusion to the Italo-Abyssinian quarrel. The occasion was that of the reading of a decree preliminary to the beatification of the Venerable Giustino de Jacobis, first Vicar Apostolic in Ethiopia, and the relevant passage ran thus : " We recall the memory of this great Italian, whom we may call an Abyssinian by adoption, at a time when, as between Italy and Abyssinia, the sky is obscured by clouds of which none can fail to mark the presence or succeed in fathoming the mysterious significance." Many Italian papers in reporting the speech omitted the above passage, perhaps because it suggested that the reasons for the Italian attitude of aggression towards Abyssinia were not clear to His Holiness. The Pope went on to enounce the dictum, so conveniently vague and so often repeated since, that he hoped for a peace consistent with truth, justice and charity.

173. On the 31st July the *Osservatore Romano*, in an article of unaccustomed vigour, against which the Duce may possibly have protested, for nothing so strong appeared in its columns again, said that the League of Nations must take strong action or show itself absurd and futile. Shortly afterwards, however, the same newspaper seemed to admit the legitimacy of Italian aspirations, if not of Italian methods, and showed it thought that Great Britain's attitude was due to her interests in East Africa.

(ii) *Threats of Aggression: Vatican Opposition.*

174. In a speech delivered at Castel Gandolfo on the 27th August, to an international gathering of Catholic nurses (a full translation of which will be found under section VI (*c*) of this report), the Pope, who seemed to be speaking on a sudden impulse, said that : " Wars of aggression are unjust; needs for expansion exist and ought to be taken into account, but do not by themselves justify war; rights of defence are limited by the need of respecting the rights of others; Italy's objects might be attained by peaceful means which should be studied; peacemakers are to be encouraged, but not those who make use of threats which can only aggravate the evil."

175. The speech was only published in garbled form in the Italian press, and on the 30th August the *Osservatore Romano* complained of the misrepresentation to which the Pope had been subjected, and insisted yet again on the facts that expansion does not constitute a right *per se*, and that the right of defence has definite limits. Incidentally, the speech in its original form is said to have been more strongly worded than in the published version, and this bowdlerisation seems to have taken place as a result of representations by the Italians, who had tried to obtain the complete suppression of the speech. Asked by the French Ambassador to the Holy See if the Italians had complained, Cardinal Pacelli replied : " Oui, ils se sont plaints, et de quelle manière ! "

176. Early in September, addressing at St. Paul's Without the Walls an international pilgrimage of ex-servicemen, the Pope, in a further allusion to

the conflict, said, *inter alia*, that he desired that the aspirations of a good and great people, which was also his own people, should be fulfilled in so far as was compatible with justice and peace. He emphasised the importance of these conditions. A little later His Majesty's Chargé d'Affaires learned from a French source that, in conversation with a distinguished foreigner, the Pope had expressed strong disapproval of the Abyssinian adventure, and had hinted at the " very serious step " which he might feel obliged to take. His Holiness was also inclined to criticise Great Britain, and especially her advocacy of sanctions.

177. On the 20th September, in a pessimistic article pointing out that things were going from bad to worse, the *Osservatore Romano* quoted with approval a passage from a sermon to the effect that the League deserved encouragement and sympathy. On the 24th September Mgr. Pizzardo said to His Majesty's Chargé d'Affaires that, for reasons of prestige, Signor Mussolini could now only give way if considerable concessions were made to him. His Excellency wondered whether Great Britain would necessarily mind a part of Abyssinia being placed under Italian control.

(iii) *October: Italian Aggression and Vatican Peace Overtures.*

178. On the 3rd October, the day on which Italian troops crossed the Abyssinian frontier, a change was noticeable in the tone of the *Osservatore Romano*, which had hitherto, though somewhat half-heartedly, supported the League. Now, a certain tenderness for Italy made itself felt. Although the first phase, that of a peaceful solution, was now admittedly over, Italy was given credit for her willingness to negotiate with Great Britain (expressed at the last meeting of the Fascist Cabinet) as also for her very natural desire to limit the scope of the conflict. Quotations were made from the Italian press to show that Italy's aggression was not unprovoked, and a then recent letter from His Majesty's Principal Secretary of State for Foreign Affairs to the French Ambassador in London, in which he spoke of " degrees of aggression," was twisted into a part-justification for Italian action. Neither then or at any subsequent date has the Vatican organ expressed a word of condemnation for what the League of Nations recognised as a clear and unmistakable act of aggression.

179. The following are further examples of the Vatican paper's attitude during October. On the 6th with a great show of impartiality it accused the League of being a collection of theorisers who would not face reality; on the 8th it defended the ringing of certain Church bells for the Fascist " Adunata " of the 2nd October; on the 14th it spoke disparagingly of pacifists as being in reality makers of war and laid great blame on the " Masonic " press; on the 23rd it criticised the Archbishop of Canterbury and said that he had received orders (presumably from the Government) to speak against Italy's war; on the 24th, under cover of blaming the press as a whole, it took particular exception to the attitude of the British press, and criticised Mr. Baldwin for not contradicting the false interpretations of his Bournemouth speech which had gained currency; on the 26th it suggested that Sir Samuel Hoare's remark that Great Britain could never play a secondary rôle might be offensive to small nations, that the concentration of the fleet in the Mediterranean was needlessly aggressive, and that an economic blockade would lead to war; at the same time General Castelnau, who had said the idea of war with Italy was absurd, was quoted as having spoken for the conscience of Europe.

180. To revert to the early days of the conflict, on the 7th October the Acting Secretary of State, Mgr. Pizzardo, in conversation with His Majesty's Chargé d'Affaires emphasised: (i) Signor Mussolini's resolve to fight to the bitter end rather than accept a humiliating peace; (ii) the danger that economic sanctions, after inflicting great misery on Italy, would eventually plunge her into Bolshevik anarchy; (iii) the strength of Signor Mussolini who might resist for years before the final collapse occurred; (iv) the alleged moral right of Italy to expand in Abyssinia and the benefits she would thereby confer on the Abyssinians. Mr. Montgomery pointed out to Mgr. Pizzardo how greatly the Duce's recourse to arms had intensified the difficulty of finding a solution acceptable to Abyssinia and the League, and said that he thought any proposals must now come from Italy.

181. On the 16th October the Acting Secretary of State told His Majesty's Chargé d'Affaires that it seemed essential in the interests of Christianity and of Western civilisation to arrive at an early solution of the conflict between the League and Italy. He did not deny Italian responsibility for the existing *impasse*, but said that the solution offered must be one which the Fascist Government could accept without humiliation. Mgr. Pizzardo then went on to suggest the main lines of a solution, which, as expanded and amended the same evening by Mgr. Ottaviani, took shape as follows :—

(1) Abyssinia to cede to Italy the Adowa district, comprising at least as much territory as the latter lost in 1896.

(2) The Somaliland frontier to be rectified in a manner favourable to Italy.

(3) A mandate over some or all of the non-Amharic territories to be granted to Italy, who would not, however, have the right to arm the native inhabitants except to the limited extent necessary for policing purposes. It was left uncertain whether Italy would consider accepting a joint League mandate for these territories, but was made clear that, if so, she would claim a predominant part in their administration.

(4) An outlet to the sea at Assab to be given to Abyssinia by Italy. It was not made clear whether there would be any territorial connexion between the port and Ethiopia.

(5) As regards Abyssinia proper, a régime to be established similar to that proposed by the Committee of Five with " suitable participation " by Italy.

(6) Abyssinia to be disarmed.

182. Overtures identical with the above were made on the same day by the Secretariat of State to the French Ambassador to the Holy See, and both M. Charles-Roux and Mr. Montgomery obtained the definite impression that the conditions in question came from the Italian Government and were being conveyed to the French and British Governments at the wish of the Duce and with the full cognisance of the Pope. This impression was shown to have been correct when the very next day (the 17th October) Signor Mussolini, in conversation with the French Ambassador to the Quirinal, put forward, though in a more exact form, conditions practically identical with the above. It is somewhat difficult to understand why the Duce should have made these overtures indirectly through the Pope if he intended on the next day to transmit them through the normal channel direct to the French, if not to the British, Government. The only possible explanation would seem to be that he wished to make sure of Vatican support beforehand.

183. In the circumstances, and as the proposals would anyhow have reached His Majesty's Government through the French Government, it seemed unnecessary to His Majesty's Principal Secretary of State, who had no desire to embark, as it were, on a double set of negotiations, to send a detailed answer to the Vatican. His Majesty's Government therefore contented themselves with sending their cordial thanks for the Vatican's good offices, at the same time making it clear that they would examine these and any future indications as to the position of the Italian Government which came to them from the same source with the greatest care. These assurances which were conveyed to the Vatican on the 23rd October by His Majesty's Chargé d'Affaires were received with relief by Mgr. Pizzardo, as rumours had been rife at the Secretariat of State as to the alleged " inflexibility " of Great Britain's attitude, and her supposed unwillingness to consider any settlement which Italy could accept.

184. The Acting Secretary of State was, however, determined to let no grass grow under his feet and took this opportunity of informing Mr. Montgomery of the alarm with which the Vatican viewed the approach of sanctions. His Excellency declared that they would arouse such violent feelings in Italy that there would be danger of an explosion. In this connexion he magnified Italy's naval air strength. Finally, he expressed the earnest hope that if the time left before the date fixed for the application of these measures proved too short for the satisfactory discussion of the Italian proposals the date of application

might be postponed. Mr. Montgomery, who did not encourage this suggestion, referred Mgr. Pizzardo to a passage in Sir Samuel Hoare's speech of the 22nd October suggesting that the time still left before sanctions could be applied should be made use of with a view to finding a solution.

185. Mgr. Pizzardo also said on this occasion how much the Holy Father would appreciate the opportunity of having a talk with His Majesty's Ambassador at the Quirinal about the whole situation; the interview, Mgr. Pizzardo thought, could be kept secret. His Majesty's Chargé d'Affaires, after informing Sir Eric Drummond of the suggestion, enquired of the Foreign Office whether his Excellency could be authorised to pay His Holiness a visit of the kind suggested. His Majesty's Principal Secretary of State replied, on the 26th October, that an audience on the lines proposed would be liable, if it became known, to misconstruction in England. Mr. Montgomery was accordingly instructed to inform Mgr. Pizzardo that the moment did not appear opportune for a conversation of the kind suggested. If, however, the situation developed favourably, Sir Samuel Hoare would not fail to reconsider the proposal. His Excellency took the decision of His Majesty's Government well, but there is reason to suppose that the Holy Father was disappointed.

186. At this time also the Secretary of State instructed His Majesty's Chargé d'Affaires to make the British point of view clearer to Mgr. Pizzardo, explaining to him that Italy, being a member of the League, deserved no credit, as he seemed to imagine, for being ready to contemplate a League solution and that the issue was not one between Great Britain and Italy, but between Italy, Abyssinia and the League. His Excellency said that he quite understood the British point of view, which, however, seemed to him unduly rigid and legalistic, and that he presented the League point of view to the Italians just as he often insisted on the Italian point of view when talking to members of sanctionist countries. As regards the needed consent of Abyssinia to any solution Mgr. Pizzardo said that the Emperor of Abyssinia could not be allowed to dictate his own terms; it was obvious that he would yield to British and French pressure if this were really exercised. As regards the necessity of League approval for any solution, the Acting Secretary of State said that a basis for a settlement, which would reconcile the Italian and League points of view, could far more easily be reached in conversations between representatives of Great Britain and France than in the course of general discussions at Geneva. In reply His Majesty's Chargé d'Affaires said that Abyssinia was a full member of the League, and that it was a mistake to exaggerate the extent of the pressure which Great Britain and France could exert upon her. As for the proposed method of finding a settlement he understood that Signor Mussolini's suggestions were actually forming the subject of Anglo-French conversations, though in their present form they seemed clearly unsatisfactory.

187. On the 28th October Cardinal Schuster, Archbishop of Milan, who was presiding by his own wish at a religious ceremony in his cathedral, organised by the local Fascists for the anniversary of the march on Rome, delivered a sermon in which he said that the Italian flag was bearing the Cross of Triumph over the Ethiopian plains, and that the intrepid army of Italy was opening the gates of Abyssinia to Catholic faith and Roman civilisation. This sermon was not reported in the *Osservatore Romano*, and the Pope's only comment on it is said to have been : " Civilisation à coups de canon ! " It was one of the first and most significant of a long series of episcopal utterances to which it will be necessary to revert later.

188. On the 31st October the Assistant Under-Secretary of State at the Vatican asked His Majesty's Chargé d'Affaires if something could be done at once to reduce the size of the British fleet in the Mediterranean. Mr. Montgomery replied that, until Italy brought more troops back from Libya or showed some other sign of goodwill, it would be difficult to take any such step. Mgr. Ottaviani went on to say that Italy's need for expansion had not been sufficiently taken into consideration, and implied that His Holiness did not approve of the policy of sanctions, for the adoption of which he (Mgr. Ottaviani) showed clearly that he thought Great Britain chiefly responsible.

(iv) November: Pro-Italian Tendencies at the Vatican.

189. On the 2nd November the *Osservatore Romano* published an article on the anti-sanctionist campaign which, though preserving an appearance of impartiality, succeeded in conveying the idea, chiefly by means of quotations from the Italian press, that Great Britain was exercising undue influence at Geneva and was herself the prime mover in the application of sanctions. On the 15th November the same paper, this time on the side of the angels, objected to a statement attributed to Catholics to the effect that sanctions were a Protestant speciality, and pointed out that Benedict XV had himself advocated a peace pact to be enforced by sanctions. On the whole, however, the paper continued to adopt an attitude which can best be described as one of benevolent neutrality towards Italy.

190. The *Civiltà Cattolica*, the well-known Jesuit fortnightly which appears in Rome and is usually taken to be an organ of Vatican opinion, went so far as to publish in its first number for November an article professing to be a review of Mr. Eppstein's recent book, *Must War Come?* in which, after alluding to the Pope's dictum that the need for expansion should be taken into account, it suggested that a satisfactory way of ending the present conflict would be to give Italy a mandate over Abyssinia. Mgr. Ottaviani, to whom Mr. Montgomery mentioned this article, assured him that it merely represented the personal views of the Father who wrote it, and said that the Pope had only seen or heard of it after publication. The next number of the periodical also gave assurances that the views expressed had been purely unofficial.

191. On the 7th November His Majesty's Principal Secretary of State, while approving the language held by His Majesty's Chargé d'Affaires to the Monsignori of the Secretariat of State, instructed him to avoid so far as was possible being drawn into discussion. The Secretary of State added that, as he found it difficult to distinguish between the attitude of the Vatican and that of the Italian Government, he felt still less ready to multiply the channels of communication which all led to one point. Mr. Montgomery was able to avoid any discussion with the Cardinal Secretary of State, whom he visited on the 9th November on the latter's return from his six weeks' holiday. On the 12th November, however, Mgr. Pizzardo insisted on reopening the subject and pressed His Majesty's Chargé d'Affaires to say what Great Britain's attitude now was and what she thought Italy ought to do. In language which was afterwards approved, Mr. Montgomery said, speaking quite personally, that nothing could be done until Italy frankly accepted her obligations under the Covenant and admitted the need for a solution which the Emperor of Abyssinia could accept. Once Italy had shown a proper understanding of the situation as it presented itself to other members of the League, he felt sure that everything possible would be done to avoid inflicting unnecessary humiliation upon her. Certainly His Majesty's Government only desired to fulfil their obligations under the Covenant and, with this proviso, were as anxious as the Vatican for an early peace.

192. During the period following on the outbreak of hostilities, His Majesty's Chargé d'Affaires had fairly frequent interviews, usually at their own request, with the French Ambassador to the Holy See and his counsellor. M. Charles-Roux, who always finds it hard to understand any point of view other than that of his country, never understood the reluctance with which British public opinion envisaged the possibility of the aggressor's being rewarded and had high hopes of the success of the Vatican overtures of the 16th October (as later of the Paris proposals). He denied for a long time that the Vatican's attitude was unduly favourable to Italy, and claimed on more than one occasion that His Holiness's objects were identical with those of M. Laval, and that the Pontifical allusions in the speech of the 27th August to those who tried to obtain peace by persuasion and not by threats were intended for the French Prime Minister. M. Charles-Roux attached great weight to the Pontiff's influence with Signor Mussolini; said that it was entirely due to His Holiness's efforts that the terms suggested in October were as reasonable as they were; and only began to falter when in December the Dictator failed entirely to act on the Pontiff's advice to adopt a conciliatory attitude and accept the Paris proposals.

193. On the 18th November M. Charles-Roux was kind enough to show Mr. Montgomery a secret memorandum which, from its allusions to the Archbishop of Westminster and to Great Britain, would appear to have been intended primarily for consumption in England and was perhaps in reality the reply to representations believed to have been made by certain English Catholic circles with a view to the Papacy dissociating itself from the Fascist cause. The memorandum, which is the only direct evidence of the Pope's views on the conflict which the Legation received after the outbreak of hostilities, pointed out that :—

(a) The Pope had in August and September spoken against war and denied that expansion justified it.

(b) Since the outbreak of hostilities His Holiness has been working for peace. This had demanded secrecy unless chances of success were to be hopelessly compromised.

(c) On account of the danger of a world war, nothing should be done to excite feeling further.

(d) Great Britain would be doing a good deed if by some *beau geste* she took into full account Italy's need for expansion.

194. On the 14th November Mgr. Pizzardo asked the opinion of His Majesty's Chargé d'Affaires on a typewritten article which had, he said, been prepared by a Catholic journalist connected with the Vatican. The article alleged, *inter alia*, that Britain had long feared a Latin *bloc* and had concluded the naval agreement with Germany as a counterblast to the Franco-Italian rapprochement. It also said that Great Britain was jealous of Italian strength in the Mediterranean; that she had restored the Greek monarchy in order to increase her own prestige in the Near East; that her only object in opposing the Abyssinian campaign was to prevent Italy expanding in Africa. Mr. Montgomery said that the article was one long tissue of falsehoods and that, if it were published under Vatican auspices, everyone in England would conclude that the Holy See was entirely under Italian and Fascist influence. Mgr. Pizzardo protested that there had never been any intention of publishing the article and that he had merely desired to have Mr. Montgomery's opinion on it, for which he thanked him.

195. On the same day, Mgr. Ottaviani denied that the broadcast from Bari, given on the 19th October, in the name of a mythical Mgr. Bellini, "Political Secretary of the Vatican," had actually come from the Vatican City. The Italian broadcasting authorities, who were consulted on this point by the Secretariat of State, also denied all responsibility. There was no confirmation of the rumours which became rife about this time that the Vatican had advised the foreign colleges in Rome to co-operate in the effort against sanctions. The General of the Jesuits did, however, issue orders to the colleges under his control to co-operate with the measures of the Government in regard to food, &c.

196. On the 19th November, in consideration of representations made by His Majesty's Government in the United Kingdom through the Legation, on the ground of imminent and increasing danger, the Vatican authorised the Vicar-Apostolic of Harrar, who had been deaf to the admonitions of His Majesty's Minister at Addis Ababa, to withdraw certain Maltese nuns from Jijiga. At an earlier date some Maltese monks had been allowed to withdraw from Dire Dawa as a result of intervention by His Majesty's Legation and Sir S. Barton had done all in his power to facilitate the repatriation of the Italian religious of the Consolata, who had been resident near Addis Ababa and whose position had become precarious.

(v) *December: The Vatican and the Paris Peace Proposals.*

197. On the 4th December, Mgr. Ottaviani indicated that in his opinion Italy would make considerable concessions in the matter of a port for Abyssinia if she were allowed to keep all the conquered territories. On the 7th December the Pope suffered from a diplomatic illness which prevented him from receiving a deputation of war nurses and mothers of the fallen who had visited Rome in connexion with one of the Duce's theatrical schemes for increasing the volume of popular resentment against sanctions. At about this time the *Osservatore Romano* excused the Cardinal Archbishop of Milan's latest imprudence by saying

that he had only recommended the giving of gold objects in churches if the needs of the poor became so desperate as to require this sacrifice.   The Cardinal Secretary of State expressed to His Majesty's Chargé d'Affaires on the 6th December his appreciation of the conciliatory tone of the speech delivered by Sir Samuel Hoare in Parliament on the 5th December, and added in confidence that the Vatican had impressed upon Signor Mussolini the need of being equally conciliatory when he spoke on the 7th December.   In fact, however, the Dictator's speech, if it closed no doors, was unhelpful and even truculent.

198.   On the 10th December the *Osservatore . Romano* expressed strong approval of the personal negotiations between Sir Samuel Hoare and M. Laval and said that the solution proposed seemed to be of the kind recommended by the Pope, *i.e.*, one which took into consideration both the rights and the necessities of those concerned, while inflicting humiliation on no one.   On the 13th December Cardinal Fumasoni Biondi (Prefect of Propaganda) said to Mr. Montgomery that the only choice for Italy lay between fascism and bolshevism; his Eminence added that much of the opposition to the Abyssinian adventure was due, not to the high motives alleged, but to Communist and masonic hatred of fascism.   All this time a certain uneasiness was growing and continues to grow, in foreign ecclesiastical circles in Rome, as to the increasing sympathy between the Vatican and the Palazzo Venezia.   In *Osservatore Romano* of the 18th December, Mgr. Vanneufville, in a clearly inspired commentary on the Pope's non-committal allocution of the 16th December (see section VI (*e*)) compared His Holiness's silence at the present juncture to that of Benedict XV during the Great War. The Pope had insisted upon the need of working for a peace which would be founded not only on justice but also on charity, and it was not his function, after having laid down the general principle that wars of conquest were wrong, to descend into the controversial arena and draw up an analysis of political responsibility.

199.   The shipwreck of the Paris peace proposals caused the greatest disappointment to the Pope, who had set all his hopes upon their bearing fruit, and though a large share of blame was no doubt attributed by the Vatican to Great Britain it is permissible to assume that much annoyance was also felt at Signor Mussolini's complete disregard of the Vatican's counsels of moderation. On the 21st December the Cardinal Secretary of State said to Mr. Montgomery that, in his opinion, the Duce ought at once to have accepted the proposals, at least as a basis of negotiation, and expressed regret at the Pontinia speech.   The *Osservatore Romano* took pains, it is true, to explain at great length the difficulties which Italy would have felt in accepting the abortive proposals, the chief drawback being apparently that Eritrea and Italian Somaliland would remain unconnected.   The same article purported also to give the objections of Abyssinia and the League, but Abyssinia's objections were limited to the one observation that she would regard cession of territory as a reward for the aggressor; and unfair play was made of the fact that the Radical press in various countries had made itself her mouthpiece.   As for the League, the paper seemed to admit that here, too, exception might be taken to such large cessions of territory; it had been hoped, however, that the view of the Laval press would be taken at Geneva, viz., that the question was really one of exchange of territory, Italy receiving large, but somewhat desert zones, in exchange for a narrow but important corridor.   On the whole, the *Osservatore Romano* seemed to consider that the proposals provided at least an equitable basis of discussion.

(vi) *The Vatican and the Italian Bishops.*

200.   The ultra-patriotic attitude of the majority of the Italian bishops, which must have surpassed all Signor Mussolini's expectations and strengthened his position considerably, was undoubtedly a cause of anxiety to the Pope.   So great was the enthusiasm of these prelates that, much to the fury of the *Osservatore Romano*, which did its ineffective best to find an adequate reply, a National Socialist paper in December actually held the Italian hierarchy up to admiration on the ground that, unlike the German bishops, they put their country before their religion.

201.   The example of the Cardinal Archbishop of Milan, whose sermon of the 28th October has been mentioned already, was fortunately not followed by any other members of the Sacred College, except Cardinal Nasalli-Rocca of

Bologna who, however, expressed himself much more mildly.   Cardinal Minoretti, of Genoa, whose words are said to have been approved by the Pope, merely exhorted his flock to be obedient to the Government, to remain patient and to pray for peace, and his example was followed by a number of the bishops.   Most of their lordships went further than this, however, speaking of Italy's civilising mission and of the trust Italians felt in their leader.   A considerable number, misled, no doubt, by Fascist propaganda went outside their sphere altogether and abused the opponents of Signor Mussolini's war of aggression in no measured terms.   Thus, the Archbishop of Brindisi spoke of the "cold-hearted egoism and arrogance of England"; the Archbishop of Amalfi referred to sanctionist "jealousy and egoism, wrapped in a cloak of unutterable hypocrisy"; the Archbishop of Sorrento paid a tribute to "the unscrupulous greed and selfishness of certain countries"; while the Bishop of San Severo said that the nations were leagued together against Italy in "swollen envy and insane pride."   These are only a few of many similar utterances and, though some bishops spoke more in sorrow than in anger and insisted chiefly on the need of prayer, it was fairly clear that they had almost to a man succumbed to the Fascist view of the situation and accepted the theory that Italy was opposed, as the Archbishop of Siena put it, by "an unrighteous coalition filled with hatred."

202.   The subject of these utterances coming up in conversation between Mgr. Ottaviani and Mr. Montgomery during November, the Assistant Under-Secretary of State said he had not noticed that any of them contained attacks on England.   At his Excellency's own request Mr. Montgomery accordingly sent him two reports of utterances mentioning England by name together with several more which were clearly directed against her.   A few days later, Mgr. Ottaviani said in confidence that a hint had been sent to the bishops to moderate their language in so far as the sanctionist Powers were concerned and, in fact, an improvement in the tone of the sermons and charges soon afterwards became noticeable.   It may be mentioned here that when the French counsellor deplored the episcopal utterances to Mgr. Ottaviani, he replied that they were no worse than those of the Anglican bishops.   It did not seem to have occurred to Mgr. Ottaviani that whereas the English bishops were condemning an unprovoked war of aggression, the Italian bishops were defending the aggressor.

203.   The bishops' enthusiasm even took tangible form and Signor Mussolini's gold fund was enriched by the crosses, episcopal rings and pastoral chains of perhaps half the Italian hierarchy.   One bishop, in an impassioned speech delivered at an agricultural prize-giving function in the presence of the Dictator, offered all the gold and the bells of the churches to the "Patria." (Whether he was speaking for his own diocese only was not quite clear; in any case his words were not presumably meant to be taken seriously.)   Apart from him, the prelate who went furthest was the Archbishop of Monreale in Sicily, who sent a circular to the parish priests of his diocese, exhorting them to give to the national fund all the gold vessels and *ex voto* offerings which could be spared from their churches.   The alienation of such objects for secular use is forbidden by canon law without prior consent by the Holy See, and the fact that no more was heard of this archbishop's *geste* and that his example was not followed shows perhaps that he was called to order by the Vatican.   It is true that a somewhat similar suggestion was made later by Cardinal Schuster, but this was subsequently explained away by the *Osservatore Romano* which said that his Eminence had merely suggested that, if the need became sufficiently great, *ex voto* offerings might have to be sacrificed in order to help the poor, but for no other purpose.

204.   The most was, of course, made of the bishop's attitude by the Fascist press, and articles appeared in various papers praising the noble gestures and "inspired" utterances of the hierarchy and alleging that never before had Italy possessed so truly national a clergy, and that never had clergy and laity throughout the peninsula been so closely united as now.

(vii) *Unfounded Rumours of Vatican Assistance to Italy.*

205.   During the last part of the year it was persistently rumoured, both in and outside Italy, that the Pope had been lending money, directly or indirectly, to the Italian Government.   That His Holiness should have been using his

English assets for this purpose would seem to be out of the question, for these consist chiefly of real property held in the name of an English registered company. It is more difficult to say what use His Holiness may have made of his investments in other countries, *e.g.*, France and the United States, but it seems unlikely, if only on grounds of expediency, that he would have employed them to support Italian finances.

206. Certainly all such rumours have been indignantly denied. On the 14th October the French paper *Humanité* was indignantly taken to task by the *Osservatore Romano* for having "dared to write" that the Holy See had concluded a secret agreement with Italy for the financing of the Abyssinian war, and a little later a *démenti* was issued of a story which had appeared in the Nazi *Völkischer Beobachter* to the effect that the Vatican was placing precious objects to the value of ten million gold francs at Signor Mussolini's disposal.

207. In December the Bâle *National-Zeitung* published a rumour that the "Peter's Pence" collected in Germany and unable to be transmitted to Rome on account of currency restrictions were, by arrangement between the Vatican and Signor Mussolini, to be placed at the disposal of the Italian Government for the purchase of war material. This story, together with a similar one which had appeared in the Paris *Information*, was indignantly denied by the Vatican newspaper.

V.—THE VATICAN.

Canonisation.

208. The chief ecclesiastical event of 1935, not only for English Roman Catholics but for the Church in general, was the canonisation on the 19th May of Bishop John Fisher and Sir Thomas More.

209. It was known early in the year that the Pope was inclined to accede to the expressed desire of the whole British Hierarchy and of thousands of British Catholics in canonising these two martyrs on the fourth centenary of their death.

210. Fisher and More, who, together with fifty-two other Catholic martyrs of the 16th century, were proclaimed blessed by Leo XIII in 1886, are the first Englishmen to have been canonised since the Reformation. There had been some hope among Roman Catholics that they would be canonised in 1929 when a further group of "English martyrs" were beatified. It was not, however, until 1930 that the cause of the two martyrs was definitely introduced as a "separate joint cause." The Holy Year of the Redemption (1933–34) brought so many English pilgrims to Rome, including a deputation which presented a monster petition for the canonisation of these two martyrs, that the Pope was pleased to take a special interest in the cause and to dispense in their case with many of the usual preliminaries. For this procedure, which is known as "equipollent canonisation" and which was first admitted, in modern times, by Pope Gregory XIII, there had been several quite recent precedents, including the canonisation of St. Ephrem in 1920 and that of St. Albert the Great in 1931.

211. In 1934 the Pope therefore committed the matter to the special section of the Congregation of Rites which deals with historical causes, and the final decision in favour of canonisation was given at a plenary meeting of this Congregation which was held at the Vatican on the 29th January, under the Pope's presidency. There had been some doubt as to whether, in view of the fact that the miracles usually required were lacking, the canonisation could be carried out *in forma solemni*. In spite, however, of the breach with precedent (Albertus Magnus had simply been proclaimed Saint by decree) the Congregation, in deference to the Pope's express desire, decided that the canonisation should be solemnly celebrated in St. Peter's.

212. Granted the theological soundness of a canonisation, there are various reasons which make each particular one opportune in the eyes of the supreme authority, and among the Pope's reasons for choosing the moment he did, it would probably be safe to number : (*a*) his wish to encourage resistance to State tyranny over the Church, as practised, for instance, in Germany and Mexico, and (*b*) his wish to pay a genuine compliment to England, while recalling that it is possible for typical and loyal Englishmen to be at the same time faithful

sons of Mother Church. His Holiness certainly did not regard the condemnation of Henry VIII which the canonisation implies as involving any sort of reflection on the British Crown of to-day; on the countrary he undoubtedly considered that he was paying the highest compliment in his power to Great Britain. That this view was shared by many Englishmen, including those who owe no allegiance to His Holiness, would seem to be clear from articles such as that entitled : "St. Thomas and St. John" which appeared in the *Times* of the 2nd February. This article, of which a translation was published in the *Osservatore Romano*, gave great satisfaction at the Vatican. Among other things it said that the vast majority of the prospective Saints' countrymen had long held them in honour and that to all alike, whether Catholics or Protestants, "the spirits of these two just men made perfect would remain an abiding inspiration."

213. The public reading of the decree *de Martyrio* took place at the Vatican on the 11th February when the Catholic Bishop of Southwark (Mgr. Amigo), who had played a leading part in furthering the cause of the two Beati, thanked the Pope for his "Fatherly good-will towards England." A similar ceremony took place on the 3rd March for the reading of the decree *de tuto*. At this Mgr. Hinsley spoke of the devotion of pre-Reformation England to the Holy See, and recalled that Cardinal Newman had attributed the revival of catholicism in England or "second spring" to the prayers of the Catholic martyrs under Henry VIII and Elizabeth. In his reply the Holy Father said that he wished to speak of the two saints-to-be "in the setting of their own country and people."

214. His Holiness went on to say that it seemed really providential that public attention should be drawn to the martyrdom of these two Englishmen at a time when the British Empire covered so large a portion of the globe. It might be said that Divine Providence had thus prepared a theatre of especial size and splendour for the glorification of these great servants and "athletes" of God.

215. The Pope went on to say that, when he had thanked The King (on the occasion of His Majesty's visit to Rome) for the benevolent treatment of Catholics in the British Dominions, His Majesty had said that the very numerous Catholics in the Empire, amounting to several millions, were among the most loyal of his subjects.

216. The Holy Father next alluded to the "happy coincidence" whereby the festivities in celebration of the beloved Sovereign's Silver Jubilee synchronised almost exactly with the fourth centenary of the death of Fisher and More. No one, he said, least of all he himself, had foreseen this coincidence at the time when the possibility of an early canonisation began to be considered.

217. The Pope went on to say that Great Britain, of all the units composing the British Empire, would naturally be the most closely concerned in the Jubilee celebrations. This, too, seemed to him providential, for it might thus be said that the two martyrs were invited to take part in the celebrations, thereby reminding the English-speaking world of the old religion and renewing the sublime words with which, on the scaffold, they thanked those through whom they obtained their heavenly crowns. Thus, having achieved celestial splendour, they deigned, said the Pontiff, to honour also that earthly crown which they always did honour, and indeed there never were, nor could be, subjects more faithful than these two who died sooner than sully their conscience or their faith.

218. The Pope concluded his allocution by giving a very special blessing to England and to all the British Empire. He said that it was not without profound emotion that, in the name of these two martyrs, he called down God's benediction on the country which had once been known as the "dowry of Mary" and "the patrimony of St. Peter." The sacrifice of the martyrs had already led to a revival of the faith in England and to a realisation of Newman's prophecy as to a "second spring," and he prayed that this spring might be rich in fragrance and in flower.

219. On the 7th April Mgr. Hinsley, who had just been appointed Archbishop of Westminster, told Sir Charles Wingfield that he knew the Pope would greatly appreciate it if The King were able to send some special mission or representative to the canonisation. His Majesty's Minister replied that, in common with other members of the Diplomatic Corps, he would himself attend

the ceremony. In view of the fact that the claim of these two Englishmen to canonisation arose out of their defence of Papal interests against the Reformation, Sir Charles Wingfield said he felt sure that His Majesty's Government would not consider that further representation was either required or appropriate and he very much hoped that His Holiness would not press the suggestion, which it would be embarrassing for The King to have to refuse. As a result of Sir Charles Wingfield's attitude and of the similar reply elicited as a result of other enquiries which the archbishop made through prominent Roman Catholics in London, the Pope seems to have abandoned the hope of welcoming a special mission to the Vatican, and no more was heard of the matter.

220.   The last of the many preliminaries to the canonisation, viz., the private and public consistories, having been held on the 1st and 4th April respectively, the final ceremony took place at St. Peter's with great pomp on Sunday, the 19th May. The long-expected event was made the occasion for the visit of many pilgrims from the United Kingdom, though there were fewer than had at one time been expected, as the recent Holy Year pilgrimages had left many who might otherwise have come without the means to do so. Nearly all the Catholic archbishops and bishops of the United Kingdom were present, as well as many abbots, minor prelates and prominent members of the Catholic laity. During the ceremony the Pope made use of a gold ewer and basin given by Queen Victoria to Leo XIII on the occasion of his sacerdotal jubilee; whilst the chalice presented by the religious of the diocese of Southwark in honour of the canonisation was used at the Papal Mass. In the evening the dome and façade of St. Peter's were illuminated. Special medals in honour of the canonisation, bearing on one side the effigy of the Pope and, on the other, that of the two new saints, were struck by the Vatican to mark the occasion, and of these, one was presented by the Cardinal Secretary of State to St. John's College, Cambridge, which, in the words of the Master, is " perpetually indebted " to its " second founder," Bishop John Fisher.

College of Cardinals.

221.   During 1935 the Sacred College lost five members, but as twenty new cardinals were added by the Consistory of the 16th December, the total gain for the year amounted to fifteen, and at Christmas the cardinals were, for the first time for very many years, only short by two of their full quota of seventy.

222.   Those who died during the year were :—

(1) His Eminence Francis Bourne, Archbishop of Westminster, who died in London on the 1st January, aged 73. (For biographical notice and other particulars, see under " United Kingdom.")

(2) His Eminence Paulin Andrieu, Archbishop of Bordeaux, who died on the 15th February, aged 85. With the exception of Cardinal Skrbensky, the former Archbishop of Prague, of whom nothing is any longer seen or heard, Cardinal Andrieu was the senior member of the Sacred College, having been created by Pius X in 1907. Before being called to the See of Bordeaux in 1909 Cardinal Andrieu had been for eight years Bishop of Marseilles, a period which coincided with the religious tension in France which eventually led to the separation of Church and State. It was to the firm stand which he made at this time for the essential rights of the Church that the cardinal owed his Hat. He was best known, however, for the uncompromising attitude which he adopted from the very beginning towards the " Action française " movement which was at first smiled upon by so many of his episcopal colleagues. For the part which he played in bringing about the condemnation of the movement by Rome, Cardinal Andrieu was never forgiven by large sections of the French Catholic laity. He seems to have been a hard, intransigent but upright man, ready to give and to receive hard knocks in a just cause.

(3) His Eminence Achille Locatelli, Cardinal in Curia, who died in Rome on the 7th April, aged 79. A namesake and fellow-townsman of the present Pontiff, Achille Locatelli studied in Rome and entered the Papal diplomatic service in 1880. Between 1906 and 1922 he was successively Internuncio at Buenos Aires and Nuncio at Brussels and

Lisbon. In 1922 Pius XI created him cardinal, and he spent the rest of his life in Rome as a member of the Curia. Having been in failing health for some time he had not of late played an important part in the counsels of the Church.

(4) His Eminence Pietro La Fontaine, Patriarch of Venice, who died at Fietta sul Grappa (Venetia) on the 9th July at the age of 75. The cardinal who had reigned over the See of Venice for over twenty years and was much beloved was, despite his French name, a native of Viterbo in Central Italy. He early attracted the favourable attention of the ecclesiastical authorities in Rome, and after working in Curia for many years with a five years' break as bishop of a small diocese in Calabria, was made Patriarch of Venice in 1914 and cardinal two years later. As spiritual head of one of the Italian provinces most affected by the war, the cardinal's task during the first three years of his patriarchate was no easy one. He devoted himself to it heart and soul, and when peace returned was responsible for the erection, on the Lido, of a votive church in memory of the thousands of soldiers who had died defending Venice. It is in this church that he was laid to rest. Among the various important missions confided to the cardinal, one of the most important and significant was that of Papal Legate to the Catholic Congress of Vienna (1933), at which the 250th anniversary of Austria's delivery from the Turks was commemorated.

(5) His Eminence Michele Lega, who died in Rome on the 16th December. He was Cardinal in Curia, Bishop of Frascati, sub-dean of the Sacred College and Prefect of the Sacred Congregation of the Sacraments. The cardinal, who was born in 1860, was chiefly known as an authority on canon law. After long years as a professor in the Pontifical Roman Seminary he became Consultor of the Commission for Canon Law, and eventually first Dean of the reformed Tribunal of the Rota. Created cardinal deacon in 1914 in Piux X's last Consistory, he, in 1926, became Cardinal Bishop of the Suburban See of Frascati. He had for many years been Prefect of the important Congregation of the Sacraments.

223. At the Secret Consistory held by Pius XI on the 16th December, the names of two dignitaries who had been created cardinals *in petto* in March 1933 were officially published, while eighteen other prelates were raised to the Sacred Purple. The Red Hats were conferred at the Public Consistory held on the 19th December.

224. The two cardinals *in petto* who have now received the full privileges and outward dignities of their rank were the following :—

Mgr. Federigo Tedeschini, Apostolic Nuncio to Spain, and Mgr. Carlo Salotti, Secretary of the Sacred Congregation de Propaganda Fide.

The eighteen other ecclesiastics who received the Sacred Purple were :—

Mgr. Ignatius Tappouni, Patriarch of Antioch.
Mgr. Enrico Sibilia, Nuncio to Austria.
Mgr. Francesco Marmaggi, Nuncio to Poland.
Mgr. Luigi Maglione, Nuncio to France.
Mgr. Carlo Cremonesi, Privy Almoner to His Holiness.
Mgr. Henri Marie Alfred Baudrillart, Rector of the Catholic Institute at Paris, Member of the " Académie française."
Mgr. Emanuel Suhard, Archbishop of Reims.
Mgr. Carl Kaspar, Archbishop of Prague.
Mgr. Giacomo Luigi Copello, Archbishop of Buenos Aires.
Mgr. Isador Gomà y Tomas, Archbishop of Toledo.
Mgr. Camillo Caccia Dominioni, for the last fifteen years Master of the Pope's Household.
Mgr. Nicola Canali, Assessor to the Supreme Congregation of the Holy Office.
Mgr. Domenico Jorio, Secretary of the Sacred Congregation of Discipline and the Sacraments.

Mgr. Vincenzo La Puma, Secretary of the Sacred Congregation of the Religious.

Mgr. Federico Cattani-Amadori, Auditor to His Holiness, Secretary of the Supreme Tribunal of the Apostolic Segnatura.

Mgr. Massimo Massimi (for the last few years Dean of the Sacred Roman Rota).

Mgr. Domenico Mariani, Secretary of the Administration of the property of the Holy See.

Father Pietro Boetto, of the Society of Jesus, for the past five years Italian " Assistant " to the Father General.

225.   Of the new cardinals, it will be observed that four are Nuncios at important posts, which (if precedent is followed) they will shortly have to leave; four (all from outside Italy) are the holders of famous primatial Sees; seven are functionaries from the different congregations of the Roman Curia; two have belonged for many years to the personal entourage of the Pope; one (Mgr. Baudrillart) is a well-known scholar; while of the remaining two, one is a prominent Italian Jesuit and the other (last, but not least) is the first archbishop of the Eastern rite to be raised to the cardinalate in the present century. He appears, indeed, to be only the fifth Eastern in the history of the Church to receive this distinction.

226.   One of the results, and many will think an unfortunate one, of the 1935 Consistory, is that it readjusts the balance of nationality within the Sacred College in a manner very favourable to Italy.   Before the Consistory there were thirteen Italian and fifteen foreign cardinals.   Now there are thirty-seven Italians to thirty-one foreigners.   The few lingering hopes which may have been entertained here and there of a foreign successor to the present Pope must thus be finally dismissed.

227.   The four Nuncios who have been raised to the cardinalate were not present in Rome for the Consistory, and their birettas were conveyed to them in December by Apostolic Ablegates specially appointed.   The birettas were actually conferred, in accordance with the precedent laid down, for Catholic countries, by the heads of the States (*i.e.*, France, Poland, Belgium and Austria) to which the Nuncios are accredited.

228.   Of the two important Church offices which were mentioned in last year's report as being still unfilled, that of Camerlengo (the official in charge of conclaves) has been conferred on Cardinal Pacelli; that of Librarian is still vacant.

229.   On the death of Cardinal Lega in December, the Holy Father appointed the newly-created Cardinal Jorio to succeed him as Prefect of the Congregation of the Sacraments.

Papal Legates.

230.   One of the innovations introduced under the present Pope is the habit of sending Legates *a latere* with great frequency to religious celebrations in various countries.   The following were sent during 1936 :—

Cardinal Pacelli to a Triduum of Prayer at Lourdes (April).
Cardinal Lépicier to Malta Provincial Council (June).
Cardinal Verdier to Prague Eucharistic Congress (June).
Cardinal Hlond to Ljubljana Eucharistic Congress (July).
Cardinal Fumasoni Biondi to Italian Eucharistic Congress at Teramo (Abruzzi) (August).
Cardinal Hayes to Cleveland Eucharistic Congress (September).

Changes in Pontifical Household and Curia.

231.   In connexion with the Consistory of the 16th December and the resulting vacancies in the Pontifical Household and Curia, the following ecclesiastical appointments were made by His Holiness :—

(i) Mgr. Arborio Mella di Sant'Elia to be Master of the Household in succession to Mgr. (now Cardinal) Caccia-Dominioni.
(ii) Mgr. Giuseppe Migone to be Privy Almoner to His Holiness in succession to Mgr. (now Cardinal) Cremonesi.

(iii) Mgr. Luca Pasetto to be Secretary of the Sacred Congregation of
        Religious in succession to Mgr. (now Cardinal) La Puma. ·
(iv) Mgr. Francesco Morano to be Secretary of the Supreme Tribunal of the
        Segnatura in succession to Mgr. (now Cardinal) Cattani-Amadori.
(v) Mgr. Celso Costantini to be Secretary of the Sacred Congregation de
        Propaganda Fide in succession to Mgr. (now Cardinal) Salotti.
(vi) Mgr. Giulio Grazioli to be Dean of the Sacred Roman Rota in
        succession to Mgr. (now Cardinal) Massimi.
(vii) Mgr. Alfredo Ottaviani to be Assessor to the Supreme Sacred
        Congregation of the Holy Office in succession to Mgr. (now
        Cardinal) Canali.
(viii) Mgr. Domenico Tardini, of the Secretariat of State, to succeed
        Mgr. Ottaviani as Assistant Under-Secretary of State (" Sostituto
        della Segreteria di Stato ").

Reorganisation of the Palatine Guard.

232. The reorganisation of the Palatine Guard of Honour, one of the four
existing corps of Papal troops, was provided for in an order promulgated on the
23rd January. The guard, which has until now consisted of one battalion
comprising four companies of 80 to 100 men each, is under the personal control of
the Cardinal Secretary of State. As a result of the new regulations, the guard
will still consist of four companies, but the number of men in each will be brought
up to 125, the whole battalion thus consisting of 500 men. The objects of the
Palatine Guard are to protect the Pope's person and to carry out the " service
d'honneur." at functions in St. Peter's and elsewhere. Only citizens of the
Vatican City or of Rome are eligible, and the age of enrolments is from
18 to 30 years. The corps takes rank after the " Guardia Nobile " and the
" Swiss Guard," and comes before the Pontifical Gendarmerie. The officers
consist of a colonel commanding the whole unit, a lieutenant-colonel, a major, an
adjutant with the rank of captain, three lieutenants, two medical officers with the
rank of major and captain respectively and two chaplains.

The Pope's Visit to Castel Gandolfo.

233. His Holiness stayed at Castel Gandolfo from the 31st July to the
30th September, *i.e.*, ten days longer than last year. It seems probable that
henceforth His Holiness and his successors will, as a matter of course, spend the
months of August and September in the country. In view of the short distance
of Castel Gandolfo from Rome, the absence of the Holy Father affects the routine
of Vatican life but little. His Holiness is only accompanied by his immediate
entourage, including a number of Papal Chamberlains and some detachments of
Pontifical troops. Certain days are set aside for public audiences, and private
audiences are given as usual, the Cardinal Secretary of State and other cardinals
and important Curia officials coming out at regular intervals. The Pope
returned to Rome on one occasion during his villeggiatura, this being in order to
say Mass for, and address, the International Peace Pilgrimage of ex-combatants
at St. Paul's on the 9th September. His Holiness did not, however, visit the
Vatican on this occasion. On the day before leaving Castel Gandolfo the Holy
Father inaugurated the new and improved observatory, which has been
transferred from the Vatican gardens to the roof of the palace at Castel Gandolfo.

The Vatican and Sanctions.

234. On the 31st October the Assistant Under-Secretary of State at the
Vatican drew the attention of His Majesty's Chargé d'Affaires to the position in
regard to sanctions of the very numerous religious, educational and charitable
establishments of a non-Italian character (including national seminaries, such as
the English and Scots Colleges) which have their seat in Rome. The Vatican,
he said, hoped that His Majesty's Government in the United Kingdom concurred
in, and would, if necessary, press the view that all religious communities of an
international character situated in or near Rome should be excluded from the
action to be taken under article 16 of the Covenant. On the 19th November His
Majesty's Chargé d'Affaires was instructed to inform the Vatican that, so far as
His Majesty's Government in the United Kingdom were concerned, any loan to
or for an institution certified by the Treasury to have a humanitarian or religious

object are exempted by the Order in Council applying proposal No. 2 of the Co-ordination Committee. The instructions also included a statement according to which, if any doubt arose about exemption in other countries of religious institutions, His Majesty's Government were prepared to urge such exemption at Geneva.

235. As a matter of law, sanctions do not, of course, apply to the Vatican City, and, although there are practical difficulties in the way of excluding the Vatican from these measures, these would not appear to be insuperable, given the goodwill of the Italian authorities, who are unlikely in the circumstances to wish to give gratuitous cause of offence to the Pope.

236. Italian restrictions and anti-sanctionist measures are not likely to affect the Vatican greatly. As regards exchange restrictions, the Pope has enough money invested abroad to pay for purchases in the currency of the country where they are made; while goods destined for the Vatican are excluded from Italian import restrictions. There would not seem to be any danger of the Vatican lending themselves to any Italian attempts to evade the embargo. The Vatican are anxious to do nothing which might appear to compromise their temporal independence, and are likely, if anything, to reduce rather than expand their imports and exports as a result of sanctions. If Pontifical colleges in Rome are in need of goods which can only be obtained abroad and the Vatican undertake to procure them, the latter would undoubtedly demand from the heads of the colleges the most explicit guarantees that the goods would be used personally and exclusively by the students.

VI.—PAPAL PRONOUNCEMENTS.

237. The following were the most important pronouncements, written and oral, made by the Pope during the year :—

(a) *The Apostolic Letter of January* 10 *addressed to the Bishop of Tarbes and Lourdes.*

238. In this His Holiness announced that he had approved a suggestion made to him by the late Cardinal Bourne and by Cardinal Verdier, Archbishop of Paris, that the conclusion of the extended Holy Year (during which, in virtue of the bill *Quod superiori anno* of 1934, the benefits of the Jubilee of the Redemption were extended from the city to the world) should be marked by a triduum of public prayer to be held in Easter Week at the Grotto of the Apparition at Lourdes. In the letter the Pope laid down that, during the whole period of the triduum, *i.e.*, for seventy-two hours, Masses would be celebrated uninterruptedly, day and night, at the Sacred Grotto. The break with tradition involved in this decision of the Pope's was considerable, for, normally, of course, Masses may only be said between midnight and noon, and never before had Masses been offered without a break for this length of time on the same spot. For the triduum, which was attended by Cardinal Pacelli as Legate, see also section III, " France."

(b) *Consistorial Allocution of April* 1 (delivered at Secret Consistory for the Canonisation of Bishop Fisher and Sir Thomas More, at which no cardinals were created).

239. The Pope said that the occasion was an auspicious one, not only for his " beloved English people," but also for all the Catholic Church, for whom the martyrs were models for admiration and imitation. He hoped this solemn act would bear special fruit for those " who shared the martyr's country, language and glory." The English had asked with insistence for this glorification of their fellow citizens, for they felt in these days more drawn than ever towards the faith of their fathers and were becoming more anxious to return to union with the Apostolic See. The desire for unity had been shown particularly during the recent Jubilee Year of the Redemption when so many pilgrims had come to Rome from England. His Holiness ended by saying that, as devotion was compatible with the highest patriotism, the two saints would doubtless obtain by their prayers an increase of prosperity for England, particularly at a time when all parts of the British Empire would be celebrating with joy the Silver Jubilee of His Majesty The King (for this part of the allocution, *cf.* the Pope's other discourse on the same subject, quoted in section V, paragraphs 214–18).

240. Turning to the world situation, the Pope said that black clouds once again darkened the horizon. If war were to break out again, the crime would be a mad one. He could not believe that the rulers of any nations could desire such slaughter and ruin, but, if they did, he would have once more to raise the prayer : " Scatter Thou the people that delight in war."

(c) *The Pope's Discourse to the International Congress of Catholic Nurses* (Castel Gandolfo, August 27).

241. As the part of this discourse which had reference to the Italo-Abyssinian conflict has been so often quoted since and has given rise to such a variety of interpretations, it seems worth while giving a full translation :—

. . . . " It is the nurses who know best of all what war is like. War, the nurses have seen it, and if any of you went through the last war, you will not have forgotten it. We ourselves have seen it, we who had to cross Europe in wartime, and we were able to take note of the ravages caused by war as we traversed Central Europe towards the destination to which obedience and Providence called us—to Poland. We reached Poland the day after the Russian evacuation whilst the traces of devastation were still smoking. That was the reality of war. . . . . Dear daughters, we would ask you to pray most particularly for this intention. Pray that war may be averted, that it may be spared to us. That is a prayer for which you have particular competence in your capacity as professional nurses. You, above all others, know what is war and what victims it claims. We wish for you the joy and the peace of Christ, that is our great desire, the object of our daily prayers and continual exhortations to God, to that God of Peace who, in the splendour of His conceptions, had ever in His heart and on His lips the word ' Peace '—*Pax Vobis*.

" Wherever He appears He announces His appearance with peace : ' *Pax Vobis*, I give you my peace, peace which belongs particularly to me, that peace which the world does not know, but which happily it will know—*Pax Vobis*.'

" And take note that if it is God's will, it is also the necessary condition for the acquisition of all the benefits of social and individual life; it is the necessary condition, too, for the good of souls. Remember how greatly the missions have suffered through war; it is tragic. The mere thought of the good of souls, even outside the missions, should make us pray for peace. Even in non-missionary countries, what spiritual troubles we have seen as a result of war, what ravages and destruction of soul. The nurses know this better than others. Yes, we desire peace, and we pray God to spare us war.

" The sole thought of war, without adding anything to it (if it is possible to add to it) makes one tremble.

" Already we notice that abroad they are speaking of a war of conquest, a war of aggression. That is a supposition on which we will not allow our thoughts to dwell, a disconcerting supposition. A war which is only one of conquest would obviously be an unjust war; something passing all imagination, something inexpressibly sad and horrible. We cannot contemplate an unjust war, we cannot admit its possibility, and we put it deliberately aside. We cannot believe it, and we do not wish to believe in an unjust war.

" On the other hand, in Italy it is said that it would be a just war, because a war of defence to safeguard her frontiers against perpetual and unceasing dangers, a war made necessary for the expansion of a daily increasing population, a war undertaken to secure and defend the material security of a country—such a war would be justified.

" It is true, however, my daughters, and we cannot help reflecting on this, that if the need of expansion exists, and if there exists the necessity of assuring the safety of frontiers, we can only hope that a solution of these difficulties may be reached by other means than that of war. How ! It is obviously difficult to say, but we do not consider it impossible. The possibility must be studied. One thing appears to us to be beyond doubt; this is, if the need for expansion is a fact which has to be taken into account, the right of defence has limits and moderations which must be observed in order that the defence should not be culpable.

" In every case we pray God to assist the activities and efforts of far-seeing men who understand the exigencies of the welfare of nations and social justice, of those men who are doing everything they can, not by means of threats which can only aggravate the situation by irritating the spirit and which render the situation daily more difficult and threatening—men who are doing what they can, not by bickerings which merely waste time, but with a really humane, really good intent—who are doing everything to pacify, to carry out a work of peace with the sincere intention of averting war. We pray God to watch over this activity, this zeal, and we ask you to pray with us."

(d) *The Pope's Sermon to the International Pilgrimage of Ex-Combatants* (St. Paul's-without-the-Walls, September 9).

242. After an appreciative allusion to the heroism shown by his hearers in the Great War and an exhortation to show equal courage in the battle of life, His Holiness proceeded to speak of the world's need for peace. He then said that, together with peace, he desired another thing, namely, that the hopes, aspirations and needs of a great and good people, which was also his own people, should be satisfied in so far as was compatible with justice and with peace. Justice must be observed, because, without it, only sin remained, and " sin makes the nations miserable "; peace must be kept because it is the essential condition of all prosperity and the foundation of all the good things of this world, including tranquillity and order. After an allusion to certain hopes (which subsequently proved delusory) that a pacific solution of the Italo-Abyssinian conflict might after all be discovered, the Pope ended by expressing his desire that Heaven would grant a peace of truth, justice and charity, in which the honour and dignity of all might be satisfied, together with the claims of right and justice.

(e) *Consistorial Allocution of December* 16.

243. The Pope began by referring to the joyful and sorrowful events of the year, among the joyful being the "triumphal demonstrations of faith" at Lourdes, Cleveland, Teramo, Prague, Ljubljana and Lima, while among the sorrowful events in Mexico, Russia and "to some extent" Germany were included. As for the other and chief source of sorrow, namely, "those conflicts which are preoccupying not only Europe and Africa but the whole world," the Pope said he did not wish to speak as his words might be misunderstood or misrepresented. His Holiness then made a somewhat testy reference to those who have criticised him on account of his silence, and said that he had done all that could properly or legitimately be expected of him. He ended by repeating to all men of goodwill that he ardently desired, and was fervently praying for, that peace which is conjoined with justice, truth and charity.

(f) *Christmas Eve Allocution to Cardinals.*

244. The Pope, after a first reference to the clouds which obscured the horizon—" dark, threatening, already tinged with blood "—made unmistakable allusion to the persecution of the Church in Soviet Russia, Mexico and Germany, though mentioning none of them by name.

245. In obvious reference to Germany, he said that, against a Christianity of catholicism, which alone merited the name, were ranged the so-called positive historical, practical, pan-Christian Christianities, monstrous shells in which nothing of true Christianity remained, but which thus endeavoured to conceal their persecution of the one true form of Christianity. Nevertheless, it was a profound satisfaction to the Pope to observe that the trials to which Catholics had been subjected in various countries had given rise to magnificent displays of Christian virtue, and that brute force had nowhere been able to triumph over the things of the spirit. Reverting to the anxieties of the moment which " keep all the world in such painful suspense," the Pope declared that within his "very limited possibilities " he had so far as he could striven to secure a settlement; and had hoped until quite recently that he would have been able to say a calm and calming word. He had been disappointed, but this did not mean that he had given up all hope. Even in the worst events it was the duty of Christians to keep on hoping.

(g) *Encyclical " Ad catholicum sacerdotium" on the Catholic Priesthood (December 24).*

246.   The encyclical, which is a treatise on the functions and duties of the Catholic priesthood, is of almost purely religious interest.   It is moderate and sensible, and shows once more that in matters concerning doctrine, education and culture the Pope is enlightened and to a large extent in sympathy with modern ideas.   The following is perhaps the most striking passage in the encyclical and emphasises a point to which sufficient importance is not usually attached by Catholics :—

> " The dignity of the office that he (the priest) holds and the maintenance of a becoming respect and esteem among the people, which helps so much in his pastoral work, demand more than purely ecclesiastical learning.   The priest must be graced by no less knowledge and culture than is usual among well-bred and well-educated people of his day.   That is to say, he must be healthily modern, as is the Church, which is at home in all times and places and adapts itself to all; which blesses and furthers all healthy initiative and has no fear of the progress, even the most daring progress, of science, if only it be true science."

VII.—LEGISLATION.

247.   The following are the laws, decrees, &c., promulgated by the Vatican since the 1st January, 1935 :—

> LIV (February 1, 1935).—Ordinance regarding issue of series of commemorative stamps for International Juridical Congress, 1934.
> LV (June 24, 1935).—Law prorogating to the 31st December, 1935, the law (No. LI) delegating to the Governor of the Vatican State legislative power for the establishment, suppression and ordering of the Governor's department.
> LVI (December 20, 1935).—Ordinance regarding the striking and issue of coinage for the year 1935.

VIII.—TREATIES, &C.

Country.	Date of Signature.	Subject.	Date of Exchange of Ratifications.	Date of Entry into Force.	Remarks.
Austria ...	Mar. 23	Exchange of notes providing for abolition of visas	Mar. 23	On signature.	
Brazil ...	Dec. 2	Exchange of notes regarding diplomatic bags	Dec. 2	On signature	Stipulating inviolability of bags, limiting weight and dimensions.
Italy ...	Dec. 26	Agreement for prorogation for 3 years of article 29 (*f*) of Concordat	Dec. 2	On signature	Regularises acts performed by ecclesiastics and religious entities previous to signing of Concordat without observance of civil law.
Yugoslavia...	July 25	Concordat	Not ratified.		

CONFIDENTIAL.

(14978)

HOLY SEE.

Annual Report, 1936.

[R 57/57/22]

Mr. Osborne to Mr. Eden.—(Received January 5.)

(No. 1.)   *British Legation to the Holy See,*
Sir,   *Rome, January 1, 1937.*
    I HAVE the honour to transmit herewith the annual report for 1936, all of
which, except the introduction, has been written by Mr. Mallet, first secretary to
the Legation.

                  I have, &c.
                  D. G. OSBORNE.

Enclosure.

Annual Report on the Holy See for 1936.

CONTENTS.

I.—INTRODUCTION.

    THE year 1936, which, for the world in general, and Europe in particular,
was a period of incessant anxiety and successive political crises, confounded the
prophets of evil by expiring in an atmosphere, if not of peace and goodwill, at
any rate of grateful realisation that many perils had been avoided, and that the

9016   [14501]   B

outlook for the future at the end of the year was by no means as black as might reasonably have been anticipated on many occasions throughout the previous twelve months.   The Holy See, however, had no cause for gratification at even such small mercy of temporary relief.   While the Abyssinian war, after months of anxiety, came to an unexpectedly early and, to patriotic Italian prelates, fortunate end, and the Pope was able in May to acclaim " the triumphant joy of a great and good people " over the peace, the French elections, the outbreak and increasing bitterness and menace of the Spanish conflict, the continuing persecution of the Church in Germany and, lastly, the serious illness of the Pope at the end of the year, allowed of no respite from preoccupation and apprehension.   The enduring pessimism of the Holy See found no relief in minor causes for satisfaction : in the fact that the advent to power of the Front commun in France was accompanied by no anti-religious movement; in the improved condition of the Church in Mexico; in the success of the American visit of the Cardinal Secretary of State; and in the excellent relations between the Holy See and His Majesty's Government and a number of other foreign Governments.   No minor ray of light or hope could penetrate the deep gloom engendered by the Vatican's obsession with the menace of communism.   Nor was this distress at all alleviated by the fact that the self-appointed champion of civilisation was a Power that was, as the Pope declared on more than one occasion during the year, an ally of communism by virtue of its similar oppression of religion.

2.   The—to the Church—alarming outcome of the French elections and the serious dangers of the Spanish situation were foreseen at the Vatican some time before the event, though perhaps even the most pessimistic prophet would have hesitated to predict the hideous tale of death and destruction overhanging the Church and its servants and adherents in Spain.   The official Vatican view is that Spain is the battlefield on which the Christian culture of Europe and the disintegrative force of Marxist materialism are locked in combat, and that, in the words of the Cardinal Archbishop of Toledo, the war is one of religion, not of class, regional differences or political systems.   This is true in so far as communism represents the anti-God front, but it is by no means the whole truth, and the Cardinal Secretary of State himself has publicly asserted that not only " the agitations of the godless " but also " the idolatry of the State " are to be combated.   Indeed, religious faith and the Church's moral mission as the guardian of the family and the instructor of youth are being undermined, not only by the active atheism of Marx, but by the reversion to tribal ritualism of the authoritarian States with their inculcation of military prowess as the basis of the education of youth, their insistence on totalitarian control of body and soul, and the deification of the dictator as the incarnate symbol and authority of the race.

3.   The silence of the Pope and the tolerance of the Church in the face of Italian aggression against Abyssinia—an attitude that did much to confirm a suspicion current among Catholics and non-Catholics alike that the policy of the Vatican was dictated, or at least influenced, by the Fascist Government of Italy, and that the Church has sacrificed its independence and universality by the signature of the concordat—were partly determined by the fear lest Italian failure in Abyssinia might lead to the fall of the régime and its substitution by communism.   And between the calamity of communism and the inconvenience of fascism there could be no choice.   But there is another consideration to which the Church is blind.   Officials at the Vatican are unable to see, or unwilling to admit, that some leftward and liberalistic movements, that are labelled " Red " or " communistic " by those against whom they are directed, may be inspired by very different motives to those governing the Comintern and the anarcho-syndicalists of Barcelona, that they may simply be overdue readjustments in the direction of social justice, economic regeneration or political development, and that, as such, they are not a menace to established religion.

4.   In the course of 1936 the Comintern adopted a new and ingenious weapon against religion in general, and the Catholic Church in particular.   For Marx's teaching that religion was the opium of the people, which had probably exhausted its appeal, they substituted the more effective argument that the Catholic Church was the ally of wealth and privilege and the oppressor of the poor and lowly.   To this the Church replies by pointing to the present Pope's encyclical *Quadragesimo Anno*, by insisting on the charitable and humanitarian

inspiration of its teaching and activity, and by declaring that those who circulate this calumny are themselves the enemies, not only of property rights, but of all human rights and liberties and the inspired agents of disintegration and destruction, as may be witnessed by their record in Spain. Catholicism is, however, on the defensive against, not only the pernicious spread of " Marxist materialism," but the post-war spirit of scepticism which is assailing all religion. Not only is it attacked on the anti-God front in Spain and Mexico, but it sees in Italy and Germany the loosening of its hold on youth and the emergence of the new racial mysticism, and in other countries a growing indifference. The world-wide organisation of Catholic Action, which is, briefly, the enlistment of lay Catholics in the ranks of the clerical army for the dissemination and defence of the faith, is the Church's newest weapon and brightest hope in the hour of its need.

5. But the outlook at the end of the year is far from favourable. And the breakdown of the Pope's health, which is without doubt largely attributable to the mental suffering caused by continuous reports from Spain of the wholesale torture and murder of priests and nuns and destruction and desecration of Church property, threatens to rob the Catholic army of its general at a critical moment. Accounts received at the end of the year suggested that it was doubtful whether His Holiness could ever be restored to his former health and energy.

II.—RELATIONS WITH THE BRITISH EMPIRE.

Death of The King.

6. On learning of His Majesty's death, the Cardinal Secretary of State, accompanied by the Under-Secretary and the Assistant Under-Secretary, called on His Majesty's Chargé d'Affaires to express the Pope's sympathy and his own condolences, and those of the Secretariat of State, on the loss which the Royal Family and the Empire had suffered. Cardinal Pacelli told Mr. Montgomery that the Pope, who had the greatest esteem for His late Majesty and was much afflicted by his death, had telegraphed a message of sympathy direct to The King. The sympathy, he added, which he had come to express had nothing conventional about it, for he felt that in his late Majesty the British people had lost a Sovereign whose devotion to duty had never flagged. The King's benevolence towards his Catholic subjects had been a constant source of satisfaction to the Holy See, which had never forgotten that it had been under King George that the wording of the Coronation Oath had been modified so as to avoid causing offence to His Majesty's Catholic subjects and that diplomatic relations had been established between His Majesty's Government in the United Kingdom and the Holy See. Among others who called at the Legation to express their condolences in person were Cardinal Pignatelli, the dean of the Sacred College, who had attended the Coronation in 1911, Cardinal Lépicier, the Protector of the English College, and Cardinal Fumasoni-Biondi, Prefect of Propaganda. On the same evening the official *Osservatore Romano*, in an article headed " Universal Regret," paid an eloquent tribute to the memory of King George.

7. A memorial service for his late Majesty was held on the 28th January in the English Roman Catholic Church of San Silvestro. The rector, who had sought permission to hold this service from the Secretariat of State, was referred by them to the Cardinal Vicar of Rome on the ground that the Secretariat of State could only interest themselves directly in a service held for a non-Catholic Sovereign if it was asked for by the Government of the country concerned. The request for permission to hold this service seems to have caused much discussion at the Vatican, since no service which could be described as official had, since the Reformation, been held in memory of a British Sovereign in a Catholic Church in Rome. Although not organised by His Majesty's Legation, the service held in the Church of San Silvestro was attended by His Majesty's Chargé d'Affaires and by the Irish Free State Minister, who sat in places of honour, while the other members of His Majesty's Legation, the majority of the Diplomatic Corps accredited to the Holy See, Cardinal Massimo Massimi, representatives of the Papal Court, of the Secretariat of State, of the religious orders and of the important pontifical institutes, the rectors and students of the English, Scots and Beda Colleges and members of Roman " black " society. were also present.

8. The report of the incident which occurred on Constitution Hill on the 16th July led His Holiness to express to His Majesty's Minister, through the Cardinal Secretary of State, his congratulations on The King's escape from danger and to renew his good wishes to the British nation and its well-beloved Sovereign.

9. In September His Majesty's Chargé d'Affaires was instructed to communicate to the Cardinal Secretary of State a copy of the King's Proclamation fixing the date of the Coronation and to state that His Majesty would be pleased to receive, as his guest, a representative of His Holiness on this occasion. The Pope's acceptance of this invitation was received at the end of the year.

10. On the 12th December, after the abdication of King Edward, the Pope addressed to Queen Mary an autograph letter, in which he expressed his deep sympathy with Her Majesty in the trying hours through which she had been passing. The Cardinal Secretary of State, to whom His Majesty's Minister communicated the official announcement of the accession of King George VI on the 14th December, stated that the wording of this letter was the Pope's and that His Holiness had given the necessary orders from his sick-bed. The cardinal went on to express his own sincere good wishes for the happiness of the new King and Queen. Mr. Osborne was instructed by telegram, on the 22nd December, to express to Cardinal Pacelli their Majesties' thanks for his good wishes, and was also furnished with the text of Queen Mary's reply to the Pope's message. The terms of this reply were communicated to Cardinal Pacelli on the 24th December. On the 31st December Mr. Osborne received a further telegram instructing him to inform the Secretary of State that King George VI was distressed to hear of the continued illness of His Holiness, and desired to offer him an expression of his anxious sympathy together with wishes for a speedy recovery.

The United Kingdom.

His Majesty's Minister.

11. Mr. F. D'A. G. Osborne arrived in Rome on the 16th February. On the 27th February he was received in solemn audience by the Pope with the customary impressive ceremonial. In presenting his letter of credence and Sir Charles Wingfield's letter of recall, Mr. Osborne addressed to His Holiness a short speech in French, expressing His Majesty's thanks for the sympathy which the Pontiff had shown on the death of his late Majesty, conveying The King's good wishes, and requesting the sympathy of His Holiness in carrying out the important task, confided to him by The King, of developing the good relations uniting His Majesty's Government and the Holy See. The Pope's reply was couched in most friendly terms. After welcoming His Majesty's Minister warmly and expressing pleasure at his appointment, His Holiness stated that the relations which he maintained with His Majesty The King were of particular importance to him, since the British Empire embraced so large a portion of the globe and in all parts of the Empire lived sons of the Catholic Church. His Majesty's Minister could count on his benevolence and cordial co-operation in fulfilling his mission. His Holiness concluded by asking the Minister, as his first task, to convey to The King, the Royal Family, His Majesty's Government and the British people his personal blessing, which was the only form in which he could give expression to his friendly sentiments.

12. At the conclusion of these remarks the Pope took the Minister to his study, where he kept him in conversation for nearly forty minutes. In contrast to the halting delivery of his formal speech, the Pope then expressed himself freely and in definite terms. After emphasising the feelings of friendship which he had entertained for King George and his affection for England, he spoke of the state of world politics, and expressed the greatest pessimism regarding the outcome of the Abyssinian affair. He had tried, he said, as was his duty, to see all sides of the question, but there was little he could do. The Minister explained the British attitude in the Abyssinian affair, and His Holiness suggested that much good might be done by making the British point of view better known in Rome.

13. On the 19th May His Majesty's Minister handed to the Pope a volume containing a series of photographs of the Middleton Manuscript which had been specially prepared and bound by the trustees of the British Museum, accompanied

by an engraved presentation address signed by the Archbishop of Canterbury in his quality of a principal trustee of the museum. The Pope was greatly interested and much pleased both with the present and with the congratulations on the anniversary of his birthday which accompanied it.

14. On the 31st August, before going on leave, His Majesty's Minister again visited the Pope at Castel Gandolfo and found that he had apparently much benefited in health by his stay in the country, in spite of the anxiety which events in Spain were obviously causing him. Mr. Osborne took advantage of this opportunity to present to His Holiness a volume containing a *memoria technica* of all the Popes in Latin hexameters, composed by Professor Lee, of All Souls, which the Librarian of the Foreign Office had had specially bound. His Holiness expressed himself delighted with the present, both as an exquisite production in itself and as a sign that in the troubled world of to-day there were still to be found men who delighted in scholarship. He later demonstrated his satisfaction by presenting Professor Lee and Sir Stephen Gaselee with the Pontifical medal for the year.

English Bishops.

15. Among members of the English hierarchy who visited Rome during the year were Archbishop Hinsley of Westminster, Bishop McNulty of Nottingham and Bishop Amigo of Southwark, who in October headed a pilgrimage of English Catholics. These pilgrims were cordially welcomed by the Holy Father, who told them that a pilgrimage from England gave him particular pleasure as no other part of the world could boast of a history such as that of the relations between England and the Holy See. Bishop Dey, the Roman Catholic Ordinary to the Armed Forces, the question of whose position and emoluments formed the subject of some correspondence between the Legation and the Vatican on one side and the Foreign Office and the Service Departments on the other, also visited Rome in the autumn.

Ecclesiastical Appointments.

16. There was a good deal of disappointment among English Catholics when Cardinal Bourne's successor in the see of Westminster was not raised to the cardinalate and when, at the Consistory in December 1935, twenty new cardinals were created, among whom were fourteen Italians, but no British. It is possible that the Pope's attitude in this matter was influenced by considerations arising out of the Abyssinian conflict, and more particularly by Archbishop Hinsley's reference to him as " a poor, helpless old man." In any case, there is no doubt that the policy followed by the Vatican during the conflict and the growing vehemence of its opposition to anti-Fascist movements gave foreigners more and more the impression that the Holy See was under the influence of the Italian Government. English Catholics, both at home and in Rome, therefore came to feel that there should be stronger British representation in the curia, congregations and Vatican service generally in Rome, and more British prelates appointed to posts in the colonies.

17. His Majesty's Minister spoke informally in this sense to the Secretary of State in June and again in November. On his return from leave in November Mr. Osborne told the Acting Secretary of State that he had noticed in England a tendency to believe that the Church was under the influence of the Fascist Government and that Church policy reflected Fascist policy. Mgr. Pizzardo took this very seriously and said that there was no justification for the belief. He explained that the Church had found a friend in the Fascist Government instead of an enemy, as in the case of former Italian Governments, with the natural result that the Italian clergy felt not only admiration for the benefits conferred by the régime on the country as a whole, but also gratitude and loyalty towards the Government. But these happy relations between Church and State did not, Mgr. Pizzardo was at pains to emphasise, imply any subservience on the part of the Church to the State in matters of policy.

18. Mr. Osborne, explaining that he was speaking on behalf of English Catholics and without any instructions from His Majesty's Government, then told Mgr. Pizzardo that he had found in London a feeling of regret that there was no important English prelate resident in Rome who could serve as an

authoritative intermediary between the Vatican and Catholic circles in the Empire. The Legation represented His Majesty's Government and the British prelates now in Rome all had their own jobs. It was not a question of the interests of the Catholics in the United Kingdom alone, but of those throughout the Empire. This need for a resident British prelate was associated, the Minister continued, with the complementary need for increased British representation in the Vatican administrative, diocesan and diplomatic services. Mgr. Pizzardo was sympathetic and expressed general agreement with Mr. Osborne's remarks, but in no way committed himself.

19. His Majesty's Minister also took up with Mgr. Pizzardo in November the question of substituting British for Italian missions engaged in educational and missionary work in the Southern Sudan. In reply to the expected answer that there were no British priests available for this purpose, Mr. Osborne expressed the hope that, as a result of the considerable increase in the number of students at the British colleges in Rome, there would soon be available more priests than were needed at home. Failing such substitution, the Minister said, it was felt essential that Italian priests appointed to these missions should study the English language and English literature and political theory and practice in the United Kingdom, where, he understood from the Archbishop of Westminster, adequate facilities were now available.

Commonwealth of Australia and Dominion of New Zealand.

20. His Majesty's Minister was instructed in June to ascertain from the Vatican the exact extent of the ecclesiastic jurisdiction of the Apostolic Delegate in Australia and New Zealand in order that the authorities in the various territories concerned might be notified. In due course the Secretariat of State communicated to the Legation the following reply which it had received from the Congregation of Propaganda Fide :—

" The jurisdiction of the Apostolic Delegate in Australia extends over all the archdioceses, dioceses, vicariats and apostolic prefectures and missions of the following countries :—

" (a) *British*.—Australia, New Zealand, Borneo, New Guinea, the Islands of the Fiji, Samoan, Phœnix, Gilbert, Solomon and Tonga groups, and all the other lesser islands of Oceania belonging to Great Britain.
" (b) *Anglo-French*.—The New Hebrides.
" (c) *French*.—All the French possessions and protectorates in Oceania.
" (d) *Dutch*.—The Dutch East Indies.
" (e) *United States*.—The American Samoan Islands.

" The Marianne, Caroline, Marshall and Haiwaian Islands and the peninsular of Malacca do *not* form part of the delegation."

India.

21. His Majesty's Government in the United Kingdom and the Government of India took a serious view of the decision reached by the Holy See as a result of the incompetence of the Archbishop of Bombay to detach, for all practical purposes, the two large districts of Sind and Gujerat from the jurisdiction of the archbishop (see annual report for 1935).

22. Sir Charles Wingfield had already, in May 1935, expressed to the Cardinal Secretary of State the objections of His Majesty's Government to this decision, and Mr. Osborne was instructed in February to inform the Vatican that His Majesty's Government could not regard the position as satisfactory and desired to express strongly the hope that the changes made would be modified. Mr. Osborne was also instructed to try and get an assurance that Mgr. Lima's successors should have effective jurisdiction over the entire archdiocese in accordance with the Padroado Agreement of the 15th April, 1928.

23. A memorandum in this sense was handed on the 6th March to the Cardinal Secretary of State by the Minister, who reminded Cardinal Pacelli that his Eminence had, in the previous May, promised Sir Charles Wingfield to consult with the Congregation of Propaganda Fide as to whether it would be possible to

meet the wishes of His Majesty's Government in this question. The cardinal said that he understood that the question had already been adjusted to meet the views of His Majesty's Government, and on the 19th March addressed to His Majesty's Legation a written reply, which stated that, instead of itself nominating and empowering the superiors of the two detached districts, the Congregation of Propaganda Fide would, under the new arrangement, " ask " the archbishop to do so, thereby, it was contended, leaving jurisdiction in his hands. Furthermore, it was stated, the title of the ecclesiastics in charge of the two districts had been changed from superior to pro-superior.

24. While this arrangement could perhaps be said to safeguard the juridical authority of Mgr. Lima and to respect the letter of the Padroada Agreement, it nevertheless seemed to impair, if not to nullify, the effective authority of the archbishop. The Prefect of Propaganda, however, argued, in conversation with His Majesty's Minister, that some such delegation of power was rendered essential by the size and nature of the diocese and by the character of the archbishop himself. This delegation of power did not, Cardinal Fumasoni-Biondi stated, involve abandonment of ultimate jurisdiction or dismemberment of the diocese.

25. After consultation between the Foreign Office and the India Office and with Mgr. Goodier, a former archbishop of Bombay, it was decided in London that the Vatican should be informed that His Majesty's Government accepted the arrangement set out in the communication of the 19th March on the under-standing that it did not in any way affect or alter the archbishop's jurisdiction over his whole diocese. His Majesty's Minister was instructed to add that His Majesty's Government would much appreciate an assurance that the prior agreement of the British authorities concerned would be obtained to any future proposals affecting the archbishop's control throughout his diocese. A communi-cation in this sense was made to the Vatican by His Majesty's Minister on the 7th August, but before this date news reached Rome of the death of Mgr. Lima. His British successor had not been appointed by the end of the year.

Malta.

Archbishopric.

26. In February the Officer Administering the Government of Malta called the attention of His Majesty's Government in the United Kingdom to the importance of formulating their policy regarding the succession to the see of Malta. Archbishop Caruana, who was not a man of strong character, was in his 69th year and in frail health, and Sir H. Luke had grounds for believing that the Vatican were considering the appointment of a coadjutor to assist him who would have the right of succeeding to the see. Sir H. Luke and the Colonial Office feared that a prelate might be appointed to this post who, through pro-Italianism or some other reason, might disturb the good relations existing between the Government and the Church in Malta. It was feared that the active element in the Church, which was the mouthpiece of Catholic Action in Malta and expressed its views through the hostile journal *Lehen-is-Sewwa*, might succeed in installing as coadjutor some prelate such as Mgr. Pantalleresco, Mgr. Galea, Mgr. Cavendish or Father Inguanez, who were felt to be hostile to the Govern-ment. Sir H. Luke suggested that Mgr. George Caruana, Papal Nuncio in Cuba, would be a man of sufficiently wide experience and moral courage, and sufficiently friendly to British rule, to be recommended should the Vatican, in fact, be thinking of appointing an assistant to help the archbishop.

27. His Majesty's Minister was instructed on the 4th April to report what steps could, in his opinion, most usefully be taken with the object of ensuring that a suitable candidate be found for the succession. On the 14th April, however, the Under-Secretary of State at the Vatican spontaneously raised this question and told Mr. Osborne that Archbishop Caruana's age and health made it necessary that he should have help in his work, and made it advisable to consider the question of his eventual succession. The Rampolla–Simmons correspondence of 1890, Mgr. Pizzardo continued, called for prior notice to His Majesty's Government of any proposed appointment to the archiepiscopal see of Malta. He had therefore been instructed to state, unofficially, that the Holy Father proposed to nominate Mgr. Gonzi, Bishop of Gozo, as coadjutor to

Mgr. Caruana with the right of eventual succession. In view of Mgr. Pizzardo's reference to the Rampolla–Simmons correspondence, Mr. Osborne enquired whether he was right in assuming that this appointment was not yet definite pending receipt of the views of His Majesty's Government, and was informed, though perhaps with some slight hesitation, that this was so. Mr. Osborne added that, though not familiar with the details of the question of the succession, he knew that it was one to which His Majesty's Government attached very great importance.

28. On the 29th April, in accordance with the instructions received, His Majesty's Minister told Mgr. Pizzardo that His Majesty's Government appreciated the courtesy of the Pope and the Secretariat of State in approaching them in regard to the contemplated appointment of Mgr. Gonzi, Bishop of Gozo, as coadjutor to the Archbishop of Malta, with right to succession; that they were consulting the Government of Malta on the subject; but that in the meantime it was not to be assumed that the appointment of Mgr. Gonzi would be acceptable to them. Mr. Osborne went on to say, speaking personally, that he had gathered from the Legation archives that Mgr. Gonzi's actions in the past might not render his appointment pleasing to the authorities in Malta. Mgr. Pizzardo replied that that had been in the past and that any difficulties that Mgr. Gonzi had raised had been on the purely religious plane and in connexion with Lord Strickland's claim to represent the Catholics of Malta. The bishop was not, however, in the least antagonistic, or even unsympathetic, to the British government of Malta; he had, indeed, expressed, on the occasion of his last visit to Rome, the opinion that British rule was essential and beneficial to the island. Leaving Mgr. Gonzi aside, Mgr. Pizzardo assured Mr. Osborne that the benefits of British rule were fully realised at the Vatican: it was felt that the culture of the island should be Italian, because the Maltese language had no literature and was incapable of serving as a cultural basis and because England was geographically remote and the English language culturally alien to a Mediterranean population, but this did not affect the question of government. British rule was beneficial and necessary and there was no sympathy at the Vatican for Fascist aspirations and no desire whatever to substitute Italian for British administration.

29. On the 4th June the Assistant Under-Secretary of State asked His Majesty's Minister whether any reply had yet been received from His Majesty's Government, and assured him that Mgr. Gonzi was a good and loyal man. In a despatch of the same date the Foreign Office, however, informed Mr. Osborne that, in the opinion of His Majesty's Government, Mgr. Gonzi would be an unsuitable person for the post in question. It was pointed out that the former Governor of Malta had considered that his political sympathies and narrowness of outlook and combative character would make for serious friction with the Imperial authorities. This view was confirmed by the present Governor and by the Archbishop of Westminster, who, in confidential conversation, described Mgr. Gonzi as "italianissimo." Mgr. Gonzi had also made so unfortunate an impression on His Majesty's Legation at the time of Cardinal Lépicier's visit to Malta in June 1935 that Sir Charles Wingfield had thought it necessary to emphasise, in his farewell interview with Mgr. Pizzardo, his unreliability and unfitness for promotion. The Foreign Office despatch further pointed out that the Rampolla–Simmons correspondence not only gave His Majesty's Government a right to be consulted about episcopal appointments in Malta, but also, by the assurance in Cardinal Rampolla's letter of the 20th March, 1890, to the effect that in the matter of such appointments the Holy Father " would have nothing more greatly at heart than also to meet with the concurrence of His Majesty's Government," made it impossible for His Majesty's Government to refrain from stating their objections when such existed. In these circumstances His Majesty's Minister was instructed to inform Mgr. Pizzardo " privately, orally and confidentially " (as stipulated in the Rampolla–Simmons correspondence) that, in view of the importance attached to the harmonious relations existing between the Government and the ecclesiastical authorities in Malta, His Majesty's Government had the strongest possible objection to the proposed appointment of Mgr. Gonzi. The Under-Secretary of State took Mr. Osborne's remarks in good part and, indeed, appeared to expect them, but, although Mr. Osborne suggested that Mgr. Gonzi's apparent bias and narrowness of outlook were due to the fact that he had spent his entire life in Malta, he was given no opportunity of putting

forward the name of the Nuncio in Cuba as an alternative appointment. On the whole, Mr. Osborne derived the impression that the Vatican would hardly proceed with the appointment in view of the very strong objections voiced by His Majesty's Government.

30.   Before this interview took place the newly-appointed Governor of Malta had had conversations with Mgr. Gonzi, as a result of which he had formed a fresh estimate of his character and had reached the conclusion that, while fanatically devoted to the Church, narrow in outlook and sympathetic to Italian ideas, he was not in favour of Italian political ambitions in Malta. While he realised that his appointment as coadjutor might lead to difficulties subsequently, Sir Charles Bonham-Carter felt that, if it should prove impossible to secure the appointment of some really suitable candidate such as Mgr. George Caruana, Mgr. Gonzi was to be preferred as coadjutor to anyone else in Malta. Shortly afterward Mgr. Gonzi came to Rome and called on His Majesty's Minister to ask his help with the Vatican in securing properly qualified teachers of English in his diocese of Gozo. This desire to promote knowledge of English, together with the unexceptional sentiments which he expressed regarding British rule in Malta, led Mr. Osborne to form the opinion that Mgr. Gonzi hoped that he might in time succeed in persuading the British authorities to withdraw their opposition to his appointment.

31.   In the course of the autumn it became clear that the Vatican considered Mgr. Gonzi to be an innocent victim of misunderstanding who was regarded as unfriendly to His Majesty's Government because he had disagreed with Lord Strickland. They therefore hoped that with the passage of time he would succeed in rehabilitating himself in the eyes of His Majesty's Government. The Governor of Malta reported that the Archbishop of Malta (whom Mgr. Gonzi had served as secretary) considered that there was no suitable alternative to the Bishop of Gozo as his successor, as Mgr. George Caruana was too senior for the post. Lest, therefore, continued opposition to Mgr. Gonzi should lead the Vatican to appoint some other candidate who could only be worse, Sir Charles Bonham-Carter advised that the objections made to Mgr. Gonzi should now be withdrawn. This advice he repeated on the 2nd September, but the Colonial Office felt both that it would be difficult to withdraw so soon the strong protest which had been made in June, and also that it might be advisable to wait and see how far the attitude then being adopted by Mgr. Gonzi was due solely to a desire to obtain the consent of the British authorities to his appointment.

32.   In November the Archbishop of Malta came to Rome. He was in need of medical treatment and assured His Majesty's Minister that he could not long continue to work without an assistant. He also made it clear that there was no candidate for the post of coadjutor other than Mgr. Gonzi whom he could conscientiously recommend. His Majesty's Minister therefore suggested to the Foreign Office on the 13th November that, as it would sooner or later be necessary to recognise that the need for a coadjutor was real and urgent and that the appointment could not be made without carrying with it the right to the succession, and inasmuch as their own candidate was unavailable, His Majesty's Government might be well advised to accept Mgr. Gonzi, making it clear that they wished to show their goodwill to the Pope, but that they intended to hold His Holiness responsible for the good conduct of his nominee.

Religious Broadcasts.

33.   Early in the year a difficulty arose in connexion with the broadcasting of religious services by the Rediffusion Company in Malta. On Sundays this company broadcast both the service included in the British Broadcasting Corporation Empire programme and a Catholic service from some continental station. On the 17th January an article appeared in the *Lehen is-sewwa*, the organ of Catholic Action, protesting against the inclusion of Protestant services in a programme which might come to Catholic ears. On the 23rd January the Archbishop of Malta suggested to the manager of the company that all religious services should be omitted from the broadcasts. The manager pointed out that, as his company always relayed a continental programme as well as the British Broadcasting Corporation broadcast, an alternative programme was always available for those who did not wish to listen to the religious service.

Mr. Whitcroft also pointed out that, as his subscribers were almost equally divided between Maltese and English, that is to say, between Catholic and Protestant, he considered that the practice of broadcasting Mass on Sunday mornings and the religious service of the British Broadcasting Corporation programme in the evening was fair to all. The latter service, he added, was even somtimes a Catholic one. His Grace, however, maintained his objections to the broadcasting of services, and the manager, afraid of exposing his company to an ecclesiastical ban, gave way under protest.

34.   Although Sir H. Luke made strenuous efforts to induce the archbishop to withdraw his demand and drew his Grace's attention to the religious toleration clause in the Letters Patent, the latter felt unable to modify his attitude, and announced his intention of proceeding to Rome to lay the question before the Vatican. His Majesty's Minister was accordingly informed of the matter and, thinking that it might be advisable to make the company's point of view known at the Vatican before a decision was reached on the basis of Mgr. Caruana's report such as might result in a deadlock, instructed the first secretary to explain the company's point of view to the Assessor of the Holy Office, the Congregation dealing with matters of this sort. Mr. Montgomery emphasised the points that an alternative programme was always available, that only three-quarters of an hour out of a weekly programme of 200 hours was allotted to Protestant devotions, and that non-Catholic subscribers only asked to be allowed to listen to their own service without being subjected to the considerable expense of buying a radio set powerful enough to receive British stations direct. Mgr. Ottaviani made it clear, as did the Secretariat of State on another occasion, that the objections of the Catholic authorities were based on two principal grounds. The first objection arose from the possibility of Maltese Catholics running the danger of hearing Protestant services either because they were trying to listen-in to the Catholic service sometimes broadcast by the British Broadcasting Corporation or because the British Broadcasting Corporation programme was transmitted by loud speakers in cafés and other public places; and the second derived from the fact that the wireless company, which exposed Catholics to this danger and thus laid itself open to the charge of conducting Protestant propaganda, was under the control of the Government and subsidised by taxation levied locally.

35.   The ban placed by Archbishop Caruana on the broadcasting of services caused dissatisfaction among Protestant subscribers, who resented the interference of a Catholic ecclesiastic resulting in their being deprived of their Sunday broadcast service. This dissatisfaction found vent in a question which was asked in the House of Commons on the 18th June, and in protests which were addressed to the Colonial Office, the Rediffusion Company and to the Government of Malta, which, being the licencee, was in some circles regarded as responsible for the ban. On the 17th April His Majesty's Minister spoke about the matter to the Under-Secretary of State, who said that he was expecting a report, and added that he believed a solution could be found on the basis of an arrangement for consecutive Catholic and Protestant services. Before going on leave in September, Mr. Osborne reminded Mgr. Pizzardo of these remarks and asked whether he had received the report, but the reply was negative. On the return to Rome of the Assessor to the Holy Office, His Majesty's Chargé d'Affaires therefore enquired of him how the matter stood. Mgr. Ottaviani expressed surprise that the matter had come up again, but, while suggesting that it might be better to let sleeping dogs lie, promised to look up the papers and speak to the Secretariat of State. In November the Foreign Office sent His Majesty's Legation a copy of a letter, in which it was stated that the Colonial Office were of the opinion that the question was one for settlement between the Rediffusion Company and the religious bodies concerned. The company was anxious that nothing should be done to offend their Roman Catholic subscribers, and the Government were unwilling to do anything which might give colour to the suggestion that they were trying to proselytise the Maltese. The Colonial Office therefore proposed that no further action should be taken in the matter for the time being.

University Theological Faculty.

36.   In February His Majesty's Legation was instructed to communicate to the Vatican the views of the Governor of Malta on the memorandum regarding the reform of the Theological Faculty which had been drawn up by the

Congregation of Seminaries in September 1935. Copies of a syllabus of studies prepared by the Faculty were communicated to the Secretariat of State at the same time. Mgr. Tardini noted with satisfaction the concessions made by the Governor regarding the formula for the conferment of degrees and promised to pass the Governor's views on to the Congregation. The reply of the latter was forwarded in a note from the Vatican, dated the 15th April. Paragraph 5 of this reply did not appear to meet the requirements of the Governor of Malta in regard to the assurance desired that, where Latin was not prescribed for teaching in the Faculty, the choice of language to be used should be at the discretion of the State authorities. His Majesty's Minister accordingly asked Mgr. Tardini, in a letter dated the 21st April, to obtain, if possible, the desired assurance from the Congregation. To this request Mgr. Tardini replied verbally on the 30th May explaining that the assurance had not been given because no such assurance was necessary. He stated that the Congregation's " Ordinationes ad Constitutionem Apostolicam ' Deus Scientarum Dominus ' " made it clear that the fact that Latin was expressly prescribed for certain subjects automatically implied liberty of choice regarding the language in which other subjects were to be taught.

37. In a despatch dated the 18th July His Majesty's Minister was instructed to take formal note of this explanation of the attitude of the Vatican in cases where Latin is not prescribed as the language of instruction. This the Minister did in a letter, dated the 4th August. Mr. Osborne also conveyed to Mgr. Tardini a revised curriculum of studies in which had been incorporated, as far as practicable, the alterations proposed by the Congregation in April, making it clear, at the same time, that there could be no question of the course preparatory to the Faculty forming the subject of any agreement.

38. Acting on telegraphic instructions, His Majesty's Chargé d'Affaires requested the Holy See on the 18th September to inform the ecclesiastical authorities in Malta that they approved of the proposal to amend the University Statute for the purpose of giving effect to the provisions regarding the language to be used as the medium of instruction in the Theological Faculty. Enquiry was also made whether the Congregation was yet in a position to concur in the revised programme of studies communicated to Mgr. Tardini on the 4th August, seeing that it was desired to complete the reform of the Faculty before the new academic year began on the 1st October. Finally, the Vatican was asked to concur in the agreement regarding the reform of the Faculty being embodied in due course in a form suitable for publication.

39. While transmitting, in their reply dated the 20th September, the observations of the Congregation on the revised programme of studies, and while concurring in the agreement reached being embodied in an exchange of notes, the Vatican made no reference to the request for a communication to the ecclesiastical authorities of Malta, and stated that, as regards the language to be used in instruction in the Faculty, it would be incorrect to speak of an agreement between the Holy See and His Majesty's Government. It was a question only of a verbal reply given to His Majesty's Minister, which could be summed up in the words : " The Regulations regarding the application of the Constitutio ' Deus Scientarum Dominus ' prescribe in article 21 the Latin language only for dogmatic and moral theology, scholastic philosophy and law. There is no regulation regarding the other subjects." This note made it clear that the Vatican intended to avoid being involved in any way with the language issue in Malta at a moment when, as a result of the introduction of the new Constitution and the repeal of the *Pari Passu* Act, this question was one of some delicacy.

Teaching Orders in Malta.

40. The desirability of increasing the number of British religious teaching orders in Malta was not lost sight of during the year. As is stated in paragraph 30 above, the Bishop of Gozo expressed to His Majesty's Minister his anxiety to help in this matter, and, in accordance with instructions received from the Foreign Office, the first secretary to His Majesty's Legation approached the English Associate to the Master-General of the Dominicans on the subject of the transfer of the Maltese Dominican Province from the jurisdiction of the Italian to that of the English Associate (see paragraph 74 of the annual report for 1935).

41. It was made clear by Father Garde, and later by the Master-General himself, that even though this change might in itself be a good one, it would be impossible to effect it without consulting the General Chapter of the Order, which might not meet for a couple of years, and that it would be impossible, at the moment, to take a step which would inevitably be interpreted as a political move to the detriment of Italy. Father Gillet stated that he would not oppose the change later, if it was supported by the majority of his subordinates, and was even prepared to sound the Maltese Dominicans as to their views in the matter. There was, however, no indication by the end of the year that any steps had been taken in this direction.

Palestine.

42. Indications reached His Majesty's Government in the United Kingdom that certain Catholic circles in Palestine were discontented with their position and felt that Catholic interests were being threatened by the policy of His Majesty's Government regarding Jewish immigration. Two articles which appeared in the Vienna *Reichspost* and a statement made by Cardinal Innitzer, Archbishop of Vienna, at a meeting organised by the Committee for Austrian Pilgrimage, emphasised the need for protecting Catholic interests. Other clerics realised, however, the advantages of British rule, and it is possible that the attempts to represent British rule as detrimental to Catholic interests were the result of the desire of certain Italian Catholics in the Holy Land, such as Mgr. Barlassina, the Latin Patriarch of Jerusalem, to profit by the existing tension in the Mediterranean.

43. On the 14th October the Secretariat of State asked His Majesty's Legation to use its good offices to prevent the requisition by the military authorities of the College of the Holy Land at Jerusalem. Representations on behalf of this and other Italian buildings and institutions in Palestine were also made at the Foreign Office by the Italian Chargé d'Affaires. On the 4th November the Secretariat of State informed His Majesty's Legation that the danger threatening the College of the Holy Land had been removed, and expressed thanks for the help given.

Seychelles Islands.

44. In June the Vatican addressed to His Majesty's Legation a note formulating a complaint by the Apostolic Delegate for the Missions in Africa against a draft Bill, which, it was alleged, would give discriminatory and unfavourable treatment to the diocese of Victoria in the matter of the right of the diocese, as a corporate body, to purchase, hold and sell landed property. In order that the arguments advanced by Mgr. Riberi might be given proper consideration it was decided by the Colonial Office to suspend action on the proposed Bill. On the 1st October His Majesty's Chargé d'Affaires was instructed to inform the Vatican that, as a result of this consideration, it had been decided to waive the provision in the proposed amending legislation requiring the consent of the Government to the purchase of immovable property.

45. His Majesty's Chargé d'Affaires was at the same time informed that the Catholic Bishop of Victoria had lately resigned. Certain differences had arisen between the Catholic Mission and the Marist Brothers, who were in charge of the chief educational institution in the island. The Governor felt it important that the outlook of the mission should be modified by British influences. His Majesty's Government were not prepared to press for the appointment of a British bishop to the See of Victoria, but Mr. Mallet was instructed to suggest to the Vatican that, when the appointment of a new bishop came under consideration, the desirability should be borne in mind of nominating a prelate who would be of sufficiently strong character to settle the dispute with the Marist Brothers and ready to co-operate with the British authorities of the island in overhauling the existing system of education.

III.—RELATIONS WITH OTHER COUNTRIES.

Albania.

46. In 1929, the year in which the Albanian Autocephalous Church came into being, a Uniate Church was opened at Elbasan under the charge of a priest of Italian nationality named Pappa Petri Scapanelli. Little was heard of this

movement for some time, but in 1936 Pappa Petri reappeared and his Church received considerable support. As the Autocephalous Church had failed to win respect or either moral or financial support his reappearance was well timed, and it seemed possible that with the encouragement of the Vatican and sympathy of the Italian Government the Uniate movement might make rapid progress in Albania.

China and Japan.

47. It was announced in July that, in consideration of certain difficulties which had arisen among Catholic converts in the Far East as a result of the conflicting exigencies of patriotism and religion, the Holy See had issued instructions which would enable converts to conform outwardly to national customs without violating their own convictions.

Colombia.

48. A serious situation was caused by the proposal of the Colombian Government to amend certain articles of the Constitution of 1886, which, they claimed, were no longer in harmony with actual conditions. The proposed reform of those articles, which concerned religious questions, was said by the Colombian clergy and Conservatives to the contrary to the concordat of 1887. In August the Colombian Minister for Foreign Affairs informed His Majesty's Chargé d'Affaires that negotiations for the revision of the concordat had been begun, but in October it was reported that the Nuncio had sent the Colombian Government a note of protest against the reform of the Constitution. This note was returned as unacceptable, and in November the Colombian bishops therefore embodied their objections in a pastoral letter.

Germany.

49. No improvement took place during the year in the position of Catholicism in Germany, and consequently in the feelings of the Vatican towards the National Socialist régime. On the contrary, the Nazi extremists intensified and developed their dual policy of trying to weaken the position of the Church by drawing attention to everything which would be likely to bring Catholicism into discredit and of making certain that the coming generation would grow up with a strong anti-Catholic, if not anti-Christian, bias.

50. Alarmed at these tendencies, the conference of Catholic bishops at Fulda issued on the 9th January a pastoral letter which contained a powerful challenge to the advocates of a national religion, such as was supposed in some circles to be more suitable for the German race than Christianity, and warned the public against reading neo-pagan literature. This pastoral provoked angry replies from the Nazi press, which claimed that, by saving Germany from communism, the régime had shown that it was the real defender of religion and accused " highly placed medicine men " in Rome of polluting Europe in alliance with Russia.

51. Early in February the registration of school children eligible for compulsory education took place in Munich and the figures showed a majority in favour of secular education. This result was achieved by the usual Nazi electoral methods, and a leading Bavarian educational official openly declared that the Reich intended to treat the concordat, which provided for the maintenance and, if necessary, increase of Church schools, in the same way as it had treated the Versailles Treaty. Indications reached His Majesty's Legation that the Vatican were contemplating denouncing the concordat, or at least publishing a white book setting out the breaches of that agreement which had been perpetrated by the Nazi Government, but apparently the Pope decided to refrain from any such action for the time being. It was thought that in reaching this decision His Holiness had been influenced by the General of the Jesuits, who was known to be even more obsessed than the Pope himself by the Bolshevik danger, but it is possible that the Holy Father was anxious to avoid giving the German Government an excuse for an anti-Catholic outburst such as might enable Herr Hitler to launch the scheme for a national Church free from Rome, which some people believed he was cherishing.

52. Speaking to His Majesty's Minister on the 13th March of the action of the German Government in denouncing the Treaty of Locarno and Herr Hitler's alternative proposals, the Cardinal Secretary of State expressed his unhappy conviction that no signature of the present German Government was worth the paper it was written on. An article which appeared in the *Osservatore Romano* on the 16th March argued that good faith among nations was the essential bulwark against the destruction of European civilisation by the corroding influence of bolshevism.

53. The position of devout Catholics called upon to vote for Herr Hitler in the election at the end of March was one of some difficulty. The bishops therefore issued declarations in which they advised German Catholics that they should " give their vote to the Fatherland, but this does not mean our consent to things of which our conscience cannot approve."

54. The announcement at the end of March by the leader of the Nazi Youth organisation that 1936 was to be the " year of the German Jungvolk," and that parents were to be asked to agree in writing to the enrolment of their children, evoked another pastoral letter, which was read in the Catholic churches, recalling that the youth organisation was in the habit of publishing articles in which the teaching and institutions of the Church were brought into contempt and reminding parents that they would be responsible to God if they failed to obtain assurances that the local youth leaders would not subject their children to influences which endangered their faith.

55. In June a fresh attack was made on the Catholic Church in Germany. A number of lay Catholics of a modern order named after St. Francis, and therefore always, but incorrectly, referred to in the press as Franciscans, were arrested for serious moral offences in a Catholic home for mentally deficient children at Coblenz. The Nazi press avidly seized the occasion to write highly coloured articles contrasting the depravity which reigned in the " Franciscan " houses with the high standard of morality ruling in the Nazi youth institutions and, deliberately ignoring the severe condemnations pronounced by Catholic bishops, attacked the Catholic authorities for failing to condemn the guilty persons. The Minister of the Interior, in a public speech at Coblenz, stated that German opinion was horrified at the abyss of vice which had been revealed, and accused the Church authorities of sharing in the guilt through failing in their duty of supervision. It was clear that the Nazis, having tried to make capital out of an alleged connexion between " political Catholicism " and Marxism, and having exploited to the full the offence of members of Catholic orders against the currency regulations, were now determined to make full use of these unhappy events to bring the Catholic Church into further discredit in the eyes of the public.

56. It was even feared that the scandal might be made the excuse for fresh legislation and that the Nuremberg Party Congress would deprive religious orders of the right to teach. These fears were not realised, but in October the official in charge of the Bavarian Ministry of Education announced that from the 1st January, 1937, steps would be taken gradually to abolish teaching by nuns in elementary schools maintained by the public authorities in Bavaria. The arguments used to justify this decision were condemned by the *Osservatore Romano* as being merely an attempt to disguise the fact that this measure was only part of the anti-Christian drive which was being carried out in Germany.

57. At the conclusion of the annual conference of Catholic bishops held in August at Fulda, three pastoral letters were issued. The first of these was embodied in a memorandum submitted to the Chancellor in which all the complaints of the Church against the régime were set out. The danger of bolshevism was recognised; the Church, however, was everywhere regarded by the Bolsheviks as their most dangerous enemy; why then, it was asked, should the national resistance to bolshevism be lessened by the attacks which were now constantly being made on religion and the Church in Germany ? The bishops stated that the Church only claimed the rights guaranteed to it by the concordat and asked why the Catholic associations, Catholic charitable institutions and the Catholic press could not be allowed to continue their valuable work. The second statement set out the Catholic point of view in the question of the confessional, and the third defended the priesthood against the accusations which had been made against it as a result of the Coblenz scandal.

58.   It was felt, in some circles, that the bishops' statement regarding the danger of bolshevism might presage an accommodation between the Church and the Government, but the Cardinal Secretary of State told His Majesty's Minister, at the beginning of September, that the persecution of the Catholics in Germany, which had been suspended during the Olympic games, had since been renewed, and that he saw no prospect of any improvement in the situation. Speaking on the 24th September at the opening of an International Congress of Catholic Journalists Cardinal Pacelli expressed his regret that no representatives of the Catholic press of Germany were present, and said that he shared with the authors of the August pastoral letters an inability to understand the necessity for the restrictions imposed on the Catholic press in Germany. The principal theme of the cardinal's speech, as of others made during the congress, was the need for combating paganism, whether it took the form of international bolshevism or of nationalistic religious movements.

59.   There were some who hoped that a common hatred of communism might form a basis of better relations between the Reich and the Vatican. Others hoped that developments in Spain would persuade the Vatican to support the fresh attack on bolshevism which was launched by the German Government in the autumn. The Nazi press made use, for this purpose, of an article in which the Austrian rector of the Teutonic College in Rome had denied that Catholicism could work more easily with bolshevism than the Vatican with the Reich. Commenting on this incident the *Osservatore Romano* issued a strongly-worded article condemning the attempts made both on the Communist side and on that of the racialists to distort the words of the Pope and to disguise, for their own ends, the fact that the Vatican condemned all threats to Christian civilisation from whatever side they came. It was, no doubt, to a desire to make this attitude clear beyond all doubt that, after the condemnations of communism which had been issued in connexion with the events in Spain, the Vatican newspaper felt obliged to issue, in October, a series of articles criticising the anti-Christian spirit and activities of such Nazi leaders as Dr. Rosenberg and Herr Baldur von Schirach.

60.   The announcement at the beginning of November that Cardinal Faulhaber had had a lengthy conversation with Herr Hitler gave rise to hopes that negotiations might be resumed which would lead to an agreement between the Reich and the Vatican. It appears that an agreement for the definition of the concordat had been drafted in June 1934, which the German Government were ready to accept. The Vatican had, however, referred the agreement back to the German bishops, and had finally declined it, making counter-proposals going far beyond what had been agreed. The terms agreed on in June 1934 have not been published, but an official of the German Ministry for Foreign Affairs stated that they would have given the Catholic Church in Germany a position corresponding to that which it enjoyed in Italy. At the beginning of 1936 negotiations had been renewed, but without result, and by the end of the year there was no indication that, in spite of the offer of the Church's support of the crusade against bolshevism which Cardinal Faulhaber is believed to have made, his interview had had better success. Herr Hitler was, it appears, unwilling to go beyond the terms which he had been prepared to accept in 1934. The Vatican, on the other hand, still insisted on more, being unwilling to admit the German contention that conditions had changed since the concordat had been signed and to recognise that its claims in respect of the training of youth, confessional schools and Catholic associations must be modified. By German officials it was maintained that the Chancellor had no intention of destroying Catholicism, but it was said that he was determined to give the wilder men of the Nazi party a free hand until the Catholic Church withdrew their claim to special privileges and to a special position in Germany. Once the Church admitted the inevitability of totalitarian State authority it would, it was said, find Herr Hitler ready to meet it and to protect it against further attacks. It seems, however, more than doubtful whether the Church can afford to surrender all authority over the training of youth into the hands of Nazi Jugendführer, in the hope that they will refrain from using that authority to attack the Church and religion. The decree issued towards the end of the year to the effect that all German boys must henceforth belong to the Hitler Jugend can only have strengthened the doubts of the Vatican.

61. The Pope, in his Christmas eve broadcast address from his sick-bed, after reiterating previous warnings of the menace of communism to world civilisation, went on to remark that there were certain self-appointed champions of civilisation against this danger who, in fact, by their own oppression of religion and, especially by trying to stamp out faith in Christ in the hearts of the young, were enhancing the influence and promoting the cause of communism.

Iraq.

62. The Apostolic Delegate, a French Dominican named Mgr. Drapier, was suspected in Iraq, rightly or wrongly, of trying to further French interests, and the Iraq Government felt that it was unfortunate that the occupant of a post in contact with many important elements among the minorities should be a Frenchman. The Iraqi Minister in Rome was accordingly instructed to suggest to the Vatican that Mgr. Drapier should be replaced by a non-Frenchman and apparently found the Cardinal Secretary of State accommodating. In virtue, however, of a Bull of the 4th June, 1638, the French Government claimed that the Bishop of Babylon or Bagdad must be a Frenchman, and as the posts of Apostolic Delegate and bishop had usually been united in one person and as there were objections to having two Latin prelates in Bagdad, it was felt that it might be difficult to appoint a non-French Apostolic Delegate.

63. During the spring relations between the Iraq Government and the Apostolic Delegate grew extremely strained. The Vatican appear to have informed the Minister at the end of June that Mgr. Drapier would be removed in the near future, but nothing happened and the Government began to consider how they could rid themselves of the unwelcome prelate. In the late summer, however, Mgr. Drapier left Iraq on leave of absence, and in November it was announced that he had been transferred to Indo-China. Nothing had been announced by the end of the year regarding his successor.

Italy and Abyssinia.

64. In the course of an address to the Pontifical Academy of Science on the 12th January the Pope spoke in a somewhat more optimistic vein regarding the international outlook. His Majesty's Chargé d'Affaires asked the Assistant Under-Secretary of State if he thought there were any specific grounds for His Holiness's optimism, but Mgr. Tardini replied that the Pontiff's hopes were based solely on supernatural motives.

65. On the 22nd January the Under-Secretary of State asked Mr. Montgomery whether he had heard anything of a *combinazione* between Great Britain, France and Italy to end the Abyssinian conflict. Mr. Montgomery replied that he had heard nothing of it and thought His Majesty's Government unlikely now to take any initiative. In reply to a request for any helpful suggestion he could make, Mr. Montgomery then reminded Mgr. Pizzardo that Sir Samuel Hoare had said that His Majesty's Government would be grateful for any indications of the intentions of the Italian Government which might reach them through the Vatican. Mgr. Pizzardo made a note of this remark.

66. On the 6th February the *Osservatore Romano* challenged the *Dépêche de Toulouse* to produce evidence in support of its statement that " the official Vatican organ has declared that Italy is the standard bearer of Christian civilisation in Ethiopia."

67. On the 26th February His Majesty's Minister drew the attention of the Foreign Office to an article which appeared on the 24th February in the *Manchester Guardian* in which the three reasons for the unwillingness of the Pope to express himself more decisively about Italian aggression were stated to be : (1) a fear of provoking a schism in the Italian Church between the Papacy and Curia on one side and the ultra-patriotic clergy on the other, (2) a fear of weakening fascism and of opening the door to bolshevism in Italy, and (3) a fear that the Fascists, if attacked, might turn and adopt Nazi methods against the Church. To these reasons might perhaps be added a fourth, viz., the Pope's feeling of inability properly to set himself up as a judge of the facts which must all be fully weighed before he could pronounce a condemnation of Italian action.

68. On the 5th March the French Ambassador told His Majesty's Minister that the Pope had urged Mussolini to accept the Geneva peace initiative. On the following day the Cardinal Secretary of State expressed himself pessimistically and implied that the threat of oil sanctions would make it difficult for Mussolini to accept. The Pope's initiative remained, in fact, without success.

69. Neither the Cardinal Secretary of State nor the Under-Secretary of State, to whom His Majesty's Minister talked on the 3rd April, entertained much hope of an early peace. On the 24th April Mr. Osborne showed Cardinal Pacelli a Fascist news-sheet called the *Diplomazia*, which asserted that information from high Vatican circles had established that Papal diplomatic agents had recently been urging the Governments of sanctionist countries not to support His Majesty's Government's proposal to intensify the application of sanctions. Cardinal Pacelli expressed indignation at the report which, he said, was not, as stated, based on information from the Vatican. In reply to a purely personal enquiry from His Majesty's Minister whether he had any idea what the Italian peace terms would be, the cardinal offered to try and find out. In conclusion, his Eminence observed that it was essential that respect for international undertakings should be restored if the world was not to relapse into barbarism and he assented when Mr. Osborne explained that this was the explanation of His Majesty's Government's policy in the Abyssinian question. Five days later the Cardinal Secretary of State told Mr. Osborne what the Italian terms had been at Easter : he could not say whether they had changed since. On the same day the French Ambassador recounted to His Majesty's Minister the various occasions on which the Vatican had tried to ascertain the Italian peace terms and to communicate them to the French and United Kingdom Governments in the hope that the latter would be able to use the information to bring about the end of the war. M. Charles-Roux thought that the Pope felt he had made real efforts to end the war; in fact, however, by the time these various supposed peace conditions reached London and Paris, further Italian successes and advances had rendered them obsolete.

70. At the opening of the Catholic Press Exhibition on the 12th May the Pope referred to the "triumphant joy of a great and good people over a peace that desires to be, and is confident of being, a valid coefficient and prelude of true European and world peace." About the same time it was asserted that pressure was being put on the Vatican to recognise Italy's annexation of Abyssinia. His Majesty's Minister informed the Cardinal Secretary of State on the 15th May that he had heard these rumours. Cardinal Pacelli in reply said that he had only an hour before been notified officially of the annexation. Mr. Osborne then said that he would like to speak to his Eminence personally and stated that if the Vatican took the initiative in recognising the annexation their action would inevitably be condemned in both Catholic and non-Catholic quarters abroad. The Cardinal replied that this was fully appreciated and Mr. Osborne derived the impression that the Vatican would make a strong resistance against any pressure put on them both by the Government and Nationalist clergy.

71. In October the Archbishop of Rhodes went to Abyssinia as Apostolic Visitor for the purpose of investigating the spiritual needs of the inhabitants and working out a programme for future organisation. On his arrival in Addis Ababa Mgr. Castellani held a pontifical mass during which he delivered an address in which he saluted "all the heroic soldiers of the army at which the world marvels, but at which Heaven has no need to marvel since it was their ally," and stated that "it will be the Roman Empire which will carry the cross of Christ into the world." In an interview given about the same time to the *Gazetta del Popolo*, Cardinal Tisserant stated that it was proposed that Italian missionaries should gradually take the place of non-Italians in Abyssinia in accordance with the tradition of the Church that missionaries should belong to the nation to whom the territories belonged in which they were to work and should, if possible, be natives of that territory.

72. In November 1935 His Majesty's representatives in the leading capitals had been instructed to furnish reports on the line adopted by the papal diplomatic representatives in regard to the Italo-Ethiopian dispute and on the effect produced on official and public opinion in the different countries by the disposition

of the Vatican to view the problem as one between Italy and the United Kingdom rather than one between Italy, the League of Nations and Ethiopia. The replies furnished by His Majesty's representatives at the end of 1935 and in January 1936 showed that there was no real ground for belief that the Holy See was engaged in propaganda on behalf of the Italian Government. None the less the failure of the Pope to pronounce clearly against the Italian aggression after the outbreak of the Abyssinian war and against the use of gas against the natives, gave to many in foreign countries the impression that the papacy was in danger of becoming an instrument of Fascist policy. This impression was increased by the ultra-patriotic position adopted during the war by many of the Italian clergy, including men so highly placed as the Cardinal Archbishop of Milan and by the attitude of the *Osservatore Romano*, the official Vatican organ. Nor were matters improved by the fact that nearly all cardinals resident in Rome, the Secretary of State and the heads of the Congregations were Italians. Some of the heads of the religious orders who resided in Rome were indeed foreigners, but none of them had any influence with the Pope except the General of the Jesuits, and he was so obsessed by the Bolshevik danger that he regarded Mussolini in the light of a Saviour. Thoughtful Catholics could not fail to regret the way in which the universal character of the Roman Catholic religion seemed to be compromised by subservience to the Italian political system. It must, however, be said that in conversation with His Majesty's Minister on various occasions, the Pope, the Cardinal Secretary of State, the Under-Secretary of State and the Assistant Under-Secretary of State all professed sympathetic understanding of the motives inspiring British policy.

Mexico.

73. Events in Mexico, which in the previous year had been a cause of grave anxiety to the Holy See, caused less preoccupation in 1936 partly because they were overshadowed by the greater disasters which fell upon the Church in Spain and partly because there were signs, during the year, that the Mexican Government were modifying their attitude of extreme hostility.

74. Some excitement was, however, caused towards the end of 1935 by the seizure, under the law promulgated in September regarding the confiscation of Church property, of buildings erected and occupied by Salesian brothers in Guadalajara on the excuse, which there is reason to believe was baseless, that they were being used for religious teaching. Two months later other buildings belonging to the same Order in the Federal district were also seized, although it is believed that they had ceased to have any religious character.

75. Nevertheless, there were indications that there was likely to be a lull in the anti-religious activities of the Government. It is believed that advice in this sense was conveyed to President Cárdenas by the Mexican Ambassador in Washington. That American Catholics continued to take a lively interest in the fate of their co-religionists in Mexico was shown by the establishment of a "Catholic Bishops' Commission for Mexican Relief" under the presidency of the Archbishop of Baltimore with the object of raising funds for supporting Catholic institutions in Mexico and relieving the needs of religious refugees. It was reported that this commission received through the Cardinal Secretary of State an expression of the Pope's commendation of their work.

76. This favourable impression of developments in Mexico was borne out by a statement published on the 18th March in the press of Mexico City to the effect that the Ministry of the Interior would not oppose the reopening of those churches which had not already been converted into schools, libraries, public offices or other secular public institutions. President Cárdenas was also reported to have stated in private conversation that he saw no reason for depriving the poor peasantry of the consolations of religion and His Majesty's Minister in Mexico City reported that it would accord with the humanitarian side of the President's character if he were to hesitate to prolong a policy which had clearly been carried too far and might have an adverse effect on his country's relations with the United States.

77. In May the Archbishop of Mexico died and was given a funeral service in the cathedral of the capital, which was attended by a vast concourse of people.

Portugal.

78. The brilliant celebration at Coimbra in July of the sixth centenary of the death of Queen Elizabeth provided a striking illustration of the change which has taken place in the attitude of the Portuguese Government towards religion since the early days of the republic, when priests and nuns were forbidden to appear in the streets in their religious garb.

Spain and Communism.

79. On arrival in Rome in February His Majesty's Minister was at once struck by the Vatican's obsession with communism. Mr. Osborne could not, however, fail to be impressed before long by the manner in which the gloomy predictions which had been retailed to him on his arrival regarding events in Spain and France were being realised.

80. On the 24th March the Papal Nuncio in Madrid told the counsellor of His Majesty's Embassy that he thought the situation far more serious than that of 1931 and, fearing that his life might be in danger from Communist elements as a result of a military *coup d'Etat* which might occur at any moment, asked whether he could, if necessary, seek asylum in His Majesty's Embassy. Whether or not they shared Cardinal Tedeschini's extreme pessimism, which later proved so fully justified, there is no doubt that the Vatican were already very alarmed at developments in Spain. On the 2nd April the *Osservatore Romano* wrote that the Spanish Government were controlled by a clique of extremists, and after the French elections the paper expressed the fear that the same cycle of developments would be seen in France.

81. On the 12th May the Pope opened an international exhibition of the Catholic press and made a speech denouncing communism. In Russia, His Holiness said, a real fury of hatred against God had destroyed all that appertains to religion . . . . " the foremost, greatest and most general danger is undoubtedly communism. Attacking openly or insinuating itself by stealth, it threatens everything, individual dignity, the sanctity of the family, the order and safety of civil society and, above all, religion. . . . . A danger promoted by a propaganda which spares nothing."

82. On the 18th March the Spanish Government issued a decree putting fresh vigour into the work of taking over and administering the property of the Company of Jesus in Spain which had been dissolved in 1932.

83. In March the Spanish Ambassador to the Holy See resigned and in the following month the historian and philosopher, Dr. Luis de Zulueta, was appointed in his place. Dr. de Zulueta, who had represented the Catalan Left in the Cortes of 1910 and was a Deputy for Madrid in that of 1919, had, in 1931, seen his *agrément* refused by the Vatican on the grounds that he was an active enemy of religion. He served as Minister of State in the second Azaña Cabinet and then as Ambassador in Berlin and, on the second application, his appointment was accepted by the Holy See.

84. Sr. de Zulueta's mission was a short one. The Spanish Ambassador to the Quirinal, having been forced to resign by his service attachés, a Chargé d'Affaires was sent from Berne to take charge of the Embassy. He, too, however, was turned out of his Embassy by the energetic attachés and took refuge with Sr. de Zulueta at the Embassy in the Piazza di Spagna. In spite of the generous guard which the Italian authorities stationed round the building he evidently soon found his position impossible and left the country. Sr. de Zulueta remained, but his position became more and more difficult. His Embassy was full of spies and he telephoned daily to the Vatican for more adequate protection. One day his cyphers were stolen so that he could no longer communicate confidentially with his Government. A little later he suddenly found himself without funds because his money which had been banked in the name of the Embassy was all withdrawn by persons claiming to represent the Embassy. On the 2nd October Sr. de Zulueta therefore left Rome. Although he did not formally resign he intimated to the Secretariat of State that he did not expect to return and Sr. de la Mora, who had formerly served as counsellor under the Ambassador, took possession of the Embassy in the name of the Junta and hoisted the Nationalist flag. The Vatican

did not, of course, recognise his position and the Assistant Under-Secretary of State was at some pains to impress on His Majesty's Chargé d'Affaires how careful the Holy See had been to preserve strict neutrality in the whole business.

85.   The pessimism shown by the Vatican in regard to the Communist danger was revealed as fully justified, when, in July, the explosion in Spain occurred. From this date onwards the Vatican was constantly receiving stories of destruction, massacre, torture and bestiality emanating from Spain.   On the 10th August the *Osservatore Romano* published an evidently inspired statement to the effect that, in order to satisfy numerous enquiries as to what action the Holy See was taking in the face of these atrocities, the writer had ascertained that strong representations had been addressed to the Madrid Government.   This semi-official admission that protests had been made was no doubt issued more with the purpose of convincing the faithful that the Church was neither condoning the barbarities nor remaining supine than with any idea of checking the Communists and Anarchists.   Indeed, the fact that the Pope himself made no pronouncement about events in Spain was probably due to a fear that the extremists would only be exacerbated thereby.

86.   On the 14th September, however, feeling perhaps that as head of a body claiming to be the secular custodian of morality, and believing, as he did, that the Spanish crisis was the crisis of Europe if not of the world, the Pope broke his silence and delivered to the bishops, priests and other refugees from Spain a long address which was widely broadcast.   After denouncing the orgy of savagery in Spain and deploring the fratricidal strife, the Pope said that the whole world had been subjected to propaganda which aimed, first at winning the masses over to absurd and disastrous ideologies, and then at throwing them against all institutions human or divine.   In a sentence which appeared to be a warning against exaggerated economic individualism he admonished his audience that this propaganda would be successful if, out of rivalry and self-interest, those who had a duty in the matter did not hasten to repair the breach.   His Holiness then issued a warning against the insidious way in which the forces of subversion sought to collaborate with Catholics on the basis of a distinction between ideas and action and between the economic and moral orders.   Next, in a passage aimed at Germany, the Pontiff declared that wherever war was being made on religion and on the Catholic Church help was being given to the forces of subversion. (This sentiment was repeated in His Holiness's Christmas eve broadcast, with evident reference to Germany.)   He then defended the Church against accusations of unpreparedness and ineffectiveness in face of such disasters as had happened in Spain.   What, he asked, could the Church do but deplore and protest when her teaching in regard to youth, the family and the masses was hampered and contradicted and the Catholic press hindered?   The beneficent influence of the Church was also paralysed by the " unceasing and dizzying swirl of contemporary life " and the general wave of immorality.   Finally, the Pope paid a tribute to the recent initiative taken by the Diplomatic Corps in Spain with the object of humanising the conflict and directed his benediction to the suffering Spanish people, especially those who had assumed the task of defending religion.

87.   As the struggle went on, His Majesty's Legation received requests, both from the Vatican and from the Dominican College of the Angelicum, for help in tracing priests whose lives were in danger and, if possible, in arranging for their escape from Spain.

88.   On the 28th October the *Osservatore Romano* protested, and not for the first time, against the attempts of certain foreign newspapers to make the Vatican appear guilty of bias against the Madrid Government and of inconsistency in its views.   It was stated, for example, that an article which had appeared in the *Osservatore Romano* of the 27th October, 1934, at the time of the Asturian revolt. emphasising that it was the Government's duty to put down rebellion and maintain order, was being used by persons of the Left as a reason for asking why the Vatican was now denouncing the legal Government.   These persons, the *Osservatore Romano* continued, evidently did not realise that what the Holy See denounced was the slaughter and torture of priests and other innocent persons and the destruction of places of worship which, in 1934, had been committed by the rebels and to-day was being carried out by those fighting for the Government.

Was it not, asked the *Osservatore*, the Red International rather than the so-called " Black International " which was showing inconsistency by now professing to be the supporter of legal government in Spain ?

89.   In December the *A vvenire d'Italia*, a Catholic paper published in Rome, printed an interview with the Cardinal Archbishop of Toledo.   In this, and in a pastoral letter published in a subsequent issue of the same paper, his Eminence insisted that the Spanish conflict was neither a civil, class, dynastic nor political war, but actually a religious war between the forces of morality, tradition and civilisation and those of disintegration and internationalism represented by Marxist materialism and led and aided by the Government of Moscow.

90.   Similar views were expressed in articles which appeared about the same time in the *Osservatore Romano*, on the subject of the Anglo-French proposals for mediation, which pointed out that, side by side with the civil war, a second war was being conducted in Spain against religion.

91.   In the message to the Sacred College and the Catholic world which was broadcast from the Pope's room on the 24th December, His Holiness issued another warning against communism.   The evil tendencies, he said, which cast a shadow over the Christmas celebrations were making in Spain a supreme effort which constituted perhaps the most serious threat ever directed against Europe, with its Christian civilisation, and the whole world.   Later, the Pope reminded his hearers throughout the world that he had on several occasions already explained what the Holy See had tried to do against this enemy and urged the faithful to do their part in combating error and evil in co-operation with the clergy by means of Catholic Action.

United States of America.

92.   The *Osservatore Romano's* article of the 10th January reviewing the reception by the European press of the message to Congress in which President Roosevelt had condemned autocracy and aggression again made clear the view of the Vatican that it would be rash unduly to decry autocratic régimes so long as bolshevism remained the only alternative to fascism.

93.   As the presidential election drew nearer the political activities of Father Coughlin caused some concern at the Vatican and in the *Osservatore Romano* of the 3rd September a notice was issued denying that the Holy See had ever expressed approval of the priest's attack on the President.

94.   There was a suggestion in America that President Roosevelt might, if re-elected, open formal diplomatic relations with the Holy See.   When, on the 1st October, the announcement was sprung on Rome that the Cardinal Secretary of State was leaving at once for New York, rumour connected his visit with this suggestion.   The Assistant Under-Secretary of State, however, told His Majesty's Chargé d'Affaires that the cardinal was going neither to open diplomatic relations nor to reprove Father Coughlin, but merely to get a holiday which he felt he would be unable to enjoy in Europe in the existing political atmosphere.   The visit, however, was far from being a holiday and resolved itself into a triumphal tour in the course of which the cardinal crossed the entire continent twice by air, visited twelve out of the sixteen Catholic provinces in the United States and inspected countless churches, religious institutes, seminaries and colleges.   On his return to the east he lunched with President Roosevelt and sailed again for Italy on the 7th November.

95.   That the cardinal went partly for a holiday there seems no reason to doubt.   Whether the question of diplomatic relations was discussed is unknown : there was no concrete indication of it by the end of the year.   The visit being the first paid to the United States by a Cardinal Secretary of State roused great interest among Catholics in America.   There is ground for believing that the Pope pressed Cardinal Pacelli to accept the invitation which he had received to visit America because he was anxious both to please loyal opinion in what is now, after Italy, the greatest Catholic country in the world and to show that the Vatican took an interest in the United States.   His Holiness may also have been influenced by the consideration that Anglo-Saxon opinion is little known in Vatican circles as well as by the fact that the United States is now the Vatican's greatest source of revenue.

96. In October it was announced that the Pope had nominated Cardinal Dougherty, Archbishop of Philadelphia, to be Papal Legate at the 33rd International Eucharistic Congress to be held at Manila in July 1937.

IV.—FOREIGN AFFAIRS—GENERAL.

European Situation.

97. In August and September the *Osservatore Romano* conducted, in its editorial columns, a laborious investigation into the causes of the European crisis. In its conclusions the Vatican organ stated that the chief negative factors threatening peace were the war of ideologies, racial intolerance, economic nationalism and the crisis of security in the four danger spots of Europe, viz., the Rhineland, Eastern Europe, the Danube Basin and the Mediterranean.

98. The *Osservatore Romano* held that in order to remedy the situation it would be necessary first to reform the League of Nations. The journal was not certain whether the separation of the Covenant from the Peace Treaty would be altogether advantageous since such separation would involve condemnation of the historical origin of the Covenant. It considered it necessary, however, to revise the treaty in the sense of removing the causes of war by "reasonable compromises" under article 19 and of eliminating opportunities for war by applying the disarmament provisions. The real problem, however, was that of exorcising the war psychology, and this was primarily a moral problem for which the solution could only be found by establishing respect for the liberties and natural rights of States and individuals. This could be achieved by developing the individual and national conscience and by reinforcing the sanctity of contract by means both of moral guarantees and of practical institutions for the delivery and affirmation of the verdicts which would result from this newly awakened conscience.

99. In a later article the *Osservatore Romano* discussed the ethical value of pacts of non-aggression. While recognising that such pacts had some practical value, the Vatican newspaper stated that they possessed no moral value beyond that of furnishing an indication of the goodwill of the statesmen engaging in them. In fact, the idea of a pact of non-aggression was really a sign of the decadence of the post-war civilisation inasmuch as the idea of non-aggression was an essential part of the ethical conscience of both individuals and nations and pledges of non-aggression should therefore be an absurdity.

Submarine Warfare.

100. In the *procès-verbal* governing the action of submarines with regard to merchant ships in time of war which was signed in London on the 6th November, His Majesty's Government in the United Kingdom were requested to communicate the rules for the action of submarines to the Governments of all Powers not signatory to the Treaty of London of 1930 with an invitation to accede thereto. Although the State of the Vatican City has no seaboard. His Majesty's Government were anxious that the rules should have general acceptance. They were further anxious to strengthen public opinion in favour of the rules by securing for them the support of the moral influence of the Holy See. His Majesty's Legation was accordingly instructed to enquire informally of the Secretariat of State whether the Vatican would be disposed to accept a formal invitation to accede to the rules in question.

V.—THE VATICAN.

The Pope.

101. The Pope left Rome for his summer residence at Castel Gandolfo on the 30th June, a month earlier than in 1935. When His Majesty's Minister visited him on the 31st August he found that he had much benefited in health by his stay in the hills. On the 30th September His Holiness returned to Rome. While there is no doubt that the change had been beneficial, it was equally clear that the anxieties roused by events in Spain and the uncertainty of the general situation were proving a severe strain. The enormous number of audiences which His Holiness gave, including the daily reception of newly-married couples and his insistence on supervising the entire work of the Vatican, must have been an

increasing strain on a man in his eightieth year. In November disquieting rumours about his health, such as had been heard in the spring, again began to circulate. On this occasion there was more ground for them inasmuch as it later became known that on the 3rd November His Holiness had been treated for blood-pressure. At the service in memory of the cardinals who had died during the year, held on the 5th November, the Pontiff had to be carried on a throne into the Sistine Chapel, and a few days later rumour said that he had suffered a heart attack. On the 5th December the newspapers announced that, as a measure of safeguard against asthma, His Holiness had been ordered to bed, and had therefore been obliged to cancel the audiences which he would otherwise have resumed after his week's retreat. This notice, coupled with the knowledge that special arrangements had been made at the Vatican for issuing bulletins to the press, roused considerable anxiety. On the following morning, however, a more reassuring notice was issued to the effect that the Pope was really only suffering from an attack of gout in the left leg, and, while keeping to his bed, would continue to receive the Secretary of State and conduct business. Later bulletins were still more reassuring and their issue was soon abandoned. Nevertheless, His Holiness was still confined to his bed at the end of the year, and reliable information reached the Legation that his condition was by no means satisfactory. He was unofficially declared to be suffering from a combination of disorders, which included heart, arterial and asthmatic conditions, and it was obvious that when a man whose robust health and strength had sustained him for eighty years of unremitting labour was finally forced to capitulate to the attrition of increasing age there was more than a possibility that his recuperative powers would be found unavailing. No surprise was therefore caused by the announcement that the Pope's usual Christmastide receptions of the cardinals resident in Rome and of the Diplomatic Corps would not take place. The dean of the College of Cardinals addressed a letter of greeting to the Pope, to which His Holiness replied in a message to the Catholic world which was broadcast from his sick-room on the 24th December.

College of Cardinals.

102. At a Secret Consistory held on the 15th June the Pope raised to the cardinalate Mgr. Giovani Mercati, Prefect of the Vatican Library, and Mgr. Eugène Tisserant, Pro-Prefect.

103. At a Public Consistory held on the 18th June the red hat was conferred on the four cardinals who had been unable to be present at the Consistory of the 16th December, 1935. These were :—

> Cardinal Tedeschini, Nuncio in Madrid.
> Cardinal Sibilia, Nuncio in Vienna.
> Cardinal Marmaggi, Nuncio in Warsaw.
> Cardinal Maglione, Nuncio in Paris.

104. Those who died during the year were :—

(1) Cardinal Binet, Archbishop of Besançon, who was born at Soisson in 1869 and created cardinal in 1927.

(2) Cardinal Lépicier, who was born near Verdun in 1863 and created cardinal in 1927. Cardinal Lépicier served for many years in the Servite Mission at Fulham and later as Apostolic Visitor to Scotland and India. He was Prefect of Religious (*i.e.*, was in charge of the administration of the religious orders) and Protector of the English and Beda Colleges in Rome.

(3) Cardinal Maurin, who was born near Marseilles in 1858 and created cardinal in 1916.

(4) Cardinal Sincero born near Vercelli in 1870 and created cardinal in 1923. He served as president of the Commission pro-Russia and as secretary of the Congregation of the Oriental Church, and was Papal Legate in Hungary in 1930 and in Sicily in 1934.

105. At the end of the year there were sixty-six cardinals, of whom thirty-seven were Italian, while the British Empire was represented solely by Cardinal Villeneuve of Canada and Cardinal MacRory of Ireland.

Catholic Press Exhibition.

106. On the 12th May in the presence of a large assembly of cardinals, Vatican officials, diplomats and journalists, the Pope opened a world exhibition of the Catholic press in the Vatican. After greeting the Catholic journalists, who had come for the occasion from forty-five countries, His Holiness deplored the " fury of hate against God," which was destroying all that appertains to religion in Russia, and regretted that " contrary to all justice and truth and on account of artificially exploited connexions and confusions between religion and politics " it had been considered undesirable in Germany that a Catholic press should exist. After then expressing his gratitude for the gallant manner in which the Catholic press continued to defend and propagate the Faith in the world, the Holy Father discussed communism, which he described as " the first, greatest and most general danger." He condemned, too, events and tendencies which threatened contemporary life and the institutions in which the individual and collective lives of man unfolded. The Church was a divine institution and could rely on divine promises of protection, but it was certain that those who assailed the life and freedom of action of the Church thereby renounced the precious contribution that only the Church could afford to public order and the public good. Such contribution involved no invasion of the purely and properly political sphere. The Church recognised the State's own proper sphere of action and enjoined and ordered conscientious respect of it; but it could not admit that politics should ignore morality, and it could not forget the command of its divine Founder to busy itself with, and take charge of morality. Finally, the Pope associated himself with the " triumphant joy of a great and good people " at the peace which had terminated the war in Abyssinia.

107. During the year various congresses and exhibitions were held in con- nexion with the Press Exhibition. Among the latter was an unofficial exhibition of the Bolshevik press organised by Père Ledit. Of the congresses the most important was the International Congress of Catholic Journalists, which was opened by the Cardinal Secretary of State on the 24th September. In his speech Cardinal Pacelli spoke of the need for resisting paganism and urged the Catholic press to combat both racialism and bolshevism, the " idolatry of the State " as well as the " agitations of the godless," and at the same time emphasised the dangers of a " rationalism which derived from the supernatural " and of the " maxims and practices of a plutocratic liberalism " which led to the exploitation of labour. Concluding his address by greeting, in seven languages, the journalists present from twenty-eight countries, Cardinal Pacelli wished to the English writers " the nobility of heart and forceful style of Newman," and some share of his gift of fellow-feeling, which had enabled him to awake in the minds of his countrymen a desire for union " beneath the shadow of the rock of Peter." The congress closed with a reception at Castel-Gandolfo by the Pope, who urged the Catholic journalists always to be active defenders of the truth and evangelists of the Papal utterances.

Encyclical.

108. An encyclical letter on the cinema was issued by the Pope on the 29th June to the United States Episcopate and other Ordinaries enjoying communion in the Apostolic See. The encyclical began by expressing apprecia- tion of the results achieved by the American hierachy in combating the evils of the cinema, while paying tribute to the latter's educational and artistic possibilities. The crusade against immoral films so far from injuring the cinema industry would, it was maintained, be of advantage to it. It was difficult to exercise a moral censorship over so vast an industry, but the bishops were urged to keep their eyes open and, when necessary, to recall leaders of the industry to their responsibility to society. Finally it was suggested that in every country Catholic Action should assist in publishing regularly lists showing which films were suitable for the public.

Pontifical Academy of Science.

109. By an Apostolic Letter in the form of a *Motu Proprio*, the Pope announced the conversion of the ancient " Accademia Pontificia," founded in 1603, into the " Pontifical Academy of Science." In this letter the Holy Father expressed his belief that real science would always work hand in hand with faith

in defending truth.   Among the seventy regular members appointed to the academy were Catholics, Protestants and Jews, laymen and religious.   Thirty-four of the members nominated were Italians, and three, Lord Rutherford of Cambridge University, Sir Charles Sherrington of Oxford, and Professor Whittaker of Edinburgh, were British.   Professor Gamelli of Milan University, a Franciscan and an old friend of the Pope, was appointed first president.

VI.—LEGISLATION.

110.   LVII (June 20, 1936).—Ordinance regarding the issue of a series of stamps in commemoration of the World Exhibition of the Catholic Press.

CONFIDENTIAL.

(15362)

HOLY SEE.

ANNUAL REPORT, 1937:

[R 1681/1681/22]

Mr. Osborne to Mr. Eden.—(Received February 23.)

(No. 24.)   *British Legation to the Holy See,*
Sir,   *Rome, February 10, 1938.*

  I HAVE the honour to transmit herewith the annual report for 1937, for which, with the exception of the introduction, I am indebted to Mr. Torr, secretary to the Legation.

            I have, &c.
            D. G. OSBORNE.

Enclosure.

Annual Report on the Holy See for 1937.

CONTENTS.

I.—INTRODUCTION.

  IN Vatican City and throughout the Catholic world the outstanding event of 1937 was the Pope's remarkable recovery and his return to vigorous leadership of the Church. Not only did His Holiness courageously assert the rights of catholicism against the attacks of international communism and German national socialism, but, in a world distracted by ideological controversies between dictatorships and democracies, capitalism and communism, abstract international ideals and concrete nationalist ambitions, he proclaimed the Church's neutrality as regards political systems and national differences, and reiterated and emphasised her unwavering support of the principles of social justice and international morality. The relations of the Holy See with Italy, in which

9759   [16832]   B

cordiality does not, as is often supposed, betoken subservience, survived the severe shock of the Rome-Berlin axis, though there is little doubt that the Vatican heartily deplored the latter, for the moral encouragement which it gave to the Nazi extremists, and would have greatly preferred an Italian *entente* with Great Britain.   Relations with France, despite the Communist complexion of the Popular Front, were cemented by the mission to Lisieux of the Cardinal Secretary of State and the honours paid to his Eminence by the French Government.   The Papal mission to the Coronation resulted in a marked and most helpful appreciation by the Vatican of British character and political inspiration and purpose. The encyclicals *Divino Redentore*, condemning communism and, to a lesser degree, statolatry, and *Mit Brennender Sorge*, addressed to the German episcopate and clergy, together with the address to the cardinals on Christmas Eve in which His Holiness stigmatised the treatment of the Church in Germany as " persecution," and the attempt to defend it on the score of the alleged political activity of the clergy as " calumny," testified to the courage and determination with which the Pope had returned to the defence of the Church.   No doubt it is easy in Rome to over-estimate the importance and effect of such pontifical pronouncements, which are deliberately suppressed by those against whom they are directed and only briefly noticed in countries not immediately concerned.   Yet their authority and appeal must be strong enough to penetrate and influence non-Catholic public opinion to some extent.   In any case spiritual and intellectual weapons are the only ones with which the Church can defend herself.

2.   Throughout 1936 the Vatican's consuming obsession was the fear of communism, not only as the arch-enemy of the Church but as a most dangerous and disintegrative influence on order and stability throughout the world. By the end of 1937 the German persecution seemed to have displaced the Communist menace as the Vatican's major and immediate cause of preoccupation. Throughout the year relations with the Reich grew more tense and embittered, the prospects of conciliation more remote and the repression of freedom of conscience and of religious worship in Germany more active and relentless, while the glorification of Rosenberg at the party congress testified to the growing power and resolution of the anti-religious extremist element in the party.   Communism, on the other hand, had displayed unmistakable weaknesses and sustained unquestionable reverses in 1937.   In Spain, which Lenin had boasted would be the second Communist Republic in Europe, the battle was almost certainly lost, if not to Franco, then to the moderates on the Republican side.   The Communist element in the French Popular Front had advertised chaos but not achieved revolution; it had not attempted to lay hands on the Church, and had even issued an appeal to Catholics for collaboration in fighting social injustice—an appeal that was an indication of weakness though not of repentance. Above all, in Russia itself the Communist experiment had been hopelessly discredited by the senseless and merciless extermination of leadership.   Thus, while in no way relaxing their vigilance against their most implacable enemy, the Vatican might well feel that they could breathe a little more freely.   And not only the Vatican.

3.   But the outlook for 1938 offers little other cause for satisfaction.   To begin with, the precarious state of the Pope's health must be a continuing anxiety, for his heart is at the mercy of any shock.   And the state of the world does not allow him or his counsellors respite from care and apprehension.   In Republican Spain worship is proscribed, 6,000 priests have been murdered, others are in hiding and in daily danger of their lives, and countless churches have been destroyed.   The offensive against religion in Germany shows no sign of abatement and the Church's powers of defence and of protection of the faithful have availed little.   In the Far Eastern war there have been casualties among the missions, and there must inevitably be further loss of life and property. Throughout the world fear, enmity and misunderstanding, and the ensuing war psychosis and competition in armaments, are a flagrant denial of the teaching of Christ and a melancholy testimony to the irredeemable folly of man.   Where the Church is not resisting open attack, she is on the defence against scepticism and indifference.   It is little wonder that the sick old Pope looks as though he were bowed down under the sins and follies of the world and that he should attach such immense importance to his Catholic Action organisation, which is in the nature of a totalitarian conscription of the Catholic laity for the defence of the Church and of its way of thinking.

II.—THE VATICAN.

The Pope.

4. A combination of cardiac weakness, arteriosclerosis, varicocele, and asthma brought the Pope near to death at the turn of the year. A bulletin announced, however, that the clarity and vigour of his mind remained unimpaired. On behalf of The King His Majesty's Minister conveyed a message of anxious sympathy and good wishes. Meanwhile His Holiness continued to give a very few private audiences. By February a notable degree of improvement was recorded and at Easter he appeared again in public at Mass in St. Peter's. In the early summer he moved out of Rome to his country residence at Castel Gandolfo, 15 miles away. Here he benefited by the altitude, the air and the avoidance of the extreme summer heat and, although by all accounts he continually insisted on doing more work than his doctors authorised, his condition continued to improve and by September he was giving frequent and large public audiences. He returned to Rome at the end of October and by December was strong enough to preside, though with manifest effort, at the lengthy functions of a consistory, and on Christmas Eve to issue personally a vigorous denunciation of the religious persecution in Germany. His recovery has been astonishing and, in His Holiness's own estimation, miraculous, but he has greatly aged and can never hope to recover his former vigour and vitality. So long as he submits to leading an invalid's life, accommodates his passion for work to his diminished resources of strength and resistance, and, above all, is able to avoid a physical or mental strain greater than his weak heart can bear, there is no reason why he should not live for some time. But he cannot hope ever to emerge from his present condition of precarious convalescence.

Pontifical Pronouncements.

5. Three important encyclicals were issued by the Pope in the course of the year. The first, dated the 19th March, combined a formidable denunciation of the communistic heresy with an admirable definition of the principles of social justice which the Catholic Church makes its own. Passages in this encyclical were directed as much against statolatry as against its ostensible rival. An even more evenly distributed impartiality characterised His Holiness's third encyclical, published in October, in which he enjoined on the priesthood and their flocks prayer to the Blessed Virgin of the Rosary as a remedy for the ills and delusions of the present day. His encyclical on the Communist danger (*Divino Redentore*) was followed within a few days by that to the bishops of Germany summarised in paragraph 32 of this report. In this document it was the Nazi idolatry of race that His Holiness denounced and condemned.

6. In this connexion it is, however, perhaps worth recording that, if for the extravagances of modern ideologies His Holiness had nothing but condemnation, it was by no means necessarily democracy that he saw as the divinely ordained *via media*. On the contrary, the basic democratic conception that sovereignty is the people's, and each national people's at that, is from the Vatican's point of view as much an absurdity as would be the contention that the individual himself is above the law. Through the mouthpiece of the *Osservatore Romano* the fallacy of distinguishing between inter-individual and inter-national moral responsibilities was repeatedly condemned. But in more than one of his pronouncements His Holiness has also had a word to say in condemnation of the moral fallacies underlying liberal economic doctrines.

College of Cardinals.

7. Cardinal Hundain y Esteban, Archbishop of Seville, died in August, and Cardinal Bisleti, head of the Congregation of Seminaries and Universities, in September. At a consistory held on the 13th December the Pope raised to the cardinalate Mgr. Pizzardo, Under-Secretary of State and ecclesiastical head of Catholic Action, Mgr. Pellegrinetti (Nuncio in Belgrade), Mgr. Piazza (Patriarch of Venice), Mgr. Gerlier (Archbishop of Lyons) and Mgr. Hinsley (Archbishop of Westminster). The College of Cardinals was thus brought to the number of 69, of whom 39 were Italians, leaving only a single vacancy.

Pontifical Academy of Science.

8. In June there was formally opened the Pontifical Academy of Sciences; this revival of an institution founded by Pius IX bore testimony to his present Holiness's insistence that between science and religion there is no quarrel.

III.—RELATIONS WITH ITALY.

Recognition of the Empire.

9. On 12th February, the anniversary of his Coronation, the Pope received from the King of Italy a telegram of congratulation. His Holiness's reply was addressed to "His Majesty Victor Emmanuel III, King of Italy and Emperor of Abyssinia," and spoke of the Queen as the "Queen Empress." On 5th April, the fortieth anniversary of the Queen's marriage, His Holiness presented to Her Majesty the Golden Rose, a traditional gift of ancient origin, once accorded to cities and shrines as well as to heads of States, but now reserved for Queens of Roman Catholic houses, and the highest honour His Holiness can bestow. In his Nuncio's special letters for the occasion the Imperial title was again employed. Asked at the Vatican whether this implied formal recognition of the Italian Empire, the Assistant Under-Secretary of State replied in the negative, observing, however, that in matters of this sort the policy of the Vatican was, while avoiding the taking of initiative, to act in accordance with realities.

Religious Policy in Abyssinia.

10. In Abyssinia, meanwhile, the Vatican were in practice not slow to fall in with Italian plans, appointing Mgr. Giovanni Castellani, Archbishop of Rhodes, an ex-army chaplain and ardent imperialist, who had long maintained close relations with the military, to be Apostolic Delegate for Italian East Africa (*i.e.*, Abyssinia, Eritrea and Italian Somaliland, territories which had hitherto formed part of the Province of the Apostolic Delegate at Cairo). Nor did they raise any open objection to the Italian Government's insistence that only Italian missionaries should henceforth work in the conquered territory, the Under-Secretary of State admitting, as early as March, when the matter was still the subject of representations by His Majesty's Government in the United Kingdom to the Italian Government, that it was improbable that in future any but Italians would be sent to that area.

Visit of the Abuna.

11. The Coptic Archbishop of Abyssinia visited Rome in June and stayed nearly a month in Italy. There was some speculation in the press as to the object of his visit. In view of the fact that in its former Emperor the Abyssinian Church had lost its spiritual head, the suggestion was not unnaturally raised that a reconciliation with Rome was under consideration; but no confirmation of this reached the Legation and the Abuna's time was for the most part taken up by the civic authorities. He did not see the Pope.

Fascism and the Rome-Berlin Axis.

12. In the domestic field relations with the State authorities remained sympathetic, the *Osservatore Romano* going so far on one occasion in March as to publish a signed article by the president of Italian Catholic Action, which in its insistence on the need for discipline, armaments and defensive measures of all kinds read like an echo of an order of the day by the Fascist Grand Council. His Majesty's Minister drew Mgr. Pizzardo's attention to it, and Mgr. Pizzardo admitted that it went altogether too far, observing in confidence and extenuation that it was sometimes necessary to "transiger." At the same time there is no doubt that higher authority in the Vatican deplored the excess of military spirit evoked by the régime, and on more than one occasion the *Osservatore Romano* condemned the growing contempt for legality in international relations. Signor Mussolini in November spoke of "a certain wavering catholicism" as one of the enemies of fascism. Mgr. Pizzardo assured His Majesty's Minister that the allusion was to an anti-Fascist Catholic element in France, but on the other hand there is equally little doubt that the Italian policy of rapprochement with Germany was regarded with serious misgivings at the Vatican. Presumably as

the result of Italian representations the Nuremberg Congress, which immediately preceded Signor Mussolini's visit to Berlin and which had been expected to prove the occasion of the promulgation of new measures against the Churches in Germany, did not mention the religious question, but the Vatican were not consulted in the matter of the action of the Italian Government, and when the congress was over they were quick to point out, both in conversation and publicly through the *Osservatore Romano*, that if on this occasion the German authorities had shown restraint it had been from tactical motives alone. It was significant that it was not from the Italians but from the French that the Vatican had first learnt of Signor Mussolini's intended visit to Berlin, and Mgr. Pizzardo admitted to His Majesty's Minister that he was a little anxious about the effect of the visit on the Duce. Meanwhile His Holiness's own German policy (see the relevant section of this report) must have been anything but welcome to the advocates of the Rome–Berlin axis.

Intervention in Spain.

13. The Italian adventure in Spain, in so far as it represented assistance to allies of the Church, enjoyed of course the sympathy of the Vatican. The *Osservatore Romano*, however, continued to maintain a difficult neutrality on the political issue, going so far on one occasion as to assert that there were two wars in Spain, one political in which the Vatican was neutral, and one against religion which was another matter. The article provoked protest from General Franco's representative to the Holy See, who contended that it did less than justice to his side's championship of the Church. The attacks on neutral shipping which provoked the Nyon Agreement were strongly condemned by the *Osservatore Romano*.

Desire for Anglo-Italian Rapprochement.

14. Meanwhile Mgr. Pizzardo repeatedly urged the necessity of a resumption of cordial relations between Italy and the United Kingdom. With the Mediterranean Agreement the opening of the year had seemed to offer some prospect of an improvement, and this was welcomed both publicly by the *Osservatore Romano* and by the Cardinal Secretary of State in conversation with His Majesty's Minister. In September Mgr. Pizzardo still professed to regard the rift as not past healing and Italian advances to Germany as not yet irreversible. As for Signor Mussolini's flamboyancy of technique, he said it must be understood that this was but "politics," defence tactics against the insidious danger of which the Front populaire in France, bolshevism in Spain and Russian influence in Czechoslovakia were the symptoms. We in England had deep-rooted traditions of democratic stability and reserves of wealth with which to blunt the edge of discontent, but in Central and Southern Europe the alternatives were grimmer and strong Governments a necessity. On the 8th October he again held similar language to His Majesty's Minister. This time he put forward a concrete suggestion.

Mgr. Pizzardo's Suggestion.

15. He was, said Mgr. Pizzardo, seriously worried about the international situation. First of all he said, and reiterated with emphasis, that Signor Mussolini was too deeply involved in Spain to be able to withdraw. He was committed to the defeat of communism and could not contemplate or tolerate a defeat of Franco. In his opinion there was no reason to question Mussolini's undertakings in regard to withdrawal from Spain, including the Balearic Islands, when the war was over, and he believed that the Duce would be ready to sign a solemn agreement to this effect. In this connexion, and again later, he referred casually to the possibility of a secret Anglo-Italian treaty which would give to both parties solemn and reliable assurances on matters in regard to which they were anxious, so as to re-establish mutual confidence for the future. One such undertaking might cover Abyssinia, and this was the point on which he spoke at most length and with most emphasis. He assured His Majesty's Minister that not only Mussolini, but also the Italian Ministry for Foreign Affairs and the Italian people in general, believed that British rearmament was largely, if not solely, designed to enable Great Britain, when ready, to take Abyssinia away from Italy, and apparently to keep it. So firmly rooted was this conviction, he

said, that there was even some hesitation about sending Italian colonists. His Majesty's Minister told him that the idea was fantastic, and public assurances by His Majesty's Ministers should have sufficed to eradicate it, if anything could. Mgr. Pizzardo assured him that anxiety and suspicion on this score were as strong as ever. Possibly, he suggested, an uneasy conscience was partly responsible. And, he went on, the first essential of a restoration of confidence and normal good relationship between the two countries was to satisfy Signor Mussolini once and for all that Great Britain contemplated no aggression or war of revenge against Italy and had not the slightest intention of taking Abyssinia away from her. Mgr. Pizzardo did not mention *de jure* recognition of the Italian Empire, and from what he said His Majesty's Minister was inclined to think that something more, either before or after recognition, would be required. And from his references to a secret treaty of mutual assurance it appeared that he believed that there were other possibilities of satisfying Signor Mussolini. Once the canker of suspicion was excised from the Italian, and above all the Mussolinian, mind, any other matters, Mgr. Pizzardo seemed to think, could be easily disposed of and the way would be clear for a restoration of the former excellent relations. Shortly thereafter both the Prime Minister and the Secretary of State took occasion publicly to reiterate that the British people and Government did not harbour thoughts of animosity or revenge against Italy.

IV.—RELATIONS WITH THE BRITISH EMPIRE.

Accession of The King.

16. On the 18th February His Majesty's Minister conveyed to the Cardinal Secretary of State a letter from The King formally announcing to His Holiness His Majesty's accession to the Throne, expressing His Majesty's earnest desire to maintain the friendship which had so long existed between the Holy See and his Royal predecessors and assuring His Holiness of the sincere amity and unfeigned respect and esteem entertained by His Majesty for His Holiness's person and character.

Pontifical Mission to His Majesty's Coronation and Mgr. Pizzardo's Conversation on Anglo–Italian Relations.

17. To His Majesty's Coronation in May His Holiness sent as his Special Envoy Mgr. Giuseppe Pizzardo, his Under-Secretary of State and one of his most trusted advisers, whom he has since raised to the cardinalate, Mgr. Godfrey, rector of the English College in Rome, and the Marchese Giulio Pacelli, Lieutenant in the Noble Guard and a nephew of the Cardinal Secretary of State. In accordance with precedent the Papal mission held themselves precluded from attendance at the religious ceremony in Westminster Abbey, but were provided with seats outside from which to view the Royal Procession.

18. Mgr. Pizzardo made use of his visit to London to petition the assistance of His Majesty's representatives in Spain on behalf of persecuted priests in that country, and had interviews with the Secretary of State, Mr. Chamberlain and Sir Robert Vansittart. The Secretary of State spoke to him frankly about the unhappy condition of Anglo-Italian relations, emphasising the eagerness with which His Majesty's Government in the United Kingdom would see an improvement in them and drawing attention to the apparently gratuitous manner in which Signor Mussolini was encouraging ill-feeling in Italy. Mgr. Pizzardo promised to repeat to His Holiness what the Secretary of State had said to him, and on his return gave every evidence of having been most favourably impressed by his reception and of an increasingly sympathetic understanding of the British point of view in relation to international problems. His subsequent promotion to the cardinalate at the end of the year necessitated, unfortunately, his transfer from the Secretariat of State. He remains, however, ecclesiastical head of Catholic Action, a position in which his influence on international problems will continue to be felt. On the 29th November His Majesty's Chargé d'Affaires called to convey to him a personal message of congratulation on his promotion from Sir Robert Vansittart. In the course of conversation Mgr. Pizzardo assured him that in his new post all his endeavours would continue to be constantly directed to the promotion of a good understanding of

England and the English, for whom he had the sincerest sympathy and a very real admiration; meanwhile his one great desire was to see an end to the estrangement between Italy and England. This was necessary, essential. The logic of converging interests compelled a revival of the traditional relationship. The Vatican's relations with Germany were going from bad to worse. For England an understanding with Italy was more feasible than one with Germany; for Herr Hitler was not a free agent, but in Italy all depended on one man.

Ecclesiastical Appointments (British).

19.   The Archbishop of Westminster was appointed a cardinal in September, thus bringing representation of the British Commonwealth of Nations in the College of Cardinals to the number of three, the other two being Cardinal Villeneuve of Canada, and Cardinal McRory of Ireland.

20.   To the Archbishopric of Bombay—see paragraphs 21 to 25 of last year's report—Father Thomas Roberts, rector of the Jesuit College at Liverpool, was appointed in August.

Theological Faculty of the University of Malta.

21.   The reform of the Theological Faculty of the University of Malta was the occasion of further correspondence between the Vatican and His Majesty's Legation during the year. On the 5th May the Legation were able to supply the Secretariat of State with a memorandum showing that all the requirements of the Sacred Congregation of Universities and Studies appeared in practice to have been met, and formally requested the Vatican's official assurance that the new scheme had their approval. The latter confirmed their reply, however, to the communication of a memorandum from the Congregation to the effect that there remained still a small point to be settled regarding the manner in which debates should be held by the theological students and their training in the preparation of theses. In August the Legation were in a position to submit a draft clause to be added to the university's regulations and to enquire whether this would meet the case. In submitting it His Majesty's Chargé d'Affaires enquired further, under instructions, whether on its promulgation the desired assurance from the Vatican would be forthcoming. The Vatican's reply received in September was that the new clause would meet the case, assuming that the second paragraph of another article, rendered irrelevant by the new clause, were deleted; and, under pressure, Mgr. Pizzardo supplemented this with a letter giving unofficial assurance that, when the Sacred Congregation's requirements on this last and very small point had been met, the desired formal assurance of approval would be given.

Archbishopric of Malta.

22.   The question of the appointment of a successor to the Archbishop of Malta, or of a coadjutor with right of succession, remained in suspense throughout the year. His Majesty's Minister reminded the Secretariat of State on more than one occasion that the candidate for the succession most favoured by His Majesty's Government in the United Kingdom was Mgr. George Caruana, Titular Archbishop of Sebastea and Papal Nuncio in Cuba. Meanwhile no appointment to the coadjutorship was made by the Vatican.

Malta Religious Orders.

23.   In June the Legation were asked to comment on views submitted by the Governor of Malta regarding the desirability of removing, as far as possible, the religious orders in Malta from Italian influence. The question was the more complicated inasmuch as any reforms would involve alterations in the administrative arrangements of the orders themselves, and His Majesty's Minister advised that to this end it would be well to secure the prior support of the Vatican. Meanwhile it was ascertained that, except in the case of the Jesuits and Salesians, the religious houses in Malta formed a separate " province " administered by a resident " provincial " or " commissioner," but that the latter's correspondence with the head of the order in Rome passed as a rule through the hands of an assistant whose district would also comprise other areas, the general practice being to treat Malta as part of the Italian Assistancy. This administrative arrangement is not peculiar to the case of Malta and Italy, considerations of geographical propinquity rather than of political allegiance normally determining.

the area comprised in each " Assistancy " ; but it was submitted that there might be advantages in securing, if possible, that the houses of the several religious orders in Malta should be placed under the same Assistancy as the houses of the same order in the United Kingdom. Further suggestions under consideration were the desirability of securing for the Governor of Malta a right of veto on the appointment of " provincials " and " commissioners " in the island and the substitution of Italian as the official language of the Church.

24. In October His Majesty's Minister visited Malta to discuss these questions with the Governor. It was agreed that as regards the first two points His Majesty's Minister should carefully consider in Rome what the prospects would be of obtaining satisfaction in respect of them, and what would be the best method of procedure. As regards the language question, the discussions in Malta had led to the conclusion that Latin and Maltese would perhaps be the most suitable as the official languages of the Catholic Church in Malta. On his return to Rome His Majesty's Minister submitted this suggestion personally and unofficially to Mgr. Pizzardo, asking for his personal opinion. Mgr. Pizzardo deprecated any attempt to raise the language question now, contending that, while Latin would be unintelligible to a large proportion of the population, Maltese was an inadequate vehicle, and that to eliminate Italian at this juncture would give rise to political misinterpretations.

Palestine: Partition Proposals.

25. Publication of the report of the Royal Commission on Palestine and the announcement of the 7th July that His Majesty's Government in the United Kingdom intended to make it the basis of their policy in that mandated area aroused at the Vatican some concern over the future of the Holy Places. Mgr. Pizzardo called on His Majesty's Minister to discuss with him the wording of the draft of a note on the subject which His Holiness wished to address to His Majesty's Government. It was to the effect that the Holy See was seriously preoccupied to learn from the report of the commission that it was proposed, not only to divide up what had hitherto been considered an indivisible whole under the name of the Holy Land, but to distinguish between Jerusalem and Bethlehem, which were to be put under the proposed new mandate, and Nazareth and Lake Tiberias, which were not considered in the report as Holy Places, while Nazareth was to be incorporated in the proposed Jewish State. The Holy See could not believe that a Christian nation would tolerate that Nazareth and Lake Tiberias should be withdrawn from Christian influence and subjected to a non-Christian authority. A further cause for anxiety was the future fate of the Christian minorities of Palestine. It was true that the report spoke of " precise guarantees," but what had happened since 1917 did not altogether reassure the Holy See. For, in spite of the assurances originally given that the rights and privileges enjoyed under the Turkish régime would be maintained, frequent representations to the British High Commissioner had been necessary to defend the reputation, property and religious practice of Catholics in the face of difficulties arising from the influence or proponderance of adversaries of the Catholic religion. And if the situation of Catholics had been difficult under the mandate, what would it be when their adversaries could do what they liked with the Catholic communities scattered over the territories of the two proposed sovereign States? Finally, the Holy See felt it to be both its right and its duty to inform other Christian States of its representations to His Majesty's Government, and to ask for their support. It was, however, confident that, in making these representations, it was not doing anything that was disagreeable to His Majesty's Government.

26. His Majesty's Minister suggested that, in view of the recommendations in the report, the Vatican's fears for Nazareth and Lake Tiberias might be excessive, that it would be well to define the past grievances and present grounds for anxiety which they had in mind in the matter of the Catholics in Palestine, and that the draft note's concluding intimation that the Holy See proposed to seek the support of other Governments for its point of view would sound less ungracious if accompanied by some such words as " provided His Majesty's Government had no serious objection." Mr. Osborne added (for it was now the 4th August and the report was already under discussion at Geneva) that he

regretted greatly that the Holy See had not acted earlier. His Majesty's Government were already confronted by objections from Arabs and Jews, and these belated representations from the Holy See would hardly ease their difficulties. To this, however, Mgr. Pizzardo replied, with great emphasis, that His Majesty's Minister must realise from the contents of the note that it was in no sense a protest against the British mandate. On the contrary, it was an expression of regret and a cry of alarm at the proposed surrender of that mandate. He added that the Pope had been under strong pressure from Catholics in all countries to address a plea to His Majesty's Government on behalf of the protection of the Holy Places.

27. In a revised form designed to meet Mr. Osborne's suggestions, the note—or rather memorandum—was finally handed to His Majesty's Chargé d'Affaires on the 6th August, accompanied by further oral assurances that it should be taken, not as carping criticism, but as evidence of the Vatican's appreciation of the manner in which His Majesty's Government had executed the existing mandate. Mgr. Pizzardo further stated orally that, as regards Lake Tiberias and the neighbouring Holy Places, he thought the Vatican would be well content if a small separate zone under British mandate, similar to the proposed Jerusalem–Bethlehem zone, but not necessarily, of course, with access to the sea, could be established for Lake Tiberias (the whole lake), Nazareth and Mount Tabor, though, of course, if Naim also could be included so much the better. As regards the Christian minorities, for whose welfare under the new scheme the note expressed anxiety, Mgr. Pizzardo said he had thought it useless to particularise too much as to the details of the Vatican's preoccupation on behalf of these scattered Christian minorities, who were, he understood, for the most part Christian Arabs, since His Majesty's High Commissioner and the Colonial Office would be already familiar with them. Finally, Mgr. Pizzardo handed to Mr. Torr a little note, unsigned, on a blank sheet of paper, saying that the Holy See would always be willing to send someone to London and to give more detailed explanations as to the substance and reasons for their anxieties should it be judged useful for them to do so.

28. His Majesty's Chargé d'Affaires was, in due course, authorised to inform Mgr. Pizzardo that His Majesty's Government much appreciated the tactful manner in which the Holy See had expressed their views, which would receive most careful attention, and that no objection would be raised if the Vatican saw fit to bring their views to the notice of other Powers.

Church of the Holy Sepulchre.

29. In Jerusalem the Apostolic Delegate had on the 5th December, 1936, submitted to the Palestine Government certain suggestions regarding proposed restoration work on the Church of the Holy-Sepulchre. The Catholic Church would, he said, be willing to bear its share of the costs, but present estimates of these might perhaps be revised; meanwhile, he submitted that, instead of restoring the old, a new and more splendid building might perhaps be raised and the existing arrangement, whereby the door of the church is kept by a Moslem family, altered. In reply, he was told that both suggestions presented serious difficulties; no objection would be raised if the Holy See, on their own initiative, explored the possibility of agreement between all the interested Christian sects on the construction of a new church; but the Palestine Government could not entertain any proposal for alteration in the traditional arrangement for the guardianship of the door.

British Rearmament.

30. The comment of the *Osservatore Romano*, the Vatican's official organ, on British rearmament was contained in an article which appeared on the 22nd February.

31. Referring to British disarmament in the past, and to the regret voiced by British Ministers over the necessity of spending hundreds of millions on rearmament, the paper argued that it was plain from these expressions of pessimistic realism that it is events that shape the destinies of man and that man can but accept the dictation of events, even though the path lead him to the suicide of civilisation. British policy must, by the nature of things, remain conservative

and defensive in the face of the claims and ambitions of others.   But the real
significance of British rearmament on a gigantic scale lay in its tacit confession of
the failure of the ideals of the League and of the experiment of collective security.
It was admitted that collective resistance to individual resort to war in pursuit of
selfish aims had proved unavailing.   Consequently security was sought in the
directly opposite paradox of individual armament sufficient to meet any coalition
of enemies.   And the predominant factor in this tragic situation was the decay
of the sanctity of international obligations and treaty undertakings.

Mr. Lansbury's Visit.

32.   Mr. George Lansbury, the former leader of the Labour party in the
House of Commons, visited Rome in July, following a previous visit to Berlin,
where he had submitted his views on the subject of the safeguarding of peace to
Herr Hitler.   After being received by Signor Mussolini, he asked also for an
interview with the Pope, but His Holiness was too ill to receive him.   Mr.
Lansbury sent him a message, begging His Holiness to appeal to the heads of all
Governments to take steps to end the current international tension.   The message
was forwarded through the Legation and the Secretariat of State.   His Holiness's
non-committal reply was to the effect that he was deeply touched, and that he
wished his paternal thanks and warm good wishes to be transmitted to
Mr. Lansbury.

V.—RELATIONS WITH OTHER COUNTRIES.

Germany.

33.   Last year's report recorded the progressive aggravation of the quarrel
between the Nazi Government in Germany and the Vatican.   The new year saw no
slackening of the tension, and on Palm Sunday, the 21st March, there was read in
all the churches of Germany an encyclical of the Pope to the German bishops and
clergy on the condition of the Church in that country.   It had been drafted and
printed in secret, and the secret had been well kept.   No foreknowledge of it had
reached the German authorities.   From its opening words, " With Deep Anxiety,"
it is commonly given the title *Mit Brennender Sorge*.   In it His Holiness declared
that it was only with misgiving that he had signed the concordat with the present
Government of Germany at all, and he frankly accused the latter of having
engaged since its conclusion in a " war of extermination " against the Church.
His Holiness then proceeded to a vehement denunciation of the Nazi deification of
race and to a vigorous reaffirmation of Christian principles, calculated to leave
the faithful in no doubt as to the possibility of compromise with existing German
policy and doctrine.

34.   On the 13th April the German Ambassador to the Holy See handed to
the Cardinal Secretary of State a note on the subject.   It was stated in the
Italian press that this note was not to be regarded as a protest against the Pope's
action, but rather as a statement of the position of the German Government as
against that taken up by His Holiness in his encyclical.   The Legation were
subsequently informed, however, that in practice the German note protested that
the encyclical was an unfriendly act, that it was political in conception and
inspired by a desire to stand well with the democratic nations and to undermine
the Nazi régime, and that the Nazi Government ought not to be so attacked, seeing
that it was the enemy of the Church's enemy, bolshevism.   None of the specific
points at issue, *e.g.*, that of religious education in the schools, liberty of the press,
or the youth organisations, were touched upon.   The Vatican reply was prompt
and uncompromising : the concordat had been broken, the Pope had acted within
his rights, they had no bias against nazism as such, they had protested only
because their rights had been violated and doctrines were being instilled into the
youth of Germany which involved issues, not of civil government but of religious
principle.   Meanwhile, the very fact that copies of the encyclical had been
confiscated in Germany was contrary to the provisions of the concordat.

35.   On the 24th May the German Ambassador in turn lodged a protest at
the Vatican in respect of a speech made in Chicago by Cardinal Mundelein, in
which the latter had *inter alia* referred to Herr Hitler as " an Austrian paper-
hanger, and a poor one at that."   The Vatican refused, however, either to
disavow or apologise for the cardinal, or even to take the matter into consideration
until the German Government should declare itself publicly on the question of

the attacks by prominent Germans on bishops, the Pope himself and religion generally. The result was a further note from the German Government stating that the Vatican's "unexpected and incomprehensible attitude in this matter had removed the conditions for normal relations between the German Government and the Curia," and Herr von Bergen, the Ambassador, took a long leave. He returned in the autumn however. Meanwhile, the Vatican had replied to his note, but again yielded no ground. On a subsequent occasion, the 20th July, the Pope went out of his way to express to a group of American pilgrims his admiration of Cardinal Mundelein.

36. Relations continued in this condition throughout the year. The Vatican's official organ, the *Osservatore Romano*, took frequent opportunity to draw attention to the gravity of the fundamental issue at stake in Germany, which was, as the Vatican saw it, nothing less than an attempt to suppress Christianity in that country and replace it by a new idolatry. In August the Cardinal Secretary of State defined it to His Majesty's Chargé d'Affaires as a war between the idea of race and the Catholic idea of universality, adding that the Germans were working against catholicism even outside Germany, and that he had heard, for instance, that they had stimulated opposition in Yugoslavia to the concordat. The Assistant Secretary of State was even more outspoken, describing the German racial cult as "a frenzy of primeval barbarism," and adding, when asked whether the Vatican had no means of reaction, *e.g.*, by the organisation of a world-wide propaganda campaign, that everything possible that could be done in that direction was being done, and that the language held to every bishop and Nuncio and to every diplomat accredited to the Holy See was the same as he was then holding.

37. As the September Congress of the Nazi party at Nuremburg approached anxiety was felt lest this might be made by the German authorities the occasion for the promulgation of some new measure against the churches. In actual practice this did not materialise. A hint had been conveyed from Italian sources that such a step would be an embarrassing prelude to Signor Mussolini's forth-coming visit to Berlin. The Vatican newspaper was quick to point out, however, that this restraint had been exercised from purely tactical motives, and that the real significance of what was going on in Germany was to be discerned in the fact that at the congress Herr Hitler had selected for a high distinction Herr Rosenberg, author of *The Myth of the 20th Century*, and had thereby formally approved its doctrines. The Under-Secretary of State went out of his way to draw the attention of His Majesty's Chargé d'Affaires to this pronounce-ment, translations of which into other languages than Italian were subsequently prepared.

38. In July the Cardinal Secretary of State had visited France to represent the Pope at the inauguration of the new cathedral at Lisieux, on his way through Paris delivering a sermon at Notre Dame, in which, *inter alia*, statolatry was condemned. The German press were quick to see in this visit an attempt to organise a political encirclement of their country. This was denied by the Vatican newspaper, and in November the Cardinal Secretary of State told His Majesty's Minister that he had even gone so far as to make it known to the Germans that he would be willing to go to Berlin to open negotiations if any useful purpose would be served thereby. But he had received no encouragement.

39. Meanwhile, the Pope himself, whenever he gave audience to German pilgrims, made use of the opportunity to deplore the anti-clerical campaign in Germany and exhort them to stand firm in their faith; and on Christmas Eve, before an assemblage of his cardinals, he delivered himself of an outspoken protest, declaring, as he said, before the whole world that on the one hand what was going on in Germany was religious persecution and nothing else (" and rarely has there been a persecution graver, more to be feared, more painful, sadder in its profound effects "), and, on the other hand, that the pretext by which the German authorities sought to justify it, viz., that the Church dealt in politics, was a calumny.

Spain.

40. In January the Holy See appointed a representative to the Government of General Franco in Spain, the Under-Secretary of State observing, in reply to enquiry, that the appointment had been rendered necessary by the emergence of

a variety of administrative questions in which co-operation with the *de facto* authorities was essential, but that it did not imply official recognition of the Nationalists' Government. The delegate selected was Cardinal Goma, Archbishop of Toledo and Primate of Spain. The official Spanish Government's representative at the Vatican, Sr. de Zulueta, had already left Rome, as reported in last year's report, and the Vatican's Chargé d'Affaires at Valencia had left Spain. Unofficially the Burgos Government was represented at the Holy See by Admiral Magaez. Though repeatedly urged by General Franco to accord him formal recognition, the Vatican refused for the time being to do so, and in May Admiral Magaez was transferred to Berlin. In August the Vatican, explaining confidentially to His Majesty's Minister that the Spanish Falangists had even used threats to force their hand, agreed as a compromise half-measure, to accept a Chargé d'Affaires, and Don Pablo de Churruca y Dotres Marquis d'Aycinena, was appointed to the post and took up his residence in the Spanish Embassy. In the Spanish Nationalists' official bulletin he was described as "semi-official Minister and Agent to the Holy See." He presented his letters on the 7th June. The Vatican meanwhile appointed Mgr. Antoniutti as their Chargé d'Affaires at Burgos; and in October he presented letters ceremoniously.

41. On the 15th May His Majesty's representatives in Paris, Berlin, Rome, Lisbon and Moscow received instructions to invite the Governments to which they were accredited to join them in approaching both the two contending parties in Spain with the object of arranging for an armistice to permit of the withdrawal of foreign "volunteers." His Majesty's Minister at this post was instructed to inform the Vatican of the substance of these instructions. The Cardinal Secretary of State a few days later informed him that while the Holy See warmly approved the initiative of His Majesty's Government and would be ready at any favourable moment to promote any endeavour to bring the civil war to an end, he was convinced that for the moment there could be no question of an armistice; for neither side would agree to it. The *Osservatore Romano* took a similar line publicly.

42. The accounts published in the English press in the spring by the Deans of Canterbury and Chichester and other Anglican clergy belittling the extent and savagery of the attacks to which the Church in Spain had been exposed were received with comprehensible bitterness at the Vatican, where, in turn, approval was given to the issue of a pastoral letter by the Spanish bishops emphasising the contrary and defining the issue at stake in the war as one between Christianity and atheism. This letter appeared in July and steps were taken to secure publicity for it among Catholics everywhere. Replies from the heads of the Catholic Churches in England, France, Ireland, Austria and other countries were in due course received, expressing sympathy and understanding of the issue as seen by the Vatican and by the Spanish bishops themselves, and were published by the *Osservatore Romano*. No doubt, too, they contributed materially to the formation of Catholic opinion in the countries from which they came. The Legation were told that the replies of the English and French cardinals had been prompted by the Vatican with this end in view. Meanwhile the *Osservatore Romano* continued to insist that in respect of the *political* issues at stake in Spain the Vatican was neutral.

France.

43. The Vatican continued to regard the Front populaire Government in France as symptomatic of a dangerous flirtation with the atheistic and materialist ideology which underlies the Communist faith and to point to it on occasion as evidence of the reality of the danger against which orderly régimes such as the Italian had to defend themselves. No important issues arose, however, though the question of religious instruction in the schools of Alsace and Lorraine aroused some local interest. The maintenance of friendly relations between the French Popular Front Government and the Holy See is largely due to the ability and influence of the French Ambassador, M. Charles-Roux.

44. In July the Pope sent as his special delegate to the inauguration of the new cathedral of Sainte Thérèse at Lisieux his Secretary of State, Cardinal Pacelli, who in the course of his visit preached a sermon in Notre Dame exhorting his hearers not to be deluded by modern heresies into forgetfulness of

the great historic rôle that was France's by tradition (see also penultimate paragraph of section on Germany).

45. The Archbishop of Lyons was made a cardinal in December, thereby filling the vacancy left by the death of his predecessor.

46. Towards the end of the year the French Communists made advances to the French Catholic workmen's organisations with a view to securing their collaboration in a united front, against poverty, social injustice and fascism. After consultation between the Vatican and leading French clergy very guarded instructions were issued through the latter : Catholics should certainly not refuse to collaborate in efforts to make an end to poverty, injustice and war, but there could be no compromise between the spiritual principles of the Church and the materialist doctrines of the Communists.

Yugoslavia.

47. A new Yugoslav Minister, Dr. Mirosevitch Borgo, presented his credentials in March, and in December the Yugoslav Prime Minister, on an official visit to the Italian Government, had audience of the Pope. But the principal feature of the Vatican's relations with Yugoslavia was a severe political crisis provoked in the latter country by the Govenment's unsuccessful attempt to secure parliamentary ratification of the concordat signed on the 25th July, 1935. This agreement would, in practice, have conferred on the Catholic Church in Yugoslavia very real advantages in respect both of doctrinal issues (marriage, schools, religious orders) and of administrative; and though the Government succeeded in securing passage for it through the Lower Chamber of the Parliament the opposition aroused was so severe that they decided to suspend its presentation to the Senate. His Holiness rewarded his Nuncio in Belgrade, Mgr. Pelligrinetti, for his efforts by making him a cardinal; and in December, when conferring this honour, expressed the conviction that the time would come when Yugoslavia's rejection of his " proffered gift " would be regretted by many —" and not only from religious reasons, but from political and social considerations too "—reluctant though His Holiness was, as he said, to speak of political considerations as his own. With Mgr. Pelligrinetti's promotion to the cardinalate the post of Nuncio at Belgrade fell vacant; and it has not yet been filled.

Czechoslovakia.

48. On the 2nd September the Pope issued a Bull incorporating in Czechoslovak dioceses certain areas which had hitherto remained in the dioceses of Hungarian bishops. The Czechoslovak Government, in return, issued a decree restoring to the Church properties which had been sequestrated since about 1920. The *modus vivendi* negotiated in 1935 was thus implemented after some delay.

49. The extent of Soviet influence in Czechoslovakia was regarded in the Vatican with suspicion. Publication of the Papal Bull was of value to the Czechoslovak Government as representing a blow to Hungarian irredentism, and the Vatican had been somewhat reluctant to proceed with it unless assured that it would not be followed by new anti-clerical measures.

Poland.

50. A new Papal Nuncio, Mgr. Cortesi, presented his letters in Warsaw in May.

51. In June an "International Congress of Christ The King" was held at Posen. The Pope sent a message denouncing in strong terms modern doctrines and modern rebels against the Divine sovereignty.

52. A dispute between the Polish Government and the Archbishop of Cracow arose over the coffin of Marshal Pilsudski, which the archbishop had *moto proprio* had removed from the Polish Royal vault to another part of his cathedral, claiming that he was within his rights in doing so. The Vatican disapproved of the attitude adopted by the archbishop and Mgr. Cortesi was instructed to negotiate a settlement, which was eventually concluded in the form of an exchange of letters between himself and M. Beck, laying it down that the

tombs of illustrious personages in the cathedral—and in particular that of Marshal Pilsudski—were inviolable unless by agreement between the ecclesiastic and governmental authorities.

53. A decision of the Catholic Bishop of Danzig to create two new parishes provoked a protest to the Vatican by Herr Greiser. The bishop suspended action in regard to his two new parishes until further notice.

54. In December an agreement was reached between the Polish Government and the Vatican regarding the disposal of former property of the Uniate Church in Poland.

55. In the same month the Polish Ambassador to the Holy See, M. Ladislas Skrvynski, died suddenly at Rome.

Belgium.

56. In the course of the Van Zeeland–Degrelle election Cardinal Van Roey of Malines issued a statement condemning the principles and methods of Rexism as a danger to the country and the Church. This proved a valuable contribution to M. Van Zeeland's fight for parliamentarism. Critics of the cardinal's intervention were condemned by the *Osservatore Romano.*

Russia.

57. The Communist menace remained, as shown elsewhere in this report, a continuing obsession of the Holy See. On conditions in Russia itself the *Osservatore Romano* published on the 7th November, the twentieth anniversary of the birth of the Soviet system, an article to the following effect :—

58. Bolshevism was born of the World War and in every future war the infection of bolshevism will be found among the vanquished and will poison the fruits of victory. Militarism contains in itself the germs of both bolshevism and imperialism, for bolshevism, born of imperialist war, is as tyrannical as its parent. It was bolshevism that has corrupted Western democracy, and the proletariat of Europe was better served by Foch than by Lenin. To-day all the artificers of the Russian revolution, intellectuals and leaders, have succumbed to the dictatorship of Stalin; there only remains the shadowy figure of Trotsky to serve Stalin as a polemical motive and a revolutionary pretext. At the age of twenty bolshevism has a history and a technique; but its appearance of strength is deceptive. The reality in Russia is not a true expression of the ideals of bolshevism, but is a tyranny which first came from the people, but now, having possessed itself of the organism of the State, is able to dominate the fate of the people. After these twenty years it is impossible to say whether the Bolshevik idea is capable of lasting. The increasing tempo of the party purges would indicate that it is on the downward curve. No new world has been born of the physical and spiritual sufferings of the Russian people.

Turkey.

59. Mgr. Tonna, a British subject of Maltese origin and Roman Catholic Archbishop of Asiatic Turkey resident in Smyrna, was boycotted by the Italian Fascists among his congregation. His Majesty's Minister was instructed in June to represent to the Vatican that Mgr. Tonna had the full support of the Maltese, French and Turkish Catholics in his community, and that the hostility to him of the Italian section appeared to be due solely to national prejudices. On learning that it was proposed shortly to transfer Mgr. Tonna to another post His Majesty's Minister warned his Excellency Mgr. Pizzardo that such action was likely to be interpreted in London as an indication of Vatican subservience to Fascist pressure. The Vatican contended, however, that Mgr. Tonna had for long past shown himself unequal to his task; and his transfer was formally announced in December.

Mexico.

60. On the 28th March the Pope addressed an apostolic letter to the Episcopate of Mexico. It began by stating that in the sorrow caused to the Pope by the grievous state of the Church in Mexico, it had been of great comfort to observe the attitude of the Mexican Episcopate

and clergy and the constancy to the Faith of Mexican Catholics at a time when the open profession of religion might call for acts of real heroism. It was to strengthen this constancy that the present letter had been written. In the present difficult situation of the Church in Mexico the most effective means of restoring Christian society lay in the sanctity of the priesthood and in the collaboration of the laity with the hierarchy in their work. Emphasis was laid on the importance of education in the seminaries; and satisfaction was expressed that the Episcopate had borne this in mind. Praise was also given to the Bishops of the United States who had come to the aid of their Mexican brethren by setting up a seminary for Mexican clergy in the United States. Turning again to the need for the collaboration of laymen in the work of the apostolate, the Pope wrote that the basis of all reconstructive work is a solid inner or spiritual training, and recommended, as among the most important tasks, the giving of religious strength and help to workmen and Indians and to Mexican emigrants abroad. Furthermore, it was necessary to apply the principles of justice and charity and to assure to all that minimum of economic well-being which is necessary to preserve human dignity and to avoid those violent changes which are harmful to society.

Colombia.

61. The Colombian Government continued to have some difficulties with the Church on educational questions during 1937, and there was talk of an attempt to secure from the Vatican a revision of the concordat. In June a new Colombian Minister, M. Echandia, presented his credentials to the Holy See.

Ecuador.

62. A *modus vivendi* was concluded with Ecuador in July re-establishing friendly relations between Church and State and arranging for the appointment of diplomatic representatives to Quito and the Vatican. The new Ecuadorean Minister at the latter post, Don Pueblo de Curruca, presented his credentials on the 27th August.

VI.—TREATIES.

63. Schedule of Treaties concluded by the Holy See with other Convernments during 1937 :—

Name of Government.	Form of Treaty.	Date of Signature.	Date of Ratification.	Date of Entry into Force.	Remarks.
Ecuador ...	*Modus vivendi*	July 24, 1937	July 26, 1937	July 26, 1937	Provides for collaboration between Church and State in education, &c.

(15668)

HOLY SEE.

ANNUAL REPORT, 1938.

[R 1519/1519/22]

Mr. Osborne to Viscount Halifax.—(Received March 6.)

(No. 43.)   *British Legation to the Holy See,*
My Lord,   *Rome, March 1, 1939.*

    I HAVE the honour to transmit herewith the annual report for 1938, for which, with the exception of the introduction, I am indebted to Mr. Torr, secretary to the legation.

                                  I have, &c.
                                      D. G. OSBORNE.

Enclosure.

Annual Report on the Holy See for 1938.

CONTENTS.

I.—INTRODUCTION.

    IN 1936 Vatican speculations and Papal pronouncements were principally concerned with the Communist danger, not only for its menace to the Church herself, but for its threat to world peace. In 1937, with the failure of the Comintern's enterprise in Spain and the non-realisation of alarmist forebodings in regard to France under the Front populaire, it was the continuing and increasing German persecution of religion that preoccupied the Holy See. In 1938, while the Communist danger continued to recede, the German menace loomed ever larger. The oppression of Catholic institutions and individuals was slowly but relentlessly intensified, and, after the *Anschluss*, was extended to Austria, while the detestable " racial heresy " was imitated and applied by Italy herself. This was a tragic blow to the old Pope and a painful disillusion to the most Nationalist of Italian cardinals. For, as the Pope and a number of eminent cardinals within and without Italy repeatedly and eloquently proclaimed, the racial doctrine was " a gross and grave error " and a flagrant affront to the essential universality of catholicism. And there was more than this in it to disgust and distress the Vatican. For it was evident that for Italy to have embraced this hideous offspring of Teutonic tribal paganism signified a growing subservience to German influence and ideology. Further, experience in Germany had revealed the intimate, even inevitable association between racial and religious

B

persecution, so that there was an implicit element of menace to the freedom of the Church in Italy. Lastly, 1938 was overshadowed, and not only for the Holy See, by the perplexities and perils of Nazi power politics, culminating at the end of September in that eleventh-hour preservation of peace for which the Pope had, in a world broadcast address, offered his life as a sacrifice.

2. It was a tragic year for the old and failing Pope. But Pius XI bore his physical and mental afflictions with a courage and hardihood that confounded his doctors and exacted the admiration of the world. He left Rome for Castel Gandolfo at the beginning of May, immediately before Hitler's arrival, although not on that account, and remained there until the end of October. As always, his health greatly benefited, but in November, a few weeks after his return to Rome, he had another severe heart attack during which his life was in imminent danger. But his astonishing resilience and powers of resistance enabled him to resume his regular heavy programme of work within forty-eight hours. Throughout the year his faith, courage and resolution allowed him miraculously to defy the ever-increasing disabilities of age and sickness, and his inflexible will, vigorous mind and extraordinary memory remained unimpaired. His most notable public utterances were his appeal for peace at the height of the September crisis, his vehement and contemptuous condemnations of " exaggerated nationalism " and " the racial heresy," and the Christmas address to the College of Cardinals, in which he denounced the violation of the concordat by the ban on mixed marriages in the Italian racial legislation, complained of Fascist interference with Catholic Action, and deplored again the display in Rome of the unholy cross of the swastika at the time of the Hitler visit.

3. Inevitably, his championship of Christianity and humanity against the intolerance and cruelty of the anti-religious policy of Germany and of the racial persecution in both Germany and Italy aligned him, at least ideologically, with the democracies against the dictatorships, just as it assured him, on humanitarian grounds, the respect and admiration of religious opponents. Yet he was careful to assert the principles of the Church's traditional political neutrality and of her impartiality towards conflicting systems of government, taking his stand on the universality of the Catholic Church and on the Catholic doctrine of the sacred and inalienable rights of the individual.

4. The appointment of an Apostolic Delegate to Great Britain in the autumn was a concrete expression of that respect and admiration for Great Britain and her Sovereigns which the Pope so frequently voiced to British visitors. Relations with France became even more amicable after the collapse of the Front populaire. With Germany they deteriorated, while in Italy itself the Hitler visit, the racial policy, with its alleged breach of the concordat, and the interference with Catholic Action combined to open a serious rift in the hitherto correct, if not cordial, relations between the Holy See and the Fascist régime. Only the future can tell whether this smouldering controversy will be resolved by the wisdom of Mussolini, or whether he will allow Catholic Italy to follow her German partner along the road that leads from racial to religious persecution. The outlook is not encouraging, either for the harassed Church and her failing but unflinching leader, or for the world in general. But, whatever the year may hold, it may well be that the Papacy, with a foot in both the democratic and the dictatorial camps, though uncommitted to either, may have an important rôle to play as an impartial, non-political, international authority, whose only worldly interests are the ensuing of peace, tolerance and justice.

II.—THE VATICAN.

The Pope.

5. The Pope's health was as good as could be expected and his intellectual vigour remained unimpaired throughout 1938. At the end of November he had a bad attack of cardiac asthma, and for a few hours his condition was serious; but thanks to his strong constitution and indomitable will he was soon again in full activity.

Organisation of the Administration of the Church in the Near East.

6. By a *Motu Proprio* issued in May the Congregation for the Propagation of the Faith was relieved of responsibility for the administration of the Catholic

Churches of the Latin Rite in the Near East. Two of the Pontifical Congregations had hitherto shared jurisdiction over the Catholic Churches in that part of the world, the Congregation for the Propagation of the Faith administering those adhering to the Latin Rite, the Congregation for the Eastern Church those following the Oriental Rite. The latter Congregation was now given sole jurisdiction over Catholics of both Rites in the Near East; and the concern of the Congregation for the Propagation of the Faith was confined to areas of the world where catholicism is still in the missionary stage.

College of Cardinals.

7. The following cardinals died during the year :—

Cardinal Capotosti.
Cardinal Minoretti.
Cardinal Serafini.
Cardinal Hayes.
Cardinal Laurenti.

No new appointments were made. The normal strength of the college being seventy, there were seven vacancies at the close of the year.

III.—Relations with Italy.

8. The year began with a much-advertised demonstration of goodwill between the Catholic clergy and the Fascist régime. On the occasion of the celebration of the " Battle of the Grain " early in January a deputation of the Italian episcopate and priesthood came to Rome to testify to their loyalty to the Duce, who in return expressed his warm approval of the manner in which the clergy had stood by the Government both in its efforts to improve the social welfare of the people and in the struggle against sanctions. This harmonious co-operation between clergy and laity was, said the Duce, one of the happy results of the reconciliation between the Church and State which had been concluded nine years previously, and the tenth anniversary of which would be happily celebrated next year. On the following day the ecclesiastics were received by the Pope, who expressed gratification that they should have deserved such high praise from so high an authority, adding that he too had no doubt that the reconciliation between the Church and State in Italy would bear abundant fruit. These happy conditions, His Holiness pointed out, provided a very agreeable contrast to those prevailing in Germany. But this exchange of compliments masked a rift which was to grow wider as the year proceeded.

9. Attention was drawn in last year's report to the disfavour with which Signor Mussolini's pro-German policy was regarded in Vatican circles. In March this policy was to lead to the abandonment of Italy's long defence of the independence of Catholic Austria. The resultant collapse of Austria was, of course, a disaster of the first magnitude from the point of view of the Church. The Vatican had endeavoured to persuade Signor Mussolini to induce Herr Hitler to hold his hand; but in reply were only told that if the Germans took forcible action the Italian Government could do nothing.

10. The enthusiastic welcome later staged for Herr Hitler's visit to Rome was also little appreciated by the Holy See, and the Pope did not hesitate to make his feelings known.

Catholic Action.

11. In the course of the summer difficulties were raised by the extreme Fascist element in connexion with Catholic Action. The terms on which this organisation was to be allowed to continue its activities in Italy had been defined in an agreement reached so long ago as the 2nd September, 1931. It was not to compete with the Fascist organisations in the fields of politics or athletics. Its aims were to be purely religious; and on this basis there had been until recently little occasion for disagreement. Now, however, with fascism tending more and more to identify itself with the extreme doctrines favoured by German fanaticism, the dividing line between religion and politics was no longer so easy to draw;

and the claim began to be put forward that membership of Catholic Action was incompatible with membership of the Fascist party. In some cases, Fascists, members of the religious organisation, were pilloried and forced to resign their posts. In August, negotiations between Signor Starace, the Secretary of the Fascist party, and the Central Office of Catholic Action resulted in a public announcement that an agreement had been reached and that it had been decided to abide by the terms of the *modus vivendi* concluded in 1931. Assurances were also given that the members of Catholic Action who had been penalised would be reinstated in their former posts; but the Government-controlled press were careful to omit any reference to this undertaking. The Vatican newspaper drew attention to the omission. Remarks made by the Pope later in the year seemed to indicate that the pledge had never been fulfilled.

Racialism.

12. In August there began the publicity campaign that foreshadowed the adoption by Italy of the German cult of racialism. The Pope was quick to denounce this as contrary to all sound Christian doctrine, and, particularly, to the essential universality of catholicism. During the summer he went in person to the missionary college adjoining his estate at Castel Gandolfo to deliver a homily on the evils of exaggerated nationalism, and he had circular instructions sent to all the training colleges on the importance of instructing candidates for the priesthood in the arguments to be used in combating the heresy of racialism. Some vague assurances were obtained from the Fascist authorities that the inculcation of the new philosophy would not be carried too far in the schools.

13. In one of his many pronouncements His Holiness had deplored the new mania for copying Germany, adding that, as a Milanese, he could not help recalling that it was not so long ago since the men of Milan had been proud to chase out "i tedeschi." The *Regime Fascista*, edited by Signor Farinacci, the chief protagonist of Italian racialism, retorted with an article to the effect that the Austrian troops in occupation on the historical occasion referred to had been Czechs, Poles, Hungarians and Croats; and Signor Mussolini, in a speech at Trieste on the 18th September, remarked that people who suggested that the Fascist Government had copied anybody in the matter were unfortunate half-wits, and he did not know whether they better deserved contempt or pity. The Pope took steps to enquire privately whether this taunt was meant as a fling at himself, and received an effusive denial. Meanwhile, His Holiness continued at his public audiences to insist on the theme that, while a sane and reasonable loyalty to one's own country is always a duty, it is much more important for human beings to remember that they belong also to the larger family of Christians.

14. Unofficially, the Vatican had taken early steps to remind the Italian Government that the proposed measures against the Jews might lead to an infringement of the concordat, under which the Italian Government was pledged to accord civil recognition to any marriage celebrated by Catholic rite. In November, however, the decree forbidding mixed marriages was published; and in an article in its issue of the 14th November, the *Osservatore Romano* disclosed that the Vatican had taken prior steps to advise the Italian Government of its point of view, and that the Pope had even gone so far as to address letters in his own hand to the King and to the head of the Government in his anxiety to avert this infringement of the concordat. The Vatican were careful, however, not to speak of the concordat as having been "violated," using instead the Latin word "*vulnus*." Faint hopes were still entertained that some accommodation might be arrived at. A little later, in a speech made before the Fascist "Institute of Culture," Signor Farinacci went out of his way to justify the persecution of the Jews on the cynical ground that this was wholly in accordance with the traditions of catholicism itself. The attitude of the Church, its tendency to drift into the same camp as Communists, freemasons, democrats and others of its declared or former enemies, was, he said, incomprehensible in the circumstances.

15. On the 24th December, addressing the cardinals assembled for the annual exchange of compliments customary on this day, the Pope took occasion

to speak his mind again. The tenth anniversary of the reconciliation between Church and State in Italy would, he said, be very shortly celebrated. This would be a joyful occasion and one for which he could not but be grateful to the noble monarch and to the incomparable minister, whose statesmanship had done so much to make it possible. Nevertheless, it was an anniversary which he approached with grave preoccupations and bitter sorrows. There had, he said, been serious and multiple provocations of his beloved Catholic Action; and the infringement of the concordat on the marriage question had most painfully and directly distressed him. So, too, had the recent glorification in Rome of the "cross that was the enemy of Christianity." His Holiness was referring here to the decoration of Rome with swastika emblems on the occasion of Herr Hitler's visit.

16. The tenth anniversary of the reconciliation falls in February of this year. Whether in all the circumstances it will be made a great occasion remains to be seen.

IV.—Relations with the British Empire.

Vatican Views of British Policy.

17. Mr. Eden's withdrawal from the Cabinet in February was welcome at the Vatican, who had for long hoped for an Anglo-Italian rapprochement. The Assistant Secretary of State said to a member of His Majesty's Legation that in their opinion it had saved peace. Hopes of the possibility of a return to something approximating to the Stresa *Entente* had not been wholly discarded. The subsequent conclusion in April of the agreement between His Majesty's Government and the Italian Government, and, indeed, the whole of the Prime Minister's efforts to promote a negotiated settlement of European differences, had also all the Vatican's sympathy.

Position of the Legation in the Event of War.

18. In the course of the September crisis arising out of the situation in Czecho-Slovakia, His Majesty's Minister enquired at the Secretariat of State as to what would be the position of the legation in the event of Italy and Great Britain finding themselves at war. The same question had already been raised by the French Ambassador, who had been informed that the case would be covered by article 12 of the Lateran Treaty of 1929, which laid down that Italy recognised to the Holy See the right of legation, active and passive, in accordance with the general rules of international law, and that the representatives of foreign Governments accredited to the Holy See would continue to enjoy in the Italian Kingdom all the privileges and immunities due to diplomatic agents in accordance with the rules of international law, *even if their countries had no diplomatic relations with Italy.* The article in question is not very precise, however, as to the position of, and the extent to which, the correspondence between the representatives of Powers hostile to Italy and their Governments would be guaranteed, nor as to the continuance of the right of the representatives of such Powers to reside in Rome. Nor is any provision made with regard to the large numbers of foreign ecclesiastics, students, &c., who reside in Rome. In these circumstances both the French Ambassador and His Majesty's Minister pressed for a clarification of these points; and on the 25th September the French Ambassador addressed a formal note to the Secretariat of State requesting a reply. Assurances were received both by the French Ambassador and by His Majesty's Legation that the matter would be discussed with the Italian Government; and in an interview that His Majesty's Minister had with the Pope on the 28th September His Holiness assured him that the Lateran Treaty provided for the retention of foreign legations in such circumstances, that relations between the Vatican and the Italian Government were good and that His Holiness was sure that every possible consideration would be given to the Vatican's representations on the matter. On the same day Mr. Osborne saw the Assistant Under-Secretary of State and repeated his enquiry, acting on this occasion under authorisation from London. He was told in reply that the Vatican had received no answer to their previous enquiries through the Italian Ambassador to the Holy See, and that in these circumstances

a further written request for an early answer had been sent off. Mr. Osborne was again assured that the Vatican were convinced that the Italian Government would do their best to meet their wishes, and that arrangements would be made for the retention of the missions with all rights and immunities, either at their existing seats in Rome or within the Vatican City or, possibly, at Castel Gandolfo, the Pope's summer residence, some twenty miles away. No formal reply was, however, ever received from the Vatican on the subject; and it is presumed that the Italian Government were reluctant to commit themselves.

Appointment of an Apostolic Delegate.

19. The Vatican made a tentative approach to His Majesty's Government during the course of 1938 with a view to ascertaining whether the appointment of a Nuncio to the Court of St. James would be agreeable, or, failing that, of an Apostolic Delegate to Great Britain who, though his primary functions would be ecclesiastic (*i.e.*, to maintain contact between the Vatican and the Catholic Hierarchy in England), might also be used as a channel of communication with His Majesty's Government in the United Kingdom in the event of the occasion arising. The appointment of an Apostolic Delegate was eventually agreed to and Mgr. Godfrey, rector of the English College in Rome, was nominated the first delegate.

Exclusion of Priests from the Legislative Council of Malta.

20. On the 28th August the Vatican addressed a note to His Majesty's Legation protesting against the proposed exclusion of priests from the Legislative Council of Malta. This, however, was coupled with a hint that, if the proposed constitutional ban on the participation of priests in the council were withdrawn, the Pope might in exchange be willing to issue an order forbidding priests to offer themselves for election. In October the Cardinal Secretary of State, in conversation with His Majesty's Minister, reiterated the Pope's objection to the principle of denying to priests political rights enjoyed by the members of their flock.

Theological Faculty of the University of Malta.

21. The Governor of Malta (see paragraph 21 of last year's report) was able to meet the last of the Vatican's desiderata regarding the statutes of the theological faculty of the University of Malta, and on the 22nd August a note was received from the Cardinal Secretary of State assuring His Majesty's Chargé d'Affaires that the statute and regulations of the university, and the text of the diplomas to be awarded to successful candidates for a theological degree, were in accordance with the general practice of the Holy See in such matters.

Archbishopric of Malta.

22. The question of the appointment of a successor to the Archbishop of Malta, or of a coadjutor with the right of succession, remains in abeyance, owing to the apparent impossibility of finding a candidate acceptable both to His Majesty's Government and to the Vatican.

Palestine.

23. Anxiety was expressed by the Vatican on the 3rd April regarding alleged restrictions on the immigration of " persons of religious occupation " into Palestine. On the 30th June His Majesty's Legation were able to assure the Vatican that vacancies were still being kept open for 200 non-Jewish immigrants in this category.

24. On the 9th November, the Vatican addressed a note to the legation stating that, according to information which had reached them, His Majesty's Government proposed to set up a Governing Council in Palestine which would be composed of eight Moslem members, four Jews and one Christian, but would provide no specific guarantee or reservation with regard to Catholic interests. The Vatican expressed the hope that His Majesty's Government would provide for Catholic representation on the council. Mr. Osborne was authorised to inform the Secretary of State that the information which had reached the Holy See was erroneous; discussions on the future of Palestine were shortly to take place

in London, and in reaching a final decision on the question His Majesty's Government would not fail to take into account the views which the Holy See had already communicated to them on the subject (see paragraphs 25 to 28 of last year's report).

Sudan Missions.

25. On the 25th May, His Majesty's Minister handed to the Under-Secretary of State a memorandum setting out the views of His Majesty's Government in regard to the administration of the Catholic missions in the Southern Sudan and advancing certain specific desiderata. In particular, it was desired that more British missionaries should be recruited for this area, that Italian priests who continued to do educational work there should take a course at the London Institute of Education, that British, or at least non-Italian, subjects should be appointed to two of the key positions, and that some arrangement should be made for improved liaison between the missions and the civil authorities. The Vatican showed commendable promptitude in meeting the first three of the above desiderata, making arrangements to recruit British missionaries for the area, appointing an Englishman and a Yugoslav respectively to the two key posts and entrusting one of the missions to the English Society of St. Joseph of Mill Hill. As regards the suggestion for some improved liaison between the civil authorities and the missions, the Vatican were unable to put forward any immediately practicable suggestions. At the end of the year His Majesty's Minister was instructed to convey to the Secretary of State an expression of His Majesty's Government's appreciation of the promptness and goodwill which the Holy See had displayed in this matter.

The King.

26. On the 28th September, Mr. Osborne was received by the Pope and had the honour to convey to His Holiness a message of friendly greeting and of congratulation on His Holiness's continued improvement in health which the King had authorised him to deliver. The Pope was evidently highly gratified by this message, and requested Mr. Osborne to convey to His Majesty the assurance of His Holiness's feeling of friendship and goodwill. He subsequently instructed the Secretariat of State to confirm these sentiments in writing, which was done; and two days later, on receiving in audience some English pilgrims His Holiness after blessing England and the English Catholics, added that he desired to extend this blessing also to their Sovereigns; for they had displayed a courteous and kindly interest in himself and in his health that had deeply moved him.

V.—Relations with other Countries.

Germany.

27. No improvement took place in the relations between the Holy See and Germany during the year. On the contrary, the anti-Catholic campaign was extended to Catholic institutions in Austria. The refusal of the Nazis to respect the old concordat with Austria, the promulgation of the new German marriage laws, the assaults on Cardinal Innitzer and on the Bishop of Rottenburg and the violent attacks on the Church made by Herr Bürckel in October served only to embitter relations.

28. On the 2nd May Hitler came to Rome on a State visit to the Italian Government. But he asked for no audience of the Pope; and the latter, who had withdrawn a few days previously to his villa at Castel Gandolfo, ordered the Vatican museums to be closed on learning that some members of Herr Hitler's suite had claimed a right of free entry thereto on the strength of passes issued by the Italian Government. The *Osservatore Romano* refrained from publishing any details of Herr Hitler's visit; and at a public audience the Pope declared that " Many sad things are happening both at a distance and near at hand, and among them this—that it is found neither unseemly nor untimely to display at Rome on the day of the Holy Cross (the 3rd May) the emblem of another cross that is not the cross of Christ." Just prior to the visit the *Osservatore Romano* had found the occasion propitious to print a number of extracts from works by

German professors, comparing the relative merits of the Mediterranean and Nordic races, greatly to the disadvantage of the former, which was depicted as voluble, shallow, sensual, lazy, cruel, &c.

Austria.

29. The threat to Austria's independence which became manifest after the meeting between Herr Hitler and Herr Schuschnigg at Berchtesgaden in February caused the Vatican grave and immediate concern. What had occurred, said the Under-Secretary of State to His Majesty's Minister, was a disaster, a disaster of which the determining factors had been German arrogance, Italian folly and Anglo-French weakness. When Herr Schuschnigg announced his intention to hold a plebiscite, the *Osservatore Romano* published a vigorous article in defence of the Austrian cause, reminding the head of the Italian Government of his previous commitments, and declaring that it was the duty of every Government sincerely interested in the maintenance of peace to bear in mind the historical, cultural, religious and social arguments in favour of the defence of Austrian independence. Despairing hopes were entertained almost to the last that it might not be impossible for France, Italy and Great Britain to unite in order to avert disaster. Once, however, the invasion had taken place, the Vatican were careful to refrain from public protest, partly from the wish not to embarrass the régime in Italy and partly from a desire not to lay themselves open to the accusation of playing politics in Germany. The *Osservatore Romano* even went so far as to publish an article differing very markedly in tone from its previous one, and contending that the Vatican had for twenty years past consistently recognised that the geographical and economic condition of post-war Austria did not provide an ideal basis for the continuance of its sovereignty and independence. The Vatican's concern in what had happened was, said the paper, confined to justifiable misgivings for the future of catholicism under the new régime. Nevertheless, the initiative of Cardinal Innitzer and the other Austrian bishops in declaring themselves favourable to the *Anschluss* and professing loyalty to the new German Reich on the strength of some flimsy promises offered by Herr Bürckel, was not approved of at all. Vatican responsibility was at once denied; and from the Vatican wireless station there was issued a broadcast denouncing the "false political catholicism" displayed in the cardinal's declaration. Official sponsorship of this broadcast was subsequently disavowed, but there is no doubt that it represented the Vatican's real feelings. Cardinal Innitzer was summoned to Rome, where, by all accounts, he was lectured very severely by the Pope. On the following evening (the 5th April) there appeared in the *Osservatore Romano* the German text of an announcement signed by the cardinal, in the name of the whole Austrian Episcopate, protesting that the bishops' previous manifesto must not be interpreted as expressing approval of anything incompatible with the laws of God and with the liberties and rights of the Church. The declaration added that, for the future, the Austrian bishops must insist that, in all matters pertaining to the Austrian concordat, there could be no question of any modification without previous agreement with the Holy See, and that in particular the religious education of the young must at all costs be safeguarded. No *modus vivendi* was, however, reached; and a few months later Cardinal Innitzer was to find himself bitterly attacked by the Nazis, his palace looted and his chaplain thrown out of the window.

Spain.

30. On the 20th March His Majesty's Legation were instructed to urge the Vatican to make representations to the Nationalist authorities in Spain urging them to desist from the aerial bombardment of Barcelona. The legation were informed in reply that the Vatican's Chargé d'Affaires at Salamanca had some time previously been instructed in the sense desired, and had constant instructions to do all he could to diminish the ferocity of hostilities. In the present instance the Pope renewed his representations, reminding General Franco of previous undertakings which he had given on the subject. In informing His Majesty's Legation of this, however, the Secretariat of State were careful to add that His Holiness must not be understood to be "associating himself with any steps that His Majesty's Government or the French Government might have seen fit to take in the matter."

31.   On the 4th May the Vatican addressed a memorandum to the legation stating that, according to reports which were reaching them, the persecution of the clergy in Catalonia, as well as of other members of the civil population, without distinction of age, sex or profession, was increasing, and that the Pope would be very grateful if any intervention by His Majesty's Government could remedy this painful situation.   Mr. Leche reported from Barcelona on the 16th May that, while it was true that police persecution in Catalonia was very severe, there was no reason to believe that the clergy were being specially singled out; indeed, their position was better than at any time previously during the war.   Mr. Osborne so informed the Under-Secretary of State on the 28th May.

32.   On the 4th May it was announced at Burgos that the Holy See had decided to recognise the Salamanca Government officially; and a decree was published readmitting the Society of Jesus to Nationalist territory and to their former properties.   A few days later the appointment of a new ambassador from the Nationalist Government in Spain to the Holy See was announced.   The Visconte di Santa Clara de Avedillo was the nominee.   As their Nuncio in Nationalist Spain the Vatican appointed Mgr. Cicognani, formerly Nuncio in Vienna.

33.   On the 6th May the Under-Secretary of State discussed with His Majesty's Minister the possibility of mediation in the Spanish war.   He was convinced that General Franco's ultimate victory was certain; he thought that, if His Majesty's Government could guarantee the safe evacuation of the Loyalist leaders, these might be more willing to treat.   The Vatican meanwhile could approach General Franco.

34.   On the 16th May His Majesty's Legation were authorised to reply to the Pope's appeal on the subject of the persecutions in Catalonia, to assure the Vatican that His Majesty's Minister at Barcelona would continue to do all that he could on behalf of the innocent sections of the Spanish population, and that he had, as a matter of fact, made very strong representations on the subject a month previously.   On the 26th May instructions were received as to the reply to be returned to the Vatican's informal suggestion of mediation.   They were to the effect that His Majesty's Government had been enquiring into the matter, with a view to ascertaining whether any action on their part would be welcome, but their information went to show that any such initiative had little likelihood of being favourably received.   They trusted, however, that the Vatican would continue to exert their influence with General Franco in this direction, and they had sent instructions to the British representative at Burgos to keep in close touch with the Nuncio.

35.   On the 4th June His Majesty's Legation received instructions to inform the Vatican of renewed British representations which had been made to the Nationalist authorities on the subject of the aerial bombardment of civil populations and to add that His Majesty's Government would appreciate any action that the Vatican might feel able to take in support of these representations. Again His Majesty's Legation were told that the Vatican had already telegraphed to their representative in Burgos to protest once more.   An official reply was also received stating that the Holy See viewed with sympathy the repeated steps taken by His Majesty's Government to endeavour to limit the bombardment of open cities.   The Holy See had not failed to make similar representations; but, " with the sole intention of not giving to its intervention even the slightest appearance of political action, and desirous of preserving in its activities that character of supernatural charity that derived from its divine mandate," it considered that it should take these steps independently of other initiatives.   Meanwhile, the *Osservatore Romano*, while deploring the bombings, was inclined also to find excuses for them.

France.

36.   There is little to be said about relations between the Holy See and France during the period under review.   The instability and extravagances of the Front populaire Government and its support of the Communist cause in Spain had been a source of grave misgiving to the Vatican, even though in France itself the Church had no cause for complaint.   Consequently, M. Daladier's advent to

power was welcomed and the former correct and friendly relations became more confident and cordial.

37. In the course of the year legislation was passed in France giving to religious missions in French colonial territories the status of juridical personality; and this, too, was welcome to the Vatican.

Czecho-Slovakia.

38. On the 31st May the *Osservatore Romano* published a short survey of the Czecho-Slovak problem, in which it made the following points: (1) The German pretension to a right of intervention in the domestic affairs of other States in the interests of its own nationals was inadmissible; (2) the racial intolerance of the Czecho-Slovaks could not be compared with the anti-Semitic policies of some other States; (3) this did not mean that the problem of the minorities was not grave: scrupulous justice for minorities was an essential condition for the maintenance of peace in Europe; but the difficulties could be easily solved if there was a spirit of mutual comprehension and a will to agreement; (4) the basis principles on which a settlement of the Sudeten problem of Czecho-Slovakia should be founded were equality of rights for all minorities, respect for the integrity of the State and regard for the necessities of European peace.

39. Lord Runciman's efforts to promote a settlement on the above lines were not, however, very optimistically envisaged at the Vatican. The Czechs, said the Under-Secretary of State to a member of His Majesty's Legation, were a slow and obstinate people; the Vatican themselves had had experience of this; and he was doubtful of the likelihood of an early settlement being reached. As for a lasting settlement, he was doubtful of that too, for Czecho-Slovakia had no natural principle of unity in it, was militarily indefensible and was surrounded by countries with claims to parts of its territory. Later, the Cardinal Secretary of State himself, deeply as he deplored the threatened spread of Nazi influence, could not but admit that, in his opinion, the mass of the Sudeten Deutsch were eager for union with the German Reich. On the other hand, the Vatican were consistently sceptical of French ability or willingness effectively to intervene should a crisis come to a head. In August, however, they became seriously alarmed by the German mobilisation. The *Osservatore Romano* published an article pointing out that Berlin had given assurances that only manœuvres were involved, but that the Reich should not be surprised at the alarm provoked, in view of the frequent vigour of its own past protests at symptoms much less grave. If the disaster of war occurred, the only victor would be that inevitable revolution which was already waiting to divide up the booty after the suicide of an era.

40. On the 22nd August the Pope paid a surprise visit to the summer quarters of the principal college for missionaries in Rome, which was adjacent to His Holiness's own summer residence at Castel Gandolfo. Here he addressed the students on the evils of exaggerated nationalism, declaring that his words were intended for all the missionaries of the world. A moderate nationalism, said His Holiness, was naturally good, but " beware of exaggerated nationalism as of a very curse. It seems to us that events may prove us only too right when we say ' a very curse,' for it is a very curse of divisions and passions and may be only too easily of war."

41. On the 23rd August the Cardinal Secretary of State told His Majesty's Chargé d'Affaires that he thought the Italian Government had their hands full enough not to want any new adventures; and he personally believed that they had some time previously told Berlin that, if the latter insisted on forcing the issue in Czecho-Slovakia, they should not count on Italy being able to back them up in the event of trouble. To the French Ambassador, however, his Eminence had used slightly different language, observing that the readiness with which the Italian Government had followed the German lead in their attack on the Jews left him in real doubt as to whether they could any longer be regarded as free agents, even in their foreign policy.

42. The Prime Minister's action in flying to see Herr Hitler at Berchtesgaden made a deep and most favourable impression at the Vatican; and the Pope so expressed himself at his audiences that morning. The *Osservatore*

Romano warmly approved the Prime Minister's generous effort, writing that the wishes of the world went with him, and that to resort to force after such a precedent would be monstrous. Ten days later, the 25th September, it was writing that the hopes of the world, which had accompanied the Prime Minister on his journey to Berchtesgaden, had changed to consternation after his departure from Godesberg. It was impossible to believe that political conditions in a few small districts were such as to necessitate the sacrifice of millions of lives, or that the problem was of such urgency as to necessitate the renunciation of pacific measures.

43. The Prime Minister's statement of the 27th September, offering His Majesty's Government's guarantee of the undertakings given for the transfer of the Sudeten territories to Germany, was communicated, on instructions from Lord Halifax, to the Vatican on the 28th September; and on the same day His Majesty's Minister, who had returned a short while previously from leave in England, had an audience with the Pope. His Holiness said that until recently he had been resolutely hopeful of peace, but that his hopes had weakened during the past two days. Mr. Osborne said that in his opinion it was tragic that there was no one to speak on behalf of the large proportion of the German and Italian peoples whose sole desire was for peace. The Pope said that he would be issuing, probably on the morrow, a statement to the Catholic people of all nations on the subject. He expressed great admiration for Mr. Chamberlain's efforts.

44. At 6·30 on the evening of the 29th September the Pope personally broadcast an appeal to the whole Catholic world to join him in prayer for the preservation of peace, offering his own life to God as a sacrifice for the occasion. On instructions from Lord Halifax, Mr. Osborne conveyed to the Secretariat of State, for transmission to its high destination, an expression of His Majesty's Government's warm appreciation of His Holiness's noble message. The *Osservatore Romano* was writing, at this time, that the Prime Minister had revealed himself as a statesman of the first order, and that the world would know to whom they owed their salvation from the appalling disaster of war.

Yugoslavia.

45. The appointment of a new Papal Nuncio to the Yugoslav Government was announced in April. Mgr. Felici, Nuncio to Chile, was chosen for the post. In the interval, on the 19th February, the Holy See had formally protested to the Yugoslav Government against the non-ratification of the concordat signed in 1935, and the refusal of the Yugoslav Government to submit the question of ratification to the Senate. In a private conversation it was admitted, however, to His Majesty's Minister that in the Vatican's view one of the principal reasons why the concordat had not met with stronger support in Yugoslavia had been the lukewarmness of the Catholic Croats themselves, who had felt that, were the agreement approved, their case for demanding political autonomy would be weakened.

Poland.

46. The Roman Catholic Bishop of Danzig, who last year had found himself attacked by the local Nazis, resigned, and a successor of German origin was appointed in his place.

47. The agreement regarding the former property of the Uniat Church in Poland was finally signed on the 20th June.

Belgium.

48. The new Belgian Ambassador, M. de l'Escaille, whose last post was Cairo, presented his credentials on the 15th March.

Roumania.

49. It was announced in December that the Roumanian representative at the Vatican would in future hold the rank of ambassador. M. Comnen, the late Minister for Foreign Affairs, is to take the post; but he has not yet arrived.

Latvia.

50. M. Munters, the Latvian Minister for Foreign Affairs, came to Rome on the 20th January to conclude an agreement with the Holy See regarding the institution of a theological faculty at the University of Riga and the adaptation of the new Diocesan Council in Latvia to certain provisions of the existing concordat. A convention was signed on the 25th January, and M. Munters left for Geneva after having been received by the Pope.

VI.—TREATIES.

51. Schedule of treaties concluded by the Holy See with other Governments during 1938 :—

Name of Government.	Form of Treaty.	Date of Signature.	Date of Ratification.	Date of Entry into Force.	Remarks.
Latvia... ...	Convention amplifying the concordat	January 25, 1939	March 26, 1938	March 26, 1938	Provides for a new diocese at Libau and a theological faculty at the Riga University.
Poland ...	Agreement regarding the confiscated lands of the Uniat Church	June 20, 1938	Not yet ratified	Not yet in force	Cedes to the Roman Catholic Church all properties at present in its possession and adds a compensation of 2,500,000 zlote.
Italy	Convention regarding the transfer of corpses for burial	April 28, 1938	April 28, 1938	April 28, 1938	

Enclosure in Mr. Osborne's
despatch No. 254 of December 31st,
1939.

POLITICAL   REVIEW   for   1939

     The Introduction to the Annual Report on the Holy See
for 1938 concluded with the suggestion that the Papacy, with
a foot in both the democratic and dictatorial camps, though
uncommitted to either, might have an important role to play
as an impartial, non-political, international authority,
whose only worldly interests are the ensuring of peace,
tolerance and justice.

     The end of the year 1939 invites an attempt to estimate
the prospects of this possibility.

     Since the report for 1938 was written two major events
have occurred: the outbreak of war between the democratic
group of countries, including the British Empire, and the
dictatorial Nazi Germany of Hitler, backed to some extent
by the dictatorial Communist Russia of Stalin; and the
death of Pius XI, who was succeeded six months before the
opening of hostilities by his Secretary of State, Cardinal
Pacelli, as Pope Pius XII.

     To these two should be added a remarkable development
at the end of the year. An exchange of formal visits between the Italian Sovereigns and the Pope (His Holiness'
return visit to the Quirinal being unexpected and unprecedented) was given the greatest publicity and significance
in the Italian press, as well as in the Vatican organ.
While these ceremonial occasions were hailed in their
superficial....

superficial aspects as putting the final seal on the Concordat, their further and wider implications were surmised
or openly declared to include a policy of cooperation in
defence of European civilization by means of resistance
to the advance of Bolshevism and the restoration of peace.
By this new Church-State axis the Vatican might almost be
said to have joined the anti-Comintern Pact while, on the
other hand, the position of Italy vis-à-vis her anti-Catholic
German ally would appear at first sight to have been inevitably compromised.

The last world war of 1914-1918 evoked on the second
day of hostilities an appeal for peace addressed to the
Catholics of the world by the saintly Pius X, when on his
deathbed, and witnessed the continuous endeavours of the new
Pope Benedict XV to arrest the war spirit, to condemn the
four fundamental evils of the day - lack of human charity,
contempt of authority, class-warfare and covetousness -, to
preach the cardinal principles of Christianity, to promote
prayers for peace, and to call for the substitution of
material force by justice and arbitration.   His last appeal
for peace was made on August 1st, 1917.   The war was only
decided fifteen months later by the military victory of one
side, and was not shortened for one day by all the efforts
of the Papacy.

Are the prospects for the present war any better?

During the war of 1914-1918, the spiritual interests
of the Papacy were more evenly divided than now: great
Catholic populations fought on both sides, and the balance
was weighted, if at all, by the Catholic Empire of Austria
against the Orthodox Empire of Russia.   Today, while the
                                        Catholic...

Catholic

Church has a better position in England and France than
twenty-five years ago, the German Government is hostile
to Catholicism, has suppressed Catholic Austria and Poland
and has transferred to its side of the scales Communist
Russia, now the arch-enemy of the Vatican. At the same
time the steady increase of the Catholic population of the
New World, compared with the relative stability of that of
the Old, has, during the last quarter of a century, made
the Vatican less dependent than formerly on Europe, and
more anxious to adopt a democratic attitude in conformity
with the spirit of America, to which indeed the Papacy may
one day have to look for its main support, financial as
well as spiritual, and to which it is significant that
Pius XII is the first Pope to have paid a visit. Finally,
the general diplomatic standing of the Papacy may be said
to have increased if measured by the number of representatives of foreign Powers accredited to the Holy See, which
has risen from sixteen in 1914 to thirty-eight in 1939.

The stage is thus more favourable for the successful
intervention of the Vatican in the present, than in the
last world war. Moreover the personality of the present
Pope should be at least as favourable as that of Benedict
XV. Both had previous diplomatic experience, but while
the latter had served only in Spain, Pius XII has the advantage of first-hand knowledge of Germany, gained as Nuncio
from 1917-1929, and of France, Hungary, the United States
and South America, all of which he has visited. More important still, the prestige and authority of the Papacy
throughout the non-Catholic world have been greatly enhanced by the fact that the late Pius XI, in his courageous

and......

and uncompromising condemnation of racialism and
neo-paganism, had voiced and interpreted the sentiments of Christian civilisation and the humanitarian
conscience, irrespective of race or creed.

During the last months preceding the opening of
hostilities in September the new Pope in fact spared
no effort to preserve peace.   From early in May,
when His Holiness proposed to address a message to the
four great Powers and Poland, appealing for peace and
urging the convocation of a conference to settle the
questions in dispute, up to the afternoon of August 31,
when he besought the German and Polish Governments to
do all in their power to avoid incidents, the Vatican
did not cease to use its considerable influence to
promote a peaceful solution by negotiation and to
avert hostilities.   All these efforts were however of
no avail against Hitler's determination to secure his
end even at the cost of war.

After the opening of hostilities indication of
the Pope's attitude were awaited with great interest,
and there was justified disappointment with His Holiness's address on the 30th September to the Polish
colony in Rome, which contained no word of reprobation
of either the German or the Russian invasion of Poland.
This produced so painful an impression that it was
found necessary later to issue an unofficial statement
explaining the danger of exposing the Poles in occupied

Poland......

Poland to new persecutions.

There was therefore the greater satisfaction with the Pope's Encyclical "Summi Pontificatus" of October 27th, the first of his reign, which in strong and clear terms condemned as the fundamental errors of the time and the ultimate causes of the war "the nefarious efforts to banish Christ, the rejection of an universal norm of morality in international relations, the usurpation by Governments of the supreme authority which belongs only to God, the exclusion of religious instruction from the education of youth, and the unilateral rescinding of treaties."   There was no doubt as to the implication of these words. That the Vatican realised that the meaning would also be clear to the German Government was shown by the fact that to Germany alone they caused the whole Encyclical to be broadcast, as otherwise they feared it would not be allowed to reach the German people.

As the war proceeds, as disaffection spreads in Germany, and as the prospect of a German military victory grows more and more problematical, such plain speaking as the above may in the end produce an effect at all events among the thirty million Catholics in the Greater Reich.

The most important role of the Vatican may, however, be reserved for the end of the war and the problems of the peace.   The preoccupation of the Vatican on this latter score is already manifest from the

Encyclical......

Encyclical.   "Will the treaties of peace" it asks,
"be animated by justice and equity towards all, by
the spirit which frees and pacifies?"   Or will there
be a lamentable repetition of ancient and recent
errors?   Victory brings triumph and with triumph
temptation.   The excitement of the people makes them
inattentive to the warning voice of humanity and equity,
which is overwhelmed in the inhuman cry "Vae victis".

From his first official pronouncement on the day
following his Election Pius XII showed his preoccupation over the gathering threat to the peace of Europe.
And just as he spared no effort to exercise persuasion
in favour of the peaceful negotiation of differences
and the avoidance of war, so he may be expected to
lose no opportunity that may present itself of contributing to a shortening of the war and a termination
of hostilities.   When peace does return he will
assuredly exert himself to secure that the settlement
and the future of international relations be based
upon that Christian ethic to the abandonment of which
he attributes the evils of the day.

Indeed in his Christmas address to the College of
Cardinals he declared that the postulates of a just and
honourable peace should be: '(1) equality of rights
of small nations and reparation in the event of their
infringement; (2) relief from the pressure of armaments and the menace of the tyrannical use of force;
(3) provision in international institutions for

                                        guaranteeing.....

guaranteeing the observance or modification of
treaties; (4) the examination, and satisfaction by
pacific revision, of the real needs and just claims
of European peoples and minorities; and (5) the
interpretation of international agreements in the
spirit of responsibility, justice and charity.

In the same address he spoke of the likelihood
that a prolonged war would mean the material ruin of
Europe and that this in its turn would involve the
spread of communism. He therefore urged the statesmen of Europe to be prepared, not only for the formul-
ation of their peace aims but also, should the occasion
arise, for the initiation of peace negotiations.

All these indications of the Pope's laudable
ambition to effect the pacification of Europe and the
salvation of Western civilisation, combinedwith the
prospect of a policy of close cooperation with the
Italian Government and with the appointment by President Roosevelt of a personal peace ambassador to the
Vatican, point to the possibility during 1940 of a
peace initiative sponsored by the Pope, the President
and the Duce and backed by the rest of the neutral
world.